EMERGING
CONCEPTS
IN
MANAGEMENT

EDITED BY

Max S. Wortman, Jr.
University of Massachusetts

Fred Luthans
University of Nebraska

EMERGING CONCEPTS IN MANAGEMENT

Process, Behavioral, Quantitative, and Systems

The Macmillan Company
Collier-Macmillan Limited, London

PREFACE

Management as a field within business administration has changed significantly during the past decade. Today the development of concepts and theories of management which will carry the field into the 1970's and 1980's is more important than the development of specific techniques. Managers and academicians are more interested today in the philosophical and theoretical foundations of management, the breakthroughs in traditional process approaches, the new concepts of the behavioral sciences as applied to management, the new quantitative techniques which improve corporate operations, the development of systems approaches which attempt to envelop management as a total system or managerial subsystems, and the formulation of solutions to new managerial problems.

Throughout the book, the major emphases are on concepts and research, rather than specific techniques, because these conceptual frameworks and empirical findings will benefit the management student more in the long run. Techniques frequently are outdated in a short time. Through an interdisciplinary approach involving economics, psychology, sociology, engineering, mathematics, and business administration, the book presents the newest orientations to management in an orderly, readable sequence.

Several criteria were used in the editing of this book. First, was the issue truly critical in one of the four major approaches to management? Or was the issue one which would lay a major foundation for the study of management? Second, was it an issue that would excite the student of management to further explore the field, in his academic studies and later as a practitioner? Third, was the issue oriented to the future or to the solution of future problems? Fourth, was the article understandable? On the basis of these criteria, the issues were selected.

This book is an attempt to integrate the recent contributions of faculty and practitioners into a cohesive whole for undergraduate and graduate students and for practitioners. Its primary purpose is to present new journal articles to

v

the beginning student in management as both primary and supplementary materials in basic management courses in undergraduate and junior college courses, although it may be used for M.B.A. students who have not previously had a management course. Executives can use the book for current information on the state of management in the United States. The materials are all from the 1964–1968 period.

The six major parts of the book provide a strong conceptual framework for management today. Part I presents the philosophical and theoretical foundations of management, and includes a section on the social responsibilities of the businessman. Part II discusses the major new thrusts in the ongoing development of the process approach to management. In Part III the behavioral approaches to management are examined. Included are individual and group behavior in the organization, the dynamics of the organization and its reactions to change and conflict, the motivational aspects of the organization, communication concepts, and specific behavior techniques being used in management. Part IV analyzes the quantitative approaches to management, including those used in decision making and planning, and the impact of the computer on management. Part V looks at the developing systems concepts and analyses being employed by management. In the last part, the future of management and some of the challenges facing management are discussed.

Each part of the book is preceded by an integrative statement on the edited materials. At the end of each part, questions are provided to stimulate class discussion of the readings and individual study, and a selected reference list is presented to encourage the student to undertake additional reading in the area.

We would like to thank all of the researchers and scholars whose contributions are reprinted in this book, and the publishers and authors who granted permission to reprint these articles. Specific acknowledgment of the authors and publishers is noted at the beginning of each selection. We would also like to thank Professor Dalton E. McFarland at Michigan State University and Professor Richard W. Brightman at Orange Coast College for their critical comments and helpful suggestions. We sincerely appreciate the assistance of Mrs. Barbara Kuehl and Mrs. Phyllis Irwin in the typing of the manuscript, and of Miss Marie Smith in preparing the materials for publication.

M. S. W.
F. L.

CORRELATION MATRIX

	Management Textbooks						
Emerging Concepts in Management	Albers	Dale	Koontz and O'Donnell	McFarland	Newman, Summer, and Warren	Richards and Greenlaw	Terry
Table of Contents				Chapter No.			
I. Foundations of Management							
A. Philosophy of Management	1, 2	1, 15	1, 4	1	1, 2	1	1, 3, 5
B. Management Theory	3	1	2, 3	1, 2, 3	1, 2	1	1, 3, 5
C. Ethics and Responsibility	3, 4, 24	15, 28	4, 32	26, 12	1	2	11
II. Process Approaches							
A. Planning	14–17	7, 22	5–7, 10	4, 7	17, 18, 21	11	10, 12, 13
B. Organizing	5–10	16–19	11–19	11, 14	3–7	7, 8	15, 18
C. Directing	11, 23	25	24, 27	25, 13, 16	23, 26	5	22
D. Controlling	20, 21	5, 26	28, 30	10, 18	27, 30, 28	12, 15	26, 27, 29
E. Staffing	25–26	23	20–23	14, 21, 20	12	14	16, 24, 34
III. Behavioral Approaches							
A. Organizational Behavior	12	25, 17	24	22, 8, 19	8, 29, 24	4, 6, 10	15, 21
B. Conflict and Change	12	20, 21	27, 10	14, 17	17, 29	2, 9, 10	19
C. Motivation	22	25	25	22, 23	2, 23	4	16, 21, 25
D. Communication	13, 18, 19	25	26	24	10, 25	10	23
E. Behavioral Techniques	25	23	6, 22, 23	5, 22, 23	19, 29, 22	2, 6	2, 21
IV. Quantitative Approaches							
A. Decision Making	4	29	8	8, 9	13, 16, 15	16, 18	6, 7, 8
B. Operations Research and PERT	16	22, 34	8, 29	9, 10	16, 28	15	8, 10, 31
C. The Impact of Computers	1, 21	33	29	10		12, 16, 18	31
V. Systems Approaches							
A. Systems Concepts	4	1	2	9, 10		3	9
B. Systems Analyses	20, 21		29	9, 10	27, 30	6, 12	
VI. Management in the Future							
A. Multinational Management	6	30–32	33	1			
B. 1970's and Beyond	1, 3, 21	35	34		19		

CONTENTS

PART III

Behavioral Approaches

PART IV

Quantitative Approaches

PART V

Systems Approaches

PART VI

Management in the Future

PART I

Foundations
of Management

For many years there have been calls from academicians and practitioners to improve the foundations upon which management is based.[1] These calls have been directed toward the philosophy of management, theories of organization and management, and management as a profession. However, until the advent of World War II, these pleas to improve the conceptual foundations of management went largely unheard. Most of the work in the field was oriented to the establishment of principles of management, and these proposed principles were seldom tested by pragmatic research. A handful of managers had begun to experiment in managerial techniques, including Frederick W. Taylor, Henri Fayol, and Frank Gilbreth. Not only did they test their hypotheses, but they began to conceptualize new foundations for -management. Just before World War II, Chester I. Barnard carried these scientific management concepts a step further and introduced some of the behavioral aspects of a modern management structure.

Nonetheless, the calls for a firmer conceptual foundation of management continued. In recent years, there have been several systematic attempts to establish a philosophical basis for the entire field of management, rather than separate philosophies of management for individual managers. These philosophical attempts have not always been related to the continuing development

---

[1] For an early statement on attempts to professionalize management, see: Mary P. Follett, "How Must Business Management Develop in Order to Possess the Essentials of a Profession?" and "How Must Business Management Develop in Order to Become a Profession?" in *Business Management as a Profession,* (ed.) Henry C. Metcalf. Chicago: A. W. Shaw Co., 1927, pp. 73–102.

1

of a science of management and its theoretical structure. Furthermore, the cries for the establishment of a profession of management have resulted in new frameworks of professionalism and ethics for managers, but frequently these frameworks have not been related to the continuing efforts to develop a philosophy and science of management.

The readings in this part attempt to provide an understanding of these steps toward an integration of the philosophy, theory, and profession of management.

The first section is a discussion of the philosophy of management. In it, Professors William D. Litzinger and Thomas E. Schaefer provide a systematic view of the various perspectives of management philosophy today, and establish a philosophy of science perspective toward management. The second selection by Professor Robert F. Pethia is an in-depth inquiry into the possible contributions of the philosophy of science to the development of administrative theory.

In the second section, Professor Maneck S. Wadia analyzes some of the positive and negative contributions of the functional school of management and the need to retain it in modern management theory. Professor Orlando Behling argues that any attempt to unify management theory is doomed to failure. In his article, he differentiates between the pragmatic and humanistic theories and discusses the reasons why they probably will not become unified into one theory of management.

In the developing efforts to increase the professionalization of management, the discussions in recent years have turned to the ethics of modern business, because of ethical breakdowns such as the price-fixing cases in the electrical equipment, steel forging, and office equipment industries. In this section, Professor Thomas A. Petit examines the need for ethical standards for businessmen and the possibility of developing a doctrine of socially responsible management for the future. In his discussion, he analyzes the relationship of profit ethics and the moral crises of modern business. In the second selection, Professor George W. England takes an empirical approach to the value systems of American managers today. Through his data-oriented approach, he views the personal value systems of managers as relatively permanent perceptual frameworks which shape and influence the behavior of the individuals. He relates his findings to the modern ethical system of business today.

A

PHILOSOPHY OF MANAGEMENT

1. Management Philosophy Enigma

WILLIAM D. LITZINGER
and THOMAS E. SCHAEFER

These observations deal with some of the variations and implications associated with the term, *management philosophy*. Any list of ambiguous words bandied about in management literature would certainly include this as one. It has been used variously to refer to a theory, a goal, a technique, a way of life with certain implied values, or a public relations gambit.

Semantic perplexity is one of the characteristics of the current stage of development in management thought. Urwick, for example, pointed out no less than twenty vague definitions for the term *management* itself in arguing for a standard glossary of terms.[1] Semantic explicitness transcends etymological con-

siderations. Koontz acknowledged this as a corollary to the disentanglement of the "jungle." [2]

Management Philosophy: What Is It?

The literature presents a potpourri of articles purporting to deal with *management philosophy*. Several different themes seem to prevail as one studies articles dealing with this subject.

THE LITERATURE AS A POINT OF REFERENCE

Although one of the first books to appear in management literature was *The*

Reprinted from *Academy of Management Journal*, Vol. 9, No. 4 (December, 1966), pp. 337–343, with permission of the publishers. William D. Litzinger and Thomas E. Schaefer are Professors of Business Administration, College of Business Administration, University of San Francisco.

[1] L. F. Urwick, "The Problem of Management Semantics," *California Management Review*, Vol. 2, No. 3 (September, 1960), pp. 77–83.

[2] Harold Koontz, "The Management Theory Jungle," *Journal of the Academy of Management*, Vol. 4, No. 3 (December, 1961), pp. 174–188.

Philosophy of Management by Oliver Sheldon,[3] the "pioneer" authors typically did not deal with philosophy in so many words. Rather, they tended to focus on technique and function and in so doing championed an approach or set of principles which was a reflection of their "philosophy." Scientific management and hints at human relations are indicative of such "philosophies."

Later, the authors begin to point to the need for a philosophy of management and then not infrequently to enumerate its components, for example, R. C. Davis:

. . . A business philosophy is a system of thought that explains basic business problems and supplies the basis for an intelligent approach to their solution. The philosophy of management is obviously the philosophy of business . . .[4]

Later, in an article enumerating the basis of a management philosophy, Davis defined it as:

. . . a body of related knowledge that supplies a logic for effective thinking for solution of certain kinds of problems.[5]

Max S. Wortman presented a somewhat more involved definition in 1958:

. . . a philosophic discipline which is the systematic study of the nature of management, especially its methods, its concepts, and presuppositions, and its place in the general scheme of intellectual disciplines.[6]

Marshall Dimock identified administration as a philosophy of integration and blending of everything that is important.[7]

Several authors raise moral and ethical questions in proposing a *managerial philosophy*.[8] Here such dangers are posited as self-righteousness, cynicism, perfectionism, compromise, control of truth, and responsibility for errors.

Some writers provide what they consider to be the basis for management philosophies.[9] Good employee relations, right of private property, collective bargaining and the like are listed as necessary foundations. Manley Jones argued that unconscious thoughts make up one's philosophy.

Still others merely present their own personal working philosophy.[10] Dignity and worth of the individual personality

---

[3] Oliver Sheldon, *The Philosophy of Management* (Englewood Cliffs, New Jersey: Prentice-Hall, Inc., 1923), pp. 27–30.

[4] R. C. Davis, *The Fundamentals of Top Management* (New York: Harper and Brothers, 1951), pp. 6–7.

[5] R. C. Davis, "Philosophy of Management," *Advanced Management,* Vol. 24, No. 4 (April, 1959), pp. 5–6.

[6] Max S. Wortman, Jr., "A Philosophy of Management," *Advanced Management,* Vol. 26, No. 10 (October, 1961), pp. 11–15.

[7] Marshall Dimock, *A Philosophy of Administration: Toward Creative Growth* (New York: Harper and Brothers, 1958).

[8] See Benjamin Selekman, *A Moral Philosophy of Management* (New York: McGraw-Hill Book Co., 1959); L. W. Norris, "Moral Hazards of American Executives," *Harvard Business Review,* Vol. 38, No. 5 (September–October, 1960), pp. 72–80; A. M. Sullivan, "Moral Responsibility of Management," *Advanced-Management-Office Executive* (April, 1963), pp. 7–10; Hurst R. Anderson, "Ethical Values in Administration," *Personnel Administration,* Vol. XVII, No. 1 (January, 1954), pp. 1–12; John F. Mee, "Management Philosophy for Professional Executives," *Business Horizons* (December, 1956), pp. 5–11.

[9] Manley Jones, "Evolving a Philosophy of Management," *Journal of the Academy of Management,* Vol. 3, No. 2 (August, 1960); L. E. Newman, "Some Philosophies of Management," *Advanced Management* (February, 1959), pp. 6–8.

[10] Wade Fetzer, Jr., "A Philosophy of Management," *Office Executive,* Vol. 33, No. 8 (August, 1948), pp. 14–15.

are offered as essential to sound operating philosophies usually.

Occasionally, the call comes forth for managers to re-examine their own philosophy in light of changes that have taken place which affect the corporation.[11] Along these lines, most recently Thomas A. Petit argues for a "social responsibility ethic." [12] This doctrine is suggested to replace the profit ethic and holds that managers must take into account the welfare of all groups in society (worker, consumer, supplier, dealer, community, and government as well as stockholders) affected by the corporation in conducting its affairs.

One of the earliest truly philosophical approaches to management was that of Chester I. Barnard:

. . . It is precisely the function of the executive to facilitate the synthesis in concrete action of contradictory forces . . . [determinism and free will] . . . to reconcile conflicting forces, instincts, interests, conditions, positions, and ideals.[13]

Carl F. Stover presented one of the more analytical approaches.[14] He first set out a definition of philosophy to include a system of ideas which does three things:

1. defines what is true;
2. determines what questions are important to ask and rules out others

(natural law, casuistic, utilitarian); 3. description of a set of values.

Using this schema, he then pointed out the importance that answers to these basic questions have on a manager's approach.

Someone outside the "mainstream" of management was the first to attempt to relate philosophy in a classical sense to management. A. R. Leys, a political scientist, wrote *Ethics for Policy Decision* in 1952.[15] The first portion of this book is devoted to an examination of the questions posed by philosophical schools (Utilitarianism, Casuistic, Stoicism). The second portion applied these questions to case examples of policy-making problems in business and government.

THE COMPANIES AS A POINT OF REFERENCE

When the managers of companies turn their attention to defining the purpose of their organization and setting down moral and ethical principles to guide their actions, a "company philosophy" or "creed" emerges. These guiding documents are referred to in a variety of ways: Basic Objectives; Our Basic Policy; Fundamental Principles; The Credo by Which We Serve; What We Are Aiming For; and more simply, Policies.[16] On occasion, companies are identified and asso-

---

[11] A. O. Ohman, "Search for Managerial Philosophy," *Harvard Business Review,* Vol. 35, No. 5 (September–October, 1957), pp. 41–51.

[12] Thomas A. Petit, "The Doctrine of Socially Responsible Management," *Arizona Review* (Division of Economic and Business Research, University of Arizona, Tucson). Series of three articles in November and December 1965 and January 1966 issues.

[13] Chester I. Barnard, *Functions of the Executive* (Cambridge: Harvard University Press, 1938), p. 21.

[14] Carl F. Stover, "Changing Patterns in the Philosophy of Management," *Public Administration Review,* Vol. 18, No. 1 (Winter, 1958), pp. 21–27.

[15] A. R. Leys, *Ethics for Policy Decisions* (Englewood Cliffs, New Jersey: Prentice-Hall, Inc., 1952).

[16] Stewart Thompson, *Management Creeds and Philosophies* (Research Study Number 32; New York: American Management Association, Inc., 1958).

ciated with a particular "philosophy." General Electric has been noted for what has been called its philosophy of decentralization. Similarly, centralized policy and decentralized administration are characterized of the General Motors philosophy of management.

Philosophy Itself as a Point of Reference

A look at philosophy and its various subdivisions will provide a frame of reference better to understand the kind of concepts and semantics associated with this term.[17] *Webster's Third New International Dictionary* presents thirteen meanings for the word philosophy. Included are: the quest for truth; study of natural phenomena; system of motivating beliefs; and personal attitude. The *Encyclopaedia Britannica* notes it popularly means any formulation of very general principles for a particular activity such as politics.

In a generic sense, philosophy represents an endeavor to discover by systematic reflection the ultimate nature of things. It is derived from two Greek words meaning a lover of wisdom and knowledge. Sometimes it is used to denote a system of speculative beliefs such as a set of convictions on important issues as when we speak of a certain man's philosophy of life.

Philosophy as taught in our colleges and universities includes the five subject areas identified in the accompanying schema.

```
                     aesthetics
                         |
metaphysics—PHILOSOPHY—epistemology
                    |         |
                  logic     ethics
```

Aesthetics deals with philosophical inquiry regarding the beautiful in nature and art. Epistemology refers to the search for a criterion for truth: the science of knowledge. Ethics is a study of the systematic behavior of the nature of value concepts, "good," "bad," "right," "wrong," "ought," and the general principles which justify us in applying them to anything. Logic deals with the forms of valid reasoning. The two major forms of logical method are induction and deduction. Metaphysics is concerned with the ultimate nature of all reality in contrast with logic, ethics, and the natural social sciences which deal with more restricted fields of inquiry. It includes ontology which deals with the nature and types of reality (materialism, idealism, dualism) and cosmology having to do with the process of reality (determinism and teleology).

Philosophers themselves are hard put to find some notion of philosophy upon which all, or at least most, philosophers can agree. However, there are two extreme views of philosophy and upon the line drawn between these two extremes, every conceivable meaning of the term can find a place. On the one hand, phi-

[17] See *Collier's Encyclopedia* (New York: O. S. Collier & Sons, 1959), Vol. 7, pp. 432–436; Vol. 15, pp. 668–670; *Dictionary of Philosophy and Psychology* (New York: The Macmillan Company, 1902), Vol. II, pp. 291–296; John Dewey, *Encyclopaedia of the Social Sciences* (New York: The Macmillan Company); Vol. XI–XII, pp. 119–128; *The Catholic Encyclopaedia,* Vol. XII (1911), pp. 25–40.

losophy can mean a totally disinterested attunement with the ultimate nature of things—a speculative enterprise which penetrates, for no practical purpose, the structure of reality. On the other hand, philosophy can mean the highest, most articulate kind of practical knowledge, the knowledge which knows how to order other knowledges for human purposes. Though too simplified, these meanings correspond to Ancient and Modern notions of philosophy. The older view saw metaphysics as philosophy's supreme expression while the more recent view repudiates metaphysics in order to free the mind from futile speculation and center it upon ends. Whereas the former seeks a knowledge of things in themselves, the latter seeks a knowledge of how things are to be used for the support and advancement of human life. In the mind of some philosophers, these two meanings are mutually exclusive. However, whether they are contradictory or compatible, the second meaning prevails today among professional philosophers.

Management Philosophy: What Meaning?

Which of these aspects of philosophy has been utilized and/or applies to *management philosophy*? Does any unity emerge from beneath the multiplicity of meanings generally ascribed to this term? We find that a single meaning does dominate and this meaning not surprisingly reflects the prevailing understanding of "philosophy" within the United States. In America, as in any land, a recognizable brand of philosophy tends to dominate the intellectual scene. The specific American philosophy is, of course, Pragmatism (the thrust of the Pragmatic position im-

plies the same sort of approach as Utilitarianism, Empiricism, or Pluralism).

One would expect, therefore, that in this country *management philosophy* means "Pragmatic Philosophy of Management." Examination of the literature confirms this. There appears little desire to erect a speculative philosophical theory of management; the chief concern is to develop a highly practice-oriented theory for control over the means and the ends of business. Philosophy here does not mean philosophy in its classical sense—a disinterested inquiry into the ultimate nature of things. Philosophy, rather refers to the correct use of knowledge for achieving a definite, practical purpose: the support and advancement of a business enterprise.

This supremely practical (pragmatic) meaning of philosophy, however, does not answer to the deepest traditional meaning of philosophy: a contemplative vision of truth for its own sake and not for the sake of any result, monetary or otherwise. Philosophy in this traditional sense finds its highest expression in metaphysics—the science of reality as reality. In a management context, metaphysics would ask not how to manage for results, but what is the meaning of management in a cosmic perspective? Metaphysics would seek to know the ontological meaning of organizational structure and control rather than the methods of sustaining and embellishing these realities. This sort of approach would seek a disinterested, non-pragmatic, strictly metaphysical knowledge of organization and/or management *in itself*, apart from any formal relationship to human passion and human desire. It would be a "Metaphysics of Management" [18] rather than a "Philosophy of How to Manage." Such a metaphysics would consider the realities

[18] Olaf Helmer and Nicholas Rescher, "On the Epistemology of the Inexact Sciences," *Management Science*, Vol. 6, No. 1 (October, 1959), pp. 25–52.

of all organizations. Only in terms of such an approach can strict reference be made to a genuine "philosophy of management" in the most ancient, rigorous sense of the term "Philosophy."

Thus *management philosophy* has come to mean knowledge of how to manage for results (pragmatism). As such, it refers to an exercise of power over the means which will be sufficient for the achievement of humanly desired goals. It utilizes available human science in an endeavor to secure the specific good it sets for itself. *Management philosophy,* American style, is concerned with knowledge for the sake of action in the human arena rather than its own sake in the arena of "divine" science (metaphysics). It eschews considering management in a cosmic context and prefers to deal with organizations in an unreservedly contextual manner. The theory of how to manage for results is, of course, a perfectly legitimate sphere of knowledge, but it is not strictly philosophical (i.e. metaphysical).

Closing Observations

The first step in dispelling confusion is to identify it, which was the task we set for ourselves in this essay. The evidence indicated a rather indiscriminate use of the term *management philosophy*. The confusion among writers on management philosophy, we observed, stems from a basic confusion about the term "philosophy" itself. On the one hand the term refers to a speculative penetration of the ultimate nature of things—Metaphysics. On the other hand certain modern thinkers, like the Pragmatists, have repudiated metaphysics in favor of an instrumentalist conception. Although these two meanings appear constantly confused in the management literature, the second meaning (Pragmatism) definitely prevails over the first (Metaphysics).

When considering management philosophy according to its pragmatic meaning, our focus is flexible and creative, centered on specific limited business goals and the most efficient method of procuring them. Any deliberation on management philosophy in its deeper metaphysical sense is more cosmic, unconcerned with control. Here management is looked at in order to understand it for itself as a perennial element of the human scene involving the deepest question of human freedom and infinite power. Some beginnings toward such a metaphysical approach were made by Barnard but these have yet to be worked out and clarified in any final way.

The dominance of the pragmatic meaning of philosophy among management writers, however, is probably not due to any conscious anti-metaphysical bias among them. Indeed, certain writers, notably Barnard, were very much at home with metaphysical concepts. Rather, the dominance of the functional or action-oriented approach to management is probably due to the prevailing focus of thought in our time. Temperamentally, we have little interest, and less time, for metaphysical questions.

Nevertheless, metaphysics is inescapable: men will always seek to know, beyond questions of efficiency, the final meaning of things in the context of the whole universe. Because of this, we can anticipate that a metaphysical meaning of management philosophy will be sought. Who is to do the job? Philosophers, as such, have shown little inclination to attempt such a task. Although several individuals have had considerable impact on the field of management, it has not been dominated by any one individual in the manner of John Dewey, M. Keynes, or M. Weber in other disciplines. Since no one can hope to contribute much to the clarification of ideas in mathematics who is not himself a mathematician and so on throughout the sciences, it seems logical to anticipate a "metaphysics of management" would need the talent of a philosopher. In like manner, a definitive work on "managerial pragmatism" would come from within management ranks. Eventually, of course, union may be possible.

In the meantime, we ought to be concerned with questions of knowledge, value, ends, and means, but it is time to stop kidding ourselves by such indiscriminate use of the word philosophy. We cannot help but profit by keeping these dual aspects of management philosophy in mind. By so doing, writers would not be tempted to slip from one usage to another, confusing their readers and robbing their work of clarity and coherence.

No *philosophy* of management worth the name can emerge without a disciplined philosophical habit of mind. One implication of this for management theory is clear. If the ageless discipline of philosophy is to have an influence on the emerging discipline of management, either those in management submit themselves to the rigors of philosophy, or a way must be found to involve philosophers in this field. For, until philosophers become managers or management people learn the power and grace of philosophy, no ultimate philosophy of management can evolve.

Any discipline must face the threat of finding its devotees talking only to each other. This appears to be the condition of management "philosophers" today: the shibboleths of a few become the *ad hoc* doctrine of the day for the many. To prevent the perpetuation of this, we would do well to recall the words of the late Professor Arthur Lovejoy, ". . . truth is more likely to emerge through the interplay and conflict of ideas resulting from the exercise of individual reason than through the imposition of uniform and standardized opinions by authority."

2. Values in Positive and Normative Administrative Theory: A Conceptual Framework and Logical Analysis

ROBERT F. PETHIA

This paper is an exercise in what might be called philosophy of science as applied to administrative theory. After giving very brief attention to definitions of the terms "theory" and "values" as used in this paper, we will explore (1) the distinction between positive and normative theory, (2) show the ways in which and the points at which values may enter into the two types of theory, and (3) consider the forms in which these values are ultimately reflected in these two types of theory. Some brief concluding remarks will follow the detailed exposition.

The term "theory" will be used to mean *a proposition or a set of propositions about some phenomena.* It is questionable whether any such thing as "administrative theory" exists if a more confining definition is used. We do not wish to become embroiled in a controversy over whether there is or is not such a thing as "administrative theory." Since propositions about administration exist in abundance, if we adopt our definition of theory, "administrative theory" clearly exists in the sense in which we will use the term.

The term "values" will be used to refer to *expressed or implied conceptions of what is good and/or desirable (and/or of what is not good and/or undesirable).* The term is being used, in other words, in the sense that we use it when we ask of someone "What are your values?" or "What values do you hold?" We are asking him in effect, "What are your conceptions of what is desirable or undesirable?" Similarly, if we ask of someone "What value judgments did you base your recommendations on?" we are asking him, in effect, "What conceptions of what is desirable or undesirable (or what convictions of 'what ought to be' and of 'what ought not to be' or what normative standards) did you use in reaching your recommendations?" This is a commonly used meaning of the term "values" as used both in philosophy and in the social sciences. There are other meanings, but we will use this one only throughout the paper.

Reprinted from *Proceedings of the 10th Annual Midwest Management Conference.* Carbondale, Ill.: Business Research Bureau, Southern Illinois University, 1967, pp. 1–19, with permission of the author and the publisher. Robert F. Pethia is Assistant Professor of Management, College of Business Administration, University of Texas.

Acknowledgment: Louis DeAlessi of Duke University and the Institute for Defense Analyses, Thomas F. Keller of Duke University (currently on a visiting appointment at Carnegie Institute of Technology), and William F. Glueck of The University of Texas provided useful critical comments on an earlier draft of this paper.

The Distinction between Positive and Normative Administrative Theory

The differentiation of theories of administration and organization into two broad categories will facilitate a discussion of values in the theories. Specifically, a distinction will be made between theories that are "positive" and those that are "normative". Not only do the two kinds of theory serve different purposes but they are constructed differently, values enter into them in different ways and at different points, and these values are ultimately reflected in markedly different forms in the two types of theories.

By a descriptive or positive theory is meant one which deals with questions of fact or knowledge, with "what is." Conversely by a normative theory is meant one which deals, in some sense, with "what ought to be." It necessarily includes some imperative or prescriptive or evaluative or ethical content of which, perhaps ideally (though, as will be shown, not practically), a positive theory will be totally free.

Positive theory deals with knowledge *about* something. Its purpose is to advance *understanding*. It gives descriptions or explanations about phenomena or makes predictions of the consequences that would be expected to follow from certain events. Positive theory deals essentially with descriptive statements, although when descriptive statements are spoken of in this sense they are not confined necessarily to statements which report direct sensory perceptions. Statements such as "grass is green" or "people work in administrative organizations" are descriptive statements. Likewise, statements of relationship, causal or otherwise, such as "X causes Y" or "Y = ⅓X + 4" or "unity of command prevents chaos" are, in and of themselves, descriptive. Explanatory statements (which might be regarded as a particular type of statement of relationship) also are descriptive. If someone says, for example, "GNP fell off because investment spending decreased due to excessive existing stocks of capital goods relative to product demand" he essentially is trying to describe *why* GNP fell. Or a positive statement might be in the form of a prediction that if some condition or state of affairs exists or is brought into existence then some other condition(s) or state(s) of affairs will result. Someone might say "if span of control is decreased, then the number of levels in the organization will increase," or "if you create a highly cohesive work group it will exhibit a smaller variability of output than will a less cohesive work group but the average level of output may be either higher or lower than that of a less cohesive work group." These two statements are meant to describe (which in this case means to predict) what the consequences resulting from certain phenomena will be.[1] A statement need not be a *correct* or "true" description, explanation, or prediction to qualify as a positive statement in this sense. Someone might quibble with the statement "grass is green," for example, on grounds that it is at best a half-truth because grass may sometimes be brown. Nevertheless the statement is intendedly descriptive, it is meant to be factual, to convey knowledge about something whether or not it is an adequate representation of the truth. In administrative theory there are scores of statements (e.g., "unity of

---

[1] A statement expressing a causal relationship, of course, contains an implicit prediction. To say "X causes Y" is, in effect, to say "I predict if X, then Y."

command prevents chaos," "specialization prevents self-actualization," "authority is a right delegated from above," etc.) which some people regard as adequate representations of the truth (i.e., of what is), while others regard them as true statements only under certain conditions and not under other conditions, and which still other persons regard as untrue under all circumstances. Nevertheless they are all meant to deal with facts, to describe what is, to convey understanding, and therefore qualify as positive statements as that term is being used here. None of these statements, taken by itself, prescribes in any sense. Nor does it, by itself, evaluate anything.

Positive theories of administration and organization are essentially theories of organizational behavior, theories which describe various components of an administrative organization or various aspects of administrative behavior and/or describe or explain relationships between these components or aspects. R. C. Davis' theory of organizational growth describes certain behavior patterns of line and staff functions as related to the size of the organization. Argyris describes some behavior patterns of people in organizations which he has deduced from some assumptions about people and from some assumptions about several characteristics of formal organizations. Simon has described some aspects of the decision-making process in organizations. Each of these theories, presumably, is designed to say something about some aspect of organizational behavior, to say *what is* rather than *what should be*. In short, these kinds of theories deal with knowledge *about* administrative organizations. Positive theories in this field may deal with a wide range of phenomena. All administrative organizations encompass a variety of individuals, work groups, formally prescribed and informally sanctioned behaviors, technological systems,

economic relationships, etc. Any or all of these may provide the substance for a positive statement.

Normative theory, on the other hand, has prescription and/or evaluation as its purpose(s). Prescriptions or recommendations that some action be taken or some conditions be brought about are made in a normative theory, and/or evaluations of the desirability or undesirability of phenomena are offered. Consequently, normative theory is characterized by either prescriptive or evaluative statements or both. For example, statements such as "authority should be commensurate with responsibility," or "objectives should be attained efficiently," or "any organization ought to concern itself with the satisfaction of its employees" are prescriptive. Statements such as "unity of command is desirable" or "authoritarian leadership styles are unsatisfactory" are evaluative. It is impossible to make either of these two types of normative statements without some assumptions, either implicit or explicit, about preferences. Until one has adopted some values, some conception(s) of what is good or desirable (or the converse) either in an intrinsic or in an instrumental sense one is in no position to make any prescriptions or recommendations or to evaluate anything. This is not to say that we need to be conscious of the bases of our valuations before we can make statements which embody an evaluation. On the contrary, casual empiricism would suggest that many people, much of the time, make many recommendations and evaluations without being very conscious of the values or, at least, of all of the values, they are adopting as standards. This does not mean, however, that the preferences are not reflected in the recommendations or evaluations nonetheless.

However, unless a normative statement is dealing with something that, in an ultimate sense, has intrinsic value in and of itself, then the normative statement is based *not only* on some assumed standard(s) of desirability *but also* on some factual assumption(s). In particular, some assumptions about causal relationships are imbedded in the normative statement. For example, if one makes a normative statement such as "happiness is the ultimate objective" then, if what is meant is that happiness is in fact good in its own right rather than because it leads to something else which is considered desirable, no assumptions of causality are being made. Rather a pure value judgment that happiness is good has been expressed. All statements dealing with ultimate objectives (i.e., with things considered good in their own right without further justification) are simply expressions of preferences. But if we take a normative statement where the desired phenomenon is, in fact, desired because of an expectation that it will lead to something else which is desirable, then not only do we have in mind some notion of what is ultimately desirable (i.e., some pure value assumption) but also we have in mind some expectation (i.e., some factual assumption) that the immediately desired phenomenon will lead, in fact, to the ultimately desired phenomenon. In a statement such as "unity of command is desirable," what is being said is either (1) "I think unity of command is desirable in and of itself without further justification," or (2) "I think unity of command is desirable because it leads to 'X' which I think is desirable." [2] If the second meaning is intended, then not only has a *value assumption* been made as to the ultimate desirability of "X" but also the *factual assumption* that unity of command does,

in fact, lead to X has been made. In short, (1) *all* normative statements, be they prescriptive or evaluative, must be based on value assumptions and (2) all normative statements except those dealing with ultimate ends are based *not only* on value assumptions *but also* on assumptions of fact.

The distinction between positive and normative theory that has been drawn here is not a novel one. In economics the distinction is of long standing. According to Hutchison:

Explicit, systematic and sustained attempts to distinguish and separate off the 'positive' propositions of 'the science of political economy' from policy recommendations and ethical and political postulates, or doctrines advocating policy objectives, can be traced back to the later classical writers of the second quarter of the nineteenth century. It is perhaps not too fanciful even to fix the actual year from which the distinction could be said to have taken root as 1836, when J. S. Mill's essay (written 1829–30) *"On the Definition of Political Economy and on the Method of Investigation Proper to It,"* and Nassau Senior's *Outline of Political Economy,* first appeared. Not, of course, that the distinction was kept clear, or was faithfully maintained, from 1836 onwards—it never has been and perhaps never will be. [3]

Hutchison goes on to point out that "anticipatory groping attempts" toward the positive–normative distinction can be traced to the seventeenth century. [4]

Similar distinctions in the literature on administrative theory are not plentiful. In the journals and in books published in the past few years there have been a number of passing references to the positive–normative distinction and several writers actually make use of the distinc-

---

[2] There may, of course, be a causal chain with more than one link in it.

[3] T. W. Hutchison, *"Positive" Economics and Policy Objectives* (Cambridge, Mass.: Harvard University Press, 1964), p. 23.

[4] Ibid., p. 23.

tion or to closely related distinctions in their analyses. Golembiewski, for example, in his *Behavior and Organization,* distinguishes between three types of theories: empirical theory, goal-based empirical theory, and utopian theory.[5] Empirical theory "has as its purpose the statement of the relations which exist in the physical or social worlds, that is, the statement of what is related to what." [6] Goal-based empirical theory "prescribes what must be done in order to attain what is desired, based upon knowledge of reality." [7] Golembiewski does not define utopian theory but says that it is unlike the two types of empirical theory in that it "is insensitive to empirical data at the same time that it deals with, or is applicable to, empirical relations . . . Either the properties of a utopian theory will not have been tested, even though it is possible to do so, or the properties of a utopian theory will not be changed, even when evidence demonstrates their inadequacy." [8] Golembiewski's empirical theory apparently is positive theory, as that type of theory has been defined here, while his goal-based empirical theory is normative theory. Since the requirement of empirical testing has not been imposed on the two types of theory as conventionally defined and as defined for purposes of this paper, it would appear that Golembiewski's utopian theory could be included within one or the other of the two types of theory defined here, de-

pending upon whether or not it is goal-directed. Shull, in his "The Nature and Contribution of Administrative Models and Organizational Research," distinguishes between prescriptive, predictive, and descriptive management models and utilizes his distinctions in his analysis.[9] Shull's prescriptive models are analogous to our normative theory. His predictive and descriptive models combined constitute an identical type with positive theory as defined here.

There are other writers, however, whose observations are sometimes confused because they fail to distinguish the two types of theory and to recognize that they are different both in structure and in purpose. Simon, for example, in his now famous chapter on "Some Problems of Administrative Theory" criticizes administrative theory for, among other things, inadequately describing administrative situations.[10] Yet, the administrative theory to which he refers is traditional prescriptive theory which makes no apparent pretense at describing administrative situations. Carzo, in his "Administrative Science and the Role of Value Judgments," [11] see-saws back and forth indiscriminately between administrative science as description and administrative science as prescription, finally highlighting the ambiguity by presenting two contiguous sentences which read as follows: "It is the task of administrative science to describe, explain, analyze, and predict human behavior as

[5] Robert T. Golembiewski, *Behavior and Organization* (Chicago: Rand McNally and Co., 1963), pp. 49–57.

[6] Ibid., p. 49.

[7] Ibid., pp. 51–52.

[8] Ibid., p. 55.

[9] Fremont Shull, Jr., "The Nature and Contribution of Administrative Models and Organizational Research," *Journal of the Academy of Management,* Vol. 5, No. 2, August, 1962, pp. 124–138.

[10] Herbert A. Simon, *Administrative Behavior* (2nd ed. New York: The Macmillan Co., 1957), pp. 37–38.

[11] Rocco Carzo, Jr., "Administrative Science and the Role of Value Judgments," *Journal of the Academy of Management,* Vol. 3, No. 3, December, 1960, pp. 175–182.

it relates to the accomplishment of organizational goals. Administrative science is concerned with efficient and effective accomplishment of organization goals." [12] In "The Management Theory Jungle" Koontz contributes to the jungle by treating a half dozen of what he chooses to call "major schools of management theory" as though they were competing substitute products whereas some are normative guides to administrative action while others are approaches to understanding organizational behavior.[13] The alleged "jungle," if it does not actually disappear, appears to contain a good deal less underbrush when this distinction is drawn.

There is other work which at first glance appears to recognize the positive-normative distinction but upon closer examination it becomes less than clear that this is the case. For example, Simon, in the book already cited, makes a distinction between scientific propositions ("statements about the observable world and the way in which it operates") and ethical propositions ("expressions of preferences") [14] which appears to be identical with the distinction drawn in this paper between positive statements and normative statements. He goes on to distinguish between a "theoretical" and a "practical" administrative science, both of which, he asserts, are concerned purely with factual statements. "Theoretical" administrative science deals with what he calls "a sociology of administration" which deals with "descriptions—with reference either to a particular organization or to organizations in general—of the way in which human beings behave

in organized groups." [15] Apparently Simon's "theoretical administrative science" is positive administrative theory as defined here. But it is not clear that he allows for a normative administrative theory. He goes on:

On the other hand, a practical science of administration consists of propositions as to how men would behave if they wished their activity to result in the greatest attainment of administrative objectives with scarce means.[16]

If the statement is taken literally to mean that a practical science deals with "how men would behave" under certain conditions, then practical science deals with *predictions about* behavior, it deals with descriptions of behavior expected to occur under certain conditions. If this is actually what Simon means, it is not clear that he has made any distinction at all between theoretical and practical science. "Propositions about how men would behave" would seem to be "descriptions . . . of the way in which human beings behave." Only if the definition is not taken literally but rather it is assumed that when he said "would" Simon really meant "should" can one conclude that his "practical science" deals with goal-directed prescriptive propositions and, therefore, is normative. There is some evidence that Simon may have meant the definition literally and that, therefore, he has not distinguished practical from theoretical science at all, nor has he allowed for a normative theory of administration. He asserts that ethical imperatives have no place in any science.[17] It might be inferred from this that neither of his two types of admini-

[12] Ibid., p. 181.
[13] Harold Koontz, "The Management Theory Jungle," *Journal of the Academy of Management,* Vol. 4, No. 3, December, 1961, pp. 174–188.
[14] Simon, *op. cit.,* p. 248. See also pp. 45–47.
[15] Ibid., p. 253.
[16] Ibid., p. 253.
[17] Ibid., p. 250.

strative science is meant to be normative.

Sociologists who are interested in administrative organizations are given to drawing a distinction between a rational or goal model of organization and a system model.[18] Superficially viewed, this distinction appears to be that between a normative and a positive approach. Closer examination raises questions as to whether or not this is the case. As Etzioni uses the notions of goal models and system models they appear to be alternative ways for evaluating the effectiveness of organizational behavior and, therefore, to be normative in both cases. The only apparent difference between the two approaches seems to be that with the goal model evaluation is made with reference to highly specific goals whereas with the system model evaluation is made with reference to the general requirements which he assumes must exist for the survival of any social system. Gouldner, on the other hand, seems to view rational models and natural system models as alternative approaches to understanding organizational behavior. If this is the case, he uses both models in a positive sense.

The intention in this discussion has not been to present an exhaustive cataloging of all of the instances where a positive–normative distinction has been or might have been drawn in administrative theory. Rather the intention has been to suggest that while some writers clearly do understand the difference between understanding on the one hand and prescription or evaluation on the other, a good many others are not at home with this distinction and do not utilize it in their work. As a consequence, some of the things that are written by students of management and administrative organization contain logical flaws because positive and normative propositions are tossed together and jumbled indiscriminately. It is essential to draw the distinction clearly for our purpose of examining values in administrative theory.

Ways in Which and Points at Which Values Enter into Positive Administrative Theory

We have just characterized positive theory as dealing with questions of fact or knowledge, as concerned with statements which describe, explain, or predict "what is." It is sometimes assumed that theory of this type has nothing to do with values or preferences, that it can be value-free and, furthermore, that it ought to be value-free. However, logical examination of the issue leads to the conclusion that any body of knowledge about any phenomena of logical necessity cannot be value-free, that it must embody some person's(s') notions of what is good, right, desirable, etc.[19]

This conclusion is arrived at by reason-

---

[18] For example see Amitai Etzioni, "Two Approaches to Organizational Analysis: A Critique and a Suggestion," *Administrative Science Quarterly,* Vol. 5, No. 2, September, 1960, pp. 257–278. Also A. Etzioni, *Modern Organizations* (Englewood Cliffs, N.J.: Prentice-Hall, 1964), pp. 16–19. Also Alvin W. Gouldner, "Organizational Analysis" in Robert K. Merton et al. (eds.) *Sociology Today* (New York: Harper and Row, Torchbooks Edition, 1959), pp. 400–428.

[19] The thinking in this section (and, to a lesser extent, the following one) owes a general intellectual debt to the following sources: C. West Churchman, *Prediction and Optimal Decision: Philosophical Issues of a Science of Values* (Englewood Cliffs, N.J.: Prentice-Hall, 1961); Morris R. Cohen and Ernest Nagel, *An Introduction to Logic and Scientific Method* (New York: Harcourt, Brace and World, Inc., 1934); Phillip G. Frank (ed.), *The Validation of Scientific Theories* (New York: Collier Books, 1961); T. W. Hutchison, *op. cit.;* Karl Mannheim, *Ideology and Utopia: An Introduction to the Sociology of Knowl-*

ing from the observation that any attempt to develop a statement of fact and/or to compile a body of knowledge about something necessarily involves making decisions. A decision involves a choice of or a selection of one thing over others based on explicit or implicit factual and value premises. (Professor Simon explored the basis for this proposition at length a generation ago.[20]) Without values or preferences (i.e., conceptions of what is good and/or desirable) there would be no basis for selecting a course of action from among available alternatives.[21] If the proposition is correct that without making decisions knowledge can neither be developed nor compiled, and if decisions necessarily are made on the basis of preferences, then what the decision-making process generates and calls "knowledge" is necessarily partly a function of the values which guided the decisions. Precisely which values guide which choices would have a great deal to do with what ultimately is called knowledge. In other words knowledge is not independent of values. Of the works consulted which are relevant to this discussion, only one—Churchman's *Prediction and Optional Decision* [22]—character-

izes science as a decision-making process and organizes the discussion in terms of the decisions that must be made by the scientist. Some others explicitly recognize that decisions are inevitable in the development of positive theory.[23] The discussions of problems of methodology offered by each of the authors could very easily be translated into these terms, however.

It may facilitate an understanding of the position taken here if some of the choices that must be made in developing and/or compiling a body of knowledge are spelled out. For convenience (1) decisions made in the research process, (2) decisions to accept or reject a proposition as "true," and (3) decisions to accept or reject a proposition as relevant for inclusion in some collection of propositions will be considered in sequence. The demarcation used is arbitrary. All of these decisions might be made by a single person, but they need not be (e.g., a researcher might simply present a report of what he did and a description of the results without deciding on the truth or falsity of some proposition, another person might look at what he considers to be relevant evidence and draw a con-

---

edge (New York: Harvest Books, 1936); William P. McEwen, *The Problem of Social-Scientific Knowledge* (Totowa, N.J.: The Bedminster Press, 1963); F. S. C. Northrop, *The Logic of the Sciences and the Humanities* (Cleveland, O.: The World Publishing Co., Meridian Books, 1959); Karl R. Popper, *The Logic of Scientific Discovery* (New York: Science Editions, 1953); Anatol Rapaport, *Operational Philosophy* (New York: Science Editions, 1953); Hans Reichenbach, *The Rise of Scientific Philosophy* (Berkeley and Los Angeles: University of California Press, 1963); Arnold M. Rose, "Sociology and the Study of Values," *The British Journal of Sociology*, Vol. VII, No. 1, 1956, pp. 1–17; Herbert A. Simon, *op. cit.;* W. Stark, *The Sociology of Knowledge* (Glencoe, Ill.: The Free Press, 1958).

[20] Simon, *op. cit.*

[21] This statement implies nothing about whether the chooser is conscious or not conscious of the values which guide his choices. Nor does it exclude random choices (e.g., made on the basis of flipping a coin). In this case a decision would have been made, on the basis of some value premise(s), that a random choice was good or at least satisfactory. A preference would have been exercised in favor of random choice and against other possible bases for choice.

[22] Churchman, *op. cit.*, p. 14.

[23] E. G., Richard Rudner, "Value Judgments in the Acceptance of Theories" in Frank, *op. cit.*, p. 33; Hutchison, *op. cit.*, pp. 53–59; Arnold Rose, *op. cit.*, pp. 9–11.

clusion about whether to accept or reject a proposition, a third person might decide which particular propositions to include in a larger scheme of propositions).

DECISIONS MADE IN THE RESEARCH PROCESS

Consider some of the decisions facing a person who is considering an investigation of something. He must decide (or must have decided at some point), first of all, whether to study something at all or not. If he decides to study something, he must decide what to study—i.e., he must exercise a preference in favor of a particular problem from among all possible problems that might have been studied. Having decided upon a general subject area for study, the investigator must choose certain concepts and definitions from among all possible concepts and definitions in terms of which to think. His choices at this stage would probably have an influence on the decisions as to which dimensions or aspects of a problem area are considered and which ignored.

The investigator must also choose a general method of carrying out his study, to adopt some "way of knowing" in preference to others. McEwen, in his *The Problem of Social-Scientific Knowledge,* suggests a number of different "ways of knowing" from among which a choice could be made:

1. "dogmatic authoritarianism" (something is taken to be absolutely true because some "authority" says so. Or, closely related to this, someone might take something to be true if there is common agreement that it is true or if it is by custom regarded as true.)

2. "mysticism" (truth is established by mystical appeal to intuitive feeling.)

3. "naive pragmatism" (something is taken to be true which has desirable practical consequences.)

4. "naive sense-impression" (that is true which is self-evident through sense-perceptions.)

5. "pure rationalism" (truth is to be established by reasoning, by logical deduction from self-evident premises.)

6. "pure empiricism" (truth is that which is directly observed under controlled conditions.)

7. "narrower operationalism" (knowledge is gained by reducing concepts to the physical manipulations of the investigator and verification through measurement of observable data under controlled laboratory conditions.)

8. "broader operationalism" (knowledge is viewed as "a system of reasonably acceptable constructs *about* observable experience" arrived at by constructing "reliable hypotheses about observable data in terms of a coherent system of explanatory and/or predictive generalizations which have causal implications that can be verified to various degrees of probability.") [24]

While McEwen's categories are arbitrary, perhaps overlapping (how different is "pure empiricism" from "narrower operationalism"?), and not exhaustive of the possibilities,[25] they do suggest a number of disparate orientations toward knowledge that an investigator might decide upon which would then mold his

---

[24] McEwen, *op. cit.,* pp. 63–132.

[25] For other views on orientations toward knowledge see Churchman's discussion of "Decision Methods of Science," Churchman, *op. cit.,* pp. 339–356; also Reichenbach, *op. cit.,* "The Search for Certainty and the Rationalistic Conception of Knowledge," pp. 27–49, "The Empiricist Approach: Success and Failure," pp. 74–94, "Predictive Knowledge," pp. 229–249, and "The Functional Conception of Knowledge," pp. 252–275; also Cohen and Nagel, *op. cit.,* on bases for beliefs, pp. 193–196.

general methodological approach to his problem.[26] One would not expect that someone whose preferences inclined him, say, toward "dogmatic authoritarianism" would conduct an inquiry in the same way as a person with a preference for "pure empiricism." The "pure empiricist" would be unlikely to go after knowledge in the hypothetico-deductive manner of the "broader operationalist." We would not expect the "dogmatic authoritarian," the "pure empiricist," and the "broader operationalist" to arrive at the same body of "truth."

If the inquirer has decided upon his problem and upon a general method for approaching it, has he now made all of the decisions necessary for determining his behavior throughout his inquiry? The answer to this question would seem to be negative. Suppose, for example, the researcher is a "dogmatic authoritarian." Would he not have to decide who are the relevant authorities? If he decides that there is more than one relevant authority and if they happen not to agree among themselves, he must decide on which one to follow or on some way of assigning weights to their various opinions. If he is a "pure rationalist" who approaches knowledge as a problem of logical deduction from self-evident premises, must he not decide which propositions are self-evident and which of these decided-upon, self-evident propositions are relevant to serve as premises for his deductions? And must he not decide upon the rules of the game for making his deductions (i.e., decide upon which rules

of logic are applicable to his problem)?[27]

If the investigator's chosen orientation to knowledge is such that observation is demanded as all or part of the process of acquiring knowledge, he is confronted with a number of additional choices. He must decide what to observe, how much observation is sufficient, and precisely which of all possible data about the observed phenomena are to be collected and which ignored.[28] He must decide whether to make his observations under controlled or uncontrolled conditions, in laboratory or in field settings. He must decide whether he will collect data using a questionnaire technique, through interviews, psychological tests, participant observation, by reading existing documents or by some combination of these and/or other techniques. Having collected some data, the investigator must decide on a way to describe what he has found (i.e., he must choose to use a language, a set of terms or concepts which may or may not have been encompassed in the language or concepts he has already adopted), he must decide how, if at all, he will classify his data, and he must decide which, if any, analyses he will perform on his data.

If the investigator has not merely set out to observe things willy-nilly, but rather has begun with a set of concepts to guide observations, he must not only have decided on which concepts but also he is faced with the decision of whether he will admit only observable (i.e., operational) concepts in his scheme or whether he will allow abstract unob-

---

[26] These general orientations to knowledge no doubt play a role also in the decision to accept or reject a proposition as true. Discussion of this point will follow below.

[27] Most deductive reasoning is probably not preceded by a painstaking consideration of the question "what are the rules of reasoning that are applicable?" Nevertheless a decision that some rules are appropriate and others not (i.e., of what constitutes "right reasoning") will have been made implicitly if not explicitly. Brief discussions of logics may be found in Rapaport, *op. cit.*, pp. 39–49 and in Reichenbach, *op. cit.*, pp. 215–228. An extensive discussion is available in Cohen and Nagel, *op. cit.*, pp. 3–187.

[28] Prior decisions may have partially or completely determined these choices, of course.

servable concepts also. If he allows for the latter, then, in order to carry out observations, he must decide on some way of connecting up, of making a jump between, his theoretically postulated abstract concepts on the one hand and some operationally defined things which can be directly observed on the other hand.[29] In an empirical study of our own, for example, it was necessary to decide on a way to bridge the gap between an abstract definition of values on the one hand and some specific things that could be observed in the body of literature to be studied on the other hand. This required making some choices. Or consider the well known Argyris model in which he reasons, on the basis of some assumptions about individuals and about formal organizations, that administrative organizations frustrate their participants.[30] Following Argyris' reasoning, organizational participants logically should exhibit behaviors which are common frustration responses. For example, on the basis of Argyris' model and assertions about frustration responses from clinical psychology one might expect organizational participants to be apathetic and/or to exhibit aggressions toward the organization. If this statement was taken as an hypothesis to be tested, how would "apathy" or "aggression" be observed? How would an investigator know when he was seeing concrete manifestations of these abstractions? He would have to make some decisions that *some specific observable behaviors* are indications of apathy and aggression and that others are not, otherwise he could not collect meaningful data. It may be worthwhile to point out that the decisions made at this point (e.g., whether dropping a wrench in a machine is or is not aggres-

sion, whether stomping the floor is or is not aggressive behavior, whether making errors in filling out a form is or is not aggressive, whether telling the boss to go to hell is or is not aggressive) could be of extreme importance in determining the way the test of the hypothesis turns out.

If the investigator formulates hypotheses to be tested, he must make a decision as to how to arrive at them. Is he to get his hypotheses by drawing inferences inductively from observations? If so, which observations, made how, under what conditions? Does he develop them as a product of pure imagination? Does he develop them through use of a deductive system in which they are deduced from axioms or postulates? If so, where do the axioms or postulates come from? How are they chosen?

No implication is intended to the effect that each of the decisions discussed is completely independent of all the others. If, for example, "mysticism" is decided upon as a general approach to knowledge, automatically a whole series of decisions is ruled out having to do with observation and data collection. The mystic simply does not make observations or collect data. Also it should not be inferred that the decisions referred to up to this point are necessarily made in the order in which they have been considered. The point is simply that the kinds of choices or decisions that have been indicated here, as well as perhaps others, are unavoidable in carrying out any investigation, that these choices are *not* determined by adherence to a vague something called "scientific method," and that, therefore, the investigator's results are necessarily conditioned by the value premises (i.e., by his conceptions of what

---

[29] A reasonably lucid discussion of this point may be found in Northrup, *op. cit.,* "Epistemic Correlations and Operational Definitions," pp. 119–132.

[30] Chris Argyris, *Personality and Organization* (New York: Harper and Brothers, 1957).

is good or bad, of what is proper or improper, appropriate or inappropriate, etc.) he employs in making these choices.

DECISIONS TO ACCEPT OR REJECT A PROPOSITION AS TRUE

The decision to accept or reject a proposition as a reasonable representation of the truth may be the final step in the investigative process. However, it may be made independently, as indicated earlier. It is discussed separately as a matter of convenience. The decision made at this point is dependent upon a number of other decisions, each of which is made on the basis of factual and value premises.

Phillip Frank, in the *Validation of Scientific Theories,* has suggested that there may be a number of reasons for accepting a scientific theory:

1. agreement with observations
2. simplicity
3. compatibility of the theory with theories that have been advanced to account for observable phenomena outside its field
4. fitness of the theory to be generalized
5. compatibility of the theory with daily life experience
6. fitness of the theory to support moral behavior [31]

No doubt all of Frank's reasons as well as a multitude of others have been advanced at one time or another as criteria for accepting a factual proposition. What is of concern here is a choice of criteria for establishing the truth or falsity of propositions. It would seem that the criteria one uses for accepting or rejecting propositions as true are very much dependent upon one's general orientation to knowledge, on whether one is inclined toward "dogmatic authoritarianism," "pure rationalism," "broader operationalism," etc. The person who believes that something is true because some "authority" said so, need look no further for general criteria of truth. He has adopted a criterion. The "pure rationalist" likewise has his general criterion of truth— that is true which is logically deduced from self-evident premises. For the "broader operationalist" the general criterion would be verification of hypotheses through observation. In other words, the same considerations which guide the steps in an investigative process [32] also guide one's choice of general criteria for accepting a proposition as factual. But just as these considerations do not completely determine all subsequent choices involved in an investigative process, so also they do not determine all decisions involved in accepting a proposition as factual. Suppose, for example, a criterion of empirical verification (i.e., of agreement with observations) is adopted. This immediately throws the investigator back to a consideration of all of the factors having to do with observation which we have already discussed (i.e., deciding what and how much to observe, under what conditions, using what procedures, etc.). In addition, it would be necessary to decide what level of attainment on the criterion is satisfactory, on how closely the proposition would have to agree with observations before one would be willing to accept it. If a probabilistic verification is being made such that one can say that the probability is

---

[31] Phillip G. Frank, "The Variety of Reasons for the Acceptance of Scientific Theories" in Frank (ed.), *op. cit.,* pp. 13–26.

[32] One reason for conducting an investigation, of course, may be to provide information for making the acceptance decision.

.95 or .75 or .99 or whatever that the proposition and the observation are in agreement, then a decision must be made as to the probability level that is good enough (in other words, to decide on the degree of uncertainty that will be accepted).[33]

Our discussion of this point has been framed in terms of a single general criterion of selection. But suppose the decision is made to use more than one criterion for judging the acceptability of a proposition as reasonably true. The investigator might wish, say, to assess it on the basis of agreement with observations *and* on the basis of its compatibility with some other propositions which, for some reason(s), are already accepted. Any such use of multiple criteria necessitates additional decisions. It would have to be decided whether to combine the individual criteria somehow into a common scale which measured acceptability or to treat them as individual constraints each of which independently must be met. If the former course is chosen, deciding on what amount of one criterion is to be treated as equivalent to a certain amount of the other is necessary. In other words, a decision would be required on how to trade off measured amounts on the individual criteria against each other and then another decision would be required on a minimally acceptable level on the combined criterion. If, on the other hand, the investigator chooses to treat the several criteria as independent constraints which must be met, then he must decide on a minimally acceptable level of attainment that must be met on each of them.

Churchman's conclusion on the verification problem is to the point:

The discussion has shown that there are multiple choices that must be made in testing [hypotheses], and none of these can be 'routinely' prescribed. Hypothesis —and theory-testing are delicate operations, and as yet in the history of science we have no very clear ideas how they should be performed. This is so, despite the many tests and manuals on testing hypotheses and the voluminous discussions in professional philosophy on "inductive" methods.[34]

DECIDING WHETHER A PROPOSITION IS RELEVANT FOR INCLUSION IN A BODY OF PROPOSITIONS

There is still a third area where value-influenced decisions may have to be made—namely, in the selection of certain propositions for inclusion in a collection of propositions. The problem of deciding which of the propositions accepted as true to a satisfactory degree and/or with a satisfactory probability is also relevant for the purpose at hand arises, for example, when compiling a textbook on a subject. The author of a text on organizational behavior would have to decide which of all the propositions he accepts as correct are significant for conveying an understanding of organizational behavior and which are not. Similarly, the developer of a theory about some phenomenon would have to decide on relevant propositions. Scott distinguishes between types of organization theories partly on the basis of the different aspects of organizations which are treated in the propositions which the theorists include as relevant.[35] Or one might have to decide on a body of relevant propositions to guide future research.

The point is that there are occasions for making decisions about the relevance

---

[33] For a view that no verification, even probabilistic verification, is possible, see Popper, *op. cit.*

[34] Churchman, *op. cit.*, p. 78. The discussion to which he refers occupies pp. 71–78.

[35] William G. Scott, "Organization Theory: an Overview and Appraisal," *Academy of Management Journal*, April 1961, pp. 7–28.

of propositions as well as for making decisions about their correctness. All propositions accepted as correct do not automatically find their way into future theories, textbooks, etc. Whether to include them or not requires an additional decision which, like all other decisions, necessarily rests on value-premises. Since much, perhaps most, of what passes for knowledge about phenomena appears in the form of collections of propositions (e.g., multi-propositioned theories, textbooks, etc.) rather than in the form of individually presented propositions, the criteria of relevance used in devising these assemblages would seem to be important mediating factors in determining the content of received positive knowledge in a field.

Ways in Which and Points at Which Values Enter into Normative Administrative Theory

Many of the considerations relevant to this section of the paper have been dealt with at various points in the preceding analysis. Much of what is said here, then, will be simply a pulling together of things which have already been examined.

Normative theories have been defined as those which deal with prescriptions and/or evaluations.[36] Prescribing something implies that the something prescribed is valued in its own right and/or that it contributes toward something else which is valued. An evaluation of something as good or bad, desirable or undesirable, and the like implies that the something in itself is valued positively or negatively and/or that it contributes to or detracts from something else that

is valued. In other words, all prescriptive statements and all evaluative statements are based on values (as we have already seen). Furthermore, they are based on *specific* values. Adoption of *different* values may produce *different* prescriptions and *different* evaluations.

In addition, all prescriptive and evaluative statements except those dealing with phenomena valued in their own right (i.e., except ultimate ends) are not only value based and value specific but also are knowledge based and knowledge specific. If someone says "do X because it leads to A" he is advocating "doing X" not only because he values A but also because he makes the *factual assumption* that X leads to A. Given the value A with a different factual assumption, say, "X does not lead to A," the prescription "do X" may no longer be made.

Furthermore, as was shown earlier in the paper, knowledge or factual assumptions are themselves value based and value specific. Adoption of different values may produce different decisions in the proposition generating research process as well as different decisions as to whether to accept or reject a proposition as true and different decisions as to whether a factual proposition accepted as true should also be accepted as relevant for a particular purpose.

In short, *all values which underlie factual propositions also underlie normative statements based on those factual propositions.* Consequently, our entire discussion of how and at what points values get into, or undergird, knowledge may be taken also as a discussion of *some* of the ways and *some* of the points at which values get into normative propositions. Whatever values influenced the development of and acceptance of the positive

---

[36] For convenience, the discussion is conducted in terms of prescriptions and positive values. It should be recognized that the discussion applies equally to proscriptions and negative values.

propositions which a normative administrative theorist embeds, explicitly or implicitly, in his work also indirectly influence his prescriptive and evaluative statements.

Apart from the values which enter into normative theory through the knowledge content it embodies, other values enter in as things valued not in an instrumental sense but in an ultimate or independent sense. This raises questions. Where does an administrative theorist get the independent values he brings into his theory and what are they? What are the goals toward which he prescribes action and in terms of which he evaluates the goodness or badness of action? Answers to these questions are not always easy to come by. It is true that in the body of normative administrative theory which we think of as "management science" or "operations research" we find explicit statements of the values or objectives or constraints which are taken to be relevant. The nature of these models demands that the value assumptions or the function(s) to be optimized be spelled out. These models say, in effect, "If you want to attain goal A, and if x, y, and z are true, do R." It is clear that the goal or value used as the criterion of effectiveness in the model is A. Unfortunately, in a much larger portion of the body of literature which we are referring to as normative administrative theory, there are few explicit statements of the values which guided the selection of prescriptions or which served as evaluative criteria. It is, in addition, seldom clear in either the management science literature or in the more amorphous normative administrative theory literature just where the particular values incorporated in the model or theory came from or why they were selected. Nonetheless, it is a matter of logical necessity that the values be there, regardless of whether or not we can identify them explicitly

and regardless of whether or not we know where they came from or why particular values were chosen by the theorist.

Forms in Which Values Are Reflected in Theory

Values need not, and typically do not, show up in positive theories in any recognizable fashion. There is nothing to prevent the theorist from disclosing the values which guided his choices, at least insofar as he is aware of what these values were. But the form of the theory requires nothing more than that he state positive propositions. To the extent that the theorist does not choose to explicitly disclose the values which guided his choices, they will be reflected in positive theory only in that some factual propositions will appear and others will not. Since values need not appear in positive theory in any overt sense, trying to determine the value content of theories of this type by examining the theories would be, at best, an extremely demanding operation, perhaps even an impossible one.

Normative theories, on the other hand, necessarily show at least some values overtly. Since, by definition, normative theories deal with prescriptions and/or evaluations at least the phenomena prescribed and/or evaluated are known. When the theorist says "do X" or "Y is bad" the reader knows at least that the theorist is favorably disposed toward X and negatively disposed toward Y. He does not necessarily know why X and Y are valued in this fashion, nor can he necessarily distinguish instrumental from independent values. It might also be pointed out that since prescriptions and evaluations reflect not only values but also the factual propositions which a theorist holds to be true and relevant, by being able to pick out the phenomena prescribed and/or evaluated, it is perhaps indirectly possible to pick up at least one aspect of the influence of the values underlying the factual propositions which, in turn, underlie the prescriptions and/or evaluations. To the extent that the normative theorist chooses to disclose his independent values by explicit assertion, by giving reasons for his prescriptive statements, or by justifying his evaluations, then a larger proportion of the value content of the normative theory is made overt. Because at least some of the value content in normative theories must appear in overt form, empirical study of at least some of the values in this type of theory would seem to be feasible.

Concluding Remarks

We have attempted to draw a clear distinction between positive and normative theory and to show that the two types of theory have different structures and purposes. We have also spelled out the ways in which values enter into the two types of theory. In the case of positive theory, what is taken to be fact is very much a function of the values adopted as decision premises in the fact generating process. In the case of norma-

tive theory, the particular prescriptions or evaluations offered are a function not only of the value-influenced facts embraced by the theorist but also of the particular independent values the theorist adopts as ends of action (i.e., as objectives) or as evaluative criteria. Finally, we briefly commented on the forms in which values are expressed in the two types of theory.

Because of the very important role played by values in both types of administrative theory, it would seem to behoove us as students of and as critical commentators on administrative theory to begin serious study in this area. As of now, the value basis of both positive and normative theories in our field remains virtually virgin territory for empirical study. In part, this is no doubt because this is a difficult area to work in. But it is no doubt also in part because we have not recognized the importance that values play in what we take to be knowledge and in the administrative actions we prescribe. It would also appear that if we are ever to deserve to be taken seriously as generators of knowledge about administration and as generators of prescriptions for administrative action we will have to devote some of our energies to spelling out the value bases of our theories much more explicitly than we have done in the past.

B

MANAGEMENT THEORY

3. The Operational School of Management: An Analysis

MANECK S. WADIA

A study of the history of management thought shows that a variety of disciplines have contributed to the ever increasing knowledge of management.[1] Engineers, economists, physical scientists, mathematicians, behavioral scientists, soldiers, politicians, professors, practitioners, and priests have all played a role in the development of administration,[2] both as a science and as an art.

Perhaps it is this varied genesis that has lead to the development of various schools of thought in management. This variety, in turn, has led scholars, especially in the past decade, to engage in a controversy over which school of thought has the right approach to management, which disciplines can contribute to management, what the proper scheme of classification is, and what should be included in and what excluded from the study of the nature and scope of management.

This controversy, in turn, has often led to the attitude that "If I have the right approach, then others may have the wrong approach." What is worse, it has sometimes led to the attitude that "*Since* I have the right approach, others *must* have the wrong approach." "Disagreement and controversy have almost reached the point where any theoretical

Reprinted from *Advanced Management Journal*, Vol. 32, No. 3 (July, 1967), pp. 26–34, with permission of the author and the publisher. Maneck S. Wadia is Professor of Management, Graduate School of Business and Economics, United States International University, San Diego, California.

This paper is partly based on the author's book entitled *The Nature and Scope of Management* (Chicago: Scott, Foresman and Company, 1966).

[1] John F. Mee, *Management Thought in a Dynamic Economy* (New York: New York University Press, 1963).

[2] The terms *management* and *administration* are used synonymously throughout.

light that has been generated has been overwhelmed by emotional heat." [3]

In the past decade, and especially since the publication of Professor Koontz's article,[4] the controversy over the various schools of thought has ranged far and wide, both among professors as well as practitioners. The controversy has crystallized around three major schools —the operational, the behavioral and the quantitative approaches to management. The operational school is accused by its critics of being outdated and is called the "traditionalist" approach; the behavioral scientists are ignored as "do gooders" by their critics; and the quantitative school is accused by its critics of generating the "new Taylorism."

This pointing of fingers and the "either-or" approach to various management schools stems partly from the fact that few scholars and practitioners are equally well qualified in more than one approach, to say nothing of being well qualified in all three. However, management is a vast field, and one need not find the various schools of thought mutually exclusive.

For all scholars and practitioners in the field of administration, the operational school offers some assets and some liabilities, as do the other approaches to management. Though there are some aspects one might reject, there are others of great significance and value. It is the objective of this article to analyze the framework of the operational school, and to further analyze the concept of functions and the concept of principles, on which this school is primarily based.

The Operational School

Define

The operational school views management as a process of applying various functions to the achievement of goals. It is this emphasis on functions that has led to the sobriquet "functional," for the operational school. Another name by which this school is often referred to is the "universalists" approach to management. This stems from the insistence of the adherents of the operational school that management has a number of principles that can be universally applied.

This school often refers to the human element and the environmental aspects of management, but this is usually lip service rather than an integral part of the operational approach.[5] In his article,[6] Professor Koontz, a strong advocate of the operational school, lists seven "fundamental beliefs" on which "this school bases its approach." The first refers to functions, the next five to principles, and the seventh to the environment, but only to say that it is not really essential to the operational school.

Basic Factors. Basically then, the operational approach looks upon management as the application of principles and functions to the achievement of goals. The approach is a systematic one and mainly involves viewing management as the operation of the factors diagrammatically presented in Figure 1.

As the diagram indicates, principles and policies apply to all the basic factors. Hence, one can have principles that apply to objectives, and to the various functions; and policies that are also ap-

[3] Waino W. Suojanen, "Management Theory: Functional and Evolutionary," *Academy of Management Journal,* VI (March 1963), 7.

[4] Harold Koontz, "The Management Theory Jungle," *Academy of Management Journal,* IV (December 1961), pp. 174–188.

[5] For further elaboration of this point, see Maneck S. Wadia, "Management and the Behavioral Sciences: A Conceptual Scheme," *California Management Review,* VIII (Fall, 1965), pp. 65–72.

[6] Koontz, *op. cit.,* p. 176.

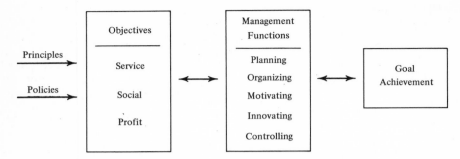

Figure 1. *Basic Factors in the Operational School.*

plicable to the various factors. Also, the objectives, functions and goal achievement are interrelated.

Various authors have expanded these basic factors. Some have added a greater variety of management functions. Others have applied the management functions to the organic functions of business—production, marketing and finance. There are others who add to these factors a rather miscellaneous category of "management techniques." These techniques range from the scientific method to operations research, but they are considered supplementary to the basic factors. These techniques are usually dealt with within the framework of one or more management functions, without in any way detracting from the belief of universally applicable principles.

The Functions of Management

The concept of management functions was first identified by the French industrialist Henri Fayol in 1916. He referred to five functions: planning, organizing, commanding, coordinating, and control-ling. In 1925, when Fayol's ideas were translated into English, the concept of management functions was transplanted to the United States, where it flourished and led to a variety of classifications. Mee has cited a list of examples that show how different authorities identify the various functions of management.[7]

Though there is disagreement over the grouping and classification of management functions, there is general agreement that certain management functions exist. As Simon has stated, scholars interested in managerial behavior are interested in management functions.[8] These functions, no matter what their variety and definitions, are concerned with the achievement of organizational purposes through human effort within the internal and external environmental of the organization.

The Process. The various functions of management, considered as a whole, make up the management process. Hence, planning, organizing, motivating, innovating, and controlling, considered separately, are management functions; when looked upon in their total approach to achieving objectives, they form a man-

---

[7] Mee, *op. cit.*, pp. 56–57.

[8] Herbert A. Simon, "Approaching the Theory of Management," in Harold Koontz, ed., *Toward a Unified Theory of Management* (New York: McGraw-Hill Book Co., 1964), p. 77.

agement process. The management process is determined by the functions, and though "there are some slight differences of opinion among the authorities, the instructors, and the practitioners on the breakdown of the subfunctions and their identifying terms, the nature of the process seems to have general agreement." [9]

The management process often has been misinterpreted by its advocates and its critics alike either as a sequence of functions that follow one another in a particular order or as a group of separate and unrelated functions. Some of the literature implies that the management process, whatever its functions, is concerned primarily with each function as a separate entity and concerned very little with its relationship to other functions or to the internal and external environment of the organization. These misinterpretations are due to the fact that the concept of functions has been borrowed from the social sciences without due regard for the theoretical complexities involved. Some scholars either fail to discuss what the concept involves or give an oversimplified definition such as "function is any distinct phase of work." [10]

The Interrelationship of Functions. Radcliffe-Brown, an eminent anthropologist, has taken a complicated but more realistic view of this concept. To him, the concept of function

involves the notion of a structure consisting of a set of relations among unit entities, the continuity of the structure being maintained by a life-process made up of the activities of the constituent units . . . By the definition here offered "function" is the contribution which a partial ac-

tivity makes to the total activity of which it is a part. The function of a particular social usage is the contribution it makes to the total social life as the functioning of the total social system. Such a view implies that a social system (the total social structure of a society together with the totality of social usages, in which that structure appears and on which it depends for its continued existence) has a certain kind of unity, which we may speak of as a functional unity.[11]

A management function is thus not a separate entity but an integral part of a larger entity made up of various functions that are related to one another as well as to the larger entity. Hence, as Gestalt psychologists have pointed out, the total is different from the sum of its parts. Only when the concept of function is viewed in this light does the management process emerge as truly dynamic.

Figure 2 shows one image of the management process created by an improper understanding of the concept of functions.

Planning

Organizing

Motivating

Innovating

Controlling

Figure 2.

Figure 3, on the other hand, shows the more realistic image of the man-

[9] Mee, *op. cit.,* p. 56.

[10] Ralph Currier Davis, *Industrial Organization and Management* (New York: Harper & Brothers, 1957), p. 23.

[11] A. R. Radcliffe-Brown, "Concept of Function in Social Science," *American Anthropologist,* XXXVII (July–September 1935).

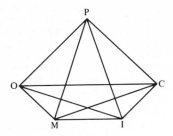

Figure 3.

without suggesting that these functions are unimportant in the management process.

The concepts of management function and management process have been most useful in developing an identifiable discipline for study and research. No scholar or practitioner has questioned that managers perform certain functions and that these functions are performed in a variety of organizations and at different managerial levels.

agement process created by the more dynamic approach to the concept of functions as expounded by Radcliffe-Brown and further elaborated by Leighton.[12] The history of social sciences teaches us not to look upon the sequence of activities as either completely random or rigidly predetermined. The process of management is a complex one, with varying degrees of interaction among the functions.

Mee has suggested that the concept of management process has lately come under strong criticism.[13] The management process, through its functions, is but the framework within which one may study the various aspects of management, however. What has come under stronger criticism is not the framework but the structure that has been built onto it and the principles that have been derived from it.

One can criticize a rigorous, step-by-step approach to planning without rejecting the function of planning; one can reject a nonempirical approach to organizing without rejecting the function of organizing; one can criticize different approaches to motivating and innovating

Management Principles

The concept of management principles has generated greater controversy [14] than the concept of management functions. Two of the firmest expressions on this controversy have been made by Simon and by Koontz and O'Donnell.

Simon is critical of principles for being contradictory. He believes that for almost every principle one can find an equally plausible and acceptable contradictory principle, leading to opposite organzational recommendations, without any indication which is the proper principle to apply under what conditions.[15] He then proceeds to cite examples.

Koontz and O'Donnell believe that even with our present state of knowledge, we have principles of management. They state a number of these principles in their book, *Principles of Management,* and write that by following these principles the manager will be in a better position to achieve his goals. "Even though the principles as stated in this book are not always established as com-

---

[12] Alexander H. Leighton, *Human Relations in a Changing World* (New York: E. P. Dutton & Co., Inc., 1949), pp. 156–161.

[13] Mee, *op. cit.,* pp. 87–92.

[14] For a more detailed analysis, see Maneck S. Wadia, "Management Principles: Fact or Fallacy," *Pittsburgh Business Review,* XXXIV (October 1964), pp. 1–3.

[15] Herbert A. Simon, *Administrative Behavior* (2d ed.; New York: Macmillan Company, 1959), p. 20.

plete causal propositions, the reader should interpret them as such. They can always be read in the sense that if this or that is done, the result will be more efficient and effective attainment of objectives." [16]

Definition. These two approaches to principles of management represent two camps, which at a cursory examination seem to be irreconcilable. However, both camps have some elements in common. Thus, both agree on a need for principles in management, and both agree that principles are not laws since we are dealing with a social science rather than a physical science.

Perhaps both camps would even agree to accept a definition similar to the following: "A principle is a fundamental truth which explains certain phenomena. If certain conditions are held to be true and the new phenomena are in accordance with those which the principle covers, then knowledge of the principle will make it possible to predict the behavior of factors in the new situation." [17]

Similar definitions are also provided by others.

The main problem, in spite of these common agreements, is the fact that in management it is well nigh impossible to have the same situation repeat itself. Hence, prediction is difficult. Though the definition and approach to principles may be acceptable to both camps, the pro-principle camp has, in most cases, failed to give any empirical evidence of being able to predict behavior.

Facts vs Generalizations. If a principle is a "general statement" as defined by many scholars, in the pro-principles camp, then just about any statement can be a principle. Thus, why is statement 1 not considered a principle?

1. "In every organization it must be decided how many subordinates a superior can manage." [18]

And why is statement 2 considered a principle?

2. "Authority should be delegated to the extent and in a way necessary for the accomplishment of results expected." [19]

Another problem with principles, as presently formulated by most management scholars, is the tendency to make generalizations before the facts have been studied. "The task of developing business theory scientifically is, first, the recording of facts; second, the arrangement of these facts into series and relationships; third, the development of generalizations which can be safely made only on the basis of such recorded facts." [20] One of the major reasons why management has not further developed as a science is because so far we have relied mainly on deductive logic whereas for a scientific point of view we need to utilize inductive logic. [21]

The overwhelming tendency among the pro-principle camp is to make generalizations, whether stated as principles

---

[16] Harold Koontz and Cyril O'Donnell, *Principles of Management: An Analysis of Managerial Functions* (3rd ed.; New York: McGraw-Hill Book Company, 1964), p. 6.

[17] Theo Haimann, *Professional Management* (Boston, Mass.: Houghton Mifflin Company, 1962), p. 11.

[18] Koontz and O'Donnell, *op. cit.,* p. 217.

[19] Koontz and O'Donnell, *op. cit.,* p. 386.

[20] Wallace B. Donham, "Essential Groundwork for a Broad Executive Theory," *Harvard Business Review,* Vol. 1, No. 1, October, 1922, p. 5.

[21] For further elaboration of this concept see: Maneck S. Wadia, "Management Education and the Behavioral Sciences," *Advanced Management,* Vol. 26, No. 9, September, 1961.

or not, without any real concern for empirical verification. In certain cases, even after the facts are available, the tendency is to maintain the generalizations as previously formulated. Thus, it is not uncommon to find a statement regarding the span of control, such as: "Students of management have found that this number is usually four to eight subordinates at the upper levels of organization and eight to fifteen or more at the lower levels." [22] This is followed by the statement that: "In a survey of a hundred large companies made by the American Management Association in 1951, the number of executives reporting to the president had as few as six or less subordinates." [23]

The first statement regarding numbers in the span of control does not in any factual way tell a manager who reads it what his span of control should be. Even the "facts" do not justify making such a statement. Empirically, there is no magic number. Yet, the tendency to generalize persists.

There are many conditions that affect this number, such as the nature of the work to be performed (for example, routine or creative), the type of subordinates one has (for example, well trained or untrained), the type of managerial leadership (for example, autocratic or democratic), the work place (for example, army or university), etc.

Before one comes up with a number, one would have to isolate and study the variables that affect the span of control. One must, however, credit the "span of management" principle for taking into consideration that "the exact number will vary in each case with the complexity of the relationships supervised and

the ability and training of managers and subordinates." [24] The principles still do not aid in prediction, nor show any causal relationships. But unlike most other principles, it does tell us something about the environmental variables that affect the size of the span.

Principles and Policies. Principles provide certain general guides to action for managers. In this respect the principles of management are like business policies. Just as policies are prescribed guides for managerial action so as to aid in the achievement of organizational goals, so are the management principles. However, management principles are considered to have a broader application, from organization to organization, whereas policies are usually particularized for a given organization. It is because of this wide application of principles as guides, that one considers them to be universal.

Thus, for example, Professor Davis, one of the pioneers of the principles approach in management, considers statement 3 as one of the more "important business principles that are associated with the business objective."

3. "The objectives of the organization must be such as to command the confidence of the public and the company's personnel. Public relations, investor relations, labor relations, supplier relations, or any other business relations depend on confidence and an effective integration of interest." [25]

How does this statement 3 of a principle differ, from a scientific point of view (such as power for greater predictability or taking more pertinent variables into consideration, or cause

[22] Koontz and O'Donnell, *op. cit.,* p. 217.
[23] Koontz and O'Donnell, *op. cit.,* p. 217.
[24] Koontz and O'Donnell, *op cit.,* p. 386.
[25] Ralph Currier Davis, *The Fundamentals of Top Management* (New York: Harper & Brothers, 1951), p. 114.

and effect relationship), for a policy statement such as 4?

4. "The behavior of all employees must be such as to command the confidence of the public and fellow employees. Public relations, investor relations, labor relations, supplier relations, or any other business relations depend on the confidence in and the effectiveness of all employees."

Is statement 4 a principle? Why? Why not? What made statement 3 a principle? Was statement 3 any more of "a fundamental statement or general truth providing a guide to action" [26] than statement 4? In the realm of management, the pro-principle camp has not shown what distinguishes a principle from other "basic guides to action" [27] or policies, and from other general statements.

The Need for Principles. One should beware of rejecting all principles as entirely valueless. That would only make us fall into the trap that Ernest Dale fell into of rejecting principles and then developing "generalizations" and "criteria" [28] similar to principles. Undoubtedly, there is a need for guides and, as such, principles may be useful. There is a tendency, however, to give principles more credit than is due them under the present state of development and knowledge in the field of management. There is also a tendency to keep formulating principles *ad infinitum*.

The present analysis does not reject the need for principles nor does it question their existence as guides. However, the analysis does reject the notion, that principles, as presently developed in management, have predictive value, and that

they demonstrate a cause and effect relationship.

As the examples cited above show, the principles are broad generalizations, which do not tell us much about particular situations. Principles should, therefore, be given the status of general guides, the degree of their applicability depending upon the conditions under which they are applied. Under these circumstances, principles can become useful tools for managers.

Conclusion

The operational school is the most widely used approach to management training. It is especially useful in the training of neophytes. For those who are about to be initiated into the challenging field of management, the operational school provides a systematic approach to the field.

For the handling of routine managerial tasks, the functional approach dissects the managerial work into readily understandable and useful categories. The principles provide general guides and permit the neophyte manager to handle the day to day duties of his job with confidence.

By maintaining its philosophy of the basic factors of management, the operational school provides a continuing approach to the field. Without changing its base, it absorbs new elements as additional factors in its philosophy.

However, combined with these assets are certain liabilities that need to be recognized. There is little agreement on what the basic functions of management

---

[26] Definition of principle as provided by George R. Terry, *Principles of Management* (Homewood, Illinois: Richard D. Irwin, Inc., 1956), p. 21.

[27] Terry, *op. cit.,* p. 171.

[28] Ernest Dale, *The Great Organizers* (New York: McGraw-Hill Book Company, Inc., 1960).

are. They can, and do, range from one function to a dozen, creating not only semantical but also operational problems. It is also unfortunate that functions are often viewed as static, step by step approaches, rather than as dynamically interrelated.

Another liability is the tendency to give principles greater credit than is due them and to formulate principles *ad infinitum*. The very asset of the operational school in handling routine tasks at the lower levels of management, turns into a liability when handling the more analytical and creative aspects of management, especially at the higher managerial levels. The confidence this school generates often turns to overconfidence and stifles research.

In an effort to maintain the univer-sality of its philosophy, the operational school has tended to neglect the environmental and human variables so important to management. Because of the lack of empirical research in this approach, the operational school continues to remain a philosophy rather than a scientific theory.

The present analysis indicates that the various schools of management are not either completely valid nor completely invalid. Each school, whether old or new, has its liabilities as well as its assets. One can well conclude with Dean Inge that—

> There are two kinds of fools. One says, "This is old, therefore it is good." The other says, "This is new, therefore it is better."

4. Unification of Management Theory: A Pessimistic View

ORLANDO BEHLING

Management and managers have, from the time of the pioneering work of Henri Fayol and Frederick W. Taylor, been the subject of study by many different individuals working from many different points of view. Engineers, accountants, economists, psychologists, sociologists, and, most recently, mathematicians have all claimed a certain expertise in regard to the human activity called management. The work of those operating within these and other frameworks and the work of thoughtful practicing managers have culminated in the publication of hundreds of articles and books by dozens of authors, each one purporting to explain management or some facet of it.

Much of this work, however, has been destructive rather than constructive. As Professor Harold Koontz pointed out in his well-known article, "The Management Theory Jungle":

> . . . . the varied approaches to management theory have led to a kind of confused and destructive jungle warfare. Particularly in academic writings, the primary interests of many would-be cult leaders seems to be to carve out a distinct (and hence original) approach to management. To defend this originality, and

Reprinted from *Business Perspectives,* Vol. 3, No. 4 (Summer, 1967), pp. 4–9, with permission of the publisher. Orlando Behling is Associate Professor of Management Sciences, College of Commerce and Administration, Ohio State University.

thereby gain a place in posterity (or at least to gain a publication which will justify academic status or promotion), these writers seem to have become overly concerned with down rating and sometimes misrepresenting, what anyone else has said or thought or done.[1]

Many authorities in the field of management would agree that some discussions of the differing approaches to the subject of management have generated far more heat than illumination. Certainly much of the infighting which has characterized supposedly dispassionate evaluations of divergent ideas about management is of little credit to any of the participants.[2]

Given fairly general agreement on this point, Professor Koontz explicitly and a number of other authorities implicitly move on to a conclusion as to the source of the problem.[3] Professor Koontz states:

. . . these intellectual cults are not drawing greatly different inferences from the physical and cultural environment surrounding us. Why, then, have there been so many differences between them and why such a struggle, particularly among our academic brethren to obtain a place in the sun by denying the approaches of others? Like the widely differing and often contentious denominations of the Christian religion, all have essentially the same goals and deal with essentially the same world.

While there are many sources of the mental entanglement in the management theory jungle, the major ones are the following: The Semantics Jungle . . . . Differences in Definition of Management as a Body of Knowledge . . . . The

Misunderstanding of Principles . . . . The Inability or Unwillingness of Management Theorists to Understand Each Other.[4]

There is little doubt that many of the disputes among students of management could be resolved by the elimination of the problems cited in the preceding quotation. They exist and are very real and very important stumbling blocks in the path of those attempting to understand the process by which men manage. The identification of these problems has led to a movement toward interdisciplinary discussions among management theorists aimed at the eventual resolution of differences and the establishment of a single "Unified Theory of Management." [5] This activity is certainly a valuable one which offers great promise of improving mutual understanding among those who study management.

Implicit in such activity, however, is an idea which bears closer scrutiny. It appears that many individuals involved in such discussions believe that a unified theory of management is, in truth, a practical possibility. That is, that the differences among management theorists have no substantive basis or that such substantive differences as do exist may be readily resolved by presently available techniques.

It is the opinion of this author, however, that fundamental and inescapable substantive differences do exist among the various approaches to the study of management, that these differences are

---

[1] Harold Koontz, "The Management Theory Jungle," *Journal of the Academy of Management,* Vol. 4, No. 3, December, 1961, p. 176.

[2] For an interesting description of one series of incidents of this type, see Lyndall F. Urwick, "Have We Lost Our Way in the Jungle of Management Theory?" *Personnel,* Vol. 42, No. 3, May–June, 1965, pp. 8–18.

[3] Harold Koontz (ed.), *Toward a Unified Theory of Management* (New York: McGraw-Hill Book Company, 1964).

[4] Douglas McGregor, *The Human Side of Enterprise* (New York: McGraw-Hill Book Company, 1960), p. 177.

[5] Koontz, *Toward a Unified . . . , passim.*

practically unresolvable, and thus that a unified theory of management is an impossibility.

To understand the logic behind this statement it is necessary to examine in somewhat greater detail the nature of theories of management. First of all it must be recognized that the various theories of management are, for the most part, theories only in terms of a most generous definition of the word. Most of them represent loose collections of ideas which lack the rigorous specification of interrelationships required of a theory in most disciplines. The term will be used throughout this paper, however, because common practice in the field calls for them to be designated as theories and because they represent the closest approaches to theories available.

Second, it must be recognized that theories of management are, by and large, prescriptive rather than descriptive in nature. That is, the primary concern of theories is not with what is management, but rather with what management should be. This contention may appear to be a logical absurdity to those who have been taught that descriptive and prescriptive theories are intertwined, with the latter growing out of the former. Such is not the case with theories of management.

Theories of management, despite the protestations to the contrary of many authors, are generally not built on detailed· empirical observation of business organizations. Rather, they tend to be exercises in logical analysis, using general premises to arrive at specific rules governing the conduct of managers in specific situations. This process is made feasible, and in many ways desirable, by the overriding concern of management theorists with the improvement of the practice of management. Theories of management are oriented primarily toward the practitioner rather than towards those seeking an abstract understanding of the nature of the process. As such they can perform a valid function by providing not so much a description of what the individual manager will encounter in the business organization, but rather by providing the basis for a common set of expectations among managers who must interact within and among firms.

It might be said that theories of management function by creating their own reality within a firm. They are certainly inadequate if they fail to relate to the realities of the physical and social environment within which they must be applied, but their success or failure is, once such a level has been attained, dependent to a large degree on the extent to which they are accepted among interdependent managers.

Theories of management are all essentially similar in one respect. They all involve consideration of three basic areas: (a) the nature and purpose of the business firm; (b) the contribution the manager can and should make, given the nature of the business organization, to the accomplishment of its objectives; and (c) the tools and techniques which best serve the manager in making such a contribution.

The first of these areas is crucial in determining the form a given theory will take. The nature and purposes established as crucial for the business firm establish the tone and prescribe the way in which the other two areas will be treated.

Based upon the way the various theories treat the first area and to a lesser extent upon the way in which they handle the other two areas, it is possible to classify the theories into two basic categories. These categories are: (a) pragmatic theories—those concerned with the business firm and the manager as tools for the attainment of some tangible profit or service objective and (b) humanistic theories—those which, while generally recognizing the validity of profit and service objectives for the firm, hypothesize additional objectives for the firm which are considered to be co-equal with, or more important than, the profit or service objectives.

While it is obvious that any attempt to summarize in a few paragraphs the theories underlying literally dozens of books and articles will inevitably involve serious oversimplification, an attempt will be made in the following pages to outline the similarities and differences between the two classes of theories.

Before beginning this, however, it should be pointed out that while certain of the statements made in regard to the pragmatic and humanistic theories might lead the casual reader to believe that this differentiation is nothing more than a re-hash of Douglas McGregor's well known treatment of Theory X and Theory Y, there is a crucial difference.[6] The analysis developed here draws from essentially the same body of information as did that made by McGregor, but classification is made along an entirely different axis. While McGregor was concerned with managerial activities and beliefs as they reflect theories of human motivation, the pragmatic-humanistic analysis is concerned with these things as reflections of theories of management and of the nature and purpose of the business firm.

The Pragmatic Theories

The pragmatic theories are, in their various guises, dominant in thinking in most developed nations today. They in fact represent the mainstream of management thought from its earliest genesis as a discipline. In the United States, they derive primarily from the works of Frederick W. Taylor in terms of historical development and from those of Henri Fayol in terms of intellectual debt. It should be noted, however, as will be demonstrated later, that this category includes much of the teachings of the self-styled arch-enemies of the traditional or managerial functions approach, the human relationists.

In regard to the nature and purpose of the business organization, implicit in the writings derived from pragmatic theories is the following idea:

The business firm as a social and economic unit exists and its existence is sanctioned by organized society not because it represents the flowering of any "herd instinct" or other innate gregarious tendency of human beings, but rather because it has proven itself an effective means for performing the basic economic functions of creating and distributing goods and services and providing profits to its owners.

There is considerable disagreement among the groups which espouse the pragmatic approach as to whether profit or the provision of service to the consumer should be viewed as the primary goal of the firm. Many writers, drawing from traditional and legal views of the business firm, consider the firm to exist primarily as a means of providing financial return in the form of profit to its owners. Others, emphasizing the right and very real ability of society acting either through governmental action or the marketplace to modify or destroy firms, industries, and economic systems which fail to serve in its best interest, consider the primary goal of the firm to be the creation and distribution of salable values. Profit, in these frameworks, represents not the *raison d'etre* of the firm, but rather a payment which is made to ensure the cooperation of a group (those whose investments provide the firm's

---

[6] McGregor, *passim.*

capital) without which the organization cannot continue to function effectively.

The theoretical implications of a choice between profit and service objectives for a firm appear great, particularly in regard to the functions of top or administrative management. Examination of differences in recommendations for management practice, however, indicates that the divergence may be less significant than it appears at first glance. The "principles of management" and the other recommendations made in profit-oriented writings and in service-oriented writings are essentially identical, particularly in regard to the middle and operative supervision levels of management. For our purposes, at least at the present level of development of these ideas, the limited differences found are not crucial.

The second basic idea of the pragmatic theories is concerned with what a manager should do within or for the business organization. Implicit in most writings derived from these theories is the idea that the differentiation of management positions varies only in degree from the operative specialization first discussed several hundred years ago by Adam Smith. Stated formally, this implicit idea of the pragmatic theories says:

The success of a business firm is measured in terms of its accomplishment of the profit or service objective established for it. In order that this objective may be accomplished certain activities must be performed which directly create or distribute salable values. Other activities which do not directly create or distribute salable values must also be performed to channel and direct operative activities toward the accomplishment of organizational goals. These channeling and direct-ing activities are what we call management and it is through their performance that the manager makes his contribution to the accomplishment of the objective of the firm.

Again, as was true in regard to the statement of the objectives of the firm, there is some disagreement within the pragmatic camp as to the proper way to name or classify these channeling and directing activities. Dozens of classification systems have been developed by various writers with varying degrees of agreement and disagreement in division points and in labels attached to the categories. Ralph Currier Davis, for example, states that the "organic functions of management" are planning, organizing, and controlling.[7] William H. Newman discusses the "basic processes of administration" which he considers to be planning, organizing, assembling resources, supervising, and controlling.[8] The United States Air Force lists five "functions of management" which are planning, organizing, directing, coordinating, and controlling.[9] Again, however, examination of writings in the field based on these different classification systems reveals only relatively minor conflicts in recommendations as to the way in which the manager's job should be performed.

The third basic aspect of the pragmatic theories concerns the tools and techniques most useful to the manager in the performance of his function within the firm. Here, in contrast to the two previous areas, we must deal with two somewhat differing premises. The first of these, which is associated with the classical, traditional or management function ap-

---

[7] Ralph Currier Davis, *Industrial Organization and Management* (3rd ed.; New York: Harper and Brothers, 1957), p. 54.

[8] William H. Newman, *Administrative Action* (2nd ed.; Englewood Cliffs, New Jersey: Prentice-Hall, Inc., 1963), pp. 4–5.

[9] Department of the Air Force, *The Management Process*, AFM 25-1, September, 1954, pp. 2–3, 6–7, as reprinted in Fremont A. Shull, Jr. (ed.), *Selected Readings in Management* (Homewood, Illinois: Richard D. Irwin, Inc., 1958), pp. 68–70.

proach to management may be stated as follows:

Since the manager cannot always personally oversee the activities of operative employees or subordinate managers, he must make his contribution to the firm by providing an environment which will effectively channel and direct employee efforts toward the objectives of the firm. This environment is physical in nature, involving the tools and conditions of work, and is also administrative, because by a careful structuring of authority and responsibility relationships within the firm the manager can substantially increase the effectiveness of operative efforts.

This idea is clear in the writings of all, or almost all, of the early advocates of scientific management as well as in those of present-day classically- or traditionally-oriented students of management. The major difference between the two is a reflection of a gradual shift in emphasis from an early concern with the physical environment of work toward concentration on the administrative structuring of authority and responsibility relationships, the major area of present-day interest.

The second assumption in regard to the appropriate tools of management is made by the human relations subgroup within the pragmatic camp. While accepting the basic validity of the pragmatic assumptions about the nature of the firm and the role of the manager in it, they vary from their classically-oriented brethren in regard to the nature of the tools which are considered most effective in making the manager's contribution to the firm.

A number of the early classical prag-

matists were apparently aware that the physical and administrative work environments were not the only determinants of the effectiveness of operative employee contributions to the firm. Mary Parker Follett, for example, anticipated much of what was later to be known as human relations.[10] In terms of practical impact, however, the human relations variant of the pragmatic theory grew from a series of studies begun in the late 1920's under the direction of Professor Elton Mayo of Harvard. These were, of course, the famous Hawthorne Studies.[11] These studies indicated that many of the techniques advocated by the followers of Frederick W. Taylor were, at least in certain situations, less effective in channeling human effort toward organizational goals than were others derived from a more complete understanding of the process of human motivation. Specifically it was discovered that the physical work environment was often less important in this respect than were the attitudes of supervisors as perceived by the workers. It was also demonstrated that a wide range of human needs affected the way in which various supervisory techniques influenced the performance of employees.

The basic thinking of the human relations-oriented pragmatists in regard to the appropriate tools for channeling human behavior toward organizational goals may be expressed as follows:

The manager makes his contribution to the firm by providing an environment which will channel and direct the efforts of operative employees and subordinate managers toward the objectives of the firm. The most important aspects of this

---

[10] See Harold F. Smiddy and Lionel Naum, "Evolution of a 'Science of Managing' in America," *Management Science,* Vol. 1, No. 1, October, 1954, pp. 1–31, as reprinted in Fremont A. Shull, Jr. (ed.), *Selected Readings in Management* (Homewood, Illinois: Richard D. Irwin, Inc., 1958), pp. 10–41.

[11] F. J. Roethlisberger and W. J. Dickson, *Management and the Worker* (Cambridge: Harvard University Press, 1939).

environment are neither physical nor administrative. Rather they are socio-psychological in nature, involving the entire spectrum of human motivation. An ideal environment is one which demonstrates to the individual that he may satisfy his dominant needs only by contributing to the over-all objectives of the firm, as viewed by his supervisor.

This idea is clearly seen in the following statement by Carl Hayel:

These arguments held that human relations had been a neglected factor in productivity; that too much attention had been given to money incentives and to impersonally engineered standards of performance; that management in general and supervisors in particular had to be much more concerned with "what made people tick," with problems of informal organizations in any working group, and with problems of communication, participation and understanding.[12]

These techniques recommended by the human relationists are far different from those espoused by the classicists and by their offspring specializing in operations research and other quantitative techniques. Yet the basic similarities of concepts of the nature and purposes of the firm and of the role of the manager in it reduce these differences to relatively minor disagreements among like-thinkers. Their underlying ideas about management and the firm are essentially similar and essentially and fundamentally different from those of the humanistic theories.

The Humanistic Theories

The humanistic theories of management are not new. They have been present in varying forms and with generally limited impact on conventional management thought for many years. Classical Marxism, for example, with its emphasis on the dissatisfaction and alienation of the industrial worker as the index of the ineffectiveness of an economic system might well be classed as a humanistic theory. In terms of direct consideration among management theorists, however, the humanistic theories are quite new, being essentially a post-World War II phenomenon. Most of the humanistic theories were developed by those who entered the study of management through other disciplines such as philosophy, anthropology, sociology, and psychology.

The humanistic theories in their treatment of the nature and purposes of the business firm establish a new objective for the firm. Basic humanistic thought in this area may be expressed as follows:

The business firm is a social and economic unit set up to accomplish economic goals. Beyond this, however, it is a dominant institution in our society, structuring the lives, feelings, behaviors and satisfactions of its employees. As such it is less than adequate for it to merely accomplish its economic ends; it is obliged to provide employees with satisfying and rewarding work and with conditions which will permit and encourage the fullest development of their individual personalities. Provision of such a work environment should not be done merely as a means of channeling employee efforts toward organizational objectives nor should it be subordinate to them. It is an independent objective which is equal to or superior in importance to the profit or service objective to the firm.

This idea is implicit in many recent writings. James Howard Cooper, for example, states:

    [12] Carl Hayel, "Changing Concepts of Human Relations," *Management for Modern Supervisors* (New York: American Management Association, 1962), pp. 44–67, as reprinted in Harold Koontz and Cyril O'Donnell (eds.), *Management: A Book of Readings* (New York: McGraw-Hill Book Company, 1964), pp. 323–334.

It is imperative that we now design man out of the repetitive, meaningless, and debilitating operations. They can make no contribution to human satisfaction. At the same time, we must reexamine our criteria of management in the light of the urgent necessity to create opportunities for individuals to reach their highest fulfillment as human beings. This will mean an imaginative reappraisal of goals and job structures, a reappraisal aimed toward giving man a proper sphere within which to achieve growth and satisfaction.[13]

Humanistic concepts appear in many other recent publications. William H. Whyte, Jr. in his book *The Organization Man*[14] presents such a concept, as do C. R. Walker and R. H. Guest in their classic study of the effect of progressive manufacture on worker satisfactions reported in *The Man on the Assembly Line*.[15] Recognition of this basic conflict between organizational objectives and human needs is also expressed by Chris Argyris in the following quotation from *Personality and Organization:*

Bringing together the evidence regarding the impact of the formal organizational principles upon the individual, it is concluded that there are some basic incongruencies between the growth trends of a healthy personality and the requirements of the formal organization . . . (employees) . . . are expected to produce under conditions leading to psychological failure.[16]

This is not to say that the pragmatic theories do not recognize the likelihood of a conflict between organizational objectives and employee needs. Many of the pragmatic theories devote considerable time and space to the consideration of the integration of employee needs and the demands of the organization. Ralph Currier Davis, for example, discusses the collateral objectives of the firm which he considers to be the provision of satisfactions to employees and other groups and individuals whose cooperation is necessary for the accomplishment of organizational objectives.[17] The crucial difference between the pragmatic and humanistic theories lies in the relative emphasis put on these aspects of the objectives complex and the reason for their consideration. Davis and the other pragmatists consider these employee needs to be secondary to the economic objectives of the firm and recommend provisions for their satisfaction primarily as a way of facilitating the accomplishment of the over-all organizational objectives. The humanists, on the other hand, consider provision for such satisfactions to be a valid *raison d'etre* for the firm in and of itself.

The second basic idea implicit in the humanistic theories defines the role of the manager in the firm. It may be stated as follows:

The manager should not merely serve to channel employee efforts toward organizational objectives. Rather his contribution is made in terms of his ability to discover and implement courses of action which will permit both the accomplishment of organizational objectives and the provision of satisfying and rewarding

---

[13] James Howard Cooper, "The Crisis in Human Relations," *Business Horizons,* Fall, 1964, pp. 31–37, as reprinted in Keith Davis and William G. Scott (eds.), *Readings in Human Relations* (2nd ed.; New York: McGraw-Hill Book Company, 1964), pp. 408–417.

[14] William H. Whyte, Jr., *The Organization Man* (New York: Simon and Schuster, 1956).

[15] C. R. Walker and R. H. Guest, *The Man on the Assembly Line* (Cambridge: Harvard University Press, 1952), p. 163.

[16] Chris Argyris, *Personality and Organization* (New York: Harper and Row, 1957), p. 66.

[17] Davis, p. 54.

work for the individual employees of the firm.

This aspect of the humanistic theories is expressed in the following statement by Argyris:

Many of the "human problems" in organizations originally are caused by the basic incongruence between the nature of relatively mature adults and healthy formal organizations. Assuming that both must "fuse," if the organization's goals are to be achieved, and knowing that both will always strive for self-actualization, it follows that effective leadership behavior is "fusing" the individual and the organization in such a way that both simultaneously obtain optimum self-actualization.[18]

The third implicit premise of the humanistic theories concerns the techniques or methods which will best serve the manager in the performance of his function within the firm. It is, in general, exemplified by the following statement:

The traditional skills of management as advocated by the Pragmatists are inadequate. The successful manager has more than mere skills and techniques for manipulating people. He must have first, an attitude which makes him "employee centered" as well as "production centered" and second, an understanding of the needs and wants of human beings either innate or derived from careful and prolonged study of the behavioral sciences.

This idea can be seen in many recent writings. James Howard Cooper, for example, states:

Any human relations endeavor must meet the test of what Peter Drucker calls the "whole man"—not merely a man who is economic, social, political and biological, but who is also purposive, rational, creative, and spiritual. Thus we can distinguish between ends and means, and equally important, between proper

ends and justifiable means. From this point of view, man's destiny in the business and industrial life of our world takes on new significance. His needs, now determined by our definition, indicate that we have short-changed work as a medium through which man can achieve his highest fulfillment as a human being. The emphasis must be upon man, and the work must be organized to fit him. No longer can we attempt to adapt man to the machine—the machine must now be adapted to the man. No longer do we dare "utilize" men, or level them down to the "average work load." Instead we must motivate them, by increasing, through higher demands, opportunities for challenge and growth.[19]

It is equally clear in the writing of C. R. Walker and R. H. Guest in *The Man on the Assembly Line:*

In this general diffusion of the techniques and knowledge of mass production, the countries and people who adopt them may make all the mistakes of our forefathers who introduced to a complacent century the tragic years of the first industrial revolution. They may even add a few mistakes of their own for good measure. But it is also possible that mankind is being offered a kind of second chance in adapting the machine to human ends. There is at least one basis for such a hope—the young but rapidly growing science of Man as it is breaking forth into such subjects as industrial psychology and sociology and cultural anthropology, together with the science, and art, of human relations in industry.[20]

The statements made by proponents of humanistic theories of management and the premises they exemplify stand in marked contrast with the premises of the pragmatic theories. Two types of theories do exist. The key problem is one of determining whether the differences between them are substantive or, as the proponents of a unified theory of management would have us believe, the prod-

---

[18] Argyris, p. 211.
[19] Cooper, pp. 417–418.
[20] Walker and Guest, p. 163.

ucts of semantics, ignorance, and misrepresentation.

The Possibility of Reconciliation

The possibility of reconciliation of the two categories of theories and, thus, the possibility of a unified theory of management, hinges on elimination of the differences between the two premises dealing with the nature and purposes of the business firm, since these premises to a large degree determine the nature of the other two pairs of premises. It is thus imperative, if we are to determine the feasibility of a unified theory of management, that we take a look at the nature of these statements and the way in which they were derived.

Careful examination of these premises reveals one important point: these premises are not based upon provable fact. Rather they are assumptions derived from value judgments of the individual theoretician or from this view of the values of the society within which the business firm must operate. The two classes of theories differ because of differences in concepts of rightness or wrongness on the part of individuals rather than because of differences in interpretation of objectively verifiable fact. Given such a condition, is it possible to reconcile the two premises and thus lay the ground work for a unified theory of management? The answer is obviously no. The two premises rest on entirely different views of our society and of what should be the role of the business firm within it. At least at our present level of understanding human values and the process through which they develop, a single unified theory of management is a practical impossibility and in all likelihood will remain so in the foreseeable future.

Discussions among students of management trained in different disciplines and holding different concepts of how the function of management should be performed within business firms can and do perform a valuable service by eliminating some of the misunderstandings that hamper progress in the development of understanding of the process by which men manage. Using such discussions as tools in a search for the philosopher's stone of a unified theory of management represents an activity doomed to failure and one which uses precious time and energy that could well be devoted to more fruitful enterprises.

C

MANAGERIAL ETHICS AND SOCIAL RESPONSIBILITY

5. The Doctrine of Socially Responsible Management

THOMAS A. PETIT

Businessmen need an ethical standard to choose between morally right and wrong courses of action. The profit ethic —the idea that business is to maximize profits—once served this purpose. It enabled businessmen to make profit maximizing decisions on moral grounds. Today this ethic cannot be used, however, since there are goals other than profit.

The corporate and managerial revolutions have led to a moral crisis in American business by undermining the profit ethic. Today's large corporation is the prime agency for organizing our social as well as economic life. Managers take into account goals other than profit. Therefore the profit ethic no longer serves as an unequivocal moral guideline for business. But without it how do managers determine which decisions and actions are morally good or bad?

The doctrine of socially responsible management emerges as a possible new business ethic. According to this ethic management takes into account the welfare of all groups in society affected by the corporation in conducting its affairs. We are concerned here with the question of whether this doctrine can take the

Reprinted from *Arizona Review*. Vol. 14, No. 2 (December, 1965), pp. 1–4; 22, with permission of the publisher. Thomas A. Petit is Professor of Management and Research Specialist, Division of Economic and Business Research, College of Business and Public Administration, University of Arizona.

place of the profit ethic and thus resolve the moral crisis of business.

Yesterday's Power-Seekers and Today's Business Moralists

Change in the roles of the corporation and the manager have brought, in turn, change in the motives and personality of men who direct American industry. At the turn of the century the businessman needed power to lead rapidly industrializing society into greater heights of productivity and wealth than ever before. Thus he became a "power-seeker."

Today the power-seeker is being replaced by a new kind of manager who underplays his power—the "business moralist." He knows that he must use power to get his job done, but he fears the consequences of its full exercise for the welfare of the corporation and himself. The business moralist may emerge as our next business hero.

What are the causes of this shift of management motives and personality? Because of his success, the businessman has created new social responsibilities for himself. When the American standard of living was low, the first order of business was to expand the flow of goods and services. The power-seeking businessman led the transformation of a rural farming society into one huge factory. For the majority of American citizens mankind's ancient foe of poverty was defeated.

The modern manager has earned his high place among the leaders of the nation. But his responsibilities have kept pace with his enlarged social role. People want other things besides goods and services from the modern corporation. More and more it is considered the manager's job to see that they get them.

There has been a decline in the broad public support of the power-seeking businessman. When the nation was first industrializing, his approach was in harmony with general ethical standards. After all, power is needed in any period of rapid mobilization of resources to accomplish broad social goals. But once these goals have been accomplished, generally there is a negative reaction to the concentration of power. The public clamors for its dispersal or control by society. During wartime the government takes over power to wage the war, but at the war's end there is a strong urge to disarm and "get back to normalcy." The early drive toward industrialization can be looked upon as a battle against poverty. That battle has been largely won. The American people no longer want managers to openly exult in their power.

Modern professional managers are well aware of this attitude. They recognize they must be careful in the use of their vast power. They no longer defend this power as the divine right of capital. They are fearful that if they do not accept the full social responsibilities which go with the power, they will lose it and probably to someone antagonistic to business management and free enterprise. Business moralists think that the reconstruction of the moral foundation of business is the most urgent problem facing American business today. This is why they are searching for a new precept to replace the old one based entirely on profit maximization. The doctrine of socially responsible management is a result of this search.

Defining the Doctrine

According to the doctrine of socially responsible management, the corporation is such a powerful institution in American life that it is socially disastrous to regard it as only a profit making organization. Whether managers like it or not, their function must change. They must accept the full responsibility for the impact of big business on society. If they do not, the corporation may not survive.

From this viewpoint, the proper function of management is to administer the enterprise not only for the welfare of shareholders but other groups as well— employees, customers, suppliers, dealers, the community, government and the like. Managers should arbitrate impersonally among these various interests.

There is evidence of the doctrine of socially responsible management: participation by executives in political affairs; corporate support of educational institutions; various employee welfare measures; community relations programs; and intensified public relations campaigns. These activities are considered essential to safeguard the position of the corporation. Sometimes they are justified on this basis alone. "A prudent regard for all the interests that merge in making the business a going concern now and in the future is, in fact, the only way to protect and to augment shareholder equity." [1]

Social responsibility of management is not merely a public relations gesture to protect the firm's profit position. "Self-conscious dedication to social responsibility may have started as a purely defensive maneuver against strident attacks on big corporations and on the moral efficacy of the profit system. But defense alone no longer explains the motive." [2] There is a sincere desire on the part of responsible executives to win respect of the general public by utilizing their power for the common good. The corporation is regarded as a multi-purpose social institution. The pursuit of profit is

secondary in importance to the public interest.

Problems of the Doctrine

Now we turn to the second aspect of the moral crisis of business—the inadequacy of the doctrine of socially responsible management. If it were able to give managers moral guidelines in making day-to-day decisions, it could take the place of the profit ethic. But at present the doctrine is more of a philosophical position than an ethical system. It is not widely accepted, largely because of its implications for the status, functions, power and control of the corporation and manager.

STATUS

Status refers to social position. The status of an organization like the corporation is defined by its relationship to other social structures.

Status of the firm in classical economics is defined by its market relations. The firm is a private organization pursuing the single goal of profit. It buys or hires resources, labor and capital and produces goods and services. Its specialized economic function limits its relations with other social entities. These relations do not go beyond the exchange process in the market.

The doctrine of socially responsible management implies that the status of the corporation transcends the market relationship, but it tells us nothing definite. The corporate revolution has turned a single-purpose economic entity into a multi-purpose social institution. The corporation's relations with government,

---

[1] Richard Eells, "Social Responsibility: Can Business Survive the Challenge?" *Business Horizons,* Vol. 2, No. 4 (Winter 1959), p. 41.

[2] Theodore Levitt, "The Dangers of Social Responsibility," *Harvard Business Review,* Vol. 36, No. 5 (September–October 1958), p. 41.

education, religion and the family cannot be defined by the exchange process alone. But the doctrine does not have a conceptual foundation which clarifies the status of the corporation in modern society.

The same kind of ambiguity surrounds the status of the manager. Separation of ownership and control has given management an autonomy difficult to fit into the concept of private property. Managers no longer seem to feel entirely responsible to stockholders. The doctrine of socially responsible management implies that somehow they are accountable to society at large. But what is the nature of this relationship? How can one occupational group holding power based neither on property ownership nor political election be related to all groups of society under its influence?

FUNCTION

Closely related to the problem of status is that of function. In recent years the corporation has expanded in function as well as size. It no longer is just a producer of goods and services. It now performs a number of political, welfare, social and cultural functions as well. Examples of the noneconomic corporate functions are:

1. *Political:* generally considered to be the responsibility of government, such as the diplomatic relations of oil companies with small oil-rich countries in the Middle East.

2. *Welfare:* corporate donations to private colleges and loaning of executives for community, charitable and civic betterment programs.

3. *Social:* meeting needs of society, such as providing social status for workers and managers based on occupation.

4. *Cultural:* influencing beliefs, values and goals of members of society; for example, application of the criteria of suc-

cess in business to nonbusiness areas of life.

Economists are opposed to noneconomic functions because they interfere with the corporation's traditional economic function. Political scientists have misgivings about corporate functions which have been traditionally the prerogative of the state. They question whether the tendency of the corporation to take on political functions is in keeping with the pluralistic tradition of American social structure and political processes.

Jurists fear that well worked out legal standards are endangered by noneconomic corporate functions and there is nothing to replace them. Cultural objections to the trend stem from a dislike for corporate values and goals becoming the common denominator in all walks of life. Opposition on social grounds is based on the fear that the open society will be destroyed and we will enter a new age of corporate feudalism.

The doctrine of socially responsible management is vague about which functions the corporation ought to perform. Should the socially responsible manager be a "business statesman" who conducts the affairs of the corporation to bring about a better world? If so, there ought to be no limitations placed on the functions performed by the corporation. Few Americans would agree to such a broad interpretation of the manager's social mandate. But if there is anything to the doctrine of socially responsible manageagement, the corporation should perform at least some noneconomic functions. But which ones and on what grounds?

POWER

Problems of status and functions would not be significant without problems posed by the great power of the corporation. There are two aspects of this problem: the concentration of corporate power and the legitimacy of management power.

Many economists believe the ideal economy is one composed of purely competitive markets in which many small firms are closely controlled by competition. The market performs the essential social task of economizing by channeling resources into their most efficient use and maintaining a check on production costs. Clearly industries dominated by large corporations cannot have decentralization of economic power. This structural characteristic is the basis of most criticism of big business by economists. They are unwilling to accept the good intentions of responsible managers in place of the rigors of market competition.

Great corporate power is therefore a precondition of the doctrine of socially responsible management. Without such concentrated power, it would not matter whether or not managers were socially responsible. Whatever their intentions, they would be constrained by market forces to behave in ways best for society.

The economists fear power not controlled by the market as irresponsible power. As Carl Kaysen put it, in the absence of market constraints "what management takes into account [in decision-making] is what management decides to take into account." Therefore, corporate power ". . . is responsible only in terms of the goals, values, and knowledge of management." [3]

The problem of the legitimacy of management power is basically political. The large corporation frequently is criticized as undemocratic. By democracy we mean a political system in which those in authority receive their power from the people and use this power according to the wishes of the majority. An organization is democratic if its leaders acquire their power legitimately and if the power can be taken away for misuse.

A few thousand top managers actively control big business in America. But who selected these men? Of course they selected themselves. Management groups of large corporations are self-perpetuating oligarchies. One of the major tasks of aging top executives is to select and groom their successors. But to whom are they responsible? There is no generally accepted answer. It constitutes the problem of the legitimacy of management power.

Lawyers argue that corporate managers must be responsible to the stockholders. They contend that if the link between owners and managers is ever dissolved management will lose the legal basis for its existence. What real claim will managers have to their positions if they do not own the company or represent the owners' interests? The implication is clear. To the extent that management is not directly responsible to the stockholders, its powers are not legitimate and big business is undemocratic. The doctrine of socially responsible management has no rebuttal to this charge.

CONTROL

Economists are uneasy about the large corporation because it seems to be running without any discernible controls. This is of more concern to them than the idea that large corporations perform poorly in the public interest.

The most sophisticated analysis of how society controls the manager has been made by Adolf A. Berle. He believes the only real control over managers is their philosophy. The source of this philosophy is the "public consensus." "This is the

---

[3] Carl Kaysen, "The Social Significance of the Modern Corporation," *American Economic Review,* Vol. XLVII, No. 2 (May 1957), p. 316.

existence of a set of ideas, widely held by the community, and often by the organization itself and the men who direct it, that certain uses of power are 'wrong,' that is, contrary to the established interest and value system of the community." [4] Public consensus furnishes the basis for public opinion. Professors, journalists, politicians and others translate public consensus into public opinion. If managers violate the public consensus they lose prestige and esteem. If this does not produce results desired by the community, more forceful penalties are invoked.

Berle's ideas about how society controls managers have been severely criticized. Economists have no faith in public consensus and question the wisdom of replacing the invisible hand of the competitive market with the heavy hand of powerful corporate management. Lawyers criticize Berle's analysis because it seems to undermine the rule of law. They want something more tangible to limit the wide scope of managerial discretion than the somewhat nebulous concepts of management philosophy and public consensus. Political scientists are critical of Berle's thesis because they have misgivings about

any check on power other than power itself.

Edward S. Mason, former President of the American Economic Association, has asked academic proponents of the doctrine of socially responsible management to produce a "managerial apologetic"— an up-to-date explanation of how society controls corporations through managers that can gain general acceptance.[5] Thus far no such explanation has appeared.

Conclusion

The doctrine of socially responsible management has been suggested as a logical successor to the profit ethic. It is in tune with the trend of the American economy in the twentieth century. Nonetheless this doctrine presently is inadequate as a business ethic. It lacks a conceptual foundation. It is more a philosophical viewpoint than a moral guide to management action. Before it can receive acceptance as the ethical system of modern business it must be able to cope with the problems of status function, power and control of the corporation and manager.

---

[4] Adolf A. Berle, Jr., *Power Without Property* (New York: Harcourt, Brace & Co., 1959), p. 90.

[5] Edward S. Mason, "The Apologetics of 'Managerialism,'" *Journal of Business*, Vol. XXXI, No. 1 (January 1958), pp. 1–11.

6. Managerial Value Systems: A Research Approach

GEORGE W. ENGLAND

For my part of this Ethics Symposium, I would like to share with you some results and implications from a study of the personal value systems of managers of American businesses. Personal values are certainly relevant to "Ethics," and managers have a great deal to do with employment relationships.

The study of the Personal Value Systems of American Managers has been reported in the *Academy of Management Journal* and it is from this source that my remarks are drawn.[1]

Background for the Research

The ideas and data presented stem from a long term research project aimed at the description, measurement and understanding of the personal value systems of managers and the impact of values on behavior. A personal values system is viewed as a relatively permanent perceptual framework which shapes and influences the general nature of an individual's behavior. Values are similar to attitudes but are more ingrained, permanent and stable in nature. Likewise, a value is seen as being more general and less tied to any specific object than is the case with many attitudes. "Value" as used here is closer to ideology or philosophy than it is to attitude.

Managers of business organizations, vitally important in any industrial society, represent individuals whose values are of particular interest. The significance and importance of studying the value systems of managers is seen when one considers seriously the following reasonable assertions and their implications:

1. Personal value systems influence a manager's perception of situations and problems he faces.

2. Personal value systems influence a manager's decisions and solutions to problems.

3. Personal value systems influence the way in which a manager looks at other individuals and groups of individuals— thus influencing interpersonal relationships.

4. Personal value systems influence the perception of individual and organizational success as well as their achievement.

5. Personal value systems set the limits for the determination of what is and what is not ethical behavior by a manager.

6. Personal value systems influence the extent to which a manager will ac-

Reprinted from *Ethics and Employment*. Minneapolis, Minn.: Graduate School of Business Administration, University of Minnesota, May, 1967, pp. 10–34, with permission of the author and publisher. George W. England is Professor of Industrial Relations and Psychology, School of Business Administration, University of Minnesota.

[1] England, G. W. "Personal Value Systems of American Managers." *Academy of Management Journal*, 10, No. 1, March 1966, pp. 53–68.

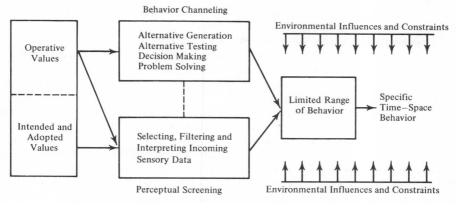

Figure 1. *Theoretical Model of Personal Value System.*

cept or will resist organizational pressures and goals.

Theoretical Model

The theoretical model underlying the present study is presented in Figure 1. Two major classes of personal values are recognized: *operative values,* or those that have the greatest influence on behavior and *intended and adopted values,* or those that may be professed but do not directly influence behavior to any great degree. The model also indicates the two primary ways in which values can influence behavior; *behavior channeling* and *perceptual screening.* Behavior channeling would be illustrated by the behavior of a manager who places a high value on honesty and integrity when he is approached with a proposition which involves deception and questionable ethics. His behavior would be channeled away from the questionable proposition as a direct result of his operative values. Behavior channeling represents direct influence of values on behavior as opposed

to the indirect influence of perceptual screening. Examples of perceptual screening underlie the common expressions, "he sees what he wants to see," "he hears only what he already agrees with," and "you can't teach an old dog new tricks." The power of personal values to select, filter and influence interpretation of what one "sees" and "hears" is well known in common experience and in the scientific study of behavior.[2]

The model further indicates that the impact of values on behavior must be considered in relation to other environmental influences and constraints before specific statements can be made about an individual behaving such and such a way at a given time and under certain conditions. Values are one part of the story, but not the whole story.

The Measurement of Values

The present attempt to "get at" a manager's values through the use of a carefully specified set of concepts was influenced by the work of Charles Osgood

---

[2] See, for example, Postman, L., Bruner, J. S., & McGinnies, E. "Personal Values as Selective Factors in Perception." *Journal of Abnormal & Social Psychology,* 43, 1948, pp. 142–154.

and represents an adaptation of his methodology.[3] Most of the research done by Osgood and his associates has been directed toward the development of an adequate measurement system for meaning. They have succeeded in showing that meaning has several dimensions which can be measured by using sets of bipolar adjectives such as good-bad, strong-weak, active-passive, to determine the meaning of a concept for an individual.

In the present study, we are concerned not with just any aspect of meaning of any concept or set of concepts. Rather it is necessary to specify a particular set of concepts and certain modes of the valuation process that are relevant to a personal value system for managers. The concepts in the PVQ were selected from the voluminous literature dealing with organizations and with individual and group behavior. In addition, ideological and philosophical concepts were included to represent major belief systems. An initial pool of 200 concepts was reduced to 96 concepts through the use of a panel of expert judges. Preliminary findings with a pilot sample of managers further reduced the concepts to the current set of 66. These concepts are categorized into the following five classes: goals of business organizations, personal goals of individuals, groups of people, ideas associated with people, and ideas about general topics. Figure 2 lists the 66 concepts in the PVQ by categories.

The development of a Personal Values Questionnaire (PVQ) was based on the rationale that the *meanings* attached by an individual manager to a carefully specified set of concepts will provide a useful description of his *personal value system*, which in turn will be related to

his behavior in understandable ways. The theoretical importance of the meanings an individual attaches to concepts is at the root of a great deal of research aimed at a better understanding of human behavior. Attitude measurement, interest measurement, personality assessment, need assessment, and verbal learning experiments, for example, lean heavily on the assumption that modes of the valuation process for individuals provide predictive clues about their behavior. How concepts are grouped; valuation in terms of like or dislike, important or unimportant, and right or wrong, whatever reactions a concept elicits from an individual—all are expressions of what the concept means to the individual and have implications for his value system and for understanding his behavior.[4]

The PVQ uses four scales to represent four modes of valuation. The primary mode of valuation used was what might be called the *power* mode of valuation (important-unimportant scale). The rationale behind the use of this scale is similar to that underlying most value measurement; the general value of objects or ideas to an individual is largely a function of how important or unimportant he thinks the object or idea is. Because of concern about the behavioral effect of values, it was necessary to determine why individuals thought certain concepts were important or unimportant. To do this, three secondary modes of valuation were used. The *pragmatic* mode of valuation was represented by a right scale; and the affect or *feeling* mode of valuation was measured through use of a pleasant scale. It was reasoned that a combination of primary and secondary

---

[3] Osgood, E. C., Suci, G. J., & Tannenbaum, P. H. *The Measurement of Meaning.* Urbana: University of Illinois Press, 1957.

[4] For a brilliant exposition of this point, see Allport, G. W. "Traits Revisited." *American Psychologist,* 21, No. 1, 1966, pp. 1–10.

Goals of Business Organizations	Personal Goals of Individuals	Groups of People
High Productivity	Leisure	Employees
Industry Leadership	Dignity	Customers
Employee Welfare	Achievement	My Co-workers
Organizational Stability	Autonomy	Craftsmen
Profit Maximization	Money	My Boss
Organizational Efficiency	Individuality	Managers
Social Welfare	Job Satisfaction	Owners
Organizational Growth	Influence	My Subordinates
	Security	Laborers·
	Power	My Company
	Creativity	Blue Collar Workers
	Success	Government
	Prestige	Stockholders
		Technical Employees
		Me
		Labor Unions
		White Collar Employees

Ideas Associated with People	Ideas About General Topics
Ambition	Authority
Ability	Caution
Obedience	Change
Trust	Competition
Aggressiveness	Compromise
Loyalty	Conflict
Prejudice	Conservatism
Compassion	Emotions
Skill	Equality
Cooperation	Force
Tolerance	Liberalism
Conformity	Property
Honor	Rational
	Religion
	Risk

Figure 2. *Concepts Used to Measure Manager's Values.*

modes of valuation would be a better predictor of the likely behavior of a manager than would either mode alone. For example, if manager A were generally pragmatically oriented (e.g., when he said something was important, he was most apt to see it as successful as opposed to right or pleasant) his behavior would be predicted best by viewing it as a joint function of those concepts he viewed as successful. On the other hand, individual B who was generally ethically-morally oriented (e.g., when he said something was important, he was most apt to see it as right as opposed to successful or pleasant) would behave in a way which is predicted by the joint function of those concepts considered important and right. In a more general sense, what is being suggested is that a manager's behavior (insofar as it is influenced by his personal values) is best explained by utilizing both those things he considers important and his personal

TABLE 1
Manager Sample Characteristics
(N = 1,072 Managers)

Type of Company	%
Agriculture	2.1
Mining	.8
Contract Const.	1.8
Manufacturing	56.6
Transportation and Public Utilities	11.8
Wholesale and Retail Trade	7.0
Finance, Insurance and Real Estate	10.0
Services (e.g. hotels. and laundries)	.7
Other	8.0
No Information	1.1

Size of Firm (No. Employees)	%
Under 100	6.0
100–499	23.0
500–999	14.6
1000–4999	21.6
5000–9999	14.2
10,000–29,999	14.3
30,000 and over	5.4
No Information	.8

Department	%
Production	8.2
Operations	9.9
Sales/Distribution	9.0
Engineering	10.3
Finance/Accounting	6.8
Personnel/IR	15.5
Public Relations/Adv.	7.5
Research and Development	11.7
General Administration	17.0
Other	3.3
No Information	1.0

Line Staff	%
Line	26.5
Staff	37.1
Combined	35.4
No Information	1.0

Organizational Level	%
Director	1.5
President	4.6
Exec. Vice President	4.0
Vice President	46.5
Levels reporting to VP	30.5
Two to Four Levels below VP	12.6
No Information	.3

Managerial Experience	%
0–5 years	17.7
6–10 years	20.6
11–15 years	21.1
16–20 years	18.4
21–30 years	14.1
Over 30 years	6.3
No Information	1.8

Age	%
20–34 years	9.0
35–39 years	12.5
40–44 years	18.6
45–49 years	18.6
50–54 years	15.8
55–59 years	13.2
60 or over	11.8
No Information	.6

Formal Education	%
Some High School	2.4
High School Degree	5.1
Some College	19.0
College Degree	40.0
Post-Graduate Education	32.7
No Information	.7

Yearly Income	%
Under $9,000	4.1
$ 9,000–11,999	8.7
12,000–14,999	12.3
15,000–19,999	16.0
20,000–24,999	15.3
25,000–34,999	18.1
35,000–49,999	13.5
50,000 or over	9.6
No Information	2.4

Job Satisfaction	%
How well do you like your job . . .	
I hate it	.2
I dislike it	0.0
I don't like it	.7
I am indifferent to it	1.3
I like it	26.4
I am enthusiastic about it	50.2
I love it	20.4
No Information	.7

mode of orientation. Symbolically, one could say $B_v \rightarrow f(I\Omega PO)$.[5]

Figure 3 shows the directions and item format that were used in the PVQ.

The Managers Studied

A national sample of 3,042 managers was selected from Poor's 1965 Directory of Corporations, Executives and Directors on the basis of three stratifying variables (size of organization in terms of employees, level of the manager in the

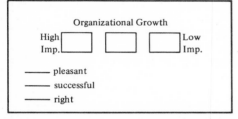

Figure 3. *Personal Values Questionnaire Format. Instructions.* Rate how important a topic is to you by placing an "X" in the appropriate box: the left box signifies high importance; the middle box, average importance; and the right box, low importance. Then specify which of the three descriptions (successful, pleasant, right) best indicates the *meaning* of the topic to you; indicate your choice by placing the number "1" on the line next to it. Then indicate which description least indicate's the topic's *meaning* to you by writing the number "3" in the space provided. Finally, write the number "2" next to the remaining description. Complete all topics in this manner and check to see that the three descriptions for each topic have been ranked in the manner instructed.

organization and organizational function of the manager). A PVQ and an accompanying letter were mailed to each manager. After one follow-up letter, 1,072 managers responded with useable data. Table 1 describes the 1,072 managers in terms of personal and organizational variables. As seen in Table 1, the managers are a relatively diverse group in terms of organizational variables (type of company, size of firm, department or function, organizational level and line-staff position) as well as in terms of personal variables (years of managerial experience, age, formal education, yearly income from their position, and job satisfaction). The personal value systems of these 1,072 American managers is of primary interest here.

Personal Value Systems of American Managers

As a total group, managers' primary orientations are pragmatic; that is, when managers view some concept as important they also tend to view it as successful. As seen in Figure 4, thirty-nine (of sixty-six) concepts are rated by the total group of managers as being of "high importance"; twenty-nine of these are likewise seen as successful. The second part of Figure 4 shows that 562 of the managers (over half) assign more of the concepts to the "high importance-successful" cell than to any of the other eight categories. In short, these data indicate that as a group managers are best described as pragmatically oriented and when considered as individuals more managers are

---

[5] This expression would be read: the behavior of a manager, insofar as behavior is a function of values, is best indicated by the joint function of those concepts he considers important and those concepts which fit his primary orientation. For a pragmatically oriented manager, behavior is best predicted by those concepts considered important and successful; for a moral-ethically oriented manager, behavior is best predicted by those concepts considered important and right; while for an affect oriented manager, behavior is best predicted by those concepts considered important and pleasant.

pragmatically oriented than are ethically-morally oriented or are affect oriented. Figure 4 also shows that managers' secondary orientation is moralistic and ethical. Of the thirty-nine concepts rated "high importance," ten also are seen as "right." Individually, 276 of the managers (about one-fourth) assign more of the concepts to the "high importance-right" cell than to any of the other eight combinations.

The data show that managers, whether considered as a group or individually, are not affect oriented; the concepts that are viewed as important by them are not viewed as pleasant.

The Value Profile of American Managers, as shown in Figure 5, allows interpretation of the responses of the 1,072 managers to the 66 concepts in value terms with implications for behavior. When one considers managers as a group and utilizes the finding that managers are pragmatically oriented, the Value Profile would suggest the following:

1) The 29 concepts which are rated as "high importance" and are viewed as "successful" represent the operative values for these managers. They are considered important and fit the primary orientation (pragmatic) pattern of the group and should influence the behavior of the managers more than the ideas and concepts in any other cell in the Value Profile. For example, the fact that managers value the characteristics Ambition, Ability, and Skill more than they value the characteristics Loyalty, Trust, and Honor would be reflected in their own behavior and in their expectations about others' behavior.

2) The 9 concepts found in the cells labeled (Adopted Values—Situationally Induced) are those that have been observed as being successful in the manager's organizational experience but which he finds difficult to internalize and view as being of high importance. Managers seem to be saying, for example,

that Labor Unions are successful (they do have a large impact on what goes on in organizations) but that they should not be considered as important as other groups such as Customers or Managers or Owners. The values represented by these 9 concepts would not be expected to influence the behavior of managers to the extent that operative values would, since managers are not as wholly committed to adopted values as they are to operative values.

3) The 10 concepts found in the cells labeled (Intended Values—Socioculturally Induced) are those that have been considered as highly important by the manager throughout most of his life but do not fit his organizational experience. Here the interpretation would be that managers, for example, have viewed "rationality" as an important criterion for behavior but that their organizational environment has not always rewarded "rationality." It is as if they were saying that we have always considered it important to be rational but don't see it as being highly useful in our organizational life. The complexities of organizational requirements do not square with individual notions of what is and what is not rational. These intended values where there is conflict between what one has learned to believe and what one sees in his accepted environment have been termed professed or talking values by a number of authors. Employee Welfare, for example, is viewed as highly important as an organizational goal by managers but it may not affect their behavior greatly because it doesn't fit their primary pragmatic orientation. It is a professed value but not one that is operative or directly influential of behavior to any large extent.

4) Finally, the 18 concepts found in the cells labeled (Low Behavioral Relevance) are those that would not be expected to influence a manager's behavior to any large extent since they are not

As a total group, Managers' primary orientation is *pragmatic*
As a total group, Managers' secondary orientation is *moralistic and ethical*
Supporting data:

	High Importance	Average Importance	Low Importance
Successful 1st Ranked	29	7	2
Right 1st Ranked	10	11	0
Pleasant 1st Ranked	0	6	1

66

The 66 *concepts* are assigned to one of the nine categories (cells) by a joint modal frequency method for the total group of managers. For example, more of the total group of managers responded "high importance-successful" than in any other category of response to each of 29 concepts. Thus, 29 concepts are assigned to the "high importance-successful" category.

	High Importance	Average Importance	Low Importance
Successful 1st Ranked	562	101	0
Right 1st Ranked	276	87	0
Pleasant 1st Ranked	12	29	5

1072

Each of the 1072 *managers* is assigned to that category (cell) that contains the highest number of concepts for him. For example, 562 managers responded "high importance-successful" to more of the 66 concepts than to any of the other eight response categories.

Figure 4. *General Value Orientation of Managers (N = 1,072).*

57

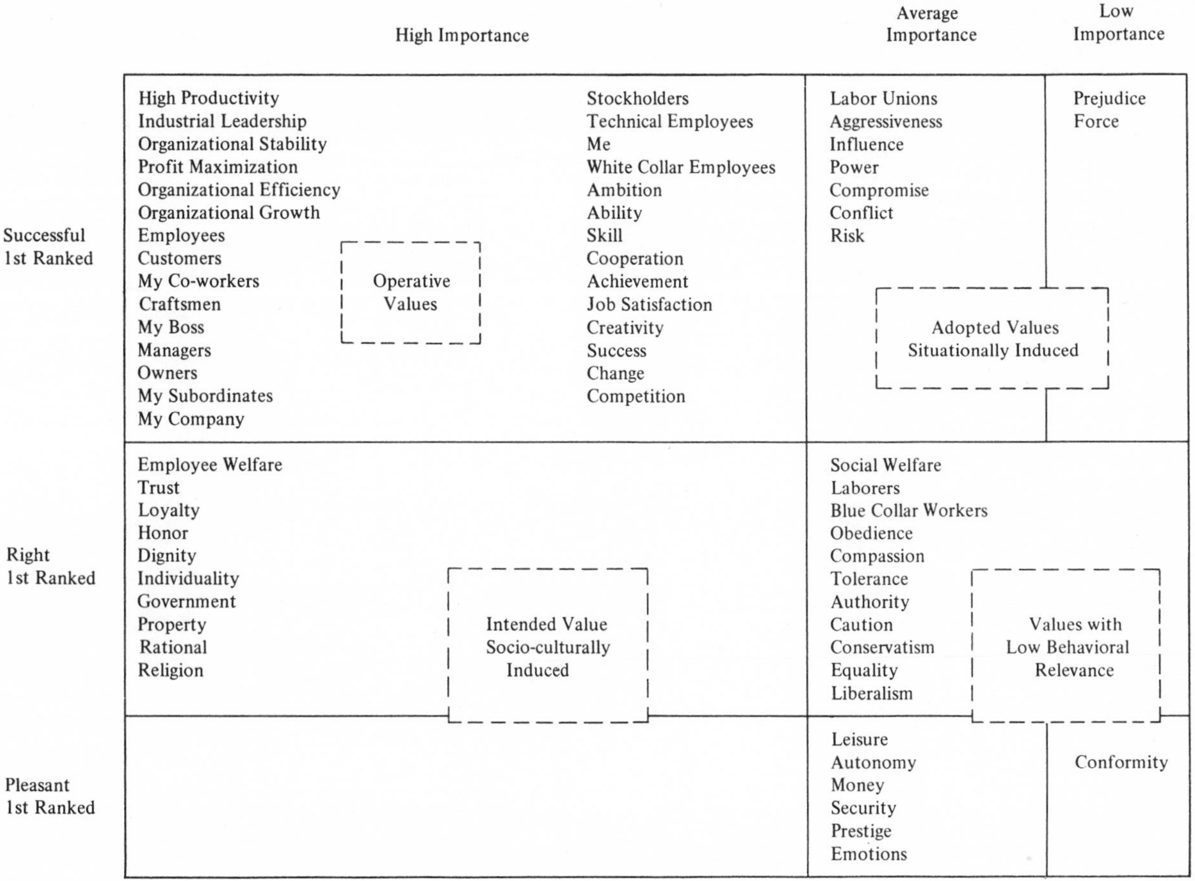

	High Importance	Average Importance	Low Importance
Successful 1st Ranked	High Productivity, Industrial Leadership, Organizational Stability, Profit Maximization, Organizational Efficiency, Organizational Growth, Employees, Customers, My Co-workers, Craftsmen, My Boss, Managers, Owners, My Subordinates, My Company	Stockholders, Technical Employees, Me, White Collar Employees, Ambition, Ability, Skill, Cooperation, Achievement, Job Satisfaction, Creativity, Success, Change, Competition	Labor Unions, Aggressiveness, Influence, Power, Compromise, Conflict, Risk	Prejudice, Force
Right 1st Ranked	Employee Welfare, Trust, Loyalty, Honor, Dignity, Individuality, Government, Property, Rational, Religion		Social Welfare, Laborers, Blue Collar Workers, Obedience, Compassion, Tolerance, Authority, Caution, Conservatism, Equality, Liberalism	
Pleasant 1st Ranked			Leisure, Autonomy, Money, Security, Prestige, Emotions	Conformity

Dashed groupings: Operative Values; Intended Value Socio-culturally Induced; Adopted Values Situationally Induced; Values with Low Behavioral Relevance.

Figure 5. *Managerial Value Profile (N = 1,072).*

considered important and do not fit the pragmatic orientation of managers.

Tables 2, 3, 4, 5, and 6 present more detailed information about each set of concepts. The columns of data in the Figures represent 1) the percentage of the total group of managers who rated each concept as "highly important," 2) the percentage of the total group of managers who ranked "successful" as best indicating the meaning of each concept to them, and 3) the percentage of the total group of managers who *both* rated

the concept as "highly important" *and* ranked "successful" as best indicating the meaning of the concept to them. As previously indicated, a useful general measure of the behavioral relevance of each concept for managers as a group is represented by the percentage in the third column of Tables 2–6. Analysis and interpretation of the data found in the Figures suggest a number of conclusions:

With respect to goals of business organizations [6] ....(Table 2)

TABLE 2
Behavior Analysis of Values (N = 1,072)

Goals of Business Organizations	% High Importance	% Successful 1st Ranked	% High Importance and Successful 1st Ranked
Organizational Efficiency	81	71	60
High Productivity	80	70	60
Profit Maximization	72	70	56
Organizational Growth	60	72	48
Industrial Leadership	58	64	43
Organizational Stability	58	54	38
Employee Welfare	65	20	17
Social Welfare	41	8	4

• The eight goals clearly constitute four subsets of goals as identified by the horizontal lines.

• The first subset includes the goals Organizational Efficiency, High Productivity, and Profit Maximization. Both the high behavioral relevance score and the content of these goals suggest that they are what Simon calls maximization criteria.[7] They are the goals which managers attempt to influence by their actions, decisions or behavior and are useful in generating alternative courses of actions or ways of behaving.

• The second subset consists of the goals Organizational Growth, Industry Leadership and Organizational Stability. The secondary position of these goals in terms of behavioral relevance and their content would suggest that they should be viewed

---

[6] For a more complete analysis of goals of business organizations, see my "Organizational Goals and Expected Behavior of American Managers." *Academy of Management Journal,* 10, No. 2, June, 1967, pp. 107–117.

[7] Simon, H. A. "On the Concept of Organizational Goal." *Administrative Science Quarterly,* IX, 1964, 1–22.

as associative goals. They generally are not sought in and of themselves (actions are not usually taken to directly influence them); rather they are utilized in alternative testing. A manager may decide on a given action to influence the "maximization criteria" goals and then check to see what the impact is on the goals in this second subset.

• The third subset of goals includes only Employee Welfare. The data suggest that Employee Welfare is a professed goal but one which will not influence managerial behavior to any great extent. Employee Welfare is considered "highly important" by 65% of the total sample

while only 20% view it as "successful." As previously indicated, Employee Welfare is an Intended Value which is socio-culturally induced but which has relatively low behavioral relevance.

• The final subset of goals includes Social Welfare which is seen as neither important nor successful by managers. In other words, it is not important and does not fit the pragmatic mode of valuation characteristic of managers; thus it would be expected to have low behavioral relevance as is shown in column 3 of Table 2.

With respect to ideas associated with people ....(Table 3)

TABLE 3
Behavior Analysis of Values (N = 1,072)

Ideas Associated with People	% High Importance	% Successful 1st Ranked	% High Importance and Successful 1st Ranked
Ability	84	72	65
Ambition	75	73	57
Skill	70	75	55
Cooperation	78	46	40
Aggressiveness	42	76	33
Loyalty	80	19	18
Trust	91	18	18
Honor	86	12	12
Tolerance	39	18	12
Prejudice	11	36	10
Obedience	30	19	8
Compassion	29	10	8
Conformity	6	23	4

• Ability, ambition, and skill are viewed as both important and successful and would be interpreted as operative values which influence a manager's behavior as well as the way in which he judges and evaluates other people.

• Cooperation and aggressiveness represent moderately important values in terms of behavior of managers. It is in-

teresting to note that cooperation and aggressiveness represent different types of values even though they have similar behavioral relevance scores. Cooperation is more of an Intended Value while Aggressiveness is an Adopted Value.

• Loyalty, trust, honor, tolerance, prejudice, obedience, compassion, and conformity represent values with low behavioral relevance. It is interesting to notice that loyalty, trust and honor have very high importance scores (80, 91, and 86 respectively) but are not viewed as successful by many managers (19%, 18%, and 12% respectively). This would suggest that these three value areas operate as Intended Values which are socioculturally induced and may have their primary effect on the behavior of man-

agers through the process of perceptual screening as opposed to behavioral channeling. It is possible, for example, that a manager is not influenced to any great extent in his own behavior by the notion of loyalty but he may judge and evaluate associates in terms of the "loyalty" of their behavior.

With respect to groups
of people . . . . (Table 4)

TABLE 4
Behavior Analysis of Values (N = 1,072)

Groups of People	% High Importance	% Successful 1st Ranked	% High Importance and Successful 1st Ranked
My Company	91	63	63
Customers	92	62	62
Managers	74	63	53
My Boss	73	52	45
My Subordinates	78	47	42
Technical Employees	63	55	42
Employees	84	44	42
Me	65	48	39
My Co-workers	67	37	32
Craftsmen	48	54	32
Owners	52	47	31
Stockholders	48	43	29
White Collar Employees	41	43	24
Blue Collar Workers	35	38	21
Government	44	29	19
Laborers	28	31	16
Labor Unions	21	42	15

• The set of concepts including my company, customers and managers represent the highest level operative values for managers and would be expected to influence their behavior most. The results indicate that managers make decisions and behave by using customers, managers, and my company as significant reference groups.
• A second set of concepts including my boss, my subordinates, technical em-

ployees, employees and me represent second level operative values. These also are significant reference groups in shaping managers' behavior but less influential than the first group.
• Concepts such as blue collar workers, government, laborers, and labor unions have low behavioral relevance for managers and do not represent significant reference groups.

With respect to personal goals of indi-

TABLE 5
Behavior Analysis of Values (N = 1,072)

Personal Goals of Individuals	% High Importance	% Successful 1st Ranked	% High Importance and Successful 1st Ranked
Achievement	83	69	63
Success	70	64	53
Creativity	70	63	50
Job Satisfaction	88	41	41
Individuality	53	29	21
Money	28	46	20
Influence	18	47	15
Prestige	21	35	14
Autonomy	20	31	13
Dignity	56	20	13
Security	29	21	12
Power	10	52	9
Leisure	11	7	4

viduals . . . . (Table 5)

• Achievement, success and creativity are the personal goals that represent high level operative values for managers. Since these goals are considered important and they also fit the pragmatic orientation of managers, it is suggested that they are keystones in the motivational structure underlying managerial behavior.

• The idea of job satisfaction as a personal goal is seen as a second level operative value. Job satisfaction approaches being an Intended Value (88% saying it is of "high importance" but only 41% considering it "successful"). A theoretical inference would be that managers may be less influenced by striving to attain job satisfaction than by striving for achievement, for example, but that they consider job satisfaction important for others. Job satisfaction, as a personal goal, may operate more through perceptual screening than through behavior channeling.

• Individuality, money, influence, prestige, autonomy, dignity, security, power, and leisure are concepts that represent lower value personal goals. Individuality and money represent another example of different types of values even though they have similar behavior relevance scores. Individuality is an Intended Value while Money is more of an Adopted Value.

With respect to general topics . . . .
. . . . (Table 6)

• Competition and change are concepts which represent operative values for managers and would be expected to be influential in shaping their behavior. The nature of these high value concepts suggests what might be described as an "action orientation" on the part of managers; doing is of primary importance.

• Risk, rational, authority, and property are second level values for managers.

TABLE 6
Behavior Analysis of Values (N = 1,072)

Ideas About General Topics	% High Importance	% Successful 1st Ranked	% High Importance and Successful 1st Ranked
Competition	66	54	41
Change	45	50	31
Risk	36	62	27
Rational	58	33	26
Authority	42	39	22
Property	45	38	21
Compromise	19	41	13
Emotions	23	24	13
Force	11	55	9
Conflict	9	46	9
Conservatism	13	28	8
Liberalism	11	26	8
Equality	29	12	8
Caution	13	30	7
Religion	40	8	7

Again, one sees concepts with similar behavioral relevance scores illustrating different types of values. Risk is an adopted value which has been organizationally rewarded but not highly internalized by managers while Rationality is an Intended Value which was brought to the organization but it is not always useful.
• Compromise, emotions, force, conflict, conservatism, liberalism, equality, caution, and religion are values with relatively low behavioral relevance. It is interesting to note the Adopted Value nature of compromise and force as compared with the Intended Values represented by equality and religion. Both sets of values suggest areas of conflict for managers but with different consequences.

Differences in Personal Value Systems

The preceding discussion and analysis has been concerned mainly with the value systems of American managers as a group. We have been interested in the extent to which ideas, concepts and values are important for managers in general. As would be expected, however, it becomes very clear that there is endless variation when we look at the personal value system of each individual manager. Value systems are like most other human characteristics; individuals differ greatly with respect to them. While it is difficult to characterize these differences briefly, the following description of some ways in which value systems of managers differ may be helpful and illustrative.[8]

As indicated earlier, the major orientations of managers differ. Some managers have a pragmatic orientation (important concepts for them are viewed as "successful") while others have an ethical-moral orientation. For these latter individuals, important ideas and values are those which are viewed as "right." A very few individuals have an affect or feeling orientation.

Some managers have a very small set of operative values while others have a large set and seem to be influenced by many strongly held values. The operative values of some managers include concepts which are almost solely related to organizational life while other managers include a wide range of personal and philosophical concepts among their operative values. Some managers have what might be termed individualistic values as opposed to group oriented values. Some managers appear to be highly achievement oriented as compared with others who seem to value status and position more highly. Finally, it is clear that some managers have a personal value system that might be characterized as "hard." Their operative values include concepts such as Ambition, Obedience, Aggressiveness, Achievement, Success, Competition, Risk, and Force. Other individuals have value systems that are often thought of as "soft" and include concepts such as Loyalty, Trust, Cooperation, Compassion, Tolerance, Employee Welfare, Social Welfare and Religion. Without attaching any personal judgment about what value system is best or most appropriate, one can appreciate the differences in behavior and in feelings of conflict

that will arise because of these value differences.

Summary and Implications

The present paper presents empirical evidence about the nature of the personal value systems of American managers and a theoretical rationale for considering the impact of values on behavior. Additional study and analyses undoubtedly will clarify the role of values in understanding managers and their behavior. It does seem safe, however, to make a few generalizations which stem from this and related studies: 1) personal value systems of managers can be meaningfully measured even though they are complex in nature, 2) there is a general value pattern which is characteristic of American managers as seen in the results of this study as well as a great deal of variation in value systems from individual to individual, 3) personal values operate at the level of corporate strategy and goals as well as at the level of day-to-day decisions, 4) the personal value systems of individual managers influence the organization in both an indirect and direct manner at the same time that personal value systems are influenced by organization life, 5) differences in personal value systems help to explain the nature of conflict between individuals in an organization while similarity of value patterns is probably responsible for much accommodation among individuals, and finally and perhaps most importantly, 6) the study and thoughtful examination of one's own personal value system may well be helpful in the effort that all must make in the "strain toward consistency" between what one believes and what one is.[9]

[8] See also, Miles, R. "Conflicting Elements in Managerial Ideologies." *Industrial Relations,* 1964, pp. 77–91.

DISCUSSION QUESTIONS: PART I

1. Is a philosophy of management which encompasses the entire field of management possible? Why or why not?
2. What are some of the most important factors in the development of a philosophy of management?
3. Differentiate between positive and normative theories. Is either more valuable in the development of a science of management?
4. How are values reflected in positive and normative theory? Give several illustrations in your answer.
5. What is the operational school of management? In what ways is it related to the development of theory and philosophy in management?
6. Distinguish between the various types of theory being used in the field of management today.
7. Do you believe that the various theories of management being used today could be unified into one theory? Why or why not?
8. Is the concept of socially responsible management related to the development of a profession of management? Explain.
9. How is the empirical research on managerial values related to: (a) managerial ethics; and (b) the development of a managerial profession?
10. How are philosophy, science, and profession related? How are they related today in the field of management? Why?

SELECTED REFERENCES: PART I

A. PHILOSOPHY OF MANAGEMENT

Bendetsen, Karl R., "A Philosophy of Management," *Atlanta Economic Review,* Vol. 17, Nos. 2–3 (February–March, 1967), pp. 6–8, 23.

Carzo, Rocco, Jr., "Administrative Science and the Role of Value Judgments," *Academy of Management Journal,* Vol. 3, No. 4 (December, 1960), pp. 175–181.

Davis, Ralph C., "A Philosophy of Management," *Academy of Management Journal,* Vol. 1, No. 4 (December, 1958), pp. 37–40.

Feigl, Herbert and May Brodbeck, *Readings in the Philosophy of Science.* New York: Appleton-Century-Crofts, Inc., 1953.

Jones, Manley H., "Evolving a Business Philosophy," *Academy of Management Journal,* Vol. 3, No. 3 (August, 1960), pp. 93–98.

Metcalf, Henry C. (ed.) *Business Management as a Profession.* Chicago: A. W. Shaw Company, 1927.

Sheldon, Oliver, *The Philosophy of Management.* New York: Pitman Publishing Company, 1965 (Original edition published 1924).

---

[9] For two excellent discussions of this point, see Learned, E. P., Dooley, A. R., & Katz, R. L. "Personal Values and Business Decisions." *Harvard Business Review,* March–April, 1959, pp. 111–120—and Bernthal, W. F., "Value Perspectives in Management." *The Journal of the Academy of Management, 5,* No. 3, December 1962, pp. 190–196.

Wortman, Max S., Jr., "A Philosophy of Management," *Advanced Management,* Vol. 26, No. 10 (October, 1961), pp. 11–15.

B. MANAGEMENT THEORY

Boddewyn, J., "Management: The Trees, the Forest and the Landscape," *Management International Review,* Vol. 7, Nos. 2–3 (1967), pp. 131–136.

Dutton, John M. and William H. Starbuck, "On Managers and Theories," *Management International Review,* Vol. 3, No. 6 (1963), pp. 25–35.

Filley, Alan C., "Common Misconceptions in Business Management," *Business Horizons,* Vol. 7, No. 3 (Fall, 1964), pp. 87–97.

Flippo, Edwin B., "Integrative Schemes in Management Theory," *Academy of Management Journal,* Vol. 11, No. 1 (March, 1968), pp. 91–98.

House, Robert J., "Research Criteria and Methods for the Development of Management Theory," *Academy of Management, Proceedings of the 1963 Annual Meeting.* University Park, Pa.: 1964, pp. 7–13.

Koontz, Harold, "The Management Theory Jungle," *Academy of Management Journal,* Vol. 4, No. 3 (December, 1961), pp. 174–188.

———— (ed.) *Toward a Unified Theory of Management.* New York: McGraw-Hill Book Co., 1964.

McFarland, Dalton E., "Theory as an Angle of Vision in Management Education," *Academy of Management, Proceedings of the 25th Annual Meeting.* Bowling Green, Ohio: 1966, pp. 3–11.

McGuire, Joseph W. *Interdisciplinary Studies in Business Behavior.* Cincinnati, Ohio: South-Western Publishing Co., 1962.

Suojanen, Waino, "Management Theory: Functional and Evolutionary," *Academy of Management Journal,* Vol. 6, No. 1 (March, 1963), pp. 7–18.

Urwick, Lyndall F., "Have We Lost Our Way in the Jungle of Management Theory?" *Personnel,* Vol. 42, No. 3 (May–June, 1965), pp. 8–18.

Woolf, Donald A., "The Management Theory Jungle Revisited," *Advanced Management Journal,* Vol. 30, No. 4 (October, 1965), pp. 6–15.

C. MANAGERIAL ETHICS AND SOCIAL RESPONSIBILITY

Carr, Albert Q., "Is Business Bluffing Ethical?" *Harvard Business Review,* Vol. 46, No. 1 (January–February, 1968), pp. 143–153.

Clark, John W. *Religion and the Moral Standards of American Businessmen.* Cincinnati, Ohio: South-Western Publishing Co., 1966.

Gilman, Glenn, "The Ethical Dimensions in American Management," *California Management Review,* Vol. 7, No. 1 (Fall, 1964), pp. 45–52.

Johnson, Harold T., "Socially Responsible Firms: An Empty Box or a Universal Set?" *Journal of Business,* Vol. 39, No. 2 (April, 1966), pp. 394–399.

Lorig, A. W., "Corporate Responsibilities," *Business Horizons,* Vol. 10, No. 1 (Spring, 1967), pp. 51–54.

McGuire, Joseph W., "Management Concepts: Fads and Fancies," *Dun's Review and Modern Industry,* Vol. 87, No. 3 (March, 1966), pp. 47–48, 80.

Towle, Joseph W. (ed.) *Ethics and Standards in American Business.* Boston: Houghton-Mifflin Co., 1964.

PART II

Process Approaches

While the scientific management school was dominating management practices in American industry in the early part of the Twentieth Century, the process approach [1] was influencing management thought in Europe. Henri Fayol, a French executive, developed the process or functional approach while managing a metallurgical company in France. He emphasized the importance of top management in carrying out certain managerial functions, including planning, organizing, commanding, coordinating, and controlling. [2] Contrary to the empirical approach of the scientific management school, the process approach was based primarily upon Fayol's observations and experience in management. Unfortunately for the field of management, Fayol's contributions were not translated into English until after his death in 1925, and were not generally available in the United States until 1949.

As the process approach became known, several other writers elaborated upon the various functions. [3] In general, the process school has been oriented

---

[1] The process approach is also called the functional or classical approach.

[2] Henri Fayol, *Industrial and General Administration*, trans. J. A. Coubrough. Geneva: International Management Institute, 1929; and Henri Fayol, *General and Industrial Management*. London: Sir Isaac Pitman and Sons, Ltd., 1949.

[3] For example, see: R. C. Davis, *The Fundamentals of Top Management*. New York: Harper and Bros., 1951; William H. Newman, Charles E. Summer, and E. Kirby Warren, *The Process of Management* (second edition). Englewood Cliffs, N. J.: Prentice-Hall, Inc., 1967; George Terry, *Principles of Management* (fifth edition). Homewood, Ill.: Richard D. Irwin, Inc., 1968; Harold Koontz and Cyril O'Donnell, *Principles of Management* (fourth edition). New York: McGraw-Hill Book Co., Inc., 1968; and Henry H. Albers, *Principles of Organization and Management* (second edition). New York: John Wiley and Sons, Inc., 1965.

to the tasks of the executive, and has attempted to establish principles which determine the ways in which the various functions should be carried out. Most of these principles have been based upon managerial experience, although a few have been derived from experimental studies by faculty members. The process approach has been applied to all levels of the managerial hierarchy in both public and private organizations.

Academic scholars and practitioners have continued to develop the process approach. This part covers some of the recent research and thought in that continuing evolution.

In the planning section, Professor George A. Steiner emphasizes the importance of long-range planning in all firms regardless of size, and develops the role of top management in those plans. In the next selection, Professor H. Igor Ansoff analyzes the importance of judgment and past experience in planning, and then points out the relationship between managerial decision-making and planning for the entire firm.

In modern organizations, the distinction between line and staff is the formal organization. In the second article on control, Mr. Gerry E. Morse describes the continuing technological change, and the computer. In his discussion of an experiment in one firm, Professor Melville Dalton attempts to clarify the line-staff relationship. By using a new set of internal organizational relationships, the company tried to minimize conflict between the line and staff. In another study, Dr. Robert E. Thompson examines some of the conceptions and misconceptions about span of control by examining some of the cost implications, the question of coordination, the need for supervisory training, and the utilization of staff services.

Professor Keith Davis discusses two types of leadership and the effectiveness of each. In his conclusions, he points out that the trend is toward a new orientation in the type of leadership being employed in industry. In the next selection, Professor J. G. Hunt describes a model of leadership and some empirical attempts to test that model.

In the control section, Professor Kenneth J. Arrow analyzes the control problem in three types of large organizations, including large corporations, governmental budgetary operations, and economic systems as a whole. He examines the roles of uncertainty and information in controlling the various parts of an organization. In the second article on control. Mr. Gerry E. Morse describes the relationship between control and the structure of the organization.

Today managers have achieved high levels of mobility between firms, between industries, and between private and public organizations. In his study of executive mobility, Professor Eugene E. Jennings explores the mobility patterns of managers, the distribution of mobile managers in organizations, and the problems which such managers encounter. In the last selection, Mr. Edward G. Matthews points out the ways in which the manpower pool within a given firm and the different skill levels within that pool can be controlled.

A

PLANNING

7. The Critical Role of Top Management in Long-Range Planning

GEORGE A. STEINER

There is no substitute for long-range planning in the development of profitable and healthy organizations. It is not, of course, the only requirement, but it is a major one. Too few companies, particularly the smaller and medium-sized ones, and too few government organizations try or do effective long-range planning.

In examining many long-range planning programs, I have come to two major conclusions. First, the fundamental concept of an effective long-range planning program is deceptively simple. Second, creating and maintaining a first-rate long-range planning program is deceptively difficult and demands, for its success,

devoted attention by chief executives. I should like to discuss these two points, but first I should like to say a few words about the importance of effective long-range planning.

Importance of Long-Range Planning

There exists in some business and government quarters surprising resistance to developing systematic and comprehensive planning. Naturally there are a great many reasons for such resistance, but failure to grasp the significance of effec-

Reprinted from *Arizona Review,* Vol. 14, No. 4 (April, 1966), pp. 5–13, with permission of the publisher. George A. Steiner is Professor of Business Administration and Director, Division of Research, Graduate School of Business Administration, University of California, Los Angeles.

tive planning is more important than it should be.

Several years ago, Mr. S. C. Beise, then President of the Bank of America, observed that for many years before World War II commercial banks did not aggressively seek savings deposits. As a result, the industry did not involve itself importantly in the related field of real estate financing. After World War II, building boomed and little financial firms grew dramatically to fill the home financing need. Mr. Beise commented:

Today these once-small savings and loan companies constitute a big industry in the United States and have given banks stiff competition for savings funds. The commercial banking industry today has made a strong comeback in the fields of savings and real estate lending, but due to its lack of foresight some twenty years ago, the banking industry gave birth to one of its own biggest competitors. I believe the industry has learned its lesson well, and it is one every industry and company should note.[1]

A recent study of the thirteen fastest growing companies in the United States revealed that all give high priority to long-range planning and manage to inspire most levels of managers to think about the future.[2]

Not only are more companies discovering the advantages of comprehensive and effective planning programs, but governments are developing organized long-range planning programs. This movement is particularly rapid among Western European governments and some developing nations. Last August President Johnson dramatically announced that the planning-programming-budgeting system introduced into the Pentagon by Secretary McNamara must

be applied throughout the government.

There are many reasons why systematic and structured long-range planning is considered so important by progressive businesses and non-business organizations. Effective planning prevents ad hoc decisions, random decisions, decisions that unnecessarily and expensively narrow choices for tomorrow. Effective planning gives an organization a structural framework of objectives and strategies, a basis for all decision making. Lower-level managers know what top management wants and can make decisions accordingly. But there are also ancillary benefits. An effective planning organization, for example, provides a powerful channel of communications for the people in an organization to deal with problems of importance to themselves as well as to their organization.

It is difficult to exaggerate the importance of effective comprehensive planning to an organization. It has, for many companies, provided that margin needed for outstanding growth and profitability.

A Conceptual Model of Long-Range Planning

A conceptual model of planning at a sufficiently low level of abstraction is a guide in establishing a complete system. The words *long-range planning* are useful in emphasizing a time dimension to planning. In describing an effective planning program, however, I prefer to speak of comprehensive, corporate or total planning.

Planning in this sense may be described from four points of view. First, a basic generic view of planning as dealing with

---

[1] S. C. Beise, "Planning for Industrial Growth: An Executive View," remarks before the Milan Conference on Planning for Industrial Growth, sponsored by Stanford Research Institute, 1963, mimeographed.

[2] Jack B. Weiner, "What Makes a Growth Company?," *Dun's Review and Modern Industry*, November 1964.

the futurity of present decisions. This means that current decisions are made in light of their long-range consequences. It means also that future alternatives open to an organization are examined and decisions made about preferred alternatives. On this basis, guidance is provided for making current operating decisions. There are also many other conceptual views of planning; one concept, for example, recognizes planning as reasoning about how you get from here to there.

Planning is also a process. It is a process which establishes objectives; defines strategies, policies and sequences of events to achieve objectives; defines the organization for implementing the planning processes; and assures a review and evaluation of performance as feedback in recycling and process.

Planning may be considered from a third point of view—namely, as a philosophy. Planning has been described as projective thought, or "looking ahead." Planning in this sense is an attitude, a state of mind, a way of thinking.

Finally, planning may be viewed in terms of structure. Long-range planning, as the term is typically used in the business world, refers to the development of a comprehensive and reasonably uniform program of plans for the entire company or agency, reaching out over a long period of time. It is an integrating framework within which each of the functional plans may be tied together and an overall plan developed for the entire organization.

Broadly, this structure includes four major elements (Figure 1). The first consists of strategic plans. These are a loose, written and unwritten set of major objectives, strategies and policies. The second is a detailed, uniform and a rather complete medium-range set of plans (two to seven, but generally five, years) covering major areas of organizational activ-

ity. The third part is short-term plans and budgets. The fourth structural part consists of planning studies which frequently are projections of things to come. A government agency, for example, may make a study of future revenues and demands for funds. A public utility may make population projections for its area. An automobile company may study changing consumer tastes, likely competitor moves and developing automotive technology. Such forecasts are not plans. The results of such studies, however, are important in actually making plans.

Long-range planning as the term is typically used in the business world does not refer so much to the future span of time covered as to the idea of management grappling systematically with future opportunities, problems and alternative courses of action. Many companies typically have the pattern of plans and the concepts of planning already defined. This can be and often is called long-range planning. But I prefer other words to describe this structure.

Long-Range Planning in Large and Small Businesses

All companies plan ahead in some degree. But not all have the sort of concept and structure noted here. While statistics on this subject are rather poor, I think it is probably true that close to a majority of the largest companies throughout the world have some sort of overall business planning program and a staff assigned to help executives do the work. Two years ago I held a research seminar at the Palais de Fontainebleau, France to discuss strategic business planning. About one hundred directors of corporate planning or top line managers of the largest multinational corporations of the world were present. One of the surprising conclusions reached at the

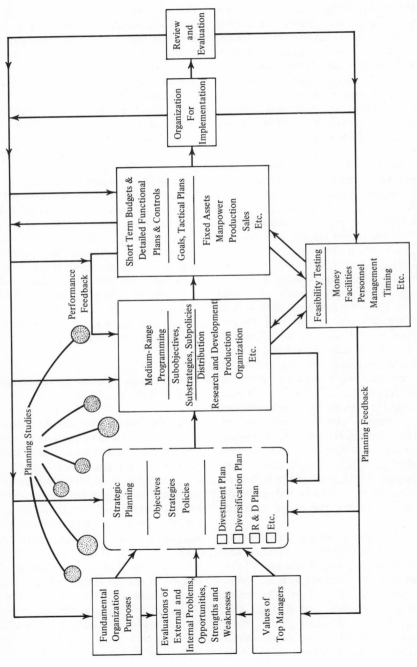

Figure 1. *A Structure and Process of Business Planning.*

seminar was that, despite the great surface diversities of planning among these companies, there was a large degree of comparability among basic planning definitions, principles, procedures and structures.[3]

There are relatively fewer numbers of medium and small-sized companies with comprehensive planning programs, but their numbers are growing. They are beginning to realize that, despite their limited resources, they have about the same fundamental planning requirements as the larger companies. Their salvation is not to ignore the problem but to develop short-cuts and rough-cut techniques for dealing with it.[4] There are many ways for a small company to get outside help at a reasonable price. Local banks can give advice. Many consulting agencies are available. Even professors are sometimes handy as consultants. Placing on his board of directors some persons who can contribute to long-range planning may also be attractive to a small businessman.

Systematic and reasonably well-structured planning programs are required by all organizations to survive and progress in the most healthy and effective manner. This is not something that only large companies need and are able to do. The requirement for effective planning exists for small companies, trade associations, industrial development agencies and for governments.

Professor Frank Gilmore of Cornell University presents the necessity for better planning in small businesses with this warning:

The swing to strategic planning in large organizations constitutes a serious threat to small business management. It challenges one of the important competitive advantages which the small company has enjoyed—being faster on its feet than the larger company in adapting to changing conditions. It is perfectly clear that mere adaptation in the short run will no longer suffice. Trends must henceforth be made, not simply coped with.[5]

His point, of course, is that strategic planning among small businesses and smaller nonprofit organizations must accompany the better planning of the larger organizations. Smaller organizations can plan ahead systematically and continuously. First, however, there must be a recognition by the chief executive that this is possible. Then the smaller organization must devise ways and means to perform planning at a cost under benefit.

Naturally, different organizations go about meeting their planning responsibilities in different ways. Many big corporations have a large central planning staff reporting to the chief executive through a senior vice president. Each of the divisions of such a company may also have a planning staff. At the other extreme are the very small firms where the chief executive does almost all the planning. As firms increase in size, the chief executive may get help by hiring a special assistant, by using his vice presidents in ad hoc advisory planning committees or by using his vice presidents and functional officers as a permanent planning staff to help him develop plans.

In a similar fashion, basic principles

[3] See George A. Steiner and Warren M. Cannon, eds., *Multinational Corporate Planning* (New York: The Free Press, Spring 1966).

[4] For suggestions about how to do this, see Roger A. Golde, "Practical Planning for Small Business," *Harvard Business Review,* September–October 1964; Myles L. Mace, "The President and Corporate Planning," *Harvard Business Review,* January–February 1965; and Raymond M. Haas, Richard I. Hartman, John H. James and Robert R. Milroy, *Long-Range Planning for Small Business,* Bureau of Business Research, Graduate School of Business, Indiana University, 1964.

[5] Frank G. Gilmore, "Strategic Planning's Threat to Small Business," mimeographed, 1966.

essential for effective planning apply to all organizations—large and small, profit and nonprofit. Precisely how the principles are applied, however, does differ among organizations and among problems and over time.

Of cardinal importance in creating and maintaining useful comprehensive planning programs is the role played by chief executives.

Top Management's Key Role in Planning

There can and will be no effective long-range planning in any organization where the chief executive does not give it firm support and make sure that others in the organization understand his depth of commitment. Yet one competent observer finds:

Probably the single most important problem in corporate planning derives from the belief of some chief operating executives that corporate planning is not a function with which they should be directly concerned. They regard planning as something to be delegated, which subordinates can do without responsible participation by chief executives. They think the end result of effective planning is the compilation of a "Plans" book. Such volumes get distributed to key executives, who scan the contents briefly, file them away, breathe a sigh of relief, and observe, "Thank goodness that is done—now let's get back to work." [6]

This, of course, shows a lack of understanding of the planning task and the responsibility of the top executive. Another competent observer says the matter is not so much a lack of understanding but abdiction of responsibility. Professor O'Donnell has said:

I think one of the outstanding facts about corporate planning at the present is that the presidents of corporations have been ducking their jobs. . . . They seem to be following the practice of setting in a fuzzy way some objectives to be accomplished in the future and establishing a committee, with the staff help of a planning group, to come up with a plan for achieving the objectives. From this point until the plan is presented to him, the president almost abdicates his responsibilities. When the plan is placed on his desk it is often too late for him to exert much influence on it. [7]

It is essential that the chief executive assume primary responsibility for his organization's long-range planning. When he hires an assistant to help him, or establishes a planning staff, he is merely extending his reach. These people are helping him do *his* job. This is a recognition that the world is too large for one man to grasp completely, and that to the extent he can get others to help him he will be more able to examine a wider range of threats to and opportunities for his organization.

Issues concerning the role of the chief executive in the development of plans are subtle and complex. I participated in one conference with chief executives where the major focus was on the relationship of the president with his staff in the development of corporate plans. These executives were dedicated to the idea of comprehensive planning but were uncertain about many matters relating to their participation. The range of alternatives is very wide. Effective planning, for example, requires that the top executive "buy it." He must believe in planning as being important to the success of his enterprise. He must give more than "lip service" to the effort. He must feel committed, and his support must be visible to others in the corporation. By his actions the chief executive will set the psy-

---

[6] Mace, *op. cit.*, p. 50.

[7] George A. Steiner, ed., *Managerial Long-Range Planning* (New York: McGraw-Hill Book Co., Inc., 1963), p. 17.

chological climate in which planning is done.

How an executive does these things will depend upon his style of management, the way his company is organized, the personalities involved and his own sense of commitment. For example, if the chief executive devotes most of his attention to short-range problems, this emphasis will not be lost on his subordinates. Even if he is interested in long-range planning, can he find the time to do it properly? I agree partly with Senator Jackson for example, when, speaking about the federal government, he observed:

. . . I am convinced that we never will get the kind of policy planning we need if we expect the top-level officers to participate actively in the planning process. They simply do not have the time, and in any event they rarely have the outlook or the talents of the good planner. They cannot explore issues deeply and systematically. They cannot argue the advantages and disadvantages at length in the kind of give-and-take essential if one is to reach a solid understanding with others on points of agreement and disagreement.[8]

While this observation does have an important element of truth in it for a large government department or a large multinational business, it has much less for a small enterprise where the chief executive must plan if any planning is to be done. But even in the largest companies and government agencies the chief executives must get involved in the substance of planning. If they do not they will clearly be abdicating one of their major responsibilities. At the very least they will be captives of their planning staffs and thereby lose some element of control of their enterprises.

But the question still exists: how shall

the chief executive participate in the substance of planning? There is no simple answer. For the first planning effort, the chief executive of any organization—large or small, profit or non-profit—ought to be deeply involved. Once the planning program has gotten on a solid footing, with periodic cycling, general understanding and acceptance, the chief executive will know more clearly at what points and how much his participation is required. If a company, for example, has just begun the planning process and is pounding out long-range objectives, the chief executive should be intimately involved. Once those objectives are established, he must help make and approve strategies to reach them. When this work is done, he may get involved in subsequent cycles of planning only with selected changes in specific objectives and strategies. Both he and his staff will know better with experience what these points are. There is no ready answer for any chief executive, however, to the question of when and how much he can delegate to and rely upon his staff—both line and functional—what are, in the end, his planning responsibilities.

It is not enough that the chief executive participate in the planning exercise. His relationship to it must be visible to others in the organization. By various methods open to him, the chief executive must have others know about and understand his interest in the process.

Developing the Plan

It is a major responsibility of the chief executive to see that the proper planning system is developed and maintained. In this effort, of course, he will have help from subordinates—both line managers and their staffs. But it is his responsi-

---

[8] Henry M. Jackson, "To Forge a Strategy for Survival," *Public Administration Review,* Vol. XIX (Summer 1959), p. 159.

bility to make sure that the system is appropriate to his enterprise, and that it is done at a cost (using this word broadly) under benefit which produces optimum values.

Many years ago I had the job of helping an organization develop its first comprehensive planning program. In preparing procedures and suggesting roles of people in the organization I ran into grave difficulties. People were not sure of their responsibilities, or did not want to assume the responsibility I suggested. Different people wanted to do different things which did not necessarily mesh. There were also other points of dispute. To solve the entire problem I prepared a letter for the signature of the chief executive which set forth the essential elements of the planning program, how it should be developed and who was responsible for what. This worked like a charm. From that day to this the top executives of that company have watched over the planning process. It is an outstanding system.

I am not saying, of course, that chief executives must get enmeshed in all the grubby details of a total planning program. What I do say is they must see that the job of planning the plan is done, that it is appropriate and put into operation.

Clarification of roles of participants in the planning process is important and raises complex issues. For example, since corporate planning staffs are direct aids to the chief executive he must see that their roles are clear and generally understood.

A staff, for example, which fails to distinguish between strategic planning and tactical planning may lose top management if it gets too deeply involved in the details of tactical planning. Top management is interested in both strategic and tactical planning, but principally strategic planning. I once knew a staff that simply could not get itself out of the morass of details involved in short-range tactical planning. It was not long before the top management and its planning staff stopped talking to one another. There have been managers who simply could not differentiate between their responsibilities for strategic as distinguished from short-range tactical planning. Their concentration on the latter got them involved in a sort of Gresham's law of planning: short-range planning tends to drive out long-range planning.

Subtle problems of staff role arise in the development of strategic plans by central planning staffs and plans and operations of divisions. Long-range plans made in one area of a company often make sense only when considered in light of other areas and of the company as a whole. In this light, corporate planning staffs inevitably get involved in this interrelationship. Their role in modification of plans to relate better to the company as a whole may result in bitter conflict with line officers if large issues are involved. No matter how clear staff roles may be this sort of conflict will arise. It is less likely to arise and less likely to be serious if roles are clearly specified and understood.

There is no question about the fact that planning should not be separated from doing. Upon examination, however, this is not as simple as it sounds. In the strategic planning area, for example, plans may be developed for divisional execution, and the divisions may not have much if any participation in their preparation. Even with close line and staff interrelations at central office headquarters, staff inevitably will make decisions. The mere choice of alternatives to present to line managers, for example, may implicitly be decision-making by staff. Problems of drawing a line of demarcation between staff and line decision-making, and planning and operations, vary from case to case in the development of plans, and from time to time. There can be no simple formula. But efforts to clarify staff role can prevent unnecessary conflict.

Even when the staff role is clear, however, difficult problems of relationships may arise. In larger companies with comprehensive planning programs, corporate functional staffs, including long-range planning staffs, review divisional plans at the request of top management. Plans are submitted up the line, but staffs help line managers review them. In one instance a president asked his director of long-range planning to review the plans of a powerful division manager. The president insisted upon a rigorous examination of the plans because of the substantial capital outlays sought by the divisional manager. The planner did so and provided the rationale for rejecting the plans. He was not very happy about his role. He had been cultivating this divisional manager for a long time in order to develop a better planning program in his division and to arrange better communications to help them both do a better planning job. Now the divisional manager felt he had been double-crossed. The corporate planner will have problems in rebuilding his lines of communication with this division.

The planning process is complex. There must be understanding of authority, responsibility, procedures and timing. The chief executive is responsible for seeing that this need is met.

Base Decisions on Plans

Comprehensive planning done with and on behalf of top management should result in operating decisions. Without decisions the planning process is incomplete. Failure to take action on prepared plans, or continuous vacillation, will weaken staff efforts. People simply will not be motivated to exert the energy, develop the creativity and use the imagination needed to make quality plans if top management ignores them or cannot seem to act upon them.

In one company I know, one month after a five-year long-range plan had been developed for the first time and approved by top management, the president announced a flat seven percent budget cut for all division budgets. This was his method to reduce costs. The announced reason was the need to bring costs within the year's anticipated revenues. With this announcement, the longer-range projects naturally were abandoned and the benefits of long-range planning cast in grave doubt.

The extent to which divisional line managers make decisions in light of strategic corporate plans raises a different type of problem. In some companies the connection between the corporate strategic plan and the divisional intermediate-range plans is very close. The two may, in effect, be prepared together. In one small company of about five hundred people making a variety of electronics equipment, there was a planning program where strategic plans were developed for the company as a whole and the divisions tied their sub-strategies and detailed long-range plans clearly and closely into the corporate plan. These were intermeshed because the two were done by about the same people and at about the same time. In other instances, the corporate strategic plan constitutes an umbrella under which the divisional plans are made but the interrelationship between the two is rather loose.

A somewhat different type of problem arises very subtly if divisional managers think that corporate planning staffs are making plans for them to execute. It can arise if chief executives do not get involved in the planning and accept staff recommendations without much or any reservation. In such cases divisional managers are likely to take this position to the corporate staff: "You made the plans, now execute them. Don't ask me to."

One of the major attributes of comprehensive corporate planning is that the structure, especially when written, permits managers down the organizational chain to make decisions with a reasonable degree of certainty they are in line with the objectives sought by higher level management. Naturally, if decisions made throughout an organization do not relate to the planning program, it will not be long before the planning program disappears.

This, of course, does not mean blind devotion to plan. Depending upon circumstances, it may be wise for a manager to make decisions which are very different than those planned. Flexibility must be injected into planning. There are a number of techniques to do this. One major method is for the chief executive to inject a philosophy and understanding of flexibility into the planning and operational decision-making process.

In sum, chief executives have an important role in assuring that decisions throughout the organization are made in light of plans and evolving circumstances —not blindly, not without reference to plans, but related meaningfully within a planning framework.

Planning Takes Time

While conceptually simple, a comprehensive long-range planning program for a large organization cannot be introduced overnight and expected to produce miraculous results immediately. Several years ago I calculated that about five years were required for a medium-sized or large company to develop an effective comprehensive planning system.[9] This was confirmed by another study.[10] Since there is so much more known today about how to develop effective comprehensive planning programs, it is possible to reduce this time span. Much depends upon the organization and what is going on inside it.

Among most initial efforts to develop comprehensive long-range planning programs with which I have been familiar, the first effort did not produce much of immediate substantive value. Yet, all those involved felt the effort worthwhile. This was so, I found, because the effort introduced a new point of view into the company which appeared to have important possibilities in future planning. It also was seen as a focal point for communicating in a common language about major problems. There are many other reasons why managements have been pleased with the first attempt at long-range planning even though it did not provide immediate substantive values. But first efforts do not always provide important bases for immediate decision.

An effective planning program of one company cannot be lifted intact and applied to another. While the fundamental process and structure may be removed from one company to another, the details of operation will vary. Furthermore, since an organization is a living, dynamic institution in a rapidly changing environment, the procedures for planning change.

---

[9] Steiner, *op. cit.,* pp. 19–21.

[10] R. Hal Mason, "Organizing for Corporate Planning," Proceedings of the Long Range Planning Service Client Conference, February 7–9, 1962, Menlo Park, Calif., Stanford Research Institute.

8. Planning as a Practical Management Tool

H. IGOR ANSOFF

For our purposes we need a quite simple, although fundamental, picture of the business firm. It can be viewed as a social organization composed of three basic resources: Physical in the form of plant, machinery, inventory; human in the form of managers, engineers, and workers; and a financial resource in money, securities, debtor obligations and borrowing power. The principal *function* of the firm is to convert these resources into goods and/or services.

Two important factors have to be recognized. All three resources are continually "used up" and need to be replenished, and the total amount of resources available to the firm at any given time is limited.

So far the social organization we have described is not particularly distinctive: There are other organizations which are also involved in resource conversion: Goodwill Industries, Army, Government, etc. A business firm is made distinctive by its motivation or what we normally call objectives. We generally recognize that a business firm's behavior is purposive and that a business firm characteristically seek to obtain the best return on its resources whatever the properties of this return may be.

The conception of the firm as a resource conversion mechanism becomes useful because we can immediately see one way in which to gain this objective. This is to optimize the firm's resource conversion efficiency: To organize, to control costs, to produce, to develop the product line, to merchandise in such a way as to get the most performance possible out of the firm's investment in its *current markets*. We will refer to this as the *operating problem* of the firm.

However, this is addressing only half the problem. A relevant question is whether the present product-market structure is the most potentially profitable allocation of the firm's resources, or whether some different produc.s and markets will produce better results.

To use a somewhat crude but descriptive analogy, in the operating problem we are seeking the best way to milk a cow, but if our basic interest is not the cow but in the most milk we can get for our investment, we must also make sure that we have the best cow money can buy.

Thus we have a second way in which the firm can solve its fundamental problem: Through allocating the firm's resources to product markets which offer the largest potential return. We will refer to this as the *strategic problem* of the firm.

Solving a Two-Level Problem

The distinction between the operating and the strategic problem is useful for several reasons. First, is the fact that

Reprinted from *Financial Executive,* Vol. 32 (June, 1964), pp. 34–37, with permission of the publisher. H. Igor Ansoff is Professor of Industrial Administration at the Graduate School of Industrial Administration, Carnegie-Mellon University.

their solution is the responsibility of the two primary levels of management. Generally speaking, the operating line management, from general manager on down, is responsible for maximizing the profitability of the resources entrusted to it on assigned products and markets. The corporate management, the president, his staff, and the Board are responsible for seeing to it that these products and markets are well chosen and that the firm is making best possible use of the various investment opportunities available to it. Secondly, the decisions involved in the two areas are different. Strategic decisions are concerned with questions such as what kinds of new business should the firm enter, which of its present products should it discontinue, how should resources of the firm be allocated between new and old business, whether to grow through external acquisition or internal development, what directions should the firm's basic and applied research take. The operating decisions deal with the questions of competition, pricing, product quality, product development, marketing effectiveness, manufacturing efficiency, inventory levels, and with the overall question of organizational efficiency.

A third reason why a distinction between the operating and the strategic problem is useful is because it highlights traditional management attitudes. Because the operating problem is a matter of day-to-day concern, because it involves all levels of management, and because managers, being human, feel more comfortable in dealing with known, tried, and familiar problems—for all these and some other reasons—top managements of a majority of firms have traditionally focussed their major attention on finding the best way of milking the cow: Of attaining the firm's objectives through maximizing the resource conversion efficiency

in pursuit of traditional markets and product lines.

Recent economic, technological, political and business trends have been such as to make exclusive concentration on the operational problem progressively less profitable and sometimes even dangerous to survival of the firm. The mechanism which causes this is a kind of two-way squeeze on the firm: (a) On the one hand, many of the basic industries are witnessing a saturation of demand which is best recognized when the rate return on earnings reinvested in traditional business begins to decrease; and (b) on the other hand, the useful life-span of products is progressively being shortened through technological innovation. The resultant instability of product markets is a problem which has been of increasing concern to business during the post-WWII era. And this means, of course, increased concentration of management attention to the strategic problem of the firm.

The Management Decision Process

With this background, let us study the relation of planning to the management decision process. According to one of the most commonly used definitions, management is "a process of getting things done through people." Two questions underlie this definition: *What* is to be done and *how* is it to be done. Or, as Peter Drucker put it, "The end products of a manager's work are decisions and actions."

While the individual styles of decision-making have an infinite variety, they can generally be categorized into two modes of behavior: What is commonly known as day-to-day or *current* decision-making and deliberate or *planned* decision-mak-

ing. The difference between the two can
be illustrated by first describing what is
meant by a planned decision. Planned decisions have the following characteristics:

• An *anticipation* of decision needs;
• A clear recognition of the desired outcome of the decision;
• Construction of several alternative decisions which can be made;
• Evaluation of each alternative with
respect to its ability to meet the purpose;
and finally
• Selection of the preferred alternative.

In brief, a planned decision involves a
*systematic prior examination of the con-
sequences* of the required decision.

The current decision, by definition,
lacks the elements of anticipation—it is
made when the need arises; and it lacks,
in most cases, a comparison of alternatives through prediction of their outcomes. It is the type of decision which a
businessman is continuously called upon
to make. In making it in his daily work
he relies on either judgment and past experience, or refers back to a precedent,
or applies a standing rule or policy of the
firm. No systematic prior analysis takes
place.

There is no ironclad proof that
planned decisions will necessarily lead to
results superior to decisions based on
outright judgments. Much depends on the
complexity of the situation and the experience and ability of the decision-
maker. However, if the decision situation
is very complex such as, for example, the
decision whether to develop a new product, or if the problem falls outside the
decision-maker's experience, such as the
decision whether to diversify, then both
intuitively, as well as on the basis of a
considerable amount of evidence, we
would feel that planning pays off.

Time-Phased Implementation

Apart from its value in making decisions the planned approach has considerable value in *implementation*. Here
the prediction of consequences takes the
form of a time-phased schedule of accomplishments and resource commitments required to meet the end goal of
the decision. Such a time-phased *program*
provides a powerful management tool for
coordination, monitoring, and control of
performance as well as for periodic assessment of whether the decision was in
fact a good one.

As a matter of fact it is exactly this
type of program document which is usually identified as *the plan* by most companies which do planning. It may have
different names: Business plan, profit
plan, management forecast, management
budget. It may vary with respect to time
horizon. Two documents are frequently
prepared: one for the forthcoming year
and another for a longer term which
varies from three to ten years. But essentially it is a time-phased spelling out of
the accepted course of action for the firm.
It will typically start with a sales forecast
by product and customer and will translate this forecast into schedules of accomplishments by manufacturing, engineering, and marketing. It will contain
associated schedules of expenditures usually classed by direct and indirect categories. The over-all picture is integrated
into a P&L forecast, cash flow forecast
and a capital budget.

Thus to the question "Is planning
practical?" the answer could be "Of
course it is, since it is a widely used management budgeting and control tool."
However, a natural rejoinder would be
to say, "If this is all there is to planning,
then why all the fuss, why have a lot of
planners around? To engage in this kind
of budgeting all the firm needs are some

competent market researchers, financial analysts, and a few good cost estimators." We would agree provided two facts were true: (a) If this kind of budgeting were *all* there is to planning and (b) if the present budgeting techniques and formats were satisfactory for the purposes for which they are used. In point of fact, neither condition exists: (a) There is much more to planning than just the management budget and (b) the techniques and the formats are creaking at the joints.

Limitations of space prevent us from a discussion of item (b). In passing it should be pointed out that the techniques and format problem arise out of their inadequacies as operational control documents. It is this kind of problem that has given rise, for example, to the PERT and PERT/COST techniques for project planning.

Planning for the Entire Allocation Pattern

We now see that the planning document discussed above is only one of several needed by the firm. That document we can recognize as addressed to the operating problem of the firm. From the new vantage point we can see that before such an operations plan is constructed, it is highly desirable to examine the entire resource allocation pattern of the firm and to make two fundamental decisions: What should be the division of the firm's effort and resources between traditional and new business areas, and what specific new business areas should the firm seek to enter? The document which embodies these decisions is what we will call the *strategic plan*. The operations plan can then follow, based on the resource allocation for pursuit of traditional business and the guidance provided by the strategic plan.

The resources allocated to pursuit of new business must also be planned. The following decisions need to be made: (a) Selection of specific types of products and markets to be pursued in new business areas, (b) choice of the means for diversification: whether to acquire, to develop with the company's own resources, or to do both, (c) means of financing: through reinvestment of earnings, borrowing additional equity, or exchange of equity. All these decisions need to be elaborated in a time-phased development program listing milestone accomplishments and allocations of personnel, money and facilities. We will call the resulting document the *development plan*.

Yet another document is needed to complete the structure. The development plan will allocate resources between external acquisition and internal development. Some of the latter will be in support of the present product line and some for new business areas. Basic decisions need to be made: What should be allocated between basic research, applied research and product development; what directions and projects will research pursue; what product development projects will be undertaken; what will be the mix between brand new and improved products.

Product development without a parallel effort to analyze and develop appropriate markets would result in what has been called "solutions in search of a problem." R&D planning activity should include, therefore, parallel decisions with respect to markets: What areas of customer needs will the firm seek to fill, what market research projects will be undertaken, what steps will be taken to establish sales capabilities for the new products.

The document which embodies the entire complex of activities in internal product research and development we will call the *research and development* plan.

The Generation of Subsidiary Plans

Starting with an analysis of the problems of the firm we have thus generated a rather complicated structure of plans, each addressed to a specific problem of the firm and yet related to one another. The job of planning does not stop here. Each of the major plans generates subsidiary plans. The development plan needs to be supported by a plan for mergers and acquisitions as well as by a plan for such divestments of existing products and markets as may be necessary. The R&D plan must be backed up by functional plans for marketing, manufacturing, finance, and administration. Similar functional plans are needed in support of the operations plan.

The structure of plans we have discussed with related inputs and outputs is shown in Figure 1.

It should be recalled that each of the boxes implies two types of planning activities. The first step is to analyze the alternatives and to *arrive at the appropriate decisions.* The second is to program the decisions: To specify results and costs over time in a way designed to expedite management action, control, and lower-level decision-making.

While these two steps are closely related they require different analytic approaches, different types of talent and different format. There is no generally accepted business terminology used to describe the respective documents. The military terminology refers to the first type of document as the "plan" and the second as the "program." Perhaps more appropriate to business would be to describe the respective steps as "plans and budgets." In this definition the standard business planning document which we discussed earlier would be referred to as an "operations budget."

Now let us return to the original question, "Is planning practical?" Since we have already agreed that the operations

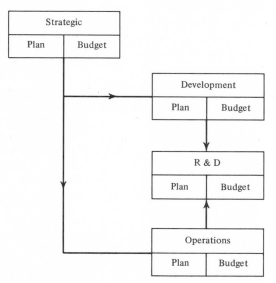

Figure 1. *Structure of Plans.*

plan has been proved by experience, the question can be rephrased into: "What kinds of plans should the firm make and how far down the organizational level should it carry them?"

Planning Must Be Responsive to the Firm's Problems

The answer to the first part is dictated by the relative management emphasis on the basic problems of the firm. If the firm is among the very few fortunate ones which can see a long path of growth in its traditional business, it can put a major emphasis on operations planning and R&D planning. The strategic plan and the development plans will be dictated largely by the evolutionary trends within the industry. While important, they will not require a major job of analysis. On the other hand, a firm in a dying industry will need to concentrate its major effort on strategic and development plans. To generalize, *the importance of strategic and development planning is directly related to the instability of the product-market demand in the firm's industry.*

The second part of the question— "How far down in organization should planning proceed?"—will vary from firm to firm depending on its size, diversification of the product line, complexity of its product and the nature of its product-market problems. However, some general rules can be suggested:

Generally, planning should be undertaken whenever the potential improvement of the operational unit (in terms of either increased output or reduced operating costs) can be shown to exceed the costs of the planning activity.

Somewhat more specifically, *planning of decisions* is appropriate at a particular level whenever it can be shown that the quality of decision-making can be improved through systematic analysis. This will generally occur when the decision problem is affected by many variables, when the outcomes of alternatives are not readily visualized, or when the decision area is new to the manager.

Planning of implementation is appropriate whenever the manager is in charge of a number of interdependent activities whose outcomes affect one another and whose relationship cannot be readily perceived.

Some qualifications are in order. The rules for deciding whether to plan are not precise formulas, but are rather intended as decision guidelines to be applied through intelligent judgment. There has been a steady growth of understanding of the meaning of social planning in general and business planning in particular, accompanied by continuous sharpening of planning tools and concepts. There is still work to be done before we have what can be called a discipline or theory of planning. However, enough tools are available now to enable planners to be of real assistance in increasing the profitability of business firms.

B

ORGANIZING

9. Changing Staff-Line Relationships

MELVILLE DALTON

This paper reports an attempt to eliminate staff and line conflict in an electronics firm. The terms "staff" and "line" continue to be controversial,[1] inadequate, and widely used. The traditional conflicts of staff and line have been reported for years,[2] and that pattern continues dominant. There are signs, however, that the older model may be changing in some industries. We can see these changes by comparing the concerns, behavior, characteristics, and situations of staff and line as I reported them earlier,[3] with those in the experiment at the Transode

Reprinted by permission from the March–April, 1966 issue of *Personnel Administration,* copyright 1966, Society for Personnel Administration, 1221 Connecticut Avenue, N.W., Washington, D.C. 20036. Melville Dalton is Professor of Sociology and Research Sociologist, Institute of Industrial Relations, University of California, Los Angeles.

I am indebted to the Institute of Government and Public Affairs, UCLA, for financial aid in making this study.

[1] They are controversial to some students because they are borrowed from the military, are too general, do not apply in all organizations, are used as catchalls by some, have become clichés—if we may use a cliché to condemn them. Despite shortcomings, the terms continue vital in industrial communication. Wilbert Moore has observed that "the line-staff division [is] the single most reliable one in any administrative organization. . . ." See *The Conduct of the Corporation,* New York: Random House, Inc., 1962, p. 136.

[2] Douglas McGregor, "The Staff Function in Human Relations," *Journal of Social Issues,* vol. 4, no. 3, 1948; George Homans, *The Human Group,* New York: Harcourt, Brace & Co., 1950, chaps. 14–15; Melville Dalton, "Conflicts between Staff and Line Managerial Officers," *American Sociological Review,* vol. 15, no. 3, 342–351; Charles A. Myers and John G. Turnbull, "Line and Staff in Industrial Relations," *Harvard Business Review* 34: 113–124, 1956.

[3] *Op. cit.* In addition to the sin of self-citation there is a weakness in treating this paper on three firms as representative of traditional staff-line problems in industry, but the continuing wide demand for it in industrial and other kinds of organizations makes it feasible for our purposes. The conditions reported are also recognized by implication in the remedial literature. See Robert C. Sampson, *The Staff Role in Management,* New York: Harper and Brothers, 1955, and Douglas McGregor, *The Human Side of Enterprise,* New York: McGraw-Hill Book Co., 1960, chaps. 11–12.

Corporation.[4] The charted polarities are qualified in the ensuing discussion and followed by details of the experiment and the unanticipated conflict that developed.

Item One. Staffs in the traditional pattern have no formal authority, except inside the staff or as temporarily delegated in the line. At Transode the technical staffs were autonomous and had authority that required the line to mirror staff theory and carry out its recommendations. Since all members of top management were staff in terms of training and were at least as concerned with staff rights and problems as with those of the line, the staff could not be challenged by middle and lower line. Authority was apportioned. Staff ideas were incorpo-

Staff-Line Characteristics

Traditional

1. Staff lacks formal authority over operations.
2. Line officers older.
3. Staff has significantly more formal education.
4. Pressures on staff to justify its existence in terms of ideas subject to rejection by the line.
5. Line salaries are higher.
6. Line tolerates staff with negative overtones.
7. Turnover of staff personnel greater than line.
8. Greater movement of staff officers to the line than the reverse.
9. Frequent sabotage or compromise of staff offerings.
10. Staff deferential to line.

Transode Corporation

1. Staff has defined authority.
2. Staff officers older.
3. Staff education not significantly greater than line.
4. Staff the dominant group. Line must accept staff ideas.
5. Staff salaries are higher.
6. Line positive toward staff.
7. Turnover of line personnel greater than staff.
8. No movement from staff to line, but limited movement from line to staff.
9. Absent.
10. Line deferential to staff.

---

[4] Fictitious name. The firm had some 1,100 personnel. Our concern here is with the 59 theoretically autonomous scientists (chiefly chemists and physicists), engineers, and related specialists who made up the "engineering" staff but who had no official hierarchy, and the 47 line officers (including 16 degreed engineers who were not called that) in a hierarchy of five levels.

I was introduced to the firm by one of the vice presidents who was a member of a non-credit seminar I gave. In the course of visiting the firm I was encouraged to look at an old interest. Casual talk with the chemists, physicists, and engineers revealed a freedom and influence on their part that required explanation. Repeated visits brought answers to my questions and opened personnel files.

Details on the number and characteristics of the top managers could identify the firm locally. But some behavior of the two most influential members should be noted to (a) counteract any impression in the paper that only impersonal "organizational" forces were at work, and (b) to recognize—without developing—the significance of what is so divergently treated under the heading of *leadership*. The two leaders had lectured in prominent universities. They read widely in the social sciences, particularly sociology, political science and economics—from the detached to the more popular and applied writings. Their experiment grew out of these readings as well as experience. Both were prepared to be autocratic to preserve democratic relations among all employees. One leader was of such influence that staff officers repeatedly referred to Transode as "his plant" or "his baby." Regarding the experiment as one to "level" all personnel, or one reflecting a collectivistic political formula, should be balanced with the fact that, as far as could be learned, all the officers were Republican in politics.

rated into the product, and staff views ordered the technology of production. On its side, the line controlled the personnel and processes of production.

Item Two. Line managers in the report of 1950 had a mean age of 48.7 as against 42.9 years for staff heads and specialists, which was a significant difference—assuming the conditions essential for such tests. Without inclusion in the staffs of several older ex-line officers, the staff statistic would have been considerably less.

At Transode the mean age of line managers was 29.0 years, that of the staff, 36.2 years. The difference, just missing .05 significance, would have been significant without inclusion of the staff-derived top managers in the line category.

Item Three. The earlier report showed the staffs to have a mean of 14.6 years for formal training as against all the line managers with a mean of 13.1 years, which was significant. At Transode, however, the staff mean of 16.2 years education was not significantly greater than the mean of 15.6 years for line managers.

Comparison of earlier and current staff groups with respect to the relevance of college training for official duties shows what is common knowledge, that education in the newer technical industries is increasingly a major criterion in hiring policy. Only 50 percent of the staff heads and assistants in the 1950 report were in positions pertinent for their training. (Again the figure would have been higher but for the presence in the staffs of older line failures with little formal education who had been dumped there sympathetically rather than released.) At Transode, on the other hand, 75.4 percent of the staff were in functions growing out of their academic specialty. The other 24.6 percent included personnel with "equivalent" practical experience, with only minor emphasis on *kind* of formal training, and some persons whom top managers had know in earlier positions and had been attracted to. Reflecting the dominant staff concern for technical training, and its influence in hiring research and all guiding personal, 75.7 percent of line managers were in charge of processes natural for their training.[5]

In large, traditional structures, the staff is likely to be used somewhat as a repository for older line officers who have lost their effectiveness and for members of local minority groups who would have smaller chance of receiving line posts. In the smaller, younger organization requiring advanced scientific knowledge in a changing, competitive field, the formal emphasis in both staff and line is on rejecting the unfit, and certainly in the staff on having no bars to competence. This was the condition at Transode. Its relatively greater spread of non-Anglo-Saxon ethnics in both line and staff than reported in earlier studies is suggested by entries in the table on ethnic composition.[6]

One might suspect that even in Transode's rational atmosphere the ma-

---

[5] The relevance of specialized training at Transode was apparently very high. In "1700 Top Executives," November 1959, pp. 138–143 and 307–308, *Fortune* reported that two-thirds of those in its sample with engineering degrees were doing work beside the point of their formal training, as were 40 percent of those with law degrees and three-quarters of those trained in research. The probable meaning is that other opportunities, personal growth and drive, wide abilities, as well as aid through friendships and related factors, weakened the training tie. Students point out that Max Weber and James Russell Lowell were trained in law, Zane Grey in dentistry, that Havelock Ellis, Elie Faure, and O. W. Holmes, Sr., were M.D.'s, etc.

[6] Ethnicity was learned by the questioning of closest informants, by study of names, and in some cases by chance.

jority ethnics would be allowed more latitude in meeting the general criterion that formal training and function should match. Possibly they were to a degree, since in both staff and line there was a slightly greater proportion of majority than minority ethnics with training not strictly relevant for their function, but the difference was far from significant (P < .40).

Item Four. In traditional structures, advisory groups must build a record to justify their existence. The line expects practical contributions presented modestly and without insistence. Where the line is difficult to deal with, successful staff members usually offer an idea so artfully that the line chief thinks—or can gracefully pretend—that it is his own. Less successful staff officers assure

Ethnic Composition

Ethnicity	Line No.	Line Percent	Staff No.	Staff Percent	Total Percent in Sample
Anglo-Saxon	25	53.1	23	39.0	45.3
German	5	10.6	17	28.8	20.7
French	4	8.5	8	13.5	11.3
Italian	4	8.5	1	1.7	4.7
Dutch	3	6.4	1	1.7	3.8
Spanish	—	—	3	5.1	2.8
Hindu	2	4.3	—	—	1.9
Japanese	—	—	2	3.4	1.9
Negro	—	—	2	3.4	1.9
Polish	2	4.3	—	—	1.9
Norwegian	2	4.3	—	—	1.9
Czech	—	—	2	3.4	1.9
Total	47	100.0	59	100.0	100.0

their failure by anxious drives for credit and acclaim from the line. Members of Transode's staffs, on the other hand, were never rebuffed, even by top line. Rather, they were consulted.

Item Five. Consistent with their deemphasis of status symbols (below), Transode's higherups hedged on giving specific comparative salaries. But they were positive in stating that staff heads —even in industrial relations, accounting, and purchasing—were paid more than the younger line officers, and that officers of the polytechnical staff of engineering received "much more" than any line officer below the top level. Fragmentary data from the interviews revealed that one of the non-engineering staff heads received a salary of $36,000 as compared with a salary of $29,000 for

a 28-year-old line officer at the middle level.

Though the 1950 study reported that line officers were more highly paid than staff, the exact salaries were not given and would in any case now be irrelevant because of progressive inflation. However, in a forthcoming study of management in 9 industries and 40 firms of national or regional importance (eight in electronics and aerospace industries), Reed M. Powell found that line officers consistently received higher salaries. For example, less than a third of the line officers received salaries as low as $25,-000, while 60 percent of the staff officers were under that amount. Eleven percent of the staff group received over $40,000, as compared with 28 percent of the line officers. Above $50,000 only 5.7 percent of the staff was included, as against 16.1 percent of the line. Staff officers in the salary levels above $30,000 were almost entirely engineers and scientists with higher degrees.

Item Six. Staff personnel still typically feel that they must yield to the line on disputed matters and wear gracious masks. But at Transode some of the scientists and technicians were secure to the point of behaving arrogantly toward the line.

The report of 1950 showed staff personnel smarting under terms implying that they were idle and ornamental— "chair-warmers" and "pretty boys." And Homans heard design engineers referred to as "temperamental" and as "prima donnas." [7] At Transode name-calling was limited, but the staff was the target. Five of six middle-line officers past age 35 who had had experience in traditional structures called some of the technicians and scientists "white tower boys," "egomaniacs," and "creativity nuts," terms which show an element of reversed staff-line conflict with the line feeling fear and reluctant deference.

Item Seven. Data omitted from the earlier paper and reported elsewhere [8] showed a turnover of staff personnel nearly three times as great as that for the line over a period of four successive years. The difference was attributed to the greater youth, education, and career drive and lower job prospects in the staffs. This contrasts with Transode, where there was practically no turnover among staff officers, as compared with a rate of 60 percent in the line over recent years.

Item Eight. Because of the typically greater income and local standing of line officers, as well as the lower career ceiling in the staffs, staff personnel with their greater youth and education are more likely to push into line officers than for line supervisors to make the reverse shift. Transferees from line to staff are often being gently released from the line as persons who have served well but are increasingly unable to deal with new developments.

Neither of these trends existed at Transode. But there were rare transfers of pertinently trained line managers to the staff.

Item Nine. The sporadic sabotage and frequent resistance to staff offerings in traditional structures was absent at Transode. However, there was apparently some wish or even overt attempt to evade staff changes or controls, for line managers occasionally boasted of "cracking down" on attempted compromises of staff theory or departure from practices set up by staff officers. In some cases this boast may have been empty and made only to impress staff officers with line alertness.

Item Ten. Where the line is dominant, staffs are deferential for the sake of acceptance, aid on the job, and career success. In the largely reversed situation at Transode, the youthful line foremen (79 percent under age 30) proudly recounted their golf games and social interaction with the scientists and high technicians. They noted the "wonderful opportunity to learn . . . almost like being paid to go to school." Indirect questioning also indicated that in any possible clash between staff and line, the foremen would support the staff.

In summary, traditional staff-line conflicts were negligible at Transode. The

---

[7] *Op. cit.,* p. 375.

[8] *Men Who Manage,* New York: John Wiley & Sons, 1959, p. 96. Turnover was determined by dividing the average number of personnel into the accessions or separations, whichever was smaller.

old question of authority was minimal because authority was defined and shared and the division enforced. With respect to age, amount and relevance of training, the kinds of organizational pressures that existed, the career blocks of personnel, their respective rates of turnover and direction of transfers in the firm, the in-groups they deferred to or disesteemed, the qualities and conditions of the two groups were either reversed [9] or markedly unlike what is typical in industrial staff and line structures.

The Experiment

Initiation of the experiment was simplified by the fact that it did not require changes in an existing organization, but was coincidental with the organization itself. Transode was founded by a group of frustrated engineers and scientists formerly associated with the staff departments of a large, traditionally structured corporation. All [10] were deeply experi-

enced with the problems and tactics for their kind of living in such organizations. And all were determined to build an organization that would allow them the relative autonomy and expression they had been without.

Toward this end the initial steps were to draw tested associates, both staff and some lower-level older line officers, from the original corporation. These recruits shortly totaled about one-fourth of the present body of officers. All were of course bound together both by personal ties and the hazards of a new enterprise.

After refining policy on division of authority, the lesser problems—to them at that point—of finance, market and sales, unique features of the product, tactics in meeting competitors, and employee recruitment were solved with minimum trouble. The daring step for our interest was the relatively successful action by the previously thwarted status-conscious staff officers to minimize visible status distinctions as the major means of reducing staff-line conflict.[11]

---

[9] Etzioni has discussed the reversal of traditional staff-line roles in professional organizations and the role of professionals in semiprofessional, nonprofessional, and administrative organizations. See Amatai Etzioni, "Authority Structure and Organizational Effectiveness," *Administrative Science Quarterly,* 4 (June 1959), pp. 43–67, and *Modern Organizations,* Englewood Cliffs, N.J., Prentice-Hall, Inc., 1964, chap. 8. As a profit organization with numerous autonomous scientists and engineers (in the staffs), with problems of communication (below) among its staffs, with some top managers holding Ph.D.'s and serving as scientific consultants at large, with a professional atmosphere and several professionals behaving unprofessionally, Transode was difficult to label with precision, but if a label is needed it could be called semiprofessional.

[10] They were but one of the many "splinter" or "breakoff" groups common in Southern California. Organizations from these groups are commonly formed in two ways: by people from several parts of the parent firm who reach unity through their shared frustrations and set up their own organization; or by an internal splinter group whose members arrived late—often brought in by an over-rational president—in the parent structure as a formal group and were never accepted by competing departments, so developed the unity to break off almost as a department after acquiring the local expertise. Transode was formed in the first way.

[11] Apparently this decision was not arrived at through equal awareness and conviction about what provokes such conflict or what corrective checks should be imposed. Responding to my comments on implied motives as to why the muting of staff-line rivalries had become a concern, one higher manager caught my guess that his group had a program from the start and declared, "No, we were not that smart." But another, with greater authority behind a lesser title, said that for him the paper of 1950 had "spelled out the problem, so the solution was clear."

The character of the experiment can be discussed under the heads of seating patterns, furniture, restrooms, parking lots, organization charts, titles, lunch situations, and dress.

Seating Patterns. Offices throughout the firm were large, unpartitioned rooms. Clerical personnel and officers of a given department were seated in no way that indicated rank or function. In some organizations seats near windows—allowing a "view"—are associated with status. This was meaningless at Transode, unless reverse snobbery was involved, for in nearly all cases personnel of lesser status were seated next to windows. The top managers also lacked a seating cluster. They were inter-shuffled with about 30 clerical and staff functionaries and were easily accessible to all. In each of the several buildings there were interconnected conference rooms without locks to which officers of all ranks might go at will for more privacy—and be interrupted at any time by others seeking the same thing. The staff of Industrial Relations had a doorless entrance that welcomed all, though a secretary seated outside in a similar open office volunteered help to any person entering the area. The only seats of isolated distinction were those of the receptionists in each building. These greeters were symbols of the firm and essentially aloof from all local groups but the top echelon.

Furniture. In all offices the desks, chairs and filing cabinets were uniform in material, size and finish and were spartan with respect to comfort. This is contrary to most industrial practices, where line officers usually have more luxurious appointments than staff, and levels in the staff are materially distinct. Thus, the example set by Transode chiefs made it possible for both staff and line groups to share the same aspect and enabled the line to reconcile seeming uniformity with the fact of its five formal levels. Functional status differences would have to find other avenues of expression, for lack of fitness could not easily masquerade behind symbols of rank.

However, lest visitors and customers feel undistinguished in this uniformity, management made one exception. After a visitor signed in he was taken to a conference room like the others except that it could be locked and had, in addition to the uniform furniture, a sumptuously upholstered armchair. Here the visitor sat, and the manager or staff officer took a plain chair. The visitor was presumably not only honored but impressed with the company's focus on unfrilled efficiency.[12]

Restrooms. Often the privacy and luxury of these facilities correlate with rank, and line opulence is greater than staff. But at Transode the uniformly stark restrooms in all offices and production sites were shared by all employees with no distinction but "men" and "women."

Parking Lots. None of the typical marks of status existed on the parking lots. There were no labeled stalls or reservations for any member of the organization. The lots were crowded, and

---

[12] Transode's use of uniform furniture as one phase of its effort to rationalize operations in the guiding group may not have historical significance but, it has a three-century-old parallel. Louis XIV's minister, Colbert, sought to make all France (excepting himself and some relatives) financially and industrially efficient, and to prevent exceptions by the privileged and highborn. As one of the 40-member French Academy of Science, Colbert was concerned to further its purpose and prevent erosion by social distinctions. When another associate, a noble, brought in an easy chair for his personal use, Colbert ordered 39 identical chairs for the other members. To class-conscious France this was so unusual that "the forty armchairs" became a synonym for the Academy.

latecomers of any rank took what was left and walked accordingly.

Organization Charts. Formal organization charts were not displayed on office walls. They did exist—in drawers and cabinets—but were deliberately kept in the background as far as employees or officers below the top level were concerned. For all their weakness, these charts were of some aid to top management's coordinative actions, but they were reserved primarily for the use of visitors and prospective customers who needed to understand the structure and who might want to tie rank and area to specific officers before meeting them in person. The charts were supplemented with a circular describing the major roles and backgrounds of officers filling them.

Titles. These were intentionally muted by being general and devoid of honorific richness. Top managers considered that any losses from use of vague titles would be compensated for by the gains. There were occasional disturbances attributable to the undefinitive titles. For example, newly graduated engineers, or persons from other organizations, sometimes raised questions about their title and job classification. Their concern apparently was to get an inkling of where they stood in the unspecified system, what latitude it allowed them, and what altitude it promised.

Though the answer to such anxieties might be uncertain, top officers remembered their former ties and theorized that job descriptions and refined titles (a) too easily lose touch with operations, (b) encourage the undesirable aspects of bureaucracy, and, worst of all, (c) stimulate concern with invidious distinctions rather than the constructive play of persons and functions. They held that more than minimal attention to charts and titles gives a misleading picture to developing leaders who must learn that neither functions nor compromised decisions

stay fixed. Transode's semi-unique product, the freedom of researchers and their continuing refinements of method, as well as ceaseless advances in the industry—all discouraged routinization.

Another condition that may have disturbed new employees, since visitors felt it, was the absence of names and titles on office doors. Where this might bewilder some, it impressed others as desirable informality, a place where the responsible faces circulated, and where diversity and change rivaled routine. Since office doors usually stood open, labels, or a formal open-door policy, would have been superfluous except for a night custodian who might wish to make his own distinctions in the care of offices.

For its desymbolization of individual and group status, Transode substituted the symbols of science, quality and service, which all officers as well as production employees could share. Outside and inside its buildings Transode placed its own unique symbol of science. On the inner walls there were photographs of (a) eminent scientists in the field, (b) kindred facilities and establishments, (c) the product and its place in the field. Enlarged charts of precision instruments and the product were both instructive and connotative. A visiting scientist described the firm as a "huge production laboratory." He might also have noted the impression that Transode gave of being a body of associates which impression was reinforced by the fact that all officers and a majority of production employees held stock in the company.

Lunch Situations. Transode was served by its cafeteria, an automat, and a mobile catering service. There were no facilities set up for or used exclusively by any specific group in or out of management. No invitations were required by anybody for entry to any service, as is often customary for admission to internal dining groups. Bag lunches, or food from the automat or catering service, were frequently carried to patios, and people sat where they chose.

Dress. This is a minor item but in a wide area of industry, as noted in the earlier report, there are customary—and functional in some cases—differences of dress in the line, and between much of the line and staff, that are related to distinctions of rank and that aggravate differences when frictions develop. At Transode there were no customary distinctions of dress. Scientists and technicians frequently wore white lab coats, as did many of the production employees and some line foremen. Similar dress concealed the actual distinctions and enabled all to seem to be scientists or engineers —exalted figures requiring no mark of status—especially to the frequent visitors.

The Conflict That Existed

To speak of conflict without reference to cooperation distorts what occurs. But a report of this kind is a focus on the unusual and assumes that cooperation is dominant or there would be no continuing organization to study. The fact that Transode's production increased over 400 percent in a relatively short time, and that outside financial reports praised the firm's successful competition with companies several times its size, indicates that hurtful conflict was subordinate to cooperative behavior.

Conflict can be discussed under (a) staff-line, and (b) interstaff and intrastaff tensions.

Staff-Line. This tension arose from the relatively greater power of the staff in plant affairs, and, as a corollary, from the lack of a safety valve to ease career rivalries in the line.

Staff "Aggression." A few suspicious staff engineers and scientists gave their female assistants or secretaries assignments as socializing observers among the many female production employees to uncover any processual improprieties in developing the product, especially those known and tolerated, or confidentially ordered, by line officers. When staff agents reported deviations, the relevant staff officers confronted the supervisors in charge. Top line of course supported the staff and made appropriate criticisms. These did not have to be extreme, for news of such events circulated quickly and in time only one meaning was given by line officers to any visit by a girl from a staff office.

A related difficulty arose when certain scientists occasionally doubted that even the staff of Quality Control was fully alert and challenged it to the extent of making personal inspections. This difficulty began as an interstaff dispute but in a sense became a staff-line issue when top line entered as peacemaker to reassure line superintendents.

Fear of the Staff. A few line officers muttered about staff weight in plant affairs. Confidential doubts were expressed about the "need of having Ph.D.'s running the show." These skeptics were technically trained officers impatient to rise in the line, but fearful that their merits might be assessed by some staff Ph.D. Their quickness and ambition were pleasing to top officers, but their wish to carry on production free of intrusion by the specialists was displeasing. Rivalries in the line became overt when temporarily appeased recipients of confidential salary increases boastfully revealed them to rivals.

Some of this disturbance was attributable to the original hope of reducing staff-line discord, in part, by putting foremen with technical degrees over line operations and allowing them (1) a free hand to motivate their employees and

(2) as specialists, to have full authority inside the line.[13] In time these officers requested the right to share in all policy-making. They were given a limited voice —more than that level of the line traditionally has—but not enough for those displeased with staff power in plant business. As we noted, the younger supervisors were gladly deferential to the staff, but their older and more traditional supervisors resented the implication that staff knowledge of production was equal to their own. Latent frictions of this kind will doubtless increasingly moderate line authority and its analogs in other organizations requiring great specialized knowledge. The rising importance of research staffs that build their knowledge into commodities (1) hypersensitive to the subtlest changes in quality of materials entering the product, and (2) requiring almost affectionate attention through every phase of production will necessarily lead them to encroach on line authority until they acquire more of their own.

Interstaff and Intrastaff Tensions

Professional Outlooks. In Transode's frictions there was evidence of the two persisting stereotypes: the engineer as the practical adapter, and the scientist as the creator and basic researcher.[14] There were exceptions, but most line supervisors with engineering degrees continued their academic bent to apply knowledge for their employer's interest. Although these officers had been explicitly instructed not to experiment or offer ideas to the research staffs, their urge to develop the practical potential of research findings was so great in some cases that line engineers covertly entered the offices of staff men at night to search their notebooks for ideas. Indirect interviewing pointed to other influences in the plagiarizing. Some line engineers resented their loss of formal recognition and title as engineers by submergence in the line organization and sought honors

---

[13] The relative success of Transode in maintaining divided authority between staff and line is highlighted by the difficulties of known attempts to break sharply away from the traditional pattern. Homans, *op. cit.,* chaps. 14–15, cites the case of an electrical equipment firm owned, staffed, and managed by engineers in which staff and line initially had equal authority. In time, however, the practical necessities of administration forced the resistive staff into a subordinate role.

One of Transode's competitors, a firm of 3,000, operated for 4 years with a traditional staff-line structure, then from losing some of its abler line officers to competitors began to fail. Its top officers replaced line heads with engineers. In the next 2 months production declined further. The firm then began pirating executives from competitors. As it succeeded, the engineers were gradually withdrawn to staffs. Production increased to a satisfactory level.

[14] Various studies have shown that engineers are less professional than scientists in that they identify less strictly with a specific task, are less interested in publication, less inclined to attend professional meetings, more interested in promotion into management, less insistent on freedom of activities, and so on. See Howard S. Becker and James Carper, "The Elements of Identification with an Occupation." *American Sociological Review,* June 1956 (vol. 21), pp. 341–348. William M. Carpenter, an engineer with 15 years' experience beyond school, studied 43 degreed engineers (of whom Carpenter himself was one) in a private firm. He found that nearly half refused to join the regional engineering association and of those who did, many were critical of the association. (Unpublished paper, 1961.) In a questionnaire study of profit and non-profit organizations given as a preliminary analysis to a seminar in May 1964, Phyllis A. Langton reported on the value orientation of 285 engineers and 292 scientists in terms of generally accepted marks of professionalism. Her findings supported the popular view but pointed to much in each role that was not covered by that view.

for themselves and degradation of chosen rivals in the staff. On their side, the staff researchers may, as alleged, have hoarded their ideas from fear of practical acuteness among the untitled line engineers.[15]

Non-staff engineers were potential rivals for honors and a threat in that they might introduce change acceptable to top line and not subject to staff control—a condition somewhat comparable to the traditional line fear of staff innovations. Staff engineers saw themselves as sole possessors of the finesse to maintain the micrometric properties of the product in the essential balance. Top managers agreed that the researchers had a "feel" for the state of the product in process that all other personnel lacked. And they approved the periodic submission of Quality Control to the wisdom of certain engineers and scientists, for without it heavy economic losses might occur before discovery of errors. This practical concern and probable willingness to top officers to accept *any* worthy idea made any able, but theoretically irrelevant, line engineer a threat to the staff.

The N.I.H. Factor.[16] N.I.H. means "not invented here." The phrase was used so frequently by top officers in analyzing their central problem that its meaning must be discussed. The problem was repeated failures between and among scientists and engineers to share their ideas and research findings toward achieving the firm's goals. Line chiefs attributed the derelictions to intellectual arrogance among a minority of the staff.

Remarks by aspirants to excellence in application of ideas and filtered comments by candidates for pure creativity suggested that the pose of the creators was that (1) ideas developed outside the firm ("not invented here") are inferior; (2) the research offerings of other departments are inferior to those of my department; and (3) the research findings and creative promise of other members of my department are inferior to mine.

As applied to the researchers, the content of the N.I.H. factor is explainable in terms of conditions in the firm and outlooks in our society. The pressure to develop new ideas was much more positive than the prohibitions against the means used. And the emphasis on creativity did not exclude the creating of personal opportunity. After all, most of the individuals were officially autonomous. Beneath the general satisfactions with colleagueship and high functional status for all, there was a current—strong enough for membership in a cult of individual honor—of ungratified desire for private triumphs among some of the professionals. Though the concept of dignity would vary from man to man, anything increasing dignity became honorable among this minority. There was too much

---

[15] In a face-to-face situation, with status to defend, the scientist may well fear a brilliant engineer whose skills he might admire if their careers were not bound together in the same organization. Physics Nobel Prize winner Sir George Thomson has said, "I am lost in admiration at the skill shown by engineers in making physical experiments reliable." See *The Inspiration of Science,* New York: Oxford University Press, 1961, p. 137.

[16] The expression did not originate at Transode and was not universally known there. The head of Industrial Relations, for example, had never heard of it. The term is rather common in the electronics and aerospace industries of Southern California. Reed M. Powell reports that 9 of 22 managerial informants he questioned gave the phrase an age varying from 2 to 12 years. But they disagreed on the context. The phrase was vaguely associated with departmental consciousness and concealment of knowledge; in some cases top managers were obliged to call on outside consultants for knowledge they believed their own researchers were withholding. My own local and more distant inquiries outside electronics and aerospace industries revealed ignorance or only hearsay knowledge of the expression.

opportunity elsewhere, too much intelligence, and too many earned honors among these aspirants to eminence for them to be "organization men," though they could seem so for other rewards. Their mixed motivation—drive for renown, commitment to Transode, sentiment for their professional societies, and, for several, success as consultants—precluded the singlemindedness desired by their academic relatives in the top administrative echelon. With similar professional backgrounds and affiliations, they were not restricted by any professional code from exalting personal honors as an end above duties to Transode. Possibly the code had never registered and technical training had been sought largely for its success potential. More probably, students have inflated the concept of professional. Professional sensibility is also dulled by task-shifting, movement from organization to organization, role compromise in the organization, and joint entrepreneurial and scientific activity.[17]

Some adverse effects were pointed to as arising from the N.I.H. complex. According to their peers as well as top managers, some scientists and engineers were not purely original. Some were taking ideas from colleagues or other sources, and, at great time and cost, seeking to disguise and deliver their plagiarisms as original contributions. Exposures were not made, but the undercurrents of jealousy, and the reluctance of administrators to offend the self-esteem of able figures, unproductively involved the sales staff and supporters of aggrieved parties —and of course reflected the growing power of staffs in these industries.

An extreme instance of this power is afforded by one of the scientists. In addition to allegedly "claiming full credit" for ideas not entirely his own, this incorrigible frequently showed his contempt for all associates and the staff of Quality Control by silently intercepting a quantity of the product en route to the shipping department and carrying it to his office for examination in his self-determined role of Supreme Inspector. Frequently distracted, he often forgot to complete his examination. When the shipping department was unable to locate the missing lot they inferred where it was. The head of production, according to an assistant, ". . . then has to take his hat in his hand and go ask Mr. God if he can have the [product] so we can meet the customer's delivery deadline."

The problem was aggravated by the fact that members of the devising groups were unequally concerned to wear the mantle of genius. Some were content to build on ideas from any source, and, if asked, to give the background of the idea or even to give others undeserved credit in their eagerness to register the practical advance. This stimulated the pure researchers to conceal ideas that might have utility beyond their own present awareness and thus weaken their position. They of course became inviting prey to the adapters who, as noted earlier, furtively sought to study the research notebooks of the withholders. Some of the adapters, usually line engineers, also sought secretly to hire new-fledged engineers from eminent schools or eminent engineers from competitors to collaborate in developing ideas. This step was attempted,

---

[17] For some aspects, see Herbert A. Shepard, "Supervisors and Subordinates in Research," *Journal of Business,* vol. 29, 1956, pp. 264–265; William Kornhauser, *Scientists in Industry,* Berkeley: University of California Press, 1963; Simon Marcson, *The Scientist in American Industry,* Princeton: Princeton University, Industrial Relations Section, 1960; James W. Kuhn, "Success and Failure in Organizing Professional Engineers," *Proceedings of the Sixteenth Annual Meeting, Industrial Relations Research Association,* ed., Gerald G. Somers, Madison: University of Wisconsin, 1964, 194–208.

but Transode was not quite large enough for it to escape detection. Even when new researchers were officially brought in there, and among its competitors, a pattern developed reflecting the N.I.H. factor. In the war of ideas and the battles for credit, entrenched researchers denied that the newcomers had any ideas, then sought to decoy them into exploitable disclosures. Newcomers typically countered that the senior group was uncooperative and was setting up obstacles. No accounting artifice could convince the managers that this kind of competition was productive.

Summary and Conclusions

Scientists and engineers are enlarging their influence and reshaping traditional staff-line structures that continue to blend cooperation with conflict over status and authority. The Transode Corporation greatly reduced staff-line friction by assigning each individual a specific authority, by obscuring status symbols and by stressing symbols of science, quality, and service that allowed all officers to share the luster of association with a vital product. These steps were supplemented by filling lower line posts with young technically-trained college graduates and giving them pay and rank uncommon for their age with the expectation that they be uncommonly cooperative and adaptable. Possibly other factors contributed to the relative staff-line harmony—the similar kinds and levels of education, for example.

This "open rank" system was not foisted on subordinates without explanation. Fresh converts to a scheme of controlled informality, the founding officers were agreed—and newcomers were gladly indoctrinated—that there should be minimum status visibility and no outbursts of status feeling. They preferred the evils attending non-scalar salary differentials and personal ranking to the restraints and apathies of documentary formalism.

The experiment was generally successful for its immediate purpose. However, two unexpected conflicts developed: (a) rivalries among younger line foremen for promotion; and (b) struggles among a minority of engineers and scientists for individual credit in discovery and refinement of products and methods. These behaviors were not peculiar to Transode, but are characteristic in our society. They can hardly be prevented or eliminated without other difficulties when so many of the personnel are supercharged by training, tradition, and example to distinguish themselves.

The conditions reflecting the N.I.H. factor could be found in most research and development groups. One might argue that zeal for individual esteem among the engineers and scientists was merely an interest in protecting their professional standards for creative research. But one would probably not say that creative license included the right to ignore their professional codes and the interests of their employer as they engaged in contests for honors leading to costly concealment of false claims to originality. Such was not typical of Transode's engineers and scientists and presumably is not general. But consequences of the practice are stimulating demand for light on how the syndrome of talent shifts from friendly to hostile rivalries akin to the potlatch spirit.

The drive for discovery and acclaim is not new or confined to industry. We know of it from before the bitter displays between and around Newton and Leibnitz over varieties of the calculus. The thing that is new in industry is the increased face-to-face living of talent in the same organization, the great volume of competitive organized research linked with profit and action, the attendant organs of publicity that quickly inform interested audiences of advances, the glorification of "creativity," and the multiplied prizes and honors that intensify and pervert rivalries as well as guide them fruitfully.

10. Span of Control Conceptions and Misconceptions

ROBERT E. THOMPSON

Span of control has long been a controversial subject. Unfortunately, discussion for the most part has been limited to consideration of Urwick's simple hypothesis: "No superior can supervise directly the work of more than five, or at most six, subordinates whose work interlocks."[1] The controversy, though bitter, has been limited to a few active participants. Among most managers the rule is widely quoted (without the final qualification) as one of the cardinal principles of management.

Rules of thumb are extremely handy, a quality that undoubtedly contributes to their popularity. But such important decisions as those involving organization structure should be guided by more than a simple rule, particularly when the basis for the rule is unknown to most. Only a full awareness of the basic issues involved will result in organization structures truly suited to the fundamental purposes of each enterprise.

Certain features of the span-of-control problem, though possibly more complex than the basis for Urwick's rule, seem closer to real management issues. I believe that broader average spans can and should be applied to today's organizations. However, this will not occur until managements in general have analyzed and discarded some of their favorite misconceptions on the subject, and until they have come to grips with the forces that militate against broader spans. These concepts and forces have been revealed repeatedly to me in personal interviews during organization analyses.

Conversation Raises Issues

In span-of-control considerations, we are concerned essentially with a manager's work load. Span of control should therefore embrace the number of individuals who report directly to the manager and who require significant planning and control efforts on his part. This eliminates secretaries and "assistant to" positions, since these functions, if anything, tend to reduce the supervisory load imposed by the other subordinates.

A typical conversation between an organization analyst and a line manager

Reprinted from *Business Horizons,* Vol. 7, No. 2 (Summer, 1964), pp. 49–58, with permission of the author and the publisher, Indiana University. Robert E. Thompson was Supervisor of Management Systems, General Precision, Inc., when this article was written.

[1] See Lyndall F. Urwick, "The Manager's Span of Control," *Harvard Business Review,* XXXIV (May–June, 1956), 39.

regarding possible changes in the manager's organization structure will raise many issues related to this subject.

Organization Analyst. I asked for some of your time today to discuss the possibility of reorganizing your department to broaden the average span of control. As you know, the company feels that certain benefits will come from such changes. Perhaps you heard that the president has already taken steps to broaden his span from two to ten.

Line Manager. Yes, I heard about that. If you ask me, the whole thing is a farce. You fellows in organization planning have been claiming that this will reduce costs. That's a good one!

Analyst. But don't you think that costs were reduced by the change the president made?

Manager. Of course not. We used to have two vice-presidents; now we've got ten. That's what I call a top-heavy organization. Just watch our overhead climb.

Analyst. I can't agree with you. The change in span from two to ten was made when the two former vice-presidents retired and the ten division directors were elevated to vice-presidencies. We now have two less executives in the organization, two less secretaries, and two available offices. How does this increase costs?

Manager. But what about the salary increases the ten got when they were made vice-presidents?

Analyst. Actually their responsibilities have not changed significantly. They still direct the same functions and the same number of people. I don't know what they got, if anything, but obviously each would have to receive an increase equivalent to more than 10 per cent of the previous vice-presidents' *combined* salaries to offset the savings. Personally, I think that's rather doubtful.

Manager. Maybe, but the change still doesn't make any sense. Back when there

were only two vice-presidents, all the operating divisions reported to one of them and the staff divisions reported to the other. Now that made a lot of sense. We in the manufacturing division had a man who could place our problems directly before the president. In other words, we were well represented at the top level. Also, since all the operating divisions reported to him, the efforts of these divisions were well coordinated.

Analyst. You mean that because all the operating divisions reported to one man, he could coordinate your activities and represent your interests to the president?

Manager. Exactly.

Analyst. But don't you still all report to one man—the president? And can't your interests be even better represented now that the manufacturing V.P.—previously the manufacturing director—talks directly to the president?

Manager. Yes, but—

Analyst. Remember the difficulties you fellows used to have with the administration division? You felt they couldn't understand your problems and were encouraging unnecessary and unjust restrictions on your method of operating.

Manager. Do I! When the two vice-presidents stopped talking to each other, the whole company seemed to be going in two different directions.

Analyst. I think that describes the situation very well. But, remember, the men in administration were having even greater difficulties with you. They were unable to get any information, cooperation, or understanding from the operating groups, simply because it was known that their boss and your boss were feuding. I know that the president was aware of the problem. Part of his wish to broaden his span stemmed from the need to pull the two parts together.

Manager. I don't see how it's going to help.

Analyst. He feels that with all the operating and staff divisions reporting directly to him, he'll be able to coordinate the activities of *all* divisions and resolve some of these difficulties. You see, he doesn't fight with himself the way the two old V.P.'s used to fight with each other. If the operating divisions are correct in the things they do, and the staff divisions are all wrong—as you undoubtedly think—he'll now have a better chance of finding that out and rectifying the situation.

Manager. Amen to that! Maybe it isn't such a bad idea at the president's level, but that still doesn't prove it's good at lower levels. For example, everybody agrees that the company needs better-trained supervisors. If you eliminate supervisory positions by broadening average spans, you're providing less opportunity for that training.

Analyst. I certainly agree that we need an improvement in the average quality of our supervisors. But we feel that increasing the average span will help bring about this improvement, even though the number of supervisory positions has been decreased. After all, there's no real need for a supervisor to be efficient when he has lots of time—as he normally has with a short span of control. He can define, redefine, and re-redefine assignments as he finds his previous definitions were not accurately or effectively communicated. He can also look constantly over the shoulders of his subordinates and work with them at every step to compensate for sloppy delegation. That isn't desirable from the subordinate's point of view.

Manager. On that last point, I certainly agree with you. I wish my boss would stop following me around. I never get an opportunity to make a decision on my own.

Analyst. Exactly. You don't get an opportunity to build the kind of independence and reliance on your own judg-

ment that is necessary for a future executive. Also, with the amount of backstopping you receive, it's very difficult to determine your potential for promotion.

Manager. Well, I can tell you my performance would be a lot better without my boss's interference.

Analyst. It seems that we agree on a few things, at least. Now let's talk about your department.

Manager. As you know, my department is rather new, so my problems are different. I needed a lot of help in getting organized, crystallizing internal procedures, and so on. So I set up a group of subordinate supervisors that I could count on. They were a big help in shaping up the operation. Now things are pretty well organized, so I delegate everything to them and spend my time thinking of ways to improve the operation.

Analyst. And what is your current structure?

Manager. I have a secretary and three subordinate supervisors; each of the supervisors has four men assigned to him.

Analyst. Some of your comments are interesting. For example, didn't you know that assistance could have been obtained from administration in setting up your department, writing the procedures, and the like? They have some highly trained specialists for that kind of thing.

Manager. Back in those days, administration was the common enemy of all operating divisions. Even if I'd wanted to, my boss wouldn't have stood still for calling them in.

Analyst. All right, but what about this idea of spending all your time thinking?

Manager. What's wrong with that? I thought that's what a manager was supposed to do. The company wants improvement, doesn't it?

Analyst. Certainly. Have you asked the Systems Department for any studies?

Manager. Actually I haven't gotten to

that point yet. Quite frankly, I've had some difficulty in determining where I should start improving things. My supervisors seem to have things well in hand; at least they tell me they're not having any problems.

Analyst. Oh, I see. But once you get under way with your improvements, will they occupy you full time?

Manager. Yes, I believe they will. You see, when I'm not thinking, I usually spend my time coordinating things with my boss.

Analyst. Wouldn't he be satisfied with a weekly meeting?

Manager. Maybe, but the other supervisor who reports to him spends a good deal of time in his office.

Analyst. Then possibly I should talk to your colleague about a weekly meeting also.

Manager. That's a good idea. If you can convince him to settle for the weekly meeting, I'll be glad to, too.

Analyst. So if your colleague would spend less time with the boss, you would too. Let's assume for a moment that this problem can be licked and consider what would happen if your three supervisors were moved to another area. This would mean then that the twelve nonsupervisors would report directly to you. The change would be advantageous to the three men who would undoubtedly be placed in the new division that's being set up. This would broaden their experience and probably provide an opportunity for a fairly rapid promotion.

Manager. Granted, it would be nice for them. But I'm concerned about the effectiveness of my department. The company won't thank you for reducing the control here.

Analyst. I don't necessarily believe that control would be reduced, even though it would be necessary to change from the concentrated personal-contact type of control to more formal means.

But even if it did cause some reduction in departmental effectiveness, this is not necessarily bad.

Manager. Now I know you're crazy. The company needs the best possible management in each department.

Analyst. Look at it this way. The company needs the best possible management, the best possible facilities, the best possible research, the best possible advertising, and everything else. Unfortunately, there isn't enough money in the state, let alone the company, to provide the best of everything.

Manager. That may be, but I'm not concerned about facilities, research, and advertising. I'm just concerned about the management of this department.

Analyst. That's true. I'm simply trying to explain why less than perfect supervision in your department may be to the company's advantage. It's quite possible, isn't it, that the $30,000 or so a year spent on your supervisors would do the company more ultimate good if spent on research or marketing—even with slightly reduced effectiveness in your department.

Manager. But that's no concern of mine.

Analyst. No, but you must admit that from the company viewpoint it is an argument for broader span. Do you see any other disadvantages to you personally if we remove these supervisors from your department?

Manager. What happens to my labor grade if the supervisors are removed from the department? The twelve nonsupervisors are all in labor grade 4; the supervisors are in grade 6, and I'm in grade 8.

Analyst. To answer your question, consider what your grade would now be had you never installed the supervisors between the men and yourself.

Manager. It would probably be less than an 8.

Obviously the conversation has not ended yet. But several significant issues have been raised.

Some Issues Examined

COST IMPLICATIONS

Most managers remain convinced that large spans increase organizational cost. How often have we heard a manager, with ten or fifteen supervisors reporting directly to him, called an empire builder? How many times have European organizations been credited with a competitive cost edge because they average only two or three vice-presidents? Unfortunately, the obvious has been missed.

Assume, for example, that a manager has fifteen supervisors reporting directly to him. What will be the effect on costs if he were to reduce the average span in this segment of the organization to three? To achieve this, he must add to his costs

the salaries of six assistant managers and arrange them in some fashion between himself and the original fifteen. (Of course, this example is somewhat idealized. It is assumed that the fifteen original supervisors will receive substantially the same pay in either situation—a reasonable assumption if the same performance is required of them.)

The theoretical manpower costs or savings resulting from changes in average spans are interesting to calculate. (The necessary formulae are explained in the section of the article entitled "Span-of-Control Mathematics.") To demonstrate their magnitude, the accompanying chart shows the annual savings in supervisory salaries and fringe benefits that might be expected for various sizes of organizations. Columns B and C both indicate the dollar savings resulting from an increase in the average span of control throughout the organization from six to ten. That is, the number of people re-

Span-of-Control Savings

(Average span increased from six to ten)

Total Organization (A)	Savings Through Supervisory Cut (B)	Savings Through Nonsupervisory Addition (C)
100	$ 74,000	$ 132,000
500	370,000	660,000
1,000	740,000	1,320,000
5,000	3,700,000	6,600,000
10,000	7,400,000	13,200,000

porting directly to each supervisor at all levels is presumed to increase from an average of six to ten. However, column B shows the savings if the increase in average span is achieved by removing supervisors and maintaining the original number of nonsupervisors. Column C shows the savings if the increase is achieved, as it would be during organizational expansion, by increasing nonsupervisors and

maintaining the original number of supervisors. Average supervisory salary plus fringe is taken as $10,000 a year. The savings indicated are substantial from any point of view.

COORDINATION

Coordination is a classical function of management. In general, it refers to the job of ensuring that different organizational components mesh both in time and function—that is, the time at which one component performs must be appropriate to the requirements of other components, and the functions performed by that component must contribute to, rather than conflict with or overlap, other components. The ease with which coordination within the organization can be achieved by the managers is of paramount consideration.

Frequently, however, the grouping of organizational components needing *close* coordination is overemphasized. The result is disregard for another equally important problem: that of achieving adequate coordination among *all* components. As management science progresses, as centralized data processing and centralized service functions become a way of life, and as management decision-making techniques are refined, organizations take on more and more the characteristics of systems. Each component becomes more closely interrelated with other components. Managements are beginning to recognize that little can be done in one component without affecting others, and therefore that the need for over-all coordination of *all* components becomes increasingly important.

This awareness should lead logically to broader spans of control. Unfortunately, human tendencies seem to militate against their acceptance. The first solution to problems of conflict between components is to group them together under one head, who can then "coordinate" them.

An experience of some years ago bears this out. In providing instruction on organization theory to several groups of industrial supervisors, I used a case example involving a six-level structure with a history of poor over-all coordination. All groups were given detailed indoctrination in the company's policy favoring broad spans, and all agreed generally on

the advisability of broad spans and few organizational levels. Following the indoctrination, each group was divided into teams to consider the case and develop an improved structure.

Typically, the teams immediately forgot the precepts and proceeded to regroup the functions in each component into smaller components, each with a new head, "for better coordination." Most of the proposed structures contained about eight levels. When confronted with the conflict between the company policy and their recommendations, the teams exhibited initial surprise, followed by chagrin. They had acted on an inner compulsion to combine without considering the effect of the combinations. Any purchase of closer coordination in one part of the organization must be paid for by a lessening of over-all coordination. It cannot be otherwise.

An interesting approach to structuring an organization starts with the structure that would provide, if managers were superhuman, the best possible coordination, and then backs off to the practical point where human managers can operate.

Assuming unlimited ability for one individual, the best possible coordination can be achieved if everyone in the organization reports directly to him. He would have unlimited visibility into the organization; he would know precisely what every individual was doing. With this knowledge, he could immediately detect duplication of effort, efforts directed to cross purposes, resource expenditures out of line with company goals, and so on. In short, he could direct expenditures and efforts to a point of extreme optimization.

The introduction of one in-between level would reduce his visibility somewhat and so limit his ability to optimize, but it brings us closer to a structure that is humanly manageable. The process of introducing levels should stop, of course, at the first practical point.

SUPERVISORY TRAINING AND EXECUTIVES

In suggesting broader spans to managers, we invariably encounter concern over the lack of supervisory training that will result. It is argued that supervisory positions should be established, even where not needed, in order to provide slots in which future managers can try their wings—as if this were the only way to provide supervisory training.

The concern is based on the idea that any training is better than no training. But certainly this is not true. Experience is the best teacher, but experience frequently teaches the wrong thing. If the experience is undemanding, the student is apt to develop faulty, inefficient methods of reacting. It is well known, for example, that reading speed and comprehension are seldom very high when students are permitted to read at their own comfortable rate. However, if the reader is consistently challenged by a stop watch and comprehension test, he will develop habits that increase his performance well beyond the average.

On-the-job supervisory training should prepare a man to delegate effectively and efficiently. It should teach him to handle different personality types, to coordinate their functions, to reconcile their differences, to make decisions without a great deal of help, and to ensure required results with a minimum of personal attention. Setting up additional supervisory positions for training purposes (and shortening average spans in the process) inevitably results in decreased training effectiveness.

If this were the only method of training future managers, the situation would be almost hopeless. Fortunately, job rotation provides a means for the effective training of any reasonable number of men without establishing an artificial and unnecessary subcomponent.

The complementary task, that of executive selection, is also adversely affected by narrow spans, because one is never quite sure who is responsible for good or bad performance. Too much supervision clouds the significance of the performance figures of the supervised. The dependent-aggressive personality, so typical of rising young executives in American business culture, is successful in the strongly supportive atmosphere of short spans of control. However, these young men usually fail to achieve expected performance when thrown into a position requiring independent judgment or the unpopular decision.

USE OF STAFF SERVICES

A flower does not burst into full-blown maturity; it requires special nurturing as a seedling, and later must be pruned carefully to reach full productivity.

Organizations are analogous. New organizations require the nurturing that can be provided only by men competent at organization design, work method structuring, personnel training, procedure writing, goal definition, and so on. After full growth is attained, unnecessary functions and unproductive steps in work methods should be trimmed periodically. Necessary adjustments in direction should be made to accommodate changes in the other functions of the business or in the business itself.

The nurturing and pruning can be performed by men assigned permanently to the organization, but, since these functions are needed only intermittently, it would seem more efficient to provide them in the form of staff assistance from the outside. Several advantages are gained; important among these are the perspective and objectivity that good outside men can bring. Centralized service groups develop a detailed knowledge of over-all operations that is extremely useful in deciding the proper relationship of a new component to others in the company—that is, for optimizing the balance of functions between them. When pruning time arrives, objectivity is an absolute necessity. The horticulturist, after all, does not ask the plant to trim itself.

Heads of new organizational components have a strong tendency to design the supervisory structure without regard for realistic requirements. Their anticipations of rapid expansion, resulting in heavy initial supervision, are usually unwarranted. Their desire for administrative control of the means of improvement is perfectly natural, but it is a luxury few organizations can afford. The short spans that result are an unnecessary burden to the company.

THE SUPERVISOR'S JOB

The philosophy of supervision that many managers seem to have been taught goes something like this: the manager's job is to set up a stable, smooth-running organization in which no problems occur. When this happy condition obtains, the manager should then sit with his feet on the desk and think about improving the operation. On the surface, the concept seems plausible, but underneath it exhibits undesirable features.

There is no real trick to establishing an organization without problems. One needs only to let it be known that no problems will be tolerated, and none will occur—at least none that become evident. With the slightest encouragement, subordinate levels of supervision can act as effective insulators between the manager and the problems.

These hidden problems seethe and grow until efficient operation becomes impossible. Direction relinquished by the manager will be exercised by others, but it will not be unifying direction, nor will it normally be the direction which the manager would have chosen had he been involved in the problems. The personal involvement of the manager in his operation is extremely important. Ernest Dale, in an article devoted primarily to this need, writes, ". . . there must be less emphasis [in management training] on delegation to the point where the manager is isolated from all practical matters affecting his company. The manager must delegate, but he must not be too devoted to keeping his desk clean to read the reports, ponder them, and pull together the ever-disunifying tendencies of his business." [2]

With a short span the manager does more than delegate work to subordinate managers; he also delegates the task of coordinating the work and so insulates himself from coordination problems, those "ever-disunifying tendencies" of his organization.

The manager *should* think. And he should arrange time to think. But few really productive managers can afford the luxury of creative thinking during working hours. Such a time is not conducive to clear, unemotional thought processes. Rather, it is then that the manager, through active participation, can submerge himself in the details of opertion and provide food for creative thought during his leisure. Usually while playing golf, washing the supper dishes, or pursuing some other purely physical pastime, perspective clears and simple solutions to complex problems occur.

Expansion of Industrial Politics

Business that is all "strictly business" is not good business. To a degree, trivial

---

[2] Ernest Dale, "Executives Who Can't Manage," *The Atlantic Monthly* (July, 1962), p. 58.

interaction between a man, his boss, his subordinates, and his colleagues is essential to the smooth functioning of the organization. It is important that a man understand the people with whom he works, that he develop insight into their capabilities, their deficiencies, their psychological problems, and their fundamental motivations. The subtle personal adjustments necessary for a group of human beings to produce the day's output absolutely depend upon this insight. Prerequisite to this insight are trivial conversations ranging from a comparison of golf scores to boasts about one's children.

Unfortunately, it is difficult to determine where productive triviality with one's boss ends and favor currying begins. To understand one's boss and to be able to anticipate his reactions are bona fide goals. To ingratiate oneself beyond this requirement can cause considerable mischief throughout the organization. Make no mistake—where one man has sufficient time (and supervisors with narrow spans frequently have sufficient time) to cross the line from productive triviality to bootlicking, other men will be watching closely to determine the boss's reaction. If the individual receives favored job assignments, promotions, confidential communications, all beyond his apparent merit, the others will usually follow suit.

In order to be free to copy the favored associate, they must separate themselves from their own operations. The simplest way to do this is to appoint one or two assistant managers who can direct operations in the manager's absence. Such action is usually justified as being necessary in order to train a replacement, a sacred management principle which few will argue with.

And so the process continues, adding more unproductive activity and more organization costs.

BALANCED MARGINAL UTILITY

One of the basic principles of business is that over-all utility (that is, value as measured by the criterion of organizational objectives) is greatest when the marginal utilities of each separate expenditure are equal. In other words, when the last dollar budgeted for marketing provides the same contribution to the organization as the last dollar budgeted for research, production, and so on, the company receives the maximum total contribution from all of its parts. If a disparity exists, then dollars should be shifted between functions until balance is achieved. Each dollar shifted raises the total contribution. Despite the logic of the principle, it is often overlooked, possibly because no one other than the president is sufficiently disinterested to be interested in over-all balance.

The principle can be applied to two dimensions of an organization structure. The horizontal dimension has been indicated above—the determination of how resources should be balanced among the various functional parts of the organization (how much to marketing, how much to production, and so on). Application to the vertical dimension implies a balance between the "coordinating-directing" elements and the "doing" elements —that is, how much for supervision and how much for nonsupervisory workers.

Obviously, since we are concerned with total effectiveness versus total cost, the two dimensions must be considered together. If greater total effectiveness is produced by a transfer of budget funds from a supervisory team to the nonsupervisors in the group, to the nonsupervisors in another group, to another supervisory team, or even to capital or expense purchases, then the transfer is warranted.

Such a transfer means, theoretically at least, that the reduced supervisory team will be somewhat less effective than formerly. To many managers, such a possibility raises a red flag. Visions of idle nonsupervisory personnel and gross unproductiveness of effort can cause considerable anxiety, but the anxiety is usually unwarranted. Competent supervisors will quickly adapt their methods to the increased work load, and the effectiveness lost will be small if the transfer of expenditures is intelligently made.

Several articles have appeared recently on the subject of methods for determining optimum spans of control.[3] My objective has been to show that certain firmly held concepts and several organizational forces frequently cause managements to structure organizations with unjustifiably short spans of control.

Analysis of the concepts reveals them to be misconceptions; identification of the forces can lead to appropriate control measures.

Much can be gained by broadening average spans within an organization. These gains include reduced cost, improved supervisory training and executive selection, better over-all coordination, more effective communication, and a higher average quality of supervision through greater utilization of the most competent supervisors available. These gains are available for the asking. No capital equipment need be purchased; no new technology need be learned; no additions to the labor force are required. Clear-headed thinking and hard-headed decisions are the sole requirements.

Span-of-Control Mathematics

For those who may be interested in the mathematics of span-of-control cost reductions, the more important derivations are presented below. Throughout these derivations the following symbols are used:

s = the number of true supervisors in the organization (group leaders, task force managers, and the like are not included)

n = number of nonsupervisors in the organization who require significant planning and control efforts on the part of their supervisor (secretaries and "assistant-to" positions are normally excluded from this group)

a = average annual salary plus fringe benefits, cost of office space, and so on for all supervisors in the organization

m = average span of control through-

out the organization (though we deal with an average for the sake of mathematical convenience, this is not meant to imply that all spans should equal the average)

Δm = increment of increase in the average span of control; for example, if average span is increased from six to ten, then $\Delta m = 4$

c = annual cost saving to the organization (a negative value for c indicates a cost increase)

First, the average span of control for the organization can be defined. Since all supervisors as well as nonsupervisors must be supervised—excluding, of course, the top supervisor—the average span is not simply the ratio of nonsupervisors to supervisors. Rather, it turns out to be:

$$(1) \qquad m = \frac{s + n - 1}{s}.$$

---

[3] See particularly Harold Stieglitz, "Optimizing Span of Control," *Conference Board Management Record* (September, 1962), pp. 25–29, and C. W. Barkdull, "Span of Control —A Method of Evaluation," *Michigan Business Review,* XV (May, 1963), 25–32.

The validity of this basic formula can be seen if we think of an organization of, say, thirteen people in which three supervisors report to the manager and three nonsupervisors report to each supervisor; $s = 4$ and $n = 9$ so, by the formula, as by intuition, $m = 3$.

Increasing m in (1) by the increment, Δm, decreasing s by Δs, and maintaining the original value for n, gives:

$$(2) \quad m + \Delta m = \frac{(s - \Delta s) + n - 1}{s - \Delta s}.$$

Substituting (1) for m and solving for Δs gives:

$$(3) \quad \Delta s = \frac{\Delta m \times s^2}{(\Delta m \times s) + n - 1}$$

where Δs represents the reduction in supervisory requirement due to the increase in average span of control. To determine the annual saving due to this reduction, we need simply multiply both sides by the average annual cost per supervisor, a, to obtain:

$$(4) \quad a\,\Delta s = c = \frac{\Delta m \times a \times s^2}{(\Delta m \times s) + n - 1}.$$

On the other hand, to determine the number of nonsupervisors who can be added without additional supervisors, assuming a given increase in span, an increment is added to n in (1):

$$(5) \quad m + \Delta m = \frac{s + (n + \Delta n) - 1}{s}.$$

Again substituting (1) for m and solving for Δn gives:

$$(6) \qquad \Delta n = s\,\Delta m.$$

To calculate the saving from organizational expansion with fixed supervisory force, increments are added to both s and n in (1), maintaining m at its original level:

$$(7) \quad m = \frac{(s + \Delta s) + (n + \Delta n) - 1}{(s + \Delta s)}$$

and Δs—that is, the number of supervisors who would normally have been added but were not because of the fixed supervisory requirement—is determined by:

$$(8) \qquad s = \frac{s\,\Delta n}{n - 1}.$$

Substituting (6) for Δn and multiplying both sides by a gives:

$$(9) \qquad a\,\Delta s = c_1 = \frac{\Delta m \times a \times s^2}{n - 1}.$$

To determine the increase in average span required to meet a predetermined annual cost saving, cross multiplying equation (4) and solving for Δm gives:

$$(10) \qquad \Delta m = \frac{c\,(1 - n)}{s\,(c - as)}.$$

C

DIRECTING

11. In the Spotlight: The Supportive Manager

KEITH DAVIS

Introduction

Historians tell us that in the 1880's when a steel mill foreman wished to hire a new hand, he went to the mill gate, surveyed the crowd of waiting applicants, and chose the one that looked the best. That man worked as long as he pleased his foreman. Whenever he did not, the foreman fired him and sent him back out the same gate. The foreman was autocratic king of his area.

Occasionally a capable employee was able to turn these insecure conditions to his advantage. For example, a number of years ago a vice-president of a major steel firm related how he kept employment with the firm where he was then vice-president, even though he was fired from his first job. In his first year with the firm, while he was a common laborer, his foreman fired him and sent him to the gate. (The term "give him the gate" arose from this practice.) Showing the ingenu-

ity which later made him vice-president, he headed for the mill gate but turned and slipped into another area where he knew several men had been hired that morning. He started working with a labor gang, and when the timekeeper appeared, gave him his name and was thus back on the payroll. The busy foreman merely assumed he was one of the men hired that morning.

Today when a supervisor works with his employees (not "hands" as in 1880), he works in an entirely different way. His work requires greater knowledge of people, social systems, and organizations. There are elaborate personnel services which he must know how to use and coordinate with specialists who direct them. There is much more investment in each employee's development and more of a long-run commitment to him. And there is often a union both criticizing from the sidelines and actively involved in influencing operations.

Reprinted from *Arizona Business Bulletin,* Vol. 14, No. 10 (December, 1967), pp. 252–256, with permission of the publisher. Keith Davis is Professor of Management, College of Business Administration, Arizona State University.

In today's environment compared with the 1880's, the supervisor's role is different, the employee's role is different, in fact, the whole system of organizational behavior is different. It is evident that ways of organizing and working with people are changing constantly as we enlarge our understanding about people and organizations. Traditional approaches to management often are insufficient for today's needs. Modern organizations require a manager who has a thorough knowledge of human behavior and can use that knowledge constructively. This kind of manager is a *supportive* manager, because he provides full psychological support for his employees in the performance of their duties. Since the supportive manager is proving to be the successful manager in modern organizations, let us further discuss his role, particularly comparing him with his autocratic counterpart 50–100 years ago.

Autocratic Managers

The management pattern of autocratic managers is well known because most of us have worked for an automatic manager sometime during our lives. We can, however, get a better understanding of his activities if we examine them in terms of the framework presented in Figure 1, which is then used to compare him with a modern supportive manager.

There are various shades of autocracy, from the extremely dictatorial boss to the more human-oriented benevolent autocrat. In each case, however, the autocrat maintains his position through power. (Words appearing in Table 1 are italicized in order to key them to that Table). The means by which he invokes power within the organization is formal, official *authority*. It gives him a right of command over those to whom it applies, but he tends to use it more as a club over

people than as a tool for accomplishing the work that needs to be done. He expects employees to do as they are told, asking a minimum of questions and giving no argument. He assumes that employees are passive and resistant to organizational needs, and that it is his task to persuade and threaten them into performance.

The motivational pattern of the autocratic boss is *negative*. To get work done he holds over the head of his subordinates such penalties rather than working.

There are occasional exceptions to the pattern of negative motivation used by most autocrats. Some autocrats are predominantly positive, emphasizing fair rewards and using their great power to dispense them plentifully and with reasonable fairness. When their motivational pattern is predominantly positive in this manner, they are called "benevolent autocrats." This exception shows that even autocracy can be used rather effectively, but the exception does not invalidate the general tendency of autocrats to emphasize negative motivational patterns.

The employee who wants to get along in an autocratic environment finds it necessary to adopt an attitude of *obedience*. He bends to the authority of a boss, not a manager. He often dreams of retaliating, perhaps like the army private who, when told to paint "the whole Jeep," painted the headlights, seats, and motor, along with the rest of the Jeep! Though he dreams of retaliating, usually he does not do so because the autocrat keeps him cowed most of the time. Further, the employee has a family to feed, so, why rock the boat? He finds it easier to develop a state of *personal dependency* on his boss, whose power to hire, fire, and "perspire" him is virtually absolute.

Under autocratic conditions the employee does not feel very motivated, but he must provide *subsistence needs* for

TABLE 1
A Comparison of Autocratic and Supportive Managers

	Autocratic	Supportive
Depends on:	Power	Leadership
Managerial orientation:	Authority	Support
Motivational pattern:	Negative	Positive
Employee orientation:	Obedience	Performance
Employee psychological result:	Personal dependency	Participation
Employee needs met:	Subsistence	Higher-order
Performance result:	Minimum	Awakened drives
Abilities primarily used:	Manager only	Whole group
Morale measure:	Compliance	Motivation

himself and his family, so he reluctantly gives *minimum performance* and hopes for a better day. There are performance exceptions, of course. Some men have autocratic role expectations of management, so they respond well when their manager acts his expected role. A few others perform well in spite of autocratic impediments because they have strong internal achievement drives, but most men in normal work situations give rather minimum performance under an autocrat. While they are giving their minimum, the autocrat may be working hard because of the many duties he has centralized in himself. The result is a department working at about half capacity because the full abilities being used are those of the *manager only*. Departmental success depends almost wholly upon the autocrat, and if he falters, his followers are unlikely to help pick him up.

The measure of morale in autocratic situations is the employee's *compliance* with rules and orders. Compliance is unprotesting assent without enthusiasm. The "good" employee is one who takes his orders and follows them without talking back.

In the extreme which has just been presented, the autocratic form of management has many obvious limitations, but we must not condemn it overzealously. Though it does not achieve the full potential that is in a work group, it does accomplish a reasonable amount of work. It did provide much of the productivity which brought the United States from relative poverty to relative affluence between 1850 and 1950. In particular, the benevolent autocrat has been effective in getting productivity, and he can develop acceptable human relationships.

Sometimes, however, the apparent productivity of autocratic management fades into a desert mirage when the long-run view is taken. An interesting example is the new branch plant manager who for two years used all sorts of autocratic devices to pressure and threaten his men into more productivity. He lost some of his key men, but achieved an excellent production record which led to his promotion to the home office near the end of his second year. Behavioral assets such as teamwork and cooperation were so depleted in the branch that productivity collapsed immediately when he left. It was restored only after two years of cleanup work by skilled troubleshooters. In the long run, therefore, the autocratic manager's high productivity was nothing but a mirage.

On balance, autocratic management

has had only limited success, and even that success was accomplished at considerable human costs. As social conditions changed and as we acquired more knowledge of human behavior, it became evident that autocratic management could be improved upon. Gradually, based on both experience and research, supportive management has developed. Today it is in the spotlight because it offers the best possibilities for productive work and satisfying human relationships in most situations.

Supportive Managers

The supportive manager is as different from the autocratic manager as the 1968 factory is from the 1868 factory. The supportive approach places a manager in a new type of role. He provides psychological and organizational support for his people as they perform their work, instead of primarily attempting to command their performance. Though this difference in role may seem small to casual observers of management, it is a significant difference.

The supportive role is described by Rensis Likert of the University of Michigan in the following words: *"The leadership and other processes of the organization must be such as to ensure a maximum probability that in all interactions and all relationships with the organization each member will, in the light of his background, values, and expectations, view the experience as supportive and one which builds and maintains his sense of personal worth and importance."* [1]

The supportive role depends on leadership, as shown in Table 1, rather than the raw power used by the autocrat. Through leadership a manager provides a behavioral climate which will help each employee grow and accomplish in the interests of the organization the things of which he is capable. The leader assumes that most workers are not by nature passive and resistant to work needs, but that they are made so by an inadequate supportive climate at work. They will take responsibility, develop a drive to contribute, and improve themselves, if given half a chance. The leader's orientation, consequently, is toward support of each employee's performance.

The supportive manager's motivational pattern is *positive*. Instead of the penalties threatened by an autocratic manager, a supportive manager emphasizes rewards, because he knows they are more effective with people. Along with traditional economic rewards, he uses psychological rewards, such as recognition, advancement, and responsibility. He is able to use these rewards effectively because of his competent knowledge of human behavior.

Research at Arizona State University and elsewhere shows that psychological rewards are particularly effective with white-collar, scientific, professional and managerial personnel. At Arizona State University, for example, a graduate research project by George R. Allen examined the causes of strong motivation among 1,014 bank employees. Particularly strong motivators were recognition, advancement, responsibility, achievement, and growth. These motivators applied to both supervisors and non-supervisors, and to both men and women.[2] Although

---

[1] Rensis Likert, *New Patterns of Management* (New York: McGraw-Hill Book Company, Inc., 1961), pp. 102–103.

[2] George R. Allen, *Testing Herzberg's Motivation-Maintenance Theory in Commercial Banks*, Unpublished Doctoral Dissertation, Arizona State University, Tempe, Arizona, 1967. The full research study is available in the University Library.

a person's salary reflects these conditions, they also stand alone as psychological motivators. The effective manager with these people is the one who recognizes the value of these conditions as psychological motivators and uses them in conjunction with economic rewards.

A study of a small group of scientists and engineers in a local electronics plant produced similar results. They were strongly motivated by the five conditions mentioned, especially by achievement in their fast moving technical fields. As a result of their type of work, they also emphasized a sixth factor. It was motivation from the challenging nature of the work itself.[3]

Since a supportive manager emphasizes achievement, responsibility, and similar conditions in the work environment, each employee is oriented toward job *performance,* instead of the simple obedience which results from an autocratic manager. The employee develops a feeling of *participation* because of his greater work involvement with his group in achieving psychological rewards. His *higher-order* needs are challenged, and he works with more *awakened drives* than he did under autocratic management. The whole pattern is one in which the employee participates and feels that his ideas are welcome and needed. The net result is that the abilities of the *whole group* are used instead of those of the manager only.

Even the morale measure changes as one adopts supportive management. Instead of determining morale on the basis of mere compliance with orders, the supportive manager measures employee morale in terms of the employee's *motivation* to contribute to his group and organization to the full extent of his

abilities. When an employee does feel supported, he will be motivated to contribute to organizational goals as a means of achieving his own goals.

Applying Supportive Ideas

Supportive management is not something which can be installed on an instant's notice. Nor can a manager go to a two-week training course and return fully capable to apply it. Supportive management is a matter of gradual growth. Increased knowledge of human behavior comes slowly, and skills in applying that knowledge are even more difficult. Consider the difficulties experienced by a brilliant scientist who managed an industrial research unit. Management sent him to a six-week development program and then gave him further training on the job for nearly a year. His blind spot was that his scientific training led him to accept only the logical content of a situation, not the feelings of the people involved. When feelings were expressed, he simply replied, "That's not true," and dismissed the matter. Since he was unable to accept the feelings of his people, he was unable to respond to them with necessary psychological support. Consequently, he never did develop strong supportive behavioral patterns with his personnel.

Even apparently small changes toward supportive management can be rewarding, and sometimes they can make dramatic improvements. An owner-manager of a laundry became interested in supportive management, even though he employed low-skilled, poorly educated workers. After considerable preparation, including visits to a manufacturing plant

---

[3] Donald A. Kunz, *A Study of Frederick Herzberg's Theory of Motivation and Maintenance Needs,* Unpublished Research Report, College of Business Administration, Arizona State University, Tempe, Arizona, 1966.

noted for its supportive climate for workers, he decided to try a small change. In his laundry the supply of work was variable, and sometimes workers became idle, especially if they were fast workers. Formerly he insisted that idle workers assist other work stations, but his approach simply caused them to work slower. Recognizing that these idle workers were mostly his faster workers, he decided to support their faster work. He began to visit with them in a friendly way as he walked through his shop. He permitted them to go to other work stations to visit, or to get soft drinks for themselves or others. The slow workers began to work faster to achieve this recognition, and the fast workers improved in order to preserve their relative position. As the fast workers visited other work stations, they developed friendships and did considerable informal training and helping of the slow workers. This manager later commented, "I am amazed by the changed attitudes of the workers and their increased productivity."

Admittedly the laundry manager had special conditions which do not apply in most work situations, but the point is that he studied the conditions of his particular group and found a way to be supportive with them. This action did pay off.

The laundry manager also had another favorable condition. Being in charge of the whole organization, he could change the climate in all of it When an individual manager in a larger organization attempts to become supportive, he may be hemmed in by surrounding conditions. His growth is much easier if the rest of his organization becomes more supportive at the same time. Most important is the need for *his own superior* to be supportive so that he can feel that his efforts to be supportive with his men will be recognized and rewarded. His peers and the staff specialists with whom he works also need to improve so that their contacts with his department will be more supportive. Even some policy and organizational changes may be necessary to build supportive conditions. However, even in the absence of these environmental changes, an individual manager can move strongly toward more supportive behavior, because autocratic management is becoming less and less effective with a large part of the labor force.[4]

---

[4] For further ideas on autocrat and supportive management, as well as two other patterns of management, see Keith Davis, *Human Relations At Work: The Dynamics of Organizational Behavior,* third edition (New York: McGraw-Hill Book Company, 1967), especially Chapters 5, 17, and 28.

12. Breakthrough in Leadership Research

J. G. HUNT

Much research has been conducted concerning the kind of leadership style needed to promote effective work performance. However, research results have not been consistent. Some studies have shown that a directive, task-oriented leadership style promotes effective group performance while others have shown that a non-directive, human relations-oriented style is best.

These inconsistent results have led some people to consider the situation in which the leader and his subordinates operate. Progressive managers have recognized for some time that the kind of leadership style which is best in one situation may not be most effective in another situation. The problem has been to develop a model for classifying situations so that the most effective style of leadership to use in a given situation can be predicted successfully.

This paper describes a model developed by Professor F. E. Fiedler at the University of Illinois which allows the kind of classification discussed above.[1] A recent test of this model in three business organizations is also discussed.

Research Background

Before describing this model it would be useful to briefly examine Fiedler's measure of leadership style and some of his research which led to the model. The leadership style measure is based on a simple scale indicating the extent to which a leader describes favorably or unfavorably the individual with whom he has been able to work least well. This "least preferred" person does not need to be someone with whom the leader is presently working, but can be (and usually is) someone with whom he has worked in the past. Such a person will usually be a worker rather than another leader.

After a great deal of research, Fiedler has concluded that the leader who favorably describes the person with whom he has been able to work least well tends to show "human relations-oriented" leader behavior. In oversimplified terms, he wants to be a "nice guy." On the other hand, a leader who unfavorably describes the individual with whom he has been able to work least well tends to be "task-oriented." He primarily wants to get the job done.[2]

Fiedler and his associates examined the relationship between leadership style and group performance in the following kinds of work groups: basketball teams, fraternity houses, surveying teams, bomber crews, infantry squads, open-hearth steel shops, farm supply service companies, and many samples of artificial laboratory groups performing a

Reprinted by permission from the September–October, 1967 issue of *Personnel Administration,* copyright 1967, Society for Personnel Administration, 1221 Connecticut Avenue, N.W., Washington, D.C. 20036. J. G. Hunt is Assistant Professor of Management, School of Business, Southern Illinois University.

[1] F. E. Fiedler, "A Contingency Model of Leadership Effectiveness," in L. Berkowitz (ed.), *Advances in Experimental Social Psychology.* New York: Academic Press, 1964.

[2] F. E. Fiedler, "A Review of Research on ASo and LPC Scores as Measures of Leadership Style," Technical Report No. 33, Urbana, Ill.: Group Effectiveness Research Laboratory, University of Illinois, 1966.

variety of creative type tasks.[3] The relationship between leadership style and performance in these groups was far from simple. Results were difficult to predict and interpret because leader-member relations, stress, and job type influenced this relationship. This problem, together with inconsistent results obtained by other researchers, led Fiedler to develop the model described.

Dimensions of Leadership Influence

The model is built around the idea of "favorableness for the leader." The important question is: "What dimensions of the group or task situation make it easy or hard for the leader to exert influence on group performance?" From his earlier research, Fiedler concluded that three dimensions seemed to be important. These dimensions are sorted into different combinations in terms of a "favorableness for the leader" axis so that the leader's opportunity to influence group performance ranges from very favorable to very unfavorable. The three dimensions are: (1) *leader-member relations;* (2) *task structure;* and (3) *leader position power. Leader-member relations* refer to the leader's feeling of acceptance by his subordinates. *Task structure* refers to the degree to which the subordinates' jobs are routine and spelled out "by the numbers" versus being vague and undefined. For instance, an assembly line worker's job would fall in the first category, while a superintendent's job would generally be relatively low in structure.

Position power refers to the power of the leadership position as distinct from any personal power the leader might have.

Figure 1 shows these three dimensions ordered into eight different combinations along the horizontal axis according to their favorableness for the leader. Situation I is the most favorable while Situation VIII is the least favorable. In sorting these dimensions Fiedler has assumed *leader-member relations* to be most important and *power* least important. He argues that a leader who is or feels himself to be accepted can often compensate for inadequacies in the other dimensions, and a leader with relatively little *power* can often be successful if he has a highly structured task.

Once the dimensions are arranged into these eight situations it is possible to plot the numerical relationship or correlation between leadership style and group performance for each of these situations and obtain the curve in Figure 1.[4]

We can interpret this curve as follows: All the points below the horizontal dividing line indicate a negative relationship (correlation) between leadership style and work performance. This means that a leader who unfavorably evaluates the person with whom he has been able to work least well obtains better performance than a leader who favorably evaluates such a person. In other words, a task-oriented leader is here more effective than a human relations-oriented leader. The opposite is true for all points above the mid-line; that is, a human relations-oriented leader is here more effective than a task-oriented leader.

Figure 1 tells us that under very fa-

---

[3] These are usually groups of college students which are set up to test a specific idea.

[4] Technical note: This curve was obtained from Fiedler's studies by plotting the average correlation between leadership style and performance obtained for each of the situations. Twelve years' worth of data from 15 studies using over 800 groups were used to plot the curve. Every point is an average correlation based on several samples, each of which consists of a number of leaders and work groups. The numbers on the vertical axis indicate the strength of the relationship with plus or minus 1.00 being a perfect positive or negative correlation and 0 indicating no relationship between leadership style and performance.

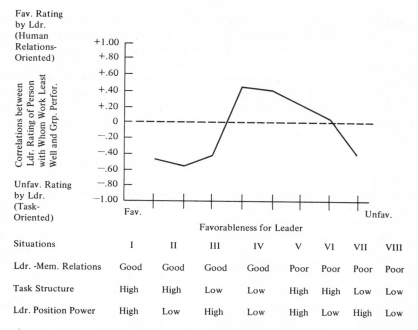

Fav. Rating by Ldr. (Human Relations-Oriented)

Correlations between Ldr. Rating of Person with Whom Work Least Well and Grp. Perfor.

Unfav. Rating by Ldr. (Task-Oriented)

Favorableness for Leader

Situations	I	II	III	IV	V	VI	VII	VIII
Ldr.-Mem. Relations	Good	Good	Good	Good	Poor	Poor	Poor	Poor
Task Structure	High	High	Low	Low	High	High	Low	Low
Ldr. Position Power	High	Low	High	Low	High	Low	High	Low

Figure 1. *A Model Which Shows the Relationship between Fiedler's Leadership Style Measure and Performance for Different Situations.*

vorable (Situations I through III) and very unfavorable (Situation VIII) conditions, the task-oriented leader is most effective. On the other hand, under conditions intermediate in favorableness (Situations IV through VI) the human relations-oriented leader performs best. (Situation VII is apparently a special case in which the nearly zero correlation shows that leadership style apparently makes little difference.) Thus, the model shows some of the conditions under which a given style of leadership is most appropriate.

Testing the Model in Organizations

The model was tested in industrial and business organizations. It was assumed that if it predicted successfully in these organizations it would have important implications for manager selection, placement and training.

Five samples were secured from three organizations. In Company X there were 18 groups of research chemists and 11 groups of skilled craftsmen. Company Y was a grocery chain where 24 grocery departments and 21 meat departments were sampled. In Company Z, a farm implement manufacturing firm, the model was tested one step higher in the organization, and 15 management teams consisting of a general foreman and his subordinate foremen were considered.

The work group supervisors' leadership style was measured by having these supervisors use Fiedler's scale to evaluate the person with whom they had been able to work least well. *Leader-member relations* were measured by asking each supervisor to rate the atmosphere of his group, using a number of eight-point scales. Fiedler used this measure in many of his studies and showed that a leader's rating of *group atmosphere* indicates the degree to which he feels accepted by his group members.[5]

Task structure was measured by having at least three raters in each company rate the structure of the jobs of the group members in the samples. The jobs were rated in terms of the following dimensions:

1. Clearness of job goals;
2. The number of ways in which a job can be performed;
3. The degree to which job decisions can be shown to be correct;
4. The degree to which there is more than one "correct solution" to job problems.[6]

These ratings were cross-checked by giving 13 business school graduate students and faculty members short descriptions of the jobs and having them rate the jobs on the same scale as the company raters. A high agreement was found between the two sets of raters, so the average of both was used to get the final rating. Finally, the scores for each *type* of job in a group (excluding the supervisor) were averaged to obtain a group *task structure* score.

Position power in each sample was measured by asking an official familiar with company policy to consider 13 questions and answer them "yes" or "no" according to this policy. The questions referred to expert, and reward and punishment power granted by the organization to the sampled supervisors.

Performance of the research chemists and shop craftsmen was measured by

using ratings of three officials familiar with their work. In the supermarket meat and grocery departments productivity figures in terms of sales per man hour were available. Finally, a ratio of actual to expected departmental productivity was used to measure the performance of the production foremen sample.

Classifying the Group

The samples were first classified on the basis of *position power* and *task structure*. All the samples were found to have leaders with "high" position power. This, of course, is what would be expected in most kinds of business and industrial organizations. *Task structure* was classified as "high" for all the samples except the production foremen and part of the research chemists.

After classification of the samples by *power* and *task structure, group atmosphere* was considered. The *group atmosphere* scores for the groups in each subsample were arranged in descending order and the mid-point was used to divide the groups into those with "good" and those with "poor" *group atmosphere*. Thus, it was possible to sample groups in Situations I, III, V, and VII of the model. These are probably the most important situations to test in industrial organizations because of the supervisor's high *position power* in most organizations of this type. Hence it is argued that this is a comprehensive test of the model in these kinds of samples.

A summary of the *average* correlations for each of these samples is shown in Figure 2. These average correlations

---

[5] F. E. Fiedler, "A Contingency Model for the Prediction of Leadership Effectiveness," Technical Report No. 10, Urbana, Ill.: Group Effectiveness Research Laboratory, University of Illinois, 1963, pp. 3–4.

[6] These are adapted from M. E. Shaw, "Scaling Group Tasks: A Method for Dimensional Analysis," Technical Report No. 1, Gainesville, Florida: University of Florida, 1963.

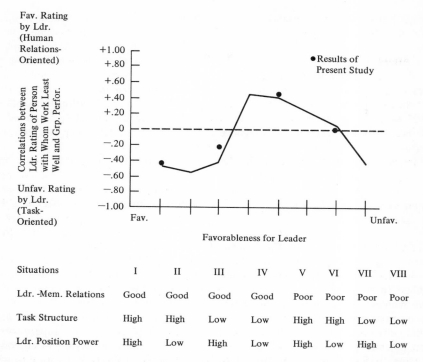

Figure 2. *Average Correlations between Leadership Style and Performance of Present Study Compared with Those Predicted by Model.*

lie quite close to Fiedler's curve based on the average correlations of his studies.[7] It was therefore concluded that the model predicts performance successfully in organizations of the kind tested here.

Importance to Management

The model provides knowledge about some of the group-task variables which apparently make a difference in the kind of leadership style that will get best results. This knowledge can be used in a number of ways. Some of these are discussed here.

Human Relations Training [8]

Available evidence indicates that human relations training given to supervisors "across the board" has typically not been very carefully evaluated, or where it has, results are disappointing.

If it is assumed that such training can effectively change the supervisor's behavior (an assumption which some people

[7] Technical note: Where appropriate, statistical tests were applied to the individual correlations from which these average correlations were obtained. These tests showed that there was only about one chance in one hundred that these results could have been obtained by chance.

[8] For a more detailed discussion of this topic, see J. G. Hunt, "Another Look at Human Relations Training," *Training and Development Journal*, in press.

question but which is not discussed here), then Fiedler's model suggests the following:

1. Give training only to those supervisors in situations calling for this kind of behavior rather than "across the board" as has typically been done.

2. Train the supervisor to diagnose group-task situations so that he can modify his leadership style accordingly.

Alternatives to Human Relations Training

Let's consider first what Fiedler has termed "organization engineering." Here one or more group-task dimensions are modified to fit the leadership style of a given manager. The primary interest is in concentrating on groups with human relations-oriented managers in Situations I and III, and groups with task oriented managers in Situation V.[9] According to Figure 2, these groups would have managers with the wrong style for their particular situation.

Now, according to the model, productivity could be improved by modifying dimensions as shown in Table 1. The effect of this modification is to change the situation in which a leader is operating to one more appropriate for his leadership style. This table shows, for example, that where there is a human relations-oriented leader in Situation I we can modify *task structure* and *position power* and place him in Situation IV, where his particular leadership style is called for. The rest of the table can be interpreted in a similar manner.

An assumption in Table 1 was made that *task structure* and *position power* can be lowered, and that it was *not* desirable to lower *group atmosphere* from good to poor. This is why it was suggested that Situations I and III with human relations-oriented leaders be changed only to Situation IV rather than to V as well. On a commonsense basis, it does not seem that *group atmosphere* should be made less favorable.

A related possibility concerns transfer or initial placement of supervisors so that their leadership style will be congruent with the group-task situation to which they are assigned. The objective is the same as the organization engineering approach but it is accomplished by moving the supervisor rather than modifying the situation. Most of the previous arguments also hold here so that little more needs to be said about this approach.

---

[9] Situation VII is not considered since the model shows an approximately zero correlation between leadership style and performance in that situation.

TABLE 1

Changes in Group-Task Dimensions Required to Improve Productivity in Situations Where Leadership Style and Dimensions Are Mismatched

| | For Human Relations-Oriented Leader | | | | | For Task-Oriented Leader | | | | |
| | Change: | | | | | | Change: | | | |
Situation	From I	To IV	From III	To IV	From V	To I	From V	To II	From V	To III
Grp.-Task Dimen.:										
Group Atmos.	Good	NC*	Good	NC	Poor	Good	Poor	Good	Poor	Good
Task Struct.	High	Low	Low	NC	High	NC	High	NC	High	Low
Pos. Pow.	High	Low	High	Low	High	NC	High	Low	High	NC

* NC = No Change.

121

D

CONTROLLING

13. Control in Large Organizations *

KENNETH J. ARROW

I welcome greatly the opportunity to address a meeting of The Institute of Management Sciences in this land where beauty and efficiency have had such a happy junction. Dr. Geisler's presidential address in Paris two years ago and this one symbolize the international character of our organization and of the needs which we hope to serve. I rejoice that we are among that small number of scientific organizations who have direct international membership—we stand together as scientific co-workers, with no labels of nationality dividing us.

In considering a topic for a presidential address, I had two motivations. One, of course, was my own interests; one cannot be interesting to others about what one is not interested in. But the second was to use the occasion to bring before you a broad and significant field of inquiry, one transcending the technical papers which are, and should be, the usual objects of our concern. Especially was I interested in speaking on this area, which is implicitly relevant to everything the management scientist does, and at the same time so poorly understood

Reprinted from *Management Science,* Vol. 10, No. 3 (April, 1964), pp. 397–408, with permission of the author and the publisher. Kenneth J. Arrow is Professor of Economics, Harvard University.

* Presidential Address delivered to the International Meeting of The Institute of Management Sciences, Tokyo, Japan, August 21–24, 1963.

This work was supported in part by Office of Naval Research Contract Nonr-225(50) at Stanford University. Reproduction in whole or in part is permitted for any purpose of the United States Government.

as an object of theoretical and practical study. There are few results to present, but many problems. If I succeed in persuading some of you of the complexity and the challenge of the issues, I will feel well satisfied.

I

The large organization, so prominent on our contemporary social landscape, is of great antiquity. If we had no other evidence, we would know that complex organizations were necessary to the accomplishment of great construction tasks —planned cities like Nara or Kyoto or Ch'ang-An, monuments like the Pyramids and temples of Egypt, irrigation systems such as those in ancient Mesopotamia or northern China. But we also know of organization for less material ends, for the preservation of law and order, the maintenance of peace or the prosecution of war—Persia, the efficiency of whose control mechanism and communication system has been so well described by Herodotus and Xenophon, and the Inca empire of Peru, where a complex and far-flung state was administered in a highly systematic manner with a technology so poor as to include neither writing nor the wheel. Truly, among man's innovations, the use of organization to accomplish his ends is among both his greatest and his earliest.

But it is perhaps only in our era, and even then haltingly, that the rational design of organization has become an object of inquiry. It is characteristic of the present day, as exemplified by the groups meeting here today, that innovation, the solving of problems, is being increasingly systematized. Whereas in the past the improvement in the choice of routes was made by insight and spontaneous inspiration, today we try to arrive at the decision by solving a transportation prob-

lem. In the same way, there is an increasing interest in studying how organizations solve their problems so that one can systematically investigate optimal organization.

Let me state the problem at hand a little more precisely; since research in this area is still in its early stages, undue exactness must be avoided. An organization is a group of individuals seeking to achieve some common goals, or, in different language, to maximize an objective function. Each member has objectives of his own, in general not coincident with those of the organization. Each member also has some range of decisions to make within limits set partly by the environment external to the organization and partly by the decisions of other members. Finally, some but not all observations about the workings of the organization and about the external world are communicated from one member to another. The word "large" in the title is meant to stress the importance of the communications element.

In this address, I wish to set forth some considerations on one aspect of the workings of an organization—how it can best keep its members in step with each other to maximize the organization's objective function. This may be referred to as the problem of organizational *control*. It divides itself naturally into two parts: the choice of *operating rules* instructing the members of the organization how to act, and the choice of *enforcement rules* to persuade or compel them to act in accordance with the operating rules. Various other terms for these two problems have appeared in the literature; a widespread usage is to refer to the operating rules as control-in-the-large and the enforcement rules as control-in-the-small. It should be noted that enforcement, here as elsewhere, includes both the detection and the punishment of deviations from the operating rules.

My point of view is rationalistic and derives, with appropriate changes, from the logic of choice as it has been developed in the pure economic theory of prices and the mathematics of maximization. The rational or economic analysis of organizations has been developing rapidly over the past fifteen years, and the present account is largely derived from the work of such innovators as Jacob Marschak, Herbert Simon, Leonid Hurwicz, Thomas Marschak, and Roy Radner. There is no intention of denying that non-rational factors, sociological and psychological, are of the utmost importance in the study and development of organizations. But a rational point of view is also needed, and indeed much of the value of studies in group dynamics will only be properly realized in the context of rational design of organizations.

I will first discuss in the very broadest outline some typical examples of control problems in modern organizations—the large corporation, government, the economic system as a whole considered as one great organization. From these illustrations, a brief statement of the essentials of the control problem will be derived. Next I will consider the price system as a solution to the problem of control; this is the solution most natural to an economist. While the price system has many values, it also has limitations. Consideration of these will bring out more clearly the basic problems of organizational control, and in particular the crucial role of uncertainty among the causes for the creation of organization. Finally, the need for some additional forms of control will be briefly examined. As can be seen from this summary, this address has as its primary function the delineation of the problem and of the present status of our understanding, not the presentation of any definitive solutions.

II

The issue of centralization or decentralization in the large corporation has received considerable attention in recent years. A large corporation contains many diverse productive activities, which have important connections with each other and yet are separately identifiable. The products of one activity are the inputs of another, and therefore it is costly to the corporation if its activities are not balanced. Some commodities have to be purchased from outside, stored, transported from one place to another among and within plants, and assigned to the activities using them; some activities produce final products which have to be transported, stored, and sold; other activities produce intermediate products, such as component parts of an automobile, which in turn enter other activities, such as assembly, which produce final products or still other intermediate products. Further, the coordination is needed not only at a single point of time but over many time periods; each activity takes time, so its product can only be used in another activity beginning when the first one ends.

What may be called the classic businessman's view is to be so impressed with the complexity of coordination that great stress is placed on the need for central control. Emphasis is placed on vertical, hierarchical relations; control is exercised by orders from above, executed in detail by those below. The coordination between managers of parallel activities is, in this view, achieved by their common obedience to the plans set at higher levels. Accounting systems and other forms of reporting provide higher echelons with all the information needed to detect violations of orders, and dismissal from employment is the punishment.

Of course, the view I have just sketched

is a caricature and was probably not held by anyone in all its rigidity. It is immediately obvious that higher management cannot literally know everything about the operations of individual activities and therefore cannot make all decisions. Indeed, management literature recognized this problem under the heading "the span of control." It was held that an official could not exercise effective supervision over more than a relatively small number of subordinates, say six. In the terminology which modern management theory is borrowing from statistical communications theory, a manager is an information channel of decidedly limited capacity. This means, of course, that the junior managers must be receiving information from their juniors which they do not re-transmit. Hence, some decisions, if only trivial ones, must be made at lower levels, since the relevant information is discarded in the process of upward transmission to avoid overloading the channels.

The recognition that individual managers will inevitably know more about their own spheres of activity than higher officials has caused decentralization of decision-making to be looked on with much more favor in recent years. It has also been recognized that decentralization can improve the allocation of responsibility; on the one hand, the subordinate has greater possibilities of initiative; on the other, his successes and failures can be more easily recognized by top management.

In the terminology introduced earlier, the operating rules under a centralized system take the form, "do this or that," while under a decentralized system they rather take the form, "do whatever is necessary to maximize a certain objective function."

But the problems of articulating more specifically the operating and enforcement rules of a decentralized organization have not been faced systematically. The objective function for the corporation as a whole may be well defined to be aggregate net worth, but its value depends on the decisions of many managers; the objective function to be maximized by an activity manager must depend in some well defined way on his decisions, to provide an appropriate set of directions to him.

Further, even when the objective function for the manager is defined, there remains the problem of enforcement. When the goal is stated in terms of an objective function, it becomes a matter of more or less, not of yes or no, as it would be if instructions were stated in terms of specific tasks. The top management can never, strictly speaking, know if the activity manager's objective function has been maximized; instead, their enforcement rules should be such as to encourage him to increase the value of the objective function as much as possible. In more usual terms, the problem is to create such incentives to activity managers for performance as will best enhance the corporation's net worth. There are (at least) two problems in devising incentive systems. (1) An effective incentive system creates new demands for information; the reward is a function of performance, so top management must have a way of measuring performance. This may be the objective function itself, or it may be some other, more easily measurable, index. If the index is something other than the objective itself, the manager's incentives may not be directed optimally from the viewpoint of the corporation; for example, if the index of the manager's performance is based primarily on output rather than profits, he will be tempted to be wasteful of inputs. However, an index which supplies better incentives may require more information; in organizational control, as in automobiles, cuisine, and every other commodity, the benefits of improved quality must always be compared with its costs. (2) Even if the index is thoroughly appropriate, the relation between the reward and the index remains to be determined. Suppose there is no difficulty in isolating the contribution of a manager to the net worth of the firm. The fullest incentive to the manager would be achieved by fixing a base salary and a target level of contribution to net worth or profits and then giving the manager as a bonus the difference between his contribution to profits and the target level. If his contribution fell below the target level, the difference would constitute a negative bonus, to be subtracted from his salary. Such an arrangement would clearly not be satisfactory in spite of its desirable effects; the corporation of course intends to share in the profits attributable to the skill of its managers and not to give them all away to him, and the manager may also be reluctant to face the risks, especially if the contribution of his activity depends in part on factors not under his control and about which his knowledge is uncertain.

III

The design of control systems in large corporations is already a formidable task, but it is several orders of magnitude simpler than the control system for a government. To keep the discussion within reasonable bounds, I will confine my remarks to one particular, though very important, phase of governmental activity, the determination of the annual budget. This is the process by which it is determined how much of the resources of society shall be diverted to the different activities carried on by government. The budgetary decisions are a major determinant of the direction of govern-

ment activities, though, of course, there are many aspects of government decision-making, for example, foreign policy, where budgetary considerations are secondary.

The governmental decision process has all the complexities of the corporate, but there are two major additions: the consumer-like character of the government, and the varied nature of its activities. Economic theory, as well as ordinary experience, tells us that the process of consumer's choice is harder to make rational than the decision-making of the corporation. In theory, the corporation maximizes a well-specified objective function, profits or net worth, with no constraints other than those imposed by its technology. The consumer, on the contrary, maximizes a subjective magnitude, under a budget constraint. This implies that the consumer cannot seriously be expected to write down in any explicit way his maximand. Rather, the process of optimization consists of a series of comparisons among alternative ways of spending marginal dollars; the utility function is revealed to the consumer himself in the process. Further, the common budget constraint means that the marginal comparisons must be made among highly disparate alternatives— travel as compared with clothing, for example.

The government's choices are analogous to those of the consumer, with the additional problem that the single utility function is replaced by the great variety of utility functions of the different groups in the political system, the final choice being the resultant of political pressures in many different directions. The government's budget to be allocated among activities is relatively fixed in any one year, though there is some opportunity for change in the total. Alternatively, and perhaps better, it could be said that society's total resources constitute the budget constraint, with the government deciding both the overall allocation between public and private activities and the allocation among public activities. In any case, the budget constraint is a basic element in the government's financial decisions.

The great scope of the government's activities means that marginal comparisons have to be made among some exceedingly remote alternatives: Is an improvement in a national park to be preferred to increased defense?

These choice problems are all institutionalized in the budget-making process. Budgetary requests are made by individual bureaus and then presented to some central agency—in the United States, the Bureau of the Budget. Symbolically, the bureaus represent the utilities of different activities, the Bureau of the Budget the overall resource constraint. But of course no simple separation is possible. The Budget Bureau has to make decisions in cutting down the total requests to the desired budget total, and these decisions involve two types of judgments: (1) the relative social value of the functions of the different bureaus, and (2) the efficiency with which the bureaus are performing their functions. The first judgment has necessarily to be made in a centralized fashion; the Budget Bureau might be thought of for this purpose as the agent of the legislative authority. It is the second type of judgment, that of the efficiency with which government activities are performed, that is more relevant to the problem of control.

For the Budget Bureau to judge efficiency would in principle require it to know as much or more about individual activities as the bureaus themselves. As the affairs of government have become increasingly complex and differentiated, the impossibility of such a concentration

of knowledge has become increasingly patent. Traditional analysis of the budgetary process tended to stress the virtues of centralized budgetmaking, strict lines of control, and avoidance of duplicating activities among bureaus. Some current writers, notably Lindblom, Enthoven, and Rowen, now argue that a good deal of apparent inefficiency and duplication are essential elements of the control process. To replace the impossible demands for knowledge on the part of the Budget Bureau, reliance is placed on the self-interest and mutual rivalry of bureaus. The bureaus act like individuals before a court; they are required to supply the information which will justify their requests, and if two bureaus have overlapping functions, the information supplied by one can be used to check on that of the other.

This theory of the invisible hand in government, though a significant contribution, is as limited a view as the earlier theory of the all-knowing Budget Bureau. The search for a more satisfactory theory of government budget control must still go on.

IV

Up to this point, the boundaries of an organization have been taken as given. The line which separates governmental from non-governmental actions, or which separates a corporation from its customers and suppliers, has been implicitly taken as well defined. But in fact we really have a nesting of organizations inside larger organizations; indeed, the whole economic system can be regarded as one large organization, and in many respects it is fruitful to do so. A socialist system is one in which the organizational unity of the economy is made explicit in its institutions, but it has long been a commonplace of traditional economics, certainly since the time of Pareto, that the apparent anarchy of capitalism conceals a complex organization fundamentally similar to socialism.

Consider the following three examples of commodity transfers: (1) An engine is placed on an assembly line to be installed into an automobile body. (2) An automobile factory receives a shipment of steel from a mill owned by the automobile manufacturing company. (3) An automobile factory receives a shipment of steel from a mill owned by a steel company. The first is certainly a transaction within an organization and is carried out in accordance with operating rules laid down by authority. The third is a commercial transaction, the result of a contract in which goods are exchanged for money, and would usually be regarded as taking place between different organizations. Yet the second, the steel shipment from a mill to an automobile factory of the same ownership, is identical to the third in its economic content and to the first in the form of the transaction.

This continuous sequence of cases shows that drawing any boundary lines for an organization has a somewhat arbitrary element. If the entire economy is thought of as a single organization, one is led naturally to think of the price system as one of the major devices for coordinating different activities, and a great deal of effort by economists has succeeded in clarifying its virtues and limitations.

The very importance of price-mediated transactions suggests that it is worth while distinguishing them from others. The boundary of an organization then will be taken as the line across which only such transactions take place. As the examples just given show, we must be prepared in such a classification to recognize that some intra-organizational transactions will have the same economic content as price-mediated transactions.

It is important and illuminating to note, however, that many transactions have both price and non-price characteristics. Professional services, such as medicine and legal services, are not carried on solely on the basis of an impersonal cash-for-service exchange. There is an expectation of personal responsibility, of fidelity and trust; physician and patient behave in many ways more like co-workers in the same organization than like a large manufacturer and his remote and unseen customers. Similar relations are typical of labor services, agents, and in general of transactions involving goods or services where quality standards are significant and not easily checkable in detail by the purchaser. Speaking broadly, these non-market relations reflect the same sort of problems that arise in control within an organization—the need for services coupled with an incompleteness of knowledge by the receiving party about the activities of the supplier.

V

From these examples of organizations, we can abstract the central problem of organizational control. It arises when two conditions hold: (1) The objective of the organization is a function of a number of interrelated decision variables concerning individual activities; (2) the different members of the organization have different bodies of knowledge. The second condition, of course, implies that the transmission and assimilation of information is costly, for otherwise each member of the organization would transmit all his knowledge to all the others.

Uncertainty is simply the complement of knowledge; when I speak of different bodies of knowledge, I could equally well speak of different uncertainties. For definiteness, let us suppose that uncertainty can be represented by probability distributions over all possible states of the world. Then the following model may serve to illuminate organizational behavior: Each member of the organization is in possession of a signal from Nature, and his probability distribution of states of the world is the conditional distribution given that signal. (The "signal" is understood to be his knowledge based on learning and experience.) Each member can, at a cost, transmit his signal, or a weaker signal compatible with it, to one or more other members of the organization. Each member who has received an additional signal appropriately modifies his conditional distribution. On the basis of the resulting distributions and the operating rules laid down by the organization, each manager makes a decision. The decisions made in turn generate further information which is transmitted in one form or another, and leads to new signals and new decisions. New signals are also coming in from outside the organization and also leading to new decisions. Finally, the messages being transmitted within the system are used to modify the operating rules and to execute the enforcement rules.

VI

It has already been observed that many of the transactions within an organization are similar to those that take place in the market. This has led both theorists and business firms to suggest that prices can be used to regulate transactions within the firm; these are usually referred to as "transfer prices." In the purest form, a price is attached to each commodity or service produced or consumed by any activity in the organization; if the commodity is sold to, or bought from, other firms, the transfer price has to be the same as the market price (with some modifications in the case of imperfect competition). The operating rule for the manager of each activity is then to maximize its profit, as computed by valuing its inputs and outputs at the transfer prices.

This is straightforward, but merely restates the control problem as that of choosing the correct prices. They have to be such that, if each manager does choose his inputs and outputs so as to maximize profits, then for each intermediate good (one not bought or sold on an open market) the total supply and demand by all activities balance.

If the organization calculates its optimum by the Lagrange method for constrained maxima, where the constraints are precisely that the activities producing intermediate products produce enough to meet the requirements of the activities consuming them, then the Lagrange multipliers are the prices. This method of determining the prices is itself centralized and does not satisfy the informational limitations which are the heart of the organizational problem. Of course, radical improvements in the techniques of constrained maximization, such as the modern work in linear and nonlinear programming, decrease the costs of centralized information handling and thereby reduce the problem of organizational control. But, as has been shown in many different forms, an informationally economical decentralization is possible if we solve the constrained maximization problem by a suitable form of successive approximations. If the prices are first set by guesswork, each manager can make a set of tentative decisions. If the resulting inputs and outputs of intermediate goods match, then the prices were indeed the correct ones; if not, the normal procedure would be to raise the prices of those intermediate goods for which demand in the aggregate exceeds supply, and lower those for which the contrary is true. Under certain assumptions as to the technologies of the activities, this process will converge to the optimum for the organization.

The price system, conceived in this way as a process of successive adjustments, is a satisfactory way of choosing operating rules when the appropriate assumptions hold. Each tentative set of rules is defined by the tentative set of transfer prices; the successive adjustments in the prices, and therefore in the rules, require information only about the supplies and demands of the individual activities, information which would have to be transmitted under almost any sensible control system; and there is a guarantee that the decisions at least tend toward full optimality for the organizations.

Though the price system for operating an organization possesses these merits, and though I believe that it is capable of much greater use than it now receives, it has intrinsic limits. Indeed, the very existence of large organizations in the commercial world is a proof of the existence of these limits. When the price system is fully operative, the large organization is equivalent to a large number of separate activities whose connections are the same as those of unrelated firms. Hence, the large organization would have no differential advantage in economic competition, and we would not expect to find it so dominant.

The difficulties in applying a price system to the control of an organization can be classified into four mutually interacting types: (1) the choice of enforcement rules; (2) the complexity of the operating rules; (3) the limits on the theoretical validity of the price system, and (4) the presence of uncertainty, which we have seen to be inherent in the problem of organizational control.

The first problem, the choice of enforcement rules, has already been discussed in some measure in the case of the large corporation. Since we have supplied each manager with an objective function, the profits of his branch evaluated at transfer prices, the most natural enforcement rule would be an incentive system; the payment to the manager should be a strictly increasing function of the branch profits. If the slope of this relation is close to one, then the branch manager is bearing most of the uncertainties due to successive revisions of the transfer prices for which, as a risk-averter, he may well require a large fixed compensation. If the slope is close to zero, then the incentive effect to the manager is small.

The second problem, the complexity of the operating rules, can be appreciated only after a little reflection on the scope of a really thoroughgoing price system. The need of coordination in time is perhaps the chief source of complications; deliveries of specific commodities have to be made at specific times, and in a pure price system there would have to be a separate price for each commodity for each possible date of delivery. One might, to take an example from the government's sphere of activity, use a price system to settle traffic problems; there would be varying prices to be paid for different priorities at intersections and in passing lanes at different moments of time. It is not hard to see the confusion such a system would cause; a traffic signal may lead to an allocation of traffic which is less than optimal in some theoretical sense but it is a far simpler system to operate.

The third problem, the limits on the theoretical validity of the price system, has received a great deal of attention in the literature of welfare economics. There are two basic conditions under which the price system is invalid, in the sense that the equilibrium prices do not represent an optimum: One is that there are increasing returns (or, more generally, non-convexity) in some of the activities, and the other is the presence of externalities, relations between the productivities of different activities which are not classified as commodity transfers. Smoke emitted by one activity may, for example, interfere with the productivity of another. Externalities are essentially a matter of classification; we can always call any externality a new commodity and attach a price to it. Indeed, the elimination of externalities can proceed much farther within an organization than in the market; there is no technically satisfactory way in the marketplace for making the smoke producer pay for his damage to others, but an organization can fix a price for the privilege of emitting smoke and order it to be paid. Of course, special enforcement rules are needed to make sure that the appropriate payments are made. Further, the elimination of externalities increases the list of commodities and thereby again complicates the operating rules.

Although the matter is too technical to be discussed in a brief space, it can be asserted that increasing returns can be handled by modifications of the price system, but these necessarily introduce some degree of centralization. There is still room for significant research to minimize the informational requirements needed for optimal allocation under these conditions.

VII

The fourth difficulty in applying the price system, the presence of uncertainty, is of major importance and yet has received relatively little theoretical study. The one case that has been studied in some detail is that in which all activity managers have the same information about the world outside the organization. Clearly, the appropriate transfer prices can easily depend on the unknown state of the outside world; the simplest illustration would be the case where production plans have to be made now for sale in the future, and at a price which cannot be known now with certainty. We may regard the organization as being faced with a probability distribution of states of the world, product prices in the example. For each state of the world, there will be a corresponding set of transfer prices, so that each activity manager will be faced with a probability distribution of transfer prices. The instructions to maximize profits is no longer meaningful; it must be replaced by the operating rule of maximizing the expected value of utility of profits, where utility is a strictly increasing function.

If the organization itself is risk-neutral, then it would want each activity manager to maximize expected profits. But now the already-mentioned problem of enforcement rules becomes even more acute. If the reward of the manager depends in some measure on his observed profits and if he is a risk-averter, he will wish to play safe by following a course which leads to more predictable profits, even if the expected value is lower. To avoid this outcome, the organization should provide insurance against unfavorable external contingencies, which the manager may buy at his option. In this way, it can be shown that the manager will be motivated to maximize expected value and at the same time have all the protection against risk that he wishes.

Such a system does really exist in the sense that a manager is not normally held accountable for unfavorable outcomes or credited with favorable ones if they are clearly due to causes not under his control. However, there is a deep problem here which is well known in insurance theory and practice under the name of the "moral hazard"; it is, in general, almost impossible to separate causes outside the organization from the efficiency of the manager himself. If an activity does badly, it may be because of external uncontrollable events, or it may be mismanagement. To distinguish between them may never be completely possible and, to the extent that it is, may require costly information. Thus, the occurrence of a fire may be partly due to failure to take precautions or may be completely independent of them; the fire insurance company will not only charge a premium but also engage in additional information-gathering in the form of inspection of premises.

Still further complications occur when the different managers have access to different amounts of information about the external world; this is the problem treated by Marschak and Radner in their theory of teams. Though operating rules can indeed be devised, the problem of enforcement has not yet been approached except in a very rudimentary case (studied by Good and McCarthy).

VIII

Even without going any further, it is clear that in the control of the typical organization, perfect decentralization is not possible because of the limitations on enforcement rules associated with uncertainty and risk aversion. The top management of the organization will always have to have some information about the internal workings of the individual activity. This is far from saying that they have to have complete information. One of the most promising lines of study is that of sampling inspection—it should be equally applicable to the control of the quality of management as to that of goods. A relatively small amount of information, properly chosen, may have large incentive effects.

The problem of organizational control is just beginning to be analyzed systematically. Already it is clear that price theory and programming methods will have to join in an unfamiliar synthesis with information theory and sampling statistics to achieve the state where the rational design of the organization becomes a reality.

14. The Swinging Pendulum of Management Control

GERRY E. MORSE

A change is taking place in management control. It is important that managers, and particularly personnel managers, be aware of this change. Employees at every level are particularly sensitive to changes in management control and to the organizational changes which result from them. So if personnel managers are to do their jobs effectively, they must understand what is happening and devise ways for their companies to meet these changes most effectively.

Reprinted from "Systems Approach to Personnel Management," *Management Bulletin No. 62*. New York: Copyrighted American Management Association, 1965, pp. 3–8, with permission of the publisher. Gerry E. Morse is Vice-President, Employee Relations, Honeywell, Inc., Minneapolis, Minnesota.

By observing the long-term trend in the organization of most human affairs, we become aware of the fact that changes do behave in a pendulum fashion. In government, for example, small states coalesce into larger nations and nations into alliances, whenever circumstances make a swing in that direction appear most advantageous. Then, as we all know from our studies of history, the movement may be in the other direction. Alliances break up, and empires or nations are subdivided. In education, small institutions grow and merge, as has been true for example in the swing from college to university status and in the great growth of the land-grant and other tax-supported schools. At the present time, however, other factors, particularly the combination of a dramatic increase in the number of students and the demand for longer periods of formal education, are causing the pendulum to swing back toward decentralized operation and even toward the re-emergence of the specialized college. In agriculture the great ranches of the West slowly gave way to the homesteader, only in more recent years to have the pendulum swing back away from the family farm and in the direction of the very large unit. Even the Christian church has witnessed the swing of the pendulum from one integrated body to a whole host of denominations. Now many forces are combining to swing the pendulum back, as illustrated by the very dramatic ecumenical conferences of recent years.

It is only natural that business organizations should behave in quite the same way as other organizations in so far as such swings of the pendulum are concerned. Therefore, it should be no surprise that the pendulum of management control swings back and forth. In the history of the United States, giant organizations, such as the Virginia Company and the Massachusetts Bay Company, were the original forms of business organiza-tion. Under the pressures of independence and of a great undeveloped, physical frontier, the swing was steadily in the direction of the individual shopkeeper and the very small production company. Later, the impetus was equally strong in the direction of consolidation, resulting in the late nineteenth century in the giant business trusts. Early in our own century, the swing was again in the direction of the small unit and the independent operator.

But the Depression, which, among other factors, called forth an increasing government involvement in business affairs and the industrial type of union, resulted in a dramatic reduction in the number of competing units in many industries, because of both the failure of the weaker units and a wave of mergers. The size and complexity of the resulting business organizations forced a re-examination of the way in which planning, decision making, and management control could best be handled. The answer arrived at in many firms was greater decentralization. The production demands of World War II moved the pendulum even further in the direction of decentralization. Decentralization or centralization are relative terms, and both are present in any organization. It is only the relative balance between the two that tends to swing one way or the other.

Perhaps one of the best descriptions of the swing of the pendulum to decentralization is the following from a research study conducted by the Stanford University Graduate School of Business:

. . . this [product-division] plan of organization affords an effective basis for decentralization of management. High-caliber divisional executives, located on the job and invested with wide responsibility and authority but guided by sound general policies, may appropriately be expected to take prompt and effective action based upon firsthand knowledge of local needs and conditions without referring any but major matters to the home office. . . . The retarding effects of absentee management and remote control are thus largely avoided. At the same time [product, division, or] regional executives are developed into all-round businessmen. . . . If a trend toward any one type may be regarded as discernible, based upon the 31 companies studied, it is perhaps in the direction of the product-division plan.[1]

Ernest Dale has made the following appraisal of decentralization:

The larger the company, the more urgent is the problem of decentralization, for an increase in size increases the number and difficulties of decisions faced by top management. Since the time and abilities of a company's top executives are necessarily limited, it becomes essential to pass on to others certain responsibilities for decision making. However, it should be noted that the need for decentralization does not necessarily increase in proportion with size. Other factors play an important role, such as complexity of operations, variety of products, and geographic dispersal. Thus a very large company, manufacturing a single, simple item might have less to gain by decentralization than a considerably smaller company manufacturing diverse types of complex, technical products which it sells in diverse markets.[2]

Dale's appraisal hinges importantly on the amount and complexity of data involved. Also, Dale developed the following list of advantages and disadvantages of decentralization. As advantages he counted:

1. Executives will be nearer to the point of decision making.
2. There may be a better utilization of the time and ability of executives.
3. The quality of decisions is likely to improve.
4. The amount and expense of paper-

work by headquarters staff may be considerably reduced.
5. The expense of coordination may be reduced because of the greater autonomy of decision making.

As disadvantages he found:

1. A lack of uniformity of decisions.
2. Inadequate utilization of specialists.
3. Lack of proper equipment or executives in the field.

It is of particular importance to note that three of Dale's five advantages and two of his disadvantages are basically matters of information. An adequate means for handling such information would tend to throw the advantage toward decentralization.

Even before the advent of the business computer, the long period of prosperity following World War II and the gradual emergence of other nations as powerful competitors in world markets began to slow the swing of the pendulum of management control toward decentralization. At first, challenges to the wisdom and effectiveness of further decentralization tended to be met more and more with two personnel arguments. The first of these was that the excess costs, if there were any, could still be justified since decentralizing increased the opportunities for development of supervisory and managerial talent, which would be to the long-run advantage of the organization. The second was that in spite of the accounting reports, costs of operation were actually lower in a decentralized setup because employee performance should be higher in response to on-the-spot management, obviously making its decisions with firsthand appreciation of the cir-

[1] Holden, Paul E., Lounsbury S. Fish, and Hubert L. Smith, *Top Management Organization and Control,* Stanford University Press, Stanford, California, 1951.

[2] Dale, Ernest, *Planning and Developing the Company Organization Structure,* American Management Association, New York, 1952.

cumstances and needs of that location. It was the result of a growing doubt as to the truth of these two views, as much as economics or line-staff difficulties or the need to respond more effectively to increased centralization in the environment, that started the swing back in the direction of centralization.

Personnel managers have to consider some difficult and worrisome questions. They must have the answers to the following questions before they decide to accept and encourage further centralization:

1. Does a more highly centralized operation afford young, high-potential individuals sufficient chance for success and advancement to assure the organization's long-run needs for top quality leadership?

2. Does it increase company success, but at the cost of individual career satisfaction?

3. Does it generate pressure for so much conformity and create so much anonymity that employee motivation and productivity are lowered to the point that they offset other advantages?

One of the first observers to publicize his answer to these difficult questions was Neil Chamberlain of Yale University:

Not only must there be an identification of goals and a consistency of means of achieving them if the enterprise is to be efficient; there should also be some method of ascertaining the *degree* to which goals are satisfied. The idea of measuring satisfaction is at present as skeptically regarded as was once the idea that manual efficiency could be measured, prior to the advent of Taylorism and scientific management. The measurement that is needed is not some psychological probing into the mental recesses

of the individual, but some objective test of the degree to which the individual possesses potentialities within the corporation for the satisfaction of his personal goals and his capacity to capitalize on those potentialities. If we are to profit from Barnard's insight that business efficiency must be considered in terms of its ability to satisfy the personal goals of those who compose the business, we can scarcely rely on faith or circumstance to realize efficiency. It must be earned by plan and design directed to the efficiency we seek, and there must be adequate means for testing the success of the planning. Such a test does not lie in production per man-hour or the total productivity of the firm, for despite an interrelationship these relate primarily to social effectiveness rather than efficiency in promoting individual objectives. The potentialities of this approach have been sensed by only a very few people. Despite the widespread discussion of "social engineering," "human engineering," and "human relations in industry," these terms have often been used to embrace a wide range of welfare sentiment, without adequate understanding of what is sought. The manager who answers that his business is not an eleemosynary institution is justified in his criticism. The same manager, however, may be quick to champion the necessity of business efficiency in terms which are all but obsolete. The successful creation of opportunities *by and for all who participate* and the satisfactory use of those opportunities is the business efficiency which must be sought. To seek it rationally, the ends to be served must be identified, the means to achieve them must be made specific, and methods of measuring the degree of business efficiency must be found. This is a program of staggering and challenging proportions.[3]

It is important to observe that Chamberlain's doubt centers largely about the difficulty of having sufficient information and the right information at the right time and the right place. He implies that if this could be done, then the clarity, directness, and precision of the highly

[3] Chamberlain, Neil, *The Union Challenge to Management Control,* Harper & Brothers, New York, 1948.

centralized organization would best satisfy all employees.

Moreover, it is also interesting to note what Chris Argyris, also of Yale, has to say about the centralized type of operation:

All organisms seem to manifest three kinds of activities. We shall refer to these activities as the *organizational core activities* or simply *core activities*. The core activities are (1) achieving objectives, (2) maintaining the internal system, and (3) adapting to the external environment. . . . The intended consequence . . . of each function is to contribute to the successful operation of the core activities . . . that is, achieving the objectives. Also, because people are finite in their capacities, the functions must be "chopped up" into manageable units. These units have been called roles or jobs. Roles or jobs are usually combined into larger units, typically labeled sections, departments, divisions, and so on. Whether one conceptionalizes the organization in terms of functions, jobs, or sections, we may say that subsystems are created and each assigned (whole or part) responsibility for the continued successful operation of a particular function. These subsystems *contribute* to the core activities by *supplying* one or more essential functions. Their degree of essentiality to the organization is related to how much they contribute to the core activities. Their contribution may vary, and thus their degree of essentiality may vary. . . . Thus every part may be considered in terms of its essentiality to the whole, its dependence on other parts, and their dependence on it. The more a part contributes to the whole and to the other parts, the more *central* it is to the organization. The less a part contributes to the whole and to the other parts, the less central it is to the organization. . . . Organic parts perform functions without which the whole cannot exist, and without the whole, the parts cannot survive. Thus, there is a state of mutual dependence among the parts and between the parts and the whole. . . . Exactly how the parts interact with one another to create a social organization is still one of the important unanswered questions. Nor do we know much about the laws that govern organizational growth. . . . the pyramidal organization can be helped to grow more with decentralization. But . . . in considering organizational growth one need not be limited to the possible flexibility of pyramidal organizations. We maintain that there are other forms of organizations which, if considered, would greatly enlarge the scope of an organization's flexibility and its freedom to change itself. . . . To summarize, let's limit ourselves to the generalization that growth in a social organization is related to the development of the "proper form" to achieve the three organizational core activities of (1) achieving the objective, (2) maintaining the internal system, and (3) adapting to the external environment.[4]

It seems quite evident that both Chamberlain and Argyris are pointing to the advantages to be gained from a swing away from decentralization and toward some new, more highly centralized form of organization. If their logic is correct, the change should give greater success not only to the company as a whole but to its various parts and to all its people.

If personnel managers consider their own personal experiences, they too may sense an increasing swing toward centralization. The heavy recruiting demands for professional engineers, the tendency to make pay and benefit change decisions largely dependent upon survey results, and the increased mobility of employees—these are some of the factors contributing to the steady trend toward greater uniformity and more standardized procedure. The reorganization announcements of many companies reflect this trend. A dramatic example, of course, was the reorganization of U.S. Steel. Honeywell has reorganized several of its product divisions. In 1964 the Temperature Controls product group, the old-

---

[4] Argyris, Chris, *Integrating the Individual and the Organization,* John Wiley & Sons, New York, 1964.

est and one of the most profitable and firmly established of all of the product lines, was more highly centralized.

This specific change in management control also has been studied and commented upon over the years by the faculty of the University of Michigan. Rensis Likert has commented:

The availability of the electronic computer can push large organizations in one of two directions at an accelerating pace: toward centralization or toward decentralization. Persons well informed about programming large computers have pointed out that the computer may reverse the trend toward decentralization and bring about much greater centralization. . . . We would predict that such a development will be accompanied by hostile attitudes and resentment not only among nonsupervisory employees, but also among lower and middle levels of management. The latter will almost surely react adversely to the substantial reduction in their sense of importance and personal worth which this development will bring about. . . . Fortunately, it is not necessary to centralize decision-making to obtain the full benefit of computers. In fact, companies operating under the newer theory would make more extensive use of computers than do companies whose operations are centralized.[5]

However, George Odiorne, also from the University of Michigan, takes the following position:

. . . change in outside conditions which affect the business accounts for the differences in results which can come through different management methods. It likewise accounts for the success of one person and the failure of another where both use the same approach. The lucky manager adopts every strategy to gain a superior position that can be protected against loss in the future. This superior position is comprised of many different features, and being lucky means knowing

what these components of a superior position are and when each should be used. . . . Such choice among alternative courses or policies of course demands a wide knowledge of trends.[6]

It is clear that both Likert and Odiorne are focusing upon information and the use of it. In fact, Odiorne also comments on:

. . . the vast amount of information which daily assails anyone in the management position. Not only have the skills and tools of the administrator proliferated, but the outside influences which impinge upon the managerial decision increase daily. Among the former are the many new tools and techniques which are being developed and which have been used successfully in many companies. The use of cost accounting, electronic data processing, computers, operations research, systems and procedures, wage and salary administration, motivation research, statistical quality control, organization planning methods, and a myriad of similar complex methods are examples of a small portion of this new technology of management and administration. While they add rationality and system to a world that needs managing, they also bring up the distinct possibility that diversion and side excursion from the principal goal of business may entrap the manager. . . . The shape of what must be for the executive is simply that the firm must work, must survive, and grow.[7]

Here Odiorne, clearly favoring centralization, comes to a conclusion opposite to that of his colleague.

As is typical with most management problems, the question of whether the trend toward further centralization of management control will be a satisfying one or one of great turmoil and grief is certainly hard to decide. On the other hand, in their jobs it is vitally important that personnel managers recognize the

[5] Likert, Rensis, *New Patterns of Management,* McGraw-Hill, New York, 1961.

[6] Odiorne, George, *How Managers Make Things Happen,* Prentice-Hall, Englewood Cliffs, N. J., 1961.

[7] *Ibid.*

trend. The immense and instantaneous amount of information which top management now may have at its fingertips; the increasing need to defend effectively against further centralization of the organizations, particularly the government and the unions, which impinge upon company operations; steadily increasing competition, both domestic and foreign; and the need to keep the economy strong in the face of the threats of international Communism—all these factors make it inevitable that certain aspects of management control will continue to become more centralized.

It would be a serious professional mistake for them to jump to the conclusion that this trend must of necessity dehumanize company operations. Quite the opposite is true. If personnel managers keep up to date, if they do the long, tedious, difficult job of retraining themselves to be effective in personnel administration in this age of technology and computers, they ought to be able to go much further in humanizing their companies than has been possible in large organizations in the past. These new tools will give management a better understanding of the individual, of his skills and potential, plus a far better measure of his progress and his job satisfactions. In fact, as far as information is concerned, these new tools offer management the opportunity, if it has the skill, the patience, and the persistence to capitalize on them, of re-establishing in a giant organization much of the same individualized and personalized attention that an employee usually receives in a very small organization. Although, as Chamberlain predicted in 1948, this is a staggering and challenging task, I believe employees have a right to expect such high accomplishment.

At this point, it may be wise to re-examine the late Douglas McGregor's view. In his book, *The Human Side of Enterprise*,[8] in which he described his Theory X and Theory Y of business management, he was careful to avoid concluding that Theory Y would be the management method of the future. As a matter of fact, he himself wrote that Theory Y was only a suggestion. In the conclusion of that monumental work, he wrote:

The purpose of this volume is not to entice management to choose sides on Theory X or Theory Y. It is rather to encourage the realization that theory is important, to urge management to examine its assumptions and make them explicit. In doing so, it will open a door to the future. The possible result could be developments during the next few decades with respect to the human side of enterprise comparable to those that have occurred in technology during the past half century.

Therefore, the challenge of the swinging pendulum of management control is clear. Management should not be afraid of this current swing toward centralization, but it should try to understand it and turn it into an opportunity for each employee to obtain in his work a greater satisfaction, a greater accomplishment, and a greater contribution than he has ever enjoyed.

---

[8] McGregor, Douglas, *The Human Side of Enterprise,* McGraw-Hill, New York, 1960.

E

STAFFING

15. Charting the Difficulties to the Top: A Study of Executive Mobility Patterns

EUGENE E. JENNINGS

Mobilography is the study of the mobility patterns of managers and executives, the distribution and number of mobile managers, and their delays and difficulties enroute. This new science can prevent and remedy problems that have been largely beyond the grasp of personnel departments of large business corporations: the talented manager lost in the corporate maze, the mobile executive going too fast up the corporate ladder, the promising manager who is without proper training and development, or the executive headed for a career crisis.

The argot of mobilography will allow the corporation to condense the careers of all of its managerial and executive personnel into a capsulized format or resumé that will allow easy inspection of differences in mobility patterns and rates. For the first time, members of a large corporation will be able to see at a glance the large numbers of men moving in all the far-flung corners of the corporation.

It is odd with all the emphasis today on developing managerial personnel that little effort is given to discovering who is progressing and regressing and at what rates. The large corporation invests millions of dollars each year on training and education of managerial personnel but does little to determine who are the real

Reprinted from *Management of Personnel Quarterly,* Vol. 6, No. 2 (Summer, 1967), Bureau of Industrial Relations, Graduate School of Business, University of Michigan, pp. 13–21, with permission of the publisher. Eugene E. Jennings is Professor of Administrative Science, College of Business, Michigan State University.

beneficiaries. The science of mobilography will bring a rare degree of precision and refinement to the process of managerial development.

Who Are the Upward-Mobile?

Mobilography is based upon the need to know who are the most upward-mobile men in the corporation and compare them with the least. A mobility audit will be both extensive and intensive in scope. By extensive we mean that all men at all levels will be surveyed to discover the kinds of jobs that they occupied during their careers in the corporation. By intensive we mean that the occupants of select positions in the corporation will be studied for as far back as twenty to thirty-five years.

Mobilography is basically concerned with the men who move into the offices of the executive suite and with their career backgrounds. The mobility audit of corporate officials for the past several decades will provide a base for evaluating relative rates of upward mobility. With these bases of comparison, managers at the many lower levels in the corporate hierarchy may be evaluated and classified into super-mobiles, sub-mobiles, and arrested mobility types, depending upon their rates of upward mobility.

Fifteen years of studying mobility patterns of executives in the largest industrial corporations has provided a few useful categories. There is a small group of business executives who are entrepreneurs, men who built their corporations from the ground up and who still preside over them as presidents. There are many more sons of entrepreneurs (SOE) who are at the top because of their birth, a large number of grandsons of entrepreneurs (SOSOE) and a few sons-in-law of entrepreneurs (SILOE). Sons, grandsons, sons-in-law and men of some other similar re-

lationship are categorized as *birth elite*. They have entirely different rates and routes of mobility than do a group of business executives called hierarchs. Hierarchs have moved from the bottom to the top without any familial or marital conditions operating for or against them. A pure hierarch is to be differentiated from a lateral hierarch who moves into the top from another corporation. Lateral hierarchs as well as birth elite have interesting and informative mobility rates and routes, but they should be analyzed and evaluated separately from pure hierarchs. Mobility studies of men who have moved into the executive suites of largest industrial corporations during the last twenty years show that a majority of executives (pure hierarchs) move through the corporate hierarchy in a predictable pattern of three stages:

1) the technical level which is nonmanagerial and subsumes the work of salesman, engineer, scientist, accountant, etc., 2) the managerial level which advances from supervising non-managers through managing managers to finally taking the responsibility of a corporate division, and 3) the executive level which is made up of the president, his immediate subordinates, and the men who report directly to these immediate subordinates. These may be either line or staff men.

The Presidential Pattern

The majority profile in mobility studies shows an S curve. The pattern of a specific executive may be a bit jagged, but executives collectively average out to form this S curve. The future president starts as a specialist in sales, personnel, engineering, accounting, etc. (i.e., in the technical or *entrance stage*). Average presidents spend no more than three years in the technical, non-managerial stage; one-fourth were spotted and elevated within a year and a half and one-fourth were spotted between three and four years. The average relative time (ART) for super-mobiles is one and one-half years, for normals two to three years, and for sub-mobiles three to four and one-half years. In the second stage of the mobility cycle, the *developmental stage,* the future president moves rapidly both upwards and laterally, through middle management. This stage is one of intense mobility and provides the corporation with well-rounded executive talent.

Because the mobile executive moves around as he moves up, he has a sort of upward spiral pattern to his career. Generally, the future president does not stay in one position more than eighteen to twenty-one months. The super-mobile stays on the average of fourteen to eighteen and the sub-mobile twenty-one to twenty-eight months.

The last stage of the mobile manager's route to the top is called *arrival.* This stage is measured by how frequently and with what duration the individual interacts with the president on a face-to-face basis. Generally he is on the arrival pad when he assists a man (line or staff) who sits on the president's first team (executive committee). One-fourth of all presidents were appointed to their office between the ages of 47–49; about a half held the reins between the ages of 50–53, and one-fourth at the age of 54 or older. Hence, the super-mobile type's ART is 49 or less, normal mobile is 50–53 and submobile is 54 and over.

From these averages we can derive an overall average relative time for each of these three stages:

	Super-Mobile	Normal Mobile	Sub-Mobile
Stage 1	0–2 years	2–3 years	3–4 years
Stage 2	11 years	14 years	15 years
Stage 3	8 years	10 years	17 years
Total	21 years	24 years	32 years
Average age when made president	47	50	54
Cutoff	49 or younger	50–54	54 or older

The author has audited mobility routes taken by pure hierarchs in specific corporations on their way to the very top. It is apparent that the development stage ends and the arrival stage begins at the level of division responsibility. A super-mobile is one who becomes division president and general manager before the age of 40, a normal mobile between 41 and 48, and a sub-mobile 48 or older. It must be noted that the ART is a basis of comparing the rate of movement of men in a corporation. This factor must ultimately be based upon data gotten from *within the corporation itself,* although national figures are helpful to compare with corporate rates and routes. Average relative times will be obtained at all levels in the corporation.

The Argot of Mobility

The next step in the mobilographic exercise is to develop a resumé for each manager and executive. This step requires an argot. Mobilography recognizes that a manager may move in one of four directions, namely, upwards, downwards, sidewards, and outwards (exits from corporation). In addition, there is a condition recognized as no movement. A condition of no movement is relative to the three conditions of movement, i.e., if a mobile manager stays in a given position no longer than two years, anyone who spends more than two years in a similar position before another upward promotion would be considered in a no-movement condition. The term for this condition is simply *stay* (S). Hence, this manager's resumé would be graphed as US (U for upward promotion, S for stay longer than the average of two years). Anyone who has received a promotion but has not yet served an average relative time (ART) would not receive an S suffix. To denote the time spent in the position beyond ART, a superscript may be added, such as S^3. An S^3 has spent 3 times as much time in the position which he occupies as a mobile manager. We say in mobilographic argot that he drew 3 stays. Or, alternatively the term U^3 indicates that the manager was promoted three times without staying longer than the ART of two years. The reader must keep in mind that the term *stay* (S) is the only letter referring to non-movement. It is assumed in mobilography that a manager who stays in a position less than ART is still mobile.

Two resumés are very commonly found in mobilographic studies: TUSD; TUSL. The letter D stands for downward movement or *demotion* and L for a sideward movement or *lateral*. If the managerial career is preceded by work in non-managerial positions, the term T may be used as a prefix. It stands for *technical* positions such as accountant, engineer, salesman, scientist, etc. If the average relative time that supermobile executives have spent performing technical work (non-managerial jobs) is five years, the letter S may be used only when the period of time exceeds five years (ART). The most appropriate term will

be TS. The first position that carries supervisory responsibility will be denoted by the term U^1. This superscript will not be used again to denote any other upward movement. Merely using U implies that the manager was promoted and if a promotion followed swiftly the term U^2 will be appropriate. The letter U^1 will be used to denote the individual's entrance into the first line managerial job. Below are some resumés that are commonly found in mobilographic studies.

TU^1LULU This individual performed technical operations (T non-managerial of any kind) but was promoted to full line management (U^1) before he completed the average relative time that mobile managers usually spend at the technical level. He stayed less than ART for men at first line management level and was lateraled (L) to a managerial job of the same degree of responsibility and difficulty. The remainder of the profile is self explanatory since it repeats the second and third terms.

$TS^2U^1S^2US^2$ This individual stayed (S) in technical operations longer than the mobile manager type, received his promotion to first line supervision (U^1) and stayed there longer than ART as he did after his next promotion. Notice must be given to the superscripts by the letters S. They stand for the amount of time that the individual stayed beyond ART for mobile men in these respective positions. The actual amount of time is of little significance to mobilographic study. Even though the ART will vary with each level in the corporation, the amount of time spent beyond ART may be meaningful and may be recorded in the format of the resumé. This manager stayed in the entrance stage (T) two years longer than a super-mobile whose ART is usually two years or less, and he stayed in the developmental stage two years longer than the super-mobile's one and one-half years. His is an up-stay pattern in contrast to the preceding manager whose is an up-lateral pattern.

TU^3 This represents an up-up pattern and, hence, this manager is extremely mobile and represents a super-mobile pattern. Mobility rates today are such that anyone who draws a stay longer than, for example, five years total (or three years beyond ART of a super-mobile) will not become president or even move into the arrival stage. An *arrested mobility type* is anyone who is performing the same job for five years or more. The probability of his not drawing a U without a stay of another five years is extremely high. Only if he could draw a U without an S could he be classified as mobile once again. He would be a partial mobile if he drew a U and L, but if he stayed in the lateral job longer than ART of a super-mobile he would become classified as a stay again. A stay after a lateral can have greater career disadvantages than a U followed by S.

TU^1SDX This case is classified as an ex-mobile. Basically this manager has an up-down and out pattern and is very commonly found in mobilographic studies. The prefix *ex-* may be attached to a super-mobile, mobile, or sub-mobile; it denotes a man who has been in the company twelve years but who has left after drawing a demotion. The usefulness of a mobility audit may be illustrated here. Suppose the most common resumé of an exit pattern is represented by TU^2LUS^2X. This was the actual case in one division of a corporation that was largely engineering personnel. The great-

est turnover of managerial talent was of super-mobiles who drew a stay about the third level, and after three years beyond ART for a supermobile made an exit from the corporation. Of all exits (X) in the developmental stage, this resumé represented about thirty per cent. The company was aghast and took steps to discover why there was such a large number of X patterns. It discovered that managers above the third level were sub-mobiles who were effectively blocking upward mobiles below them. Steps were taken to move men whose resumés approximated TU^2LUS^2 to other divisions in the company to keep their career aims alive. The X rate was sharply reduced and good men were saved from leaving the company for mobility opportunities elsewhere.

TU^1Xi One of the most common exit patterns is identified by the resumé commonly referred to as a TUX. Here is a young man who stayed in the technical level about the time of a super-mobile, was promoted to first level supervision, and in a year exited voluntarily from the corporation. Mobility studies are beginning to spot a higher frequency of inter-corporation mobility during the last few years among men who fit this resumé. This is called *leveraging* and is signified by the letter Xi. It appears that leveraging has increased about three-fold during the last ten years. Men use a promotion to garner another one in another corporation because they feel they can be promoted faster.

The Mobilographic Resumé

EA	Mobility Pattern	PA	$TMP/CA = MR/PA = MQ$				
23	(TU^1LULU)	32	37	9	4.11	32	128

A mobilographic resumé traces the *mobility pattern* of an employee (promo-

tions, demotions, laterals, and stays), the age when he becomes a first-level manager

(*Entrance Age,* EA), and his *present age* when the mobility audit was taken (PA).

The *pattern* may be evaluated numerically by referring to the mobility points assigned to each move. Generally, T = 10, U = 5, L = 3, S = 2, and D = −5. (Full details of the variance cannot be presented here, but they will appear shortly in the book upon which this article is based.[1]) From these, the *total mobility points* (TMP) are calculated and held for further reckoning. The *career age* (CA) is the difference between the employee's entrance age and present age, that is, the length of his managerial career in the firm. The *mobility rate* (MR) is derived by dividing the total mobility points by the career age (MR = TMP/CA). The mobility rate represents the average num-

ber of mobility points that the individual has gained during each year of his managerial career. This rate is especially useful because it allows the auditor to project mobility. The *mobility quotient* (MQ) is based upon reasoning that mobility is a kind of test given to a manager when he starts to manage. The amount of points that he gets during a given career time (CA) is comparable to the score he gets on an intelligence test during the period for which the test is given. TMP divided by CA (TMP/CA or simply, MR), when divided by present age (PA), will produce the mobility quotient (MQ = MR/PA). By multiplying by 100, the auditor may derive whole numbers. Following are some additional samples of resumés:

EA	Mobility Pattern	PA	TMP/CA		= MR/PA	= MQ
25	(TU[1]LULU)	32	31	7	4.43 32	138
26	(TU[1]SLLU)	35	23	9	2.56 35	73
28	(TU[1]SLDX)	38	13	10	1.30 38	34

The resumé also includes a reckoning of the *average career time unused* (ACTU) and *total expected mobility points* (TEMP). The mobility audit will determine the average age when executives are

made president. If it is about 51, as is the case in many corporations, the present age of the manager subtracted from the *average age when made president* (AAWP) will give the average career unused

---

Sample:

EA	Pattern	PA	TMP/CA		= MR/PA	= MQ		ACTU	TEMP
32	(TSU[1]SL)	46	16	14	1.14 46	25		5	8 + 16 = 24

This is a repeat of 4 of the previous samples, with the ACTU and TEMP added:

EA	Pattern	PA	TMP/CA		= MR/PA	= MQ		ACTU	TEMP
23	(TU[1]LULU)	32	37	9	4.11 32	128		19	78 + 37 = 115
25	(TU[1]LULU)	32	31	7	4.43 32	138		19	84 + 31 = 115
26	(TU[1]SLLU)	35	23	9	2.56 35	73		16	41 + 23 = 64
28	(TU[1]SLDX)	38	13	10	1.30 38	34		13	17 + 13 = 30

---

[1] *The Mobile Manager: A Study of the New Generation of Top Executives* (Ann Arbor, Mich.: Bureau of Industrial Relations, University of Michigan, 1967).

(ACTU). The total expected mobility points (TEMP) follow the ACTU on the resumé and are calculated by multiplying MR by ACTU and adding TMP. It is most relevant when an average of the TMP for presidents is determined. If the average total mobility points garnered by presidents and/or vice-presidents is 75, a TEMP of 70 will suggest that the manager could go all the way. The TEMP is useful to predict in advance if the manager will become president or vice-president. If he tops out at lower levels, this fact is particularly instructive.

Strategy Shifts the Channels

Mobility and strategy are highly related. The routes and rates of mobility change with the strategy of the corporation. The change from a manufacturing emphasis to a marketing orientation may enlarge the number of managers moving to the top in marketing and sales and from these kinds of backgrounds. As research and development budgets have increased, the number of people at the top with scientific and engineering backgrounds has increased. They number about 18 per cent but are growing in number rapidly.

As the corporation has increased the emphasis placed upon planning, evaluating, problem analysis, research and advisory activities, staff positions have become developmental. From 1948–1953 only 25 percent of the presidents had *not* had at least five years during their managerial careers in staff work of some kind. It is no longer believed that only line managers provide presidential stock.

The route to the top has also changed as the corporation has developed a multinational orientation. From 1948–1953 few presidents had three or more years in foreign operations. By 1966 one out of three presidents of the 500 largest industrials had been three years or more in foreign subsidiaries and divisions.

Men at the top strengthen the mobility routes they have themselves used, since they tend to bring with them crucial subordinates who have largely the same mobility patterns. Routes become strengthened by and through the successes of men who have created them. However, men at the top may be replaced by men from other routes because of changes in corporate strategies (although these do not occur suddenly, partly *because* of the threat to existing routes of mobility). The dependent variable seems to be corporate strategies; for this reason, corporations often adopt new strategies long after the facts warrant changes.

How Mobile Are the Competent? How Competent Are the Mobile?

It has often been noted in mobilography that success is more than merely turning in consistently high performances. Upward mobility is partly dependent upon being in a fast route. There are many good men in slow moving routes to the top, i.e., accounting and personnel: these routes produce the fewest of the pure hierarchs who go to the top.

Nevertheless, there is a strong relationship between mobility and competency. Mobilographic studies tend to show that many, if not most, managerial positions can be learned in a year and a half or less. That is to say, the basic elements of the job can be grasped. Mobile executives have an 80/20 orientation toward most positions, i.e., 20 percent of any job counts for 80 percent of the learning. If they can get the 20 percent under their belts and move on to another job, the learning curve is constantly rising. If they were to stay in the job longer, they would be completing the 80 percent of the job that counts for only 20 percent of the learning. Besides, much of the 80 percent can be mastered easily from the transfer knowledge that has accumulated during previous managerial experiences. Only about 20 percent of a new job is actually new and developmental. The manager who can move into a position, grasp its essential uniqueness and master the new responsibilities and assignments and move to another job is apt to gain more competency. Many managers are doing their jobs out of the backs of their pockets after a year and a half and each additional year decreases their mobility rate, increases lost career time, and slows down their developmental curve.

There is a basic difference between the new breed of manager and his predecessor. Before 1950, American business largely thought talent would automatically surface, much as cream comes to the top of milk. Each aspiring executive was on his own more or less. A second belief was based on the notion that practice makes perfect. This belief may have been useful in teaching piano, but it was definitely a liability when applied to developing executive talent. Men were kept in jobs long after they had learned them. Consequently, men overlearned their jobs on each rung of the corporate ladder. They were not only slow in arriving at the top, but many were old men with much of their enthusiasm and brilliance wrung out of them.

Today, things are becoming radically different. Promising managers are moved before they get bored. If anything, they practice underlearning. They have to be mentally alert to get into a job and learn quickly the fundamentals and move to another job.

Growing in a Growing Firm

Mobility is highly related to growth. The firms that have had spectacular growth patterns have had high rates of mobility of all kinds. They have had high functional mobility. Men move up fast through the functions of business, i.e., accounting, finance, personnel, manufacturing, marketing, sales, research, and development. In response to a growth need, they started in the early fifties to move managers across functions, from engineering to sales, from accounting to manufacturing, etc. Now these growth corporations realize that men who stay in one functional route all the way up suffer from route vision, seeing the whole corporation from the various visions of their functional routes. Growth firms have also increased divisional and geographic mobility. Managers are moved to different areas of the corporation to expose them to similar responsibilities in different social, economic, and political environments of the corporation and society. They often substitute geographic mobility for positional mobility.

In the arrival stage, assignment mobility is often substituted for positional mobility. In growth firms, the executive may stay in a position longer than he did in managerial levels, but he will get three to four times the number of special assignments of task-force responsibilities. For this reason, an executive who draws a stay is penalized less than a manager.

Promotion: Trust and Trailers

Mobility is largely a relationship between two or more people. Few men arrive at the top who are not trusted by somebody already there. Executives move up by being sponsored by someone who has the power to promote or recommend promotion. They move up in twos and threes, bringing their trailers with them. Such subordinates are considered crucial to their superior's effectiveness and mobility, for they know how to make their bosses look good and how to keep them moving ahead. This way they move ahead too. A crucial subordinate must not only keep the superior mobile, he must extricate himself from the relationship if the superior's mobility becomes permanently arrested. The act must be done with care for the upward mobile manager cannot afford to offend this immobile superior. The latter cannot help him but he can hurt him. After all, this upward-bound manager may need him on the way down.

A new kind of president is emerging. He is the project type. He is the man who is asked to do a particular job after which he turns the baton over to the next executive in the relay race. This means that he stays in the job about five years or less. Ten years was the average tenure of presidents in our base period (1948–1953). The trend is such that by 1970, 50 percent or more will be project presidents.

Executives become presidents because corporate situations require their talents. A corporation has a kind of rhythm of its own that determines the movement of talent. To execute project assignments successfully, the manager must know how to organize teams of limited purposes and to draw talent from the far corners of the company. As a project manager, he must motivate people who have their loyalties attached to other superiors and functions.

Arrival: Your Age in Salary

Mobility is related to entrance age. A few mobilographic studies reveal the distinct possibility that the large industrial corporation is placing its scarce chips on a particular kind of individual. He is one who displays a capacity to manage early in his career. There are six times as many early arrivals today as there were in

1948–1953. The most mobile managers are relatively young for their salary level and positional level. The early arrival makes his age in salary: that is, if he is 35 years old, he makes $35,000. The chances of making thirty thousand dollars a year are four times as great for the man who gets out of the technical or entrance stage in two years as for a man who stays there five years or more.

Contrary to what some people believe, the men who fail at the top are not the men who came up fast. An *early terminal* (ET) is a president who stayed in the job less than one-half the average relative time. This is about two years. Any president who has stayed two years or less has usually been summarily relieved of his job. Of some thirty-six early terminals studied, only one-fourth could be classified as having been early arrivals and super-mobiles. Most were delayed arrivals, having spent too much time in middle management jobs. They overlearned their jobs, spent too much time on the theme that practice makes perfect. They showed in their managerial styles while president an inability to adapt quickly and respond to change and crisis. There is something deadly about staying in middle management too long. The biggest step in the corporate ladder is from executive to president. This last step cannot be approximated by any prior training except perhaps throwing managerial assignments to a promising manager just as fast as he can absorb them.

The Over-Mobile Manager

Of course, mobility may exceed skill and self-confidence. One of the bad effects of the last fifteen years of economic growth and high managerial mobility is that many managers have moved up faster than they have acquired skill and self-confidence. The number of executives and managers who were once very mobile but who now sit on shelves is large. But, of course, not all can or should be mobile. The corporation needs men who can manage well at all levels. Not everyone can go to the top or maintain upward mobility.

Mobility is not directly related to college grades or technical competency. When the young accountant, engineer, salesman, or personnel specialist is promoted to a supervisory job, he is at the threshold of his managerial career. The first six to nine months will be the most crucial of his life. The number of men who move up to first level management jobs and down again within one year is very great. In some firms it is as high as two out of five. This high up-down rate serves as a screening device that separates the men who can manage from those who serve better as technicians or specialists. The fact that the up-down rate is high suggests several other possibilities. One is that preparation for sales, engineering, accounting, personnel, or some other technical or specialized role does little to prepare people for managerial responsibility. Another implication is that managers who are responsible for selecting first level superiors do a very poor job of separating the men from the boys at the point of promotion. If this suggestion is valid, it follows that actual screening occurs after performing the managerial role for a while rather than before entrance into it.

Beginning a Mobile Career

The question that is uppermost at this point is why the first six to nine months of a novitiate is crucial to a whole managerial career. As an accountant, engineer, salesman, personnel specialist, or scientist the manager is supervising men of his own kind. This is not to suggest that he was the best technician or specialist before he was promoted to supervisor.

A better key to the reasons for his promotion is his skill in handling technical people who are his peers, knowing how they think and react. In short, a desire to achieve managerial proficiency is a greater key to promotion than a desire to achieve technical proficiency. Of course, the young man out of college must take seriously his technical assignments and achieve technical competency. But it is commonplace to find that men who have been well trained in college in some professional area like accounting, engineering, or science, hope to pursue their careers in as pure a form as possible. Many professionally-trained people have aspired to their vocations as early as ninth grade. Many years of hard work under rigorous educational situations reinforced in their minds the professional halo that gradually took over command of their adult personalities. This hold upon them by their professional images is keenly seen when the young engineer, scientist, or accountant discovers upon entry into the business world that so much of what he has been taught is not practiced or useful in business. The author has watched the agony experienced by young men who discover that business and industry do not really use engineers in the way that they have been trained. The struggle to maintain one's professional identity is a story that has not been adequately told. The well-educated engineer, scientist, or accountant conceives managing as alien to his interests, and may not respect managers because they do not measure up to his high standards of technical competency.

The Technical Man, an Upstay

We have mentioned the up-down rate as critical and high at the point of the first-level supervisor. There is also the up-stay rate. This is the number of people who are promoted to first level and stay there for five years or longer and never receive a higher promotion. The young man who identifies almost totally with his technical skill and chooses not to become disassociated from it may prove to be an effective first-level superior. Here he has a chance to stay close to his identity because he can see the technical work being performed and can engage in it frequently. But why may he not be promoted to a second- or third-level manager? One reason is that his over-identification with maintaining his technical competency and being the most technically competent of his staff dilutes his energies for giving careful attention to developing his managerial style. At the second level he will be evaluated by how expert are the technical people who supply him with answers. His job will be to find and develop managers who can directly supervise technical men and keep him properly advised and informed. If he has to wait until the second level to develop a proper technical-managerial mix, he will be forced to do it without the experience of prior successes and failures. His chances of failing are greater than for the individual who began to utilize a mix weighted toward management in the first-level supervisory position.

The fact is that the route to the top is not found in technical competency. Management does not ask where a person got useful technical ideas and solutions as long as they are in abundant enough supply. When a first-level manager fails to apply proper technical ideas, he does not expose his technical gap but his managerial ineffectiveness. His superiors will wonder why he has not utilized the technical competency of his staff or acquired technically competent people. They may inquire if he knows how to draw out the technical competency of his staff and they may suspect that he is trying to be a know-it-all and has stifled creative responses of his staff. At most he will be held responsible for enough technical knowledge to know how to screen the technical chaff from the wheat, but this amount of knowledge is almost a prerequisite for moving into a first-level managerial job. If he does not have the prerequisite technical knowledge, he is not at fault as much as his superiors who erroneously promoted him. Since they will be reluctant to admit mistakes, he must assume the blame solely and totally. He will receive a demotion with an inscription next to his name on the personnel record, "Not ready for management responsibility."

The author is reminded of a bright young accountant who became technically proficient in computer systems. He was asked to computerize an accounting process and did the job with dispatch and authority. However, the first thing he did upon completion of the job was to train two men in computerization and programming. He was promoted to a project to computerize the whole division, at which time he hired two men who were more competent than he was. The project was not entirely completed before he was promoted to corporate staff to advise the various executives of finance, the comptroller, and the treasurer on computerization possibilities for the whole company. He took with him to this job one of the men he hired and hired another from the outside. He completed assembly of a fine staff, all of whom came to a high point of proficiency that excelled his level. While at corporate staff he obtained visibility with the general managers of the eight company divisions and they came to ask him to help them computerize various parts of sales, manufacturing, and marketing. This young man never did have all of the best answers. He knew where they were and how to get them. At age thirty-four, this executive was made a vice-president and placed in charge of all technical processes except research and development. From his staff have come large numbers of technically proficient people, some of whom have left the corporation. But his outstanding trade mark is that he also developed extremely fine managers who have fanned out to all parts of the corporation assuming management jobs at many and diverse levels. At a recent meeting of corporate staff he was asked a question and his answer was that of a manager, "Well, off the top of my hat I would say that you should follow the solution we used last year in the organic division. However, if you let me consult my staff, I'll get a much better answer for you."

Mobility is creating mobicentric managers. Mobilographic interviews and studies reveal a manager whose central concern is for mobility itself. Success is mobility; it is less position, title, salary, or exceptional performance. Success is moving and movement. In mobicentric circles, it is not power or money or position, but the *acquiring* of these things that counts.

The profile of a mobicentric is a manager whose style of managing is predicated upon rapid movement from position to position. He never expects to complete a job, is prepared to depart soon after he arrives, is impatient in doing the finishing stages of an assignment, is preoccupied with the mobility of people about him, is quick to feel mild anxiety when he stays in a job too long, rejects the belief that a person can move up too fast, definitely does not believe that he has moved or is moving too fast, relates himself psychologically to people several levels above him who are fast climbers, tends to be somewhat aloof with superiors who are slow climbers, demands a great deal from subordinates and sees a direct relationship between their efforts and his mobility rate, and tends to seek and accept assignments that give him high visibility.

16. Controlling Skill Mix in Large Organizations

EDWARD G. MATTHEWS

Most large organizations control manpower for locations or divisions simply by designating manpower ceilings, but these attempts to set limits on numbers of people, without simultaneously controlling skill, educational level, or other fundamental personnel characteristics, can be wasteful and inefficient. Such a control measure virtually invites the operating manager to staff with overqualified people—a tendency to which he is already prone because of his natural desire to insure against the demands of an unknown future by obtaining people

Reprinted from *Personnel,* Vol. 44, No. 3 (May–June, 1967), pp. 16–21, with permission of the publishers. Edward G. Matthews is Manager of Plans and Controls, Systems Development Division, IBM, Poughkeepsie, New York.

with a high upper range of capabilities.

The insurance is bought, however, at a premium in terms of salary costs to the company and of professional underutilization of the employee. The practice leads eventually to the atrophy, or at best the obsolescence, of employee skills and knowledge. Other consequences of packing organizations with persons having educations, skills, or experience substantially in excess of job requirements appear in the frequency and number of requests for transfer and resignations.

Controlling the Mix

One approach to treating the source of these symptoms involves the use of multipliers of manpower count to get a balanced skill mix. The multipliers are selected to control average skill mix in large units, such as plants, laboratories, or divisions of a company. The quantifying multipliers are chosen to reflect general education or skill level, though other personnel characteristics could be used as well, depending on what the user wanted to control.

Table 1 shows a typical manpower counting system where mix is not a factor. The numerical ceiling is the only control number against which management is measured.

TABLE 1

Employee Classification	Number
Professional	200
Technical	60
Clerical	40
Ceiling 300	300

Here, the control criterion has been met, but without mix control almost certainly there is a disproportionate number of overqualified people. Furthermore, if the ceiling were reduced, it's a pretty sure bet that staff whittling would be primarily among the technical and clerical employees.

It may be argued that salaries could be used as a means of controlling manpower mix, and that is probably true, but the use of salaries to manipulate manpower mix is an inappropriate and marginally effective management tool for this purpose. It is inappropriate because salary should be fundamentally compensation for services performed. It is marginally effective because in many large organizations salaries are averaged when operating costs are evaluated, and reductions or reallocations of effort in successful companies are most often carried out in terms of people, rather than in terms of salary. A manager, in reducing the size of his group, will almost always transfer the least skilled or lowest paid employee first, if he has the option.

"Pricing" the Job

Table 2 shows a manpower counting system in which both number and mix are used as control factors. The mix has been designed to put a premium on the "count cost" of professionals and to induce the manager to use clerical workers because of their low "count cost." (Of course, the premium could just as well have been placed on clerks or technicians if the executive wanted to include more professionals.)

In this example, one of the control criterion—number—has been met. However, the count cost, which is a product of number and multiplier, has exceeded the ceiling by 32.

At this point the manager may choose among several alternatives to bring his count cost down to 300. If he insists on

TABLE 2

Employee Classification	Number	Multiplier	Count Cost
Professional	200	1.2	240
Technical	60	1.0	60
Clerical	40	0.8	32
Ceiling 300	300		332

retaining all 200 professionals, he must make his reductions in the other categories—for example, as indicated in Table 3.

In this case the manager has maintained the maximum number of professionals, but at the cost of having 35 people fewer than his manpower ceiling

TABLE 3

Employee Classification	Number	Multiplier	Count Cost
Professional	200	1.2	240
Technical	40	1.0	40
Clerical	25	0.8	20
Ceiling 300	265		300

allows. Moreover, it would undoubtedly prove extremely difficult to run the department efficiently with this kind of skill mix; the sharp reduction in technical and clerical workers would inevitably mean that many professional employees would be forced to do work that was far below their level of ability. The problems of morale and turnover that this kind of mix would generate are obvious, and the manager would be constrained to reject this solution in favor of a more workable alternative.

One such alternative would be to maximize the number of people in the department, but at the same time retain as many professionals as possible. This can be accomplished by making the necessary

reductions among the professional group, bringing their count cost down to 208 $(240 - 32 = 208)$.

As indicated in Table 4, the manager now has struck a balance between maximizing the number of professional employees and the number of employees in the department, but he still has 27 people fewer than his manpower ceiling allows.

Another alternative is for the manager to concentrate solely on maximizing the number of people in his organization. To do this, he would make further reductions among professionals, since they incur major count costs, and increase clericals, whose count costs are lowest. As Table 5 indicates, this solution bal-

TABLE 4

Employee Classification	Number	Multiplier	Count Cost
Professional	173	1.2	208
Technical	60	1.0	60
Clerical	40	0.8	32
Ceiling 300	273		300

ances the count costs with the manpower ceiling, maximizing the number of people in the organization.

From these examples, it appears that the manager is forced to choose between maximum professional strength with less

TABLE 5

Employee Classification	Number	Multiplier	Count Cost
Professional	120	1.2	144
Technical	60	1.0	60
Clerical	120	0.8	96
Ceiling 300	300		300

than a full manpower contingent, or a full staff at the sacrifice of maximum professional strength. That may be so, but whether the forcing is appropriate in its extent or nature depends on the correctness of the original mix, and that, of course, is not evident here.

The examples do, however, show how a manager may respond to a weighting system and how the executive who allo-

cates the weightings can determine the ranges within which the manager can maneuver in selecting personnel. For instance, if the executive had chosen to reduce the ranging of the manager around the established ceiling of 300, he might have selected multipliers as shown in Table 6.

In this case, the manager's mix is already almost perfectly optimized, and few

TABLE 6

Employee Classification	Number	Multiplier	Count Cost
Professional	200	1.1	220
Technical	60	0.9	54
Clerical	40	0.7	28
Ceiling 300	300		302

changes would be necessary. After the system of controls through weighting has been introduced in this way, the executive can, by changing the weightings, force a change in the mix if he thinks it should be adjusted.

At this point another objection to weighting systems may arise: Won't the managers spend a good deal of time trying to beat the system, to improve their position in it? The reply, of course, is that they will—but this is exactly what should be done. The manager's attempts to find the best skill mix for his department require painstaking analysis and thought. In the allocation of an expensive and often scarce resource, this can hardly be called objectionable.

The success of any system for modifying demand, whether manpower, material, capital, or time is involved, rests on the selection of an appropriate value for weighting units. In a sense, executives act as a Federal Reserve Board for their companies when they establish discount rates for whatever is being counted.

Establishing Weights

Any specific suggestions for establishing weights would probably have a usefulness in inverse proportion to their detail, since the personnel elements that should be selected for weighting and the weights that should be assigned to them depend on factors peculiar to each company or organization. However, six fundamental steps in arriving at the specifics of a weighting system can be listed:

• Defining and sizing the job to be done by the organization.
• Establishing the tasks required to do the job.
• Evaluating the types and amounts of skills needed to perform the tasks.
• Describing the desired mix.
• Identifying the existing mix.
• Assigning weightings to move from existing to desired mixes.

The temptation to apply weightings for the control of skill mix to small units of an organization should be resisted; attempts to adjust the skill mix in small departments or groups are rarely successful. But the mix in individual departments can be influenced when senior executives are charged with responsibility for obtaining an average mix in their larger groups. In this way, the organizations involved have the freedom to work out their own internal approach toward mix distribution and still meet assigned goals.

Weighting systems provide executives with a tool for substantial control over average manpower mix, which is important for several reasons. In most businesses, payroll is a major expense; if the payroll is $10,000,000, for example, an improvement of 1 per cent in productivity by reduction of "packing" practices saves $100,000. And aside from direct savings, optimized employment of personnel can result in operational and professional efficiencies and all that an environment of opportunity for growth implies for employee morale and output.

DISCUSSION QUESTIONS: PART II

1. What role should top management play in long-range planning? Why?
2. Discuss the function of long-range planning in large, medium, and small firms. Are there differences? If so, what are they? If not, why not?

3. Distinguish between operating and strategic problems. How are these problems related to long-range planning?
4. Why does conflict between staff and line exist? What types of conflict?
5. In what ways could you resolve line-staff conflict?
6. Describe the major conceptions and misconceptions about span of control. What methods could be employed to handle these misconceptions in a firm?
7. Compare the autocratic and supportive styles of management. Under what conditions could each be used? Illustrate.
8. What major problem areas in leadership need to be researched today? Why?
9. How is control extended in large organizations?
10. Discuss the relationship between the price system, uncertainty, and control in large organizations.
11. Does managerial control move through cycles of centralization and decentralization in an organization? Explain.
12. After analyzing the concept of mobilography, in what ways could you improve the original concept?
13. Is the technique of controlling the skill mix viable in all types of organizations? Why or why not?
14. After examining the recent research and thought in the process approach, what other major problems need to be explored in this area?

SELECTED REFERENCES: PART II

A. PLANNING

Ackoff, Russell L., "The Meaning of Strategic Planning," *Management Review,* Vol. 55, No. 10 (October, 1966), pp. 20–24.

Anderson, T. A., "Coordinating Strategic and Operational Planning," *Business Horizons,* Vol. 8, No. 2 (Summer, 1965), pp. 49–58.

Dale, Ernest, *Planning and Developing the Company Organization* (second edition). New York: American Management Association, 1965.

Dwyer, Henry E., "Departures from Tradition in Organization Planning," *Personnel,* Vol. 40, No. 4 (July–August, 1963), pp. 18–22.

O'Donnell, Cyril, "Planning Objectives," *California Management Review,* Vol. 6, No. 2 (Winter, 1963), pp. 3–10.

Reynolds, William H., "The Edsel Ten Years Later," *Business Horizons,* Vol. 10, No. 3 (Fall, 1967), pp. 39–46.

Warren, E. Kirby, *Long-Range Planning: The Executive Viewpoint.* Englewood Cliffs, N.J.: Prentice-Hall, Inc., 1966.

Weinberg, Robert S., "Improving Corporate Planning Through E.D.P.," *Management Bulletin No. 79.* New York: American Management Association, 1966, pp. 33–43.

B. ORGANIZING

Brooker, Michael, "Does Traditional Organizational Theory Conflict with Theory Y?" *Personnel,* Vol. 41, No. 5 (September–October, 1964), pp. 65–68.

Gelfand, Jack E., "The Optimum Degree of Centralization in Organizational Structure," *Economics and Business Bulletin,* Vol. 18, No. 2 (December, 1965), pp. 25–34.

Huddle, F. P., "Coordination," *California Management Review,* Vol. 9, No. 2 (Winter, 1966), pp. 9–16.

Koontz, Harold, "Making Theory Operational: The Span of Management," *Journal of Management Studies,* Vol. 3, No. 3 (October, 1966), pp. 229–243.

Logan, Hall H., "Line and Staff: An Obsolete Concept?" *Personnel,* Vol. 43, No. 1 (January–February, 1966), pp. 26–33.

Moore, Franklin G., "Is Divisionalization on the Way Out?" *Michigan Business Review,* Vol. 16, No. 3 (May, 1964), pp. 26–32.

Read, William H., "The Decline of the Hierarchy in Industrial Organizations," *Business Horizons,* Vol. 8, No. 3 (Fall, 1965), pp. 71–75.

Zald, Mayer N., "Decentralization—Myth vs. Reality," *Personnel,* Vol. 41, No. 4 (July–August, 1964), pp. 19–26.

C. DIRECTING

Albers, Henry H., *Principles of Organization and Management* (second edition) Chapter 23. New York: John Wiley and Sons, Inc., 1965.

Hodgetts, Richard, "Leadership Techniques in the Project Organization," *Academy of Management Journal,* Vol. 11, No. 2 (June, 1968), pp. 211–219.

Likert, Rensis, *New Patterns of Management.* New York: McGraw-Hill Book Co., 1961.

McCormack, James S., "Communication and the Organization," *Advanced Management Journal,* Vol. 33, No. 1 (January, 1968), pp. 63–67.

McGregor, Douglas, *Leadership and Motivation* (eds.) Warren G. Bennis and Edgar H. Schein. Cambridge, Mass.: M.I.T. Press, 1966.

——— *The Professional Manager* (eds.) Caroline McGregor and Warren G. Bennis. New York: McGraw-Hill Book Co., 1967.

Zaleznik, Abraham, "The Human Dilemmas of Leadership," *Harvard Business Review,* Vol. 41, No. 4 (July–August, 1963), pp. 49–55.

D. CONTROLLING

Bonini, C. P., R. K. Jaedicke, and H. M. Wagner (eds.), *Management Controls: New Directions in Basic Research.* New York: McGraw-Hill Book Co., 1964.

Buck, Vernon E., "Too Much Control—Too Little Quality," *Business Horizons,* Vol. 8, No. 3 (Fall, 1965), pp. 34–44.

Jones, R. L. and H. G. Trentin, *Budgeting: Key to Planning and Control.* New York: American Management Association, 1966.

Livingston, John L., "Management Controls and Organizational Performance," *Personnel Administration,* Vol. 28, No. 1 (January–February, 1965), pp. 37–43.

Luthans, Fred, "Faculty Promotions: An Analysis of Central Administrative Control," *Academy of Management Journal,* Vol. 10, No. 4 (December, 1967), pp. 385–394.

McGregor, Douglas, "Do Management Control Systems Achieve Their Purpose?" *Management Review,* Vol. 56, No. 2 (February, 1967), pp. 4–18.

Raia, Anthony P., "A Second Look at Management Goals and Controls," *Management Review,* Vol. 55, No. 8 (August, 1966), pp. 65–69.

E. STAFFING

Alfred, T. M., "Checkers or Choice in Manpower Management," *Harvard Business Review,* Vol. 45, No. 1 (January–February, 1967), pp. 157–169.

Burke, Maurice O., "The Clinical Method of Managerial Selection," *Business Horizons,* Vol. 8, No. 1 (Spring, 1965), pp. 83–94.

Dunnette, Marvin D., "Predictors of Executive Success," in *Measuring Executive Effectiveness* (eds.) Frederick R. Wickert and Dalton E. McFarland. New York: Appleton-Century-Crofts, Inc., 1967, pp. 3–43.

O'Donnell, Cyril J., "Managerial Training," *Training and Development Journal,* Vol. 22, No. 1 (January, 1968), pp. 2–11.

Scott, William E., Jr., "The Actuarial-Clinical Controversy in Managerial Selection," *Business Horizons,* Vol. 7, No. 4 (Winter, 1964), pp. 89–99.

Stolz, Robert K., "Executive Development—New Perspective," *Harvard Business Review,* Vol. 44, No. 3 (May–June, 1966), pp. 133–143.

Tagiuri, Renato (ed.), *Research Needs in Executive Selection.* Boston: Division of Research, Graduate School of Business Administration, Harvard University, 1961.

Tosi, Henry L. and Robert J. House, "Management Development Beyond the Classroom," *Business Horizons,* Vol. 9, No. 2 (Summer, 1966), pp. 91–101.

PART III

Behavioral
Approaches

The major initial impetus for the use of behavioral approaches in management began with the extensive study of human behavior at the Hawthorne Works of Western Electric Company in the 1920's.[1] These studies borrowed techniques from psychology and sociology to study managerial problems at the operating level. When the researchers had concluded their work, they decided that the contribution of social and human factors to productivity is frequently more important than the physical environment surrounding the workers. The Hawthorne experiments were followed by intensive research into human behavior in organizations. Many different facets of individual and group behavior were analyzed, including the impact of group norms, the factors contributing to individual job satisfaction, the importance of informal groups and leaders within the organization, and the role of status within the organization.

As the research efforts continued, the behavioral science approach to management slowly became better defined. In 1962, Professor Wilmar F. Bernthal stated that the behavioral science approach could be defined as an approach which explains man's behavior in productive organizations—specifically, the behavior of individuals in a social system designed to achieve particular objectives through cooperative effort.[2] This approach involves the analysis of the environmental setting in which individual and group behavior occurs by historians,

---

[1] For discussion of these experiments, see: F. J. Roethlisberger and William J. Dickson *Management and the Worker*. Cambridge, Mass.: Harvard University Press, 1939. For a later evaluation, see: Henry A. Landsberger *Hawthorne Revisited*. Ithaca, New York: Cornell University Press, 1958.

[2] Wilmar F. Bernthal, "Contributions of the Behavioral Science Approach," *Academy of Management, Proceedings of the 1962 Annual Meeting,* University Park, Pa.: 1963, p. 22.

economists, political scientists, and anthropologists, and the examination of organizational behavior by psychologists, sociologists, social psychologists, and applied anthropologists.[3] Although some of the research and conceptual efforts in the behavioral approach to management are interdisciplinary, many of them are initiated within one discipline.[4]

The behavioral sciences have made several major contributions to the field of management, including (1) *conceptual,* the formulation of abstract concepts and explanations about human behavior in the organization; (2) *methodological,* the empirical testing of these concepts; and (3) *action,* the formulation of managerial policies and decisions based on these concepts and on research on human behavior.[5] These contributions have led to an increasing acceptance by management of the behavioral approach.[6]

Today the behavioral sciences are examining such problems as the factors, other than salary, which determine the levels of motivation and performance in organizations; [7] the integration of minority groups into the structure of an organization; the impact of the manager himself upon the organization; and the environmental constraints upon individual behavior. Indirectly, the behavioral approach has forced managers to examine some of the ethical questions which are related to human behavior in the organization.[8] This part of the book examines some of the conceptual, methodological, and action issues in the behavioral approach to management.

In the first section, Professor Mason Haire examines some of the reasons why the social sciences have made few contributions to the practice of management. The second reading, by Professor James L. Gibson, challenges management practitioners and academicians to express explicitly their assumptions about human behavior and to carry out research on human behavior in actual organizations. Professor William M. Fox discusses the impact of human relations in industry in several different settings in his attempt to stress the failure of human relations when it become an end rather than the means to success in the organization.

Through the behavioral approach, managers have begun to realize that not all conflict in an organization is bad for the organization. In the first selection on conflict, Professor Joseph A. Litterer examines the utility of conflict in modern organzations, and the ways in which conflict can be controlled. In the second, Professor Warren G. Bennis analyzes the methods by which modern organiza-

---

[3] Bernthal, p. 22.

[4] William G. Scott *Organization Theory: A Behavioral Analysis for Management.* Homewood, Ill.: Richard B. Irwin, Inc., 1967, p. 3.

[5] Scott, p. 4.

[6] For other reasons why the behavioral approach is achieving more influence in management circles today, see: Scott, pp. 17–18, and Bernthal, pp. 21–28.

[7] For example, see: Lyman W. Porter and Edward E. Lawler, III *Managerial Attitudes and Performance.* Homewood, Ill.: Richard D. Irwin, Inc., 1968.

[8] Bernthal, p. 28.

tions structure their changes and the ways in which the behavioral sciences can be applied to help in the implementation of the changes.

At one time many managers felt that one of the primary ways in which to motivate individuals to higher productivity was through some type of incentive system. Few of these managers were concerned about non-monetary motivators. Professor Herbert Zollitsch considers the various types of factors that affect productivity in the plant, including environmental conditions, the needs of the employee, and social conditions. In the second reading, Professor Harold J. Leavitt discusses some factors, other than motivation, which he considers important in the operations of a firm.

Another major concern of the behavioral scientists has been the question of communication within the organization. After presenting an incisive analysis of managerial communication, Professor Jack R. Gibb debates the merits of persuasion and problem solving approaches to communication problems which are related to organizational effectiveness. In the next article, Mr. John Anderson presents a possible framework for analyzing factors that inhibit the upward flow of communications in an organization. In the last reading, Professor Wayne Baty stresses the factors that affect effective communication between receivers and senders in the organization.

As a result of the continuing conceptual and research efforts by behavioral scientists interested in the administration of organizations, many new behavioral techniques have evolved. The first reading by Mr. Walter S. Wikstrom discusses one of these techniques, sensitivity training, and its impact upon management. Professor Richard E. Walter evaluates the relative merits of two different designs for obtaining worker participation in the management of the organization. Lastly, one of the major behavioral approaches to the evaluation of managerial performance, management by objectives, is presented by Mr. Dale D. McConkey.

A

ORGANIZATIONAL BEHAVIOR

17. The Social Sciences and Management Practices

MASON HAIRE

The one thing which, more than any other, seems to keep the social sciences from being socially useful is the lack of developmental research. By "developmental research," I mean a kind of work midway between the rarified aloofness of laboratory tests of theoretical propositions and the somewhat pebble-picking particularity of applied research. It is the research that asks the question, "If this proposition is true in principle, how does it find expression in the operational context of action?" It is the second half of research and development programs in industry and the military services which looks for the detailed means for translation to use after the theoretical basis is clear. It is properly a "development" of theoretical concepts. It differs from applied research in just this way, that it flows from theory and is the developmental extension of theory toward practice. Applied research, on the other hand, tends to take the operating problems and work backward toward theory, scanning the possibilities for concepts and methods which will solve or ameliorate the particular problem. This latter route lacks the leverage of broad theoretical concepts and, as a result, usually fails to develop any generality.

The absence of this kind of developmental research creates a frustrating, powerful, and potentially dangerous gap between the social scientist on the one hand and the practitioner on the other. One of them says (to himself and, smugly, to his colleagues) "with all the advances we've made in understanding social phenomena, they still fail to take any advantage of it. The case is probably hopeless." The other—the enlightened

Reprinted from the *California Management Review*, Vol. 6, No. 4 (Summer, 1964), copyright by the Regents of the University of California. Mason Haire is Professor of Psychology and Industrial Relations, Institute of Industrial Relations, University of California, Berkeley.

executive, for instance—says, "For all the theory and research and exciting possibilities they talk about, I don't see the possibility of doing anything substantially different or better than we've been doing all along. The case is probably hopeless."

Developmental research would be directed exactly toward the problem of helping people to see, given new theoretical insights, how something could be done substantially differently or better.

The following example is hackneyed; it has been used to cover everything from the marketing of a new shaving cream to pedagogical innovations. Much used and worn, it will serve again. In the summer of 1939, Einstein signed a letter which was delivered to President Roosevelt by Alexander Sachs on October 11, 1939. It said, in part,

Some recent work by E. Fermi and L. Szilard, which has been communicated to me in manuscript, leads me to expect that the element uranium may be turned into a new and important source of energy in the immediate future. . . .

This new phenomenon would also lead to the construction of bombs and it is conceivable—though much less certain—that extremely powerful bombs of a new type may thus be constructed.

The historical steps form a classic model. Here was an idea, generated by theory and supported by laboratory tests in circumstances far removed from any possible use. The power of the idea, if it could be brought into practice, was clear. By implication, the letter asked for developmental research. That is, research which would explore whether the idea could be recast into processes and materials that would make it capable of use in various situations. Its application was not at all perfectly clear. That it had application was likely. What was needed was to find out how one could do this thing on a quite different scale from the laboratory, and if

one could, what could be done with it. The initial research was not applied research on how to make atomic bombs. It was work on how to use the power of the concept (and the uranium).

Roosevelt, convinced by a variety of reasons, authorized the developmental research. I hope the foundations will forget that he initially committed only $6,000 to the project. Even the fact that Vannevar Bush later put up another $20,000 from other funds makes our budget proposals for exploratory research seem ludicrous. Much better for them to remember the total cost of the whole developmental project. Much better for them, and for the executive or other potential user of social scientific concepts, to remember the years of work that went into the question, "Can this idea be translated into materials and processes that can be used?"

All of the work until some time after the first Los Alamos explosion properly belongs in the category of developmental research. After it became clear, first in principle and then in practice, that it could be done, the developmental phase ended. The question became one of finding more efficient and less expensive production methods, of producing standardized units in quantity, and of tailoring the product more exactly to the requirements of its final use. These are properly the engineering or applied phases of the work. In these phases the problems arise not so much from the nature of the idea behind the phenomenon but from the particular problems of the product itself, and they are solved on this somewhat specific level. This, of course, is not a complete either-or distinction, but a large and important difference in emphasis.

It is not only in a dramatic field like the atomic bomb that this separation of theoretical possibility, developmental research, and applied research becomes clear. In most of the cases where new concepts have found expression in practice, each of the steps is apparent. The theoretical basis of semi-conductors existed and was well understood for a long time before the important developmental research showed the possibility of making transistors in practice. This was the necessary bridge between the power of the idea and the continuing applied research that goes along with production. Similarly, the gas turbine engine for automobiles is now presumably in a developmental phase where an attempt is made to find out whether the idea, which is clear, can profitably be brought to the engineering phase.

Neglected Middle Step

It is exactly this middle step in the process, the developmental phase, that we have tended to overlook in social science research.

It would be fatuous to raise the question of whether the social sciences offer any concepts whose potential is of a magnitude equal to Einstein's letter to F.D.R. However, it seems clear that tremendous possibilities lie untapped in some of the theories. Let us take an example or two.[1] Rensis Likert, in his recent book, *New Patterns of Management*,[2] suggests quite simply in theoretical terms, along with some research data to support the notion, that the total amount of influence or authority in a social system can be expanded by particular kinds of decentralization. Put in other terms, the amount of influence a superior has over his subordinates depends, at least in part, on the amount of influence his subordinates can have on him. Or in still

other terms, if the superior relinquishes part of his authority to the group, his authority is not diminished thereby, but may actually be increased. It is a simple enough concept, but one of tremendous potential.

In general, industrial organizations have been built on the implicit assumption that the total amount of influence or authority in the system is a finite commodity, ultimately grounded outside the firm in ownership, and vested, through the medium of the board, in the chief executive officer. He then delegates authority by carving out a piece of the finite pie with which he was originally endowed, to pass on to a subordinate, who does the same thing and so on down. At each step, however, if one considers authority thus to be a finite pie to be split among the members, it is necessary to be sure to keep a little more than one gives away, to retain a kind of voting control. The amount of influence, plotted by level, thus is negatively accelerated, rapidly approaching zero as a limit, and the amount of effective decentralization that is possible is sharply limited by the necessity to retain a working control. It is just this limit which, in the theory of the firm, provides the diminishing returns with growth. The finite chief executive in a single firm, compared with the virtually infinite supply in the industry, is soon stretched beyond capacity. If Likert's concept can find application, then, with effective group-influence systems the total amount of authority in the system can be increased and the limitation of size either disappears or is pushed back beyond the horizon to factors that are presently not considered.

[1] If my choice of examples seems biased and narrowly concerned with my own field of interest, I happily admit it. Nothing would please me more than to have someone else illustrate the point more tellingly with other examples.

[2] Rensis Likert, *New Patterns of Management* (New York: McGraw-Hill Book Co., Inc., 1961).

Likert's research and theory have some suggestions about how this might be done. They are, however, just guidemarks for developmental research to explore. He suggests an organization built with substructures on the model of the human group; the development of social skills in group membership as well as leadership skills, commensurate with the task; and techniques for a continuous inventory of the level of shared objectives and mutual confidence which provide the integration of the group. These suggest where one might work in trying to see how this concept could find expression in practice, but they do not solve the problem. The developmental research still needs to be done.

Likert's idea is potentially even more revolutionary in a sphere far beyond the organization of a company. When England considered membership in the Common Market, one of the most widely heard reactions was the almost instinctive response, "If we join the group we will have to give up some of our sovereignty." Similarly, in the United States, the considerable body of opposition to participation in international organizations is still based on the idea that we must surrender our individual sovereignty if we join a group of nations. If it is true that the amount of influence a nation has is increased by the degree to which other nations in the group can influence it, the calculus is quite different, and the discovery of the ways to make this an effective working reality is at least as important as nuclear energy.

Let's take another example. Douglas McGregor [3] has suggested the application of some motivational concepts to management philosophy. To oversimplify, following suggestions by Maslow, there may be classes of needs which are hierarchically arranged in such a way that until a lower order reaches a certain level of satisfaction the higher needs find little or no expression, and, on the other hand, once the lower levels are reasonably secure in satisfaction, the needs appear at higher levels, and satisfaction is only effective at these levels. To put it in business terms, the basic needs—for security and the satisfaction of physical demands —are largely met by the first levels of pay. Once these are satisfied and there is some security in their future satisfaction, the system progresses to demands for social satisfactions, for example, of affiliation and loyalty, to egoistic satisfactions of esteem, understanding, and recognition, and, finally, to a demand for self-actualization and growth.

Theory of Needs

In a time of unemployment and low living standards, pay is what is important. Satisfactions in the form of a bigger desk or the title "Lubrication Engineer" to replace "grease monkey" are not effective. On the other hand, with job security and reasonable levels of pay, money incentives lose effectiveness and the demand is for satisfactions at the levels at which the needs are expressed. Trying to pay enough to make up for a deficit in social or egoistic needs is likely to be an expensive process of chasing an ever-receding goal. The implications in the form of the satisfactions afforded by membership in a powerful well-integrated union, or in terms of personnel policies appropriate to a loose labor market or to professionalism are clear. What is not clear is exactly how these ideas can and

---

[3] Douglas McGregor, *The Human Side of Enterprise* (New York: McGraw-Hill Book Co., Inc., 1960).

should be translated into practice. The developmental phase of the research is missing. The appropriateness and power of these ideas in the industrial situation stand out at once. They have been underutilized largely because it is not perfectly clear how to use them.

As is the case of Likert's concept of expanding influence, McGregor's motivational concepts apply more broadly than to industry. To the extent that it is true that needs are felt for higher order satisfactions only after there is a reasonable level of satisfaction and some future security of basic physical needs, McGregor's concepts provide guides to a country's foreign policy. An attempt to export ideals of freedom, equality, and democracy to underdeveloped countries whose primary need is food is bound to be unsuccessful. The need must be met and satisfied on the level at which it is felt. After some security in basic needs, the higher order needs can be satisfied. We can't realistically plan for others in terms of our own level of need-satisfaction. There is an Indian saying that "even Allah wouldn't dare to appear to a starving man except in the form of bread." The same thing is true of foreign policy. The trick is to know how to do it. This is the developmental job.

These two concepts are picked to illustrate the thesis that:

• The social sciences have powerful relevant ideas to guide the practitioner in social action.
• These ideas are underutilized largely because little effort has been invested to make it clear how to use them.

These are certainly not the only such concepts available, and may not even be the best for the purpose. But the fact remains that the resource exists and the failure to tap it is glaring and socially expensive.

Apparent Difficulties

The difficulties of utilizing social science research are everywhere apparent. The Air Force once set up a research project on how to overcome the lack of utilization of research results. (The possibilities of this move for infinite regression are staggering.) In the last fifteen years, there has been a tremendous boom in a sort of lecture tour in which social scientists talk to groups of managers about research and theory. It is a kind of latter-day evangelism, partly replacing Émil Coué and perhaps Billy Sunday. In these meetings we (for I must admit I have been among them) exhort the semifaithful, explaining the bright possibilities at a theoretical level with a few well-chosen illustrations from a mundane industrial context. What happens if someone should say, "Wonderful! I'm convinced, what do I do now?" In general, we have stood back grandly and washed our hands of the matter in a somewhat Pontius Pilate fashion (if not with Freudian overtones) and said, "That's your business. You are the man of action. I'm a social philosopher. How you do it is your domain." And so, as in *The Crock of Gold,* the philosophers went on philosophizing all day long.

This is, of course, slightly caricatured, and a little bit harsh, but not much. It is not at all unusual for a borderline convert, a little more resistant than the rest, to say, "It sounds good, but if it's so darn good, how come everyone isn't doing it?" The question is so staggering to the speaker that it is a little bit of a gaucherie to raise it even in the permissive atmosphere that is part of the point of view. There are a variety of lines of answer to the question. At least one of the very important ones is that no one has shown them how to do it. There are also some difficulties grounded in the nature of the case. Organizational difficulties arise in practice; several companies have made tentative tries without outstanding success. But the main stumbling block is that, with rare exceptions, very little effort has gone into how to put these ideas into practice.

One of the built-in difficulties, of course, is that in most changes considered by management, management decides that someone else should change; in general, the social scientific concepts suggest that management change. Related to this is the fact that change-programs are often instituted with the approval of top management but without their complete understanding of the concept. When mistakes occur, as they're bound to do, the man in charge is in an exposed position. The safest—and most frequent—solution is to put the blame on the idea, jettison the program, or compromise it out of recognition. These forces pinch particularly hard since the new practices usually ask a man to give up the ideas and behaviors that have led to his present success and to operate in an uncomfortable darkness with only the light of hope at the end. The group of reasons clustered around these problems means that the developmental task associated with social scientific concepts is very much harder than is usually the case with hardware innovations. More developmental research is needed, not less, to find out how it can be done.

A group of companies, notably G.E. and A.T.&T. and all three military services, have made formal efforts in the social sciences. It seems to me that they are not as successful as one might hope. Certainly they are not as successful as the dazzling prospects in the situation-papers usually prepared for the decision to institute such programs. In the companies, they run into special organization problems. Hardware research can be put off to one side of the organizational chart and the result brought in only when a product or process change is ready for consideration. Social research, on the other hand, must usually take place in an ongoing part of the organization. It already upsets things. Where to put it? Since it deals vaguely with people, the first thought is usually to attach it somehow to the Personnel Department. Now its experimentalists come in conflict not only with past practices, but with the prejudices and hopes and machinations that run just below the surface. Projects can be too easily subtly sunk at the start or doomed with heavy-handed cooperation. Furthermore, many projects can be delicately distorted to become instruments for undercover spying. A series of interviews on performance evaluation, for instance, provides the personnel head with a tempting bag of information on the way executives operate.

All of these problems associated with the difficulty of introducing behavior-change into a behavior system expose social science concepts to particularly perilous difficulties. The head of the program, too, meets some special pressures. Laboring with the vagueness and frustrations of a grand concept, some of his friends tell him the company is getting dissatisfied; he'd better do some small things that are immediately useful to the company and prove that the program is worthwhile. (A phrase grew up, I think in wartime, to describe this: "quick and dirty" research. Obviously this doesn't describe research at all, but tactical maneuvers to bolster a position.) Faced with this reported dissatisfaction, he turns part of his force to the most applied research possible: Why is the turnover rate so high in shipping clerks? What are the characteristics of a good maintenance supervisor? Now his resources are divided hopelessly between two courses, neither of which will bring fruit from the social sciences. His "basic" wing may add to the sum of human knowledge, though it is not clear that a company is as convenient a place for this as a university. Moreover, lacking the developmental research to lead it into action, this work tends to remain as sterile as the outside research. His "applied" research, on the other hand, puts out local fires, and gets the merited criticism of being no different from and no bigger than that they've been doing in the past.

Contact with Reality

The services have met the same problem, but, being more monolithic, took more ponderous unidirectional lines. The Air Force Psychological Program began as an intensely applied job of selection. It expanded to research on training, human engineering, and studies of groups and attitudes. The pressing situation eased and the demand for selection refinements diminished. The broader studies had produced some splendid professional papers but little change in the Air Force. Much of the program folded. The Navy, on the other hand, largely provided financial support for basic research projects in universities. The range and diversity of research articles with the footnoted statement of indebtedness to the U.S.N. is amazing. There is, however, equally little evidence that the Navy is much changed by them.

The Navy can't be blamed for the lofty ideal of "refilling the pipelines of basic concepts." The phrase was borrowed largely from the experience with the physical sciences. Actually, the pipeline of social scientific concepts is still chockfull; very little has been withdrawn. However, we professors have gone on selling basic research because it is part of the academic ideal. We have concerned our-

selves primarily with theoretical connectedness, construct validity, and logical consistency. For theory-building this is fine. We also need, however, application, external validity, and coordinating definitions. Truth as coherence may well be the ultimate nature of the article, and enough publications embodying it serve admirably for academic promotion. To make the social sciences socially useful, however, we need some explorations of truth as correspondence. How do the theories make contact with reality, not only in the laboratory but in practice?

At this point, one is bound to want a good clear example of what developmental research is in the social sciences. It seems to me that there is none; if there were some, it would be less necessary to insist on the need for it. Instead we'll have to settle for some things that approach it and some hints about what could be done in other fields.

McClelland's studies [4] of the achievement motive in businessmen in different countries belong in the category: "basic." They extend previous research and theory. They make possible a cultural interpretation of the need for achievement. When he goes on to investigate ways in which the drive for achievement can be increased, he is doing developmental research. It is not applied because it it not limited to specific problems—changing shoe salesmen in a retail outlet or life insurance salesmen. It is not basic because its primary aim is a step toward the application of the basic concept. The work sheds more light on the fundamental problem; lots of developmental research does. That's not the criterion of basic research.

On the other hand, there are a series of experiments dealing with group-structure and communication which are often

---

[4] David C. McClelland, "Business Drive and National Achievement," *Harvard Business Review,* July–August 1962.

referred to.[5] They add measurably to basic understanding, but they leave us wondering what to do. We know how people behave when organized as a circle, a star, a wheel, or a straight line. We know it is difficult (if not impossible) to maximize productivity and morale simultaneously. But we still don't know what to do in a firm. There is no developmental bridge from theory to practice. At the other extreme, the Tavistock Institute has given us some splendidly insightful applied work. Trist and Bamforth[6] ingeniously showed how group structure influenced behavior in coal mining and what could be done about it; Rice did the same kind of thing in the Indian textile mills.

These studies are remarkably ingenious applications of their general notions about socio-technical systems at work. But, again, what does one do? If one's problem is not coal mining or textile production, it is not clear how the power of the principle can be brought to bear without calling consultants in and hoping they will be as insightful as Trist, Bamforth, and Rice were. The communications experiments are too general to be easily applied to a group of problems in companies. The Tavistock work is too specific to be easily transferred to other problems. Both need developmental research to make it possible to use the lineage of the general principles behind them.

Let us turn to some research that hasn't been done. Most psychologists would agree, as a result of a host of studies, that knowledge of results is one of the most powerful of all principles in modifying behavior. The awareness of the consequences of behavior greatly facilitates changing behavior. In the absence of knowledge of results, changes tend to be randomly distributed around the (stable) original average. The general notion is used in many business practices —discussing performance evaluations, returning data on production cost to the producing unit, and the like. Yet it seems likely that this learned-by-experience application of the principle is not being used in full force. We have laboratory studies in the hundreds on the effects of knowledge of results. We need the developmental bridge. What should one do?

It seems clear from laboratory studies that the effectiveness of knowledge depends on the clarity and relevance of the information, its immediacy, and the degree to which the behavior in question can be modified. Sometimes it isn't clear to the subject what he's doing that produces the effect; sometimes it's clear to him what he's doing but not what the effect is. Sometimes either or both of these is clear but the information comes too long before the next trial (too soon) and he loses interest; or it comes after he's repeated it so many times that it is ineffective (too late). Some of his behaviors are more easily modified than others. For example, if we say to him, "that wasn't a tactful remark," he may not easily be able to change. These guidelines of application, too, probably exist in everyone's fund of general experience, but not in precise formulation or in a careful weighting of how they relate to one another.

In a developmental program one might take a general class of managerial problems—say, supervision of first-level su-

---

[5] H. Leavitt, "Some Effects of Certain Communication Patterns on Group Performance," *Journal of Abnormal and Social Psychology,* XLVI (1951), 38–40; H. Leavitt and R. Mueller, "Some Effects of Feedback on Communication," *Human Relations,* 1953, pp. 151–173; G. Heise and G. Miller, "Problem Solving by Small Groups Using Various Communication Nets," *Journal of Abnormal and Social Psychology,* XLVI (1951), 327–335.

[6] E. L. Trist and V. Bamforth, "Some Social and Psychological Consequences of the Longwall Method of Coal-Getting," *Human Relations,* IV (1951), 3–38.

pervisors—which is relatively free of specific job content. Within this framework one asks "What kind of behavior is desired? What modifications do we seek? What kind of information is possible?" With the answers to these, research could begin on the meaning to the supervisor of clarity and relevance of each of several general classes of knowledge of possible results. Each of these kinds of knowledge probably has its own constants for immediacy. Some of them may belong just after one has done something; some of them just before one does it again. Some of them relate to specific acts; some help shape the perception of general goals. Further, some of the behavior is easily modified, some is not. For some, specific skill training may be necessary, for others only the realization of the connection. After such a program —and, obviously, it would lead into areas not specified here—the social scientist would be in a very different position in answering the question: "How can the principle of knowledge of results be used in managing?" The material would be general enough for a range of applications. On the other hand, if the applied (specific) work were done first, it might be difficult to see—as in the coal-mining case—how to generalize it to other operations.

The example from knowledge of results may serve to illustrate the meaning of "developmental" as an adjective in this context. It, of course, by no means exhausts the field where such research is needed. For example, we recognize the power of participation as one of the tools of leadership but we have relatively little detailed knowledge of its operation— wage and salary systems are built on motivational concepts (incidentally, knowledge of results, too) but we have surprisingly little research on them. Group cohesiveness, attitude formation and change—all these and many others—

are areas where the basic principles seem potentially fruitful, but where their contribution to practice is limited by the lack of a developmental bridge.

That we need the fruit of social science concepts in society and that the social sciences have something to offer are matters of faith to me. The difficulties seem largely a matter of administrative organization. Our universities are set up to encourage and support basic research and theoretical development. The research worker gets his rewards for these things. The task of investigating the way in which these developments can be expressed in practice is long, difficult, and expensive. The universities are not well set up to support, direct, and reward this. Indeed, except in a few cases of schools of technology, it is probably not a proper function for them. On the other hand, the experience with operating institutions— with companies' research organizations in the social sciences and with the military —is discouraging. Organizational difficulties on the one hand and problems inherent in the subject matter on the other both tend to push them toward one of the two extremes of very basic or very applied research, avoiding the developmental work that is necessary.

We are at a point like the one shortly after Einstein's letter to Roosevelt. The idea is clear; we need a Manhattan project (in type, not in size or money) and an Argonne Laboratory to implement it. Such a laboratory—or two or three of them—should be set up in a university. If it were put in a single company, it would come under the crippling pressures already mentioned. If three or more companies supported it, their joint commitment to the idea would make it much harder for organizational pressures and prejudices to divert it. It would have to be supported not only with money, but with a clear understanding of its purposes at the very top of the company and with a firm agreement to permit and facilitate research within their organizations.

Executive Concern

Is there any possibility of this? Probably there is. The social-science-lecture-circuit I spoke of somewhat slightingly before has had a real effect on managerial thinking. Many people see the possibilities and are anxious to see them in practice. Initially this realization was largely at the level of the personnel man, and led to several frustrating attempts at change in companies when they met unchanged upper levels. The concepts are now much more common at policy-making levels. The next step is to see that developmental research in the social sciences in industry is research on the managerial philosophy of the company and as such is the concern of the chief executive. It needs a special dotted-line staff co-ordinator at that level. It does not belong under subordinate staff specialists where it competes with day-to-day operating policies. The concepts challenge the most basic ways of organizing and operating, and as such, their consideration belongs at the top. Later their product may be delegated to appropriate functions for action, but the initial impact is in helping the chief executive frame an organizational philosophy.

If several companies joined at this level to support a laboratory, its chances seem good. Staff coordination at the top would put the concepts where they belong organizationally. The plurality of support would prevent a single company's inadvertently distorting or misdirecting the research interest. Placed at a university— or universities—the laboratory could draw on all the resources of skill and talent that are available without raising the personnel problems—which have seemed almost insurmountable to some

companies—of wooing social scientists to leave academic life to work for a company. They could work, say, half-time, single-mindedly on the question "How can the social sciences be made useful to social action?" The companies' commitment to provide research situations would free scientists from fictitious small groups or from communications experiments involving bits of paper passed from hand to hand dealing with how many marbles are in an urn. Basic research would go on elsewhere; applied research would go on elsewhere. Such an institution would be devoted to developmental research.

We go through a series of long historical cycles in the evolution of the problems of management. At one point in history the problem was capital formation; at another it was production. Neither of these is the pressing problem at the moment. Today the problem of organizing and managing coordinated human effort is paramount, and it is just here that the social sciences find their point of impact. To meet present problems we need their contributions.

Great Potential

In broader terms, the image of American know-how is in production technology and management. The first Sputnik completely destroyed the idea that America is unassailable in technological innovation. The remaining ground is the contention that we still can organize and operate our society and its productive institutions better than alternative forms. If my job were to try to attack this notion, I would try to organize a management spectacular by focusing efforts on two or three areas to produce the most advanced management possible. If this were done without parallel effort on our part, it would be as easy to destroy, in many eyes, this picture of a free world's advantage as it was for the U.S.S.R. to orbit a satellite first.

Both the social scientists and the managers have been too modest in their hopes for the results from the application of new concepts. We tend to think about improvements on the order of four or five hundred per cent. Lincoln made a campaign speech to a group of Illinois farmers whose land was producing about twenty bushels of corn to the acre. He said,

The soil has never been pushed to one-half its capacity. [We need] deeper plowing, analysis of soils, experiments with manures, with varieties of seeds, and with the observance of seasons.

This is the kind of statement that is accepted as the pardonable hyperbole of the politician. Probably even he thought the phrase "one-half its capacity" was a loose exaggeration to make the point. Today anyone who can't get four times the yield can't afford to hold the land. The Illinois farmer would have had difficulty seeing that only a 400 per cent increase in productivity would keep his land an economic unit. We have difficulty in seeing the same thing in the corporation. But the potential of the social sciences applied to management seems as great as the contribution agronomy made to farming. An adequate developmental research program will help to realize this potential.

18. Organization Theory and the Nature of Man

JAMES GIBSON

A recent contribution to the literature of organization theory raises serious questions about the nature of men who participate in organizations.[1]

If Anthony Downs' hypotheses are correct, William H. Whyte's quietly-conservative, status-conscious and security-seeking organization man has been replaced by a new variety whose characteristics are even less admirable than those of his predecessor. If Downs is cor-

rect, the organization man of today is suspicious, distrustful, jealous, deceitful, self-centered, apathetic, and immature. He is intolerant of differences, unable to communicate in depth with his fellows, and short-sighted. In short, here is a man whose integrity and moral fiber should be seriously questioned.[2]

Downs, however, is not the only writer to introduce some interesting organizational characters. Robert Presthus devel-

Reprinted from *Academy of Management Journal*, Vol. 9, No. 3 (September, 1966), pp. 233–245, with permission of the publisher. James Gibson is Associate Professor of Management, College of Business and Economics, University of Kentucky.

[1] Anthony Downs, "A Theory of Bureaucracy," *American Economic Review, Papers and Proceedings* (May, 1965), pp. 439–446.

[2] Downs does not make such harsh indictments of the nature of man; he states only that officials distort information and orders, fear investigations of their activities, champion the status quo, seek consensus of goals, and perform acts that would be embarrassing if publicly known. The adjectives that I use to describe the behavior are my own. The reader is invited to study Downs' paper and draw his own conclusions.

oped three personality types to be found in organizations which he called the up-ward-mobiles, the indifferents, and the ambivalents.[3] Victor A. Thompson and others suggest similarly evocative concepts to describe some of the more irrational behavior of organizations (bureaupathology) and to portray the behavior of some individuals in organizations (bureausis).[4]

If the views of these writers are correct, there is need for a great deal of research and study directed at finding ways of making life in modern organizations more meaningful. I share the value system of those who believe "that work which permits autonomy, responsibility, social connection, and self-actualization furthers the dignity of the human individual, whereas work without these characteristics limits the development of personal potential and is therefore to be negatively valued." [5] And I value negatively the behavior of organization members who "inevitably distort information which they relay upwards to their superiors or downward to their subordinates," [6] or who "distort the orders they receive from their superiors, interpreting them to their own benefit . . . as they develop the implications of those orders for their subordinates." [7]

To say the least, the conclusion from the above statements is simply that some organization men are dishonest; to the extent that organizations create conditions which encourage and reward such behavior, to that extent, organization theorists should be concerned.

In the remainder of this article, I outline the development of organization theory in terms of its underlying assumptions regarding the nature of man. My purpose is to stimulate thought and action on two fronts:

(1) To urge organization theorists and practitioners to express explicitly their assumptions about the nature of man; and,

(2) To urge more analysis of ongoing organizations to determine the causes of behavior which Downs, Presthus, and Thompson describe.

This discussion seeks to add to the literature on the philosophy of organizations by emphasizing the value premises which underlie some of the major strands of thought.

The vehicle used to develop the literature is a classification system of three categories: the *mechanistic tradition;* the *humanistic challenge;* and, the *realistic synthesis.* An essential feature of the literature classified in the mechanistic tradition category is the view of man as a constant without peculiar features and malleable without incident into the organization structure; man is characterized as a machine—predictable, repairable, and replaceable. The literature of the humanistic challenge is characterized by an awareness of man as a unique element in the organization structure; man is viewed as having a need structure and individual differences are tolerated. The literature of the realistic synthesis is not easily characterized, but its essential feature is to treat man as one of a number of variables in the organization all of which are interdependent and interacting.

---

[3] Robert Presthus, *The Organizational Society* (New York: Alfred A. Knopf, 1962).

[4] Victor A. Thompson, *Modern Organization* (New York: Alfred A. Knopf, 1961) and Marshall E. Dimock, *Administration Vitality* (New York: Harper and Brothers, 1959).

[5] Robert Blauner, *Alienation and Freedom* (Chicago: The University of Chicago Press, 1964), p. 15, fn. 1.

[6] Downs, *op. cit.*, p. 443.

[7] *Ibid.*, pp. 443–444.

Man is seen as being acted upon and as acting on the organization environment.

The Mechanistic Tradition

The writers of the mechanistic tradition focused on *two* aspects of organization theory.

At *one level,* Frederick W. Taylor and others analyzed the basic tasks of the individual members. The objective of Taylor and his followers was to reduce the contributions of each workman to the smallest, most specialized unit of work possible and to eliminate any uncertainty about the expected outcome. Elementary to such analysis were (and are) work simplification studies which break down manual labor tasks into definite repetitive movements and motion and time studies which establish time standards for the accomplishment of each movement. As Taylor himself said:

Perhaps the most prominent single element in modern scientific management is the task idea. The work of every workman is fully planned out by the management at least one day in advance, and each man receives in most cases complete written instructions, describing in detail the task which he is to accomplish, as well as the means to be used in doing the work. And the work planned in advance in this way constitutes a task which is to be solved, as explained above, not by the workman alone, but in almost all cases by the joint effort of the workman and the management. This task specifies not only what is to be done but how it is to be done and the exact time allowed for doing it.[8]

To assure that each task is performed according to the plan, the worker is paid on an incentive basis which rewards him for meeting the expectations of the organization and punishes him if he does not. The application of scientism tended to reduce the skills of craftsman to routine, procedural, predictable sequences of movement; workers were to be as interchangeable as the cogs in Eli Whitney's cotton gin.

Underlying the procedural prescriptions of scientific management were definite assumptions about the nature of man. Taylor said:

A reward, if it is to be effective in stimulating men to do their best work, must come soon after the work has been done. But few men are able to look forward for more than a week or perhaps at most a month, and work hard for a reward which they are to receive at the end of this time.[9]

Later, in discussing the reasons for the failure of profit sharing schemes, he said: "Personal ambition always has been and will remain a more powerful incentive to exertion than a desire for the general welfare."[10] The view that man is motivated solely and predictably by economic considerations and is an isolated factor of production independent of social and group pressures guided the development of scientific management theories and practices.

The postulates of scientific management were quite appealing to those who were concerned with administrative aspects of organizations—the *second level* of analysis.

Wolin suggests that Saint-Simon[11] laid the foundations of organization theory "with the conscious intent of establishing a defense against political instability and

---

[8] Frederick W. Taylor, *Scientific Management* (New York: Harper and Brothers, 1911), p. 39.

[9] *Ibid.,* p. 94.

[10] *Ibid.,* p. 95.

[11] See Henri de Saint-Simon, *Social Organization, The Science of Man, and other Writings,* edited and translated by Felix Markham (New York: Harper and Row, 1965).

social disorder" in the aftermath of the French Revolution.[12] However, it was one hundred years later before a theory of organization structuring was articulated.

The most prominent writers of what is often called "Classical Organization Theory" were Luther Gulick,[13] Henri Fayol,[14] James D. Mooney and A. C. Reiley,[15] and L. Urwick [16] all of whom wrote from the perspective of business or military organizations. These writers owe an intellectual debt to Max Weber who provided the "ideal type" of administrative organization which he called a bureaucracy.[17] Even though Weber's model is based primarily on the European methods of organizing the civil servants (chiefly the Prussian experience), the characteristics of his "ideal type" are illustrative of the main features of classical organization theory.

According to Weber, the essential characteristics of the "ideal type" are as follows: [18]

1. All tasks necessary for the accomplishment of the goals are broken down into the smallest possible unit; the division of labor is carried out to the extent that specialized experts are responsible for the successful performance of specified duties.

2. Each task is performed according to a "consistent system of abstract rules" [19] to assure uniformity and coordination of different tasks. This uncertainty in the performance of tasks due to individual differences is theoretically eliminated.

3. Each member or office of an organization is accountable to a superior for his or its decisions as well as for his or its subordinates. The authority is based on expert knowledge and is sanctioned and made legitimate by the ultimate source of authority—the chief official at the top of the hierarchical pyramid.

4. Each official in the organization conducts the business of his office in an impersonal, formalistic manner. He maintains a social distance between himself and his subordinates and between himself and the clients of the organization. The purpose of this impersonal detachment is to assure that personalities do not interfere with the efficient accomplishment of the mission.

5. "Employment in the bureaucratic organization is based on technical qualifications and is protected against arbitrary

---

[12] Sheldon S. Wolin, *Politics and Vision* (Boston: Little, Brown, and Co., 1960), p. 376.

[13] Luther Gulick and L. Urwick (eds.), *Papers on the Science of Administration* (New York: Institute of Public Administration, 1937).

[14] Henri Fayol, *General and Industrial Management* (London: Sir Isaac Pitman and Sons, 1949).

[15] J. D. Mooney and A. C. Reiley, *Principles of Organization* (New York: Harper and Brothers, 1939).

[16] L. Urwick, *The Elements of Administration* (New York: Harper and Brothers, 1943).

[17] Max Weber, *The Theory of Social and Economic Organization,* translated by A. M. Henderson and Talcott Parsons (New York: Oxford University Press, 1947). Michel Crozier in *The Bureaucratic Phenomenon* (Chicago: University of Chicago Press, 1964), a study of the French experience in organization of the civil service, points out three usages of the term bureaucracy: (1) The "traditional usage" is the political science concept of government by bureaus but without participation by the governed; (2) the Weberian usage is the sociological concept of rationalization of collective activities; and, (3) the vulgar usage is the laymen's concept which implies the dysfunctional nature of "bureaucratic" organizations, i.e., red tape, procedural delays, frustrations of agents and clients, p. 3.

[18] Weber, *ibid.,* pp. 329–340. For more reflective analyses of the "ideal type" see Peter M. Blau, *Bureaucracy in Modern Society* (Chicago: University of Chicago Press, 1956), pp. 27–56 and Victor A. Thompson, *op. cit.,* pp. 12–21.

[19] Weber, *ibid.,* p. 330.

dismissal." [20] Promotions are based on seniority and achievement. Because employment is considered a career and the vagaries of making a living are eliminated, a high degree of loyalty for the organization is engendered in the members.

The inherent logic of the bureaucratic structure led Weber to believe that the bureaucratic form of administration is "superior to any other form in precision, in stability, in the stringency of its discipline, and in its reliability. It thus makes possible a particularly high degree of calculability of results for the heads of the organization and for those acting in relation to it." [21] Thus Weber presented the case for bureaucratic administration on precisely the same grounds that the Taylorites presented the case for Scientific Management. In fact Weber himself drew the analogy: "The fully developed bureaucratic mechanism compares with other organizations exactly as does the machine with nonmechanical modes of production." [22]

The bureaucratic form of organization was (and is) prominent in business practice. The proponents of its use in this context formulated "principles" which are obviously in the Weberian tradition. Haynes and Massie have codified these principles as follows: [23]

1. The Unity of Command principle: No member of an organization should report to more than one superior.

2. The Span of Control principle: No superior should have responsibility for the activities of more than five to eight subordinates.

3. The Exception principle: A superior should delegate responsibility for routine matters to subordinates.

4. The Scalar principle: Every organization should have a well defined hierarchical structure.

One is struck by the prescriptive nature of these principles, by their similarity to the characteristics of Weber's ideal type, and by their concern for order and certainty in carrying on the activities of the organization.

The evidence supplied in the foregoing discussion suggests the assumptions regarding the nature of man underlying scientific management and classical organization theory. March and Simon observe that two "views" of organization members are pervasive: "First, in general there is a tendency to view the employee as an inert instrument performing the tasks assigned to him. Second, there is a tendency to view personnel as a given rather as a variable in the system." [24] Mason Haire has been less polite: "These are the implicit assumptions about man on which classical organization theory seems to me to be based: He is lazy, short-

[20] Blau, *op. cit.,* p. 30.

[21] Weber, *op. cit.,* p. 334.

[22] *From Max Weber: Essays in Sociology,* translated by H. H. Gerth and C. Wright Mills (New York: Oxford University Press, 1946), p. 214 and quoted in Blau, *op. cit.,* p. 31.

[23] W. Warren Haynes and Joseph L. Massie, *Management* (Englewood Cliffs, N. J.: Prentice-Hall, Inc., 1961), pp. 39–43. Other writers notably L. Urwick, *op. cit.,* pp. 119–129 have lengthened the list, but the four here seem to be primary. Herbert A. Simon refers to such principles as "proverbs" in *Administrative Behavior* (New York: The Macmillan Co., 1945), pp. 20–36 because they have neither empirical verification nor universality of application.

[24] James G. March and Herbert A. Simon, *Organizations* (New York: John Wiley and Sons, 1958), p. 29.

sighted selfish, liable to make mistakes, has poor judgment, and may even be a little dishonest." [25]

From another perspective, William F. Whyte argues that there are three assumptions underlying the theory: First, it is assumed that "man is a rational animal concerned with maximizing his economic gains," second, "each individual responds to economic incentives as an isolated individual," and third, "men, like machines, can be treated in a standardized fashion." [26]

The Humanistic Challenge

It was only in the 1930's that these assumptions and their implications for organization theory and practice were seriously challenged. The body of concepts that developed during the initial thrust of the industrial revolution and which I have characterized as mechanistic was soon confronted with evidence that seriously challenged its validity. This challenge (which I call the humanistic challenge) came from two sources:

(1) There were those who questioned the basic assumptions of the scientific management approach regarding the motivation of men; and,

(2) There were those who questioned the efficiency of the bureaucratic form of organization.

Although the two sources of challenge were seemingly unrelated, the emphasis of both was the same, namely: the participants of organizations are not constants and cannot be regarded as givens; and, a large mass of empirical evidence was soon available to show that participants adjust the environment to meet their individual and group needs. And part of this adjustment process is related to motivations, as some industrial engineers were to discover.

In 1924, engineers at the Hawthorne Works, a division of the Western Electric Company in Chicago, began a series of tests to determine the relationship between certain variables and the rate of production.[27] A number of frustrating experiments caused the scientists to reject their original hypothesis (that a high and positive correlation exists between working conditions and the rate of output) and they formulated alternative hypotheses. The major sources of data for testing the revised hypotheses were the voluminous recordings of interpersonal conversations that the experiments had accumulated. These conversations between workers and the scientists revealed

---

[25] George B. Strother (ed.), *Social Science Approaches to Business Behavior* (Homewood, Illinois: The Dorsey Press, Inc., 1962), p. 175. And lest one think that contemporary organizations are free of such assumptions, consider this statement by E. F. Scoutten, Vice-President, Personnel, Maytag Company: "Operating management has long since known what academic experts appear to reject. Many people, perhaps the majority, prefer to accept instruction, direction, and order without question, and in fact are uncomfortable and, therefore, resist being placed in situations where they are required to evaluate or otherwise exercise independent thought." Mason Haire, (ed.), *Organization Theory in Industrial Practice* (New York: John Wiley and Sons, 1962), p. 86.

[26] William F. Whyte, *Money and Motivation* (New York: Harper and Brothers, 1955), pp. 2–3.

[27] The Hawthorne Studies are reported in T. N. Whitehead, *The Industrial Worker*, 2 volumes (Cambridge, Massachusetts: Harvard University Press, 1938), Fritz J. Roethlisberger and William J. Dickson, *Management and the Worker* (Cambridge, Massachusetts: Harvard University Press, 1947), Fritz J. Roethlisberger, *Management and Morale* (Cambridge, Massachusetts: Harvard University Press, 1941), and Elton Mayo, *The Human Problems of an Industrial Civilization* (New York: The Macmillan Co., 1933).

that the workers were members of closely knit work groups and that these work groups had established acceptable patterns of behavior for the members. These patterns of behavior, in turn, were based on the sentiments of the members of the group, but these sentiments were easily disguised and difficult to isolate. Nevertheless, the scientists discarded their statistical techniques and "denuded of their elaborate logical equipment" [28] they went into the shop to learn the things that were important to the workers.

The findings of the Hawthorne studies challenged the basic assumptions of earlier organization theory, namely the social isolation of the worker and the primacy of economic incentives. For these two assumptions, the human relations school substituted the view that man desires "first, a method of living in social relationship with other people, and, second, as part of this an economic function for and value to the group." [29] Thus man (according to Mayo and his followers) "is a uniquely social animal who can achieve complete 'freedom' only by fully submerging himself in the group." [30] Based on the notion of man as a gregarious animal, the human relations school included in their ideology a view of a society in which man could best achieve his freedom. But the industrial society is not such a society and in fact the process of industrialization destroys the cultural traditions of former times which had enhanced social solidarity. The results of industrialization are social disorganization and unhappy individuals.

According to Mayo the responsibility for restoring the bases for social stability belongs to administrators of large industrial firms. With leadership that is human-oriented rather than production-oriented the prospects for social stability and its concomitant, a meaningful life for the individual, are enhanced. In fact Mayo has said: "If our social skills (that is, our ability to secure cooperation between people) had advanced step by step with our technical skill, there would not have been another European war." [31] Thus the ideology of the founders of the "human relations" approach consisted ðf three parts: (1) a view of man as a social animal, (2) a view of industrial society as incompatible with the basic nature of man, and (3) a view of the solution to man's dilemma as resting with industrial leaders.

The findings of the Hawthorne experiments were exceedingly important to those members of society primarily concerned with rational industrial supervision.[32] It had long been a mystery why workers would restrict output and produce far below standards established by exacting analyses. The Hawthorne studies provided both diagnosis and prescription. The practical application of human relations theory required careful consideration of the informal organization, work teams, and symbols that evoke worker response. Unions were viewed in a new dimension and were seen as making a contribution to effective organization rather than as the consequence of malfunctions in the organization.[33] Participative management, employee education,

---

[28] F. J. Roethlisberger, *ibid.,* p. 16.

[29] Mayo, *op. cit.,* p. 18.

[30] Clark Kerr, *Labor and Management in Industrial Society* (Garden City, New York: Doubleday and Co., Inc., 1964), p. 54.

[31] Elton Mayo, *The Social Problems of an Industrial Civilization* (Boston: Division of Research, Graduate School of Business Administration, Harvard University, 1947), p. 33.

[32] Burleigh B. Gardner, *Human Relations in Industry* (Chicago: Richard D. Irwin, Inc., 1945) is a "classic" of this tradition.

[33] See William F. Whyte, *Pattern for Industrial Peace* (New York: Harper and Brothers, 1951).

junior executive boards, group decisions and industrial counseling became important means for improving the performance of workers in the organization. Industrial leaders were spurred on by researchers whose findings indicated that "every human being earnestly seeks a secure, friendly, and supportive relationship and one that gives him a sense of personal worth in the face-to-face groups most important to him." [34] Thus, in practice, the "herd hypothesis" replaced the "rabble hypothesis."

The research methodology, the ideology, and the practice of human relations have been attacked on several points. The methodology of the supporting research is criticized for dealing with only immediate variables and for ignoring the external environment; the work is viewed as static and subject to little change over time. The findings of single case studies do not provide sufficient data for the construction of a rigorous theory of man and his organizations. But at a more fundamental level, the ideological view of man is attacked. "They (the human relations advocates) begin by saying that man dislikes isolation and end by consigning him to the care of the managerial elite for his own salvation." [35] Thus by losing his identity man becomes free or so assert the Mayo-ites. [36]

Critics of the practice of human rela-tions have pointed to a number of defects. Most vehemently criticized has been the use of human relations techniques as means of manipulating workers to accept the superior's view of reality. Indeed, one has said: "I am totally unable to associate the *conscious practice of human relations skill* (in the sense of making people happy in spite of themselves or getting them to do something they don't think they want to do) with the *dignity of an individual person created in God's image.*" [37]

This tendency toward manipulation is, at least in part, due to a misunderstanding of the purpose of the social sciences, "to the belief that the function of the social sciences is the same as that of the physical sciences, namely, to gain control of something outside." [38]

A second misunderstanding, and one springing directly from the ideology of human relations, is the belief that the business firm is a total institution which provides for all the needs of its members and that such an institution has the "right" to demand total loyalty. The attempt to gain total loyalty underlies much of personnel and human relations work; administrators frequently use the tags "loyal service" and "loyal employee" to describe the record of a retiring organization member. On this point Peter Drucker has said: "It is not only not compatible with the dignity of man, but it is not permissible

---

[34] Rensis Likert, *Motivation: The Core of Management* (New York: American Management Association, 1953). Reprinted in Harry Knudson, *Human Elements of Administration* (New York: Holt, Rinehart, and Winston, 1963), p. 81.

[35] Kerr, *op. cit.,* p. 57.

[36] It is not quite fair to say that Mayo "asserts" in this connection. In *Human Problems of an Industrial Civilization, op. cit.,* he analyzes various traditional cultures and presents as evidence of the social nature of man the many practices designed to achieve social integration, e.g., ritual, custom, codes, family and tribal instincts.

[37] Malcolm P. McNair, "Thinking Ahead: What Price Human Relations?" *Harvard Business Review* (March–April, 1957), pp. 15–23. Reprinted in Harold Koontz and Cyril O'Donnell, *Readings in Management* (New York: McGraw-Hill Book Co., Inc., 1959), p. 279.

[38] Peter Drucker, "Human Relations: Where Do We Stand Today?" in Knudson, *op. cit.,* p. 364. The purpose of the social sciences is to gain understanding of one's self as Drucker explains.

to believe that the dignity of man can or should be realized totally in a partial institution." [39] The present state of human relations theory might be expressed as follows: "Let's treat people like people, but let's not make a big production of it." [40]

The findings of post-Weber studies of bureaucratic behavior are similar to the findings of the Hawthorne studies—the reaction of individuals to organizational factors is not always predictable.[41] Merton,[42] Selznick,[43] and Gouldner [44] suggest that treating people as machines not only leads to unforeseen consequences but can actually reinforce the use of the "machine model." Each researcher studied some form of procedure designed to control the activities of the members of the organization.

Merton analyzed the organizational need for control and the consequent concern for reliability of member's behavior. In order to get the desired results, the organization implements standard rules and procedures. Control is achieved by assuring that the members are following the rules. Merton points out three consequences that result from concern for reliability of behavior: (1) officials react to individuals as representative of positions having certain specified rights and privileges; (2) rules assume a positive value as ends rather than as means to ends; and, (3) decision-making becomes routine application of tried and proven approaches and little attention is given to alternatives not previously experienced.[45] The organization becomes committed to activities that insure the status quo at the expense of greater success in achieving organization objectives.

Selznick studied the consequences of a second technique for achieving control and reliability—the delegation of authority. As intended, the specialized competence required to carry out the delegate tasks has the positive effect of achieving organization goals, but there are unintended consequences. Delegation of authority "results in departmentalization and an increase in the *bifurcation of interests* among the subunits in the organization." [46] Members of the organization become increasing dependent upon the maintenance of subunits and there is a growing disparity between the goals of the subunit and the goals of the organization. The content of decisions is increasingly concerned with subunit objectives and decreasingly concerned with organization goals, except that there must not be too great a disparity between the two. Subunit officials seek to make legitimate their activities by squaring their decisions with precedent. Again there seems to be an inherent tendency in the bureaucratic structure toward conservatism and the maintenance of the status quo.[47]

Gouldner gives additional support to

---

[39] *Ibid.,* p. 364.

[40] McNair, *op. cit.,* p. 285.

[41] This discussion is based on March and Simon, *op. cit.,* pp. 36–47.

[42] Robert K. Merton, "Bureaucratic Structure and Personality," *Social Forces,* Vol. 18, (1940), pp. 560–568.

[43] Philip Selznick, *TVA and the Grass Roots* (Berkeley: The University of California Press, 1949).

[44] Alvin W. Gouldner, *Patterns of Industrial Bureaucracy* (New York: The Free Press of Glencoe, 1954).

[45] March and Simon, *op. cit.,* pp. 38–39.

[46] *Ibid.,* p. 41.

[47] Such is the thesis of Robert Michels, *Political Parties* (Glencoe, Illinois: The Free Press, 1949), whose concept of the "iron law of oligarchy" is a classic description of the tendency of organization to become conservative as the demands for more specialized competence intensify.

the thesis that organizational techniques designed to implement control often entail unanticipated results. In his study of industrial organization he found, among other things, that the improvisation of rules to assure control results in the knowledge of *minimum acceptable levels of behavior* and that members of organizations gear their activities to these minimum levels of behavior if there is a high level of bifurcation of interest. As officials perceive this low performance, they react by increasing the closeness of supervision and by enacting additional rules and procedures. Again, the unintended consequences are increasing tension among members, increasing non-acceptance of organization goals, and increasing the use of rules to correct matters.[48]

To summarize, the essence of the humanistic challenge is that man in organizations is socially oriented and directed. He has multiple needs which affect and are affected by the work environment; he reacts unpredictably, yet predictably, to stimuli encountered in the organization. The "unintended consequences" of bureaucratic methods imply that man may be incompatible with organization needs. The scene is set, then, for contemporary organization theorists to devise a synthesis of the two polar positions.

The Realistic Synthesis [49]

An important feature of modern organization theory [50] is the systems approach which treats organizations as complex sets of mutually dependent and interacting variables. In this framework the participants are one set of variables which act on all other variables. Because this paper is concerned only with the place of man in organization theory, I will outline the feature of the systems approach (which I term the realistic synthesis) and then return to the discussion of man as a variable in the system.

The systems approach to organization theory presents the opportunity to view the organization as a totality. The emphasis is on the parts of the system, the nature of interaction among the parts, the processes which link the parts, and the goals of the system.[51] The key parts are the individual and his unique personality, the formal structure of jobs, the informal groups, the status and role patterns within the groups, and the physical environment. Relating these parts are complex patterns of interactions which modify the behavior and expectations of each. The basic parts are linked together by certain organizational processes including structured roles, channels of communication, and decision-making. These processes provide

---

[48] March and Simon, *op. cit.,* p. 45. Those studies are classics in the development of our knowledge of organizational behavior. It is obvious that many of Downs' hypotheses are suggested by this literature, particularly the hypotheses that organizations value status quo solutions and consensus and that the content of decisions is limited to precedents.

[49] Some third dimension as a basis for synthesis and the criteria for its selection are a concern to many students of organization theory. The work of Warren B. Bennis and many others could be cited. The focus of this paper, however, is on *values* more than the whole panorama.

[50] Some presentations of modern organization theory are March and Simon, *op. cit.;* Mason Haire (ed.), *Modern Organization Theory* (New York: John Wiley and Sons, 1959); Albert H. Rubenstein and Chadwick J. Haberstroh, *Some Theories of Organization* (Homewood, Illinois: The Dorsey Press, Inc., 1960); Joseph A. Litterer, *The Analysis of Organizations* (New York: John Wiley and Sons, 1965); and Theodore Caplow, *Principles of Organizations* (New York: Harcourt, Brace and World, Inc., 1964).

[51] William G. Scott, "Organization Theory: An Overview and an Appraisal," *Academy of Management Journal* (April, 1961), pp. 7–26. Reprinted in Joseph A. Litterer (ed.), *Organizations: Structure and Behavior* (New York: John Wiley and Sons, 1963), p. 19.

means for overcoming the centrifugal tendency of the parts [52] and for directing the parts toward the ultimate goals of the organization—growth, stability and social interaction.[53]

The systems approach is a realistic synthesis because it views the individual as only one of many parts, because it allows for modification of the parts, because it views conflict within the organization as a natural by-product of group endeavor, and because it anticipates dynamic rather than static patterns of interaction.

The realistic view of man in the organization acknowledges the contributions of the Hawthorne experiments, but it has added certain ideas that go beyond "human relations." The basic premise seems to be that man's needs and the organization's needs are inconsistent.[54] Man's behavior is seen to be motivated by a hierarchy of needs and once the most basic needs are satisfied, the individual turns to the ultimate source of satisfaction—self-actualization. But to achieve self-actualization requires that the healthy individual be "independent, creative . . . exercise autonomy and discretion, and . . . develop and express . . . unique personality with freedom." [55] The organization, however, presents barriers to this development of self-actualization and requires that the individual be dependent upon others for goal-setting and direction and conform to norms far below the level

of his ability or expectations. The results of this conflict are immature behavior and frustration-oriented activities, the overt expression being determined by the unique personality of the individual. Argyris' studies indicate that an organization member experiencing frustration and conflict may behave in any one of the following ways.[56]

a. He may leave the organization.

b. He may work hard and become president.

c. He may adapt through the use of defense mechanisms.

d. He may adapt by lowering his work standards and by becoming apathetic.

Other students of organizational behavior also perceive basic conflicts between the organization and the individual. Presthus argues that the reactions of members can be characterized by three bureaucratic types: the upward-mobiles; the differents; and, the ambivalents. The upward-mobiles are those who react positively to the organizational requirements and by adopting the sanctioned behavioral patterns succeed in it.[57] The indifferents are the great majority who view their jobs as means to secure off-work satisfactions and who neither seek nor expect on-job satisfaction.[58] The ambivalents are a small minority who are unable to play the organizationally defined role which would enable them to realize their ambitions.[59] The

---

[52] John M. Pfiffner and Frank P. Sherwood, *Administrative Organization* (Englewood Cliffs, N. J.: Prentice-Hall, Inc., 1960), pp. 116–117.

[53] Scott, *op. cit.*, p. 22.

[54] This view is developed by Chris Argyris in *Personality and Organization* (New York: Harper and Brothers, 1957) and more recently in *Integrating the Individual and the Organization* (New York: John Wiley and Sons, 1964).

[55] George Strauss, "Some Notes on Power-Equalization" in Harold J. Leavitt, editor, *The Social Science of Organization* (Englewood Cliffs, N. J.: Prentice-Hall, Inc., 1963), p. 46.

[56] *Personality and Organization* . . . pp. 78–79.

[57] Robert Presthus, *op. cit.*, pp. 164–204.

[58] *Ibid.*, pp. 205–256.

[59] *Ibid.*, pp. 257–285.

similarity between these three patterns of behavior and the adaptive responses which Argyris lists is evident.

Thus, the contemporary view of the nature of man in organizations recognizes the essential conflict that exists. Whereas: the mechanistic tradition considered conflict to be dysfunctional to organizational purposes and felt that it could be neutralized by monetary payments; and, the humanist challenge viewed conflict as dysfunctional but believed that human relations techniques could control it; the realistic synthesis assumes that conflict is a normal aspect of organization life.

The problem posed then is how to harness the energies of conflicts such that both organizational and individual needs are realized. Given the problem, we can accept at the outset that neither will be met perfectly—this being the essence of the conflict.[60] And whether conflict or cooperation is the *essential* nature of man does not seem to be relevant,[61] since research indicates that many organization members are *in fact in conflict* with the requirements of the organization.

Assumptions Have Consequences

I offer no final conclusions as to where recent efforts in organization theory and organization structuring will lead us; [62] all the evidence is not in and final arguments have not been heard. However, it is not difficult to concur with Haire's statement:

> Whenever we try to plan what an organization should be like, it is necessarily based on an implicit concept of man. If we look . . . at the outline of a "classical" organization theory and some more modern alternatives, we begin to see the change in the concept of man.[63]

Of course, to point out the importance of the assumptions which underlie organization theory is my major purpose. Anthony Downs would, perhaps, argue that these modern alternatives are not being tried since his findings indicate that much of classical organization theory is still with us. Perhaps again, the reason for its continued use is that those of us who study organizations have not given sufficient attention to questions that are value-laden.

Specifically, in what kinds of organizations do men behave in the very unattractive ways which Downs depicts? Or more basically, do we consider such behavior to be unattractive? What are the particular features of ongoing organizations that create the climate for such behavior? What variables are controlling and controllable? Or can we dismiss the problem by suggesting that the pressure-packed and anxiety-ridden culture of the times is the real culprit? But if it is concluded that such behavior is a necessary concomitant of organizations, I for one will count it a cost.

---

[60] Conflict and struggle for power in organizations lead to patterns of behavior that are political in nature. Melville Dalton in *Men Who Manage* (New York: John Wiley and Sons, 1959) analyzes organizational politics.

[61] Nor is there a final answer since some men (e.g. Thomas Hobbes) have viewed the essence of man to be conflict while others (e.g. John Locke) have viewed man as essentially cooperative. Realization of the individual through the group is not characteristic of Rousseau.

[62] See William W. Cooper, Harold J. Leavitt, and Maynard W. Shelly, *New Perspectives in Organization Research* (New York: John Wiley and Sons, Inc., 1964) for some indications.

[63] Strother, *op. cit.*, pp. 170–171.

19. When Human Relations May Succeed and the Company Fail

WILLIAM M. FOX

While the title of this article may sound facetious, it is meant in earnest. The concept of human relations in industry, like many other worthwhile movements, has been subjected to oversimplification and perversion.[1] Among the guilty are "human relationists" with an inadequate concept of human relations, who mistakenly preach participation, permissiveness, and democracy for all, and those employers who confuse popularity with managerial effectiveness and misinterpret the Golden Rule in dealing with their subordinates.

This article should not be construed as an attempt to discredit the findings of behavioral science. My purpose in writing is to demonstrate that a problem arises when the concept of human relations is misunderstood and misapplied in business organizations.

Part of the problem lies in lack of clarity as to the role "good human relations in an organization" should play. Many mistakenly regard it as an "end" toward which the organization should endeavor rather than as what it should be— a "means" for achieving the organization's primary service objectives. I define primary service objectives as the firm's chief objectives which not only specify how a firm hopes to create and distribute salable utilities profitably but also how it will justify its existence in a competitive

milieu. Good human relations—along with policies, rules, plans, procedures, specifications, functions, organization structure, etc.—should serve as a tool, a means, for the achievement of these objectives. There are at least five rather common situations in industry when good human relations are regarded as an end rather than as a means.

1. When elimination of conflict becomes a primary goal of the organization.

Few of us enjoy the prospect of unpleasantness with another human being —especially when we must initiate it. We hate to fire or discipline an ineffective employee who has an attractive family and tries hard to please us, and we find it most distasteful to face the possible rejection or disapproval of subordinates when we feel that duty demands that we fly in the face of their sentiments. Nor do we enjoy the anxiety generated by the prospect of able young men bringing new ideas and new skills into the organization which may threaten our status and feelings of competence.

There is strong temptation for peace of mind to settle for being popular rather than effective and for hiring only those who fit in with our scheme of things and

Reprinted from the *California Management Review,* Vol. 8, No. 3 (Spring, 1966), copyright by the Regents of the University of California. William M. Fox is Professor of Industrial Relations and Management, College of Business Administration, University of Florida.

[1] See, for example, James V. Clark, "Distortions of Behavioral Science," *California Management Review,* VI:2 (Winter 1963).

offer little likelihood of ever "rocking the boat." A striving for complete harmony and absence of stress in a large company can be rationalized into respectability with the "custodial" philosophy of management. Under this philosophy, it is felt that the firm has completed its entrepreneurial-expansionist phase and that the major functions of the management team are to traditionalize and perpetuate the "winning combination," to instruct neophytes as to its mysteries, and to protect it at all costs against the subversive influences of change.

In the absence of control afforded by the vigilance of large stockholders, it is surprising how long a group of noncompetitive "custodians" can coast on the momentum of a formerly successful corporation, milking its assets via unwarranted bonuses for years before they are found out. This can be quite pleasant as long as it lasts, but the future failure of the company is virtually assured in the process.

It is instructive to observe how few of the most successful companies of 1900 are still extant and to hear of the misfortunes and close calls of those who momentarily thought they were competition-proof. No—the function of human relations in an organization cannot be the elimination of conflict, for this will create a state of dormancy and lead to eventual disaster. The legitimate function of human relations in an organization is to facilitate the introduction of change with a minimum of conflict.

2. When there is no "price of admission" (i.e., individual and group goals are permitted to conflict with company goals or be unrelated to them).

Employees can be quite happy and team minded as they do nothing or as they actively subvert an organization. There is no natural law which assures a relationship between high morale and the effective pursuit of an organization's primary service objectives. A number of researchers seemingly have been startled by this discovery. Actually, the absence of such a relationship is not too surprising. A source of misunderstanding has been the tendency to use the word "productivity" in one context only—the efficient creation of goods or services for the firm. Yet a widely accepted concept of high morale is that it exists to the extent that individual group members are willing to subordinate their immediate convenience or interests to the achievement of group goals. If we think of the productivity of a group as the efficiency with which it achieves its goals, then the relationship between high morale and productivity becomes apparent and tautological.

In other words, employees can be quite productive by striking well as a team, by withholding production well as a unit, and so on. The challenge to management is to create good group morale and concurrently to see to it that group goals are consistent with company goals. Or, to put it another way, to demonstrate to employees that the satisfaction of their diverse individual needs can and will take place to the extent that they discharge their obligations to the firm and to the extent that such activity does not detract from the achievement of company goals.

A good analogy, perhaps, is afforded by the Marine Corps. Its primary objective is, presumably, to fashion one of the finest fighting forces in the world, an organization prepared to tackle military assignments that impose personal hardships and risks greater than those which an average military organization could or would impose on its members. Is it likely that the typical Marine is looking for an improved opportunity to have his head blown off? Hardly! It seems much more plausible to argue that the Corps functions in such a way as to satisfy important personal needs of its members—for feelings of acceptance, worthwhileness, etc.—in the process of preparing to carry out, and in carrying out, its hazardous assignments. The "price of admission" for Marines to stay in the Corps—and to continue to enjoy the satisfaction of needs that they believe only the Corps can satisfy so well—is to do the work of the Corps and identify with its objectives in a manner consistent with its high standards of excellence.[2]

3. When certain "good works" need not be justified in terms of contribution to primary service objectives.

This can happen, for example, when the rehabilitation of personnel rather than the effective utilization of personnel becomes a primary goal. Sometimes the latter will encompass the former, but this is more the exception than the rule. Take the case of the dependent subordinate who has strong emotional needs for assignments well within his competence, close supervision, and personal acceptance. For many routine assignments he can become a productive, dependable, and loyal employee. It might be argued that such an individual would be better off if he could be weaned from his dependency needs through appropriate counseling and guidance, and this is probably true. However, normally, unless organizational needs warrant it, the company cannot justify the diversion of its resources to this type of therapy.

Or consider the maladjusted troublemaker who is so insecure and hostile that he will not respond to positive supervision. He is compelled by his neurotic needs to subvert and challenge the authority of the formal leader. In fact, he tends

to perceive positive leadership behavior either as appeasement—the leader is afraid of him—or as an attempt to put something over on him. Though such individuals may be helped by professional counseling, supervisors do not have the time, skill, or justification for administering it. They must protect their own integrity with their groups and make every effort to eliminate disruptive influences in them. If a troublemaker does not respond to negative sanctions, he should be fired! For good human relations in an organization must pay its way through contribution to company goals. Any worthwhile undertaking, whether it has to do with the rehabilitation of personnel or some other desirable practice, must operate within this framework if the firm is to succeed.

Danger lies also in an overexpansion of benefits and services. This may result from an excessive desire to please—even competitors—or from a desire to dodge the responsibilities of leadership through "committeemanship" or undue reliance upon the opinions of specialists. Cameron Hawley reports some startling data brought back by American executives after visits to counterpart operations in Europe.[3] "Until I got on the inside," said one executive, "I thought they had us licked over here because of wage rates. I know differently now. For every penny they're saving in direct labor costs, they've got us whipped by three cents in general overhead and burden. Inside the plant it's about a stand-off . . . but when you get to the office, they make us look like fools." He pointed out that his company and the European firms are about the same size in terms of units produced. His company has about 1,200 hourly workers

[2] For further discussion of the relationship between individual needs and organizational goals, see Chapter 8, *The Management Process,* William M. Fox (Homewood, Ill.: Richard D. Irwin, Inc., 1963).

[3] "The Quality of Leadership," *Personnel,* May–June, 1960.

in the plant, the overseas firm 1,300. But the contrast in salaried employees is a different story: 912 in the United States *vs.* 221 overseas.

Hawley hypothesizes that a lot of the "organizational fat" which plagues some of our companies may have resulted from the whipping-boy role that American employers were cast in during the great depression. Many young executives determined then that when their turn at the wheel came they would win public approval by introducing real democracy into business. With time, this evolved into substituting group-thinking for one-man-rule and trying to keep everybody happy. And in the process of hiring ten men to make one man's decisions, needed discipline and internal surgery went by the board—and with them the possibility of adherence to high standards of performance.

As part of the problem, the number of staff specialists has been increased without adequate justification. In the area of selection, for example, much effort and money are expended each year on the administration of tests and interviews which have little if any validity (that is, no one has bothered to base their usage upon statistically demonstrated ability to predict success or failure on the job).[4] Elaborate counseling, training, and public relations programs have been established and expanded with little evidence as to ability to pay their way through contribution to company goals.

4. When there is adherence to "the bubble-up theory" (good theory and practice at lower levels do not square with what is practiced at the top).

Sound human relations training can backfire. Or in medical terms it can be very iatrogenic, i.e., it can cause more harm than the difficulties it is designed to overcome. An organization cannot be reformed from the bottom up. Yet this is what is often attempted when lower level supervisors are instructed in philosophies and practices of management which are incompatible with the values and behavior of their superiors. Research has uncovered several cases wherein foremen have been less effective after good training in human relations than they were before—and in comparison with their colleagues who did not receive the training.[5]

This result is not too surprising. For when we move from training designed to impart information to that designed to alter basic behavior, we move toward the necessity of a preceptor system. There are several ways in which supervisory behavior may be altered. One is to structure the "compulsions" of the environment—formal sanctions, group pressures, role assignments, etc.—to produce the desired behavior. Another is to help the individual gain insight into his behavior and then to support and encourage him in experimenting with more productive modes. And closely related to the first two is the process of identification wherein a "junior" individual adopts the values and behavior of some "senior" individual whom he admires and wishes to emulate.

Harry Levinson of The Menninger Foundation goes so far as to hypothesize that "one of the significant differences between those who become executives and those who do not lies in the presence or absence of certain kinds of identification

---

[4] Among more than 100 companies interviewed by *Fortune,* only one noted any difference in ability between graduates hired over the counter and recruits painstakingly selected as the "cream of the crop." See Herrymon Maurer, "The Worst Shortage in Business," *Fortune,* April 1956, or William M. Fox, ed., *Readings in Personnel Management from Fortune* (New York: Holt, Rinehart and Winston, Inc., 1963), p. 26.

[5] For an example, see Harold E. Burtt, "Why Most Supervisor Training Fails," *Management Methods,* Jan. 1958, p. 28.

models." [6] He points out that every human being in later life tends to repeat unconsciously those modes of behavior which he learned in the family. Consequently, organizations of people tend to assume qualities like those of the family. In the same way that a boy grows and matures through identification with authority figures, a supervisor or junior executive will grow in stature and competence to the extent that his superiors provide models with which he can identify. It is interesting that Levinson and his colleagues found support for this concept in their intensive study of a large utility company. [7]

Top management, far more by its action than its pronouncements, will establish a "climate" for supervisory behavior. Autocratic managers are better advised to prescribe standards of supervision for their organizations which both they and their subordinates can accept and practice than to risk the disruptive effects of a "double standard." They should not expose their subordinate managers to human relations training until they, personally, can understand, accept, and practice the substance of such training—or step aside to make room for others who will. The right theory is "the trickle-down theory."

5. When "intelligent autocracy" would have been more productive for the organization.

Democratic, consultative leadership, based upon participation, effective two-way communication, and nondirective counseling, which we associate with the expression "good human relations," is superior for the majority of employees in a wide range of organizations and in most instances. But there are important exceptions. I have already discussed the need for more directive, unilateral supervision for the dependent employee and for the maladjusted troublemaker. There are two other situations which deserve our attention.

First, time is required for a supervisor to gain acceptance and build the kind of relationship with his subordinates which will ultimately lead to higher productivity and long-term individual growth. If a temporary work group or committee is composed of mature people who share and practice a positive philosophy of leadership, then it will probably function best under such leadership. However, in other temporary work group situations, positive leadership may well be less productive than intelligent authoritarianism. For example, consider a group of casual common laborers hired for a period of three months to do road work. Because of their lack of education and skill, they require close supervision. They perceive this particular job as a stopgap, offering little opportunity for growth, enhanced self-esteem, advancement, or lasting security. It seems likely that motivation of such a group in terms of negative sanctions would be superior to an attempt to develop positive values that are largely precluded by the character of the workers and the work environment.

Second, a situation which deserves our attention has to do with a firm, or part of a firm, which can operate more effi-

---

[6] "A Psychologist Looks at Executive Development," *Harvard Business Review,* Sept.–Oct., 1962, p. 70.

[7] See *Men, Management, and Mental Health,* Harry Levinson, Charlton Price, Kenneth Munden, Harold Mandl, and Charles Solley (Cambridge, Mass.: Harvard University Press, 1962), esp. Chapter 4, "Interdependence." In his book, *Personal Adjustment* (New York: Macmillan Company, 1963), p. 140, Sidney Jourard asserts that "It is by means of *identification* that we acquire our most important values, and it is through identification that we change our values from time to time throughout life."

ciently under centralized autocracy. When a company is operating in a relatively stable environment with little competition (e.g., a railroad during the years before the advent of good roads, busses, trucks, and planes), centralized management can reduce its load to manageable proportions through the extensive use of rules, procedures, and standard practices. This is feasible because centralized management will be confronted for the most part with predictable situations. The security-minded, dependent-type employee can be attracted, held, and effectively utilized in this environment, because there is little need for fast, innovative local action to cope with unforeseen developments. In fact, given well-conceived goals by those at the top and a well-drilled and disciplined organization, centralized autocracy can spare top managers the problems of dealing with the centrifugal tendencies generated by decentralized, autonomous units staffed with creative and ambitious young men.

The cult of "excessive permissiveness" has been seen in progressive education and also among certain overzealous "human relationists." There are those who imply that sweetness and light will conquer all and that any form of negative motivation is self-defeating and outmoded. There is little question that positive motivation is superior to negative motivation when it is appropriate. But there are instances when it is not, and negative motivation—intelligently applied—is definitely superior to no motivation. Reference has been made to certain situations for which a positive, permissive approach is inappropriate—with dependent or transient employees and maladjusted troublemakers, and for certain stable, predictable organizational environments. In addition, one must have the time, rapport, skill, or insight to make a positive approach productive.

Not only is time necessary for a super-visor to gain acceptance from his subordinate and to build useful relationships with them, time can also be a major limiting factor in many specific situations. No one expects an infantry platoon leader caught with his unit in an ambush to confer with his subordinates as to the best course of action; it is his job to give the right orders and to give them quickly and concisely. Actually, any attempt on his part to be consultative on such an occasion might diminish the respect of his men and jeopardize his effectiveness with them in the future. In fact, unilateral leadership is the only appropriate mode for the occasion and—in this context—is positive leadership.

Positive motivation is based upon accurate perception of subordinate needs and upon effective interpersonal communications. It is difficult for a supervisor to perceive the needs of a subordinate or effectively to communicate with him if he cannot establish rapport with him—a relationship of mutual trust. Often this is not easy, even with the best of intentions for, if we find it difficult to "warm up" to a person, it is virtually impossible to establish such a relationship with him. Also, a supervisor will not perceive subordinate needs if he lacks the skill or insight required. It is not surprising that most of us lack this skill in dealing with those individuals who are themselves incapable of perceiving their own needs. And even when rapport, perception, and effective communication have been achieved, the supervisor must attempt satisfaction of the subordinate's needs within the framework of organizational constraints. At times, this will not permit the supervisor sufficient flexibility to deal in a positive manner with a particular case.

In real life situations, the use of negative motivation is inescapable. One of the significant differences between a good human relations environment and a poor one is that, in the former, negative motivation is used only when necessary and then in a goal-oriented, nonpunitive manner.

Five common situations in industry when human relations tends to be regarded as an end rather than a means for the achievement of company objectives were examined. These were:

• When elimination of conflict becomes a primary goal of the organization.
• When there is no "price of admission" (i.e., when individual and group goals are permitted to conflict with company goals or be unrelated to them).
• When certain "good works" need not be justified in terms of contribution to primary service objectives.
• When there is adherence to "the bubble-up theory" (when good theory and practice at lower levels do not square with what is practiced at the top).
• When "intelligent autocracy" would have been more productive for the organization.

I have examined instances in which the application of sound human relations may lead to company failure. When will successful human relations lead to company success?

• When the concept of human relations is seen as a tool, or means, for the achievement of the firm's goals.
• When it is properly integrated with other key tools. Among these are well-defined goals and high standards of performance—arrived at whenever possible through consultation and enforced with the aid of a system of rewards and penalties which responds to every important facet of activity.

When top management can lead the organization to internalize high standards of performance and make them part of the organization's culture, its battle for excellence will be largely won. For it will have sown the seeds of continuous regeneration, founded in the basic psychological truth that "we value more those things we must strive for, and we value ourselves more for having made the effort."

B

ORGANIZATIONAL CONFLICT AND CHANGE

20. Managing Conflict in Organizations

JOSEPH A. LITTERER

This paper deals with a few things on conflict which have not previously been given much attention in research, but which are becoming increasingly important. First, on reading some of the current literature concerning conflict, at least conflicts internal to an organization, one can see an important change taking place. Not too long ago, the normal posture in writing and thinking about conflict in organizations was that it was undesirable, and the standard decision rule was to eliminate it. More recently, it would appear that people are beginning to accept the idea that conflict makes important contributions to the organization.

This shift in thinking about conflict in organization seems to parallel closely changes which have recently taken place in the field of personality psychology. At one time, it was thought that people were motivated when tension was reduced. More recent thinking seems to be that tension has a proper place, that the normal or "healthy" personality is one that tends to maintain a certain level of tension, that when tension is low, tension-building situations may actually be sought out. There is not only a parallel between these two changes, but actually, an important connection between the two ideas, for conflict is an important source of tension.

The writings of Boulding, some of the later things by Argyris, and certainly some of the writings of Melville Dalton

Reprinted from *Proceedings of the 8th Annual Midwest Management Conference.* Carbondale, Ill.: Business Research Bureau, Southern Illinois University, 1965, pp. 27–31, with permission of the author and the publisher. Joseph A. Litterer is Professor of Management, College of Commerce and Business Administration, University of Illinois.

and Peter Blau, discuss some of the positive contributions of conflict in organization. This is certainly a major step: to bring conflict from its previously condemned position into one where it is accepted. However, it opens up several new and very difficult questions. What are the circumstances under which conflict is acceptable or useful? What are the ranges of permissible or useful conflict? A review of the literature at least does not reveal much, if anything, to guide us in answering these questions. I should like, however, to review briefly what the literature does contain and to suggest some partial answers to these questions.

The first step is to examine briefly what people see as the utility of conflict. Dalton, among others, shows that conflict stirs *invention* or certainly the search for ways to eliminate, reduce, or compensate for the conditions leading to conflict. A second product of conflict is that the people feel a tension and this impels them to act; or, it gives them an impetus to do something. Hence, conflict can be looked upon as an *energizer* of activity. Some call it a motivator; yet, upon examination, what conflict seems to do does not quite fit the usual concepts of motivation, and leads me to use the term above—energizer. A third function of conflict is that it develops what might be called protection for something else in the organization. For example, it has been observed by a number of people that when there are conflicts between units or positions on the same hierarchical level, those in conflict will have little time, opportunity, or energy to take action against people or units or institutions at different hierarchical levels. Turned around, this is the old political axiom that in order to dominate a country or political sphere, one should "divide and conquer." Hence, this point must be looked at in two ways: that parties in conflict will be both more easily controlled and dominated and less able to exert influence over others. Lastly, conflict can be viewed as serving as an element in a cybernetic system. For a system in the steady state, conflict functions as a red flag and indicates that here something is not right. Conflict may not, and often does not, indicate what is wrong, but it does indicate that something needs attention, thus providing the signal for analysis and corrective action.

These are the principal functions or utilities of conflict which one finds in the literature. There are doubtless others, and one could make a useful research project of the search for them.

Recognizing that conflict does have uses as well as disadvantages opens the important question of what is to be done about it. There is the important issue of what the permissible range of conflict is. Unfortunately, the literature throws little light on this, and there is not time here to develop even this small amount. There is another question to which attention should be directed, however; that is how conflict can be kept within the bounds that can and should be tolerated. In short, what are the handles and levers which are used to manage conflict? A quick answer seems to be that there are many. An attempt will be made to group them according to the major organizational variables which are involved, or, more accurately, intervening states or situations.

The first of these is what I would call the *incompatible goals situation*. People and units within organizations can have incompatible goals for many reasons. Often these reasons emanate from deliberately contrived organizational situations. Perhaps one of the most common of these is the win-lose condition. Such a condition exists when two parties are placed in a system where, as one achieves his goal, the other automatically loses or is excluded from obtaining his goal. It may be surprising, but organizations have many such situations. A very common one centers around the position of the inspector. It is the inspector's job to find things which are not right according to organizational standards or norms. Every time he does this, his existence is justified. He is filling his role. On the other hand, as soon as he does this, some other person has been shown to be doing something wrong. His position or his tenure in his position is threatened, and he is shown not to be succeeding. Organizations have many positions which function as inspectors. Most obvious, of course, are those of quality control inspectors in production. But many aspects of accounting, and, in fact, most staff departments have some inspection activities attached to them.

Inspection positions are not the only ones, however, which are in the situation of having goals incompatible with those of others. Some people find themselves in this situation because of a combination of poorly designed reward and work-flow systems. One illustration is a problem which developed in a major airline a few years ago. The symptoms were considerable conflict between the regional sales manager and the regional ramp service manager. The ramp service manager is in charge of servicing the plane when it is on the ground on everything except maintenance. He, therefore, is concerned with cleaning the plane, getting luggage off and on, getting passengers off and on, etc. This airline had attempted to decentralize as much as possible and had installed a bonus system for the manager of personnel down to the regional level. The regional sales manager received a bonus based in part upon his sales volume. The ramp service manager received a bonus likewise based in part upon how well he kept down the costs of servicing aircraft. The sales manager, an imaginative man, had developed a number of schemes to increase sales over the years, a number

of which unfortunately required action on the part of the ramp service manager. The ramp service manager, however, was rather firm about not taking action upon these plans when, to his mind, they increased his costs and thereby diminished his chances for a bonus. The frustration of the sales manager and the defensiveness of the ramp service manager led to considerable conflict. In organizational terms, here were interdependent positions whose occupants were part of a reward system which gave benefits in accordance with individual performance. There are many situations in organizations which innocently are producing conflict through incompatible goals.

A second category or situation producing conflict which appears in other literature centers around what might be called *incompatible means* or *incompatible resource allocations.* As an introductory point, let me recall that Schacter and his associates found that there is a greater disruption of group cohesiveness and more conflict when there are strongly differing opinions over the means to an end than over the ends themselves. Hence, in organization, differences over the means to be used or who is to have the means can be chronic and serious sources of conflict. Such situations are, needless to say, many. There is, for example, the all too frequently cited conflict which develops when department managers have to go to a single source of resources, such as to a finance department, for funds or to a personnel department for their share of limited numbers of highly specialized employees.

A third organizational situation which leads to a great deal of conflict and has been cited many times occurs when there are *status incongruities.* This rests on the common observation that one of the things people continually try to do is to determine "where they stand" in some status hierarchy. This would be a serious, but not a particularly complex, issue if there were but one status hierarchy; however, since there are many such hierarchies and since many decisions made in organizations influence a person's position on several of these at the same time, often in different ways, almost any administrative decision is likely to lead to a situation of status incongruence, and thereby lead to stress and conflict. Also, many problems arise in this area from conditions almost beyond the control of any manager, or, for that matter, of management as a whole. For example, there is the not at all uncommon problem of managers who joined their company 20 or 25 years ago, who have worked hard and intelligently, and who think they will gradually be promoted to a higher position, but who now find that some of the more choice positions around and above them are being filled by young men, 10 to 15 years their junior. This often comes about because the decisions managements often must make now require a high level of technical sophistication. Men more recently in undergraduate and graduate university programs may have this sophistication, but men two or three decades away from their formal education do not. So these men find themselves in a position where their age and seniority suggest that they be at one level, but who hardly equal or are even below men considerably younger and with far fewer years with their organization. It is understandably a source of conflict but there is no easily understandable solution. There are many sources which lead to status incongruities and therefore to conflict. Many of these sources of conflict are the result of conscious managerial decisions such as the design of work-flows, reward systems, or selection and placement of personnel.

The last source of conflict to be discussed might be called *differences and perception*. The perception differences that are of concern here are those which occur or develop as a result of differences and organizational position. The perceptual differences of people at different hierarchical levels are frequently described. But there often are, also, substantial differences in perception between people at the same hierarchical level when they are in different functional areas. The classic disputes between marketing and production are all too common to need much elaboration.

These, then, are four types of situations which can develop in organizations and lead to conflict. These are also situations which, by and large, develop as a result of decisions made about organizational structures or practices. They are, therefore, controllable by these same decisions, but this list is useful not only for identifying some of the ways in which conflict can be controlled or, for that matter, increased or decreased, but also for providing a tool to analyze more deeply some properties of conflict, or more accurately, these conflict-producing situations.

A number of researchers, especially those who have been involved with studies in bargaining, have pointed out that when a person gets into a win-lose type of situation or the first category, incompatible goals, there is, in a sense, a situation in which it is extraordinarily difficult to achieve resolution. Mediation in this kind of dispute is usually hopeless, or at the very least is extraordinarily difficult. Mediation is therefore usually abandoned for arbitration. In short, one way of handling conflicts from this source is to take away the possibility of resolution from the people directly involved and turn it over to someone else who will make an arbitrary decision.

The other conflict situations, particularly the second (incompatible means) and the third (status incongruities), do seem frequently to lead to resolutions by the people involved, and it seems that these types of situations are those which are most likely to have important functional qualities for an organization. Examination further suggests that the fourth situation (differences and perceptions) along with the first (incompatible goals) is likely to be the least rewarding or useful to an organization.

One interesting and potentially difficult point is the possibility of shifting from one to another type of situation. Merton, in his study of bureaucracy, has pointed out that means can be transformed into ends; hence, a situation in which the conflict was over means could be transformed into one where there was actually conflict over ends or, to put it another way, it could move from being a situation in which the parties involved could find a solution for themselves to one in which it would be virtually impossible for the parties themselves to be reconciled.

The last general issue that should be dealt with is what can be done about conflict. Perhaps a simpler recommendation which both the literature and common experience suggest is to separate the parties, or bring about a disengagement. We do this in many ways, and often, it would appear, almost unconsciously. One of the most frequently cited illustrations in the literature is that described by White in his study of the restaurant industry where, in order to reduce conflict between cooks and runners, the runners were instructed to write messages on a slip of paper and then place the paper on a hook from which the cook could take it. Thus, the need for direct spoken contact between cook and runner was eliminated and, consequently, the conflict was reduced. Actually, rather than call this disengagement, it would be better to say that buffers are being erected between people; if you wish, you may consider space as a buffer. But with this term and concept, many other things can be considered also; such

as an illustration above, having messages written and transmitted through some mechanical means or using formalistic language which we often witness developing in tense or uncertain situations.

Another way of reducing conflict which is often suggested is to help the people in the situation cope more adequately with both inward and outward conflict or competitive situations. Work, for example, in T-group training is to a considerable part directed to helping individuals cope with a tension they feel, and helping them cope with things directed to them by other people. Even if such knowledge and skill does not permit tension to be eliminated, it may well keep it from escalating.

A third way of handling conflict is consciously to recognize that many conflict situations arise from the design of the organization and that this is the thing which needs attention and adjustment. This has been proposed by many people— perhaps the most widely quoted reference is Worthy in his classic paper on decentralization. It is, in part, his conclusion that the product type of structural form is more likely to lead to harmonious relationships than is the functional type.

In conclusion, from an examination of the literature, it would seem that conflict may be useful in organizations; that it is controllable; and that it should now be moved forward as a topic for major analysis and investigation. Having been neglected for so long, it poses a rich field for research. It is an interesting topic and one about which relatively little is known, at least from the point of view of considering it as a useful and acceptable element in an organization. If someone wanted a fruitful area of investigation for at least several lifetimes, he could easily take up the topic of the management of conflict in organizations.

21. Theory and Method in Applying Behavioral Science to Planned Organizational Change

WARREN G. BENNIS

What we have witnessed in the past two or three decades has been called the "Rise of the Rational Spirit"—the belief that science can help to better the human condition (Merton & Lerner, 1951). The focus of this paper is on one indication of this trend: the emerging role for the behavioral scientist and, more specifically, the attempts by behavioral scientists to apply knowledge (primarily sociological and psychological) toward the improvement of human organizations.[1]

Many signs and activities point toward an emerging action role for the behavioral scientists. The *manipulative standpoint,* as Lasswell calls it, is becoming distinguishable from the *contemplative standpoint* and is increasingly ascendant insofar as knowledge utilization is concerned.[2] Evidence can be found in the growing literature on planned change through the uses of the behavioral sciences (Bennis, Benne, & Chin, 1961; Freeman, 1963; Zetterberg, 1962; Gibb & Lippitt, 1959; Leeds & Smith, 1963; Likert & Hayes, 1957; Glock, Lippitt, Flanagan, Wilson, Shartle, Wilson, Croker, & Page, 1960) and in

such additions to the vocabulary of the behavorial scientist as action research, client system, change agent, clinical sociology, knowledge centers, social catalysts. The shift is also reflected in increased emphasis on application in annual meeting time of the professional associations or in the formation of a Center for Research on the Utilization of Scientific Knowledge within The University of Michigan's Institute for Social Research.

It is probably true that in the United States there is a more practical attitude toward knowledge than anywhere else. When Harrison Salisbury (1960) traveled over Europe he was impressed with the seeming disdain of European intellectuals for practical matters. Even in Russia he found little interest in the "merely useful." Sailsbury saw only one great agricultural experiment station on the American model. In that case professors were working in the fields. They told him, "People call us Americans."

Not many American professors may be found working in the fields, but they can be found almost everywhere else: in

---

Reprinted from *Journal of Applied Behavioral Science,* Vol. 1, No. 4 (October–November–December, 1965), pp. 337–360, with permission of the author and the publisher. Warren G. Bennis is Professor of Management, Alfred P. Sloan School of Management, Massachusetts Institute of Technology.

[1] Drawn from keynote address presented at International Conference on Operational Research and the Social Sciences, Cambridge, England, September 1964.

[2] For an excellent discussion of the "value" issues in this development, see Kaplan, A. *The Conduct of Inquiry.* San Francisco: Chandler, 1964, Chapter 10; and Benne, K. D., & Swanson, G. (Eds.) "Values and Social Issues." *J. Soc. Issues,* 1960, p.

factories, in the government, in under-developed countries, in mental hospitals, in educational systems. They are advising, counseling, researching, recruiting, devel-oping, consulting, training. Americans may not have lost their deep ambivalence toward the intellectual, but it is clear that the academic intellectual has become *en-gagé* with spheres of action in greater numbers, with more diligence, and with higher aspirations than at any other time in history.

It may be useful to speculate about the reasons for the shift in the intellectual climate. Most important, but trickiest to identify, are those causative factors bound up in the warp and woof of "our times and age" that Professor Boring calls the *Zeitgeist*. The apparently growing dis-enchantment with the moral neutrality of the scientist may be due, in C. P. Snow's phrase, to the fact that "scientists cannot escape their own knowledge." In any event, though "impurity" is still implied, action research as distinguished from pure research does not carry the opprobrium it once did.

Perhaps the crucial reason for the shift in emphasis toward application is simply that we know more.[3] Since World War II we have obtained large bodies of re-search and diverse reports on application. We are today in a better position to assess results and potentialities of applied social science.

Finally, there is a fourth factor having to do with the fate and viability of human organization, particularly as it has been conceptualized as "bureaucracy." I use the term in its sociological, Weberian sense, not as a metaphor *à la* Kafka's *The Castle* connoting "red tape," im-potency, inefficiency, despair. In the past three decades Weber's vision has been increasingly scrutinized and censured,

Managers and practitioners, on the one hand, and organizational theorists and researchers on the other, are more and more dissatisfied with current practices of organizational behavior and are search-ing for new forms and patterns of orga-nizing for work. A good deal of activity is being generated.

Unfortunately, no viable theory of soc-cial change has been established. Indeed it is a curious fact about present theories that they are strangely silent on matters of *directing* and *implementing* change. What I particularly object to—and I in-clude the "newer" theories of neo-conflict (Coser, 1956; Dahrendorf, 1961), neo-functionalism (Boskoff, 1964), and neo-revolutionary theories—is that they tend to explain the dynamic interactions of a system without providing one clue to the identification of strategic leverages for alteration. They are suitable for *observers* of social change, not for practitioners. They are theories of *change,* and not of *changing*.

It may be helpful to suggest quickly some of the prerequisites for a theory of changing. I am indebted here to my col-league Robert Chin (1961, 1963):

a. A theory of changing must include manipulable variables—accessible levers for influencing the direction, tempo, and quality of change and improvement.

b. The variables must not violate the client system's values.

c. The cost of usage cannot be prohibi-tive.

d. There must be provided a reliable basis of diagnosing the strength and weakness of conditions facing the client system.

e. Phases of intervention must be clear so that the change agent can develop esti-mates for termination of the relationship.

---

[3] For a recent inventory of scientific findings of the behavioral sciences, see Berelson, B., & Steiner, G. A. *Human Behavior*. New York: Harcourt, Brace & World, 1964.

f. The theory must be communicable to the client system.

g. It must be possible to assess appropriateness of the theory for different client systems.

Such a theory does not now exist, and this probably explains why change agents appear to write like "theoretical orphans" and, more important, why so many change programs based on theories of social change have been inadequate. This need should be kept in mind as we look at models of knowledge utilization.

Planned change can be viewed as a linkage between theory and practice, between knowledge and action. It plays this role by converting variables from the basic disciplines into strategic instrumentation and programs. Historically, the development of planned change can be seen as the resultant of two forces: complex problems requiring expert help and the growth and viability of the behavioral sciences. The term "behavioral sciences" itself is of post-World War II vintage coined by the more empirically minded to "safeguard" the social disciplines from the non-quantitative humanists and the depersonalized abstractions of the econometrictists. The process of planned change involves a *change agent,* a *client system,* and the collaborative attempt to apply *valid knowledge* to the client's problems.[4]

Elsewhere I have attempted a typology of change efforts in which planned change is distinguished from other types of change in that it entails mutual goal setting, an equal power ratio (eventually), and deliberateness on both sides (Bennis *et al.,* 1961, p. 154).

It may further help in defining planned change to compare it with another type of deliberate change effort, Operations Research. I enter this with a humility bordering on fear and a rueful sense of kinship in our mutual incapacity to explain to one another the nature of our work. There are these similarities. Both are World War II products; both are problem-centered (though both have also provided inputs to the concepts and method of their parent disciplines).[5] Both emphasize improvement and to that extent are *normative* in their approach to problems. Both rely heavily on empirical science; both rely on a relationship of confidence and valid communication with clients; both emphasize a *systems* approach to problems—that is, both are aware of interdependence within the system as well as boundary maintenance with its environment; and both appear to be most effective when working with systems which are complex, rapidly changing, and probably science-based.

Perhaps the most crucial difference between OR and planned change has to do with the identification of strategic variables, that is, with those factors which appear to make a difference in the performance of the system. Planned change is concerned with such problems as (1) the identification of mission and values, (2) collaboration and conflict, (3) control and leadership, (4) resistance and adaptation to change, (5) utilization of human resources, (6) communication, (7) management development. OR practitioners tend to select economic or engineering variables which are more quantitative, measurable, and linked to profit and efficiency. Ackoff and Rivett (1963), for example, classify OR problems under (1) inventory, (2) allocation, (3) queuing,

[4] For a fuller discussion, see Lippitt, R., Watson, J., & Wesley, B. *The Dynamics of Planned Change.* New York: Harcourt, Brace & World, 1961; and Bennis *et al.,* 1961.

[5] For a brilliant exposition on the contributions of applied research to "pure" theory, see Gouldner, A. "Theoretical Requirements of the Applied Social Sciences," in Bennis *et al.,* 1961. Pp. 83–95.

(4) sequencing, (5) routing, (6) replacement, (7) competition, (8) search.

A second major difference has to do with the perceived importance of the relationship with the client. In planned change, the quality and nature of the relationship are used as indicators for the measure of progress and as valid sources of data and diagnosis. Undoubtedly, the most successful OR practitioners operate with sensitivity toward their clients; but if one looks at what they *say* about their work, they are clearly less concerned with human interactions.

A third major difference is that the OR practitioner devotes a large portion of his time to research, to problem solving. The change agent tends to spend somewhat more time on implementation through counseling, training, management development schemes, and so forth. Fourth, planned-change agents tend to take less seriously the idea of the *system* in their approaches. Finally, the idea of an interdisciplinary team, central to OR, does not seem to be a part of most planned-change programs.

One thing that emerges from this comparison is a realization of the complexity of modern organization. Look through the kaleidoscope one way, and a configuration of the economic and technological factors appears; tilt it, and what emerges is a pattern of internal human relations problems. It is on these last problems and their effects upon performance of the system that practitioners of planned organizational change tend to work.

To develop what George Kelley refers to as a "focus of convenience" for planned organizational change, I want to make two key aspects clearer: the notions of "collaborative relationships" and of "valid knowledge." I see the outcome of planned-change efforts as depending to some considerable extent on the relationship between client and agent. To optimize a collaborative relationship, there need to be a "spirit of inquiry," with data publicly shared, and equal freedom to terminate the relationship and to influence the other.

As to valid knowledge, the criteria are based on the requirements for a viable applied behavioral science research—an applied behavioral science that:

a. Takes into consideration the behavior of persons operating within their specific institutional environments;

b. Is capable of accounting for the interrelated levels (person, group, role, organization) within the context of the social change;

c. Includes variables that the policy maker and practitioner can understand, manipulate, and evaluate;

d. Can allow selection of variables appropriate in terms of its own values, ethics, moralities;

e. Accepts the premise that groups and organizations as units are amenable to empirical and analytic treatment;

f. Takes into account external social processes of change as well as interpersonal aspects of the collaborative process;

g. Includes propositions susceptible to empirical test focusing on the dynamics of change.

These criteria must be construed as an arbitrary goal, not as an existing reality. To my knowledge, there is no program which fulfills these requirements fully. In this focus of convenience, I have arbitrarily selected change agents working on organizational dynamics partly because of my greater familiarity with their work but also because they seem to fulfill the criteria outlined to a greater extent than do other change agents. My choice of emphasis is also based on the belief that changes in the sphere of organizations—primarily industrial—in patterns of work and relationship, structure, technology, and administration promise some of the most significant changes in our society. Indeed it is my guess that industrial society, at least in the United States, is more radical, innovative, and adventurous in adapting new ways of organizing than the government, the universities, and the labor unions, who appear rigid and stodgy in the face of rapid change. If space permitted, however, I would refer also to change agents working in a variety of fields—rural sociology, economics, anthropology—and in such settings as communities, hospitals, cultural-change programs.[6]

Let us turn now to some of the "traditional" models of knowledge utilization.

It is possible to identify eight types of change programs if we examine their strategic rationale: exposition and propagation, élite corps, human relations training, staff, scholarly consultations, circulation of ideas to the élite, developmental research, and action research.

I should like to look at each of these programs quickly and then refer to four biases which seem to me to weaken their impact.

Exposition and propagation, perhaps the most popular type of program, assumes that knowledge is power. It follows that the men who possess "Truth" will lead the world.

Élite corps programs grow from the realization that ideas by themselves do not constitute action and that a strategic *role* is a necessity for ideas to be implemented (e.g., through getting scientists into government as C. P. Snow suggests).

Human relations training programs are similar to the élite corps idea in the attempt to translate behavioral science concepts in such ways that they take on personal referents for the men in power positions.

Staff programs provide a source of intelligence within the client system, as in the work of social anthropologists advising military governors after World War II. The strategy of the staff idea is to observe, analyze, and to plan rationally (Myrdal, 1958).

Scholarly consultation, as defined by Zetterberg (1962), includes exploratory inquiry, scholarly understanding, confrontation, discovery of solutions, and scientific advice to client.

Circulation of ideas to the élite builds on the simple idea of influencing change by getting to the people with power or influence.

Developmental research has to do with seeing whether an idea can be brought to an engineering stage. Unlike Zetterberg's scholarly confrontation, it is directed toward a particular problem, not necessarily a client, and is concerned with implementation and program. (I would wager that *little* developmental research is being done today in the behavioral sciences.)

Action research, the term coined by Kurt Lewin, undertakes to solve a problem for a client. It is identical to applied research generally except that in action research the roles of researcher and subject may change and reverse, the subjects becoming researchers and the researchers engaging in action steps.

These eight programs, while differing in objectives, values, means of influence, and program implications, are similar in wanting to use knowledge to gain some socially desirable end. Each seems successful or promising; each has its supporters and its detractors. Intrinsic to them all, I believe, is some bias or flaw which probably weakens their full impact. Four biases are particularly visible.

Most of the strategies rely almost totally on rationality. But knowledge

---

[6] For a fuller exposition of these ideas, see my paper, "A New Role for the Behavioral Sciences: Effecting Organizational Change." *Administrative Sci. Quart.,* 1963, 8, 125–165.

about something does *not* lead automatically to intelligent action. Intelligent action requires commitment and programs as well as truth.

Change typically involves risk and fear. Any significant change in human organization involves rearrangement of patterns of power, association, status, skills, and values. Some may benefit, others may lose. Thus change typically involves risk and fear. Yet change efforts sometimes are conducted as if there were no need to discuss and "work through" these fears and worries (e.g., F. W. Taylor's failure to consider the relationship between the engineer with the stopwatch and the worker, or Freud's early work when he considered it adequate to examine the unconscious of his patients and tell them what he learned—even to the extent on occasion of analyzing dreams by mail).

This refers to strategies which rely on the individual while denying the organizational forces and roles surrounding him. There is, however, simply no guarantee that a wise individual who attains power will act wisely. It may be that *role corrupts*—both the role of power and the role of powerlessness. In any event, there is no guarantee that placing certain types of people in management—or training them or psychoanalyzing them or making scientists of them—leads to more effective action. Scientists act like administrators when they gain power. And graduates of human relations training programs tend to act like non-alumni shortly after their return to their organizational base.

The staff idea, proposed by Myrdal, is limited by the unresolved tensions in the staff-line dilemma noted by students of organizational behavior and by the conflicts derived from the role of the intellectual working in bureaucratic structures. The élite strategy has serious drawbacks, primarily because it focuses on the individual and not the organization.

My major quarrel here is not with the formulation: insight leads to change, though this can be challenged, but with the lack of provision of variables accessible to control. It is not obvious that insight leads directly to sophistication in rearranging social systems or making strategic organizational interventions. Insight provides the relevant variables for planned change as far as personal manipulation goes, but the question remains: How can that lead directly to the manipulation of external factors?

In the October 7, 1963, edition of the *New York Times,* a classified ad announced a search for change agents. It read:

What's a Change Agent? A result-oriented individual able to accurately and quickly resolve complex tangible and intangible problems. Energy and ambition necessary for success. . . .

The change agents I have in mind need more than "energy and ambition." They are *professionals* who, for the most part, hold doctorates in the behavioral sciences. They are not a very homogeneous group, but they do have some similarities.

They are alike in that they take for granted the *centrality of work* in our culture to men and women in highly organized instrumental settings; in their concern with improvement, development, and measurement of *organizational effectiveness;* in their *preoccupation with people* and the process of human interaction; in their interest in changing the relationships, perceptions, and values of *existing personnel.* They may be members of the client system, arguing that inside knowledge is needed, or external agents, arguing that perspective, detachment, and energy from outside are needed. They intervene at different structural points in the organization and at different times.

Though each change agent has in mind a set of unique goals based on his own theoretical position and competencies as well as the needs of the client system, there are some general aims. In a paradigm developed by Chris Argyris (1962), bureaucratic values tend to stress the rational, task aspects of work and to ignore the basic human factors which, if ignored, tend to reduce task competence. Managers brought up under this system of values are badly cast to play the intricate human roles now required of them. Their ineptitude and anxieties lead to systems of discord and defense which interfere with the problem-solving capacity of the organization.

Generally speaking, the normative goals of change agents derive from this paradigm. They include: improving interpersonal competence of managers; effecting a change in values so that human factors and feelings come to be considered legitimate; developing increased understanding among and within working groups to reduce tensions; developing "team management"; developing better methods of "conflict resolution" than suppression, denial, and the use of unprincipled power; viewing the organization as an organic system of relationships marked by mutual trust, interdependence, multigroup membership, shared responsibility, and conflict resolution through training or problem solving.

Discussion here will focus on three broad types of change programs that seem to be most widely used, frequently in some combination: training, consultation, and research. Training is an inadequate word in this context, as its dictionary meaning denotes "drill" and "exercise." I refer to what has been called laboratory training, sensitivity or group dynamics training, and most commonly, T-Group training.[7] The idea originated in Bethel,

Maine, under the guidance of Leland Bradford, Kenneth Benne, and Ronald Lippitt, with initial influence from the late Kurt Lewin. The T-Group has evolved since 1947 into one of the main instruments for organizational change. Bradford has played a central role in this development as director of the National Training Laboratories. Growth has been facilitated through the active participation of a number of university-based behavioral scientists and practitioners. Tavistock Institute has played a similar role in England, and recently a group of European scientists set up a counterpart to the National Training Laboratories.

The main objective at first was *personal change* or *self-insight*. Since the fifties the emphasis has shifted to *organizational development,* a more precise date being 1958, when the Esso Company inaugurated a series of laboratories at refineries over the country under the leadership of Blake and Shepard (Shepard, 1960).

Briefly, laboratory training unfolds in an unstructured group setting where participants examine their interpersonal relationships. By examining data generated by themselves, members attempt to understand the dynamics of group behavior, e.g., decision processes, leadership and influence, norms, roles, communication distortions, effects of authority on behavioral patterns, coping mechanisms. T-Group composition is itself a strategic issue. Thus the organization may send an executive to a "stranger laboratory" which fills a "seeding" function; "cousin laboratories" may be conducted for persons of similar rank and occupational responsibilities within the company but from different functional groups; "diag-

---

[7] For a popular account of laboratory training, see Argyris, C. "T-Groups for Organizational Effectiveness." *Harvard Bus. Rev.,* 1964, 42, 60–74. For a theoretical background, see Bradford, L. P., Gibb, J. R., & Benne, K. D. (eds.) *T-Group Theory and Laboratory Method.* New York: Wiley, 1964; and Schein, E. H., & Bennis, W. G. *Personal and Organizational Change via Group Methods.* New York: Wiley, 1965.

onal slices" may be composed of persons of different rank but not in the same work group or in direct relationship; and "family laboratories" may be conducted for functional groups. The more the training groups approach a "family," the more the total organization is affected.

The change agent *qua* consultant, perhaps best exemplified in the work of the Tavistock Institute, operates in a manner very like the practicing physician or psychoanalyst: that is, he starts from the chief "presenting symptom" of the client, articulates it in such a way that causal and underlying mechanisms of the problem are understood, and then takes remedial action. Heavy emphasis is placed on the strategy of *role model* because the main instrument is the change agent himself. Sofer (1961) reveals this when he suggests that psychotherapy or some form of clinical experience is necessary preparation for the change agent. Argyris, as consultant, confronts the group with their behavior toward him as an analogue of their behavior *vis-à-vis* their own subordinates.

If the role of the consultant sounds ambiguous and vague, this probably reflects reality. Certainly in the consultant approach the processes of change and the change agent's interventions are less systematic and less programmed than in training or applied research programs. A word about the latter.

I refer here to research in which the results are used systematically as an *intervention*. Most methods of research application collect information and report it. Generally, the relationship ends there. In the survey-feedback approach, as developed primarily by Floyd Mann (1957) and his associates at The University of Michigan's Institute for Social Research, this is only the beginning. Data are reported in "feedback" meetings where subjects become clients and have a chance to review the findings, test them

against their own experience, and even ask the researchers to test some of their hypotheses. Instead of being submitted "in triplicate" and probably ignored, research results serve to activate involvement and participation in the planning, collection, analysis, and interpretation of more data.

Richard Beckhard, too, utilizes data as the first step in his work as change agent (in press). In his procedure the data are collected through formal, nonstructured interviews which he then codes by themes about the managerial activities of the client for discussion at an off-site meeting with the subjects.

It should be stressed that most planned-change inductions involve all three processes—training, consulting, researching—and that both agent and client play a variety of roles. The final shape of the change agent's role is not as yet clear, and it is hazardous to report exactly what change agents do on the basis of their reports. Many factors, of course, determine the particular intervention the change agent may choose: cost, time, degree of collaboration required, state of target system, and so on.

More often than not, change agents fail to report their strategy or to make it explicit. It may be useful to look at two quite different models that are available: one developed by Robert Blake in his "Managerial Grid" system, and one with which I was associated at an Esso refinery and which Chris Argyris evaluated some years later.

Blake has developed a change program based on his analytic framework of managerial styles (Blake, Mouton, Barnes, & Greiner, 1964). Figure 1 shows the grid for locating types of managerial strategies. Blake and his colleagues attempt to change the organization in the direction of "team management" (9, 9 or high concern for people and high concern for production). Based on experience with 15

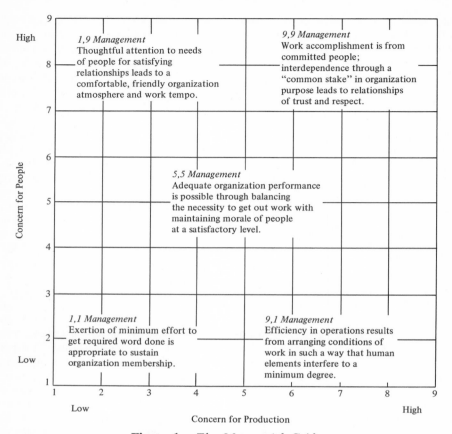

Figure 1. *The Managerial Grid.*

different factories, the Blake strategy specifies six phases: off-site laboratory for "diagonal slice" of personnel; off-site program focused on team training for "family" groups; training in the plant location designed to achieve better integration between functional groups; goal-setting sessions for groups of 10 to 12 managers.

Blake and his colleagues estimate that these four phases may require two years or longer. The next two, implementing plans and stabilizing changes, may require an additional two years.

Figure 2 (Argyris, 1960) presents another strategy: a change program used in a large oil company to improve the func-

tioning of one of its smaller refineries. A new manager was named and set to a T-Group training session to gain awareness of the human problems in the refinery. The Headquarters Organizational Development staff then conducted a diagnosis through a survey and interview of the managerial staff (70) and a sample of hourly employees (40/350). About that time the author was brought in to help the headquarters staff and the new manager.

It was decided that a laboratory program of T-Groups might be effective but premature, with the result that weekly seminars that focused on new develop-

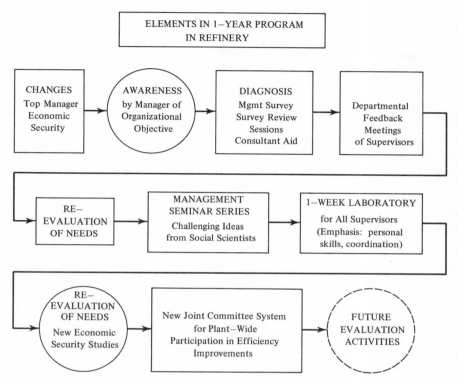

Figure 2. *A Change Program.*

ments in human relations were held with top management (about 20). A one-week laboratory training program followed for all supervisors in diagonal slices, and then another re-evaluation of needs was undertaken. Some structural innovations were suggested and implemented. During the last phase of the program (not shown in the figure), the Scanlon Plan was adapted and installed (incidentally, for the first time in a "process" industry and for the first time that a union agreed to the Plan without a bonus automatically guaranteed).

Though it cannot be said with any assurance that these two strategies are typical, it may be helpful to identify certain features: (a) *length of time* (Blake estimates five years; the refinery program took two years up to the Scanlon Plan); (b) *variety of programs* utilized (research, consulting, training, teaching planning); (c) *necessity of cooperation* with top management and the parent organization; (d) approaching the organization *as a system* rather than as a collection of individuals; (e) *phasing program* from individual to group to intergroup to over-all organization; (f) intellectual *and* emotional content. How and why do people and organizations change, and what is the nature and source of the power exerted by the change agent? We have to make inferences because change agents themselves tend to be silent on this. It is not *coercive power*, for the change agent generally does not have the ability to reward or punish. Moreover, he would prefer, at least intellectually, not to wield power at variance with his normative goals. Further, there is some evidence that coercive power is less durable than are other kinds of power, except under conditions of vigilant surveillance.

Traditional power? Almost certainly not. The change agent is, in fact, continually working without legitimization. *Expert power?* Possibly some, but it is doubtful whether his knowledge is considered "expert" enough—in the sense that an engineer or doctor or lawyer is seen as expert. *Referent* or *identification power?* Apparently so. Sofer, for example, attributes some influence to the client system's ability and desire to emulate the change agent. Still, this will vary from a considerable degree to not at all.

This leaves us with *value power* as the likeliest candidate of the possible sources of power. Most change agents do emit cues to a consistent value system. These values are based on Western civilization's notion of a scientific humanism: concern for our fellow man, experimentalism, openness and honesty, flexibility, cooperation, democracy. If what I have said about power is correct, it is significant (at least in the United States) that this set of values seems to be potent in influencing top management circles.

For the most part, the client systems appear to be subsystems of relatively large-scale international operations who find themselves in increasingly competitive situations, in rapidly changing environments, subjected to what have been called "galloping variables." Often the enterprise was founded through an innovation or monopolistic advantage which is thought to be in jeopardy.

Then there is some tension—some discrepancy between the ideal and the actual —which seem to activate the change program.

Finally, there is some faith in the idea that an intermediate proportion of organizational effectiveness is determined by social and psychological factors and that improvement here, however vague or immeasurable, may improve organizational effectiveness.

Until very recently, change agents, if they did any evaluation research at all, concentrated almost exclusively on attitudinal and subjective factors. Even so-called "hard" behavioral variables, like absentee rates, sickness and accident rates, personnel turnover, and so forth, were rarely investigated. Relating change programs to harder criteria, like productivity and economic and cost factors, was rarely attempted and never, to my knowledge, successful.

And again, the research that was conducted—even on the attitudinal measures —was far from conclusive. Roger Harrison attempted an evaluation study of Argyris' work and found that while there was a significant improvement in the individual executive's interpersonal ability compared with a control group, there was no significant "transfer" of this acuity to the real-life organizational setting. In short, there was a fairly rapid "fade-out" of effects obtained in T-Group training upon return to the organization (Harrison, 1962). This study also shows that new tensions were generated between those individuals who attended the training program and those who did not—an example of the lack of a *systems* approach. Shepard's evaluation on the Esso organization shows that the impact of laboratory training was greatest on personal and interpersonal learnings, but "slightly more helpful than useless" in changing the organization.

More recently, though, some studies have been undertaken which measure more meaningful, less subjective variables of organizational effectiveness. Blake, Mouton, Barnes, and Greiner (1964), for example, conducted an evaluation study of their work in a very large (4,000 employees) petrochemical plant. Not only did they find significant changes in the values, morale, and interpersonal behavior of the employees, but significant improvements in productivity, profits, and cost reduction. David (in press), a change agent working on a program that attempts to facilitate a large and complicated merger, attributed the following effects to the programs: increased productivity, reduced turnover and absenteeism, in addition to a significant improvement in the area of attitudes and subjective feelings.

While these new research approaches show genuine promise, much more has to be done. The research effort has somehow to equal all the energy that goes into developing the planned-change programs themselves.

The work of the change agents reported here is new and occurs without the benefit of methodological and strategic precedents. The role of the change agent is also new, its final shape not fully emerged. Thus it has both the advantage of freedom from the constraints facing most men of knowledge, and suffers from lack of guidelines and structure. Let us touch quickly on problems and criticisms facing the change agents.

I can identify six dimensions of organizational effectiveness: legal, political, economic, technological, social, and personal. There is a good deal of fuzziness as to which of these change agents hope to affect, and the data are inconclusive. Argyris, who is the most explicit about the relationship between performance and interpersonal competence, is still hoping to develop good measures to establish a positive relationship. The connection has to be made, or the field will have to change its normative goal of constructing not only a *better* world but a more *effective* one.

The values espoused indicate a way of *behaving and feeling;* for example, they emphasize openness rather than secrecy, collaboration rather than dependence or rebellion, cooperation rather than competition, consensus rather than individual rules, rewards based on self-control rather than externally induced rewards, team leadership rather than a one-to-one relationship with the boss, authentic relationships rather than those based on political maneuvering.

Are they natural? Desirable? Functional? What then happens to status or power drives? What about those individuals who have a low need for participation and/or a high need for structure and dependence? And what about those personal needs which seem to be incompatible with these images of man, such as a high need for aggression and a low need for affiliation? In short, what about those needs which can be best realized through bureaucratic systems? Or benevolent autocracies? Are these individuals to be changed or to yield and comply?

The problem of values deserves discussion. One of the obstacles is the emotional and value overtones which interfere with rational dialogue. More often than not, one is plunged into a polarized debate which converts ideas into ideology and inquiry into dogma. So we hear of "Theory X vs. Theory Y," personality vs. organization, democratic vs. autocratic, task vs. maintenance, human relations vs. scientific management, and on and on.

Surely life is more complicated than these dualities suggest, and surely they must imply a continuum—not simply extremes.

Up to this point, I have used the term "organizational change" rather loosely. In Argyris' case, for example, organizational change refers to a change in values of 11 top executives, a change which was not necessarily of an enduring kind and apparently brought about some conflict with other interfaces. In most other cases of planned organizational change, the change induction was limited to a small, élite group. Only in the work of Blake and some others can we confidently talk about organizational change—in a systems way; his program includes the training of the entire management organization, and at several locations he has carried this step to include wage earners.

Sometimes the changes brought about simply "fade out" because there are no carefully worked out procedures to ensure coordination with other interacting parts of the system. In other cases, the changes have "backfired" and have had to be terminated because of their conflict with interface units. In any case, a good deal more has to be learned about the interlocking and stabilizing changes so that the total system is affected.

It may be useful, as peroration, to state in the most tentative manner some generalizations. They are derived, for the most part, from the foregoing discussion and anchored in experience and, wherever possible, in research and theory.

First, a forecast: I suspect that we will see an increase in the number of planned-change programs along the lines discussed here—toward *less* bureaucratic and *more* participative, "open system" and adaptive structures. Given the present pronounced rate of change, the growing reliance on science for the success of the industrial enterprise, the growing number of professionals joining these enterprises, and the "turbulent contextual environment" facing the firm, we can expect increasing demand for social inventions to revise traditional notions of organized effort.

As far as adopting and acceptance go, we already know a good deal.[8] *Adoption* requires that the *type* of change should be of proven quality, easily demonstrable in its effects, and with information easily

available. Its cost and accessibility to control by the client system as well as its value accord have to be carefully considered.

Acceptance also depends on the relationship between the change agent and the client system: the more profound and anxiety-producing the change, the more collaborative and closer relationship required. In addition, we can predict that an anticipated change will be resisted to the degree that the client system possesses little or incorrect knowledge about the change, has relatively little trust in the source of the change, and has comparatively low influence in controlling the nature and direction of the change.

What we know least about is *implementation*—a process which includes the creation of understanding and commitment toward a particular change and devices whereby it can become integral to the client system's operations. I will try to summarize the necessary elements in implementation:

(a) The *client system* should have as much understanding of the change and its consequences, as much influence in developing and controlling the fate of the change, and as much trust in the initiator of the change as is possible.

(b) The *change effort* should be perceived as being as self-motivated and voluntary as possible. This can be effected through the legitimization and reinforcement of the change by the top management group and by the significant reference groups adjacent to the client system. It is also made possible by providing the utmost in true volition.

(c) The *change program* must include emotional and value as well as cognitive

---

[8] See, in particular, Rogers, E. *The Diffusion of Innovations.* New York: Free Press, 1962; and Miles, M. (ed.) *Innovation in Education.* New York: Bureau of Publications, Teachers College, Columbia Univer., 1964.

(informational) elements for successful implementation. It is doubtful that relying solely on rational persuasion (expert power) is sufficient. Most organizations possess the knowledge to cure their ills; the rub is utilization.

(d) The *change agent* can be crucial in reducing the resistance to change. As long as the change agent acts congruently with the principles of the program and as long as the client has a chance to test competence and motives (his own and the change agent's), the agent should be able to provide the psychological support so necessary during the risky phases of change. As I have stressed again and again, the quality of the client-agent relationship is pivotal to the success of the change program.

References

Ackoff, R. L., & Rivett, P. *A Manager's Guide to Operations Research.* New York: Wiley, 1963, p. 34.

Argyris, C. *Organization Development: An Inquiry into the Esso Approach.* New Haven: Yale Univer., 1960.

Argyris, C. *Interpersonal Competence and Organizational Effectiveness.* Homewood, Ill.: Dorsey, 1962, p. 43.

Beckhard, R. "An Organization Improvement Program in a Decentralized Organization," in D. Zand (ed.), *Organization Development: Theory and Practice,* in press.

Bennis, W. G., Benne, K. D., & Chin, R. (eds.). *The Planning of Change.* New York: Holt, Rinehart & Winston, 1961.

Blake, R. R., Mouton, Jane S., Barnes, L. B., & Grenier, L. E. "Breakthrough in Organization Development." *Harvard Bus. Rev.,* Vol. 42, No. 6, 1964, pp. 133–155.

Boskoff, A. "Functional Analysis As a Source of a Theoretical Repertory and Research Tasks in the Study of Social Change," in G. K. Zollschan & W. Hirsch, *Explorations in Social Change.* Boston: Houghton Mifflin, 1964.

Chin, R. "The Utility of System Models and Developmental Models for Practitioners," in W. G. Bennis, K. D. Benne, & R. Chin (eds.), *The Planning of Change.* New York: Holt, Rinehart & Winston, 1961, pp. 201–214.

Chin, R. "Models and ideas about changing." Paper read at Symposium on Acceptance of New Ideas, Univer. of Nebraska, November, 1963.

Coser, L. *The Functions of Social Conflict.* New York: Free Press, 1956.

Dahrendorf, R. "Toward a Theory of Social Conflict," in W. G. Bennis, K. D. Benne, & R. Chin (eds.), *The Planning of Change.* New York: Holt, Rinehart & Winston, 1961, pp. 445–451.

David, G. "The Weldon Study: An Organization Change Program Based upon Change in Management Philosophy," in D. Zand (ed.), *Organization Development: Theory and Practice,* in press.

Freeman, H. E. "The Strategy of Social Policy Research." *The Soc. Welf. Forum,* 1963, pp. 143–160.

Gibb, J. R., & Lippitt, R. (eds.). "Consulting with Groups and Organizations." *J. Soc. Issues,* 1959, 15.

Glock, C. Y., Lippitt, R., Flanagan, J. C., Wilson, E. C., Shartle, C. L., Wilson, M. L., Croker, G. W., & Page, H. E. *Case Studies in Bringing Behavioral Science into Use.* Stanford, Calif.: Inst. Commun. Res., 1960.

Harrison, R. in C. Argyris, *Interpersonal Competence and Organizational Effectiveness.* Homewood, Ill.: Dorsey, 1962. Chapter 11.

Leeds, R., & Smith, T. (eds.). *Using Social Science Knowledge in Business and Industry.* Homewood, Ill.: Irwin, 1963.

Likert, R., & Hayes, S. P., Jr. (eds.). *Some Applications of Behavioral Research.* Paris: UNESCO, 1957.

Mann, F. "Studying and Creating Change: A Means to Understanding Social Organization." *Research in Industrial Relations.* Ann Arbor: Industr. Relat. Res. Ass., 1957, Publication No. 17..

Merton, R. K., & Lerner, D. "Social Scientists and Research Policy," in D. Lerner & H. D. Lasswell (eds.), *The Policy Sciences: Recent Developments in Scope and Method.* Stanford, Calif.: Stanford Univer. Press, 1951.

Myrdal, G. *Value in Social Theory.* New York: Harper, 1958, p. 29.

Parsons, R. T. "Evolutionary Universals in Society." *Amer. Sociol. Rev.,* 1964, 29, 339–357.

Salisbury, H. E. *To Moscow and Beyond.* New York: Harper, 1960, p. 136.

Shepard, H. "Three Management Programs and the Theory Behind Them," in *An Action Research Program for Organization Improvement.* Ann Arbor: Foundation for Research on Human Behavior, 1960.

Sofer, C. *The Organization from Within.* London: Tavistock, 1961.

Zetterberg, H. L. *Social Theory and Social Practice.* Totowa, N. J.: Bedminster, 1962.

C

MOTIVATION

22. Motivation for Productivity

HERBERT G. ZOLLITSCH

The secret of how to motivate people to work as efficiently as they are capable is a problem as old and as complex as society. There are no universal or simple answers. There are only theories and principles which need to be individually applied in much the same manner that a physician cures each patient of his illness.

The need to motivate employees to greater productivity is everywhere about us. It is the general belief of many industrial engineers that day workers (those being paid on the basis of a time unit, like an hour or a week) are generally not strongly motivated and thus they exert only a minimum degree of effort on their jobs. This minimum effort produces only about one half of what they are capable of producing. Incentive workers (those being paid on the basis of their output or pieces produced) are more strongly motivated and generally exert a medium degree of effort to produce from one third to one half more than the day worker.[1] This means that day workers, who are not fully motivated, do not produce as much as incentive workers who are strongly motivated.

Reprinted from *Proceedings of the 7th Annual Midwest Management Conference*. Carbondale, Ill.: Business Research Bureau, Southern Illinois University, 1964, pp. 63–68, with permission of the author and the publisher. Herbert G. Zollitsch is Professor and Chairman, Department of Industrial Management, Robert A. Johnston College of Business Administration, Marquette University.

[1] Langsner and Zollitsch. *Wage and Salary Administration*. Cincinnati: South-Western Publishing Co., 1961, pp. 520–521.

It has been said that people are the main difference in plants which have varying degrees of production. The emphasis has been placed on people as the key factor because it is through people that new machines, methods, and increased productivity is accomplished. Most all well established companies have enough money to buy the same machines, materials, and other facilities needed to produce products. The real difference in companies then is the effectiveness or efficiency of the workers. Much of the effectiveness of both the workers and their companies is due to the degree that the workers are motivated.

Since it was indicated earlier that there are no fixed or standard solutions to this problem, any more than there is a standard remedy for the common cold, this paper will attempt to present an overall picture, or frame of reference, relating motivation to productivity. The attempt will identify the main factors that researchers have indicated have a bearing on productivity. Some guidelines through which the factors may be better utilized to produce greater motivation and greater productivity will then be suggested.

Productivity has generally been understood to mean the amount of output per employee per unit of time. It is considered one of the more important business goals of a firm in the United States today because when productivity increases at a greater rate than the population, the standard of living rises. The rapid rise in population in the United States has emphasized the need to increase productivity. The American labor movement is dedicated to the continual advancement of the worker's standard of living. Management is dedicated to increased productivity because this can result in lower prices.

Thus, there are many valid reasons for increasing productivity.

Basic Factors Affecting Productivity

If we think of productivity as one of the main targets or goals in business we could say that there are two broad factors that affect production, namely: the technical factor and the human factor. The technical factor includes those facilities which may be available to workers to increase their efficiency and output such as: tools, machines, materials, methods, etc. The technical factors have been reported to be responsible for increases of productivity up to 200 percent.[2] The human factor refers to the job performance of every employee in a company. Employees may be highly efficient, highly inefficient or somewhere in-between.

Productivity then is a result of these two factors, either of which may be the more important in a given situation. It would appear that, generally, employee job performance is the more influential factor on productivity in companies where manual work predominates. The technical factor, however, becomes more influential as mechanization and automation become predominant. In this paper we are primarily concerned with the human factor. We are concerned with the improvement of the employee's job performance through motivation so that productivity in turn is increased.

If we examine the employee's job performance we could say that it is based on two sub-factors, motivation and ability (assuming his tools and facilities are adequate). An employee who has little or no ability cannot be expected to produce

---

[2] Argyle, Gardner, Cioffi. "Supervisory Methods Related to Productivity, Absenteeism, and Labor Turnover." *Human Relations.* Vol. 11, No. 1, 1958, p. 24.

much or to increase his productivity. For the moment, let us assume he has ability and is capable of increasing productivity. This leaves motivation then as a key factor in increasing employee job performance and productivity.

Factors Affecting Motivation

If we continue our analytical approach to the subject, we could say that the positive or negative motivation of employees is related to and dependent upon three interacting forces: (a) the physical conditions present in the factory, (b) the basic needs of each worker, and (c) the social conditions present in the factory. Each of these forces will now be discussed.

A. FACTORY PHYSICAL CONDITIONS

Fifty years ago in the industrial management movement in the United States, it was commonly believed by industrial engineers and psychologists that the physical conditions in a factory (such as ventilation, lighting, safety, etc.) were a key factor in motivating employees to increased production. This belief continued until the Hawthorne plant studies of the Western Electric Company in Chicago, Illinois, failed to show any significant relationship between physical conditions and rate of output.[3] This does not mean that physical working conditions can be ignored by management but rather that if poor physical conditions are unavoidable, the worker is likely to produce as well as if he had better conditions—as long as he believes that management has done the best it can to provide him with good physical conditions. Good physical working conditions today in the United States are the rule rather than the exception. This means that satisfactory physical conditions are pretty much taken for granted and therefore generally have little motivating force.[4] The Hawthorne studies revealed also that the subjective feelings of the employees and the way they view things appeared to influence motivation. Employee feelings are related to the basic needs of the individual. These will be discussed next.

B. MAN'S BASIC NEEDS

Satisfying man's individual needs and desires has long been considered one method of motivating employees. One of the assumptions of personnel management is that if the management of a company can help workers satisfy their needs the workers, in turn, are more likely to reciprocate and help the management meet the goals of the company. A popular theory of human motivation based on man's needs is the Maslow theory.[5]

The Maslow theory groups all of man's needs into five basic categories: physiological, safety, love, esteem, and self-actualization. Because of the limited time available, we shall consider physiological and safety needs combined under physiological; love as a social need; and esteem and self-actualization under egoistic needs.

---

[3] Mayo, Elton. *The Human Problems of Industrial Civilization.* New York: Macmillan Co., 1933; Whitehead, T. N. *The Industrial Worker.* Cambridge: Harvard University Press, 1938, 2 Vols.; and Roethlisberger and Dickson. *Management and the Worker.* Cambridge: Harvard University Press, 1939.

[4] Sutermeister, Robert A. *People and Productivity.* New York: McGraw-Hill Book Company, 1963, p. 12. (This book was used as a reference for the organizational framework of the concepts expressed in this paper.)

[5] Maslow, A. H. "A Theory of Human Motivation." *Psychological Review.* Vol. 50, 1943, pp. 370–376.

Physiological needs may be thought of as those very basic needs of self-preservation such as food, clothing, shelter, air, water, and the like. These necessities are mainly achieved through money and security on the job. They must at least be partially fulfilled before a person gives much thought to any other needs. As the physiological needs are fulfilled, a person tends to place increasing emphasis on the social and egoistic needs. In the United States about 80% of those persons who are employed are likely to have their physiological needs well satisfied. A satisfied need does not motivate behavior.[6] We cannot assume, therefore, that more pay or more security will automatically lead to improved job performance. In fact, they may provide very little motivation because the struggle to satisfy subsistence needs has been won.[7] On the other hand, if higher pay fulfills an egoistic need for recognition and status, it could lead to greater job performance. When pay and security are adequate to satisfy physiological needs, management should turn its attention to the social and egoistic needs of the employees, if the employees are to be motivated to improved job performance.

Social needs are represented by man's desire to "belong" and to "be accepted" by others. Social needs include such group needs as friendship, identification with the group, teamwork, helping others and being helped.[8] Social needs are satisfied by contacts with others such as with fellow employees, the union representatives,

management personnel, and friends on and off the job. No doubt many employees have their social needs already satisfied off the job. When this is true, further satisfaction of the social needs on the job is not likely to serve as a strong motivator.

Egoistic needs are those which enable a person to be highly satisfied with himself. Man wants to achieve status, be respected, be honored or recognized, and be a master of something. To maintain a high estimate of ourselves, most of us regularly need reassurance that we are held in esteem by others.[9] This means that we continue to seek daily satisfaction of our egoistic needs, in spite of the fact that they may have been satisfied quite well the day before. This differentiates egoistic needs from physiological and social needs which, when satisfied, cease to motivate. Many people feel that the physiological and social needs are largely satisfied when a person has a job (at least in the United States). The continuing satisfaction of egoistic needs, then, would seem to offer the best opportunity to motivate employees to better job performance.

The Maslow theory of human motivation described above has many adherents. However, in the last five years or so there has been a great deal of theorizing, experimentation and research which would appear to indicate that when man's individual needs are satisfied, he is not necessarily motivated to perform better on the job.[10] The research studies at the University of Michigan (Survey Research Cen-

---

[6] McGregor, Douglas. *The Human Side of Enterprise.* New York: McGraw-Hill Book Co., Inc., 1960, p. 36.

[7] Zaleznik, Christenson, and Roethlisberger. *Motivation, Productivity, and Satisfaction of Workers.* Cambridge: Harvard Business School, Division of Research, 1958.

[8] Strauss and Sayles. *Personnel: The Human Problems of Management.* Englewood Cliffs: Prentice-Hall, Inc., 1960, p. 8.

[9] Sutermeister, p. 14.

[10] Argyris, C. "Employee Apathy and Non-Involvement: The House That Management Built." *Personnel.* Vol. 38, No. 4, pp. 8–14.

ter) failed to prove that a high level of job satisfaction (or morale) assured high productivity.[11] On the other hand, it appears safe to assume that the chances of improving employee performance and increasing productivity are greater when man's needs are being satisfied than when they are not (other things being equal).

On the surface, the Maslow theory appears a reasonable approach to motivation of an employee, however, it can be a complex method because of the numerous factors that affect the individual's needs. For example, if a worker doesn't have much ambition or a personal goal, he isn't likely to be motivated by any approach. If the group the worker is a member of has radically different goals than the worker's goals, the pressure of the group may greatly affect his motivation. Likewise, education, training, and cultural background may influence the degree of motivation. Whether the worker is a man or woman also affects the person's perspective. It should be apparent then, that although man's individual needs can be a source of motivating him, the satisfaction of his needs are only a part of the total motivating process. It is only within the last decade that the influences of the social conditions present in the factory have received close attention. A brief account of these influences will now be made to round out the overall picture of motivation.

C. SOCIAL CONDITIONS IN THE FACTORY

The major factors present in the factory which establish the social conditions in the factory are the *company leaders,* the *formal* and *informal organization* of the plant, and the influence of the *Union* (if one exists). The *company leaders* set the tone of employee-employer relations by an acknowledgement (or lack of it) of company responsibilities and employee responsibilities. The leaders have to be of whatever type (autocratic, democratic, or other) that is needed to get the most from the type of persons employed. They have to have the ability to plan well and to establish rapport with their employees if employees are to be spurred on to greater performance and productivity.

The company leaders need to consider the organizational efficiency of the plant. This calls for some degree of *formal organization* in which company goals, job duties, responsibilities, standards of performance and company policies are formally established and communicated. Highly important to the motivation of employees are the personnel policies of the company. These policies need to be such that they will result in attracting, selecting, hiring, training, motivating, rewarding and retaining competent employees.

Every organization has an *informal structure* which influences the performance of the employees. By informal organization is meant the relationships the employee encounters in his work which are not formally planned as such. In other words, most every employee is influenced by the daily contacts he has with individuals and various groups. These individuals and groups have their own goals, ambitions, needs, satisfactions and interests. They may be in harmony or in conflict with those of an individual employee. These associations and influences cannot help but affect the motivation and job performance of every employee. Where informal organizations or groups exist with effective control over their members, the problem for manage-

---

[11] Kahn, R. L. "Productivity and Job Satisfaction." *Personnel Psychology.* Vol. 13, 1960, pp. 275–287.

ment is clear. If it wishes to change human behavior, its attack must be made through the group.[12]

If a company has a *union,* its influence on the employee depends to a great extent on the strength of the union. A strong union can be as powerful an influence as management. A strong union can hold down production or help production by accepting or rejecting the technology available along with the human relations involved. Unions can encourage, support, or oppose company policies and goals. When the motivation of employees is tied to the union, the influence of the union needs to be examined and understood.

Summary of Factors Affecting Employee Motivation and Productivity

Productivity depends not only on employee performance but also on the technical factors of production. Employee job performance depends not only on the ability of a person but also on his motivation. The motivation of an employee generally depends very little on the physical working conditions but more so on the social conditions interacting with employee needs. Every employee has basic needs which may differ in importance to each employee. A satisfied need is no motivator of behavior. Egoistic needs appear never to be completely satisfied and so never lose their motivating power. We know the least about the real effects of social conditions as motivators. Much research is also needed in the area of group motivation.

Figure 1 was intended to show the more important factors affecting employee motivation and productivity. These factors are complex and interrelated. It cannot be assumed that a change in a factor in an outer rectangle will directly cause a change in employee performance. More likely, a change in one factor in an outer rectangle would be accompanied by changes in other factors, so that any change in employee job performance (and ultimately in productivity) would be the net result of all the changes occurring throughout Figure 1.

Some Guidelines to Effective Motivation

At the beginning of this paper it was indicated that motivating employees was no simple task and that there are no standard cure-alls. However, before closing, I would like to offer some suggestions which may help make the motivation of employees easier. It would appear that anyone seriously interested in effectively motivating employees needs to do the following:

1. Understand the complicated factors involved.

2. Constantly analyze and be aware of the individual needs of the workers hired and the ever changing state of the conditions which affect motivation and job performance.

3. Communicate the goals of the company and what the worker can expect from a career with the company, and

4. Show sincerity and integrity in carrying out personnel policies which are designed to attract, select, hire, train, motivate, reward and retain competent employees.

---

[12] Brown. *The Social Psychology of Industry.* Baltimore: Penguin Books, Inc., 1954, p. 126.

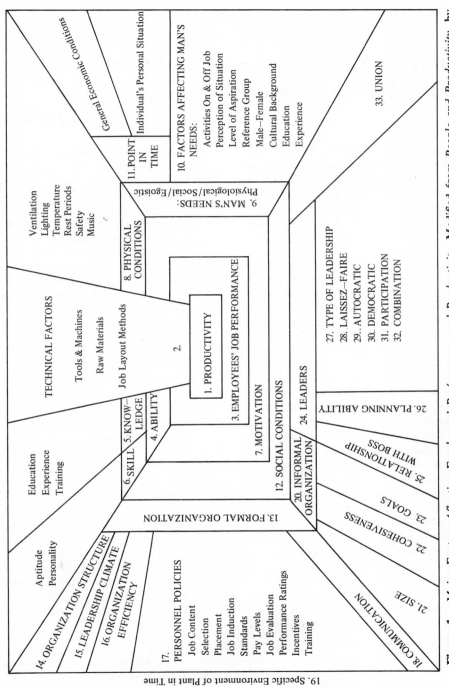

Figure 1. *Major Factors Affecting Employees' Performance and Productivity.* Modified from *People and Productivity,* by R. A. Sutermeister, McGraw-Hill, N. Y., 1963, p. 24.

217

23. It's a Valuable Management Tool, But . . . Motivation Is Not Enough

HAROLD J. LEAVITT

Please don't let the title of this article fool you. When I say motivation is not enough, that's all I mean. It's big, it's important, it's necessary, but it's not enough. The *not enough* part is worth special emphasis only because motivation is so much in the spotlight these days that some of us have come to believe motivation *is* management. I submit that motivation is a large *part* of management. An important part. But not the only part.

When ideas are new and stimulating, as ideas about motivation have been in the last few years, it's understandable that we sometimes run off in all directions. There's a rather well-known case that appeared in the *Journal of Psychosomatic Medicine* back during the war that's apropos here. It was written by a psychiatrist and at that time the notion of *psychosomatic* medicine was even more stimulating in medical circles than the notion of motivation is in management circles today.

The patient described in the case was a woman who complained to her psychiatrist about a series of rashes that showed up on her face every few weeks. Then they would disappear again after a few days. The psychiatrist searched around for a long time to see if she could relate these rashes to any emotional problems. She finally uncovered something.

The patient had a boyfriend who was a traveling salesman. Whenever the boyfriend was in town, the rashes appeared. Shortly after he left town on a trip the rashes disappeared. And that, of course, set the psychiatrist to thinking about tensions and incompatibilities in the relationship between this woman and her boyfriend. Obviously the situation was psychosomatic.

Then, quite by accident, the psychiatrist discovered something else. The girl was allergic to the after-shave lotion her boyfriend used.

Not All Problems Are Motivational

Sometimes we are apt to define all problems of management as problems in motivation when there may be simpler alternative answers. For the past ten years or so, we have been on a strong motivational kick. Perhaps it's been too strong a kick. But remember we are not the only ones to have been oversold on our own ideas. Long before the psychologists appeared on the scene, back in the teens and 20's, there was another group of experts in management, raised in another neomilitary tradition. For them the control problem of management was the logical definition of an organization structure. They were bugged on *scientific man-*

Reprinted from *Stanford Graduate School of Business Bulletin*, Vol. 35, No. 2 (Autumn, 1966), pp. 21–27, with permission of the author and the publisher. Harold J. Leavitt is Walter Kenneth Kilpatrick Professor of Organizational Behavior and Psychology, Graduate School of Business, Stanford University.

agement. Motivation was the farthest thing from their minds. In those days, the preferred way to solve human problems was to go out and find square human beings that could be plugged into the neat square holes that the methods men had so happily laid out on their drawing boards. These draftsmen of organization charts were as oversold on their approach as we motivators are on ours. And ahead of us both we can already see the computer boys beginning to make the same mistakes. Their panacea is information technology. Both organization structures and motivation are old-hat, horse-and-buggy activities to them.

But it's not all bad that experts who have committed themselves to a field often get hooked on their own drugs. Perhaps they should. For by their enthusiasm, their tendency to interpret the world in the light of their ideas, they speed up the development of those ideas and contribute to knowledge. That they are oversold is a danger. Perhaps it is precisely that danger that the manager needs to watch out for. For if staff experts tend to see the world through their own rose-colored glasses, the line manager should not. He, presumably wise and fatherly, can step back and understand the untempered enthusiasms of the bright young men. He should be able to set it in perspective.

If the Experts Differ, Are They All Wrong?

That's what he *should* do. I am afraid that what many managers *do* do is not that. Instead of having wise farsighted views, they are more likely to behave in a way that is even more silly than the behavior of the experts. The manager may be ensconced in his own traditional style of doing things the way he has always done them by the seat of his own pants; con-

vinced that his wisdom and judgment can never be surpassed by the steam drill or the computer. So instead of learning from these hot, energetic stimulating new fields, he is apt to take blind and foolish comfort in the belief that if the experts differ among themselves then obviously they must all be wrong. Then the manager can feel justified in denying them all, and in denying the need to progress and change. But the presence of disagreement is not a license for continuing old ways. It is a license to learn new ones.

So one theme of this article is that the idea of motivation is not enough. But another theme is that each new set of ideas represents a real contribution to managerial knowledge providing the manager with the challenging and important job of tempering, combining, and testing each contribution as it begins to come into the realm of practical application.

Let me go on to push these themes:

Consider the following example: If, as a manager, you have a rather complicated problem you may want to call in a consultant for help. Suppose the problem is a typically hard one: one of your larger units is turning in much poorer results than all your forecasts had predicted.

The Rose-Colored Blinders of Consultant "A"

So you call in the partner in charge of the local office of Company A. A is a reputable, older consulting firm—the largest in town. They contract to take on the problem and send some people out to the unit to collect information.

When they finally come in with a report, you scan it and then turn to the recommendations. They recommend the following: (1) You need tighter controls. (2) Job relationships need to be reorganized and redefined; job descriptions need to be rewritten with greater precision (to get rid of squabbles about overlapping authority). (3) The functional form of organization they now have down there ought to be switched over to a product form. (4) In fact, that unit has grown so big that it ought to go through a partial decentralization itself, with a lot more authority given to the product managers. (5) You need a thorough methods analysis. The number of reports that are being generated now is excessive. There is wasteful duplication of effort and communication. You ought to streamline the organization's procedures. (6) And you may have to move a few people out, too. There is too much fat in the organization, and so on.

If you are a manager with an experimental turn of mind and a pocket full of money, you will decide not to act on this consultant's report yet. You decide, instead, to knock on the door of Company B, another consultant, and obtain a second independent assessment of your problem.

The Rose-Colored Blinders of Consultant "B"

You had gotten to know Firm A by now. You had found that their people were active in the Society of Advancement of Management, and highly experienced in business organization. You note, with some discomfort, that this second firm, Company B, professes different allegiances and displays other pedigrees. This second group is active in the Operations Research Society, and the Institute for Management Sciences. Its experiences in industry really are not as extensive as those of Firm A, but it has done a lot of recent military work, and its senior people all have Ph.D.'s. It looks like a group of whiz kids. But they have cut their hair and they sound reasonable, so you hire them to look into the same problem.

They send their people out to the unit and they, too, come up with a report. But their conclusions are different. Instead of recommending modifications in the *structure* of the organization, they recommend modifications in the *technical* and *analytic* methods being used. They are technologists who think technological improvement is the means to the best of all possible worlds. They want to linear program the inventory control methods being used in that division and to automate the purchasing operation. They want to modify the information flows, so that decisions can be made at different points in the organization and faster. And instead of job descriptions and organization charts as their tools, their pockets are full of computers and long equations. You will have to hire some hot-shot college boys if you want to carry out their recommendations because neither you nor any of your top people can fully understand them.

The Rose-Colored Blinders of Consultant "C"

But if you are really an experimental manager, and if your pockets are really full of gold, and if you don't satisfy easily, you call in the only other consulting firm in town, Company C. Its members are Ph.D. types, too. Their offices aren't very elaborate, either. Their affiliations are different, again. They are members of the American Psychological Association, and/or members of the consultant network of the National Training Laboratories. They are clinical or social psychological types. They don't carry computers in their pockets, or write job descriptions, or draw organization charts. Their favorite tools are the meeting, the discussion, the face-to-face group, and the open-ended interview.

So you hire Company C, and let them

take a look at your difficult unit. And they, too, come in with a report. But their report is different again. Company C argues that the solution to division X's problem lies in changing the attitudes and interrelations of the people in that unit. Morale is low, they say. Apathy is high. People are constricted, anxious, afraid to speak up or take risks. What your organization needs is more *openness*, more *participation*, more *involvement*, more *creativity*.

So C's recommendation is that you work on the *people* end of the problem. They want you to set up a series of "laboratory" training programs, in which you take groups of your people from division X out to a country club for a week at a time to talk things over; to open up valid communication among themselves; to express what they really feel; and to develop much more mutual trust and confidence.

On What Would You Base Your Opinion?

Probably you could go on experimenting, but the board members are giving you strange looks by now, and the people in division X are really up in the air. So you decide to stop there and take a look at what you have. Which of the three firms' recommendations should you follow up? Since you are the manager, we'll leave it to you to answer that question.

Now if we would stop there, some managers would argue that all we have shown is that these three kinds of experts can't agree and that, therefore, there is no use using experts at all. The best thing to do is go back and fly by the seat of your pants the way we always have. Or else just pick the consultant that has the prettiest receptionist.

But remember that you could have made the same argument if you had encountered differences in opinion among experts in other fields. After all, when you build your new house, the gas people argued for gas heat and the electric people argued for electric heat and they couldn't agree between themselves; the only reasonable thing to do then was to throw them both out and go on heating your kitchen with a good old reliable wood-burning stove. And then, while sitting with your feet in the oven, you could at least take comfort in the fact that the old ways were good ways and all these newfangled ideas just made life too complicated.

Is Being Different Being Wrong?

But one can take another, less primitive, view of our consulting example. It's true that the three experts A, B, and C may offer different recommendations. But instead of interpreting the conflict as an excuse to throw all three rascals out, one can argue that they are are all partially right.

First, the fact that you can go and hire three different kinds of firms represents a real advance in the amount of knowledge about management that is available now, as compared to forty years ago. Just as the fact of medical specialists has complicated the world of medicine, the fact of highly specialized people with knowledge in management has complicated the world of management. But while we may bewail the good old days of the general practitioner, most of us also recognize that people seem to live longer now. The debates among surgeons, internists, neurologists and psychiatrists make sensible decisions about our appendixes more likely. So the existence of the structuralists, the technologists, and the people-oriented experts indicate enough knowledge so that debate is possible. They need not mean empty conflict.

Second, it is true that the addition of new fields of knowledge into the managerial library over the last forty years has complicated the manager's job. But some managers greet this enlargement of knowledge a little bit like small children who wish they had lived a thousand years earlier because then their history books would have been thinner.

And third, the fact that our three hypothetical consultants offer three different solutions suggests that maybe there are interactions among the three that are different parts of the same elephant. For if we can solve organizational problems in the A way (by manipulating structure), or the B way (by manipulating technology), or the C way (by working on human relations), then maybe these three are tied together in important ways. Perhaps, that is to say, when one hires the people-oriented consultant C, he will not only change the way the job gets done in the organization but he may at the same time be changing the A part, organization structure, as well. And similarly when we take A's advice, and rewrite job descriptions, it may be that we will not only affect the way jobs are done, but also C's part of the picture, the relationships between people. If we take B's advice, and add a computer, perhaps we will also be changing both our structure and our people, as well as solving the inventory problem.

Synthesis Factor: The Well-Rounded Manager

At precisely this point the manager himself becomes a valuable contributor to progress in the art and science of management. For although each expert wears the blinders of his own special interest and knowledge, the manager does not. It is the manager who can enlighten the expert on the *total* picture. For it is the manager

who can see better than anyone else that when he starts re-designing his organization structure, things also begin to happen on the people side of the system. When he plugs in a new computer, the old, well-defined structure begins to totter and creak. It is the manager who knows that when he modifies his organizational system from any of the three positions, A or B or C, bells will begin to ring and lights will go on in lots of places that each consultant doesn't know anything about.

Turn One Valve and You May Blow the Others

In the 20's our early A people, the scientific managers and industrial engineers, were sure they would achieve the best of all worlds by measuring and specializing and by setting up just the right system of incentives. And they did it. They put the stopwatch on every job they could reach. They time-studied and they motion-analyzed. And by so doing they were going to increase production, and they did that too.

But we didn't know very much about people in those days. We didn't have C-type consultants. And we didn't foresee at least one large, unexpected cost. We didn't realize that people were going to get mad and unhappy, and mad and unhappy people were going to slow down and hide the jigs and even beat up the guy who didn't go along with their war against the new system. Now we know more about people and about human motivation. We know that despite the obvious logic of specialization and centralization we'd better slow down and think about the effect of such structural changes on people; and we look for changes that will have positive instead of negative people effects.

But the pessimist will not be impressed

by this argument. For all we have done now is to complicate life. "Mr. Manager," we experts seem to be saying, "you can turn lots of different valves in your organizational system. You can turn structural valves, technological valves, and people valves. And all we can tell you is that you'd better watch out because if you turn any one you're apt to blow the others." So how does all this new knowledge have any practical pay-off? Why bother with it? Such a pessimistic argument is partly right and entirely useless. We cannot deny new knowledge. We cannot be afraid of seeing the world in a way that is as complicated as the world really is. Denying the complications does not make organizations simple. It just makes us blind.

And in fact, we know a little bit more than just that organizations are complicated. We have some general ideas about when to turn one set of valves instead of another. We can begin to relate valves to jobs to be done. For the kinds of jobs that our organization is trying to do is one key to the decision about which consultant—structural, people, or technological—to hire. We can manage, that is, *according to task*.

Consider, for example, the kinds of tasks which can be best tackled structurally, humanly, or technologically. It begins to look as though the structural valves are great when tasks are clear and routine, when the organization knows what it wants to do and how it wants to do it.

Turning the Structural Valve

Your first reaction to that one may be to say, "Well, our organization always knows what it wants to do and how it wants to do it." So the structural valves are for us. But if you are saying that to yourself, I will just have to say that I

think you are wrong. For although the textbooks on business organizations often picture them as having clear, well-defined objectives, that is mostly just mythology.

Some *parts* of some organizations know pretty well what they want to do and how to do it. Typically, routine manufacturing operations are like that. When you have an order for X tons of Y-type pipe, the production superintendent probably can say—and this time he is not full of baloney—that he now knows what he wants to make and how he ought to go about making that pipe. In such situations the structural valves are pretty good ones to turn. In those cases we can specify operations and the order in which operations should take place; we can institute controls; we can set time standards; and we can do all the other myriad things that will increase the quality and speed of production.

But it is also in just those situations that we ought to watch out for signals indicating trouble on the *people* side of the system. For when we tighten up on structure, people are apt to feel squeezed. So if we decide that what we need is more controls, clearer rules, more instructions, we'd better also be ready with better rewards, higher payoffs and other devices to compensate people for having to work in a less free world.

Turning the Technological Valve

Let's turn now to the second set of valves—the technical valves. When should one try to change one's organization primarily by turning them on? Let me try what may seem an odd answer to that one. Technological valves, especially computers, are great when an organization wants to move some of its parts from a people orientation to a structural orientation. Because one thing computers do very well is to help convert open-ended, ill-defined tasks into clearly structured and well-defined ones. Computers are great devices for taking problems out of the realm of human judgment and into programmed, systematic analysis. If people valves are the ones to worry about when tasks are unprogrammed, and structural valves are good when tasks are highly programmed, then technological valves become useful when you want to convert unprogrammed to programmed tasks—from people to structure.

But when you do that, watch out again. And this time watch out for bells and lights going on *all over* the system. For human beings are apt to get very itchy when the computer comes along; it looks like a giant new stopwatch. It threatens to reduce the range of their activity. And the existing structure is apt to crack wide open as you begin to convert from human to computerized information systems.

Turning the People Valve

Now when are the people valves likely to be most helpful? When should we worry most about improving communication and mutual trust? I think they are apt to be most useful when the tasks are exactly opposite from the routine; when tasks are novel and complicated,—when we don't know exactly what we're doing. Now where and when do we find such situations? We find them when we try to innovate in new areas, when the world changes, or the government begins to get tough, or foreign competition enters the market, or when the aluminum people put zip tops on cans. Curiously enough, those kinds of situations seem typically to confront *higher* levels of management. All of which is to say that it is top management that most often doesn't know what it is doing.

I submit that what I just said is a fair and healthy statement, and in no way disparaging to top management; for another way of saying the same thing is to say that the tough problems are the ones top management is there to tackle; often the ones in which we can't even identify the problem, let alone solve it. The reason we need bright and experienced and level-headed senior executives is precisely because we know they are going to face uncharted tasks—problems in which neither they nor anybody else can know with any certainty what they are doing. The people valves are the valves of choice in these situations because in 1966 the very best tool we have for solving such problems is a set of savvy human brains.

Notice I said a *set* of "savvy" human brains. Because when such wide-open problems get large enough, they get too big for a single individual. So the people issue becomes not only selecting the very best man for the big job, but also the issue of combining several good men, of effectively using the human group. Hence relationships, interpersonal trust, feelings of security and self-respect become important issues if top management groups are to function effectively.

Motivation Most Needed by Top Management Groups

These are motivational issues: So I am suggesting that the toughest motivational problems are problems of the motivation of higher-level management. I know that sounds odd. For usually when we talk about motivation we think about motivating unwilling production workers, not eager executives. Perhaps the problem of motivation is more obvious at these lower levels because our over-specialized structures generate so much resistance. We think about motivating workers in quite negative terms. We think of motivation as a problem of overcoming resistance and apathy.

At higher levels there is ordinarily no such problem. Executives work hard. Nobody worries very much about making them work harder. Yet there is, I argue, an important motivational problem here. The problem is motivating them *jointly* toward common goals instead of toward individual and competitive ones. At higher levels the problem of motivation becomes a problem of the *group*, not of the *individual;* a problem of resolving conflict among hard-working people, not a problem of getting people to work hard. So I commend to you the people valves when the problems are big, open problems; and I commend them especially for the groups at the top of organizations.

In Summary

Let me go back now and try to summarize. I noted that human motivation is terribly important but it is not enough. I suggested that when we usually think of human motivation in organizations, we think of motivating "lazy" workers in clerical and blue collar jobs. I've implied that we worry about motivation at those levels because we were so structure-conscious in the past that we killed human motivation in the process of building our neat organization chart. And so we had to look for gimmicks to bring dead motivation back to life, gimmicks like suggestion systems and incentive schemes. On the other hand, we haven't worried very much about motivation in top management on the assumption that management groups are automatically motivated. In many senses they are. But the fact is that top managements are no longer made up of individuals but of groups. Motivation of groups, the establishing of good healthy open relationships among groups, is one

large motivational problem that is very much alive.

I have suggested that managers have at least three sets of valves they can use in trying to move their organizations along. One is the people valve—the motivational valve—a second is structural, a third technological. At least three openings into the organizations are available. The problem is that when we enter from any one of these points, in order to try to get the job done, we also influence the other two. So that we may have to trade off advantages in one against costs in the other. We may have to give up some structural advantages as if we are to earn motivational advantages. Highly motivated groups are not likely to be very well disciplined or very orderly. And computerization of an organization may change the existing structuure—perhaps causing it to centralize further than it originally intended.

But I also tried to say something a little more positive than just that the whole situation is complicated. I suggested that the manager—trying to decide whether to change his structure or his people or his technology—ought to look first at *the task* that his organization is trying to do. If it is already a pretty well defined task, then it is probably sensible to think about how one can build a better structure. But if the task is wide open, novel and unclear, then the human valve is the very best tool the manager has.

Finally let's not forget that the large complex organization will continue to be large and complex even after computers. And that there will continue to be unstructured, ill-defined problems that will keep the problem of human motivation up near the top of the list of important managerial problems. Human motivation will not be enough in the future, just as it is not enough now. But it will continue to make managerial life both interesting and frustrating.

D

COMMUNICATION

24. Communication and Productivity

JACK R. GIBB

Communication is a process of people relating to other people. As people relate to each other in doing work and in solving problems they communicate ideas, feelings and attitudes. If this communication is effective the work gets done better and the problems are solved more efficiently. Thus, in one sense, at this level of abstraction, there is an obvious relationship between communication and productivity.

Work and problem solving can each be viewed as the taking of appropriate roles at appropriate times as the task or problem evolves. Role taking *is* communication. This apparent and real relationship has caused management to take an increasing interest in all phases of communication. Books are written, training courses are devised, and communications specialists are created and demanded. The rapid growth of literature and programs has far out-distanced the relevant research and the clear knowledge that management can use in making decisions about communications programs. The literature is confusing, contradictory and voluminous.

Although in the most global sense it is fairly obvious that communication is related to productivity, it is very difficult to find satisfying evidence of clear relationships between specific communicative programs or acts, on the one hand, and measures of productivity, profit or corporate vitality on the other. Most studies of communication are short term in na-

Reprinted by permission from the January–February, 1964 issue of *Personnel Administration,* copyright 1964, Society for Personnel Administration, 1221 Connecticut Avenue, N.W., Washington, D.C. 20036. Jack R. Gibb is a Consulting Psychologist in private practice.

ture and relate aspects of communication to various personal and group variables that are perhaps assumed to be related to productivity in the long run, but whose relationships are tenuous at best.

It is the purpose of this paper to look at the over-all problem from the standpoint of managerial decision making. What does top management or the individual manager do? The paper is organized around 9 fundamental communication issues that confront management in today's corporate world. These issues grow out of research, theory and management experience. While it is true that in both practice and theory there are many and varied legitimate positions on each issue, it is possible to distinguish two clusters of related managerial behaviors that are fairly consistently antithetical on each of the fundamental issues. In Table One are summarized the extreme positions of the conflicting views—the views of the "persuasion manager" and of the "problem-solving manager"—on each of the nine issues. Each issue is stated in more detail at the beginning of each of the nine sections of the paper. The issues are practical, overlapping and in general are worded in the language of management

rather than in the language of the specialist.

In general, the *persuasion approach* to communication tends to assume that it is the responsibility of management to regulate the flow of fact and feeling through the organization, to use such regulation as a convenient managerial tool, to build staff roles to work on communication problems, to spend a great deal of time and energy building "communications" programs, and to show a high concern about the information flow in the organization, particularly about verbal and written messages downward.

An alternative approach, designated for convenience as the *problem-solving approach,* is to assume that effective communication is an intrinsic component of effective work and efficient problem solving, that if communications problems exist they are symptoms of aberrant organization or poor line management, that communication is improved by more adequate line management action and problem solving rather than by staff action, and that by creating a managerial climate in which trust and openness is a norm appropriate facts, attitudes and feelings tend to be spontaneously fed into the process of getting the job done.

TABLE 1

Two Alternative Views of the Communication Processes

A Persuasion Approach— The Focus Is On:	A Problem-Solving Approach— The Focus Is On:
1. Remedial programs	1. Diagnosis and etiology
2. Staff responsibility	2. Line responsibility
3. Morale and hygiene	3. Work product and job requirements
4. Persuasion	4. Problem solving
5. Control of communication flow	5. Trust and openness
6. Verbal communication	6. Management action
7. One-way messages	7. Interaction and climate
8. Knowledge and logic	8. Attitudes and feelings
9. Output and telling	9. Input and listening

In each of the following sections a focus or viewpoint consistent with each of the two above approaches is discussed.

1. Symptom or Cause

Is communication seen primarily as a symptom of more basic organizational processes or as itself a fundamental factor to be manipulated by management in the quest for greater productivity and organizational vitality? Is communication best viewed as a symptom or as a cause?

A manager with what might be termed a persuasion approach to management sees communication primarily as a management tool to be used in getting people to get the job done. When he sees some defect in the work pattern that must be remedied he tends to attempt to manipulate the flow of communications as a remedial action. Communicative distortion is seen as a basic cause of poor work or problem solving and is worked on directly by altering managerial communications.

A manager with what might be termed a problem-solving approach to management tends to see communication primarily as a symptom or indicator of more basic organizational or managerial inadequacy. Information about communicative distortion is used as diagnostic data which will guide the manager in taking new managerial actions, reorganizing work patterns, or achieving new attitudes toward the organization or the people in it.

The evidence is fairly clear that when people are in an effective problem-solving or work relationship with each other they tend to communicate relevant feelings, ideas and perceptions with each other. When there is goal ambiguity, poor supervision or role inadquacy then communicative distortion occurs as a symptom of these more basic problems.

An analog occurs in the concurrently flowering field of human relations. Human relations can be viewed as a symptom or as a cause. The growing awareness of human relations and communications problems is symptomatic of growing feelings of inadequacy on the part of management, and of a growing awareness of basic inadequacies in both management and organization theory and practice. When people have trouble getting along with each other and understanding each other, it is probably an indication that somehow they have been unable to create satisfactory jobs or a satisfying and effective work organization. The way to improve human relations and communications is to evolve new job prescriptions and more adequate work organizations—to change managerial actions. It may be a temporary solution to build human relations training programs and communications workshops—but this is at best a *temporary* or intermediate solution, a step that is getting at symptoms rather than more basic causes, and that is working on the shadow of the problem rather than on the problem itself.

2. Staff or Line

Who is primarily responsible for effective communication—staff or line? The persuasion manager tends to emphasize the staff role in improvement of communications. The problem-solving manager tends to build responsibility for communications and human relations directly into the line functions.

A differentiating characteristic between the persuasion manager and the problem-solving manager is his emphasis upon one of two paths. The persuasion manager tends to build a communications staff with many responsibilities for studying communications, instituting programs, managing information and data flow within the organization, training people to communicate, and using various media to *persuade* people to change behavior or to communicate more adequately.

The problem-solving manager makes the assumption that communication is a direct line responsibility, that communication *must* occur in the process of doing work, solving problems, controlling distribution, or getting the job done. He works directly on the line causes of communicative errors. He works with others towards recomposing work groups, changing organizational patterns, reorganizing work space, or creating more adequate man-job relationships. He tends to change his behavior rather than his speech. He tends to control actions rather than to control talk.

It seems well at this point to call attention to the fact that we are describing two extreme typologies of management. In one sense the two types of managers being considered are hypothetical or "ideal" cases. The pure cases do not exist in the natural state. However, anyone with wide experience on the industrial scene can recognize the *genre*. The intent is to sharpen assumptions and to focus attention upon the implications of communications research for management practices. In practice individual managers tend to show mixtures of the above patterns.

3. Hygiene or Production

If there is a "communications program" is it primarily centered upon the requirements of the job and the product or is it primarily remedial in nature? Is it directed toward morale, hygiene and human relations or is it directed toward work and productivity?

The persuasion manager tends to direct the communication program toward improvement of morale and hygiene around the plant. He fights fires, drops verbal bombs where they are presumed to do the most good, centers upon remedial aspects of the situation, and directs plant and company campaigns toward curing ills such as absenteeism and waste.

The problem-solving manager tends to have no special communication program as such. When he does create such a program he tends to deal with analyses of job requirements, production schedules, goals of the enterprise, information storage and retrieval, efficiency of work flow, and other aspects of communication flow that are directly relevant to job performance and problem solving.

Hygiene-centered communication programs tend to send out information that is irrelevant, distorted to fit management goals, camouflaged to cover management errors, sent in too great a quantity, irrelevant to the concerns of the moment that *grow out of* task and problem demands or out of spontaneous group maintenance demands. Such programs are often met with suspicion and apathy, and may be seen as propaganda or as attempts to meet management needs rather than work needs or worker needs.

There is some evidence that communication is best when it is in response to natural interaction on the job between people who are learning appropriate trust, when it is in small groups or face-to-face situations, when it is asked for, and when it is between members who do not have too great psychological or hierarchical distance. The most effective communication thus tends to arise spontaneously out of situational demands.

Effective communication tends to be best in work units, where line managers and co-workers are learning a degree of trust appropriate to their relationship, and are learning to send and receive attitudes, feelings and information that are necessary for appropriate job performance. The interrelated assumptions here are that people like to do meaningful work, feel good when they have satisfactory job relationships, have good morale when they do challenging work that is related to their own choices, goals, and abilities, and that effective communication is a residual property of effective work and problem solving.

4. Persuasion or Problem-Solving

Is the communication program focussed upon persuasion of people or upon individual and team problem solving?

The persuasion manager tends to see communication as primarily an influence process through which people can be changed, controlled, guided, or influenced. Communication becomes education, propaganda, leadership, or guidance. Managers try to sell ideas, or to motivate others to work harder, feel better, have higher morale, and be more loyal.

The problem-solving manager sees communication primarily as a necessary adjunct of the process of doing work or solving problems. In order to solve the problem or get the job done certain information must be obtained, certain feelings must be expressed, and a certain amount of interpersonal perceptions must be exchanged in order for a team to be a healthy work or problem-solving unit. Job demands or team maintenance demands determine the amount and kind of communication that is necessary. Communication *is* problem solving.

The difference in the two approaches is one of *focus*. Communication is *both* influence and problem solving. The emphasis and the approach are the significant things. Persuasive communication tends to produce resistance, distrust, circumvention, or counter-persuasion. It is seen by the worker or subordinate as "news management", as propaganda, or as an effort to get him to do what he may not want to do. Research has shown persuasion-centered communications programs to be discouragingly ineffective in accomplishing management goals.

Problem-solving communication is subordinate to the demands of the job or the problem. The nature of the job or the problem calls forth certain bits of information, feelings or perceptions that are relevant to job accomplishment or problem solution. In general, the research shows that when conditions are created which produce relevant *emergent* communications out of the work situation, that communications problems are reduced. Thus, face-to-face communications in small groups tend to be superior to other forms of communication because there is a greater likelihood that communications will emerge from interactive job and problem demands.

5. Regulation or Trust

Does one trust the manager and the worker or does one regulate the communication flow?

An increasingly clear body of evidence indicates that communication is related to the trust level in the relationship or in the organization. People who trust each other tend to be more open with each other. With high trust people are free to give information and feelings and to respond spontaneously to questions, are less apt to devise control strategies to manipulate others, are less apt to be closed and devious, are less apt to manufacture rumors or distortions, perhaps have less need to engage in extra communication, and thus they lay the groundwork for higher productivity. With low trust, people use more strategy, filter information, build interpersonal facades, camouflage attitudes, deliberately or unconsciously hold back relevant feelings and information in the process of interpersonal in-fighting, distort feedback upward in the direction of personal motivations, engage in extra communication, and thus indirectly sabotage productivity.

Managers tend to regulate the communication flow when distrust is high and tend to be more spontaneous and open with feelings and information when distrust is low. The persuasion manager tends to regulate communication flow—both in his personal actions and in his managerial policies. The problem-solving manager tends to create trust by allowing communications to follow the demands of the work situation. The openness-trusting stance is antithetical to the persuasion stance. Experimentation indicates that work and problem-solving efficiency is dependent upon the spontaneous flow of information and feelings through the system. Trust and openness are related to productivity.

6. Talk or Action

Does a manager talk or act? Given a choice of where to focus effort, does management spend energies getting the problems solved and the jobs done or deciding what kinds of communications to send to the subordinate and the worker?

With articulate people words can become a fetish. What shall we say to the worker? What can I tell my subordinate? How shall I word the message? Part of this word-focus habit arises from a naive confidence that people will take the words at face value, part of it perhaps from an unconscious protest to one's intuitive understanding that talk will make little difference and that people won't listen at all. Interviews with managers indicate bimodal reactions of naive trust or equally naive cynicism about the effectiveness of words in communication.

Experimental and field studies can be interpreted to show that actions are more significant than words in communication. Gestures, bodily attitudes, empathic postures, and management actions communicate a great deal more than words do. A manager who says verbally that he trusts a subordinate and then proceeds to require detailed and frequent reports, or to make frequent checks on the subordinate's work, usually is *perceived* as distrusting the subordinate. Actions take priority over words in the communication channels.

The persuasion manager tends to ascribe an inordinately high value to words, symbols, pictures, and formal communications. Most people would perhaps agree that both words and actions communicate. The difference in management technologies lies in the relative emphasis in day to day management decision. The problem-solving manager tends to rely upon actions to communicate rather than upon words. He tends to use words more for information than for influence.

7. Traffic or Climate

Is the "communication problem" basically a climate problem or a traffic problem? Do we focus attention upon refining the messages we send or upon creating a climate in which "messages" are decreasingly necessary? Is communication primarily directional or is it an interaction among people doing a job? Is the management problem one of creating a climate for interaction or one of regulating the message traffic?

The persuasion manager tends to be a traffic man, usually centering attention upon the one-way channels down the hierarchy or command channel. Great attention is paid to the mass media, refinement of the message, timing of the presentation, organizing the campaign, hitting at the psychological moment, and devising an appropriate propaganda strategy. Public relations, advertising and visual aids are in great demand. The problem is control of the traffic patterns of communication. Communication is often one-way.

The problem-solving alternative to such action is to focus upon the interactive climate of work, to rely upon face-to-face interaction in line units who are working or solving problems together, to give all relevant information to line managers with maximum openness, to arrange the geography of work in such a way as to optimize relevant interaction, and to encourage questions, criticisms and all forms of informal interaction. Group discussions, small, flexible and overlapping work teams, and open channels are seen as communication tools. The problem is seen as one of creating a climate for work and problem solving. Communication is seen as flowing in a field of interaction, rather than as occurring on a one-way street—or even on a two-way street. Communication is a relationship.

8. Knowledge or Attitude

Which is more central in determining effective communication—information and logic or attitudes and feelings? If communication is seen as poor does the manager direct his energies toward refining the flow of information or toward changing the attitudes of persons engaged in communicating? Which is a more critical "leverage point" in adequate communication—knowledge and logic or attitudes and feelings?

The persuasion technologist tends to place an emphasis upon information and upon getting the "facts" to the right people. He tends to assume that information will change attitudes and behavior, and that information can be transmitted with acceptably high reliability through formal channels.

The evidence seems to point to the relative importance of attitudinal and motivational factors over informational factors in management and in behavior change. Campaigns to increase information usually accomplish considerably less than management would hope. Information does not necessarily change attitudes, value systems, or even perceptions. People tend to perceive information or reinterpret data in the direction of their motivations and wishes. People hear what they want to hear. They forget what they want to forget. There are various motivational reasons why people select from available information, ignore posters and pamphlets, overperceive or underperceive the "facts", and in general add their own distortions to the information that they receive.

The communication of intangibles like warmth, acceptance, respect, and trust are complex processes which are poorly correlated with the words people use and the information that is conveyed. The problem-solving manager tends to place emphasis upon feelings and perceptions of people, and to focus upon the work climate which will determine the way information is received and which may make special communication decreasingly necessary.

9. Output or Input

If something goes wrong does the manager start telling or listening? If a manager wishes to take a diagnostic stance toward the communication problem in his company does he accomplish more by refining the outputs or the inputs? Supposing we knew no other information about the alternatives than the titles of the courses, which management development course would we keep going: "Management Public Speaking" or "Management Listening"?

The persuasion manager tends to think in terms of output. He tends to talk of getting the message across, telling subordinates about the goals of the company, motivating people to work, seeing that people understand what management is trying to do, and putting out the message efficiently and quickly with a minimum of effort.

The problem-solving manager tends to think more in terms of input. He may ask himself such questions as the following. What information is needed? How do others look at the problem? What other solutions are there to problems that face us? How can we get more data? How can we interpret what information is available? What cues are we failing to process?

In examining the above clusters of management behavior we find that tradition and precedent are on the side of the persuasion manager. Most of the scientific evidence where it is available is on the side of the problem-solving approach. The skills and habits of persuasion are readily available. The skills, habits, and attitudes appropriate to the problem-solving approach are less easily acquired. The paths to creative problem solving are unclear. The managerial rewards are presumably very great.

References

1. Gibb, Jack R. "Defensive Communication." *J. Commun.*, 1961, 11, 141–148.
2. Gibb, Jack R. "Climate for Trust Formation," in Bradford, Leland P., Gibb, Jack R., and Benne, Kenneth (eds.), *T-group Theory and Laboratory Method*. New York: Wiley, 1963.
3. Jackson, Jay M. "The Organization and Its Communication Problems." *J. Commun.*, 1959, 9, 158–167, 189.
4. Johannsen, James R., and Edmunds, Carolyn Y. *Annotated Bibliography on Communication in Organizations*. La Jolla, California: Western Behavioral Sciences Institute, 1962.
5. Mellinger, G. D. "Interpersonal Trust As a Factor In Communication." *J. Abnorm. Soc. Psychol.*, 1956, 52, 304–309 .
6. Schutz, William C. "Interpersonal Underworld." *Har. Bus. Rev.*, 1958, 36, 123–135.

25. What's Blocking Upward Communications?

JOHN ANDERSON

When the subject of poor upward communications is discussed in management circles, analysis of the problem often turns to the concept of "effective vs ineffective listening." The idea is that many managers don't listen very effectively to what people are saying to them, and this not only deprives them of valuable information, but is also bad for employee relations in general. So the solution sought is a way of helping managers develop their "listening skills."

In this article I want to present a framework for analyzing factors that may inhibit effective upward communication in an organization. There is little doubt that ineffective listening is often an important *part* of the communication problem. Many people do not listen very effectively, and even the most effective "receivers" are likely to have bad periods. But if an organization has problems with the quantity and quality of its upward communications, there may be several causes that have little to do with getting the beans out of management's ears.

First of all, to simplify the question with a model situation:

1. Suppose that B works for A.
2. B knows something that A needs to know, but doesn't.
3. This "something" might be knowledge of a current, developing, or potential problem in A's area of responsibility that A is unaware of. It might be factual information or a creative idea that could help solve a problem A *is* already aware of. It might be no more than a feeling of personal satisfaction or dissatisfaction with some situation that A is unaware of, but that may be affecting B's motivation on the job, or his ability to work effectively with A. Or it might be any combination of the three.

4. So the question is: "Under what circumstances will B probably communicate to A what he knows, and under what circumstances will he probably not?"

The task for any manager interested in improving the quality of communications coming up to him, then, would seem to be to look for these circumstances in his own organization, and in his own relationships with subordinates, and see which ones he might do something about.

From B to A: Possibilities

In considering the likelihood of B's passing his information to A, one classification of requirements might be:

1. It must *occur* to B that he should tell A.
2. If he thinks of it, he must *choose* to do it.

3. If he chooses to tell, he must find an *opportunity* to do so.

4. If he finds an opportunity and takes it, A must *listen* to him.

5. Having listened to him, A must *act* on what he hears (at least sometimes) in ways recognizable and encouraging to B, or the next time around they will be right back at step 2 and B will choose *not* to bother. Now, what obstacles might get in the way at each step, and what might A do about each if he were aware of it?

1. *It must occur to B that it matters whether he says anything.*

a. B may not realize that the information he possesses has any value. For example, the cleanup man in a warehouse may see Product X stacked 8 high but not say anything because he doesn't know the stacking limit is 7. The more a man understands of the *sense* of his job, and the jobs of people around him (the whys of operating procedures, cost, quality, safety information, and salient department goals) the more likely he is to know when his observations are worth passing on. So, the solution for this obstacle to upward communication will usually be better downward or lateral communication through better initial job training, or continuing education on current departmental operating concerns.

b. B may know the information he has is important, but he may think A already has the information, too, from his own observations or reports he receives from someone else. If erroneous assumptions of this sort ("Why, I thought you knew!") are often an obstacle to effective upward communication, a manager should check whatever systems he has for keeping informed for gaps and overlapping reporting responsibilities that could cause confusion.

2. *Once aware that he has significant information, B must choose to pass it on.*

a. B may realize his information is im-portant and that management doesn't have it, but he may still not pass it on because "it's not his job" to do so. If he has a narrow enough view of his job responsibilities (i.e., the organization's expectations of him), there may be several kinds of things he wouldn't think of talking about openly—for example, questioning his boss's judgment on anything to his face or making any kind of creative suggestion for solution of a problem himself. If he considers his management-expected role that of someone who does what he is told, suffers in silence, and questions or criticizes management judgment only privately with friends or through mechanisms provided in the union contract, he won't "communicate upward" in a way you might like him to because he doesn't think you would *want* him to. Corrective action for this obstacle probably lies initially in orientation and training practices, and then in the way individual managers respond when a B does volunteer information (see paragraphs under 4 and 5 below).

b. Another consideration B will think about is who might be helped by his information, and who hurt, if he reveals it. If he thinks it might hurt his own pay, or the interests of someone he likes, or perhaps make life easier for a boss he *doesn't* like, this will encourage him to keep his mouth shut. Suggestions for management in avoiding this obstacle fall in areas of (1) consideration, fairness, and basic man-manager relationship development, (2) incentive system design that minimizes situations in which individual and organizational needs are at cross purposes, and (3) education again to broaden the perspective from which people view their responsibilities.

3. *B must have an opportunity to make his information available to A.*

a. If B doesn't have access to A, he can't communicate with him even if he wants to. One requirement is time. If

B is so busy he can't find time, or if A is so busy, B can't find him, or if their available times don't coincide sufficiently for them to get together, B will often forget the whole thing.

    b. A second requirement is a place to talk. Some kinds of things B might like to pass on to A he may not wish to unless it can be done privately (and "privately" may include out of sight, out of hearing, out of telephone access by others, or all three). The extreme example of a manager whose only desk is in a bullpen area may limit upward communications he receives regardless of his skills or his people's motivations.

    4. *If B does speak, A must be able to receive his message.*

Once B has taken the step, placed himself in A's presence and started talking, the rest is up to A. In attempting to understand what B has on his mind, A must be able to compensate for any hesitancy or lack of clarity on B's part :

    a. by his (A's) ability to set aside other pressing problems on his mind and concentrate his attention on B and what B is saying now;

    b. by his own knowledge of B (his strengths, weaknesses, hopes, and concerns), and, therefore, his ability to see things from B's viewpoint and sense any pressures B may feel in the situation;

    c. by his knowledge of technical aspects of B's job and how B's job relates to the department;

    d. by his ability to question—to probe for information B doesn't clearly reveal —that is, to help B to get everything out that needs to be said. This implies both knowing what additional information to ask for to get at the heart of the problem, and how to ask (i.e., in a manner that is patient, interested, non-evaluative, appreciative—in general, supportive);

    e. by his ability to keep his head in a situation where B's emotions might start to carry him away;

    f. by his ability to summarize and keep straight in his mind the key points of B's message, even when it has been presented in a disorganized fashion.

What, then, can be done to build a management team with the ability to do these six things (a–f) well? First, ability in all six areas will be determined partly by well set and change-resistant qualities a manager brings to the company that hires him. So, selection and placement criteria will be important. Beyond this, however, factors that will affect managerial behavior in these areas, and that are within the control of management at some level, are:

• *Management work load.* If a manager is pressed by a work load beyond his capacity, his performance in factors a and e will be strained.

• *Pre-job training.* Gaps in technical-operational aspects of pre-job training will affect his capacity in factor c.

• *Special training and coaching.* Insight and ability in factors b, d, and f can be improved during pre-job training and/or after takeover by other special training programs now available to management.

• *Job tenure.* Finally, since preformance in factors a, b, c, and possibly d and e, will depend at least partly on the manager's experience in the area, too rapid job rotation can be deterimental.

Without even considering the time required to develop efficient administrative and technical competence in a department, the building of a man-manager relationship that is close, open, and trusting takes time, and some kinds of upward communication just won't take place unless and until such a relationship has had time to develop. Other things being equal, this means that larger numbers of people reporting to a manager, and such practices as shift rotation of managers and people on different schedules, as well as brief management job tenure, are going to have a negative effect on upward communications.

5. Having listened to and understood B's message, A needs to act on it.

If B doesn't see that anything *happens* once in awhile as a result of his communication to A (and results that please B, or at least don't displease him), he will probably not bother to give A the benefit of his thoughts as often, thereafter, and he may stop altogether (at least just short of what he needs to communicate to stay out of personal trouble).

The suggestion for A, then, is to make results plainly visible to B, or let B know quickly and plainly why he wasn't able to act. A's own manager should also recognize that if A is to continue to be a channel for good upward communications from B's, A must be seen as influential in the organization by B's. If A's manager can't support that image, A's effectiveness as an upward communications channel will be hampered or destroyed, no matter how effective a "listener" he may be.

Summary of Obstacles to Upward Communications (When B Didn't Communicate to A)

1. B didn't think of telling A what he knew because:

• B didn't know that what he knew was important.
• B thought A knew it already.

2. B choose not to tell it to A because:

• B didn't think it was his job to tell it.
• B thought if A learned of it, it might help (or harm) someone B wished not to help (or harm).

3. B couldn't get to A because:

• A was too busy.
• B was too busy.
• There was no good place for B to talk to A about it.

4. B tried, but A didn't get the message because:

• A was thinking about something else while B talked.
• A couldn't empathize with B's concerns, so he misunderstood and B gave it up (for a while).
• A didn't know B's job (or his own) well enough to understand or appreciate what B was talking about.
• A couldn't interview (question, probe) B well enough to get all the facts out clearly.
• A didn't like what he thought he was hearing so he got mad.
• By the time B finished, A had confused or forgotten important parts of the message.

5. B talked and A listened:

• But A didn't do anything about it.
• And he forgot to tell B why.
• So B didn't talk to him anymore.
• He talked about A sometimes, but to somebody else.

26. Vital Factors in Interpersonal Communication

WAYNE BATY

The process of transmitting a message from one person to another (interpersonal communication) is often inefficient. To illustrate this point, students in a business communication class at Arizona State University were asked to examine the following drawing:

Then, they were given this problem: "Assume that you want another student to reproduce the drawing. You cannot demonstrate. You must write a set of instructions that will (if followed correctly) result in an accurate reproduction."

Students in one class tried to follow the instructions written by students in another class. Although 67 per cent of the reproductions were reasonably accurate, here are some of the inaccurate results:

Some of the inaccuracies appeared to be the fault of those who *wrote* instructions; others, of those who *followed* instructions.

When a businessman *sends* a spoken or written message that appears in his mind as

it must be *received* in the other person's mind as

Otherwise, the results can be catastrophic.

Administrators in business and industry reportedly spend between 75 and 95 per cent of their time communicating (either sending or receiving messages).[1] They cannot afford the 33 per cent error experienced by these students.

So important is accuracy in transmitting ideas that Peter Drucker (well-known consultant and professor of management), says, ". . . ability to express oneself is perhaps the most important of all skills a man can possess." [2] Yet, lack of this ability to express ideas is widespread. Personnel recruiters have difficulty in finding the right men for open positions. A recent survey of sales managers showed that they are looking pri-

Reprinted from *Arizona Business Bulletin,* Vol. 14, No. 4 (April, 1967), pp. 98–103, with permission of the publisher. Wayne Baty is Professor of Business Communications, College of Business Administration, Arizona State University.

[1] Lee O. Thayer, *Administrative Communication* (Homewood, Ill.: Richard D. Irwin, Inc., 1961), p. 3.

[2] Peter Drucker, "How To Be An Employee," *Fortune,* May, 1952, p. 126.

marily for recruits with a college background and high communication skills.[3] Another survey of marketing managers reported that ". . . the recruiters felt the greatest weakness in applicants did not stem from 'how to do it' courses, but from the inability of college students to express themselves clearly." [4] Regardless of whether communication is written or oral, some of the factors that result in failure can be attributed to the *sender;* others, to the *receiver;* and others, to either or both.

Factors That Apply to Both Senders and Receivers

Both sending and receiving are greatly influenced by (1) reputation, (2) rank, (3) metacommunications, and (4) grammar.

REPUTATION

What a businessman *says* or *writes* is strongly influenced by what he *is* and by what his listeners or readers *think him to be.* T. M. Higham, an industrial psychologist, says,

. . . if a person dislikes or mistrusts us, he is not likely to be receptive to what we have to say, and his version of our words is likely to be distorted by his personal opinions of us or his preconceived notions about our motives.[5]

The following incident illustrates how a receiver's evaluation of a sender's reputation can influence the message.[6] A cartoon "The Four Goals of Labor" was clipped from the CIO newspaper and

photostated. A new legend was added at the bottom: "From the June 3 N.A.M. Newsletter." Twenty laborers were asked for their reactions to the goals stated. Four agreed with the statements. Two could not decide. Fourteen condemned them as "loaded," "patronizing," "paternalistic," and "makes you want to spit." No wonder the *Fortune* writer believes that "Only with trust can there be any real communication, and until that trust is achieved the techniques and gadgetry of communication are so much wasted effort." [7]

Implications for the sender. To communicate effectively, be the right type of person—have a reputation for such qualities as integrity, industry, and efficiency. "You will not get any reception if you are not trusted." [8]

Implications for the receiver. To understand effectively, try hard to concentrate on the message itself—resist the temptation to vitiate a message just because the reputation of the sender is negative. A receiver can profitably keep in mind, also, that he could have been wrong in his evaluations of negative qualities in the sender.

RANK

One who can communicate effectively with others of his own rank may have difficulty in communicating with a superior or a subordinate. Schuyler Dean Hoslett accurately describes the problem:

It is well known that the subordinate tends to tell his superior what the latter

[3] "Communication Skills Outrank College Background in Sales Trainee Recruiting," *Marketing Insight,* February 20–24, 1967, p. 3.

[4] Robert E. Linneman and George L. Herpel, "On Marketing Curriculum: Does the Personnel Office Practice What the President Preaches?," *Collegiate News and Views,* Oct., 1966, p. 6.

[5] T. M. Higham, "Basic Psychological Factors in Communication," *Occupational Psychology,* Jan., 1957, p. 2.

[6] "Is Anybody Listening," *Fortune,* Sept., 1950, p. 82.

[7] *Ibid.*

[8] Higham, *loc. cit.*

is interested in, not to disclose what he doesn't want to hear, and to cover up problems and mistakes which may reflect on the subordinate.[9]

Likewise, superiors often feel that they cannot confess to subordinates any problems or crises that reflect on themselves as superiors. Whether a sender is in the role of subordinate or superior, he runs the risk of revealing more than he thinks he should. Awareness of this risk may interfere with his ability to say what he means. When he is in the role of receiver, the same awareness may interfere with his ability to understand what another means. As a distracting factor in a communication, the influence of rank can be reduced if the following attitudes are cultivated: (1) willingness to expect and accept criticism, and (2) recognition that—even though communicating with a superior or to a subordinate—one is also communicating with a *person*.

METACOMMUNICATIONS

In a speech on the ASU campus in 1963, Dr. S. I. Hayakawa said, "With every communication goes an accompanying metacommunication." [10] That is, with every idea that is expressed in words goes an additional idea that is not expressed in words. The following incident involves a typical metacommunication: [11] A superintendent and his foreman were standing outside the latter's office. Upon hearing the girls in the office burst into loud laughter, the superintendent said, "The girls seem happy this morning the way they are talking and laughing." That was his *communication*. From this sentence, the foreman got one or more of the following messages: "Your secretaries are loafing on the job." "Your secretaries do not take their work seriously." "You are not exercising proper control." Later, the foreman reprimanded the girls and changed their working stations (at the expense of good morale).

At the end of a class hour, a student said to his teacher, "I'll have to be absent tomorrow. Will we be doing anything important?" The teacher replied, "Certainly. Everything we do is important." Along with his message, the student had conveyed this *metacommunication*: "From my experience in the class thus far, I note that some things are important and that others are trivial." The teacher was offended. What the student really wanted to know was whether a test would be given.

The sender needs to keep the following points in mind: (1) Metacommunications are always present. (2) Receivers may pay more attention to the metacommunication than to the communication itself. (3) Communications can be so presented that their accompanying metacommunications work *for* the sender, not *against* him.

The receiver needs to keep the following points in mind: (1) Try hard to concentrate on the idea that is put into words. (2) Remember that a negative metacommunication may have been accidental. (3) If the communication is oral, a receiver can easily verify whether he has understood the communication and whether a metacommunication has been properly interpreted.

GRAMMAR

If one person is to understand another, both must have a basic knowledge of the language used. So essential is this knowledge that Peter Drucker says courses

---

[9] Schuyler Dean Hoslett, "Barriers to Communication," *Personnel,* Sept., 1951, p. 109.

[10] Dr. Hayakawa is author of *Language in Thought and Action* (New York: Harcourt, Brace & World, Inc., 1949).

[11] Burleigh B. Gardner and David G. Moore, *Human Relations in Industry* (Homewood, Ill.: Richard D. Irwin, Inc., 1955).

in English really are strictly vocational courses because they teach one to express himself.[12]

Among the common grammatical causes for misunderstandings are errors in the use of compound adjectives, participal phrases, modifiers, and superlatives. Although businessmen may have a better command of grammar than college freshmen, here are the results of a test given to 74 students at ASU. The students were asked for interpretations of the following sentences:

1. We need six-foot soldiers for this assignment.

(25.7 per cent incorrectly concluded that six soldiers were needed—that they were to be *foot* soldiers instead of any other type. 74.3 per cent correctly concluded that the soldiers needed were to be six feet tall.)

2. After helping with the balance sheet, George asked John to do the statement of profit and loss.

(28.4 per cent incorrectly concluded that—if the sentence meant what it said—*John* was helping with the balance sheet. 71.6 per cent correctly concluded that *George* was helping with the balance sheet.)

3. She is the best typist.

(17.6 per cent incorrectly concluded that two typists were being compared. 82.4 per cent correctly concluded that at least three typists were being compared.)

Such sentences are so common in business that both senders and receivers need to be familiar with the grammatical principles involved. A sender must be sure that his sentences are grammatically correct. (Errors can introduce distracting and uncomplimentary metacommunications; such as "Since he makes errors in English, he probably makes errors in judgment.")

If for any reason a sender recognizes that a sentence (even though grammatically correct) can be misunderstood, he should revise for clarity. A receiver must fight against being distracted by an error, he needs to know what the sentence means as written or spoken, he needs to use judgment sometimes to determine whether a literal interpretation is sensible, and he should be sure to ask for clarification when he is in doubt.

Factors That Apply Primarily to Senders

Those who initiate communications frequently make errors in their selection of words, in failure to take the receiver's reaction into account, and in conveying messages at the proper time.

WORDS

Anyone who knows English is well aware that one word may have many different meanings. For example, the word "fast" has at least 14 different meanings. Of the 500 most commonly used words, there are over 14,000 different dictionary definitions.[13]

The young or immature person may sometimes yield to the temptation to use a big, unusual word for the sake of impressing others. He soon learns, however, that his message is either not understood or misunderstood. He may learn, too, that he did make an impression—a bad impression.

Even relatively common words are frequently misinterpreted. Carson reports about a questionnaire sent to field staff

---

[12] Drucker, *op. cit.,* p. 127.

[13] Wiliam V. Haney, *Communication Patterns and Incidents* (Homewood, Ill.: Richard D. Irwin, Inc., 1960), p. 48.

members of the Bureau of Old Age and Survivors Insurance.[14] About 20 per cent of the field staff had misunderstandings of instructional materials sent to them from headquarters. Link reports that of 69 articles from 13 representative employee papers, 37 were on a readability level too difficult for more than 67 per cent of the adult population.[15] (Some of the difficulty could have resulted from complicated sentences as well as words.)

Businessmen are encouraged to rely on the short, simple word; however, even these words can be misinterpreted.[16] [17] [18] A grocery clerk turned to her manager and said, "This fellow is demanding my money from the cash register." When the manager replied, "Let him have it," the robber shot both the manager and the clerk. To him, "Let him have it" meant "Shoot him." An engineer in a local firm instructed a subordinate to "Let the motor run continually." The subordinate erroneously let the motor run and run, without stopping at all (continuously). True, the subordinate did not follow instructions; but the engineer could have avoided the misunderstanding by choosing words that would be more readily understood; such as, "The motor is to run while the door is open; the motor is to remain stopped while the door is closed."

A sender's chances of doing his part in the communication process is improved if he (1) relies mainly on the short, simple word, (2) uses them in the way his receiver would normally expect them to be used, and (3) restates in different words any ideas that he thinks might be misunderstood. In addition he needs to create an atmosphere of cordiality in which his receiver will not be reluctant to ask for clarification.

RECEIVER REACTION

Just as engineers are expected to plan before they build and writers are expected to outline before they write, communicators need to plan their messages before presenting them. If the receiver can be expected to be happy with the message that is about to be sent, the task is simple. Tell him the big idea that will make him happy; then, supply the details.

The problem of anticipating receiver reaction is especially important when the receiver is about to be sent some bad news. For example, assume a superior is planning to tell a subordinate that the latter's promotion will have to be delayed a year. Two ideas must be conveyed: (1) the fact of delay, and (2) the reasons for it. The *reasons* are very important. If they are thoroughly understood by the receiver, a noticeable loss in morale may be avoided. If they are not, the employee may either leave the firm or lose enthusiasm for his work. Since the reasons are so important, the sender must present his message in such a way as to insure that the receiver actually listens while the reasons are being given.

If the sender should present the fact of delay first, the receiver may become emotionally involved or angered to such an extent that he will not listen to the reasons

---

[14] John Carson, "Weak Links in Chain of Command," *Public Opinion Quarterly*, Fall, 1945, pp. 346–349.

[15] Henry C. Link, "How to Get Listeners," *The Management Review*, February, 1951, pp. 62–63.

[16] Rudolph Flesch, *The Art of Readable Writing* (New York: Harper and Row Publishers, 1949).

[17] Robert Gunning, *The Technique of Clear Writing* (New York: McGraw-Hill Book Co., 1952).

[18] Donald R. Murphy, "Test Proves Short Words and Sentences Get Best Readership," *Printers Ink*, Jan. 10, 1947, pp. 61–62.

regardless of how good they may be. The chances of getting the reasons across are greatly improved if they are given first, if the reasons lead up to the denial.[19] [20] Kermit Rolland says, "If you can say *yes,* say it at once. If you must say *no,* take a little longer." [21]

TIMING

A company on the West Coast was forced to reduce the pay of its employees. They had known for some time that the firm was in serious financial difficulties. However, when management sent a memorandum informing them of the reduction in pay, they ignored the memorandum because it was dated April 1! The memorandum would have been taken seriously at any other time.

Even though a sender can do his part of the communication task perfectly, his message may not be received if the timing is improper. If the receiver has just recently been jolted with an unexpected assignment, reprimanded, promoted, granted a vacation, or informed that his income tax form is being reviewed, he may have considerable difficulty in concentrating on any message he received.

Factors That Apply Primarily to Receivers

Even though a sender may do his job skillfully, communication may be ineffective if the receiver has difficulties with concentration, expectancy, and interest.

CONCENTRATION

Although one aspect of intelligence is the ability to hold important information in one's mind, another significant aspect is the ability to *exclude* everything except that which is being considered at the moment. This power to concentrate is to some extent innate, but it can also be developed through cultivation of good listening habits. Nichols lists six bad habits that prevent effective listening: (1) Faking attention, (2) listening so hard for the small details that major points are missed, (3) refusing to listen when the subject matter is difficult, (4) dismissing a subject prematurely as uninteresting, (5) criticizing delivery or physical appearance of the sender, and (6) yielding to distractions.[22]

Many people in group discussions pride themselves in being able to make a well polished contribution when their turn to speak comes (or when they can manage to cut in!). Yet, the contribution loses much of its impact when in the process of talking the speaker reveals that he was not listening to the preceding comments made by others; instead he was concentrating on how best to phrase his thoughts for maximum impact.

Rogers and Roethlisberger report an effective technique for forcing concentration in group discussions.[23] The members of a group are requested to follow these rules: "Each person can speak up for himself only *after* he has first restated the ideas and feelings of the previous speaker

[19] W. Wilkinson, J. H. Menning, and C. R. Anderson, *Writing for Business* (Homewood, Ill.: Richard D. Irwin, Inc., 1955), pp. 71–75.

[20] William C. Himstreet and Wayne Murlin Baty, *Business Communications* (second edition; Belmont, California: Wadsworth Publishing Co., 1964), Chapter 7.

[21] Kermit Rolland, "Letters Can Say No but Keep or Make Friends," *Printers Ink,* Oct. 7, 1949, p. 46.

[22] Ralph G. Nichols and Leonard A. Stevens, *Are You Listening?* (New York: McGraw-Hill Book Company, Inc., 1957), pp. 104–113.

[23] Carl Rogers and F. J. Roethlisberger, "Barriers and Gateways to Communication," *Harvard Business Review,* July–Aug., 1952, pp. 46–52.

accurately and to that person's satisfaction." Although the technique is time consuming, its value in settling arguments is astonishing. When participants are forced to listen and understand, chances of genuine differences of opinion are greatly reduced.

EXPECTANCY

Students in a class at ASU were being given some step-by-step instructions to draw a rectangular solid (but they had not been told what the finished drawing was to be). They had already received instructions that resulted in a drawing that looked like this:

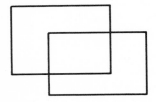

The next instruction was to make a line from A to B.

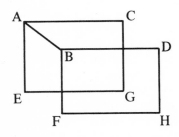

Before further instructions were given, a few students were observed to draw similar lines from C to D, E to F, and G to H. Because they had anticipated remaining instructions, they quit listening and continued drawing.

Those who are listening or reading must learn to resist the temptation to tune themselves out just as soon as they *think* they know what the remainder is to be. It may be vastly different from the expected.

INTEREST

If the receiver has no interest in a message, effective communication is unlikely. As an experiment to see how much distortion occurs in communication, Higham started rumors and then checked to see how much change had occurred after the rumors had been passed along to several people.[24] Typically, the rumors underwent considerable change as they went from one person to another. Then, he started a rumor about a test that a fellow faculty member was supposedly planning to give. This rumor had special interest to the students involved, for they were also taking the other teacher's class and their grades would be affected. Even though the rumor was passed through many students, there was almost no distortion. The differences in distortion were statistically significant. The receiver's problem is simplified if he is interested. If he is not, he should either get interested or strenuously resist the temptation to let his mind wander.

Summary

Businessmen, employees, and students are frequently criticized for their lack of ability to communicate.

When two people fail in their efforts to communicate, either the sender or the receiver may be at fault. The sender may be so concerned with his own *reputation* or *rank* that he does not say or write exactly what he should. The receiver may

---

[24] T. M. Higham, "The Experimental Study of the Transmission of Rumour," *British Journal of Psychology*, 1951, pp. 42–55.

be so concerned with the sender's reputation or rank that he inaccurately interprets the sender's perfectly prepared message. The sender sometimes transmits a *metacommunication* that gets more attention than the message itself. If either the sender or the receiver lacks a basic knowledge of *grammar,* serious misunderstandings may result.

The one who initiates a communication (the sender) makes a serious mistake if he chooses *words* that the receiver might not understand, or if he chooses words that can be readily misunderstood. If the sender does not anticipate a *receiver's reaction* and plan his message accordingly, the receiver may be so disappointed about one part of the message that he will not listen to the other parts. If a sender's *timing* is poor, the receiver may have difficulty in keeping his mind on the message.

The one who receives a communication makes a serious mistake if he attempts *concentration* on two ideas at once. He needs to exclude everything from his mind except the message he is now receiving. Because the receiver is in a state of *expectancy* (of knowing what he thinks the remaining message is to be), he may commit a serious error if he stops listening. Likewise, if he stops listening because of a lack in *interest,* he may miss a message that is vital to him and to the entire business.

The foregoing factors are not all-inclusive; others could be added. If interpersonal communication is to be effective, both senders and receivers must take such factors into consideration.

E

BEHAVIORAL TECHNIQUES IN MANAGEMENT

27. Sensitivity Training

WALTER S. WIKSTROM

One of the newer training methods that has attracted attention in recent years is something called "sensitivity training." As the name suggests, the goal is to make men more sensitive to themselves and others, to make them aware of how, consciously and unconsciously, they affect others and others influence them. Its role in management development is based on the assumption that a manager will do a better job of achieving results through the efforts of others if he has this heightened sensitivity to others.

Many popular articles have suggested that it is an experience in which executives vent their hostility upon one another; other reports have suggested that it is training in being kind and helpful. Both of these extreme views are correct—but only partially so.

The professional practitioners of sensitivity training concede that it is extremely difficult to give an accurate description of this type of training. But their writings, couched as they are in the technical jargon of educational and clinical psychology, have not made it easier for most laymen to understand what sensitivity training is all about.[1]

Under the circumstances, it is not sur-

Reprinted from *Studies in Personnel Policy, No. 189*. New York: National Industrial Conference Board, Inc., 1964, pp. 90–94, with permission of the publisher. Walter S. Wikstrom is a staff member in the Division of Personnel Administration, National Industrial Conference Board.

[1] The practitioners also differ considerably among themselves. This section presents a general view of the training method rather than giving a detailed account of the beliefs and techniques of any of the "schools" of sensitivity training. The description given by Dr. Chris Argyris in *Interpersonal Competence and Organizational Effectiveness* (The Dorsey Press, Inc., & Richard D. Irwin, Inc., 1962) was a valuable guide in preparing this section.

prising that the method has not become widespread. In the Board's survey, only slightly over one third of the cooperators reported using sensitivity training. Significantly, however, of those firms that have experience with it, over 80% intend to continue its use; indeed, a third of them plan to give it an even more prominent place in their management development programs.

The Rationale for Sensitivity Training

The format and procedures used with sensitivity training are unlike anything that is normally thought of as "training." These unconventional procedures can be understood only in terms of the rationale that is the basis for the goals of this technique.

This rationale begins with the belief that all men are the product of their cultures. From the culture, men absorb concepts and values concerning themselves and their relationships with others. Most men are not aware of and do not question the assumptions upon which these concepts and values are based. This is as true of the business world as it is of any other part of the culture.

Among the widely accepted values and concepts with which sensitivity training is concerned are the following:

• An effective man controls his emotions and does not ordinarily express his feelings, especially his negative feelings, toward others.
• A "boss" is needed if a group is to accomplish anything.
• Authority in an organization always flows down from above.
• Purely rational processes are the most effective for reaching decisions.

One of the reasons these beliefs are widely accepted is that they work fairly well—most of the time. However, there may be occasions when these beliefs, and actions based upon them, do *not* work for an individual or a group.

For example, a manager may have difficulty with a subordinate because of unexpressed feelings that both men harbor. The boss may fear that the subordinate is trying to show him up; the subordinate may resent what he considers too tight supervision. Neither feels free to discuss their relationship. Their work suffers.

Another example: A boss may be confused by his employees' "unreasonable" resistance to changes that he has ordered. The employees may be less concerned with the changes than with the way they were introduced. They think: "He can't make me do this," and their attitude may destroy the effect of his authority formally delegated to him. The change is finally carried out, but it does not produce the results that were anticipated.

When failures such as these occur, there is a tendency to find out whose "fault" it is. Sensitivity training contends that no one person may be at fault. All the people involved may have been hiding from one another (perhaps even from themselves) the feelings and reactions that could explain just what was going on in their relationships.

The purpose of sensitivity training, then, is to help men achieve a greater awareness of how human beings relate to one another. It accomplishes this by bringing to the surface, for conscious examination, the normally unquestioned assumptions about human relations.

Requirements for Sensitivity Training

Since the values and assumptions tend to be unquestioned in normal social and business situations, it follows that a normal training situation cannot be used to bring them to the surface. In fact, trainers contend that a normal training situation may have the effect of reinforcing existing values and assumptions. Formal training procedures involve a "boss" (in the person of the instructor) with greater knowledge or formal authority. There are "subordinates" (in the form of students) who accept his authority. Participants expect the instructor to "give them the word." They expect to learn about and to talk about their understanding of a subject, rather than their own insightful response to a situation.

In sensitivity training the boss-subordinate atmosphere is avoided. The instructor uses his position and knowledge to create a situation where the assumptions cannot go unrecognized and unquestioned. The training session becomes, in effect, a laboratory in human relationships.[2]

Some of the characteristics of this "laboratory" are the following:

• No one has formal authority over the group and the participants are robbed of their status. No titles are used and the participants are usually strangers to one another.
• There is no established agenda for the training sessions.
• There is no established goal for the group to work toward—other than the goal of learning more about how individuals and groups function.
• There is no prescribed way for the group to reach decisions.
• The instructor (often called the "trainer") does not instruct the participants.

Groups set up in this fashion are called "T-groups"; the "T" stands for training.

The T-group is the core of sensitivity training, although other training experiences are incorporated in most programs.

Three to four dozen men participate in the typical program of sensitivity training. They are assigned to three or four T-groups that meet concurrently, each with one or two trainers. Most programs last two weeks. The men live together at some spot remote from their families and business associates; communication with home is permitted only in emergencies. During the two weeks, the participants assemble for lectures, illustrative motion pictures, or for experiments in group behavior. But once or twice a day for several hours at a time, they meet in their assigned T-groups.

What Happens to a T-group?

Participating in the first session of a T-group is an extremely frustrating experience for all concerned. It is hard for the strangers in the group to get started when they have no agenda or goals, when the trainers refuse to provide leadership, and when their only introduction to the experience has been the warning that the training will probably be different from what they anticipate.

The announced agenda for a T-group session is "whatever you want to talk about." And, typically, participants have trouble deciding what to talk about. They may have trouble deciding how to decide. Usually they also have trouble providing themselves with leadership. One or more members of the group may try to assume a leadership role; this seldom succeeds in the early sessions. All of this is quite frustrating to the successful business executives who participate in these training programs. After all, their success is based

---

[2] In fact, some sensitivity programs are called "management training laboratories" or "group dynamics laboratories."

upon "getting things done." And now, nothing seems to be happening—let alone getting done. Most experienced trainers consider this initial frustration a necessary, though unpleasant, part of sensitivity training. Through this experience, the participants soon realize that their effectiveness in the past has depended in large measure upon their established relationships and upon their formal authority to command. Stripped of these, many of the participants have difficulty creating and maintaining working relationships with other men. Only as they become aware of this are they ready to question their assumptions about human relationships. They learn emotionally (not just intellectually) that there may be something more they need to know if they are to be effective when normal relationships break down.

However, the participants not only learn that old ways may not always work, they also try new ways of relating to one another. This usually begins quite tentatively. It may be one man's blurted admission that he doesn't yet trust the other men in the group. A man may say that he has always found it good practice to keep somewhat aloof from associates in order to gain their respect. Someone else may question whether these attitudes are helping this group accomplish anything. Gradually the participants begin to be more open and honest about their feelings and reactions to one another.

Is It a "Blood Bath"?

Participants may express their reactions to one another quite bluntly. This has led some writers to call sensitivity training an emotional "blood bath." But the majority of participants say that this is not true, although they admit that the going can get rough. A man who has prided himself on his dignified manner and impressive utterances may hear that one of the other men considers him pompous. A man who has considered himself a forceful leader may learn that others resent the way he tries to railroad his own point of view. At the moment of hearing this, it can be a distinct shock, no matter how helpful the insight may seem later.

On the other hand, men learn that their fellows appreciate the constructive things they do that help to move the group along. A good question, an honest admission of feelings, even a joke that is timed to relieve tension, may gain the approval of the men.

The fact that the participants are strangers makes giving and receiving this feedback somewhat easier. It has often been noted that a man may tell an understanding stranger things that he would not reveal to even his closest friends. But the feeling that "we're all in this together" probably helps the most. Initially, the men accept one another as fellow participants in an unusual experience; gradually, they begin to accept one another as individuals. A man learns that others may not value him for what he has considered his good points but that they do not dislike him in spite of having seen his bad points. And, as a man learns that others can accept him as he is, he begins to accept himself. Ever since the Greeks coined the motto: "Know thyself," this has been acknowledged as the beginning of wisdom.

Is It Psychotherapy?

The techniques and procedures of the T-group resemble closely those that are used in group psychotherapy. Almost all trainers stress that there is a difference although they disagree on how closely sensitivity training must approach psychotherapy in order to be effective.

The difference lies primarily in the purposes of the two experiences. The goal of psychotherapy is greater insight into one's own personality, greater understanding of the self and its inner motivations. The goal of sensitivity training, on the other hand, is greater understanding of how groups operate and how individuals (including oneself) function in them.

Indeed, almost all experienced trainers agree that sensitivity training is intended for the healthy, not the sick. They say that a man should be emotionally stable enough to take the jolts that he will probably get if he participates. The neurotic manager needs other types of help.

Preventing the T-group from becoming group psychotherapy is one of the chief responsibilities of the trainers, many of whom are experienced therapists. They do this principally by controlling the depth of the probing that goes on. The trainers try to keep the group's focus on observable behavior rather than on inferences about motives.

For instance, in a T-group, the trainer would not interfere if one man said to another: "I get mad as hell when you try to steamroller the rest of us." He might well interject himself if, instead, someone said: "You try to steamroller us to cover up your own feelings of insecurity." He would probably point out that the speaker has no way of really knowing why the other man behaves as he does. The speaker can know, however, how he reacts to the other man's behavior.

Thus, sensitivity training remains near the surface of the personality. Its purpose is to help healthy men function more effectively with others, not to help sick men function more effectively within themselves.

The T-Group Becomes Effective

If the T-group remained rambling and ineffective, the participants would not learn much that would be useful to them on their jobs. Obviously, this isn't the case. The men learn to trust one another and become more open and communicative. The men decide more easily what they want to do and how to do it. They are better able to achieve a consensus that recognizes both majority and minority viewpoints. They learn to seek the leadership they need and to accept it from one another as it is offered. They develop effective ways to control the members who need to be restrained and to invite into the discussion the members who may be holding back.

It is not unusual for a participant to say, near the end of the two weeks, "If we only had a bunch of guys like this back home, we'd set the world on fire."

The value of the T-group comes from the fact that the unusual structure of the experience makes almost anything the group does stand out clearly. Therefore, the members can see what procedures work under different sets of circumstances. In effect, they increase their understanding of what *does* happen in groups and they broaden their repertoire of skills for dealing with group situations.

Is the T-group All There Is?

While the T-group experience is the heart of sensitivity training, other training methods are also employed. The trainers usually lecture to the participants assembled as a total group. The topics of the lectures are usually closely geared to what is taking place in the T-groups. For instance, during the first few days when the participants are still strangers, there might be a lecture on "The Problem of the Stranger in a New Group." These lectures are intended to provide insights that can help the members to articulate what they are experiencing in their groups.

Motion pictures are sometimes used. For example, "Twelve Angry Men," a film about a jury trying to decide upon a verdict in a murder case, has been used to show how groups can struggle with problems. Other films may be used to pose questions about the use of power, the legitimacy of formal authority, or the difficulties of communicating.

In some cases, sensitivity training incorporates experiments in group behavior. For instance, T-groups may be pitted against one another to show the effects of competition upon group morale. Another experiment may be set up to demonstrate the difficulties involved when a representative for a group has to negotiate with representatives of other groups. Such experiments are considered additional ways to provide insight into the roles of individuals in groups.

Sensitivity Training Evaluated

One of the few concrete indicators of the value of this training method is the experience of companies that have used it: While few have used it, almost all (80%) that have, plan to continue with it.

There are some former participants who vociferously denounce this training as a complete waste of time. The majority consider the experience very valuable. And quite a number of former participants have become enthusiastic advocates of sensitivity training. Almost no one, however, is able to say precisely how the experience has helped his work as a manager.

Former participants tend to use rather vague generalizations to explain how they have benefited: "I seem to get more co-operation from others now." "Since my T-Group, I really search for the other fellow's viewpoint; usually I'm able to get him to see mine, too. This seldom happened before." "I no longer get annoyed when meetings don't seem to be getting anywhere. Now I try to figure out what is getting in our way and often I can get us back on the track again." "I'm not sure exactly how I was helped but I know I'm a better manager; my boss says so too."

Sensitivity training is an unusual training experience, time-consuming and somewhat unpleasant in its early stages. But for the emotionally healthy manager, apparently it is an extremely effective means for deepening his understanding of how individuals work together to accomplish their purposes.

28. Contrasting Designs for Participative Systems

RICHARD E. WALTON

Two Designs for Participation

These two designs are contributed by different groups of social scientists. The approach of social scientists who advocate worker participation via leadership style is related to their more general interest in group dynamics and organizational relationships. Other social scientists, who perceive a formal plan as instrumental to participation, have come to their views through a larger interest in labor-management relations. Central to both designs is the ideal of democratic principles.

LEADERSHIP STYLE

The writings of Likert (1961), Argyris (1964), McGregor (1960) and others report on instances in which managers have modified their pattern of supervision in ways that allowed and encouraged workers to make more decisions for themselves and to participate more in planning and policy making functions. A participative leadership style involves sharing more information with subordinates, eliciting their ideas, encouraging interchange among them, employing general rather than close supervision, and engaging in

a supportive interpersonal pattern. Emphasis is placed on the handling of face-to-face relationships. An attempt to adopt more participative patterns is often accompanied by training in the skills of face-to-face relationships.

FORMAL PLAN

Labor unions have been a mechanism for subjecting hours, wages, working conditions and other terms of employment to joint decision-making. Occasionally, however, unions have joined employers in social experiments providing for broader worker participation in the functions of management and in direct support of firms' goals.

Slichter, Livernash and Healy (1960) have reviewed these formal plans of union-management cooperation in the United States and Canada.[1] Several thousand joint committees to promote production were established during the Second World War, but most of these, if they functioned at all, disappeared after the war. There have been more significant and enduring plans in the railroad industry, notably Canadian National Railways and the Baltimore and Ohio Railroad, and

---

Reprinted by permission from the November–December, 1967 issue of *Personnel Administration*, copyright 1967, Society for Personnel Administration, 1221 Connecticut Avenue NW., Washington, D.C. 20036. Richard E. Walton is Professor of Administrative Science, Herman C. Krannert Graduate School of Industrial Administration, Purdue University.

[1] In some European countries the labor movements have as a goal co-determination or joint consultation with respect to all aspects of the enterprise, and in some cases the law supports this pattern.

in the T.V.A. More recently, a number of plans have been established in the needle trades and automotive parts industry. Finally, the Scanlon Plan has been used in a variety of industrial situations, including LaPointe Machine Tool, Stromberg-Carlson, and others.

In almost all of these plans individual workers participate through joint union-management or worker-management committees that encourage, collect, and pass on suggestions for improving productivity. In most cases there is some explicit scheme for sharing between workers and management the fruits of increased productivity. Although formal plans with these characteristics have typically been developed in a union-management context, they should be considered on their merits independent of a collective bargaining relationship.

Explicating the leadership style and the formal designs, respectively, are two books—*New Patterns of Management,* by Rensis Likert (1961), and *The Scanlon Plan,* by F. Lesieur (1958). A comparative analysis of these two approaches to participation reveals both common aspects and important differences.

SIMILARITIES

Both approaches reflect optimistic assumptions about the typically untapped potential of workers to make contributions to productivity. First, it is assumed that workers have the knowledge, skill and ingenuity that can improve the design of the production process. Second, it is assumed that an opportunity to contribute ideas will have further motivating effects increasing the energy available for production and increasing worker sense of responsibility for product quality. Third, it is assumed that the predicted increase in involvement and commitment to company goals will have the further effect of increasing worker readiness to

accept technological change and other modifications in his work environment.

CONTRASTS

Mechanisms for Participation: Interpersonal Relations versus Structure; and Single versus Dual Hierarchies. The supervisory style approach emphasizes face-to-face discussions among members of the immediate work group, including the supervisor who is employing the participative style. A worker's influence and participation beyond his work group occurs, if at all, through his supervisor. There is sometimes an explicit assumption that the supervisor will "represent" his subordinate group as a member of the next higher participating group. Likert has termed this the "linking pin" concept. If there is not a participative group at this higher level, the supervisor will simply serve as a communicator to his supervisor on a one-to-one basis.

The formal plans place more emphasis on the structure and procedures for participation. The structure is more likely to provide for participation through selected representatives. The procedures are designed to ensure that ideas get processed to a top level screening committee with representatives of both workers and management.

The formal approach does not rely exclusively upon the same hierarchical channel for downward instructions and allocation of individual rewards and penalties and also for upward communication of ideas and influence. (See Figure 1.)

Motivators: The Process Itself versus Tangible Rewards and Economic Justice. The two approaches place primary emphasis on different motivators. The leadership style approach emphasizes the social and psychological satisfactions a worker can derive directly from the participative process itself. The process al-

Linking Pin Organization

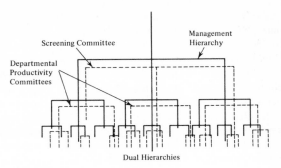

Dual Hierarchies

Figure 1.

lows the individual to use more of his skills, to exercise upward influence, and to enjoy membership in a task group. These opportunities are gratifying and enhance the worker's individual self-worth. Economic rewards are not often stressed, nor is the social-economic-legal concept of an equitable sharing of the productivity gains resulting from participation given much explicit attention.

Those who approach participation through the formal plan reverse the above emphasis. They stress the economic rewards which can result from participation. In some cases, the benefits are greater job security through improvement in the market position of the company. More frequently, bonuses for the total work group are tied to some measure of productivity. The bonus is more than an economic incentive; it is a means for achieving an equitable sharing of the fruits of the participative efforts. The worker's sense of social-economic justice which results is assumed to be an important source of reinforcement for their efforts.

Scope and Pervasiveness of Each Approach. The two approaches also differ in the extent to which they involve widespread participation under similar ground rules.

The leadership style approach is more likely to be local option, used in only one of many work groups or in only one or two of several levels in a given chain of command. Where it is a generally accepted pattern throughout an organization, even if it was initiated at the top, it is typically adopted by a consensus process. This process of adoption is necessary and consistent with the basic assumptions underlying this particular participative approach: it is a fundamental value that supervisors should be able to determine their respective leadership styles; and because of the importance of the face-to-face process they should not be encouraged to use a style that is not authentic.

A significantly different type of influence process for gaining acceptance and involvement in a participation pattern is employed in connection with the formal plan, and the pattern which results is broader in scope and more pervasive. The formal plan is usually created by top officials of management and union. Although one consideration of the decision is the current attitudes by lower level supervision and officials, the top officials are likely to base their decision on many other considerations and then try to get compliance and genuine participation after the plan is formally adopted. They are also likely to use organizational authority to "encourage" cooperation of lower level officials. Often they encourage workers to determine which supervisors are not cooperating and to supply pressure to induce more cooperation.

II. Obstacles to Participation at the Worker Level

Certain forces tend to operate against the development of an effective participation pattern at the worker level of the organization. This fact is made obvious by comparing the worker and middle management organizational levels in terms of certain factors critical to the success of participation.

1. *Factors which inhibit the boss.* Compared with higher management, first line supervisors tend to be more concerned about narrowing the status differences between themselves and their subordinates and about losing disciplinary control. Also, first line supervisors can less afford to spend time in talking activities, the medium of participative management. Both factors inhibit participative approaches by foremen.

2. *Skill factors which limit the boss.* Compared with middle managers, first line supervisors are less likely to have the verbal and human relations skills requisite for participation. Thus, even the willing foremen's capabilities may be too limited to make participation work.

3. *Factors which inhibit or limit subordinates.* Compared with subordinates at the middle management level, workers tend to be more concerned about being induced to work harder and about eliminating their own or others' jobs. As a result, workers are likely to be more cautious or even suspicious in their response to participative overtures.

The typical worker has less aspiration to either enlarge his job, increase his skills or take his superior's job and is less responsive to the values of individual freedom and self development in the job context. Where he is unionized, the worker who has such aspirations has another status and power hierarchy available apart from management which provides him with an alternative source of recognition and influence.

What are the implications of these limiting and inhibiting factors? The first conclusion is the obvious one: a participation pattern is more likely to be successfully initiated at middle management level than at the first line supervisory level.[2] The second implication emerges from the analysis developed in the next part: namely, that the formal plan minimizes the adverse effects of these potential limiting and inhibiting factors.

III. Advantages of Formal Plan Design

An evaluation of the contrasting features of the two plans, especially against the background of the inherent or potential obstacles to participation at the worker level, suggests the following advantages of the formal plan.

Committee Structure and Prescribed Procedures Are More Realistic. Because it is hard for both first line supervisors and workers to initiate and maintain a pattern of open participation when this runs counter to all of their previous experience, a structure and set of procedures which prescribe their respective roles and behaviors are important aids.

An informal local choice approach places the greater demands on the behavioral skill of the supervisor. He must initiate, reinforce, and evaluate participa-

[2] Also see further analysis by George Strauss. "Some Notes on Power Equalization," in *The Social Science of Organizations,* edited by Harold Leavitt, Prentice-Hall, Englewood Cliffs, N.J. 1963.

tion. In contrast, under a formal plan the supervisor is more in the position of adapting to the requirements of a structure and responding to the production oriented, participative initiation of the workers, who in turn are encouraged by an incentive. This is a relative matter because either plan requires a higher level of behavioral skill than normally is manifest in supervisory organizations.

Parallel Hierarchy Gives Workers More Independence. A special hierarchy of committees with worker membership and whose primary purpose is to screen and pass on productivity suggestions is more likely to get top level consideration for a worker idea than is the regular line hierarchy, even if the latter has the best of intentions. The individual worker has more power and independence because he does not have to rely exclusively upon his immediate supervisor either for upward or downward communication. Among other things, he can be more sharply critical of poor supervision when he participates in or is represented by another worker on a departmental and over-all screening committee.

Emphasis on Financial Incentives Is Realistic. Because workers, compared with middle management subordinates, don't identify as closely with higher officials and the management function and have less self-development aspiration, they require more extrinsic incentives to participate in higher organization activities. Workers have less upward mobility and the incentives must be in financial terms rather than in increased promotability. Managers, however, may be content with the knowledge that their chances for promotion have increased as a result of the value of their contributions.

Exclusive reliance upon monetary or tangible incentives is inadequate. However, total work group incentives in the context of the other participative features of the formal plan tend to create a congruent set of motivational forces.

Productivity Bonuses Serve Other Purposes. The explicit linking of bonuses with improvements in productivity has several advantages.

First, this characteristic faces up to the classic problem of simultaneously increasing total joint gain and allocating this resource among contributors. A recent article by McKersie and the author (1965) analyzed interpersonal, interdepartmental and interorganizational relations to illustrate the generality of the dilemmas involved and to demonstrate the importance of their solution to the viability of a social relationship. Briefly, if a person perceives himself to have low influence over decisions on how to allocate gains created by collaboration, or if there is considerable uncertainty involved in the allocation process, the person is less likely to enter into the collaborative process of creating joint gain. In terms of that analysis, the ratio used in the Scanlon Plan is a very imaginative attempt to allow for periodic, rational allocation decisions in a way which interferes least with the collaborative processes which increase joint gain. The plan provides for the occasional review and revision of the ratio, based upon specified criteria or factors—product mix, technological investment, different raw material.

Thus, an important feature of the formal plan is that as much attention is paid to the problem of equitable sharing in the fruits of improvement as to structures for creating and processing ideas for improvement and then implementing the ideas. This contrasts with an emphasis on the personal values, behavioral styles and skills, and attitudes of a superior in his dealing with his subordinates. The prominent place of the ratio increases the results-mindedness of managers and workers alike, whereas without specifically developed measurements with a clear understanding of all of the factors which can offset performance there is a tendency to judge effectiveness by the process itself and the satisfaction it generates.

These formal plans require and insure that employees' representatives become educated in important factors relating to bonuses. Controllable cost factors must be stressed particularly. Concepts of work flow, delays, bottleneck factors, pay-back period. etc. come to be shared by employee committee members.

The Costs of Local Option by Supervisors Are Too Great. The localized or piecemeal characteristic of many instances where the leadership style approach has been tried has been an important liability to the effort. Apart from the differences in the output or rewards which may accompany localized use of participation, there are important differences in the accepted patterns of worker behavior; the participative workers are given more freedom, initiative and latitude in the way they go about their work and in the way they deport themselves. They are likely to be less deferential to others in authority, to follow rules less literally, and to criticize otherwise accepted procedures and practices. If they continue with "deviate" patterns, they may cause severe resentment in other groups; if they are controlled, they may be discouraged about participation in "such a rigid system."

Since the formal plan officially covers all groups and provides for participation mechanisms in addition to the worker-supervisor relationship, a worker can participate in spite of a reluctant supervisor. Although under the formal plan there is less local choice for the individual supervisor, there is *more* freedom for the *individual worker* to participate as much or as little as he likes. Under a participative leadership style, the leader often treats all

of his subordinates as members of a group, involving them all in meetings, decisions, subtask assignment, etc. With or without intent, group norms often develop, *requiring* members to participate. Under the formal plan, some employees become very active in terms of submitting suggestions, others are active in departmental or screening committee work, still others may not get involved in either type of activity. They easily choose their own level and kind of participation. The nature of the structure and procedures of the formal plan makes this differentiated participation easy and natural.

IV. Conclusions

The above analysis leads one to be pessimistic about the use of the leadership style approach to participation at the worker level; but more optimistic about the formal plan approach for this class of employees. In addition, it is impossible not to be impressed with the potential of the leadership style approach where higher organizational levels are involved.

The matrix on page 258 summarizes the implications of this analysis.

The above conclusions about participation at the level of first line supervision emerge from a more or less theoretical analysis, rather than empirical studies. These should be treated as hypotheses subject to more detailed comparative study of actual experiences under the two approaches.

The two approaches have been treated at times as if they were strictly alternatives. This is useful in clarifying the different emphases involved. Actually, I believe the most fruitful approach is to *start* with structure of a formal plan and then try to develop the leadership and other interpersonal skills.

Type of Approach.

		Leadership Style	Formal Plan
Level of Organization:	Middle Management	Optimistic	Not Appropriate
	First Line Supervisor-Workers	Pessimistic	Optimistic

References

Argyris, Chris. *Integrating the Individual and the Organization,* John Wiley and Sons, Inc., New York, 1964.

Lesieur, Frederick G. *The Scanlon Plan: A Frontier in Labor Management Co-operation,* The Technology Press of Massachusetts Institute of Technology and John Wiley and Sons, Inc., New York, 1958.

Likert, Rensis. *New Patterns of Management,* McGraw-Hill Book Company, New York, 1961.

McGregor, Douglas M. *The Human Side of Enterprise,* McGraw-Hill Book Company, New York, 1960.

Slichter, Sumner S., James J. Healy, and E. Robert Livernash. *The Impact of Collective Bargaining on Management,* The Brookings Institute, Washington, D.C., 1960.

Strauss, George. "Some Notes on Power Equalization." in Harold Leavitt (ed.), *The Social Science of Organizations,* Prentice-Hall, Englewood Cliffs, N.J., 1963.

Walton, Richard E. and Robert B. McKersie. "Behavioral Dilemmas in Mixed Motive Decision-Making," Institute Paper #108, Institute for Research in the Behavioral, Economic and Management Sciences, Purdue University, April 1965.

29. Management By Objectives:
How to Measure Results *

DALE D. McCONKEY

Today's highly competitive business climate is intolerant of mediocrity on the part of its managers, as has been evidenced several times within the past two years by the removal of the chief executives of half a dozen major corporations and the reshuffling of the top command in others. In at least two of these instances, the executives concerned were well recognized and had been hired because of their outstanding records—yet they failed to achieve the results demanded of them. Since the results achieved by the chief executive are essentially the sum of the results achieved by each of his managers, it appears only equitable to attribute much of the blame for top-level failure to comparable failures on the part of subordinates.

Today's professional manager often finds it difficult to measure the results of his subordinates, lacking as he does a thorough knowledge of all activities of the business and the intuitive judgment usually developed by constant exposure to the same business. Indeed, traditional measures do not afford him an accurate gauge of the activities or results of his managers.

The difficulty of measuring results is compounded by the growing size and complexity of business. Where the executive was formerly able to direct personally many of the activities of the business, now he is forced to delegate much of the operation and responsibility to his subordinates. However, he still bears ultimate responsibility and cannot fully relinquish his control. He must know how to break up the responsibility among many, maintain the necessary coordination and control, and evaluate the effectiveness of the delegation.

How does a company determine just who in the enterprise is responsible for its successes or failures? In many companies there is only one profit and loss center—the total company—and only one man is accountable for results—the chief executive.

One-Man Accountability

What is a one-man profit center? For the purposes of this article, it can be defined as a company in which the managers on various levels cannot be held responsible for results because of the vague definitions of their function, and therefore only one man—the chief executive—can be held responsible for the performance of the entire enterprise. If the enterprise succeeds, all is well; if it fails, he alone is responsible. Countless managers up and down the line who contrib-

Reprinted from *Business Horizons*, Vol. 7, No. 3 (Fall, 1964), pp. 47–54, with permission of the author and of the publisher, Indiana University. Dale D. McConkey is Vice-President and Assistant to the President, United Fruit Company, Boston.

* For a more complete treatment of the subject, see Dale D. McConkey *How to Manage by Results* (revised edition). New York: American Management Association, 1967.

uted to the failure remain relatively immune from justice because their responsibilities were never enumerated, and thus the effectiveness of their efforts cannot be measured. This is true particularly in highly centralized organizations in which almost all major decisions are made at the top, with little or no authority delegated down the line—organizations in which there are no subsidiary profit and loss centers or other established means for measuring managers at all levels. It is equally true for less highly centralized companies in which the responsibilities and accountabilities of the various managers have not been clearly defined.

Many companies mistakenly believe they have established multiple levels of accountability when in reality they are operating as one-man profit centers. These companies point with pride to fat job descriptions which state in lofty terms that a vice-president of purchasing "is responsible for formulating, establishing, and administering an effective purchasing program." A prodigious amount of paper and effort could be saved if they merely said "he purchases," and most of them would lose little by this two-word abbreviation because these descriptions say little more than this anyway. Certainly they do little else than state the particular functional area or activity for which the manager is responsible. They do not enumerate the results for which the manager is accountable.

Levels of Accountability

The alternative to the one-man profit and loss center and single accountability is to establish multiple levels of accountability; all levels of supervision—from first line through top management—are held responsible for achieving results for portions of the enterprise.

While many companies are fond of bragging of their "management team" and the degree to which they have delegated authority, there is a real question with respect to just how much authority has, in fact, been delegated and by what method the effectiveness of the delegation is measured. It is one thing to give an executive responsibility for production, permit him to run production, and evaluate him based on how well he actually runs production. It is an entirely different matter to delegate production to him and then run production from the front office. It is yet another matter to delegate production, let the manager run it, and fail to measure and control the results achieved by that delegation.

Thus, if multiple levels of accountability are to be truly achieved, responsibilities must be both delegated and controlled through all levels of the organization.

Kinds of Measuring

TRADITIONAL MEASURING

Traditional measuring has taken the form of performance appraisal or merit rating, which might be termed "personality" measuring. These typically follow a civil service type of measurement; that is, emphasis is on effort expended rather than output achieved (results). The writer has reviewed many of these forms and appraisal processes, including those in current use by many large corporations. These forms usually rate the individual according to a series of factors ostensibly designed to measure his effectiveness. Factors frequently used include initiative, grasp of function, cost consciousness, health, judgment, potential for advancement, ability to deal with others, and so forth. At best, these are weak measuring devices because they do not actually measure results, and it is, after all, results that determine the success of an enterprise. For example, a particular executive could be bubbling with initiative, know his function well, be especially cost conscious, have the best of health, possess superb judgment, be a real comer, and get along well with others, and still not make any contribution to company profit.

One leading nationally known company has changed its appraisal form four times in as many years and is currently working on the fifth modification—all because actual results achieved by the executives do not bear out the glowing words included on their appraisal forms. What better testimony is needed to show that merit rating forms, while probably good as guides for training and development, are a poor measure of results. These appraisal or merit rating forms have other faults. In many companies they supply the basic premises on which merit increases are granted, promotions are based, bonuses are awarded, efficiency awards are made, and a whole host of other rewards are "justified."

Critical analysis of their use demonstrates that traditional measures have failed primarily because they attempt to measure before their users know what they are supposed to measure. To illustrate, let's take one of the more common factors appearing on managerial appraisal forms, that of cost consciousness. This factor is usually spelled out in terms such as "Degree to Which the Manager is Cost Conscious." In an attempt to guide the person doing the rating, the factor is usually further broken down into degrees: "Manager is especially cost conscious," "Manager is below average in cost consciousness," and "Manager is poor in cost consciousness." These are indefinite, highly relative terms. In view of the fact that many of these companies do not have any precise standard against which to measure the manager, use of the words "appraisal," "rating," or "measurement" is obviously ridiculous. For ex-

ample, take the case of a plant manager who spends $50,000 on plant maintenance during the year. Is he especially cost conscious, above average, below average, or poor? Naturally, without much more knowledge of the given situation, no one in possession of all of his faculties would attempt to answer the question. Yet we attempt this stab in the dark when we endeavor to appraise or measure without first knowing precisely what we are measuring.

MANAGEMENT BY OBJECTIVES

One effective alternative to this largely inadequate traditional approach is a method that establishes definite results which a manager is expected to achieve during a particular period. This method of measuring is called management by objectives, goals management, or management by results. The last term is preferred because it emphasizes the positive aspect of managerial performance, that is, results; the method is important, not the label, and in a properly formulated and administered plan the terms may be used interchangeably.

One of the most critical aspects of this method is the superior's evaluation of the objectives. It is important that the goals be set for measuring at a particular future time. The superior must evaluate each objective in these terms:

1. Does the objective represent a sufficient task for the manager during the measuring period?
2. Is the objective a practical and attainable one?
3. Is the objective clearly stated in terms of the task? The measuring period? The method of measuring to be used?
4. Is the objective compatible with the company's plans for the period?

If an objective is approved that is too easily attainable or is an insufficient task for the measuring period, the company and the manager will suffer. The company will not have received value due for the period, and the manager's development will have been impeded since his objective has not put demands on his full capacity.

Choosing such a goal is more complicated than setting work standards in rather routine, highly repetitive production operations, and this is one of the most difficult aspects of the problem. Once the superior has put his approval on the manager's objectives, the manager has every reason to accept those objectives as being his mandate and operating procedure for the length of the measuring period. Then, if the manager has satisfactorily completed his objective at the end of this measuring period, he has every right to believe he has done a good job.

But take, for example, an objective to be completed in two years, but for which a period of twelve or eighteen months was a realistic period for completion. Does this mean that a manager who took the full allowable two-year period was "goofing off"? Not altogether. The manager knows he has two years to complete the objective, and so he schedules each phase of the task for completion during a certain interval within the period. If he completes one phase ahead of schedule, he is likely to use his time and that of his staff to work on other matters which he considers to be important.

MEASURING BY OBJECTIVE

There is little doubt but that the better method for setting objectives is the one in which the objectives are drafted and recommended by the individual managers and then approved by their superiors. After a general briefing by the chief executive as to the company's objectives for a specified future period, the manager applies these corporate goals to his department, and determines objectives his department will have to achieve to contribute to the over-all goal. After approval by the chief executive, the departmental

goals become the manager's directive of required action and standard against which he will be measured and rewarded or removed.

To be effective, measurement by objectives should not be limited to the top managers. By the same techniques, each manager must measure the supervisors under his jurisdiction, in order to achieve multiple levels of responsibility. Thus the total enterprise is being held accountable for results. This method has the further advantage of leading naturally into good forward planning, since each manager is required to set future objectives and work toward them. In combining the managers' objectives, the chief executive establishes the forward planning for the total entity.

Certain theoreticians advocate that only a limited number of objectives should be set for any manager and that a responsibility should not be included as an objective unless it constitutes a certain minimum percentage of the time required for the over-all task for the period. Thus if a particular responsibility constitutes only 5 per cent of the total task for the period, it should not be included because (1) it might detract from the more important objectives, or (2) several small items might be substituted for a few more important ones.

I quarrel with this school of thought on two counts. First, in applying measurement by objectives to all levels of management, one cannot follow any standard format; the number and percentage weights of objectives must be dictated by the nature of the job. Second, the time required to accomplish a particular objective is not indicative of the importance or contribution of that objective to the company; that is, a task requiring only 10 per cent of an executive's time may be worth infinitely more to the company than one requiring 30 per cent of his time.

An effective system should also provide for measurement of the manager's performance at interim periods within the total time allowed for accomplishment of the objective. This has two distinct advantages. It serves as a further check on the validity of the original objective and it permits corrective action before an improperly conceived objective or a poor manager has gone beyond the point of no return.

QUANTITATIVE AND QUALITATIVE MEASURING

The measurement of the line managers is infinitely easier since the line is engaged in activities of a tangible nature, which lend themselves to quantitative measuring. Although they have some responsibilities that may be measured in qualitative terms, the means of measuring line managers is quantitative as contrasted to staff managers where measurement is primarily qualitative.

The contributions of line managers are measured by these rules: profit and loss centers, cost centers, return on investment, units of sales, cost of sales, and net income. Budgetary control should be used with caution as a quantitative measure. Although very desirable for other valid business purposes, many budgets are little more than a historical reporting of what has happened as compared to what someone projected would happen. Unless budgets are tied in accurately with well thought out and approved objectives, they do not measure what should have happened and therefore, by themselves, they do not measure a manager's accomplishment with respect to what he should have been responsible for accomplishing during a given period.

Breech has said, "In the case of staff activities, whose relation to profit is far less capable of definition, top management must find its own guidelines to minimize unnecessary costs and achieve the best possible results." [1]

Continuation of the traditional difficulty or reluctance in measuring staff activities becomes quite critical in view of the rapidly increasing ratio of staff to line activities. The growing complexity of business requires more and more sophisticated "advice and counsel," for example, guidance in the increasingly frustrating area of antitrust. Growth in size of corporations has expanded the role of staff activities from general staff in the headquarters to smaller counterparts down the line at subsidiary, division, and plant levels. Increasing technology has created whole new groups of staff people—computer engineers, programmers, systems experts, and so forth.

Industry had a chance to see the dimensions of this problem a few years ago when a large corporation took a strike of twenty-two weeks over its insistence that it be permitted to establish time standards for its indirect workers. Direct workers in this company had worked under time standards for years without objection from the bargaining representative. Why then should the union suddenly object to the point of prolonged strike over the issue of timing indirect workers? It appears that both the company and the union suddenly awoke to the fact that indirect workers were concertedly outnumbering direct workers.

The lack of accurate qualitative measurement for staff managers results in waste when their work, self-generating and self-perpetuating, and involving many employees and high costs, bears no relation to the company's objectives and needs. Ineffective managers may adopt policies that have worked for other companies but are not adaptable to their own. This leaves a vast and growing segment of business management immune from accountability just because it cannot be measured completely in quantitative terms.

---

[1] Ernest R. Breech, "New Role for the Financial Man," *Think* (April, 1963), p. 5.

Examples of Quantitative and Qualitative Measuring
of Typical Management Positions

Quantitative Measuring	Qualitative Measuring

Plant Manager

1. Complete construction and equipping of approved addition to new plant within cost of $20,000.
2. Produce X number of units of Y product at Z costs.
3. Install and have operational approved XYZ packaging line.

1. Conduct monthly management development sessions for superintendents in techniques of standard cost program.
2. Select and train agreed upon cadre of supervisors for new Texas plant.
3. Install system for more effective expediting of "drop orders."

Industrial Relations Director

1. Reduce costs of recruiting research Ph.D.'s from $1,000 to $750 each without sacrificing quality.
2. Formulate a full-strength, one-for-one incentive system for packaging department designed to lower unit labor costs by 3 per cent.
3. Maintain cafeteria costs at 1962 levels without loss in food quality.

1. Prepare and distribute industrial relations policy manual.
2. Prepare prenegotiation bargaining strategy sessions with all plant managers.
3. Prepare and make final recommendation for a restricted stock option plan for employees in Grade 18 and above.

Research Director

1. Reduce costs of fertilizer application by 5 per cent.
2. Complete development of ABC product and make available for production.
3. Apportion research costs on basis of 25 per cent basic and 75 per cent applied.

1. Reduce orientation period for Ph.D.'s from 24 to 18 months.
2. Undertake to more closely ally research efforts with product needs.
3. Improve appearance packaging and design of products.

Quality Control Director

1. Reduce by 5 per cent the quantity of rejects of ABC products.
2. Reduce quality control labor costs by 15 per cent by centralized rather than decentralized inspection.
3. Reduce inspection time on X items by 35 per cent by installation of electronic measuring devices.

1. Establish system for tracing substandard products back to their originating point.
2. Prepare quality control manual for supervisors.
3. Improve statistical reports to reduce time lag between production and the date of reports.

Controller

1. Reduce clerical accounting labor by $100,000 by installation of electronic data processing equipment.
2. Reduce by seven days the time lag in preparation of standard cost follow-up reports.
3. Reduce by 25 per cent working cash required in bank deposits.

1. Install cost accounting system that can be used by supervisors for effective cost control at the first level.
2. Provide monthly investigation and analysis of budget variances.
3. Install a standard cost program for XYZ product line.

Quantitative Measuring	Qualitative Measuring

Sales Director

1. Increase sales of *ABC* product by 3 per cent.
2. Hold private label sales to 7 per cent of sales.
3. Maintain advertising promotion expenses at last year's level.

1. Establish sales quotas for all outside salesmen.
2. Prepare and recommend incentive compensation plan for regional managers.
3. Switch advertising emphasis from wholesalers to consumers.

General Counsel

1. Reduce by 10 per cent the cost of outside legal services.
2. Increase international legal staff by 15 per cent.
3. Hire and train two antitrust specialists at cost of $35,000.

1. Conduct working seminars with field sales personnel re antitrust aspects of selling.
2. Present plan for compliance with Blank consent decree.
3. Prepare program for patent protection.

Public Relations Director

1. Reduce costs of holding regional PR seminars by 10 per cent.
2. Hold direct mail program costs to $.05 per unit.
3. At cost of $20,000, conduct survey of company's public relations posture and needs.

1. Develop community relations program for Rochester plant.
2. Prepare and distribute an internal public relations manual.
3. Recommend a corporate identification program for parent company and subsidiaries.

Corporate Secretary

1. Reduce cost of shareholder mailings, decreasing the frequency and making more comprehensive.
2. Complete all arrangements for annual meeting thirty days prior to meeting.
3. Hold cost of annual report printing to $25,000.

1. Prepare program for welcoming and orienting new shareholders.
2. Prepare weekly analysis reports of changes in stock transfer books.
3. Install central file system for official company records.

Engineering Director

1. Complete construction and place boiler #2 on line.
2. Reengineer package line #10 to provide for one-hour surge facility.
3. Complete rewiring of plant #6.

1. Complete program for first echelon maintenance of company delivery trucks.
2. Investigate feasibility of installing higher speed wrapping machines on line #2.
3. Undertake skill training sessions to upgrade technical abilities of instrumentation engineers.

Qualitative measures can now be applied to staff measurement if a definition of quality can be agreed upon. These three basic aspects should be considered in the qualitative measurement of staff: cost of the activity, consistency with company goals, and contribution to company goals.

The failure to recognize a cardinal difference between the measurement of line and staff will render useless the qualitative measurement of staff. A line manager's performance in a profit and loss center, for instance, is measured by the end results of that center, and not by the results of one particular component of the center, say production, marketing, or research. Any attempt to apply the same inclusive measurement to staff would be not only fruitless but also distorting and misleading. If we merely say that an industrial relations director is responsible for the successful formulation, installation, of an effective industrial relations program, we have stated the final result expected, but by the same token we have made it impossible to measure this manager's performance. Actually, this method of stating responsibility may permit excellence in one major area to overshadow lack of accomplishment in another, with the result that the manager is considered satisfactory when in reality his performance may have been only fair or poor in terms of all of the other activities for which he was responsible. Thus, to measure the total performance of this industrial relations director we must specifically state and specifically measure each of the activities that together make up his performance. We must break down and measure his objectives in the areas of wage and salary administration, labor relations, training, recruiting, and so forth.

On the preceding two pages are examples of quantitative and qualitative measuring of ten jobs, both line and staff, under the results-oriented approach to measuring managers.

How to Begin

The executive who adopts management by results should begin on a modest basis regarding the organization unit to be measured, the measuring period, and the objective itself. A good kick-off point for the uninitiated is to select one department or division of the company and use this as a workable, moderate-sized guinea pig. After gaining experience on this limited basis, the scope of the experiment can be extended a department at a time until the enterprise is fully covered. A relatively short measuring period of three to six months should be used at first. The exact length of this period depends on the objectives and must be sufficient to permit measurable progress. The objectives selected should be relatively simple, so as not to confuse the beginner or cloud the ability to measure. With the completion of each measuring period, the executive will build confidence and experience in this method and will soon be able to use it to its maximum effectiveness.

The weaknesses of the traditional approach to measuring and the strong points of the results approach are illustrated by comparing the measuring of a particular job using each of the two approaches. In the traditional method, a typical job description spells out the manager's job in broad generalizations extensively intertwined with vague personality traits. Any appraisal or evaluation of the incumbent's performance must be general and vague because the standards in the "rating scale" are similarly general and vague. We cannot measure the nebulous in precise and definitive manner. I submit that the type of managerial appraisal which many companies now use is tantamount to measuring running water with a micrometer. It cannot be done.

In contrast, a statement of accountability, precisely oriented to the results desired, tells the manager what is expected of him and the criteria against which he will be measured. No verbose, pretentious appraisal form is required to measure his performance when accountability is clearly spelled out. A simple comparison of results with expectations is enough to measure achievement.

The time has come for industry to concentrate full time on improving the performance of its management. We must determine and formalize the exact results for which an incumbent will be held responsible and let him have no doubt about what they are. We must stop trying to measure performance in terms of vague personality traits or broad generalizations about attitudes. We must stop acting like pseudo-psychoanalysts and concentrate on the hard business of getting results. We must start moving away from one-man accountability toward a more effective type of management—multiple levels of accountability.

DISCUSSION QUESTIONS: PART III

1. Why have the social sciences contributed so little to the practice of management? How would you improve the relationship of the social scientists to industry? What types of research do you think industry would be interested in having social scientists complete for them, if any? Why?

2. Abstract each of the following in a paragraph: the mechanistic tradition; the humanistic challenge; and the realistic synthesis. Is the "realistic synthesis" a reasonable approach to organization theory? Explain.

3. Define a "good" human relations? In what types of situation should it be used? List several possible research projects which could be used to determine what "good" and "bad" human relations are.

4. What is the utility of conflict? Examine each of the possible conflict situations. What are the ranges of permissible conflict?

5. Describe the major types of change programs? If you were planning a major change in an organization (such as the elimination of large numbers of white-collar clerical jobs due to the advent of a new computer), what steps would you take to minimize organizational conflict and confusion and what type of change program would you use? Why?

6. Analyze the criteria for valid applied behavioral science research. Could you improve them? If so, how? If not, why not?

7. What are man's basic needs? How are each of these needs related to the work situation? Explain.

8. Discuss the major factors affecting productivity. Which of these do you consider to be the most crucial? Why?

9. Why isn't motivation sufficient in running a company? How would you reconcile the views of Consultants A, B, and C in the Leavitt article?

10. Differentiate between the persuasion and problem-solving approaches. After establishing a set of criteria for evaluating these two approaches, which one would be the most effective? Why?

11. Why are upward communications frequently blocked?

12. In communications, what factors affect both senders and receivers? Senders only? Receivers only? In what ways could you improve communications in a firm? Why would you take those steps?

13. What is sensitivity training? When should it be used in industry? Is it psychotherapy?
14. Distinguish between the two designs for achieving worker participation in management. In what ways are they similar or different? If you were going to adopt one of these two designs, which one would you adopt and why?
15. Describe "management by objectives." What are the assumptions underlying "management by objectives?" List the major advantages and disadvantages of such a method as you see them.

SELECTED REFERENCES: PART III

A. ORGANIZATIONAL BEHAVIOR

Applewhite, Philip B., *Organizational Behavior*. Englewood Cliffs, N.J.: Prentice-Hall, Inc., 1965.

Berelson, Bernard and Gary A. Steiner, *Human Behavior: An Inventory of Scientific Findings*. New York: Harcourt, Brace and World, 1964.

Bernthal, Wilmar F., "Contributions of the Behavioral Science Approach," *Academy of Management, Proceedings of the 1962 Annual Meeting*. University Park, Pa.: 1963, pp. 21–28.

Davis, Keith, "Evolving Models of Organizational Behavior," *Academy of Management Journal,* Vol. 11, No. 1 (March, 1968), pp. 27–38.

Fisk, George (ed.), *The Frontiers of Management Psychology*. New York: Harper and Row, 1964, pp. 41–108.

Herbst, P. S., "Problems of Theory and Method in the Integration of the Behavioral Sciences," *Human Relations,* Vol. 18, No. 4 (November, 1965), pp. 351–359.

Knowles, H. P. and B. O. Saxberg, "Human Relations and the Nature of Man," *Harvard Business Review,* Vol. 45, No. 2 (March–April, 1967), pp. 22–40; 172–178.

Leavitt, Harold J., *Managerial Psychology* (second edition). Chicago: University of Chicago Press, 1964.

Litterer, Joseph A., *Organizations: Structure and Behavior*. New York: John Wiley and Sons, Inc., 1963.

———— *The Analysis of Organizations*. New York: John Wiley and Sons, Inc., 1965.

March, James G. (ed.), *Handbook of Organizations*. Chicago: Rand McNally and Company, 1965.

Zaleznik, Abraham and David Moment, *The Dynamics of Interpersonal Behavior*. New York: John Wiley and Sons, Inc., 1964.

B. ORGANIZATIONAL CONFICT AND CHANGE

Bennis, W. C., "A New Role for the Behavioral Sciences: Effecting Organizational Change," *Administrative Science Quarterly,* Vol. VIII, No. 2 (September, 1963), pp. 125–165.

Boulding, Kenneth E., "A Pure Theory of Conflict Applied to Organizations," in *The Frontiers of Management Psychology,* (ed.) George Fisk. New York: Harper and Row, 1964.

Dennis, Jamie, "Managing Change," *Personnel Administration,* Vol. 28, No. 5 (September–October, 1965), pp. 6–11.

Greiner, Larry E., "Antecedents of Planned Organizational Change," *Journal of Applied Behavioral Science,* Vol. 3, No. 1 (January–February–March, 1967), pp. 51–85.

Pondy, Louis R., "Organizational Conflict: Concepts and Models," *Administrative Science Quarterly,* Vol. 12, No. 2 (September, 1967), pp. 298–320.

Prell, Arthur E., "Conflict Theory: Its Basic Sociological Elements," *Proceedings of the 8th Annual Midwest Management Conference.* Carbondale, Ill.: Business Research Bureau, 1965, pp. 5–10.

Scott, William G., *The Management of Conflict.* Homewood, Ill.: Richard D. Irwin, Inc., 1965.

Shull, Fremont A., "Managerial Conflict in Administered Organizations," *Proceedings of the 8th Annual Midwest Management Conference.* Carbondale, Ill.: Business Research Bureau, 1965, pp. 11–26.

C. MOTIVATION

Chung, Kae H., "Developing a Comprehensive Model of Motivation and Performance," *Academy of Management Journal,* Vol. 11, No. 1 (March, 1968), pp. 63–74.

Gellerman, Saul W., *Motivation and Productivity.* New York: American Management Association, 1963.

Herzberg, Frederick, *Work and the Nature of Man.* Cleveland, Ohio: World Publishing Co., 1966.

Katz, Daniel, "The Motivational Basis of Organizational Behavior," *Behavioral Science,* Vol. 9, No. 2 (April, 1964), pp. 131–146.

Myers, M. S., "Conditions for Manager Motivation," *Harvard Business Review,* Vol. 44, No. 1 (January–February, 1966), pp. 58–71.

Rodney, Thomas C., "Can Money Motivate Better Job Performance?" *Personnel Administration,* Vol. 30, No. 2 (March–April, 1967), pp. 23–29.

Scanlan, Burt K., "Motivation Today—Toughest Part of Management's Task," *Factory,* Vol. 124, No. 9 (September, 1966), pp. 78–81.

Vroom, Victor H., *Work and Motivation.* New York: John Wiley and Sons, Inc., 1964.

D. COMMUNICATION

Geneen, H. S., "The Human Element in Communication," *California Management Review,* Vol. 9, No. 2 (Winter, 1966), pp. 3–8.

Haney, William V., *Communication and Organizational Behavior* (rev. ed.). Homewood, Ill.: Richard D. Irwin, Inc., 1967.

Marcus, Edward E., "The Basis of Effective Human Communication," *Public Personnel Review,* Vol. 28, No. 2 (April, 1967), pp. 110–114.

McCormack, James S., "Communication and the Organization," *Advanced Management Journal,* Vol. 33, No. 1 (January, 1968), pp. 63–67.

McMurray, Robert N., "Clear Communications for Chief Executives," *Harvard Business Review,* Vol. 43, No. 2 (March–April, 1965), pp. 131–147.

Melcher, Arlyn J. and Ronald Beller, "Toward a Theory of Organization Communication: Consideration in Channel Selection," *Academy of Management Journal,* Vol. 10, No. 1 (March, 1967), pp. 39–53.

E. BEHAVIORAL TECHNIQUES IN MANAGEMENT

Blake, Robert R. and Jane S. Mouton, "The Managerial Grid in Three Dimensions," *Training and Development Journal,* Vol. 21, No. 1 (January, 1967), pp. 2–5.

———— *The Managerial Grid.* Houston, Texas: Gulf Publishing Co., 1964.

Davis, Keith, "The Case for Participative Management," *Business Horizons,* Vol. 6, No. 3 (Fall, 1963), pp. 55–60.

Howell, Robert A., "A Fresh Look at Management by Objectives," *Business Horizons,* Vol. 10, No. 3 (Fall, 1967), pp. 51–58.

Kuriloff, Arthur H. and Stuart Atkins, "T-Group for a Work Team," *Journal of Applied Behavioral Sciences,* Vol. 2, No. 1 (January–February–March, 1966), pp. 63–93.

Odiorne, George S., "The Trouble with Sensitivity Training," *Training Directors Journal,* Vol. 17, No. 10 (October, 1963), pp. 9–20.

Paine, Frank T., "Management Perspective: Sensitivity Training: The Current State of the Question," *Academy of Management Journal,* Vol. 8, No. 3 (September, 1965), pp. 228–233.

PART IV

Quantitative Approaches

Probably the newest approaches to management have evolved from mathematics. During World War II, many quantitative methods were developed to analyze and solve military problems (e.g., the assignment of personnel and the deployment of submarines). Immediately following the war, managers began to use these mathematical techniques and models in organizational decision-making. Many of the problems which previously had been solved by managerial intuition and experience were now resolved by these quantitative methods. In the next decade, with the advent of computers, mathematical solutions to increasingly complex problems were rapidly made available to executives. In many instances, instead of having one or two possible alternatives in solving a problem, these new methods provided several solutions.[1]

The quantitative approaches to management have generated operations research techniques, program evaluation and review technique (PERT), models, and simulation techniques. Through such techniques, managers have had available more and better alternatives for dealing with the complex operating problems of modern industry, and frequently have been given insights into the consequences of particular decision.[2] Although the quantitative approach does not offer the optimum solution to all the problems of management, it certainly has aided in pinpointing the actual problems and in resolving them.[3]

---

[1] Max D. Richards and Paul S. Greenlaw, *Management Decision Making*. Homewood, Ill.: Richard D. Irwin, Inc., 1966, pp. 8–9.

[2] Phillip G. Carlson, *Quantitative Methods for Managers*. New York: Harper and Row, 1967, p. vii.

[3] For additional information on quantitative methods in management, see Arthur F. Veinott, Jr. (ed.), *Mathematical Studies in Management Science*. New York: The Macmillan Co., 1965.

Closely allied with the development of increasingly sophisticated quantitative methods in management has been the continued evolution of faster and better computers. Computer experts have predicted that the number of middle management jobs will decline and that those that remain will become more specialized, quite specific, and highly programmed.[4] At the top executive levels, managers will be less involved in details and will have more time to be innovative and creative in their approaches to implement the objectives of the organization and to the problems of the organization itself. These top level executives will have almost instantaneous information on the operations of the business from the computer, which may in fact increase the effectiveness of employee performance, because it will provide them with a sense of participation and continuous feedback on the individual performance of each part of the business. These developments may humanize rather than dehumanize business.

The computer will reduce the importance of such middle-management functions as pacesetting, work pushing, and expediting, because decision-making will become more automated and rationalized. Problems will be better structured and easier to handle, because most of the managers will see the problem as it truly is. This part of the book covers some of the mathematical techniques being used in industry and the impact of the computer upon the organizations.

In the first section on decision-making, Professor Robert K. Jaedicke states that all types of business problems can be analyzed by modern mathematical analysis. In the second article, Professor Robert C. Pickhardt discusses the use of simulation in businesses of all sizes and the ways in which problem simulation can lead to informed decision-making. Professor Robert C. Meier concludes the section by demonstrating the uses of a computerized management game to improve decision-making in the long run.

In the next section, Mr. John Ott examines operations research techniques in industry, and shows the value of such techniques in predicting the consequences of deciding on a particular solution to a problem. Professor Peter P. Schoderbek describes the historical development of PERT and how this technique can be employed by managers.

During the past decade, computers have become increasingly important to executives. They handle everything from production scheduling to manpower forecasting and market simulation problems. Professor Herbert A. Simon analyzes computers as a factor of production, and predicts that a Second Industrial Revolution may be occurring—the revolution of information processing. In the next article, Mr. George Glaser discusses the impact of some of the new problems being posed by the technological development of the computer. Lastly, the modification of occupations, decision-making methods, and the organization by the computer are analyzed by Professor Roger G. Vergin. In his concluding remarks, he speculates about the future impact of the computer upon the organization.

---

[4] Gilbert Burck, *The Computer Age and Its Potential for Management.* New York: Harper and Row, 1965, pp. 17–18.

A

DECISION MAKING

30. Current Analytical Techniques Useful in All Decisions

ROBERT K. JAEDICKE

Probably the single most important change in business decision-making in the last two decades has been the introduction, development, and use of mathematical (analytical) models. Such terms as linear programming, inventory and queuing models, and simulation are all familiar to the modern-day manager. If a manager is not familiar with the techniques themselves, the chances are good that he is either trying to learn about them or he is trying to hire someone who can make use of the new technology for him.

A study of the new mathematical techniques now occupies a major part of the curricula of many graduate schools of business. These developments in technol-

ogy are major factors in the evolution of a new type of manager. The emergence of the "new breed" of quantitative manager is unmistakable. The quantitative sophistication of the breed is frightening and regarded with suspicion by many who have not had this advantage.

This situation brings up a very important question of the usefulness of analytical techniques (the new technology) in decision-making. Heretofore, most attempts to appraise the usefulness of this new technology have been limited to identifying those decision problems on which analytical techniques can be used; but here we take a different approach. *The main hypothesis here is that analytical*

Reprinted from *Stanford Graduate School of Business Bulletin,* Vol. 34, No. 2 (Autumn, 1965), pp. 2–6, with permission of the author and the publisher. Robert K. Jaedicke is Associate Professor of Accounting, Graduate School of Business, Stanford University.

273

techniques are useful in all *decision problems.* Hence, instead of finding problems to fit techniques or instead of attempting to identify those particular decision problems which are amenable to quantitative analysis, I will try to show that the analysis can play an important role in *any* decision problem. First, the approach will be to identify and discuss the main characteristics of mathematical (quantitative) analysis. Then the main requirements of the decision-making process will be identified; and many of the requirements of this process will be matched with the characteristics of quantitative analysis. In this way I hope to show the real power of the new analysis that makes it a potent addition to the managers' tool kit for dealing with his decision problems.

Abstraction—A Powerful Method Analysis

The basis of mathematical analysis is the notion that if the problem at hand is too difficult to permit a solution, a simpler problem will be solved in its place. That is, if a complex problem is given to a mathematician and if he cannot solve it, he is likely to reply, "I can't solve this problem but I can solve a simpler one." This may sound very amusing but it is the basis of much of mathematics. The idea is to *abstract* from the complex problem that cannot be solved to a simpler problem that can be solved. Then, having solved the simpler problem, the mathematician will try to proceed toward a solution of the complex problem. Sometimes the complex problem will defy solution and the best that can be done is to solve the complex problem subject to certain simplifying assumptions.

In the process of abstraction, the main trick is to retain as much as possible of the complexity of the main problem. In

so doing, the mathematician, once he has solved the simpler problem, will have less of a "gap to bridge" to get back to the complex problem.

Sometimes it is possible to abstract very little and yet the abstracted problem may be much easier to solve than the more complex problem. When this happens, the process of abstraction is at its best. This can be illustrated by a very simple example. Suppose that I must find the number of years in the period January 1, 1952 to December 31, 1965. Personally, I can never remember whether the answer is 13 years, 14 years or 15 years. I can, of course, count the years, one at a time. I can also abstract and ask how many years there are in the period January 1, 1952 to December 31, 1954 and then I only have to count to 3. Having done this I find the general rule is to subtract the smaller number from the larger number and add one. Hence there are 14 years in the time period that I'm really interested in. This is a simple problem, but I think the power of abstraction is well illustrated.

Decision-Making—A Process of Abstraction

Now, let us examine the decision-making process. Decision-making is basically a process of abstraction—of first solving simpler problems than the ones presented. Except in the most trivial decisions, how many times do decision-makers solve the problem *exactly* as it is given to them—without any assumptions or simplification? This happens *very infrequently* indeed. The usual case is that decision problems are so complex that some abstraction from reality is necessary even to get started toward a solution. Having solved a simpler problem than the one given, the decision-maker tries to move toward a solution for the real problem. Usually, even the final decision (solution) is based on some simplifying assumptions.

Let me illustrate the above discussion in some detail. Assume the decision problem is whether or not to introduce a new product. The decision-maker may be fairly certain of the production and marketing costs. He estimates the variable cost per unit at $5 and the increase in fixed cost to be $100,000 per year. Assume also that the facilities to produce the new product could be devoted to producing more of an existing product. If this were done, a $200,000 profit per year would be earned. However, the decision-maker is highly uncertain on what price to charge for the new product and how many units will be sold. Since he cannot solve the exact problem he is given—whether or not to introduce the new product—a useful starting place is to abstract from the complex problem and solve a simpler one. That is, it may not be possible to say whether the new product will be more or less profitable than the alternative use of the facilities but he can solve a simpler problem. *He can find the number of units that must be sold at each price in order for the new product to be equally as profitable as the existing product.* That is, he may not be able to specify the market demand function that does exist for the new product, but he can solve for the demand curve that defines his indifference between the two alternatives. If a price of $10 is charged, then more than 60,000 units will have to be sold in order for the new product to be more profitable than the existing product:

$$\frac{\$100,000 + \$200,000}{\$10 - \$5} = 60,000 \text{ units.}$$

Repeating this calculation for different prices, a "breakeven" demand curve can be calculated as shown in Figure 1.

The breakeven demand curve is really a line of equal profit. Any combination of price and quality on the line will give a profit of $200,000. Hence, for any price-quantity combination to the right of the equal profit curve, the best decision from a quantitative viewpoint is to introduce the new product; for any price-quantity combination to the left of the equal profit line, the best decision is to use the facilities to produce more of the existing product.

Now the decision-maker has not solved his real problem but he has solved a simpler problem. The problem which has been solved is how many units of the new product *must be* sold at various prices in order for the introduction of the new product to be a wise decision. This solution is based on certain assumptions:

1. The variable cost of the new product,
2. the increase in the fixed cost associated with the new product, and
3. the alternative profit that can be earned from the facility.

Having solved a simpler problem than the one given, the next series of steps should be to move closer to the real problem. The decision-maker may do this by asking his sales manager a series of questions such as: "If we charge a price of $10 do you think we will sell more than (or less than) 60,000 units?" In this way, he may ultimately be able to solve the real problem. However, notice that the final solution (1) will have been reached through an initial process of abstraction; and (2) will be based on certain assumptions.

Now, if it is true that abstraction is a basic feature of the decision process, then the decision-maker should want to abstract in such a way that the importance of the assumptions can be tested. Abstraction typically involves the use of

Breakeven Demand Curve

Figure 1.

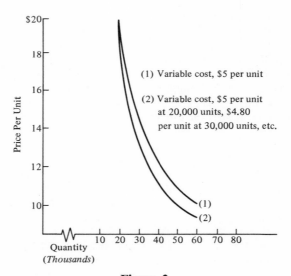

Figure 2.

assumptions; hence, when the simpler, abstracted problem is solved, the decision-maker may very well want to see the effect of relaxing or otherwise bringing the assumptions closer to reality. That is, he may wish to test the sensitivity of the solution to changes in the assumptions and parameters. Herein lies another advantage that analytical models can bring to any decision problem. The basis of the abstraction process in developing analytical methods *is a precise and rigorous statement of the assumptions that have been made.* This rigor should permit the decision-maker to experiment in order to determine how sensitive the solution is to changes in the assumptions of the model.

Returning to the new product decision problem given above, note that an assumption was made on the variable cost per unit. That is, the variable cost was estimated at $5 and it was assumed that this amount was constant per unit, no matter how many units were produced. Stated another way, the *total* variable cost was assumed to vary in direct proportion to changes in volume. Having made this assumption and having estimated the variable cost at $5 per unit, the decision-maker calculated the equal profit curve shown in Figure 1. Since quantity and price are uncertain, it may be useful to see how sensitive the equal profit line is to the assumption of cost proportionality as well as the variable cost estimate of $5. In this particular example, sensitivity analysis would be carried out by simply recalculating the equal profit line under different sets of conditions. For example, Figure 2 shows the effect on the equal profit line of an assumption that the unit variable cost of $5 decreases by 20¢ for every 10,000 unit increase in volume over 20,000 units.

This type of analysis should aid the decision-maker in deciding whether the proportionality assumption is of critical importance in his decision problem. In this particular case, change in the cost proportionality assumption (above) changes the correct decision very little; that is, the two equal profit lines are very close together. I think this fact is not obvious; hence, the analysis should be useful to the decision-maker.

In many mathematical models, the effect on the answer of changes in the assumptions or the parameter values can usually be tested analytically. It is often more efficient to carry out sensitivity analysis by using analytical methods rather than using the recalculation process demonstrated above. However, in those instances where analytical methods are either difficult or impossible to use, it is often possible to use a recalculation method with the assistance of a computer.

The Answer to "What-If"-Type Questions

The process of experimentation described above is aimed at answering "what-if"-type questions. That is, *what will happen* to the required volume *if* variable costs decrease? Or, how will the required volume change *if* selling price changes? Since the decision-maker must abstract and since he can rarely solve the exact problem he faces, the answer to the "what-if" type of question is a powerful method by which he can discover which variables are really critical to his decision. This type of analysis will rarely "make a decision" but it is a great help in considering the quantitative aspects of a decision.

Just as experimentation is an important part of decision-making it is also an important aspect of mathematics.[1] That is, once a problem has been solved, it is quite natural for the mathematician (or the person who is analytically inclined) to begin to experiment (some refer to this as "playing around") with the solution to the problem under different sets of conditions. This type of curiosity which is highly useful in decision-making has led

---

[1] In the preparation of this paper for the General Management Seminar, Howard Raiffa, Visiting Ford Research Professor on leave from the Harvard Business School, made this point. The author is indebted to Professor Raiffa for his help on much of the succeeding material.

to the development of much of mathematics. The following two interesting examples (taken from *Mathematics,* a volume in the Life Science Series, by David Bergamini and the editors of *Life*) illustrate this point:

Apparently, much of topology, a special kind of mathematics concerned with the ways in which surface can be twisted, bent, pulled or otherwise deformed from one shape into another, has developed by experimentation. Network theory, one of the practical forms of topology, which has application in electrical circuitry and economics, was originated by Leonhard Euler some 200 years ago. He was motivated by a puzzle involving the bridges of Königsberg. Apparently it had long been a tradition among the townspeople that the seven bridges could not all be crossed in a continuous walk without recrossing the route at some point. Euler set out to find a mathematical explanation and showed why the tradition was true.

Also, the origin of modern probability theory is attributed to Blaise Pascal and Chavalier de Méré who, finding themselves on a trip together, began consideration of a problem of how to split the pot in a dice game which has to be discontinued.

This problem was posed by de Méré, a worldly nobleman, to Pascal who was interested in philosophy and religion. Pascal, after pondering the problem for about two years, relayed it to another Frenchman, Pierre de Fermont. In the celebrated correspondence which followed, Pascal and Fermont began by agreeing that the pot in a discontinued dice game should be divided according to the prospects each player has of winning. The analogy of the problem to probability theory, used today in business decision problems, is clear.

In Summary

Mathematical or analytical models are frequently criticized because they are ab-

stractions and therefore will not fit every aspect of the empirical (real) situation with which they are intended to deal. Yet the fact that they *are* abstractions is the most powerful aspect of these models and methods of analyses. As has been pointed out, the decision-maker is forced to abstract. It is impossible for him to deal effectively with real-life complex business problems without making abstractions. In fact, when a decision-maker attempts to deal with complex business problems without abstracting, he is simply not using one of the most powerful decision techniques available to him.

So, given that abstraction is both necessary and desirable, it should be done in such a way that (1) the assumptions are clearly stated; and (2) the decision-maker can experiment with changes in the assumptions and parameter estimates to help him find those variables which are critical in his decision.

This entire process can be diagrammed, as shown in Figure 3. As can be seen by the diagram, mathematical analysis cannot *make* a decision. It is always necessary to bridge the gap between the mathematical (analytical) conclusions and the real or physical world. This process is referred to above as "interpretation." Generally, the more that can be learned about the problem through experimentation with the mathematical system, the better will be the interpretation and the better the decision. In conclusion, whereas the qualitative aspects and judgment and intuition will never be eliminated from a decision, neither will the quantitative aspects. Mathematical (analytical) models are too powerful a method for dealing with the quantitative aspects of a decision to be overlooked by decision-makers. "Quantitative Management" is here and it is here to stay!

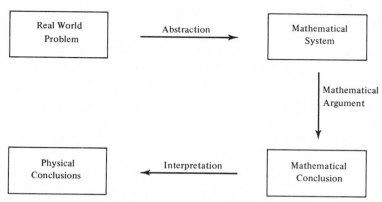

Figure 3. *Bridging the Gap.* Based on a diagram (and discussion) which can be found in: C. H. Coombs, H. Raiffa, and R. M. Thrall, "Some Views on Mathematical Models and Measurement Theory" in *Decision Processes,* R. M. Thrall, C. H. Coombs, and R. L. Davis, Editors, John Wiley & Sons, Inc., N. Y., 1954, p. 20.

31. Decision Making Versus Strategy Determination: A Gaming and Heuristic Approach

ROBERT C. MEIER

Since the introduction of business games about ten years ago, they have become a widely used tool for business education and management development. A large variety of games have been developed with different emphases as to complexity, functional areas included, and degree of competitive interaction.

Regardless of the specific structure games normally have been formulated to operate on a period-by-period basis. That is, the participants or players in the game make decisions, these decisions are evaluated or scored under the rules of the game (in many cases using a computer because of the complexities and volume of calculations), and the results for one period of operation of the game are returned to the participants. In most games competitive elements are present so that the decisions of the participants interact in determining the results, and there also may be random elements included which affect the results. Following the receipt of the results for one period, the participants evaluate their positions, make a new set of decisions, and the cycle is repeated.

Reprinted from *University of Washington Business Review,* Vol. 25, No. 4 (April–June, 1966), pp. 34–41, with permission of the publisher. Robert C. Meier is Associate Professor, Graduate School of Business Administration, University of Washington.

I. A Game Focusing on Long-Run Strategy

The focus in the play of business games is on the immediate problem of making a decision for the following period. Long-run strategy over a larger number of future periods is, of course, a consideration, but not one which need be made explicit by the participants.

A properly constructed business game, however, can provide a vehicle for explicit consideration of long-range strategy determination rather than immediate, short-run decision making. To do this, we have developed a computerized business game in which the participants write game-playing subroutines which play the game repetitively period after period *without* intervention of the participants each period.[1] In this way emphasis is shifted from the immediate *decision* for one period to a consideration of strategies which will be effective over a larger number of periods. Structures of this general type have been used before in computerized checker-playing programs [2] and for military games,[3] but there has been little application of the concept to business games. The differences in play between a normal computerized business game and the game which we have developed are shown schematically in Figure 1.

The game is a simple one, since the complexities of writing game-playing subroutines even for a limited number of decision variables are great. The hypothetical environment of the game is a competitive market for a single product whose price is in the $5.00 per unit range. The market is structured so that the total market available to the teams is a function of an economic index, the industry marketing expenditures, and industry average price. The total market behaves in a conventional way—rising with increases in the economic index, or increased marketing expenditures, or decreased average price, and falling conversely. Company market shares are determined by the company price level and marketing expenditures relative to those of competitors. Both the total market behavior and behavior of the company market shares are determined by functions in the computer program which are set to yield realistic results.

II. Playing the Game

The game was developed and tested using manual scoring and by playing it in the conventional way as shown in Figure 1(a).[4] Using the structure shown in Figure 1(a), the players make five decisions each period:

1. Price per unit
2. Marketing expenditures
3. Production rate
4. Additional plant and equipment purchases
5. Loan repayments

The first step in the scoring after the decisions are made is to determine whether the scheduled production rate is consistent with plant capacity; if not,

[1] The general structure of the game was designed by the writer. Mr. H. Richard Burson wrote the computer program as part of his master's work at the University of Washington.

[2] See A. L. Samuel, "Some Studies in Machine Learning Using the Game of Checkers," *IBM Journal of Research and Development,* July, 1959, pp. 211–229.

[3] See E. S. Quade, *Analysis for Military Decisions* (Chicago: Rand McNally & Company, 1964), p. 78.

[4] The game was first tested with a group of executives in attendance at the Advanced Management Seminar of the Concrete Products Association of Washington held at Lake Wilderness Lodge, March 21–25, 1965.

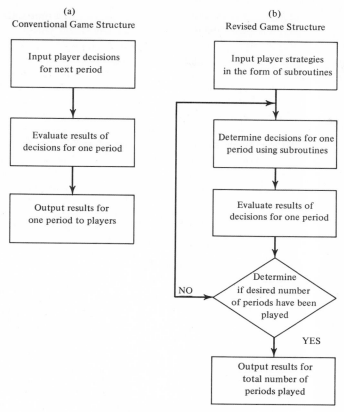

(a)
Conventional Game Structure

(b)
Revised Game Structure

Figure 1.

production rate is reduced to plant capacity. The total market in each company's share is then determined together with the ability of the company to fill its demand from inventory and production. If the company cannot fill its share of market demand, any shortage is distributed to the other companies unless they cannot fill this demand, in which case the demand is assumed to be lost. A *profit and loss statement, statement of cash flow, balance sheet,* and *summary of industry data* are then prepared for each company and returned to the players for use in making the following period's decisions.

While the computerized game can be played in the manner just described, the computer program for the game was specifically designed to provide for the use of game-playing subroutines rather than input of decisions for each period. Under this concept, as shown in Figure 1(b), each player works out a decision *strategy* for each of the five decision variables. This strategy is then converted into a computer program, a subroutine, and the subroutines play each other for as many periods as are desired without further intervention on the part of the players.[5] As the play proceeds automatically from

---

[5] In actuality, the number of periods is determined by the number of values of the economic index which are given to the program as input data.

period to period, profit and loss statements, statements of cash flow, balance sheets, summaries of industry data, and summaries of company decisions are prepared for each period so that the events taking place and relative standings of the companies can be traced. Table 1 is an illustration of the data prepared each period for each team.

The use of the game-playing subroutines as just described changes the emphasis in the game from *decision making.* each period to the selection of an effective *strategy.* While it is not difficult to play a game such as this when making ad hoc decisions on a period-by-period basis, it is quite a different matter to select a strategy for each of the five variables which will be effective against the strategies of competitors, whatever these may be.[6]

Since we have found no mathematical techniques which would enable a team to win [7] the game (or, for that matter, even play the game), the subroutines which we have devised thus far for playing the game fall under the broad class of techniques

TABLE 1

Company 4 Period 5

Profit and Loss Statement			*Statement of Cash Flow*		
Sales—			Sales	$266,000.00	
50,000 units at			New bank loan	0.00	
$5.32 per unit		$266,000.00	Total cash		
Less—			provided		$266,000.00
cost of goods			Less—		
sold	$150,000.00		material and		
depreciation	17,600.00		labor	150,000.00	
marketing			marketing		
expenditures	23,000.00		expenditures	23,000.00	
administrative			administrative		
expense	42,000.00		expense	42,000.00	
interest paid	1,000.00		interest paid	1,000.00	
Total current			federal income		
expenses		233,600.00	taxes	16,200.00	
Net income before			additional plant,		
federal income			equipment	0.00	
taxes		32,400.00	loan repayment	0.00	
Federal income					
taxes		16,200.00			
Net income after			Total cash		
federal income			outlay		232,200.00
taxes		$16,200.00	Net cash flow		$33,800.00

[6] One strategy which we have ruled out is that of industrial espionage. Since all data concerning the industry and companies are available in common storage in the computer memory, it would be possible to obtain perfect information about the other companies. Although it is doubtful that even this information would permit a company to select overwhelmingly successful strategies, we have established the ground rule that a company will use only its own company data and general industry data as shown in Table 1.

[7] "Winning" in the context of this game is in itself an ambiguous concept since the criteria for evaluating success are not as clear-cut as in games such as checkers or chess.

Balance Sheet

Assets		Liabilities		
Current assets—		Current liabilities—		
Cash	$408,391.00	Total liabilities	$50,000.00	
Inventory	0.00	Long term liabilities	50,000.00	
Total current assets	$408,391.00	Loans outstanding		$100,000.00
		Net Worth		
Fixed assets—		Capital stock	320,000.00	
Plant and equipment	880,000.00	Retained earnings	600,391.00	
Less—				
depreciation	268,000.00			
Total fixed assets	612,000.00	Total net worth		920,391.00
		Total liabilities and net worth		
Total assets	$1,020,391.00			$1,020,391.00

Industry Data

	Previous Period	This Period
Economic index	105.0	107.0
Industry weighted average price	$5.07	$5.07
Industry marketing expenditure	$73,000.00	$76,000.00
Total market (units)	220,000	224,000
Company average profit after taxes	$17,658.12	$18,373.87

Company Decisions		Other Data	
Price per unit	$5.32	Sales lost (units)	15,090
Marketing expenditures	$23,000.00		
Production rate	50,000		
Additional plant, equipment	$0.00		
Loan repayment	$0.00		

known as heuristic methods.[8] That is, player strategies as programmed in the game-playing subroutines are heuristic in that they involve selection of values for the decision variables from a very large number of possibilities in somewhat the same way that a human decision maker might make the selection. This use of heuristic methods is different from the use of analytical methods such as game theory, linear programming, or calculus optimization models, none of which appear to be directly useful in playing the game.

Our experimentation with this form of game structure is in its earliest stages, and only the simplest game-playing subroutines have been devised thus far. These have, to date, been principally of the type that look at the data from the last period only and make decisions on that basis. Other obvious possibilities would be to

---

[8] For a discussion of heuristic methods, see Herbert A. Simon, *The New Science of Management Decision* (New York: Harper & Row, 1960), pp. 21–34.

employ data from a number of previous periods and incorporate learning in the selection of decision procedures within the subroutines, both of which would make greater use of the power of the computer. However, it is difficult enough to conceive of sensible strategies when the game is viewed in the most elementary fashion, and we have not yet advanced to the point of experimenting with truly sophisticated game-playing subroutines.

III. Strategy Determination

Before we move on to more sophisticated subroutines of this nature it is necessary to gain some experience with and understanding of some of the simpler possibilities, and this alone is a substantial task.

PRICE STRATEGIES

To illustrate, for one of the five decision variables, price, it is not difficult to conceive of a substantial number of possible (and reasonably sensible) decision strategies. Among the most elementary are:

1. Hold price constant at some value.
2. Set price at the previous industry average.

3. Set price at some multiple or fraction of the previous industry average.
4. Select price at random from a specified distribution.
5. Increase the price if sales are above the last period industry average, and decrease it if sales are below.

These and many others are eligible candidates for strategies for just the one decision variable, price, and their effectiveness must be weighed in conjunction with the specific selection of strategies for the other four decision variables.

LACK OF THEORY OF STRATEGY DETERMINATION

As we have begun to work with this problem of selecting a set of decision strategies for playing the game, it has become apparent that there is a lack of adequate theory to use as a guide and that available techniques are inappropriate or inadequate. However, the absence of theories, or even suggested approaches, is probably only indicative of the fact that the problem has not been made explicit before since neither the real business world nor previously developed models provide the proper sort of controlled environment in which concepts of competi-

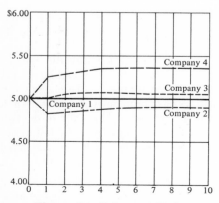

Figure 2. *Price per Unit*

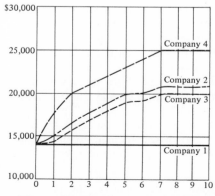

Figure 3. *Marketing Expenditures*

tive strategy determination in a dynamic situation can be evolved and tested. The business game just described provides a useful vehicle for exploring this question of *strategy determination* as opposed to *decision making* and is a significant extension and elaboration of the gaming technique. In addition, the unique structure of the game permits the exploration of certain aspects of the question of automated managerial decision making, a subject which is gaining increasing importance with the advent of the computer age. It also affords the opportunity for investigating questions of competitive equilibrium and market strategy in a dynamic fashion which was not possible using previously available tools of analysis.

IV. Conclusions

Because our results and experience to date are quite limited, the purpose of this article is not to draw conclusions about the relative merits of various strategies. However, to demonstrate the operation of the game, we include in Figures 2–5 summaries of a portion of the results from a trial run of the game with four companies playing for 10 periods. In this run the

major emphasis was on price and marketing strategies while the production capacity remained constant and equal for the four companies. Company One's strategy was essentially a "do nothing" strategy in which price and marketing expenditures were held constant at $5.00 per unit and $14,000 per period respectively. Company Two set its price at 97 percent of the previous period's industry average and marketing expenditures at 105 percent of the previous period industry average. Company Three's strategy was to "follow the crowd" and set both price and marketing expenditures equal to the industry average. Company Four set price at 105 percent of the industry average and marketing expenditures at 125 percent of the industry average. While these strategies are both elementary and extremely naive, the results are still interesting. By the end of the 10 periods, a condition of relatively stable equilibrium in the game has been reached, a situation which is somewhat unexpected in view of the four divergent strategies. We anticipate that further experiments with the game in the future will enable us to increase considerably our understanding of problems of strategy determination, automated decision making, and competitive equilibrium.

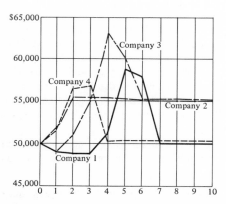

Figure 4. *Sales (Numbers of Units)*

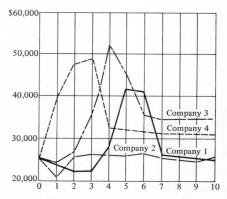

Figure 5. *Profit per Period (before Taxes)*

B

OPERATIONS
RESEARCH AND PERT

32. The Challenging Game of Operations Research

JOHN OTT

Shakespeare's "Hamlet" has been described as the story of a man who can't make up his mind. Throughout the play, he is presented with so many alternatives, each with its own set of consequences, that he is torn with anxiety, almost totally incapable of reaching a decision:

Although Hamlet's situation and subsequent solution may have been unique, the problem he faced was not. The process of making a decision has always been an agonizing one and, throughout history, those willing to accept the responsibility for making important decisions have been held with respect, even a degree of awe.

Information, in one form or another, has usually been considered essential. If one could only get the relevant facts, or so the reasoning went, one could make a sensible decision based upon experience. And so, the emphasis in the decision-making process is more and more upon the collection and analysis of significant data and a reliance upon the lessons of past performance. This has generally worked out pretty well, provided the consequences of an error were not disastrous.

There is the widely quoted remark that a man who makes the right decision 51 per cent of the time is a good executive. Today, this rule of thumb no longer applies.

It does not apply in our economy where a combination of more analytic manage-

Reprinted from *Electronic Age*, Vol. 24, No. 4 (August, 1965), pp. 15–18, with permission of the publisher. John Ott is on the RCA corporate staff.

ment and keener competition will no longer support such a marginal ratio. It does not apply in government where the consequences of even a slight error in the planning and implementation of a major domestic program may result in the waste of millions of dollars and the misuse of precious national human resources. It certainly does not apply to our vast national defense complex where there is a shrinking tolerance for any miscalculation in the deployment of nuclear capabilities.

With the consequences of faulty judgment as grave as they are in business, in government, in the management of our military establishment, there is an urgent need to fashion techniques designed to reduce the risk of error in the decision-making process. Experience, intuition, and even the most painstaking staff support are simply not enough for those who manage today's complex society. They need more efficient analytic tools to help them evaluate judgment situations.

Fortunately, these tools and the techniques to go with them are being developed by a relatively small and uncommon breed of specialists who work in a discipline known as operations research.

O.R. men, as they call themselves, are not strictly advisers or management consultants attempting to uncover the absolute best solution to a problem. An Oriental potentate, on the other hand, sitting in a council of state surrounded by his viziers, did exactly that. The evidence of factual information was weighed against experience, and recommendations were made for a particular decision. The decision was expected to be the right one. If his recommendation led to a reversal, the grand vizier's future was gloomy.

Today's operations research practitioners sensibly adopt a more cautious approach. They begin by defining, as precisely as possible, the nature of the problem as well as the ultimate objective. They recognize that certain actions will probably result in certain patterns of behavior, and they attempt to take into consideration all factors that might influence the structure of the situation. They then determine the probability of certain occurrences under all conditions. This is totally different from recommending a course of action. It is saying, instead, if you do so-and-so, here is the statistical probability of your return and risk. All possible courses of action are plotted in the same way, and the over-all picture is presented for selection.

This admittedly oversimplified description of operations research procedure suggests that the field is essentially a modern application of quite a venerable tradition in mathematical inquiry, that of probability theory or, as it is sometimes known, game theory. Such a view is very close to the truth.

One O.R. man credits the eminent 18th century French mathematician Pierre Simon Laplace with being one of the first operations research practitioners to boast a consulting service and a regular clientele. Recognized throughout Europe as the greatest living mathematical theoretician, Laplace was retained by members of the nobility to act as a consultant at the gaming table. Watching the progress of a card game, Laplace would advise his clients on the wager and play with the greatest probability of maximum return with least risk. If the client elected to take a plunge, Laplace was prepared to calculate the discouraging probability of his meeting with success. The final decision was always left to the client.

What Laplace did was to provide a mathematical description of the probable consequences of alternative choices of capital investment, a function that is widely performed by operations research people today. But modern operations research did not find its first significant application in business strategy. That occurred during World War II when mathematicians were enlisted to solve several military problems, the most famous one being the determination of the safest method of transporting men and supplies across a hostile ocean.

Allied intelligence could predict, more or less, how many enemy submarines were engaged in Atlantic patrol at any given instant. But there was no way to fix their positions. Still, the Atlantic is a vast expanse and enemy patrols could not be expected to cover it all. Intuition led to the conclusion that the least loss to shipping would result if vessels were widely scattered, traveling singly or in very small groups. There would be some loss, of course, but a target, if found, would be a limited one. This reasoning seemed sound, but losses were still disturbingly high. Military men began to have second thoughts about their intuition and turned the project over to mathematicians for a more orderly study.

This type of problem was especially well suited for operations research analysis. The objective was clear: obtain a maximum flow of transport at a minimum risk. There were several known quantities and a number of variables. Within the environment, the task was to select, among many possible combinations, the traveling pattern with the greatest probability of a safe crossing. The O.R. solution led to the development of the modern convoy concept and resulted in a significant reduction in shipping loss.

Having written this success story, O.R. was given additional wartime assignments, such as the scheduling of bombing strikes for maximum effect, optimum selection of alternative targets, and the development of effective search patterns to locate small objects moving in vast areas. All these problems had one factor in common. Their solution rested upon the mathematical consideration of a number of variables in order to establish the most likely statistical occurrence of a predetermined future objective.

It took no great imagination to realize that O.R. techniques could be adapted to a wide variety of peacetime uses, especially in business management. One of the major problems facing any management has always been anticipating the future. What will people really want five years from now? How much will they be able to spend? Will traditional marketing concepts be sufficient for this new market? Will current distribution systems be adequate? When, where, and how will advertising be most effective?

The answers to these questions were normally sought through sampling techniques. But this was not a very reliable tool. A small error in the quality of the sample can cause a gross error in the prediction. It was thought that O.R. analysis could be brought to bear upon this problem. But, although the techniques of operations research analysis were theoretically adequate to meet the requirements of business management, the problems themselves proved too cumbersome and complex.

It is, for example, a relatively simple matter to draw up a probability table for a throw of dice. The most likely outcome is a combination that results in a seven. The least likely outcome is either a pair of sixes or a pair of ones. But this is based on a cast of only two six-sided dice. The problem is tremendously more complex if each dice has, say, 100 sides and there are eight dice. Yet this situation is comparable to an analysis of business investment where there may be scores of variables that must be taken into consideration. Without question, operations research had the methodology to solve the problem, but the sheer number of calculations that had to be made seriously reduced the effectiveness of using such analysis.

This state of affairs changed radically

with the advent of the commercial computer. Suddenly, all restrictions were removed. Calculations no longer had to be made manually; they could be performed electronically, and at speeds that could accommodate even the most complex problem. Operations research as a practical management tool had finally come of age.

RCA became extensively involved in the area of operations research in 1957 when the company set up an O.R. activity at the David Sarnoff Research Center in Princeton, N.J., under the direction of Dr. Franz Edelman.

Operations research can take several forms, but Dr. Edelman defines his function as "the development of mathematical models that provide for the evaluation of the economic consequences of alternatives for planning and operations in quantitative terms." Dr. Edelman's reference to the construction of a mathematical model means precisely that. He sees a business activity as a series of relationships all of which can be described algebraically.

When Dr. Edelman and his associates are asked to build a model, their first step is to confer at length with key divisional managers who have an intimate knowledge of the activity. Together, the two groups dissect the total operation, reducing each relationship to the form of an equation. For example, it is possible to state mathematically product price as a function of the price of raw material. Product price, of course, ultimately depends upon many factors, all of them potentially variable. But an equation can be, and is, written for each one.

As each succeeding relationship is identified and various interdependencies are discovered and expressed algebraically, the model grows more complex. A mathematical simulation of a company's total business may contain hundreds of equations. But even that, Dr. Edelman points

out, is only the beginning. The model is presumably to be used for something. Perhaps the purpose is to determine the desirability of increasing production facilities in order to meet an anticipated expansion of the existing market.

Faced with the prospect of an imminent market growth, it is not necessarily the best response to expand production facilities. The sales curve may go up, but there is the possibility that added costs will weaken the net profit figure. If, on the other hand, it is decided to respond by increasing production, there is the question of how much to expand.

At this point, certain qualitative judgments must be introduced. What is the best estimate of the size of the expected market expansion? What will be the company's share of this new market? Will it remain constant or drop? Will it be proportionately higher and, if so, by how much?

These questions are painfully familiar to most business managers. The accuracy of their answers is often the yardstick by which performance is measured and, consequently, many anxious hours are ordinarily invested before an opinion is hazarded.

Dr. Edelman and his group offer a comparatively pleasant alternative by framing their questions differently. What is the probability, they ask, that the market will expand by 10 to 14 per cent? What is the probability of it being between 15 and 18 per cent? Requesting an informed estimate of the probability of a range of possible outcomes, rather than demanding pinpoint predictions, actually results in improved analytic procedures. For one thing, the manager being queried is not tempted to modify his assessment in the interest of self-protection. Almost invariably, he gives accurate judgments within the assigned possibility limits.

These probabilistic predictions about

future environment are mixed into the model, together with the complete set of algebraic equations describing the total business. These are then converted into a computer code for programming. The operations research team is now almost ready to manipulate the model, running through as many combinations and permutations of variables and fixed relationships as are desirable or practical.

But first, one final all-important step must be taken. The model must be verified. This is done by programming sample runs based on historical data. Next year's environment, for example, may be a variable, but last year's is a matter of record. These historical data are fed into the model, and the results are compared with what actually happened. If the two match, then the model is valid. If there is a discrepancy, the model' must be taken apart and each equation reexamined. This, Dr. Edelman says, can be a frustrating experience, but one that forces management into an extremely precise examination of business relationships that had previously been assumed as understood.

Business management is by no means the only area in which RCA employs the resources of operations research. Norman S. Potter, Manager of Systems Analysis in SEER (Systems Engineering Evaluation and Research), an activity under the direction of Dr. H. J. Watters, Chief Defense Engineer of Defense Electronic Products, reports that O.R. techniques are regularly used in a wide variety of systems design and control problems.

The design of a communications system to balance traffic flow against circuit requirements is essentially an operations research inquiry. SEER has conducted analyses for the Department of Defense to determine the optimum inventory level for spare parts. The defense establishment ordinarily maintains an enormous stockpile of spares to support its widely dispersed weapons systems. Since this is an investment that runs into many millions of dollars, highly sophisticated purchasing schedules, based on many years of experience, were perfected. Still, using the operations research approach, SEER developed purchasing and inventory programs that resulted in savings of 50 to 75 per cent.

The manpower assignment problem is another that lends itself to operations research analysis. Skilled technical personnel is in short supply and is expensive. How to make the best use of available personnel to perform a particular task at the least possible cost is a problem that is being probed by Mr. Potter's group. In one RCA activity, involving several hundred engineers, it was discovered that conventional methods of selecting and assigning supplementary personnel called for the employment of five to six times as many people as was necessary. SEER's methods are now under consideration by the National Aeronautics and Space Administration in an effort to make the most efficient use of NASA's technical and professional manpower pool.

There is a growing appreciation for the effectiveness of operations research methods in a wide variety of endeavors—in hospital administration and planning, urban transportation, education, general finance, banking, portfolio analysis—in any activity, in fact, that involves an evaluation of the consequences of alternatives.

Even that most unpredictable variable of all, man himself, has been subjected to operations research study. In the behavioral sciences, researchers have speculated on the likelihood of predicting the statistical probability of group behavior under varying conditions. This, of course, leads to the alarming specter of a controlled and guided society.

But Dr. Franz Edelman discounts that possibility. "Operations research," he points out, "dictates no particular course of action. All it does is to express the likely consequences of any choice in a reasonably clear and precise manner. Ultimate selection is still the responsibility of the decision-maker.

It seems, then, that reaching a decision will remain the agonizing process it has always been. Perhaps even more so, since there will be less excuse for a misinterpretation of information. Just like Laplace's client, there may still be the executive with the inclination to take a long shot. But before he makes the plunge, operations research will be able to quote him the odds. The consequences of this could be far-reaching, indeed.

33. PERT—Its Promises and Performance

PETER P. SCHODERBEK

For the smooth functioning of modern complex industrial society new management planning and control techniques have recently been introduced. Of these, one of the better known, more useful, and now widely accepted is PERT, an acronym standing for Program Evaluation and Review Technique.

From its inception in 1958, PERT (originally developed by the Navy for the aerospace industry) has aroused widespread interest in the business community and has won willing acceptance by a growing segment of private industry. For years industry had been seeking more realistic and more sophisticated approaches to the conventional managerial functions of planning and control. Here finally was a technique designed not only to improve project planning and control of the most varied and complex proportions but also one which has actually proven its ability to do so. So successful, in fact, has the Defense Department found this technique that it now requires all prime contractors to use it.

From the United States PERT has moved into Canada, crossed over into Great Britain and the European continent, and penetrated behind the Iron Curtain. The Canadian Government also now requires many of its contractors to use PERT or other similar methods. Although Great Britain began using PERT only a few years ago, their enthusiasm for this method has already been felt throughout Western Europe where they are promoting and endorsing this technique.

The real value and importance of PERT, however, can probably be more justly appraised by the extent of its adoption by those corporations not contractually obligated to use it. In the past several years, industrial applications have appeared at an ever increasing rate so that PERT is now no longer solely used for complex industrial and defense projects but is employed also by small firms for such tasks as book publishing, house building, theatrical production, marketing, and making organizational changes.

That PERT is already revolutionizing the planning and control function of management in many industries is a phenomenon familiar to many. Yet as the technique matures through imaginative use and guided experimentation, the added refinements that are bound to result will

Reprinted from *Michigan Business Review,* Vol. 17, No. 1 (January, 1965), pp. 25–32, with permission of the publisher. Peter P. Schoderbek is Associate Professor, Production Management, College of Business Administration, University of Iowa.

help usher in the day of the automated control system whereby management will become even more an operating reality rather than a textbook ideal. Herein lies PERT's long-range value to society.

Historical Development of PERT

In 1957 when Morgan R. Walker of E. I. du Pont de Nemours & Co. and James E. Kelley, Jr. of Remington Rand introduced the network method of depicting the project plan and of supplying time estimates for the completion of each job segment, it became possible to identify the job parts which were critical for the completion of the over-all project. This method became known as the Critical Path Method (CPM) and is the civilian counterpart of PERT.

In January, 1958 Willard Fazar of the Special Projects (SP) Office of the Navy Bureau of Ordnance, together with representatives of the consulting firm of Booz, Allen, & Hamilton, and of Lockheed Missile Systems Division began the development of a network system for managing the Fleet Ballistic Missile (FBM) program. They originally named their network system the Program Evaluation and Research Task—later changed to Program Evaluation and Review Technique. They developed this technique because, with advances in technology, the complexity of the Navy weapon and support system had increased significantly. The research and development and the actual production and installation of the above-mentioned systems had also assumed prodigious proportions. Since some 2,000 contractors were involved in the FBM program, a new managerial technique was evidently required to integrate the major program tasks upon which so many subordinate ones depended.

While the list of PERT users is growing rapidly, most users are in the two major areas of application—research and development, and construction. The use of PERT in the construction industry is especially appropriate since the myriad requirements, related interdependencies of projects segments, and the over-all coordination needed in this industry fit nicely into the PERT framework. It is interesting to note that for the 1964 World's Fair almost all of the major exhibitors have used the network approach for planning, scheduling, and controlling progress on the projects. Although the construction industry uses the Critical Path Method (CPM), there is essentially little difference between it and PERT. PERT uses three time estimates—the Optimistic Time, the Most Likely Time, and the Pessimistic Time—while the CPM utilizes only one time estimate—the Expected Time.

The Basics of PERT

As originally conceived, PERT's prime objective was to provide management, through an integrated system of forced planning and evaluation, with on-the-spot control at any point in time and at the proper organizational level. A notable weakness of many current reporting tools is the time lag in the reporting of timed data and the evaluation of the possible effects of such belated data on the successful outcome of the project. With PERT, however, it is possible to observe the effects of any one activity upon the total performance. Because PERT is a dynamic reporting tool, it can call attention to trouble spots requiring immediate remedial decisions if deadlines are to be kept. This progress reporting can be done as often as management desires, although many users have found a bimonthly report sufficient.

PERT highlights critical activities with the end result that trade-offs in manpower or other resources may profitably be resorted to. If, for instance, a breakthrough occurs in one part of a network—less time is consumed than was expected—then it is possible to utilize this manpower and equipment on other major activities either to shorten their completion dates or, if behind schedule, to bring them up to their expectancies. PERT accepts project uncertainties as part of the system and is consequently readily adaptable to unforeseen changes in the program. By its very nature it forces the development of a logical and comprehensive plan for program completion and permits realistic rescheduling to meet the exigencies of the situation.

Basically, PERT is concerned with the formulation and development of a sequential network consisting of the totality of activities required for implementing the final objectives. Each activity is carefully analyzed so that a realistic estimate of the time required for completion can be made. But since PERT is so often used on the construction of devices never before produced, the time estimates must necessarily be somewhat uncertain.

To cope with this uncertainty factor PERT utilizes a weighted time average, the Expected Elapsed Time, calculated from the three time estimates for every activity. Given these three time estimates, a computer can be used to compute the expected completion dates for each activity (or this can be done manually) and to calculate the Latest Allowable Date on which events must be completed if the key objective is to be reached.

PERT Network

The PERT Network is a "flow diagram consisting of the activities and events which must be accomplished to reach the program objectives, showing their logical and planned sequences of accomplishment, interdependencies, and interrelationships." [1] It is important to notice that the network comprises not only events and activities but also the interrelationships that exist between them. Fundamental to an understanding of the network are the concepts of *events* and *activities*.

An event is a "specific, definable accomplishment in a program plan, recognizable at a particular instant in time. Events do not consume time or resources." [2] Each accomplishment in a specific program is an event and is usually represented visually as a circle or as a rectangle. Typical events might be "Start training personnel," "Start production," etc.

Events are related to one another by activities. Each activity is a time-consuming task connecting events, but the beginning or end of an activity (an event) is assumed to be instantaneous, i.e., not to consume time. Activities utilize resources—manpower, equipment, materials, etc.; therefore, they represent work to be done. Since activities connect events, they are bounded by two events: the Beginning Event which is the starting point of the activity and the Ending Event or Successor which is its terminus. On the

[1] *PERT Fundamentals* (Washington: PERT Orientation and Training Center, 1963), Vol. III, p. 16.

[2] Definitions of PERT concepts can be found in many government publications now generally available from the Superintendent of Documents, Government Printing Office, Washington, D. C. See Bibliography.

network diagram, activities are represented by arrows pointing in the direction of the time flow—toward the Ending Event. Figure 1 shows that events numbered 6 and 8 are related, i.e., the activity connecting these two events cannot begin until event No. 6 is completed nor can event No. 8 take place unless the activity is completed.

Figure 1. *Event-Activity Relationship.*

In the case where several activities lead up to an event, all activities must be completed before the event comes into existence. For instance, the network activities

number 8–11, 9–11, 10–11 in Figure 2 must all be completed before event No. 11 can "instantaneously" occur.

An actual example of the preceding schematic is illustrated in Figure 3. While an activity implies doing or acting, events are usually expressed as a state of being, e.g., tested, developed, completed, or started. However, since the completion of several activities leading up to the same event could occur simultaneously, the events by themselves cannot always specify all of the activities which are connected to them.

The network also serves as an external communications device as well as an internal control vehicle. The need for scheduled dates can be realistically impressed upon a supplier or a sub-contractor by showing him the deleterious effects his delay will have on the entire project. When many sub-contractors are involved

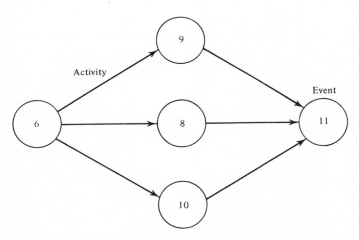

Figure 2. *Network Schematic.*

in a complex project it becomes imperative that they meet delivery dates on time if the project is to proceed as planned.

While the network functions admirably as a control device, its greatest value perhaps comes from its usefulness as a plan-

ning aid. Planning involves the determination of what tasks are necessary to achieve the end objectives and the sequence in which they should be performed. The network allows one to plan at whatever level or depth he feels is nec-

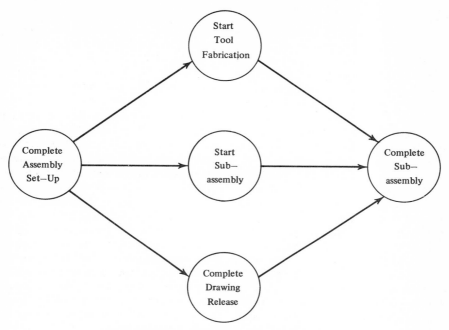

Figure 3. *PERT Network Diagram.*

essary for the proper management of the project. If desired, the events in a project can be broken down into still smaller events, thus forming a longer and more detailed network. The value of this further breakdown is that it enables the manager to look at specific segments as through a magnifying lens.

Time Estimates

Because of the uncertain nature of the activities involved, PERT usually requires three time estimates for each activity. If the time required to complete an activity could be estimated accurately, there would be no need for three time estimates; one time estimate would be sufficient. However, when a company is involved with activities of an exploratory nature, with non-repetitive activities, three time estimates are most desirable.

There is still much debate over the merits of using only one time estimate instead of three. Those advocating the use of one time estimate believe that the statistical manipulations that need to be performed only add computational work to the efforts already put forth. Also, many persons doubt that the use of three time estimates actually improves the accuracy. On the other hand, with the increased complexity of research and development projects and with the inherent uncertainty of these fallible forecasts, project engineers hesitate to commit themselves to the one time estimate. For they know well that the completion of an activity can be affected by many factors over which they have no control whatsoever.

The three time estimates (usually expressed in calendar weeks) employed in estimating activity time are the following:

Optimistic Time: The least amount of time that an activity can take. It is assumed that everything "works" the first time. This time can be expected to be accomplished in only one out of a hundred cases.

Most Likely Time: If only one time estimate is required, this is it. It is the expected time for an activity if the activity were repeated many times under identical conditions, or that most often given if many qualified persons were asked to give a time estimate.

Pessimistic Time: The maximum amount of time that an activity can take. It is the expected time if unusually bad luck were experienced. Maximum time estimates should include the possibility of initial failure followed by a fresh start.

In the PERT network the three time estimates are usually entered above the activity arrow to which they apply in the following order: the optimistic time, the most likely time, and the pessimistic time.

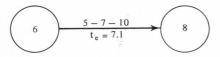

Figure 4. *Network Segment.*

Figure 4 shows that the optimistic time, the most likely time, and the pessimistic time of the activity (6–8) are 5, 7, and 10 weeks respectively.

From the optimistic, most likely, and pessimistic times the Expected Elapsed Time (t_e) can be obtained by statistical techniques. These three time estimates are related to the Expected Elapsed Time by the formula:

$$t_e = \frac{a + 4m + b}{6}$$

where
$$a = \text{optimistic time}$$
$$m = \text{most likely time}$$
$$b = \text{pessimistic time}$$

In arriving at the expected time, the most likely time estimate is given four times as much weight as the optimistic and pessimistic estimates. The Expected Elapsed Time in our example is 7.1.

Earliest Expected Time

The Earliest Expected Date (T_E) of an event is the earliest calendar date on which an event can be expected to take place. (Dates are predicted of events, times of activities. Symbolically, the former are generally represented by upper-case letters, the latter by lower-case letters.) The T_E value for a given event can be calculated by summing all activity times (t_e) through the most time-consuming chain of events from the beginning event to the given event and this path is called the critical path. In Figure 5 there are two paths from Event zero to Event No. 5. One is via Event No. 1, and the total of the T_E value is 8. The other is via Event No. 3 and the total T_E value is 19. Similar reasoning shows that there are two paths from Event zero to Event 6. One, via Event 3, has a T_E of 11. The other via Events 2 and 4 has a T_E of 17. Therefore, the larger figure, 17, is the most time-consuming path, and must control.

Critical Path

In Figure 5, a network is depicted within which there is one path composed of activities which, if delayed, would affect the expected completion date of the entire project. This is the most time-consuming path through the network and is designated on the diagram by a heavier line. The path itself is called the critical path and the activities located on the path are termed critical activities. Since no ending event can be completed until all activities leading to it have been completed, it can be readily seen that Event

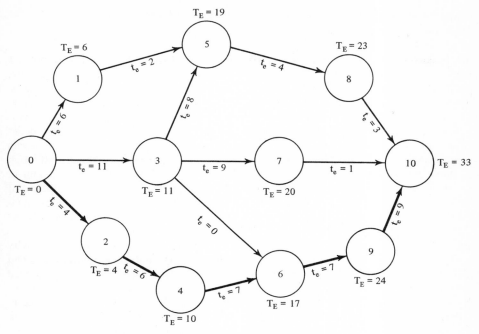

Figure 5. *Critical Path.*

No. 10 cannot occur before all activities located on the critical path have taken place. The earliest completion date for an ending can be no sooner than the time required for the most time-consuming activities along the critical path to occur.

Since the critical activities are the most time-consuming activities in the network, there is no leeway, no "slack" possible in their case. Therefore, the critical path is often defined in terms of slack as "that particular sequence of events and activities in a path that has the greatest negative, or least positive, algebraic slack; that is, the longest path through the network." All other paths in the network are called "slack" paths; they have some slack.

Slack Determination

Slack exists in a network system because of multiple junctions which arise when two or more activities contribute to a third. The slack for an event is a measurement of the "excess" time available. It is calculated as the difference between the latest allowable date (T_L) and the earliest expected date that the activity can be completed (T_L-T_E). The Latest Allowable Time is the latest calendar date on which an event can take place without affecting the scheduled completion date of the project. When computing the T_L for an event, it is necessary to work back from the final event in the network. You subtract the value of the t_e following the event from the value of the T_L of the succeeding event. For example, the T_L for event number 8 in Figure 5 is 30 (33–3).

The critical path has no positive slack since it is already the most time-consuming path in the network. Since slack may be negative, zero, or positive it is characteristic of all network paths. In the previous figure, the earliest expected date (T_E) that the project can be completed is 33 weeks. If you wanted to complete the project in 30 weeks there would be three weeks of negative slack; if the project deadline were 38 weeks away then five weeks positive slack would exist. One of the advantages of PERT is that resources can often be interchanged whenever slack exists somewhere in the network. Thus it is possible to divert manpower resources to those areas where negative slack exists so as to be able to complete the project on time.

PERT Simulation

Despite rigorous efforts to adhere to any set, definite plan, it sometimes becomes virtually impossible not to deviate from it. Regardless of whether the changes that bring this about are intentional or not, some method for an orderly and efficient plan revision is absolutely necessary. Naturally enough, these adjustments should be made with a minimum of disorganization, confusion, frustration, and wasted effort.

Inherent in the PERT system are the means whereby alternative courses of action can be simulated and evaluated even before action is actually undertaken. This simulation of activities becomes extremely important when serious trouble occurs unexpectedly. Some type of corrective action is then definitely necessary, sometimes almost immediately. It is this ability to assess rapidly the possible impact of a proposed change that makes simulation such a great aid to decision-making.

Simulation is also useful in the initial planning stages of a program. Alternative methods of realizing events by means of different resource combinations or of various techniques can be tested. Even alternative network plans can be tested and evaluated through simulation.

PERT Problems and Limitations

1. *Acceptance.* One of the significant problems associated with PERT is due, not to the inadequacy of the technique, but rather to the failure of top management to support its acceptance. Top management has done little in selling the benefits of PERT to the operational managers and the technical personnel. Although these engineers are often instrumental in the initial introduction and installation of the PERT system, they lack an appreciation of its benefits and an awareness of its limitations.

2. *PERT Logic.* Another difficulty with PERT is that some programmers and data processors have become mesmerized with their own ability to modify the PERT system, and as a result, it is becoming increasingly and unnecessarily complicated. These complexities hinder the operating managers from utilizing this technique as they should. Many of the modifications made by programmers are intellectual exercises rather than improvements in the system. Coordination must be achieved between these programmers who view PERT as a toy or a management systems concept and the line operating personnel who view it as another, though more effective, reporting tool.

3. *PERT Mis-use.* PERT at times has been misused. Although it was developed as a planning and control device for use on complex research projects, and even though PERT users have extended its application to many new areas (it has recently been used by one company in their recruiting efforts), its main strength still lies in the forced planning of one-time complex projects in contradistinction to repetitive or routine projects.

4. *Resistance to Change.* One obstacle standing in the way of initial adoption and of full utilization of the PERT system can be characterized as "resistance to

change." It is almost axiomatic that workers resist attempts by management to alter work procedures and to modify existing work regulations. The pages of history are replete with the activities of organizations that have fought tooth-and-nail against superior innovating practices. But somehow modern man often fails to notice that the problem has more than historical interest. It too can assume a modern garb (as it has with PERT) and appear in a twentieth-century managerial milieu.

When analyzing resistance to change one must keep in mind that the factors favoring this state of affairs are not one but many; that one factor may out-weight another, and that, generally speaking, no single factor infallibly and of itself will bring about or hinder change. The cumulative effect, therefore, will decide the direction in which the scale will finally tilt—toward acceptance of change or toward rejection. For despite the many potential advantages inherent in the PERT system, these are ultimately diminished when the system itself is not utilized at its utmost efficiency.

Another reason for the lack of practical interest in a proposed change is the fact that at times the advantages associated with it are neutralized or even outweighed by the disadvantages. It is the task of management, and a not too difficult one at that, to interest the would-be PERT personnel in the tangible advantages and present rewards flowing from the PERT system. It goes without saying that they themselves must not only be "sold" on the system but also must be thoroughly conversant with it, with its merits and its inherent limitations.

PERT/Cost

Recognizing the benefits and future of the PERT technique, the Department of Defense and the National Aeronautics Space Administration have recently developed a uniform PERT/Cost system which measures not only the physical but also the financial progress of a project.

In the PERT system as originally developed it was found impractical to try to integrate both time and cost considerations since in the scheduling process the critical path often ignored the availability of resources. Before the emergence of a PERT/Cost system much experimentation was necessary with respect to the use of one cost estimate, three cost estimates, single costs, direct costs, total costs, etc.

The incompatibility of time and cost data also posed problems. Since activities often cut across normal accounting periods, cost analysis required the measurement of the costs of activities in progress and an estimation of the value of the work performed. Current accounting systems for the estimation of manpower costs, skill classifications, time/cost trade-offs, and optimum cost schedule were inadequate. Only through much trial and error has an adequate PERT/Cost system been developed.

The use of PERT/Cost greatly facilitates the assessment of project status and its bearing on financial planning, the interrelationship of time and costs, and the financial effect on the project of possible changes in resources and/or schedules. PERT/Cost also allows for the comparison of progress data from multiple sources of information and provides a single report by which financial status can be evaluated against physical status.

Stripped of all its paraphernalia, PERT/Cost is concerned with the accumulation of cost data and the summarization of reports which integrate time and cost information on a single framework. The resource dimensions which are added to basic PERT include labor man-hours, material, subcontracting costs, and travel costs.

By integrating PERT/Time and

PERT/Cost one can determine whether the managers at various levels are meeting their committed schedules and cost estimates; and, if not, how resources can be utilized so as to minimize premium costs and how additional resources will affect the over-all program.

In measuring the progress of a project, a direct comparison can be made between the sum of actual costs to date and funds authorized and the estimated cost to complete the project. This comparison will reveal potential cost overruns and/or cost underruns and will pinpoint those segments of work where these can occur.

The Future of PERT

A survey of the 200 largest industrial corporations, made by the author, indicated that although the use of PERT is related to the size of the firm, i.e., the larger firms tend to employ it more, an increasing number of small firms are adopting the technique. No longer is the use of the method limited to large, complex projects; its usefulness has been demonstrated on projects as short as two weeks. Such diverse activities as the taking of inventory, monthly closing of accounting books, college recruiting, maintenance, book publishing, and even weddings have been PERTed.

Nor is the use of PERT limited to those companies with computers. While a network containing over a hundred activities becomes cumbersome to work with manually, it can be managed. Much of the benefit of PERT is derived from the detailed planning that is required in the initial preparation of the network.

A certain amount of mysticism surrounds the PERT system, which is probably due to the statistical underlying assumptions of the concept. However, a mathematical orientation is not a requisite for using PERT. In the study referred to above, only one-half of the companies had formal training programs in PERT and no company had any specific education requirement for participation in the PERT training program.

As the technique matures and as further experimentation and refinements occur, PERT will bring management a more useful tool for the planning and control of small projects as well as large ones.

Selected Bibliography

1. Kelley, James E. R. and Walker, M. R., *Critical Path Planning and Scheduling—An Introduction,* Fort Washington, Pennsylvania: Mauchly Associates, 1959.
2. Miller, Robert W., *Schedule, Cost and Profit Control with PERT: A Comprehensive Guide for Program Management,* New York: McGraw-Hill Book Company, Inc., 1963.
3. *PERT Fundamentals,* Washington: PERT Orientation and Training Center, 1963, Vol. III.
4. Stilian, Gabriel, et al., *PERT: A New Management Planning and Control Technique,* Edited by Jerome W. Blood, New York: American Management Association, 1962.
5. Tebo, K. M., *PERT COST, Advanced PERT COST Course,* New York: American Management Association, 1963.
6. U. S. Department of the Navy, *PERT Summary Report,* Phase 2, Washington: Special Projects Office, Bureau of Naval Weapons, 1958.
7. U. S. Department of the Navy, *PERT Summary Report,* Phase 1, Washington: Special Projects Office, Bureau of Naval Weapons, 1958.

C

THE IMPACT
OF COMPUTERS

34. Programs as Factors of Production

HERBERT A. SIMON

As a member of that rapidly growing happy band who spend our days trying to find ways of inducing computers to do interesting new things, I feel a good deal of responsibility for understanding the probable economic and social consequences of introducing these new devices into our society and widening the range of their applications. From an economic and social standpoint, are computers and automation something new under the sun or are they, to paraphrase Clausewitz, simply "a continuation of the Industrial Revolution by other means"? Do they call for a new chapter in the economic textbooks or are they merely details in the chapters on capital and distribution?

In a series of essays published under the title of *The Shape of Automation,*[1] I explored some of the macroeconomic aspects of these questions—in particular, the implications of automation for full

Reprinted from the *California Management Review,* Vol. 10, No. 2 (Winter, 1967), copyright by the Regents of the University of California. Herbert A. Simon is Richard King Mellon Professor of Computer Sciences and Psychology, Graduate School of Industrial Administration, Carnegie-Mellon University.

This is an address given in December 1966 to the Industrial Relations Research Association meeting in San Francisco, California.

[1] (New York: Harper & Row, 1965). I have been reinforced in the conclusions reached in those essays by noting their agreement with the subsequent report of the National Commission on Technology, Automation, and Economic Progress, *Technology and the American Economy* (Washington, D.C.: United States Government Printing Office, 1966), and the recent book by Charles Silberman, *The Myths of Automation* (New York: Harper & Row, 1966).

employment, real wages, and the demand for unskilled labor. I will not repeat my conclusions here except to observe that I ended my investigation with more optimism than I began with. From the standpoints considered, automation does, indeed, seem a natural continuation of the Industrial Revolution, fully compatible with full employment, creating a high probability that labor will reap all or most of the gains of rising productivity.

The present essay is an inquiry in a different direction. It begins with the observation that what we generally call a "computer" includes both a hardware component and a software component— both a collection of electronic gear and a collection of programs and data that are stored in the hardware memory. During the first five years that computers were obtainable commercially, to buy or rent a computer meant to buy or rent the hardware. Since that time, during the last decade or so, the merchandise on the market has generally included a substantial software as well as hardware component. In fact, the software represents a steadily increasing part of the total purchase or rental cost, and no computer of any size could be marketed today without being accompanied by appropriate software. Categories of software include:

• Monitor programs and scheduling algorithms, to make the system available to a multitude of users and to allocate and schedule its facilities among them.
• Programming languages, such as assembly languages and user-oriented languages (e.g., FAP, FORTRAN, COBOL, SIMSCRIPT).
• Utility routines, such as linear programming algorithms, standard statistical packages, and programs for solving differential equations.

For the most part, computer users either employ these precooked programs, or write their programs in user-oriented languages. Few users program in machine language, and almost none in large installations run their programs outside monitor and scheduling systems. Some current suggestions that, because of economies of scale, large central computing hardware systems will take on the character of public utilities will, if realized, accentuate and hasten these trends.

If computers, regarded as a factor of production, are to be classified with capital, they are capital with a difference. To be sure, there are precursors, such as the Jacquard loom, which was as truly programmed as the most modern solid-state machine. But the software component of modern computers is so prominent in comparison with anything that went before that we must treat the difference as having qualitative significance.

An alternative to regarding computers as a new form of capital is to regard them as *a new form of labor*. This, too, is a familiar idea used to denote their applicability to a widening range of humanoid tasks. I would like to introduce an allegory for exploring further the reasonableness and limitations of regarding computers as labor. Like most allegories, this one will simplify real life.[2]

In the time of Columbus, devices for ocean transportation incorporated both a hardware component—a sailing ship— and a software component—a navigator. A shift in the production function for ocean transportation could result from an improvement either in sailing ships or in

---

[2] The technological developments that underlie the possibilities of using human and computer programs interchangeably in a wide range of tasks are discussed in my paper, "Decision Making as an Economic Resource," in Lawrence H. Seltzer, ed., *New Horizons of Economic Progress* (Detroit: Wayne State University Press, 1964), pp. 71–95.

the skills of navigators. Improvements in hardware were incorporated in the production function as new ships were launched. I suppose that the economics of the matter were handled by using Terborgh-like replacement formulas to determine when ships had become obsolete and should be replaced by improved ones.

Improved navigational technology, however, could be incorporated in the production function either by replacing navigators or by retraining the present ones. At a cost, an experienced navigator might be trained to use a magnetic compass to find north or, some centuries later, a chronometer to determine his longitude.

One important *difference,* then, between the hardware and software components in ocean navigation lay in the greater opportunities for revising and improving the latter without complete replacement. One important *similarity* was that, even in the absence of technological change, both hardware and software gradually wore out and had to be replaced anyway. In both cases, the replacement cost was not negligible. Ships were obviously costly to build, and navigators could only be produced by years of training and experience.

Let us now introduce an automated navigator into this technology, in the form of a programmable computer. Only one thing has changed in the economic structure of the situation, but a rather significant one thing: Many technological changes in the art of navigation can now be introduced, almost without cost, by replacing the present program in the automated navigator with a copy of a program incorporating the improved method. The automated technology is an example of a technology that can be copied almost without cost.[3] To understand the significance of the difference,

we must consider the economics of copying.

The significance of cheap copying processes is that when they are available, the cost of developing improvements need be paid only once. Darwinian evolution is as much a matter of multiplication of the fittest as it is survival of the fittest. Genetic material, DNA and RNA, is organized as a copying mechanism, permitting improved organisms to be multiplied in number at no higher cost than would be required to produce the old, unimproved ones. Like improvements in the ship, however, and unlike improvements in the navigator, the superior technology cannot be introduced into existing organisms but must wait until they are removed by obsolescence and wearing out. As a matter of fact, copies continue to be made of the unimproved as well as of the improved organisms until competition gradually weeds out the former.

A second instructive example of a copying process is the one used by animals, but especially by man to transmit culture from one generation to the next by training, instructing, and educating progeny. This particular copying process can hardly be called "cheap," since in human cultures it commonly occupies a span of years nearly as long as the period during which the adult is fully productive. It is worthwhile—even necessary—precisely because man has reprogrammable software and can improve on the programs that he copies genetically from his parents. We might even say that these latter programs provide him with little more than a monitor system and an assembly language—that is, capabilties for acquiring performance programs.

The peculiarity of this particular copying technique and the reason why it is costly is that the program to be copied

---

[3] *Ibid.,* pp. 91–93.

cannot be inserted directly into the human head, but must gradually be grown there by those poorly understood processes we call education and experience. Copying is by no means synonymous, by the way, with memorization: you can memorize a page of Hoyle to the point where you can recite it perfectly, without being able at all to play the game described there. As a result, also, of the indirectness of the copying process, an exact copy is almost certainly never produced. In general, we can expect degradation in copying, the quality of the program being restored only by new improvements after experience in use.[4]

In order for knowledge and skills to be transmitted from one generation to another, they have to be stored reliably by memory. Until about five hundred years ago, the two major storage depositories were human memory and man's artifacts. Although writing has been known, of course, for some thousands of years, it was used to only a very limited extent to store the information needed to transmit skills from one generation to the next. One reason, undoubtedly, was the high cost of providing children with the programs (i.e., reading skills) needed to retrieve information from this memory source. A second was lack of knowledge about how to communicate "how-to" information in words generally, and in writing in particular. A third, and the most obvious, was the high cost of producing copies so that the information would be widely available.

Artifacts were a more interesting memory device. Houses were not built to teach people how to build houses, but were built to shelter them. Nevertheless, the houses were always present and available for inspection as a source of information on how to build houses. Hence, the existence of houses greatly reduced the cost of copying houses (as compared, say, with what the cost would have been if the builders only had oral or written descriptions of houses, or even pictures).

Five hundred years ago, the invention of printing greatly reduced the cost of copying verbal information, as well as the cost of copying pictures and diagrams. It provided an important new cheap, reliable memory device. For a long time, however, it appeared to be used far more for remembering abstractions and intangibles than the concrete particulars of everyday life and its technology. I would conjecture that these concrete particulars were already recorded in artifacts better than they could be in the verbal expressions (oral or written) available at that time.

Thus, among the crucial events in human evolution have been the introduction of five important advances in the technique and copying and storing information: organismic reproduction with duplication of genetic material; indirect programming through learning; preservation of artifacts; writing; and printing. Each of these has its characteristic structure of costs. None of them allows "instant" reprogramming of existing hardware. The third and fourth are simply storage devices; the fifth allows cheap copying; but all these last three contribute to production only through the second—learning—hence do not avoid its costs.

Direct copying of computer software has characteristics, therefore, quite different from any of these earlier copying techniques. When an improved program has been invented for the automatic navigator, it can not only be installed in new navigators at no addition to cost, but it can also be provided to existing naviga-

---

[4] "The Economic Implications of Learning by Doing" are examined in Kenneth Arrow's well-known essay with that title, *Review of Economic Studies,* XXIX (June 1962), 155–173, and in the reference cited there.

tors instantly and substantially without cost. The comparative advantage of automatic navigators relative to human navigators will increase in any field where the technology is advancing rapidly, since improvements can be incorporated in the former sooner than in the latter. The economics of the matter are developed more fully in the Appendix.

In the case of any copyable technique, there is a problem of how the costs of developing improvements are to be recovered. In the absence of adequate opportunity for recovery, there will, of course, be underinvestment in research and development. In a competitive economy, the problem becomes the more severe the less expensive and the more rapid the copying process.

Patent and copyright laws are the usual modern procedures for returning rewards to the authors of technological advances that can be copied. Secrecy is another method still widely used, but not applicable when the improvement can be copied from antifacts embodying it. (Study of artifacts may permit copying not only the objects themselves, but even improved methods of manufacture, evidences of which are preserved in the manufactured object.) At an earlier point in history (and even today in the military sphere), governments intervened to prevent the export of technological improvements, whether in the form of machinery or of programs recorded in the memories of artisans.

Because of the cheapness of the copying process, and the potential value of even single exemplars, the protection of inventors' interests in improved computer programs is a matter of great technical difficulty. Here we must distinguish programs written to run on a particular type of machine, on the one hand, from programs written in higher-level languages

that are easily transferred to different machines. The machine manufacturer can recover investments in software developments of the former kind, since they can only be used with his machines. On the other hand, the improvements are then not used everywhere they might be, and competing manufacturers must duplicate development investments, both sources of misallocation of resources.

With progress in software technology, programs have tended to become more independent of hardware. Hence, the problem from a social point of view appears to be to secure a sufficiently high rate of investment in software development.

Labor's contribution to production is achieved by the coordination of a system of sensory organs—eyes and ears—with a system of effectors—principally hand and mouth—by means of those stored programs we call "skills." [5] In our Columbian ocean transport technology there are both the skills of the navigator—whether human or automated—and the skills, or technical know-how, of the shipbuilders. Evidence from wartime destruction shows that an economy that has lost most of its physical capital but retained its pool of technology can restore previous levels of productivity relatively rapidly.

As was pointed out earlier, the stored skills in a pre-computer economy must be replaced each generation, even if there is no technological change, since these skills must exist in human brains in order to be useful for production. The replacement costs are by no means the same as the costs of formal education in the economy. In the first place, the entire time, not just the school time, of children prior to their entrance into the labor market should be charged as part of the replacement cost. Whether in school or out, children learn to speak, become acquainted

---

[5] "Decision Making as an Economic Resource," *op. cit.*, pp. 80–82.

with the common artifacts of their culture, and, at least in simple economies, learn one or more relevant production technologies.

In the second place, in societies with formal educational systems, a large part of what is taught and learned in the schools has no productive significance. This is certainly true of most of the curriculum of the contemporary American school system. Schooling is best regarded, under such circumstances, primarily as a consumption good that has as a small byproduct the storage of a certain amount of production skill.[6] If I were given a contract, at a fixed price, to produce research scientists, I would certainly turn the finished product out of my educational institution at an age earlier than 25!

In the third place, much of the transmission of programs takes place through on-the-job training and experience. These training costs do not show up in the social accounts, but are hidden as direct costs of production.

In a peasant culture, the avoidable cost of replacing programs each generation is probably very small, because by the time children are physically capable of doing hard manual work they have already learned most of the skills they will use. On the other hand, the absence of mechanisms for cheap transmission and reliable storage of programs probably operates to slow technical progress or even cause the loss of discoveries, so that improvements need to be repeatedly re-invented.

We observe, for example, that there was only minor technological advance in peasant cultures from pre-Christian times to the Industrial Revolution. We may conjecture that the technologies of these cultures remained in a state of dynamic equilibrium—they were able to maintain just that level of technology at which the forgetting from one generation to the next was balanced by re-invention. Increases in the density of population and improvements in the security or economy of travel and transportation would allow increases in specialization, hence permit a larger stock of programs to be transmitted. Nomadism, on the other hand, through increasing the difficulty of retaining numerous physical possessions, would decrease the stock of the culture's artifacts, hence degrade an important store of technological information.

It is not my purpose here to rewrite cultural history in terms of the problems a society faces in maintaining and transmitting stored programs. The notion of a learning-forgetting equilibrium of technology is not relevant, however, only to peasant cultures. It is equally applicable, for example, to the problem that a university department faces in remembering its own policies and all of the subtle considerations that went into their formulation. As faculty come and go, secretaries marry and are replaced, files are lost, and conditions change, the subtleties vanish, and the policy tends to reduce to a few general (though not necessarily sound) principles, plus some specific regulations that happen to have been recorded in documents that continue to be referred to. Often, the documents themselves become inoperative because the "retrieval" programs that would cause them to be re-

---

[6] My intention here is simply to state a fact, not to offer social criticism. In particular, I do not mean to argue that transmission of production programs should be the sole, or even a major, goal of formal education. I simply observe that it is easy to jump to the conclusion that this is what education is all about. The jumping has been encouraged by studies of American education that have made much of the largely spurious correlation between the amount of education and earnings. The correlations are spurious because they have been uncorrected, or inadequately corrected, for differences in ability, in ambition, and in family status.

ferred to on appropriate occasions are lost.

In sum, the costs of maintaining a store of human programs over periods during which personnel turnover is substantial are very large. Storing technology in the form of computer programs rather than human programs opens up new possibilities for greatly reducing such costs.

Learning is needed not only to transmit programs from generation to generation and to modify programs to incorporate new technology, but also simply to adapt programs to problems posed by a constantly changing environment. The economic gains to be realized from cheap copying will be inconsequential if new programs have to be devised ad hoc for each small change in circumstances.

The program of the navigator may make use of large amounts of information about tides, currents, winds, coastlines, and harbors in different parts of the world. The program, to be workable, must be factorable into two parts:

• A store of information that can be augmented readily by simple processes of memorization and by simple programs for consulting available reference sources.
• A general purpose program that can apply appropriate parts of this data store to any given specific navigational problem.

The economy of automated programs will depend on their having comparable features. They must be learning programs, at least in the sense that they can apply new information to new situations and probably also in the stronger sense that they are capable of some adaptive modification in their own structures. Without such features, each program would be applicable to only a narrow range of situations; hence little would be gained from the availability of cheap means for producing copies.

The ocean transportation technology of our allegory depends both on the programs stored in the navigator and on the programs for the manufacture of ships. All of our discussion of the costs of programming and improving the programs of human or automatic navigators applies quite as well to the programs of human or automated shipwrights.

Technological advance requires the invention of new techniques, but also the development and storage of the programs necessary to apply these techniques. For any extensive technological change, a whole series of "reprogramming" decisions have to be made—by managers, engineers, and workmen. In evaluating these decisions, numerous externalities will be encountered, because the effectiveness of the new technology in comparison with the old will depend on what programs have already been stored. Thus, the productivity of capital in the form of automobiles will depend on the commonness of driving and mechanics' programs in the population, as well as the presence or absence of such material artifacts as roads and gas stations.

One particular difficulty in the diffusion of new technologies is that the new programs have to be ingested, at least in considerable part, in order to evaluate them. Hence, much of the reprogramming cost must be borne before an accurate evaluation can be made—or acceptance of the new technology must be postponed until its advantages are obvious even to the untutored eye. To the extent that the programs of the new technology are computerized, the costs of developing the programs will have to be borne, but not borne anew in each application. We would expect more rapid diffusion of new technologies under these conditions.

Automation of the programs that constitute a technology will make explicit not only the problem of modifying programs to take advantage of advances in knowledge, but also the problem of using existing programs in relevant situations.

Specialization increases the repertory of programs that are available within the economy taken as a whole. It does not guarantee, however, that the sophisticated programs stored in the specialist's brain will be used whenever relevant. Someone, at the point of problem impact, must note the relevance and must have an effective procedure for locating the specialist. Even when he has been located, there may be difficult problems of compatibility between his programs and those of the persons consulting him—what we call now an "interface" problem. The specialist may fail to understand the problem properly, and those consulting him may fail to understand his solution or how to combine his knowledge with aspects of the problem that fall outside his specialty.

There is much talk today about the "knowledge explosion" and how this explosion makes it more difficult to locate relevant knowledge. Much of this alarm is ill-considered, for the advance of knowledge is not primarily an additive (or multiplicative) accumulation of knowledge. It is primarily the reorganization of knowledge to make it more parsimonious and more applicable. To become a research chemist should involve less learning today than it did fifty years ago, because physical chemistry and quantum mechanics have provided such powerful tools for organizing facts, and indeed making them derivable from theory.

In this age, as in any other, an important part of the programs that define the technology are programs for retrieving knowledge from its storage places. Among the important prospective consequences of automation are its consequences for retrieval techniques.

The cost of retrieving relevant programs depends, first, on finding them; second, making them usable in the application situation. Finding costs depends, in turn, on the structure of available indexes and on the power of the available search programs. As illustration, consider the boxed problem.

In spite of the apparent simplicity of a scheme for retrieving specialized information, retrieval in our present technology is by no means a perfected art. A good example of the inadequacies is provided by the lag between the level of sophistication of the statistical techniques applied by data users and the level of sophistication among experts in statistics. The more sophisticated programs are not retrieved when they would be appropriate because

• The user is not aware of their potential relevance.
• His access to the existing knowledge through appropriate inquiry procedures has not been institutionalized. (Among other things, he may have no way to recompense the expert properly for his time and trouble on a problem that is only a matter of "application," hence not of direct professional interest to the technique-oriented expert.)

Automation of technologies will cause the problem of retrieving relevant programs from the stock of existing ones to become more explicit than it has been in the past. The computer technology—both hardware and software—will also provide new means for retrieval. It will also create interesting new problems for economists, relating to the design of efficient retrieval systems.

One question that will arise repeatedly is the question of how far information should be processed when stored, and to what extent, on the other hand, it should be processed on demand. Should executives, for example, have "instantly" available the answers to large numbers of questions they might conceivably ask, should they have available the programs that will seek out and compute the answers in a short time, or should they have available programming languages that will allow them to write programs that, in turn, will find the answers? The cost structures of automated information systems are so different from those of manual systems that all of these issues will have to be rethought as the new technology develops.

Conclusions. A technology exists largely in the minds of its labor force and in the future will be distributed between those minds and the memories of computers. If programs, stored in one or the other of these forms, constitute the core of a technology, then important consequences are likely to follow from the fact that automation greatly decreases the cost of making copies of such programs.

One of the obvious consequences of cheaper copying is that there will be underinvestment in program improvement unless steps are taken to reward inventors of programs or to subsidize invention. A second consequence is that the comparative advantage of automation will tend to be particularly great in situations where frequent and rapid program change is called for, and will tend to be relatively less in areas where only a few copies of a program can be used. Since human programs are at least modestly capable of on-the-job learning and adaptation to specific situations, the range of feasible automation will depend heavily on the extent to which similar learning and adaptive features can be incorporated in automated programs.

The concept of technology as consisting of stored programs gives us a somewhat novel framework for theory about the rate of technological progress and the rate of diffusion of new technology. The level of technology that a society can maintain will depend heavily—indeed, in the past may have depended heavily—on the costs of transmitting programs from each gen-

eration to the next. It will depend also on the possibility of economizing transmission costs through specialization.

To the extent that there is specialization of programs within an economy, retrieval programs for locating relevant knowledge and skill become an important element in productive capacity. When copying costs are high, locating a relevant specialist will be useless if his time is fully occupied. With techniques for copying programs cheaply, the numbers of specialist programs will respond flexibly to demands, hence retrieval programs will take on an even greater importance than they have at present.

The automation of programs will have many consequences beyond those I have identified. If there is anything we can say with confidence about a new technology, it is that we will not really understand its implications until we have lived with it for a few generations. Now that we have perhaps achieved some understanding of the First Industrial Revolution—the revolution of power—we are already in the midst of the Second—the revolution in the processing of information. It is important that we identify the salient characteristics of the new technology and their consequences for the economy.

Appendix

The argument in the text with respect to the effect of cheap copying on technological change can be made more rigorous by a simple mathematical model. We assume that invention is an autonomous activity, as a result of which there exists at any given time, t, a most efficient technology. This technology takes the form of programs (e.g., programs for navigators and shipwrights) and is implemented by copying these programs and installing them in place of existing programs. (It should be observed that, in contrast to the "learning by doing" theories of Arrow and others, we assume that application of the new technology does not increase the rate of invention. A more complete theory would combine the "learning by doing" mechanism with the copying mechanism discussed here.)

Navigational technology. Let $R(t)$ be the net revenue per year (exclusive of program-copying costs) produced by a ship that employs the best navigational technology available at time t. Let P_n be the cost, assumed constant, of a navigator's program. If navigators' programs are replaced, on the average, every T years, then the average age of the technology in use will be $T/2$. The net revenue will average:

$$\bar{R}(t) = \frac{1}{T}\int_{\tau=0}^{T} R(t-\tau)\,d\tau. \quad (1)$$

Assume that invention produces a constant rate of increase in net revenue returnable by the best technology:

$$R(t) = A + Bt. \quad (2)$$

Then, from (1) and (2):

$$\bar{R}(t) = \frac{1}{T}\int_{\tau=0}^{T}\left[A + B(t-\tau)\right]d\tau$$

$$= A + B\left(t - \frac{T}{2}\right) = R\left(t - \frac{T}{2}\right).$$

$$(3)$$

The cost of replacing navigators' programs every T years will be, per ship per year:

$$C_n = \frac{P_n}{T}. \quad (4)$$

Hence, the revenue, net of this cost, will be:

$$\bar{R}(t) - C_n = R(t) - B\frac{T}{2} - \frac{P_n}{T}. \quad (5)$$

We wish to choose the replacement interval, T, so as to maximize revenue, for given $R(t)$ and P_n. Setting the first derivative of (5) equal to zero, we get:

$$\frac{d(\bar{R}(t) - C_n)}{dT} = -\frac{B}{2} + \frac{P_n}{T^2} = 0. \quad (6)$$

Whence,

$$T^* = \sqrt{\frac{2P_n}{B}}. \quad (7)$$

That is to say, the optimal replacement interval for programs, T^*, will vary directly with the square root of copying costs and inversely with the square root of the technological change coefficient. Substituting T^* in the revenue function (5), we get:

$$\bar{R}(t) - C_n = R(t) - 8\sqrt{P_nB}. \quad (8)$$

The second term on the righthand side of (8) is the penalty for failing to use the best available technology. This penalty is larger the greater the cost of copying programs (because the lag will then be greater) and the more rapid the improvement in technology.

Suppose there are also rental costs associated with navigators, human (C_H), or automatic (C_A). Then if human and automated navigators are just competitive:

$$\bar{R}_H(t) - C_{NH} - C_H =$$

$$\bar{R}_A(t) - C_{NA} - C_A. \quad (9)$$

That is:

$$-\sqrt{P_{NH}B} - C_H =$$

$$-\sqrt{P_{NA}B} - C_A. \quad (10)$$

Presumably, $P_{NH} > P_{NA}$, and $C_A > C_H$, so that:

$$C_A - C_H = \sqrt{P_{NH}B} - \sqrt{P_{NA}B}$$

$$= (\sqrt{P_{NH}} - \sqrt{P_{NA}})\sqrt{B}. \quad (11)$$

Now if the rate of invention increases (B larger), the cost balance will be tipped in favor of automated navigators. If human learning can be made more efficient (P_{NH} reduced), the balance will be tipped in favor of human navigators.

Shipbuilding technology. The argument is easily extended to deal with optimal replacement rates for ships and for shipwrights' programs. The average age of the technology embedded in ships will be $\frac{1}{2}(T_W + T_S)$, where T_W is the replacement period for shipwrights' programs and T_S the replacement period for ships. Ignoring navigation, we have, analogously to (3):

$$\overline{R}(t) = R\left(t - \frac{T_W}{2} - \frac{T_S}{2}\right). \quad (12)$$

Assume that the number of shipwrights required is proportional to the number of ships built. If the improvement in technology is linear, as before, then, for each ship:

$$\overline{R}(t) - \frac{P_S}{T_S} - \frac{P_W}{T_W}$$

$$= R(t) - B\frac{T_S + T_W}{2} - \frac{P_S}{T_S} - \frac{P_W}{T_W}. \quad (13)$$

Maximizing, we obtain:

$$T_S{}^* = \sqrt{\frac{2P_S}{B}}, T_W{}^* = \sqrt{\frac{2P_W}{B}}. \quad (14)$$

35. Plain Talk About Computers

GEORGE GLASER

A decade or so ago, at the dawn of the computer era, writers of Sunday-supplement articles were fond of describing the mysterious new electronic gadget as a superbrain possessed of nearly magical powers. More recently it has become fashionable to point out, rather disparagingly, that the computer can do only. what it is programmed to do. This sounds a lot more sophisticated, but it misses a crucial point. In the words of Herbert Simon, the observation that the computer can only follow instructions is "intuitively obvious, indubitably true, and supports none of the implications that are commonly drawn from it." [In *The Shape of Automation* (New York: Harper & Row, Publishers, 1965).] For the fact is that the computer's capabilities, though not supernatural, far exceed any use yet made of them.

The computer is, first of all, a dutiful and tireless slave in processing huge volumes of paper work—subscriber billing, insurance premium accounting, credit card invoicing, and on and on. Second, it can deal with problems of complexity— problems that are literally insoluble, in any practical sense, by manual methods. Typical problems of complexity are satellite tracking and impact prediction, economic models for long-range corporate planning, and optimization of petroleum refineries. Third, the computer can provide extremely rapid response to external events. This capability of the computer, a relatively recent development, has led to airline reservation systems, on-line monitoring of hospital patients, process control (in the petroleum, paper, and chemical industries, for example), and

Reprinted from *Business Horizons,* Vol. 10, No. 3 (Fall, 1967), pp. 33–38, with permission of the author and the publisher, Indiana University. George Glaser is a principal with McKinsey and Company.

most important, perhaps, to time-sharing and the much-discussed computer public utility.

Technological Developments

Most of these applications would have taxed our imagination ten years ago. Today we accept many of them as routine. And we see a continuing series of new developments in computer technology—both hardware and software—that opens up entirely new horizons to us.

Massive files, storing hundreds of millions of characters of data and retrieving them in millionths of a second, are being installed. Only months ago a computer manufacturer announced a memory device that will allow storage densities of one million bits per square inch, approximately the amount of information on six pages of a four-column telephone directory. For some time we have had photographic techniques that would reduce these six pages to one square inch of film, but the data stored using the new technique can be retrieved, manipulated, and stored again. This new capability is only one of many developments now being explored.

Computer memory specifications are no longer stated in microseconds but in nanoseconds. A nanosecond—one billionth of a second—is a difficult figure to comprehend, but try this: There are as many nanoseconds in one second as there are seconds in thirty years, or as many nanoseconds in 2.5 seconds as there are seconds in a person's lifetime.

These changes in the internal workings of the computer are difficult to understand and appreciate. More obvious changes are occurring in input/output equipment; these changes for the most part are intended to increase human access to the machine. We see increased use of graphic techniques for all kinds of engineering

applications. The automobile industry is using graphic display systems to design cars; the areospace industry is using them for aeronautical engineering and for shortening the production lead times of new types of aircraft.

Communication capabilities now allow the computer to switch both data and normal message traffic. In the planning stage are public computing utilities that will provide access to computing power over communication circuits by widely dispersed users, each paying only a fraction of the system's cost. A single computer now can handle multiple programs, processing several independent applications at the same time. This development has led to the introduction of time-sharing systems. Forty or more users in as many different companies may each sit at a typewriter-like console connected by teletype or telephone to a computer located miles, or thousands of miles, away. The computer's response time is so fantastically quick that it can serve forty masters at once without strain. For each user, it is precisely as if he alone had sole and complete access to the computer. For all practical purposes, he does.

COST TRENDS

Despite these fantastic increases in the power and complexity of hardware, hardware costs are falling. In the past few years, they have declined from 50 to 40 per cent of the total cost of a typical data processing installation. With further progress in low-cost mass storage and high-speed microcircuitry, indications are that the trend will continue. Cost-performance curves show a steady improvement in output per dollar, and no leveling-out is in sight.

Software and applications development costs, on the other hand, have continued to rise despite the best efforts of equipment manufacturers and software houses to develop higher-level languages. These efforts, for the most part successful, have greatly eased the burden of the programmer in translating systems logic into operating instructions for the computer, but they have not reversed the upward trend of costs. There are two reasons for this. First, the systems themselves are more complex, span larger portions of the business enterprise, and thus increase the difficulty of analysis and design. Second, the severe shortage of experienced systems design and programming personnel has rapidly driven up their salary levels.

PERSONNEL TRENDS

In terms of immediate practical effects, people—not technological trends—are the overriding issue of tomorrow. Already the supply of talented programmers and systems analysts is far short of the demand, and the gap is widening inexorably. For the foreseeable future, there is literally no possibility that we shall have enough trained people to go around. All three categories of special skills needed to use the computer effectively are in short supply:

1. *Operations researchers and management scientists,* who apply mathematical and statistical techniques directly to the problems the decision maker faces and to the information he needs to run his business. They also must determine the means for providing management with the best alternatives on which to make decisions.

2. *Systems analysts,* who design the complex mechanisms for applying the computer to the detailed activities of the entire operation.

3. *Computer programmers,* who translate the work of the operations research and systems analysis into the language of the computer.

There are somewhat more than 100,-000 qualified computer specialists in America today. By the end of 1970, roughly 300,000 will be needed—an increment of well over 50,000 each year between now and then. Quite obviously, this is not going to happen. Alarmingly, however, company managements are acting and thinking exactly as if it were.

We asked a few leading computer users to compare the number of computer personnel on their staffs in 1965 with the number they had employed in 1960 and with their anticipated requirements for 1970. In aggregate, these companies had more than tripled their computer staffs between 1960 and 1965. Between 1965 and 1970, they were planning an increase of another 50 per cent.

In this sample, the company with the longest computer history and the largest and slowest-growing staff will have recorded a personnel increase of 200 per cent from 1960 to 1970. By way of contrast, two companies that did not become active computer users until 1960 have increased their staffs since then by ten times and fourteen times, respectively, and will have increased them by about twenty times by 1970—*if* their present plans are realized. Clearly, a five-year-old company computer effort has not yet come of age. Observation suggests, in fact, that maturity and stability seldom come until about the ten-year mark.

The scramble for skilled computer personnel in private industry will be seriously aggravated by competition from federal, state, and local governments, whose rate of growth in computer activity almost certainly will exceed that of private industry in the next few years. This, of course, means a further intensification of demand for trained OR specialists, systems analysts, and programmers in the biggest business of all.

Clearly, the competition for talented people is going to get fiercer—and management's use of computer systems five years hence will probably be seriously hobbled by a lack of competent people to analyze applications and program their machines. Companies leading the field today will, in all probability, continue to attract the best people available, thereby extending their lead. The rich, in other words, will get richer, while the company attempting to build an organization from scratch will find itself at a very serious disadvantage—not least because it will have trouble convincing high-talent people that it is a progressive company to work for.

The frustration of being unable to find and hold enough qualified specialists to develop needed systems will almost surely impel many companies to pressure their operating executives into taking an important hand in systems design and development. Yet, the more complex the new applications become, the dimmer is the hope of salvation offered by this alternative. To see why, let us look at the nature of some of the changes now occurring.

Applications

In just a few years, the nature of computer applications has changed dramatically. In most companies, the first applications were designed to process routine transactions, mostly in accounting. Here the computer proved itself a swift, accurate, and insatiable processor of mountains of paper work. In many cases, clear-cut savings were achieved by reduction of clerical costs. These routine applications could be justified economically by relatively straightforward extensions of known cost factors, and apart from some procedural adjustments, little in the company had to change.

The next era of computer applications saw the rise of business systems for inventory control, production scheduling, cash management, and the like. At the time these applications were designed and implemented, they were considered very complex. Their designers took consider-

able pride in making them work—and a few resounding fiascoes resulted. But, in general, these systems brought about lower inventory levels, faster deliveries to customers, and smoother production. Their benefits, however, were harder to estimate. On occasion, managements authorized these efforts without any guarantee of dollar results appearing on the profit-and-loss statement.

Significantly, companies began to realize that these more complex systems could raise sticky issues of corporate policy. What, for example, is the objective of inventory control: reduced working capital, improved customer service, or lower production costs? Can all these objectives be satisfied at once? Top executives had to help answer such questions. It became apparent that computer systems were introducing a new dimension of difficulty. Close coordination of the individual requirements of several functional and staff departments had become necessary.

Today, with increased hardware and software capabilities, we see opportunities for tackling still more important business problems on a still higher level of complexity. Our new goal is the most ambitious yet: to improve management's decisions. In terms of potential benefits— better planning, better allocation of resources, more timely decisions, explicit consideration of risk and uncertainty— these systems offer an economic potential far greater than the most successful paperwork processing applications of a few years ago. But they are far harder to justify on a straightforward cost-saving basis, far more difficult to design, and far more painful for the organization and its people to assimilate.

Management information systems (especially the "total" or "integrated" variety) are currently much in vogue. The ultimate objective of such a system, in grossly oversimplified terms, is to collect all the data pertaining to a company's operations and to amass it in vast computer files from which any information and all reports can be readily extracted. Of course, only a few zealots would seek to realize this objective literally. More practical systems designers realize that it would be technically impossible and economically untenable to collect *all* the relevant data. Their approach is to integrate certain closely related functions of the business—inventory control and production scheduling in a manufacturing company, for example. Such systems are now being designed, but not even the most expert of systems analysts would argue that they all offer clear sailing.

By definition, a system consists of interrelated parts functioning together toward a single goal or objective. A television set is a system that receives a signal, processes it, and displays a picture; similarly, an automobile ignition system responds to a signal and delivers electrical energy to the spark plugs. Such electrical and mechanical systems have a completely unambiguous objective; their design is single-purpose and they are relatively reliable. We are not so blessed in the case of business systems. Business systems involve people—and people, with their individual designs and conflicting objectives, are of questionable reliability from the systems designer's point of view.

Most of the functioning computer systems of today were designed for a single purpose; in many cases, they served only a single user department. Their design and implementation, accordingly, posed relatively few problems. Now, however, we are designing systems that affect entire organizations; every operating function of the business will be part of the information system needed to control it. And, since systems are characteristically susceptible to the failure of their weakest link, a management information system may be crippled or wrecked if just one

operating manager providing data to the system does his job poorly.

It would seem that the applications now confront us with an entirely new level of difficulty. First, the technical problems are considerably more difficult, a point that can easily be confirmed by asking any data processing manager how many of his people are qualified to modify the operating system that controls the flow of programs through third-generation computers. Second, it is becoming increasingly difficult to estimate the expected benefits as problems deal more and more with factors that cannot be quantified in advance. Third, the new applications require far more organizational discipline and coordination than did the earlier single-purpose systems.

Feasibility

A data processing project should be considered an investment; benefits are expected, costs will be incurred, and risks are involved. On the basis of an evaluation of these costs, benefits, and risks, the company allocates resources of manpower, equipment, and time to specific projects. In principle, this approach is not very different from any other investment of resources, but in practice a computer systems proposal poses special complexities that call for detailed analysis. This analysis is usually conducted as part of a feasibility study.

Three aspects of feasibility—technical, economic, and operational—should be evaluated in a feasibility study. They deal, respectively, with (1) whether the project can be implemented, given existing constraints on known technology and the company's ability to exploit it; (2) whether the economic benefits will outweigh the costs, and whether they represent the best available return for the resource investment; and (3) whether the implemented system will function successfully in the given environment.

Technical feasibility, primarily the province of the computer systems staff, involves defining alternative approaches to the problem and specifying the technical resources each approach will require. Given today's advanced equipment and software, few business systems are likely to prove technically impossible, but their feasibility, in terms of available corporate resources, often cannot by any means be taken for granted. And the "best" technical approach can seldom be identified without imaginative and painstaking systems analysis.

Economic feasibility cannot be determined by the systems staff alone. To be sure, they can and should weigh the economic benefits of the proposed system, as estimated by the line managers for whom it would be developed, against predictable development and operating costs. But these calculations, although necessary, are not sufficient—the same resources invested in a different project might have produced a greater return. Assessment of the opportunity cost of a particular application is the key to the question of economic feasibility.

Operational feasibility, though seldom formally evaluated, is no less important. Because the constraints on operational feasibility are motivational and organizational, they frequently are overlooked by managers and technicians alike.

Computer systems do not operate in a vacuum; they serve and are served by people. Unless the people involved are sold on the system, want to make it work, and are eager for the help it can give them, its technical and economic feasibility are simply irrelevant. The necessary motivation, in turn, depends on whether the system will enable the people affected to perform better in ways that are rewarded by the company's established value system. The most detailed computer-aided sales analysis and reporting system, for example, will fail to achieve its objective of concentrating salesmen's attention on profitable accounts and lines if their compensation plan continues to reward them solely on the basis of volume.

Again, how enthusiastic will the head of one department be about incurring additional costs to supply another department with data that will enable it to make a significant added contribution to overall company profits? The answer depends entirely on how Department A's performance is evaluated.

If the sole yardstick is control of departmental expense—if, in other words, the responsible executive is paid to be myopic about matters outside his immediate authority—his department may well prove to be the reef on which the entire project goes aground.

Only top management is really in a position to insure operational feasibility. The analysis need not be formal, but it had better be thoughtful and thorough, for the pitfalls in this area are many—and some are far from obvious.

What the Manager Can Do

No set of rules will guarantee success with any undertaking as complex as a corporate computer systems effort, but a few guidelines for the individual can be formulated.

1. He should identify how his job is related to the objectives of the company. This obligation, of course, applies to every manager, quite apart from any consideration of the computer effort. But it applies with singular force to the manager whose company is pushing ahead into strategic applications of the computer.

2. He should consider how the computer can contribute to performance in

working toward these objectives. In doing so, he should seek the help of the data processing department. If the manager identifies an opportunity to use the computer, he must be willing to put a value on it—but not confine his search to applications that will generate a measurable dollar return, in reduced clerical costs, for example. Even if these applications develop as anticipated, the effort may consume valuable developmental resources that would be better spent on projects of more strategic significance.

3. He should insist on helping to design the system and on approving the costs/benefit trade-offs—shorter development time vs. better system performance, for example. Such trade-offs arise in any major system development, and since the data processing staff cannot really evaluate potential benefits, they should not be compelled or permitted to make the trade-off decisions.

4. He should encourage his people to use installed systems well. If a system does not work as it should, he should recommend changes. The manager can complain if he does not like the results, but he is not to carp; if the system does not live up to expectations, it may be his fault. He, after all, is an integral part of any system he uses.

5. Finally, he should agree to an audit of the results after systems are installed. This aspect is most important in systems development. It will help not only the manager but the data processing depart-ment to do a better job the next time.

The computer is synonymous with change—changes in the way business is conducted, in its internal organization, and in the decision prerogatives of its managers. Those companies, and those managers, who have the ability to accept and take advantage of change generally use the computer well and find it a powerful and profitable adjunct to their operations. Those who shrink from change and revere the *status quo* generally find it difficult to absorb the computer's impact on their operations.

The computer requires more than toleration, or the attitude that "it's here to stay and we may as well learn to live with it." Companies that are living with the computer begrudgingly are usually unhappy with the results, and will be for a long time. The computer is a mechanical beast, and its master, the human, is a fantasically complex and wonderful creature possessed of powers to think, reason, judge, and feel. So if an intelligent human being decides to scuttle the computer, it is generally no contest. A good systems designer tries to make his system not only foolproof but *idiot*-proof, since the odds are that the system will, in fact, have to ward off a few attacks by idiots. But this kind of preventative is not enough. The company that expects to use the computer effectively must not only accept change, but reach out and grasp it. And managers —not technicians or hardware—will determine its success.

36. Computer Induced Organization Changes

ROGER VERGIN

Since the computer first appeared as a business tool a short decade ago, business and academic journals have been replete with predictions and assertions about its eventual use and impact. Both businessmen and management scholars alike have predicted that wide and drastic changes in the organization of the firm, the decision-making process, and management positions and duties are likely to occur as a result of the computer.[1]

While occasional reports have been issued about such changes in individual firms [2] (usually in the guise of "success stories" describing the application of electronic data processing), little attempt has been made to systematically gather empirical evidence describing the general pattern of such changes. This report presents such an attempt.

In order to provide a foundation for statements about the general pattern of computer induced organization adjust-

ments, observations were made in a variety of business organizations of diverse sizes, with diverse objectives, and operating in varying environments. Research was undertaken in eleven firms [3] in the Minneapolis-St. Paul area, ranging in size from 89 to 23,000 employees, and using computers ranging from small to large scale. Interviews were held with people in the following positions: manager of the data processing department, manager of the systems and procedures department, programmers and system analysts within these departments, managers of departments affected by the computer system, and senior executive officers. Additional data were obtained through the study of the computer information systems and other material such as organization charts and job descriptions.

In actuality, the changes that occur in a firm as a result of computerization

Reprinted from *MSU Business Topics* (Summer, 1967), by permission of the publisher, the Bureau of Business and Economic Research, Division of Research, Graduate School of Business Administration, Michigan State University. Roger C. Vergin is Associate Professor of Management and Organization, Graduate School of Business Administration, University of Washington.

[1] See, for example, Harold J. Leavitt and Thomas L. Whisler, "Management in the 1980's," *Harvard Business Review*, XXXVI, 6 (1958), 41–48; and Robert E. Slater, "Thinking Ahead: How Near Is the Automatic Office?" *Harvard Business Review*, XXXVI, 2 (1958), 27–36.

[2] See, for example, J. Douglas Elliot, "EDP—Its Impact on Jobs, Procedures and People," *The Journal of Industrial Engineering*, IX, 5 (September–October, 1958), 407–410; and Wesley S. Bagby, "Planning for Electronic Data Processing," *Proceedings of the Ninth Annual Industrial Engineering Institute,* University of California, Berkeley and Los Angeles, February, 1957, pp. 3–12.

[3] At least one firm from each of the following types: insurance, banking, public utility, wholesaling, wholesaling-retailing, manufacturing-wholesaling, retailing, processing, transportation, and investment.

are not easily separable into a series of neat, distinct subcategories such as decision-making changes, formal organization changes, or decentralization changes, but rather they collectively form a pattern of reaction to the introduction of this new technological innovation. Thus, they defy classification into any simple quantitative or even qualitative terms that can be used as the basis for the construction of a normative model. Yet, separation and classification is necessary if consideration of the changes is to ensue. Therefore, the changes which are actually inseparable in the operating systems will herein be treated independently insofar as possible in order to facilitate their discussion. First, the computer's effect on decision making will be considered. Next, changes in the formal organization structure, with particular emphasis on middle management positions and the decentralization issue will be examined. Then, the position of data processing in the organization will be discussed and resistance to organizational change will be noted. Finally, comment will be made on the impact of the computer in the future.

Decision-Making Changes

The decision-making process has received considerable attention by social scientists in recent times. With the adoption of computers by business firms, attention quickly focused on its potential effect on the decision process in business organizations. The research in the eleven firms revealed that the computer substantially improved the decision-making process in some firms but that, frequently, its capabilities had been underutilized. Many of the eleven firms treated the computer as merely a fast calculating device and applied it to perform the same tasks previously done by simpler tabulating machines and by clerical workers.

The cost savings resulting from the computer's enormous computing advantage justified its installation. In such firms, the managerial decision process was practically unchanged with perhaps occasional small improvements resulting because the information was more accurate and more timely. Computerized payroll processing typifies the above approach.

More substantial decision-making improvements occurred in a minority of firms which took a broader view and focused their system design efforts on providing the information required for decision making rather than on "using the computer" to cut costs. In such cases the power of the computer was used to provide pertinent decision-making data which were previously either technologically impossible or uneconomical to obtain, and to assist in the coordination and integrated operation of previously independent operating units. To conclude that the resulting decision-making changes constituted improvements required, in many cases, that managers' subjective evaluations of their decision processes be accepted at face value since measurements of the quality or profitability of decisions before and after the computer were impossible to obtain. In other cases, however, direct measurements were obtained which confirmed managers' assertions about decision improvements. These decision-making changes will now be considered along a number of dimensions.

The computer enabled a wider view to be taken in decision making. In a few instances, computerized decision models were developed which explicitly considered operations throughout large segments of the firm in making department-level decisions. While completely integrated decision systems have not yet been developed, some of the firms were taking a broad systems view of at least portions of their organizations and developing analyses far more sophisticated than any previously seen. For example, a processing firm was making decisions daily on the quantities of goods to be bought, processed, and sold, and the coordinated movements of these goods among over a hundred facilities throughout the country. The computer made possible an increase in the information considered and the alternatives explored. Under the traditional data-process system, the firm had been limited to evaluating the alternatives at each location almost independently.

More commonly, a broader view of the firm was obtained merely through improved dissemination of information. In a typical system, each department manager was provided with the current status of all related departments. Thus, for example, when the marketing department head was considering a special sales promotion, he could gauge its effects on other segments of the firm by information supplied to him concerning present inventory and production status, financial position, raw material availability, and the like. While such information could be gathered under any data processing system, the comparative ease with which it was done under the computer system made such information dissemination standard operating procedure.

With up-to-date information, management was able to take corrective action or begin investigation of problems on the basis of problem indicators such as minute changes in costs, profits, ability to meet delivery dates, accounts payable, and accounts receivable. Consequently, action was possible before difficulties reached great magnitudes or even before they previously would have been suspected. This increased the frequency of decisions since managers made frequent minor adjust-

ments in order to avoid dysfunctional problems rather than waiting until the problems reached serious proportions.

In some firms it was possible to precisely measure the value of reduced information time lag. A wholesaling firm reduced inventory from 25 to 19 days' supply. In a transportation firm, computerized data processing reduced rolling stock, construction materials, etc., by 20 percent, resulting in the freeing of several million dollars. At the same time stockouts were reduced by 25 to 50 percent because of perpetually accurate inventory records.

With the computer systems, managers were using decision information which previously was too costly, took too long to process, or was literally beyond human capabilities to obtain. For example, one firm, with over a million accounts, was making decisions based on statistical data which previously were impossible to obtain without tying up both the accounts and the data-processing equipment for an extended period of time, thus prohibiting the transaction of regular business. Similar new decision opportunities were found in almost every firm. One EDP manager estimated that 50 percent of the data processing was for applications which were performed only because the computer made them feasible.[4]

The computer also provided a tool for solving those problems which had long been quantifiable but computationally too complex or too time-consuming for human calculating effort. Firms were solving problems which would have taken months to solve manually. Production scheduling, blending, investing, and other activities were being reevaluated daily on the basis of current information. This re-

---

[4] In a few instances, it appeared that new analyses were being undertaken not because the produced information was needed but only because it could now be obtained with the computer. That is, the new applications seemingly were developed at least partially to justify the introduction of a computer.

sulted in shorter planning periods, since previously such decisions were made weekly, monthly, or even just annually on information that was already obsolete by the time the decisions were reached.

In several instances, the computer improved the decision process by forcing management to examine critically its decision-making methods. While managers had often been content to evaluate many decisions in general terms and with a great deal of subjectivity, the computer forced them to specify the criteria being optimized, the important variables, and the method by which they should be analyzed. Managers then frequently found to their amazement that they were failing to even consider many important factors. In other instances, decisions which managers felt depended on *judgment* and were consequently made at high levels in the organization were actually found to be made by simple *rules of thumb*. Such decisions were then either programmed for the computer or moved to a lower level manager.

Computerized decision-making was not without some added risks. One serious problem revealed in the research was a lack of flexibility of the decision systems. This rigidity was particularly felt in the difficulty of revising the system to include new variables or add new functions. Even though most firms had programming time allocated to program maintenance, changes or new data which would have been readily absorbed by human decision makers were simply shunted aside until there was a large enough accumulation to justify a system revision since reevaluation could have resulted in a considerable reprogramming effort.

Another frequently revealed shortcoming was that decisions were overly simplified in order to make them suitable for computerization. Quantified variables were given 100 percent weight when qualitative information should have retained

some importance. In most such cases, however, the economies achieved by the substitution of the computer for human decision makers more than offset an occasional less than satisfactory decision resulting from a lack of complete information.

Organization Structure Changes

The organizational revisions viewed in the eleven firms were much less extensive than those forecast in many predictions of the past decade. In the firms where the computer was installed as merely a fast calculating device, practically no changes occurred. In other firms that were developing integrated decision systems, some corresponding organizational integration was achieved. Most such instances of change were due to increased administrative efficiency in handling information. For example, an insurance firm, which had previously had three departments organized around three record files, consolidated all of the information into one file and was then able to handle all of the work within one administrative unit. Also, a wholesaling firm which had maintained parallel departments in several geographic locations was able to dissolve the regional departments and make decisions centrally because of the accessibility of complete and current information.

While few major organizational revisions occurred, there was substantial evidence of continual minor changes in several firms. As the computer systems expanded from the original cost reduction applications into more complex operations with some degree of integration, subtle, sometimes almost unnoticed, structural revisions were made. In time, the accumulated changes sometimes reached significant proportions. Managers who originally flatly stated that no organizational revisions were caused by the computer, later upon close examination of their pre-computer and present organizations pointed out major differences.

Overall, it appeared that the greater the importance of data processing in the total operations of the firm, the greater the organizational revision. That is, firms such as banks and insurance companies revealed larger changes than firms in manufacturing, processing, and transportation.

Although the organization changes in most of the eleven firms were not substantial, there were indications that larger changes are likely in the future. In general, the firms which had installed their computers most recently had gone the farthest toward achieving integrated information systems and, thus, exhibited the largest structural revisions. In fact, the firm which underwent the largest transformation was one which had first tried to install a computer to gain cost reductions almost without any consideration of the long-run total information requirements of the firm. In trying to fit a hastily chosen computer into the going system, so many problems arose that the original computer had to be abandoned before the system ever achieved operational status. But, because of this failure the firm then conducted an intensive study of its data requirements and eventually installed a successful integrated information system which required major organizational changes. As experience in computer applications grows, firms are continuing to progress from the early piecemeal cost reduction application to systems incorporating more sweeping changes.

The eventual magnitude of structural changes depends in large measure on advances in the art of programming and model building. It can be expected that as more sophisticated integrated simulation and decision models are developed there will be an accompanying amalgamation of organizational units. At the same time, as more decisions are shifted from managers to computers, the managers will be able to increase their span of control and administer larger, more complex units.

Middle Management Positions

There has been frequent discussion concerning the possibilities of programming the activities of middle management, thus reducing or eliminating this segment of the organization.[5] A substantial portion of the duties of middle management consists of activities properly classified as routine decision making, such as deciding what quantities of materials to purchase, scheduling work to be processed, assigning individuals to jobs, and establishing job priorities, regardless of the type of business involved. In addition, middle managers are concerned with problems of motivating employees and coordinating work within the department and with outside organizational units.

Thus, it would seem logical that the computer, with its acknowledged computational superiority, has the potential to take over many of the routine tasks of middle management. And, in the firms in the sample, this was happening to some extent. In companies handling inventories, computers were deciding when to place orders, with whom to place them, and what quantity to purchase. In manufacturing firms, computers were establishing schedules and routing orders. In all of the firms some of middle management's decisions had been abrogated by the computer.

---

[5] See, for example, George J. Brabb and Earl B. Hutchins, "Electronic Computers and Management Organization," *California Management Review*, VI, 1 (1963), 40; and Martin Shubik, "Approaches to the Study of Decision-Making Relevant to the Firm," *Journal of Business*, XXXIV, 2 (April, 1961), 114.

Yet there were no cases of middle managers either being eliminated or suffering financial downgrading because of the shift of duties to the computer, although a few were placed at lower levels in the organization.[6] It should be pointed out, however, that the process of computerized decision making was only in the very early stages of growth in most of the firms. Typically the very routine low-level clerical operations which held the greatest potential for cost reduction were first programmed. The only middle management decision functions programmed were those that accompanied such operations. For example, in a wholesaling firm where the principal EDP operation was customer billing and inventory recording, inventory ordering decisions were incorporated into the computer system. Thus, only a few of the many potentially programmable middle management decisions had thus far been included in the computer systems.

For those middle managers whose positions were most affected by the computer, the major change was not in the elimination of some decisions but rather that their task of motivation and coordination was reduced. This occurred because the number of subordinates in their departments decreased as the clerical work which they had performed was transferred to the computer. Thus, their jobs were made less demanding and those who held the jobs sometimes viewed their positions as being downgraded even though no salary reductions occurred.

Centralization Trend

Undoubtedly the largest and most visible organization change resulting from computer use in the eleven firms was a move toward recentralization of decision making. Much of the decentralization move of the 1950's was undoubtedly negatively motivated because of the difficulty of centralized management when corporations became large and complex. The computer, with its ability to synthesize data, eliminated much of the need for decentralized decision making. Instances of recentralized movement of decisions were found in virtually every firm in the sample. For example, an insurance firm which previously was making decisions on rates for special policies in field offices shifted the task to central offices; a banking firm shifted some of its loan evaluation decisions from the branches to the central bank; and a wholesaling-retailing firm moved many of the decisions concerning sales promotions and stocking from the retail store managers to a central staff.

There was also a major trend toward a complementary yet distinct type of centralization—centralization of the information gathering and processing function. This resulted in a physical movement of personnel and equipment. For example, the check processing and accounting for a multi-office banking firm was consolidated at one location; a wholesaling institution performed data processing and customer billing for several regional warehouses at a central location; another firm actually closed a regional office because it found that the computer enabled it to perform all of the regional office's functions centrally. Another corporation found that, despite increasing volume, it was able to operate from one national office; without the computer, regional offices would have been required. All but one of the eleven firms experienced either a major move toward physical centraliza-

---

[6] In some cases, it appeared that managers were being retained only to prevent opposition to the EDP changeover. For example, in one firm it was stated that when suitable positions could be found for two managers whose positions were affected by the computer, they would be transferred and their former positions eliminated.

tion or the elimination of the need for a major move toward decentralization with increasing volume because of the computer. The remaining exception was a small, single-unit firm which had always had centralized operations.

The cost pattern of computerized systems reenforced the trend toward centralized data processing. The EDP systems had a high fixed cost to develop and operate as compared to traditional data processing systems but little added cost for increased volume of processing. This processing centralization often caused some accompanying centralization of decision making simply because of the data proximity.

Data Processing

In addition to the organizational impact of the computer on the remainder of the firm, the data processing division itself often experienced a sharply changed position. Under traditional data processing systems, it generally was placed in approximately the same organizational category as other facilitating functions such as purchasing or personnel. With the introduction of the computer, however, data processing assumed responsibility for designing the information system and was often given authority to coordinate activities among other functional areas. With these new duties, movement from an obscure low-level location in the accounting division to independent status under a top-level executive was common.

The amount of change appeared to depend in large measure on the capabilities and even the "empire building" motives of the individual in charge of the computerized data processing section. As with most newly emerging positions, his duties as well as those of the new computerized data processing department were usually not precisely defined. In firms with capable, energetic individuals in charge of the computer effort, there seemed few bounds on the amount of activities undertaken, and the data processing manager usually achieved a high organizational position for his department. Conversely, in those firms where the data processing manager was content to merely apply the computer to the obvious cost-saving applications, the data processing department rarely exhibited an appreciable upward movement.

In several firms, the computer was a pet project of one or more top executives. Their impetus was also instrumental in securing a top-level position for the department.

Resistance to Change

There was remarkably little evidence of reluctance to accept changes caused by the computer on the part of either management or labor. The type of destructive resistance to change often cited in factory automation was simply not present in the move to computerized data processing. Since almost all of the firms applied a policy of handling job reductions by natural attrition and communicated this policy to employees, the fear of job loss due to the computer was not an important factor.[7]

Firms most successful in averting hostilities were those in which the managers whose departments were affected by the computer were involved in designing the computer system and planning the changeover.[8] The few firms who turned

---

[7] For a report of employment changes caused by the computer in the eleven firms, see Roger C. Vergin and Andrew J. Grimes, "Management Myths and EDP," *California Management Review*, VII, 1 (1964), 64–65.

[8] They also, in general, had better EDP systems.

this task completely over to the EDP department appeared to have a disproportionately large share of opposition. Most of the active opposition to the computer by managers came from an expected source—those managers whose personal positions were adversely affected through curtailment of part of their responsibilities or by placement at a lower organizational level. Several EDP managers stated that opposition was much less than had been expected.

The few cases of employee resistance to change could perhaps be better classified as skepticism. During conversion to the new computer system and for a time afterwards, some employees persisted in returning to the old data processing system or concluded the computer was wrong whenever an abnormal condition arose. One such example occurred in a wholesaling firm when the warehouse personnel frequently could not locate stock that the computer system indicated was on hand. They claimed the computer was in error and proceeded to mark the item as out-of-stock. Management followed up such discrepancies and in almost every case the goods were found. Nevertheless, the designer of the computer system had to remain in the warehouse investigating the problems for a month before this resistance was overcome.

Future Computer Impact

While speculation concerning the computer's impact in business has somewhat subsided in recent years, numerous and varied predictions continue to be heard. Despite the failure of present evidence to support the conjectures, there can be little doubt that the computer has the *potential*

to cause far more substantial changes than have occurred thus far. Recognizing this potential, many have concluded that it is just a matter of time until the computer completely revolutionizes the management process as well as the firm itself. Many of these predictions have come from ivory tower academicians who have never actually been involved in developing computer systems and therefore fail to fully perceive the sources of inertia and opposition which must be overcome. Major barriers are imposed by human opposition and system development difficulties.

Designing and programming large-scale integrated decision systems is a difficult job. Scholars who have attempted to build laboratory models of relatively small subsystems of the business enterprise can attest to the enormity of the task. As integrated systems are developed it is necessary to describe interrelationships that exist among variables and departments which previously have only been treated subjectively. As these relationships are incorporated into the system each addition increases the complexity of the model not linearly but exponentially.

Even if the model building problem could be conquered, the models still must be translated into machine language. This task is usually assumed to be inconsequential by those prognosticators who lack any exposure to programming. Yet with programmers in short supply, training periods as long as a year before reasonable productivity is achieved, rapid turnover, and a high failure rate upon programmers, there is currently an extreme shortage of people qualified for programming. Add to this the considerable length of time required to program even simple clerical operations and the programming barrier becomes imposing.[9]

---

[9] For a discussion of recruitment, training, turnover, and failure rates of programmers and programming times, see Roger C. Vergin, "Staffing of Computer Departments," *Personnel Administration*, XXVIII, 4 (July–August, 1965), 6–12.

A second often overlooked retarding factor is human opposition to computerization. Thus far, managers' resistance has been slight because the impact has not been severe and few positions have been challenged. Should the computer begin to revise management positions by moving decision making from managers to the computer and from lower and middle managers throughout the organization to a centralized top management group, more serious revolt is likely to occur. If managers are placed in a position of only carrying out decisions which they once made, their reaction may be similar to the reaction of production workers to "scientific management." Certainly much of the militant unionism of the 1920's and 1930's must be blamed on dissatisfaction resulting from the elimination of participation in planning and the regimentation of factory work. Participation in decision making is even more ingrained in managers of the present era, a portent of the active opposition that may occur. At the same time, the top management group may not be entirely receptive of its new burden. Many managers have filled large portions of their days with routine decisions and busy-work. They will find it difficult to adjust to placement in planning groups where creative decision making and planning are expected at all times and where there is no opportunity to renew their energies while occupied with routine administrative details.

What then is the probable future impact of the computer? It will largely be confined to clerical replacement for the next several years with decision-making applications gradually increasing in importance as the clerical applications are completed. Firms will continue to make noises about "integrated systems," but their applications will remain piecemeal. The time and expense of developing complex systems combined with pressures for immediate cost reducing programs will continue to keep the level of sophistication of applications far below the level of available technology.[10] Furthermore, the task of maintaining and adjusting programs to internal and environmental changes will continue to occupy a large portion of the time of programmers—who will remain in short supply.

Thus it appears that advances in computerization will be limited by economic and personal barriers rather than technical capabilities. As these barriers are reduced and management begins to give full attention to the development of information systems, it is inevitable that management duties will change, decision making will improve, and the organization will undergo modification. It seems unlikely, however, that the computer will cause startling changes in business organizations in the next decade.[11]

---

[10] While some writers mention that cost reduction is not of prime importance and many firms actually find costs increased with EDP, every one of the eleven firms in the study demonstrated major cost reductions. The sample may, of course, have been biased since it included only firms with operational systems, not those which may have attempted EDP, found it unsuccessful, and abandoned the computer. Of thirteen firms contacted for the study, one refused to be included and another was somewhat hesitant and was dropped after an unproductive preliminary interview. Both of these firms had very recently installed their computers and were having acknowledged difficulties in operating their EDP systems. It is quite probable that these two firms had not reduced costs at that stage.

[11] This report was written under a grant from the Ford Foundation to the Graduate School of Business Administration, and administered through the Center for Research in Management Science, University of California, Berkeley. The study was begun under a grant from the School of Business Administration, University of Minnesota.

DISCUSSION QUESTIONS: PART IV

1. Are analytical techniques useful in all decision problems? Why or why not?
2. How are mathematical models used in solving managerial problems? List the chief advantages and disadvantages in using mathematical models to solve management problems.
3. Describe simulation. In what ways can simulation techniques be used to solve organizational problems? What is the Monte Carlo technique? What types of problems can be solved by the use of the Monte Carlo technique? Give an example of each type.
4. Discuss the development and use of games in industry.
5. What is operations research? What steps would you take to use a particular operations research technique? Why? Describe several problems which could readily be solved by some type of operations research technique?
6. Explain how PERT works. What types of problems should be handled by using PERT?
7. Differentiate between computer software and computer hardware. Why has the development of computer software been important? Will computer software develop more rapidly in the future than computer hardware or vice-versa? Defend your answer. How is the knowledge explosion related to the computer?
8. List the major types of uses of a computer. Which of these do you feel is currently most important? Why? What are some of the major problems in expanding the capabilities of computers? If you were attempting to determine the feasibility of buying a new computer for your company (which previously has not had a computer), what steps would you take? If you were evaluating the feasibility of buying a larger computer than the one your company presently owns, what steps would you take?
9. How does a computer modify the structure of an organization? In the future, what impact will the computer have upon industry? What problems will probably occur as the result of the increased use of computers throughout industry? What types of research should be implemented to reduce the impact of the computer upon organizations?

SELECTED REFERENCES: PART IV

A. DECISION-MAKING

Bierman, Harold, Jr., *et al. Quantitative Analysis for Business Decisions* (rev. ed.) Homewood, Ill.: Richard D. Irwin, Inc., 1965.

Drucker, Peter F., "The Effective Decision," *Harvard Business Review,* Vol. 45, No. 1 (January–February, 1967), pp. 92–98.

Hein, Leonard W. *The Quantitative Approach to Managerial Decisions.* Englewood Cliffs, N.J.: Prentice-Hall, Inc., 1967.

Hoggatt, Austin C. and Frederick E. Balderston (eds.) *Symposium on Simulation Models: Methodology and Applications to the Behavioral Sciences.* Cincinnati, Ohio: South-Western Publishing Co., 1963.

Magee, John G., "Decision Trees for Decision Making," *Harvard Business Review,* Vol. 12, No. 42 (July–August, 1964), pp. 126–135.

Miller, David W., "The Logic of Quantitative Decisions," in *Scientific Decision-Making in Business.* New York: Holt, Rinehart and Winston, Inc., 1963, pp. 313–332.

Richards, Max D. and Paul S. Greenlaw, *Management Decision Making.* Homewood, Ill.: Richard D. Irwin, Inc., 1966.

B. OPERATIONS RESEARCH AND PERT

Carlson, Philip G., *Quantitative Methods for Managers.* New York: Harper and Row, 1967.

Davis, P. Michael, "From Scientific Management to PERT—An Evolution," *Nebraska Journal of Economics and Business,* Vol. 5, No. 2 (Autumn, 1966), pp. 34–46.

Hare, Van Court, Jr., *Systems Analysis: A Diagnostic Approach.* New York: Harcourt, Brace, and World, Inc., 1967.

Kaufmann, Arnold, *Methods and Models of Operations Research.* Englewood Cliffs, N.J.: Prentice-Hall, Inc., 1964.

MacCrimmon, K. R. and C. A. Ryavec, "An Analytical Study of the PERT Assumptions," *Operations Research,* Vol. 12, No. 1 (January–February, 1964), pp. 16–27.

Paige, Hilliard W., "How PERT/Cost Helps the General Manager," *Harvard Business Review,* Vol. 41, No. 6 (November–December, 1963), pp. 87–95.

Schoderbek, Peter P. and Lester A. Digman, "Third Generation in PERT Systems," *Academy of Management, Proceedings of the 27th Annual Meeting.* State College, Pa.: 1968, pp. 195–200.

Simone, Albert J., "A Dynamic Programing Approach to the Maximization of Output from Production Processes of Varying Efficiencies," *Academy of Management Journal,* Vol. 10, No. 2 (June, 1967), pp. 129–143.

Veinott, Arthur F., Jr. (ed.), *Mathematical Studies in Management Science.* New York: The Macmillan Co., 1965.

C. THE IMPACT OF COMPUTERS

Borko, Harold, *Computer Applications in the Behavioral Sciences.* Englewood Cliffs, N.J.: Prentice-Hall, Inc., 1962.

Brabb, George J. and Earl B. Hutchins, "Electronic Computers and Management Organization," *California Management Review,* Vol. 6, No. 1 (Fall, 1963), pp. 33–42.

Burck, Gilbert, *The Computer Age and Its Potential for Management.* New York: Harper and Row, 1965.

Dean, Neal J., "The Computer Comes of Age," *Harvard Business Review,* Vol. 46, No. 1 (January–February, 1968), pp. 89–91.

Feigenbaum, Edward A. and Julian Feldman, *Computers and Thought.* New York: McGraw-Hill Book Co., Inc., 1963.

Jenecks, Stephen F., "Machines That Can Think," *The Harvard Review,* Vol. 3, No. 2 (Spring, 1965), pp. 36–45.

Rico, Leonard, *The Advance Against Paperwork: Systems, Computers and Personnel.* Ann Arbor, Michigan: The University of Michigan, 1967.

PART V

Systems
Approaches

Although the process, behavioral, and quantitative approaches have been widely adopted, a growing group of practitioners and academicians have felt that another approach which would encompass most, if not all, of these segmental approaches was necessary.[1] They felt that a systems approach would encompass the subsystems emanating from each of the other approaches.

The systems approach has been viewed from several perspectives, from the specialized systems such as wage and salary systems, accounting, computer programming, and electronic control systems, to the highly generalized systems such as philosophical systems, value systems, and mathematical systems.[2] As a result of these specialized and general efforts, several major steps have been taken to strengthen both general systems and management systems concepts.

"Systems analysis is the selection of elements, relationships, and procedures to achieve a specific purpose."[3] In other words, a system covers many different possible concepts. Ludwig von Bertalanffy in 1951, and Kenneth Boulding in 1956 began to lay the modern foundation for general systems theory.[4] Such a

---

[1] For example, see Jay W. Forrester *Industrial Dynamics*. Cambridge, Mass.: The M.I.T. Press, 1961; Richard A. Johnson, Fremont E. Kast, and James E. Rosenzweig *The Theory and Management of Systems*. New York: McGraw-Hill Book Co., Inc., 1963; Stanley Young *Management: A Systems Analysis*. Glenview, Ill.: Scott, Foresman and Company, 1966; and Van Court Hare, Jr. *Systems Analysis: A Diagnostic Approach*. New York: Harcourt, Brace, and World, Inc., 1967.

[2] Hare, p. ix.

[3] Hare, p. ix.

[4] L. von Bertalanffy, "General System Theory: A New Approach to the Unity of Science," *Human Biology* (December, 1951), pp. 303–361; and Kenneth Boulding, "General Systems Theory: The Skeleton of Science," *Management Science,* Vol. 2 (April, 1956), pp. 197–208.

theory is concerned with the development of a systematic, theoretical framework for the description of general relationships of the empirical world.[5] Upon this foundation of general systems theory, managers and scholars have developed the systems approach to management.

Several authors have defined the systems approach to management. Professor Stanley Young stated that "A management system can be defined as that subsystem of the organization whose components consist of a subset of individuals (man to man) whose duties are to receive certain organizational problems (inputs) and thereupon to execute a set of activities (process) which will produce organizational solutions (output) for either increasing the value of return of the total organizational activity (satisficing) or for optimizing some function of the total organizational inputs and outputs."[6] Systems are deliberate, rational human inventions to achieve certain objectives. Because they can be modified as time passes, the systems frequently increase in value to the users of the system.

In industry, managers are necessary to manipulate human, technological, and capital resources into an effective organization. Management is the process through which these resources are integrated into a system which accomplishes the objectives of the organization. When an organization is structured according to the systems approach, the necessity for the basic functions of management is not eliminated. There is a change of emphasis. Each management function no longer operates as an individual entity, but must be coordinated into the operation of the system. All operations and functions carried out by employees and machines are thus oriented to the objectives of the organization.[7] This part of the book examines systems concepts and systems analyses.

In the first section on systems concepts, Professors Richard A. Johnson, Fremont E. Kast, and James E. Rosenzweig discuss general systems theory and the ways in which management systems and general systems are related. In the next selection, Professor Stanley Young describes the organization as a total system and the design of such a system. Mr. W. M. A. Brooker attacks the total systems concept because of its assumption that this approach is the most important approach to management and discusses the ways in which this attitude is expressed by systems analysts.

On the basis of the systems concepts which have been developed during the past decade, many managers have turned to the development of specific systems and subsystems within organization. In the fourth article in this section, Professor Jay W. Forrester analyzes the progress of the industrial dynamics movement as one approach to corporate policy design and as an evolving theory of structure in systems. Professor Aharon G. Beged-Dov stresses information system design in the organization, while Professor Paul S. Greenlaw outlines a system view of management development. In the last article, Professor Bertram M. Gross establishes a general systems approach to corporate planning.

---

[5] Richard A. Johnson, Fremont E. Kast, and James E. Rosenzweig, "Systems Theory and Management," *Management Science,* Vol. 10, No. 5 (January, 1964), pp. 367–384.

[6] Young, p. 15.

[7] Johnson, "Systems Theory . . . ," p. 376.

A

SYSTEMS CONCEPTS

37. Systems Theory and Management

RICHARD A. JOHNSON, FREMONT E. KAST,
and JAMES E. ROSENZWEIG

Introduction

The systems concept can be a useful way of thinking about the job of managing. It provides a framework for visualizing internal and external environmental factors as an integrated whole. It allows recognition of the proper place and function of subsystems. The systems within which businessmen must operate are necessarily complex. However, management via systems concepts fosters a way of thinking which, on the one hand, helps to dissolve some of the complexity and, on the other hand, helps the manager recognize the nature of the complex problems and thereby operate within the perceived environment. It is important to recognize the integrated nature of specific systems, including the fact that each system has both inputs and outputs and can be viewed as a self-contained unit. But it is also important to recognize that business systems are a part of larger systems—possibly industry-wide, or including several, maybe many, companies and/or industries, or even society as a whole. Further, business systems are in a constant state of change—they are created, operated, revised, and often eliminated.

What does the concept of systems offer to students of management and/or to

Reprinted from *Management Science,* Vol. 10, No. 5 (January, 1964), pp. 367–384, with permission of the authors and the publisher. Richard A. Johnson, Fremont E. Kast, and James E. Rosenzweig are Professors of Management, Graduate School of Business Administration, University of Washington.

practicing executives? Is it a panacea for business problems which will replace scientific management, human relations, management by objective, operations research, and many other approaches to, or techniques of, management? Perhaps a word of caution is applicable initially. Anyone looking for "cookbook" techniques will be disappointed. In this article we do not evolve "ten easy steps" to success in management. Such approaches, while seemingly applicable and easy to grasp, usually are shortsighted and superficial. Fundamental ideas, such as the systems concept, are more difficult to comprehend, and yet they present a greater opportunity for a large-scale payoff.

Systems Defined [1]

A system is "an organized or complex whole; an assemblage or combination of things or parts forming a complex or unitary whole." The term system covers an extremely broad spectrum of concepts. For example, we have mountain systems, river systems, and the solar system as part of our physical surroundings. The body itself is a complex organism including the skeletal system, the circulatory system, and the nervous system. We come into daily contact with such phenomena as transportation systems, communication systems (telephone, telegraph, etc.), and economic systems.

A science often is described as a systematic body of knowledge; a complete array of essential principles or facts, arranged in a rational dependence or connection; a complex of ideas, principles, laws, forming a coherent whole. Scientists endeavor to develop, organize, and classify material into interconnected disciplines. Sir Isaac Newton set forth what

he called the "system of the world." Two relatively well known works which represent attempts to integrate a large amount of material are Darwin's *Origin of the Species* and Keynes's *General Theory of Employment, Interest, and Money*. Darwin, in his theory of evolution, integrated all life into a "system of nature" and indicated how the myriad of living subsystems were interrelated. Keynes, in his general theory of employment, interest, and money, connected many complicated natural and man-made forces which make up an entire economy. Both men had a major impact on man's thinking because they were able to conceptualize interrelationships among complex phenomena and integrate them into a systematic whole. The word system connotes plan, method, order, and arrangement. Hence it is no wonder that scientists and researchers have made the term so pervasive.

The antonym of systematic is chaotic. A chaotic situation might be described as one where "everything depends on everything else." Since two major goals of science and research in any subject area are explanation and prediction, such a condition cannot be tolerated. Therefore there is considerable incentive to develop bodies of knowledge that can be organized into a complex whole, within which subparts or subsystems can be interrelated.

While much research has been focused on the analysis of minute segments of knowledge, there has been increasing interest in developing larger frames of reference for synthesizing the results of such research. Thus attention has been focused more and more on over-all systems as frames of reference for analytical work in various areas. It is our contention that a similar process can be useful for managers. Whereas managers often have been focusing attention on particular

---

[1] For a more complete discussion see: Johnson, Kast, and Rosenzweig [3], pp. 4–6, 91, 92.

functions in specialized areas, they may lose sight of the over-all objectives of the business and the role of their particular business in even larger systems. These individuals can do a better job of carrying out their own responsibilities if they are aware of the "big picture." It is the familiar problem of not being able to see the forest for the trees. The focus of systems management is on providing a better picture of the network of subsystems and interrelated parts which go together to form a complex whole.

Before proceeding to a discussion of systems theory for business, it will be beneficial to explore recent attempts to establish a general systems theory covering all disciplines or scientific areas.

General Systems Theory

General systems theory is concerned with developing a systematic, theoretical framework for describing general relationships of the empirical world. A broad spectrum of potential achievements for such a framework is evident. Existing similarities in the theoretical construction of various disciplines can be pointed out. Models can be developed which have applicability to many fields of study. An ultimate but distant goal will be a framework (or system of systems) which could tie all disciplines together in a meaningful relationship.

There has been some development of interdisciplinary studies. Areas such as social psychology, biochemistry, astrophysics, social anthropology, economic psychology, and economic sociology have been developed in order to emphasize the interrelationships of previously isolated disciplines. More recently, areas of study and research have been developed which call on numerous subfields. For example, cybernetics, the science of communication and control, calls on electrical engineering, neurophysiology, physics, biology, and other fields. Operations research is often pointed to as a multidisciplinary approach to problem solving. Information theory is another discipline which calls on numerous subfields. Organization theory embraces economics, sociology, engineering, psychology, physiology, and anthropology. Problem solving and decision making are becoming focal points for study and research, drawing on numerous disciplines.

With these examples of interdisciplinary approaches, it is easy to recognize a surge of interest in larger-scale, systematic bodies of knowledge. However, this trend calls for the development of an over-all framework within which the various subparts can be integrated. In order that the *interdisciplinary* movement does not degenerate into *undisciplined* approaches, it is important that some structure be developed to integrate the various separate disciplines while retaining the type of discipline which distinguishes them. One approach to providing an over-all framework (general systems theory) would be to pick out phenomena common to many different disciplines and to develop general models which would include such phenomena. A good approach would include the structuring of a hierarchy of levels of complexity for the basic units of behavior in the various empirical fields. It would also involve development of a level of abstraction to represent each stage.

We shall explore the second approach, a hierarchy of levels, in more detail since it can lead toward a system of systems which has application in most businesses and other organizations. The reader can undoubtedly call to mind examples of familiar systems at each level of Boulding's classification model.

1. The first level is that of static structure. It might be called the level of *frame-*

works; for example, the anatomy of the universe.

2. The next level is that of the simple dynamic system with predetermined, necessary motions. This might be called the level of *clockworks*.

3. The control mechanism or cybernetic system, which might be nicknamed the level of the *thermostat*. The system is self regulating in maintaining equilibrium.

4. The fourth level is that of the "open system," or self-maintaining structure. This is the level at which life begins to differentiate from not-life: it might be called the level of the *cell*.

5. The next level might be called the genetic-societal level; it is typified by the *plant,* and it dominates the empirical world of the botanist.

6. The animal system level is characterized by increased mobility, teleological behavior, and self-awareness.

7. The next level is the "human" level, that is, of the individual human being considered as a system with self-awareness and the ability to utilize language and symbolism.

8. The social system or systems of human organization constitute the next level, with the consideration of the content and meaning of messages, the nature and dimensions of value systems, the transcription of images into historical record, the subtle symbolizations of art, music and poetry, and the complex gamut of human emotion.

9. Transcendental systems complete the classification of levels. These are the ultimates and absolutes and the inescapables and unknowables, and they also exhibit systematic structure and relationship.[2]

Obviously, the first level is most pervasive. Descriptions of static structures are widespread. However, this descriptive cataloguing is helpful in providing a framework for additional analysis and synthesis. Dynamic "clockwork" systems, where prediction is a strong element, are evident in the classical natural sciences such as physics and astronomy; yet even here there are important gaps. Adequate theoretical models are not apparent at higher levels. However, in recent years, closed-loop cybernetic, or "thermostat," systems have received increasing attention. At the same time, work is progressing on open-loop systems with self-maintaining structures and reproduction facilities. Beyond the fourth level we hardly have a beginning of theory, and yet even here system description via computer models may foster progress at these levels in the complex of general systems theory.

Regardless of the degree of progress at any particular level in the above scheme, the important point is the concept of a general systems theory. Clearly, the spectrum, or hierarchy, of systems varies over a considerable range. However, since the systems concept is primarily a point of view and a desirable goal, rather than a particular method or content area, progress can be made as research proceeds in various specialized areas but within a total system context.

With the general theory and its objectives as background, we direct our attention to a more specific theory for business, a systems theory which can serve as a guide for management scientists and ultimately provide the framework for integrated decision making on the part of practicing managers.

Systems Theory for Business

The biologist Ludwig von Bertalanffy has emphasized the part of general systems theory which he calls open systems

---

[2] Boulding [2], pp. 202–205.

[1]. The basis of his concept is that a living organism is not a conglomeration of separate elements but a definite system, possessing organization and wholeness. An organism is an open system which maintains a constant state while matter and energy which enter it keep changing (so-called dynamic equilibrium). The organism is influenced by, and influences, its environment and reaches a state of dynamic equilibrium in this environment. Such a description of a system adequately fits the typical business organization. The business organization is a man-made system which has a dynamic interplay with its environment—customers, competitors, labor organizations, suppliers, government, and many other agencies. Furthermore, the business organization is a system of interrelated parts working in conjunction with each other in order to accomplish a number of goals, both those of the organization and those of individual participants.

A common analogy is the comparison of the organization to the human body, with the skeletal and muscle systems representing the operating line elements and the circulatory system as a necessary staff function. The nervous system is the communication system. The brain symbolizes top-level management, or the executive committee. In this sense an organization is represented as a self-maintaining structure, one which can reproduce. Such an analysis hints at the type of framework which would be useful as a systems theory for business—one which is developed as a system of systems and that can focus attention at the proper points in the organization for rational decision making, both from the standpoint of the individual and the organization.

The scientific-management movement utilized the concept of a man-machine system but concentrated primarily at the shop level. The so-called "efficiency experts" attempted to establish procedures covering the work situation and providing an opportunity for all those involved to benefit—employees, managers, and owners. The human relationists, the movement stemming from the Hawthorne-Western Electric studies, shifted some of the focus away from the man-machine system per se to interrelationships among individuals in the organization. Recognition of the effect of interpersonal relationships, human behavior, and small groups resulted in a relatively widespread re-evaluation of managerial approaches and techniques.

The concept of the business enterprise as a social system also has received considerable attention in recent years. The social-system school looks upon management as a system of cultural interrelationships. The concept of a social system draws heavily on sociology and involves recognition of such elements as formal and informal organization within a total integrated system. Moreover, the organization or enterprise is recognized as subject to external pressure from the cultural environment. In effect, the enterprise system is recognized as a part of a larger environmental system.

Since World War II, operations research techniques have been applied to large, complex systems of variables. They have been helpful in shop scheduling, in freightyard operations, cargo handling, airline scheduling, and other similar problems. Queuing models have been developed for a wide variety of traffic- and service-type situations where it is necessary to program the optimum number of "servers" for the expected "customer" flow. Management-science techniques have undertaken the solution of many complex problems involving a large number of variables. However, by their very nature, these techniques must structure the system for analysis by quantifying system elements. This process of abstraction often simplifies the problem and takes it out of the real world. Hence the solution of the problem may not be applicable in the actual situation.

Simple models of maximizing behavior no longer suffice in analyzing business organizations. The relatively mechanical models apparent in the "scientific management" era gave way to theories represented by the "human relations" movement. Current emphasis is developing around "decision making" as a primary focus of attention, relating communication systems, organization structure, questions of growth (entropy and/or homeostasis) and questions of uncertainty. This approach recognizes the more complex models of administrative behavior and should lead to more encompassing systems that provide the framework within which to fit the results of specialized investigations of management scientists.

The aim of systems theory for business is to develop an objective, understandable environment for decision making; that is, if the system within which managers make the decisions can be provided as an explicit framework, then such decision making should be easier to handle. But what are the elements of this systems theory which can be used as a framework for integrated decision making? Will it require wholesale change on the part of organization structure and administrative behavior? Or can it be woven into existing situations? In general, the new concepts can be applied to existing situations. Organizations will remain recognizable. Simon makes this point when he says:

1. Organizations will still be constructed in three layers; an underlying *system* of physical production and distribution processes, a layer of programmed (and probably largely automated) decision processes for governing the routine day-to-day operation of the physical *system,* and a layer of nonprogrammed decision processes (carried on in a man-machine system) for monitoring the first-level processes, redesigning them, and changing parameter values.

2. Organizations will still be hierarchical in form. The organization will be divided into major subparts, each of these into parts, and so on, in familiar forms of departmentalization. The exact basis for drawing departmental lines may change somewhat. Product divisions may become even more important than they are today, while the sharp lines of demarcation among purchasing, manufacturing, engineering, and sales are likely to fade.[3]

We agree essentially with this picture of the future. However, we want to emphasize the notion of systems as set forth in several layers. Thus the systems that are likely to be emphasized in the future will develop from projects or programs, and authority will be vested in managers whose influence will cut across traditional departmental lines. This concept will be developed in more detail throughout this article.

There are certain key subsystems and/or functions essential in every business organization which make up the total information-decision system, and which operate in a dynamic environmental system subject to rapid change. The subsystems include:

1. A *sensor subsystem* designed to measure changes within the system and with the environment.

2. An *information processing subsystem* such as an accounting, or data processing system.

3. A *decision-making subsystem* which

---

[3] Simon [4], pp. 49–50. (Italics by authors.)

receives information inputs and outputs planning messages.

4. A *processing subsystem* which utilizes information, energy, and materials to accomplish certain tasks.

5. A *control component* which ensures that processing is in accordance with planning. Typically this provides feedback control.

6. A *memory or information storage subsystem* which may take the form of records, manuals, procedures, computer programs, etc.

A goal setting unit will establish the long range objectives of the organization, and the performance will be measured in terms of sales, profits, employment, etc. relative to the total environmental system.

This is a general model of the systems concept in a business firm. In the following section a more specific model illustrating the application of the systems concept is established.

An Illustrative Model of The Systems Concept

Traditionally, business firms have not been structured to utilize the systems concept. In adjusting the typical business structure to fit within the framework of management by system, certain organizational changes may be required. It is quite obvious that no one organizational structure can meet operational requirements for every company. Each organization must be designed as a unique system. However, the illustrative model set forth would be generally operable for medium- to large-size companies which have a number of major products and a variety of management functions. The primary purpose of this model is to illustrate the application of systems concepts to business organizations and the possible impact

upon the various management functions of planning, organizing, communication and control. The relationships which would exist among the top management positions are shown in Figure 1.

The master planning council would relate the business to its environmental system, and it would make decisions relative to the products of services the company produced. Further, this council would establish the limits of an operating program, decide on general policy matters relative to the design of operating systems, and select the director for each new project. New project decisions would be made with the assistance and advice of the project research and development, market research, and financial groups. Once the decision was made, the resource allocation committee would provide the facilities and manpower for the new system, and supply technical assistance for systems design. After the system had been designed, its management would report to the operations committee as a major project system, or as a facilitating system.

Facilitating systems would include those organized to produce a service rather than a finished product. Each project system would be designed toward being self-sufficient. However, in many cases this objective may not be feasible or economical. For example, it may not be feasible to include a large automated mill as a component of a major project system, but the organization as a whole, including all of the projects, might support this kind of a facility. A facilitating system, would be designed, therefore, to produce this kind of operating service for the major project systems. The output of the facilitating system would be material input for the project system and a fee should be charged for this input, just as if the input had been purchased from an outside source.

A soap manufacturer could have, for

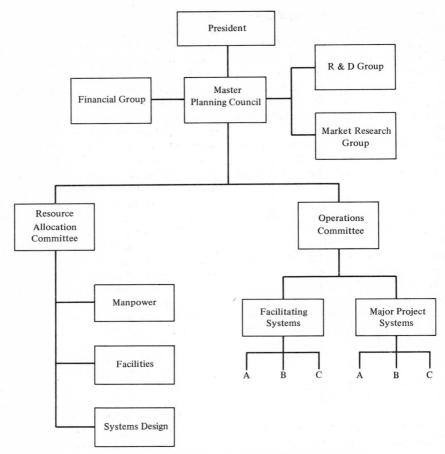

Figure 1.   *The Systems Model: Top Management.*

example, major project systems in hand soap, laundry soap, kitchen soap, and toothpaste. A facilitating system might be designed to produce and *sell* containers to the four project systems.

OPERATING SYSTEMS

All operating systems would have one thing in common—they would use a common language for communicating among themselves, and with higher levels of management. In addition, of course, each system designed would be structured in consideration of company-wide policies.

Other than these limits, each operating system would be created to meet the specific requirements of its own product or service. A model of an operating system is shown in Fig. 2.

Figure 2 illustrates the relationship of the functions to be performed and the flow of operating information. The operating system is structured to (1) direct its own inputs, (2) control its own operation, and (3) review and revise the design of the system as required. Input is furnished by three different groups: technical information is generated as input into the

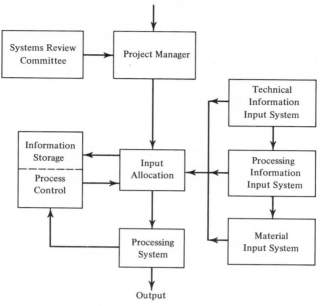

Figure 2. *An Operating System Model.*

processing system, and in addition, technical information is the basis for originating processing information. Both technical and processing information are used by the material input system to determine and supply materials for processing. However, corrective action, when necessary, would be activated by input allocation.

This model can be related to most business situations. For example, if this represented a system to produce television sets, the technical information would refer to the design of the product, processing information would include the plan of manufacture and schedule, and the material input would pertain to the raw materials and purchased parts used in the processing. These inputs of information and material would be processes and become output. Process control would measure the output in comparison to the standard (Information Storage) obtained from input allocation, and issue corrective infor-

mation whenever the system failed to function according to plan. The design of the system would be reviewed continually and the components rearranged or replaced when these changes would improve operating efficiency.

Basically, the operating systems would be self-sustaining with a high degree of autonomy. Therefore, they could be integrated into the over-all organizational structure (Figure 1) with a minimum of difficulty.

Systems Concepts and Management

Managers are needed to convert the disorganized resources of men, machines, and money into a useful and effective enterprise. Essentially, management is the process whereby these unrelated resources are integrated into a total *system for objective accomplishment.* A manager gets things done by working with people and physical resources in order to accomplish the objectives of the system. He coordinates and integrates the activities and work of others rather than performing operations himself.

Structuring a business according to the systems concept does not eliminate the need for the basic functions of planning, organization, control, and communication. However, there is a definite change of emphasis, for the functions are performed in conjunction with operation of the system and not as separate entities. In other words, everything revolves around the system and its objective, and the function is carried out only as a service to this end. This point can be clarified by reviewing each of the functions in terms of their relation to the model of the systems concept illustrated previously.

PLANNING

Planning occurs at three different levels in the illustrative model. These levels are shown in Figure 1. First, there is top level planning by the master planning council. Second, the project and facilitating systems must be planned and resources allocated to them. Finally, the operation of each project and facilitating system must be planned.

The master planning council establishes broad policies and goals and makes decisions relative to the products or services the company produces. It decides upon general policy matters concerning the design of the operating systems and selects the director for each new program. It is the planning council which receives informational inputs from the environmental and competitive systems. It combines these inputs with feedback information from the internal organizational system and serves as the key decision-making center within the company. Much

of the decision making at this level is non-programmed, unstructured, novel, and consequential. While some of the new techniques of management science may be helpful, major reliance must be placed upon mature assessment of the entire situation by experienced, innovative top executives.

Once these broad decisions have been made, the planning function is transferred to the resource allocation and operating committees. They plan and allocate facilities and manpower for each new system and supply technical assistance for individual systems design. At this planning level it is possible to utilize programmed decision making—operations research and computer techniques.

The third level, planning the operations of each project or facilitation system, is concerned primarily with the optimum allocation of resources to meet the requirements established by the planning council. This planning can most easily be programmed to automatic decision systems. However, the project director would still have to feed important non-quantifiable inputs into the system.

Under the systems concept of planning there is a direct relationship between the planning performed at each of the three levels. The first planning level receives informational inputs from the environment and competitive system and feedback information from within the organization. It translates this into inputs for the next planning level which in turn moves to a more detailed level of planning and provides inputs for the third or project level. One of the major advantages of this systems model is to provide a clear-cut delineation of the responsibility for various types of planning.

This concept facilitates integrated planning on a systems basis at the project level within the organization. Given the inputs (premises, goals, and limitations) from the higher levels the project managers are delegated the function of integrated planning for their project.

ORGANIZATION

Traditional organization theory emphasized parts and segments of the structure and is concerned with the separation of activities into tasks or operational units. It does not give sufficient emphasis to the interrelationships and integration of activities. Adapting the business organization to the systems concept places emphasis upon the integration of all activities toward the accomplishment of over-all objectives but also recognizes the importance of efficient subsystem performance.

The systems basis of organization differs significantly from traditional organization structures such as line and staff or line, staff, and functional relationships. As shown in Figure 1, there are three major organizational levels, each with clearly delineated functions. The master planning council has broad planning, control, and integrative functions; the resource allocation committee has the primary function of allocating manpower and facilities, and aids in systems design for the facilitating or project systems. One of the major purposes of this type organization is to provide an integration of activities at the most important level— that is the individual project or program.

Staff specialization of skills is provided for the master planning council through such groups as financial, research and development, and market research. Their activities, however, are integrated and coordinated by the planning council. There are specialists at the operating level who are completely integrated into each project system. Thus, the activities of these specialists are geared to the effective and efficient performance of the individual project system. This type organization minimizes a major problem associated with staff and functional personnel—their tendency to associate their activities with specialized areas rather than with the optimum performance of the over-all operation. Yet, under the model the importance of initiative and innovation are recognized. In fact, the major function of the master planning council is planning and innovation. Specific provision for receiving information inputs from product and market research are provided in the model.

There are other advantages of the systems concept. Business activity is dynamic, yet the typical organization is structured to perpetuate itself rather than change as required. There is generally resistance by the various specialized functions to change in order to optimize organization performance. For example, Parkinson's Law states that there is an ever increasing trend toward hierarchies of staff and functional personnel who are self-perpetuating and often do not contribute significantly to organizational effectiveness, or in extreme cases may be dysfunctional. In contrast, a system is designed to do a particular task. When the task is completed, the system is disbanded.

Systems are created from a central pool of resources. Facilities, machines, and manpower are assigned to specific projects or programs. The approach is to create and equip the project system with a complete arrangement of components to accomplish the job at hand. This may result in the duplication of certain activities in more than one operating system; however, this disadvantage is not as serious as it may seem. For example, it may be more efficient to have several typewriters assigned to each system rather than a center pool of typewriters. In the first instance, the typewriters may be utilized less than 100 per cent of the time, but the problems of scheduling the work at the central pool, delays, accountability, measurement of contribution, etc., would soon offset the advantages of centralizing equipment. Too much effort may be spent in creating processing information which accomplishes no objective other than keeping the machines utilized. A reasonable amount of redundancy or extra capacity will provide more flexibility, protect against breakdowns, reduce flow time, require less planning, eliminate many problems associated with interdepartmental communication, and reduce the amount of material handling.

Obviously, there are situations when it is impractical to decentralize a particular facility, because individual systems cannot utilize it sufficiently to warrant its incorporation into each separate operation. In these instances, a facilitating system would be created which would sell its services to any or all of the major project systems. These service systems would have to justify their existence and compete with outside vendors as suppliers to the major project system.

One of the great advantages of the systems concept for organizing pertains to the decentralization of decision making and the more effective utilization of the allocated resources to the individual project system. This has the merit of achieving accountability for performance through the measurability of individual systems of operation.

CONTROL

The systems concept features control as a means of gaining greater flexibility in operation, and, in addition, as a way of avoiding planning operations when variables are unknown. It is designed to serve the operating system as a subsystem of the larger operation. Its efficiency will be measured by how accurately it can identify variations in systems operation from standard or plan, and how quickly it can report the need for correction to the activating group.

We must conclude that error is inevitable in a system which is subject to variations in input. When the lag in time between input and output is great, more instability is introduced. Feedback can reduce the time lag; however, corrective action which is out of phase will magnify rather than overcome the error. Every system should be designed to make its own corrections when necessary. That is, a means should be provided to reallocate resources as conditions change. In our model the Systems Review Committee (see Figure 2) should be aware of any change in operating conditions which might throw the system "out of control." Replanning or redesign may be required.

In controlling a system it is important to measure inputs of information, energy, and materials; and outputs of products and/or services. This will determine operating efficiency. In addition it may be important to establish points of measurement during critical or significant stages of processing. Such measurements would be used principally to help management analyze and evaluate the operation and design of individual components. The best approach is to spotlight exceptions and significant changes. Management can focus their attention on these areas. One important thing to remember is that the control group is not a part of the processing system—it is a subsystem, serving the operating system. Cost control can be used as an example to illustrate this point. The cost accountant must understand that his primary objective is to furnish managers with information to control costs. His task is to inform, appraise, and support; never to limit, censure, or veto. The same principle applies to every control group serving the operating system.

COMMUNICATION

Communication plays a vital role in the implementation of the systems concept. It is the connecting and integrating link among the systems network. The flow of information, energy, and material—the elements of any processing system—

are coordinated via communication systems. As shown in the model (Figure 2) the operating system requires information transmission to ensure control. Communication systems should be established to feed back information on the various flows—information, energy, and material. Information on the effectiveness of the planning and scheduling activities (as an example of information flow) would be helpful in adjusting the nature of this activity for the future. Similarly, reports on absenteeism are examples of communication concerning the energy flow (the people in the system) to the processing activity. Information on acceptance inspection is an example of information stemming from the material flow aspect of an operating system. All of these feedback communication systems provide for information flow to a sensor and a control group. Comparison between the information received and the information stored (the master plan for this particular operating system) would result in decisions concerning the transmission of corrective information to the appropriate points.

Relationships within and among various project systems and between the levels of the system as a whole are maintained by means of information flow which also can be visualized as a control device. Moreover, any operating system maintains contact with its environment through some sensory element. Referring to Figure 1, the sensory elements in this case are the groups reporting to the master planning council. The master planning council makes decisions, concerning the product or service the organization will produce, based on information gained from market research, research and development, and financial activities. In a sense, these activities function as the antenna of the organization, maintaining communication with the external environment. The master planning council melds

the information received through these activities with other premises covering the internal aspects in order to make decisions about future courses of action. Here again, communication or information flow can be visualized as a necessary element in controlling the course of action for the enterprise as a whole. Based on the feedback of information concerning the environment in general, the nature of competition, and the performance of the enterprise itself, the master planning council can continue its current courses of activity or adjust in light of developing circumstances. Thus, communication or information flow facilitates the accomplishment of the primary managerial functions of planning, organizing, and controlling.

Communication by definition is a system involving a sender and a receiver, with implications of feedback control. This concept is embodied in the lowest level projects or subsystems, in all larger systems, and in the system as a whole. Information-decision systems, regardless of formal charts or manuals, often flow across departmental boundaries and are often geared to specific projects or programs. The systems concept focuses on this approach and makes explicit the information-decision system which might be implicit in many of today's organizations.

The systems concept does not eliminate the functions of management, i.e., planning, organizing, control, and communication. Instead, it integrates these functions within a framework designed to emphasize their importance in creating more effective systems. Because of the great diversity of operations and environments, particular missions of organizations differ and each system must be unique or at least have some unique elements. Nevertheless, the illustrative model and its application to the management functions of planning, organizing, controlling, and communication can serve as a point of departure in systems design.

Pervasiveness of System Concepts

Many of the most recent developments in the environment of businessmen and managers have involved systems concepts. For example, the trend toward automation involves implementation of these ideas. Automation suggests a self-contained system with inputs, outputs, and a mechanism of control. Yet the concept also recognizes the need to consider the environment within which the automatic system must perform. Thus the automated system is recognized as a subpart of a larger system.

The kinds of automation prevalent today range in a spectrum from sophisticated mechanization to completely automatic, large-scale production processes. Individual machines can be programmed to operate automatically. Large groups of machines also can be programmed to perform a series of operations, with automatic materials-handling devices providing connecting links among components of the system. In such a system, each individual operation could be described as a system and could be related to a larger system covering an entire processing operation. That particular processing operation could also be part of the total enterprise system, which in turn can be visualized as a part of an environmental system.

Completely automated processing systems such as oil refineries are also commonplace today. In such cases the entire process from input of raw material to output of finished products is automated

with preprogrammed controls used to adjust the process as necessary, according to information feedback from the operation itself.

The systems concept is also apparent in other aspects of automation. The above examples deal with physical processing; another phase which has been automated is information flow. With the introduction of large-scale, electronic-data-processing equipment, data-processing systems have been developed for many applications. Systems concepts are prevalent, with most applications built around the model of input-processor-output and with feedback control established within the instructions developed to guide the processing of data. Here again, there is an entire spectrum of sophistication leading from simple, straightforward data-reduction problems to elaborate, real-time data-processing systems.

Physical distribution systems have received increasing attention on the part of manufacturers and shippers. The concepts of logistics, or materials management, have been used to emphasize the flow of materials through distribution channels. The term *rhochrematics* has been coined to connote the flow process from raw-material sources to final consumer.[4] In essence, these ideas embrace systems concepts because emphasis is placed on the total system of material flow rather than on functions, departments, or institutions which may be involved in the processing.

In recent years increasing attention has been focused upon massive engineering projects. In particular, military and space programs are becoming increasingly complex, thus indicating the need for integrating various elements of the total system. Manufacturing the product itself (a vehicle or other hardware) is quite com-

---

[4] Rhochrematics comes from two Greek roots; rhoe, which means a flow (as a river or stream), and chrema, which stands for products, materials, or things (including information). The abstract ending -ics has been added, as for any of the sciences.

plex, often involving problems of producibility with requirements of extremely high reliability. This is difficult to ensure for individual components or subsystems. In addition, each subsystem also must be reliable in its interrelationship with all other subsystems. Successful integration of subcomponents, and hence successful performance of a particular product, must also be integrated with other elements of the total system. For example, the functioning of the Nike-Zeus antimissile missile must be coordinated with the early warning system, ground facilities, and operating personnel. All elements must function as an operating, integrated whole.

The previous discussion has emphasized the mechanistic and structural aspects of the systems concept. Yet, we cannot forget that business organizations are social systems; we are dealing with man-made systems. Obviously, a great deal could be said about the possible consequences of applying systems concepts to human relationships, but such a task is beyond the scope of this article. However, in discussing the impact of the systems concept it should not be assumed that people basically resist systems. Much of man's conscious activities since the dawn of history has been geared to creating system out of chaos. Man does not resist systematization of his behavioral patterns per se. Rather, the normal human being seeks satisfactory systems of interpersonal relationships which guide his activities. Without systematization, behavior would be random, non-goal-oriented, and unpredictable. Certainly, our complex, modern, industrial society demands more systemized human behavior than older, less-structured societies. A common characteristic in a rapidly advancing society is to make systems of interpersonal relationship more formal. While many of these systems have been implicit in the past, they are becoming more explicit. This remains one of the basic precepts of our systems model; systematic interpersonal relationships are necessary for accomplishing group objectives and an effective organizational system should be designed to meet this need.

Summary

General systems theory is concerned with developing a systematic, theoretical framework for describing general relationships of the empirical world. While a spectrum, or hierarchy of systems can be established over a considerable range, the systems concept is also a point of view and a desirable goal, rather than a particular method or content area. Progress can be made as research proceeds in various specialized areas but within a total system context.

The business organization is a man-made system which has a dynamic interplay with its environment—customers, competitors, labor organizations, suppliers, government, and many other agencies. In addition, the business organization is a system of interrelated parts working in conjunction with each other in order to accomplish a number of goals, both those of the organization and those of individual participants. This description parallels that of open systems in general which maintain a constant state while matter and energy which enter them keep changing; that is, the organisms are influenced by, and influence their environment and reach a state of dynamic equilibrium within it. This concept of the organization can be used by practicing managers in order to integrate the various ongoing activities into a meaningful total system. Regardless of specific adjustments or organization arrangements, there are certain subsystems or essential functions which make up a total information-decision system. However, the exact form utilized by a particular organization may depend upon the task orientation. We have presented a generalized illustrative model which indicates an approach that may be appropriate for a large segment of modern business organizations.

Managers are needed to convert disorganized resources of men, machines, and money into a useful, effective enterprise. Essentially, management is the process whereby their unrelated resources are integrated into a total *system for objective accomplishment*. The systems concept provides no cookbook technique, guaranteed to provide managerial success. The basic functions are still planning, organization, control, and communication. Each of these activities can be carried out with or without emphasis on systems concepts. Our contention is that the activities themselves can be better accomplished in light of systems concepts. Furthermore, there can be a definite change in emphasis for the entire managerial process if the functions are performed in light of the system as a whole and not as separate entities.

The business organization as a system can be considered as a subsystem of a larger environmental system. Even industry or inter-industry systems can be recognized as sub-elements of the economic system, and the economic system can be regarded as a part of society in general. One of the major changes within business organizations of the future may be the breakdown of traditional functional specialization geared to optimizing performance of particular departments. There may be growing use of organizational structures designed around projects and information-decision systems. The systems concept calls for integration, into a separate organizational system, of activities related to particular projects or programs. This approach currently is being implemented in some of the more advanced-technology industries.

The breakdown of business organizations into separate functional areas has been an artificial organizational device, necessary in light of existing conditions. Management-science techniques, computer simulation approaches, and information-decision systems are just a few of the tools which will make it possible for management to visualize the firm as a total system. This would not have been possible two decades ago; it is currently becoming feasible for some companies; and it will become a primary basis for organizing in the future.

References

1. BERTALANFFY, L. VON, "General System Theory: A New Approach to Unity of Science," *Human Biology,* December, 1951, pp. 303–361.
2. BOULDING, K., "General Systems Theory: The Skeleton of Science," *Management Science,* April, 1956, pp. 197–208.
3. JOHNSON, R. A., KAST, F. E. AND ROSENZWEIG, J. E. *The Theory and Management of Systems,* McGraw-Hill Book Company, Inc., New York, 1963.
4. SIMON, H. A., *The New Science of Management Decision,* Harper & Brothers, New York, 1960.

38. Organization as a Total System

STANLEY D. YOUNG

Increasingly, organizations are being considered from a systems point of view in both a descriptive and normative context.[1] Ashby's work would exemplify some of the descriptive work. System's Development Corporation, Strategic Air Command, and Lockheed are effectively using the systems concept to redesign major phases of organizations in an operational and normative sense.[2] Many companies have expended similar efforts to certain subsystems such as steel-rolling mills and oil refineries.[3]

What appears to be occurring is that our conception of the organization is changing from one of structure to one of process. Rather than visualize the organization in its traditional structural, bureaucratic, and hierarchical motif, with a fixed set of authority relationships much like the scaffolding of a building, we are beginning to view organization as a set of flows, information, men, material, and behavior. Time and change are the critical aspects. This change in construct will become more pronounced in the future

because (and this is an assertion which I will not attempt to defend) I believe the systems approach is more productive. If we consider organization from a normative point of view, there is another reason for this trend which is of more immediate concern and is the working hypothesis of this paper. Only when the organization is designed (Organizational Planning) from a systems orientation will it be able to take full advantage of the new and emerging managerial technologies which include quantitative methods, the computer, information sciences, and the behavioral sciences. Although I will not attempt to prove this proposition in the rigorous sense, the balance of this analysis will be directed toward demonstrating how this might be accomplished.

However, before taking up this thesis, let us note the problems which currently exist that hinder the effective utilization of managerial technology. One problem relates to the absence of a construct as to how the new technology is to be used in an integrated and systematic manner; or

Reprinted from *Proceedings of the 9th Annual Midwest Management Conference.* Carbondale, Ill.: Business Research Bureau, Southern Illinois University, 1966, pp. 20–31, with permission of the author and the publisher. Stanley D. Young is Professor of Management, School of Business Administration, University of Massachusetts.

[1] For example see: Litterer, Joseph, *Analysis of Organizations,* John Wiley, New York. 1965; Macmillan, Claude, and Gonzalez, Richard, *Systems Analysis,* Richard Irwin, Homewood, Illinois, 1965, Ch. 11–14; Ashby, Ross, *An Introduction to Cybernetics,* John Wiley, New York, 1958, Ch. 10–14; McDonough and Garrett, *Management Systems,* Richard Irwin, 1964; Johnson, Richard, Kast, Fremont, Rosenzweig, James, *The Theory and Management of Systems,* McGraw-Hill, New York; Beer, Stafford, *Cybernetics and Management,* English Universities Press, London, 1959.

[2] For example see: Malcolm, Donald G., Rowe, Alan and McConnell, Larimer, *Management Control Systems,* John Wiley, New York.

[3] See Leondes, Cornelius, *Computer Control Systems Technology,* McGraw-Hill, New York, 1961, Chs. 15–20.

consider it as the absence of a meaningful gestalt or whole into which such a technology would logically fit. What does exist might be categorized as a tool chest or "bits and pieces" state.

For example, let us suppose that a personnel manager has what he believes is a problem—excessive absenteeism. Given the external and internal environment of the firm, the organizational constraints he has as a manager, and a set of behavioral information and managerial tools, how does he reduce the absenteeism rate? He knows something about psychology—perception, cognition, learning and motivation theory—social psychology, attitude formation, and resistance to change. From sociology he recalls group theory; he can calculate the median, mean and mode, run a correlation and find a derivative. In other words, he is a qualified MBA student. Specifically, what should he do to reduce the absenteeism rate? The students and practitioners are given a tool chest filled with bits and pieces: a little math, a little psychology, a little sociology, and the manager is then admonished to build a better house. How is the application of the technology to be integrated so that the manager can be relatively assured that he is achieving a desired result? What is missing is the bridge or discipline between tools and organizational results. That those of a more traditional bent remain somewhat skeptical of the newer managerial technology is understandable.

Although one can raise many serious questions as to the reality, validity, predictability, and effectiveness of the classical principles approach, nevertheless, it can be said that it roughly holds together as a whole or single unit, and its parts are related in a logical fashion. Starting with the concept of private property and the delegation of authority, the organizational chart is drawn; authority is allocated; a division of labor is specified; the functions of management are outlined and planning, organizing, and staffing are conducted. A certain internal logic is present, not unlike the economist's model of perfect competition. The parts are related to each other in a particular manner. Viewed as a single construct, a traditional model is understandable and operational to students and practitioners alike.

The same cannot be said for the newer managerial technology. The General Management or Organization Theorist's domain is the whole. One is concerned with the problem of organization space, or the distance between subfunctions, subprocesses, tools, and techniques—the interface problems. To those who are concerned with the whole, the "bits and pieces" approach of the new technology is disconcerting. Where and how do all these parts fit together and what is the relationship between one piece and another? Sprinkling behavioral and quantitative courses about a business curriculum is of questionable effectiveness and has not, I believe, changed the basic manner in which organizations are managed. Therefore, as far as the newer technologies are concerned, a gestalt or general model has been missing which will integrate all the bits and pieces meaningfully. I am suggesting that the systems approach will provide this model.

Another problem which has emerged requiring the organization to be designed as a total system, is that all too frequently the organizational context into which the newer technologies are placed tend to be inappropriate. We are attaching sophisticated techniques to a primitive vehicle, the bureaucratic structure. Organizations should be designed around the technology; technology should not be forced to fit an existing structure. Thus some corporations, to be fashionable, have created operations research departments which, fact, have been given little or nothing to do. One case was reported in which the primary duty of the O.R. official was to solve the school math problems of the Corporate President's daughter.

In the history of innovation one frequently finds that when a new device is invented, it is attached to the existing model. For example, when the gasoline motor was first invented, it was connected to a buggy. However, as additional innovations occurred, the vehicle itself eventually had to be modified. If advantage was to be taken of additional improvements, obviously one could not unite a 300 horsepower motor to a light shay with wooden wheels and axles. If innovation follows its normal course, we can expect the new managerial techniques to force a modification in the traditional organizational arrangements. This, indeed, has been taking place. The exploitation of the computer, particularly when utilized in an on-line capacity, has led to

a weakening or abolishment of the tradition divisional or departmental lines of authority. Improvements in the control and measurement of operations have the same consequences.

The hypothesis that a more sophisticated managerial technology can be fully utilized only when the organization has been designed as a total system, will be examined in accordance with the following model.

In this presentation, my approach will be analytical, or a successive breakdown of the whole into increasingly smaller parts.

Organization As a Total System

In Figure 1, the business organization is presented in its most simplified form. The basic input is economic resources,

Figure 1. *Organization as a System.*

the organization is the process, and the output is economic welfare. Other organizations can be represented by changing inputs-outputs. For example, a hospital has a human input (sick patient) and a human output (healthy patient).

In Figure 2, the control or feedback mechanism is added to the organization which is represented by management. Or, in terms of control theory, the management segment constitutes the basic control element of the organization. Thus, given a certain welfare objective or expected welfare output (a profit incre-

ment), actual welfare is measured against expected welfare. If a difference exists, then a problem is indicated. This information is sent to the management segment which formulates a solution that becomes an input in the organization process. This feedback device will operate until the actual and expected welfares are approximately equal.

In Figure 3, the control unit is further broken down into a series of parts in order to provide an adaptive capability for the organization.[4] Given a change in certain environmental inputs, one initially

---

[4] For a review of adaptive systems see Mishkin, El. and Braun, Ludwig, Jr., *Adaptive Control Systems,* McGraw-Hill, New York, 1961, and Westcott, J. H., *An Exposition of Adaptive Control,* Macmillan Co., 1962.

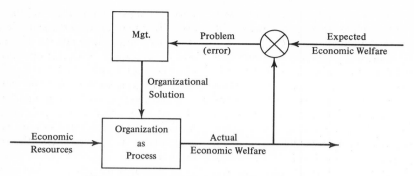

Figure 2. *Organization with Control Unit.*

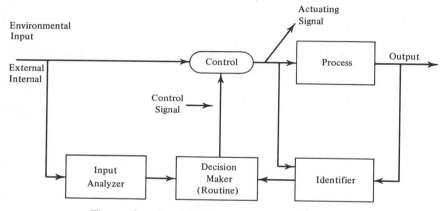

Figure 3. *Organization as an Adaptive System.*

has an input analyzer which indicates the nature of such changes. This is an information gathering or sensory device; and somewhat analogously, market research might be so categorized in terms of sensitizing the organization to some of the external variables as accounting functions for the internal changes. One also has a display device or identifier which indicates the state of the organization or any of its subprocesses at any given time. Hence, if the subprocess was a production plant, the identifier at a given time might indicate the productive capacity, current running capacity, order backlog, inventory conditions, orders in process, production lines in operation, and machine break-

down. Such information is fed to a decision-making unit along with the information from the environment. We assume that a set of rules has been programmed. One of these rules will be selected, given a particular environmental input, and given the state of the process at some given point of time in order to achieve a certain output.

For example, if the initial input is a large order with a required completion date, the rule may be to go to overtime. This information is called a control signal and is sent to the control unit. The control unit is that element which actually changes the input before it enters the system or the process itself. The order could have been put into a queue. Such information is simultaneously sent to the identifier. Therefore, at any given time, the identifier tells us what inputs have entered the process, the state of the process, and its outputs.

Because the control signal and the control unit are frequently confused, the difference between the two should be noted. The example that is usually given is that of driving an automobile. If one wants to stop an automobile by pressing on the brake pedal, information is relayed to the brakes of the car. It is not the brake pedal that stops the car, but the brakes which constitute the control unit. Similarly, in a man-to-man system, the control signal, and the control unit might appear as in Figure 4.

Let us suppose that the total employee population is the basic system and we want a higher work output. Further as-

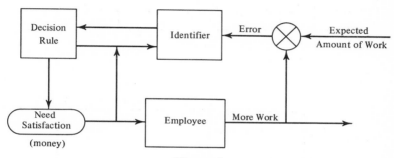

Figure 4.

sume that we know exactly what the relationship is between need satisfaction input and expected work output. Given the figure for expected work output, the decision-maker will increase or decrease the amount of need satisfaction (for example, money) by a control signal to the financial department where need satisfaction is stored in the form of money. This department would release funds until the expected work output was achieved. The control element constitutes the reservoir and release of funds, not the decision to increase work output, its relay to the employee, or even the decision to pay more. In other words, money may be to the employee what brakes are to an automobile.

For our particular purposes, those subparts of the organizational control mechanism, input analyzer, and so on, give the process an adaptive capability: the ability to adapt to changing inputs in order to maintain a desired or expected output.

In Figure 5, the organization is further broken down into a series of major subprocesses: marketing, production, and so on, each with its own adaptor. The adaptor consists of an input analyzer, decision rules, identifier, and control for each subprocess. Moreover, it is assumed that each of these subprocesses can be identified and separated from other subprocesses. A super adaptor applies a series of decision rules for subdecision makers to assure appropriate adjustment between processes. It is further assumed that each subsystem's adaptor has this same capability concerning sub-subprocesses. Consequently, the production system may have such subsystems as purchasing, inventory control, and maintenance. The inputs and outputs of these subsystems would have to be controlled appropriately with the proper decision rules.

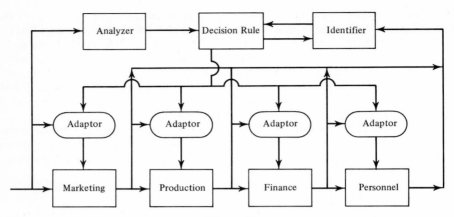

Figure 5.

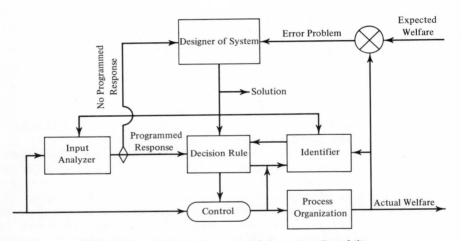

Figure 6.   *Adaptive System with Learning Capability.*

In Figure 6, a learning capability in the form of a designer is added to the adaptive system. A learning capability can be thought of as the ability of the system to redesign itself or learn from past mistakes in order to improve system performance. However, although the environmental state of the system and the application of what is thought to be the correct rule is given, the expected output may still not be produced. This indicates design problems.

The designer would receive information as to system performance. Then, in order to increase welfare output, he would attempt to improve the adaptive mechanism by formulating more effective decision rules for the decision-making routine; by improving the identifier in terms of more and better information; by achieving a more rapid response in information from the input analyzer; by improving the sensory devices; and by improving the control mechanism.

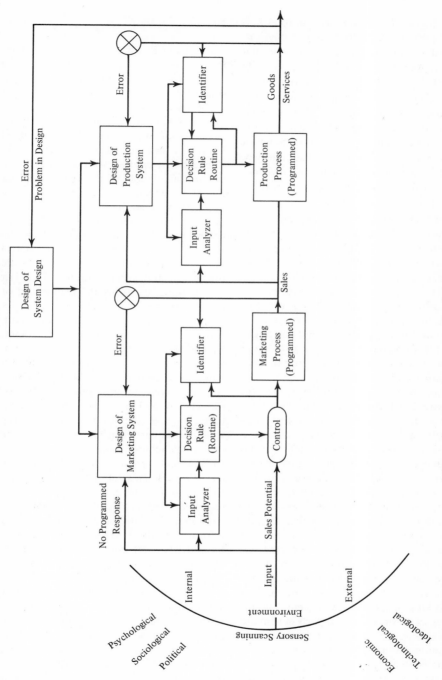

Figure 7. *Organization as a Total Adaptive System.*

353

In Figure 7, we now see the total system in some detail. We have our environmental inputs on the left, both external and internal: psychological, sociological, etc. Two basic subsystems are shown, marketing and production, in which the marketing output becomes a production input. Each of these subsystems has its own adaptor and, although not shown, a coordinating adaptor to integrate the two. Further, each subsystem has its own design capability. The only new feature of the schematic is the box at the top, "Design of System Design." This particular function would integrate the work of sub-designers. For example, if the organization is viewed as an aircraft, design coordination is required for such areas as weight and structures, air frame, power, and information systems. Moreover, this function would advise as to design technique and strategy, and ideally, one might be able to reach a stage in which the actual design of subsystems could be programmed and routinized.

Thus, in looking at Figure 7, we see, in some detail, the organization as a total system that is self-regulating and self-learning and at least partially closed; a system in which the environment can be detailed and in which subsystems are integrated. Further, the adaptor provides for appropriate internal adjustments between subsystems. In other words, the organization, without too much difficulty, can be considered as a total system. All of its essential elements can be incorporated into a design. Also, with an appropriate index, one could detail the subsystems; each subsystem could be broken down into its sub-subsystems, etc. The indexing of the system's subparts schematic to assure appropriate usage is not an insurmountable problem. For example, it is estimated that the blue prints for a new aircraft may finally weigh two or three tons—more than the aircraft itself!

System Design

In Figure 8, we can briefly go through the design process which further analyzes the function of the designer. Given a statement of the problem or the type of system with which one is concerned, the next and key step is the construction of a model of the system. Such a model (which I believe should be essentially stochastic in nature) would stipulate the output, or mission, of the system and the inputs, of which there are three: 1) the input upon which the process is to operate or that input which enters the system, 2) environmental inputs which affect the process, and 3) instrumental or control inputs which modify the operation of the process or the process itself. (This last set of inputs concerns the technology of processing the load inputs.)

For example, in a marketing subsystem, if the initial input is a potential customer, he has to be processed through the subsystem so that a sale is secured. The system's logic relates to the set of decision rules or, given certain inputs, the state of the system and a certain control capability, such as the extent of advertising, what particular decision rule should be utilized to achieve some expected output? Information requirements relate to the classification, amount, and timing of information for the system to operate as expected. Concerning the environmental variables, it is necessary to know what information about which variables should be gathered and how often, how much, and how soon this information has to reach the decision rule.

At the outset, it would be a highly worthwhile investment to construct a fairly complete stochastic model of the proposed system in which output is the dependent variable and environmental and instrumental inputs are the independent variables. For example, one might be concerned with a personnel selection

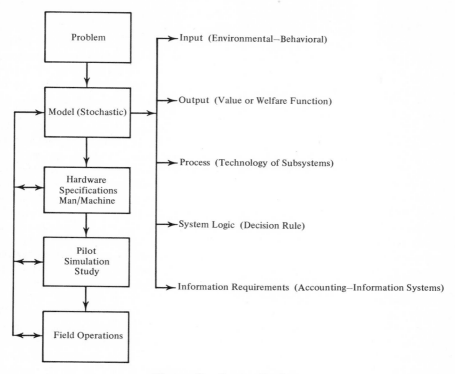

Figure 8. *System Design.*

subsystem in which the output is a certain number of qualified employees. The environmental inputs might include labor demand for certain occupations, amount of unemployment, and the number of graduates. The instrumental variables might include the recruiting budget, the number of recruiters, and the training program.

What is being suggested is that it is more efficient to construct one model to which various decision rules can be applied than to construct a new model every time a new decision rule is formulated. With the latter approach, one would always be reconstructing the model when there is a change in tools.

Assuming the model can be constructed, the research and development begins. One can experiment and try dif-ferent decision rules and different hardware specifications, which lead to the next two steps in the design process. Given a new rule on a pilot basis, one can apply it to actual hardware. Naturally, one has to be sure that the data from pilot studies are meaningful in terms of the total system with which one is concerned. Experimentation is costly and uncertain, but there is little doubt that the payoff is greater than using an intuitive approach.

If it is successful, the new rule can be applied and data can be fed back regularly to the designer so that he can continually improve and refine his initial model. Although one may begin with a relatively unrefined model, with successive experimentation and field experience, hard data will constantly flow back to the designer. This will enable him to improve his model in terms of the nature of variables, the preciseness of the parameters, and predictability.

As for hardware specifications, apart from the consideration of costs, one is concerned with providing components that will execute the operations as specified. In Figure 8, Schematic, the hardware problem how to convert what is essentially a paper model into something that approaches operating reality is of particular concern. (It seems to me that this is the area of greatest deficiency as far as the state of the arts is concerned.) We can construct reasonably good stochastic or econometric models, which can be used to simulate different decision rules, but the conversion of those models into operating reality with appropriate hardware is a different matter.

In operating context, the stochastic model or identifier becomes an information panel for a decision or rule-maker. In terms of hardware, what is needed are information collection or sensory devices which survey the environment and send such data to a central location so that the values of the variables of the model can be displayed. An example of this is the control room in a public utility in which the operator continually watches the changing values of significant variables. Only with such a display can appropriate action be taken. However, wiring such a system is a particularly difficult task.

For example, I am a member of a team that has been given the responsibility of designing a metropolitan poverty program as a total system. The primary inputs are poverty families and the output is supposed to be self-sufficient economic units. Although there exists some technical assurance that a stochastic model can be constructed, we have not been able to reach this design step because we are at the very primitive stage of inventing sensory mechanism that will give us some running idea of the nature of our changing inputs. In this instance the changing inputs are the changing mix of the characteristics of our poverty family inputs. This program appears in Figure 9.

Another area that requires additional work is the control element, which actually modifies the operation of the system. In a man-to-man system, we do not have sufficient information about which variables to vary and the degree of variation necessary to achieve the desired human behavior. The crude reward and punishment system that we have all too often gives us dysfunctional results. Presumably, in the design process, when serious deficiencies arise, research and development should be directed to those areas.

Managerial Technology as Utilized in System Design

Although this view of an organization as a total adaptive system and the design process has been brief, perhaps it has been sufficient to indicate how one can take advantage of the newer managerial techniques in the use of system analysis.[5] It is necessary to know where and how these techniques fit in terms of the system presented. As for the behavioral sciences, our environmental inputs or variables are behavioral in nature. To build a model, and eventually a display panel, such knowledge is essential. In the decision box we would utilize our various decision rules such as Linear Programming, Game Theory, Dynamic Programming, and PERT.

Because system design requires eventual concern with a total subsystem such as marketing, we will probably become in-

---

[5] For a more complete review, see Goode, Harry H., and Machol, Robert, *System Engineering,* McGraw-Hill, New York, 1957.

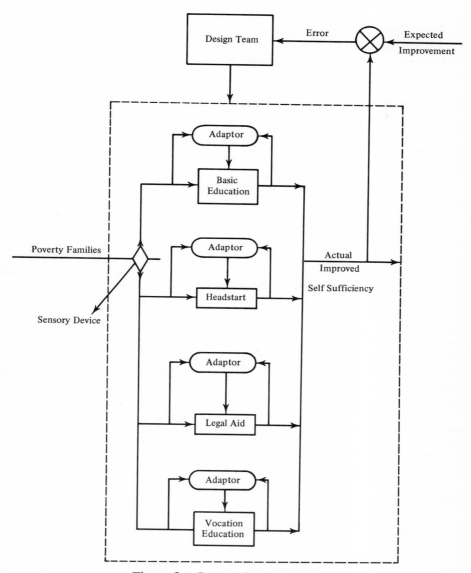

Figure 9. *Poverty Program System.*

creasingly concerned with the problem of combining various decision rules. For example, Gerald Thompson has indicated that we must combine appropriate decision rules to achieve the most satisfactory system output. We must know under what conditions it is advisable to move from Linear Programming to rule of thumb and then back to Linear Programming. There is an over-concern with single decision rule, and we must learn how to use different combinations of rules under a variety of operating conditions. As professor Thompson has noted, "We need to develop heuristics about using heuristics. That is, an executive program that would accept a problem and then decide which of a list of heuristics (decision rules) should be employed to give its solution." [6]

The information sciences relate to the input analyzer, collection, manipulation, and relay of information. Here we have all of our data, collection, and processing problems. The control element relates to the relatively new area of control theory; specifically, the direction of human effort. Finally, in designing a specific subsystem, such as personnel or marketing, we should have some knowledge with regard to the technology of these systems. For example, we should be able to use employment tests correctly in the selection process.

In designing an organization as a total system, it would appear that we would have to be familiar with and capable of using, a wide array of reasonably sophisticated managerial techniques and knowledge. The understanding and use of managerial techniques is an integral part of the design process. This is a counter-distinction to the bureaucratic structure, which merely attaches such techniques to the system with little purpose or place.

Design Criteria

Design criteria are rules which are utilized to evaluate the acceptability of designs. Given a number of designs, we must determine which one is the best. Although there are numerous rules, the most widely used are measurability, feasibility, optimality, reliability, and stability. We will consider only the first three. Measurability is the system's ability to evaluate its performance. If its performance cannot be measured, a sysem's desirability or undesirability cannot be established and its particular excellences or deficiencies cannot be known. When models are measurable, the superior system can be inferred from the specific measuring devices used in each. In the model which I have suggested, the identifier as a display panel is the primary measuring mechanism since we would know the actual inputs, process, outputs, and decision rules. If the model is not working as expected, the errors would be fed to the designer on a more or less continual basis so that the system could be redesigned for more effective results.

One of the most serious weaknesses of the bureaucratic design as a management system is that it lacks measurability. When the bureaucratic system is redesigned from a product to a functional arrangement or when the line of command is lengthened by the introduction of additional levels of managers, no measuring devices exist, either in the previous or subsequent design, that will indicate what improvements, if any, have occurred.

Feasibility relates to the question of whether or not the model will operate as planned. A model must be realistic; it must be capable of being installed, of achieving expected payoff, and of performing its task requirements within the environment of the system. If a particular quantitative decision-making tool is suggested, we must be reasonably certain that it can be employed in an operational context.

The use of pilot studies or experimental models relates to the question of feasibility. Given any managerial device, we want to know whether it will increase organizational payoff when it is utilized; whether stockholders, employees, and

---

[6] Thompson, Gerald L. "Some Approaches to the Solution of Large Scale Combinatorial Problems," Carnegie Institute of Technology, Pittsburgh, working paper, p. 25.

consumers will be better off than before. Organizations are normative systems. All too often, the student and practitioner are exposed to quantitative manipulations and behavioral research that is interesting, but either no directions are provided as to how these findings are to be incorporated into the operations of the firm, or no measuring devices are suggested that will actually establish the quantity of welfare that the research results will actually produce. Frequently, we are highly impressed with the elegance and sophistication of the research and the virtuosity of the analyst, and then discover that the extent of research usefulness is limited.

The end purpose of the manager, as it is viewed in this analysis, is to design subsystems which will actually increase human well-being. The manager is not, per se, a mathematician, statistician, sociologist, or psychologist. However, he must rely on these disciplines in much the same way as the engineer has to rely on physics.

This does not mean that continuous research is unnecessary in these disciplines, but it does mean that such research will not automatically lead to improvements. It is only when the designer is able to incorporate findings into an operating reality that he can achieve the full value of the research.

A corollary to the feasibility criterion relates to balance between parts of the system. All parts of the system must not only be integrated, but also mutually consistent. We would not put a primitive input analyzer into practice and follow this with a complex regression analysis in the identifier. The final system output would be no more productive than the least productive part of the system. Each part acts as a constraint on all other parts. Consequently, the identifier can never be any better than the input analyzer, and so on.

The absence of integration and/or balance is self-defeating. For example, we frequently find information systems personnel providing voluminous data; that is, the input analyzer is well developed. However, the rest of the system may be missing—there is no identifier, set of decision rules, etc. In other instances, we may have an analysis of the use of a single decision rule, as linear programming, but nothing else.

As long as we find this "bits and pieces" type of analysis, managers will always revert, out of necessity, to the most primitive part of the total system because this part represents the primary constraint. In such a context, increasing sophistication will not meet the criterion of feasibility. Even if it is used, no increment in organizational payoff will result.

For example, in the design of the poverty program system previously mentioned, the staff's initial impulse was to design an econometric model of the program, including exogenous variables. We immediately ran into the constraints of the rest of the system and realized that until we had a relatively effective input analyzer, a set of decision rules, and a control element, we could not move to the sophisticated model we wanted. In other words, when we design a total system, we are generally forced to start with a fairly elementary model. Then, when all the parts are developed, we can progress to a more complex system.

It seems to me that we are overly concerned with the optimality criterion in the "management sciences," while we tend to ignore such other criteria as measurability and feasibility on the assumption that, if one has an optimal solution, there is little else that has to be done. But unless all criteria are considered, we will not get the hoped-for results. To have a solution that is optimum but not feasible is meaningless. Obviously, a solution has to be measurable, feasible, and reliable before we can consider its optimality. For the most part, operating managers stress the feasibility criterion. At the outset, they want something that will work and actually function at this stage. They are not overly concerned with optimality. In dealing with a complex system, I am not sure of what constitutes an optimal solution. Engineers, for example, have told me that they really don't know what an optimal aircraft would be like.

Russell Ackoff has said, "One of the things Operations Research has learned about putting results to work is having considerable effect on its methods. This means the team must either translate elegant solutions into approximations that are easy to use, or side-step the elegance and move directly to a quick and dirty decision rule. Operations Research is learning that an approximation that is used may be a great deal better than an exact solution that is not." [7] Because design methodology imposes a specific discipline on the designer, we can be assured that new techniques will be effectively utilized.

Some Implications

While this has been a rather broad treatment of the organization as a total system, nevertheless, certain implications can be inferred. First, on a normative basis, organizations should be viewed as a total system if we are to increase organizational output. Different organizations, corporations, universities, poverty programs, and so on, can be so categorized.

Further, although this is by and large an article of faith, some empirical evidence does exist; certainly in the area of complex weapons systems. If organizations are viewed as a total system, better results will be obtained. We are in the initial stages of this development and, at this time, we can only block out the basic characteristics of total systems. I am quite convinced, for example, that the poverty program on the local metropolitan operating level can only be designed as a total system.

Second, I have attempted to demonstrate that the systems approach is a highly conducive vehicle for the incorporation of current managerial technologies, unlike the bureaucratic structure. Irrespective of the developing managerial concepts, the bureaucratic structure itself represents such a serious constraint that only minimal advantages would occur.

Third, when viewed in this context, the essential role of the manager is that of designer of organizational or behavioral systems, just as the engineer is the designer of machine systems. The design of a large complex system will, however, necessitate a team effort of mathematicians, psychologists, and information specialists. But, as in the case of large machine systems, system specialists will be required to integrate the team effort. There is little reason why efforts cannot be organized to design a marketing system in the same fashion as the F-111 aircraft was designed.

If we were to speculate about the future, eventually the organization might be divided into two basic divisions, planning and operations. The computer, behavioral scientists, information specialists, and quantitative personnel would comprise the planning unit. This planning division would be comparable to the engineering division currently found in organizations. The organization of the poverty program, for instance, is divided between planning and control on the one hand, and operations on the other. Planning has the primary responsibility of total system design.

---

[7] Russell L. Ackoff, "The Development of Operations Research as a Science," in *Scientific Decision Making in Business,* Abe Shuchman, ed., Holt, Rinehart, and Winston, N.Y., 1963, pp. 59–60.

This unit is an interdisciplinary team under the direction of a systems specialist. This is in contrast to the typical operations research arrangement in which a line manager may use operations research for assistance if he has a problem. In the poverty program, the manager is viewed as the operator of the system developed by the team.

Similarly, if the organization is to fully utilize the systems approach, the first step would be to establish a design team with planning responsibility. Also there is no reason why a particular team has to be concerned entirely with one subsystem, such as marketing or personnel. Once the development work has been done regarding one subsystem, the team should have the capability of designing any other subsystem. In the poverty program, the same team is dealing with headstart, legal aid, health, and manpower training subsystems.

There are educational implications suggested by this analysis; namely, a division of business education into two relatively distinct areas. One would represent the traditional bureaucratic approach and contain the basic principles, material and functional areas. The other would stress the organization as a total system (the alternative to principles), and would be the basic course upon which the newer management technologies (as exemplified by such courses as statistics) would be systematically built and integrated. At the University of Massachusetts, we have moved in this direction on the graduate level.

Thus, rather than offer behavioral and quantitative courses in a curriculum with little rhyme or reason, the new technologies can be integrated in the systems fabric. This is a rational program for the student because he now knows why and where the parts fit, why he has to be able to construct a stochastic model, and so forth.

In all probability, the two basic approaches—bureaucratic and systems—will exist side by side in the curriculum over a number of years. Gradually, however, one would expect the bureaucratic material to be phased out in order to reflect changes in the real world. In form, organizations may continue as bureaucratic structures; in substance, they will take on systems orientation with a continual integration of operations and elimination of authority boundaries.

My final observation concerns the ultimate development in systems. It is hoped that, in the long run, the systems approach will result in a more "human use of human beings" in an organizational setting which the Father of Cybernetics, Norbert Wiener, suggested.[8] The ultimate goal of the designer of man systems is to increase the human welfare of the organization's membership. This will occur because the nature of the design process is to continually create a system that most closely fits the basic material of the system—man himself. I certainly concur with Chris Argyris' comments upon the non-human characteristics of bureaucracy.[9]

The ideal organization or system would be a cybernetic one—a self-regulating mechanism in which individuals adjusted and adapted to their environment because they were self-motivated to do so. Such an organization would have the characteristics of the purely competitive economic mode. Yet, if we are to reach such an ideal state, such systems will have to be invented. To observe that the traditional bureaucratic structure has serious

---

[8] See Wiener, Norbert, *The Human Use of Human Beings,* Doubleday, 2nd Ed. Revised, Garden City, New York, 1954.

[9] Argyris, Chris, *Personality and Organization,* New York, Harper, 1957.

drawbacks, or that principles of management are not very vigorous, is not enough. If the present hierarchical scheme is deficient, then only a better one will rectify the situation. There is little question that

we are at last in a position to invent better social systems. I have attempted to demonstrate, when we view the organization as a total system, we have taken the first step in this forward direction.

39. The Total Systems Myth

W. M. A. BROOKER

The purpose of this article is to examine critically the value of the total systems concept and to make predictions on the effects of its applications. As is implied in the title, the author does not regard the concept itself as having the practical value claimed by its followers. On the other hand, the belief in this concept is a powerful motivating force among those who have accepted it as a frame of reference.

Why and what is untrue about the total systems concept? The basic error in the total systems concept is the assumption that the total systems approach is the most fruitful; that systems analysis in any situation is the most powerful kind of planning that can precede planned and profitable change for a company.

This article will discuss the foundations of the systems concept, the value of this concept and the limitations of its application. These limitations amount to an inadequacy as to the totality of pervasiveness of the approach, notwithstanding its value in an auxiliary role. We shall then discuss the requirements of an overall

approach and outline an alternative in which systems theory occupies a significant but auxiliary role.

Foundations of the Systems Concept

The foundation of the systems concept seems to rest on the work of von Bertalanffy, who apparently coined the term "general systems theory." Hall, who is referred to by Bertalanffy, defines the system as . . . "a set of objects with relationships among the objects and among their attributes. Objects are simply the parts or components of a system." [1]

More specifically, systems are defined in terms of flows. According to Forrester: The business system is . . . "a system in which the flows of information, materials, man-power, capital equipment and money set up forces that determine the basic tendencies toward growth, fluctuation and decline." [2]

The flows of business system, according to Optner, are in the form of a closed

---

Reprinted from *Systems and Procedures Journal*, Vol. 16, No. 4 (July–August, 1965), pp. 28–32, with permission of the publisher. W. M. A. Brooker is a sociologist with a leading Canadian corporation in Montreal.

[1] Arthur D. Hall, *A Methodology for Systems Engineering*, Van Nostrand, Toronto, 1962, p. 60.

[2] J. W. Forrester, *Harvard Business Review*, July–August, 1958, p. 52.

system which . . . "can be defined as one which is free of variation or distur-

bance . . . the concept of the black box" [3] of which the basic model is thus:

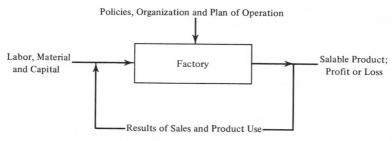

Policies, Organization and Plan of Operation

Labor, Material and Capital → Factory → Salable Product; Profit or Loss

Results of Sales and Product Use

In its business form, this model becomes:

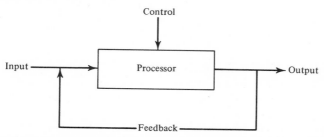

Control

Input → Processor → Output

Feedback

An advantage of the systems approach is that it focuses attention on broader issues than may be contained in a single department. This is because of the emphasis on inputs and outputs. What goes on *inside* the black box is of secondary importance. Naturally this has a healthy effect on any departmental narrowness of viewpoint.

The second advantage of the systems approach is that it aids in the formulation of purpose or objectives for a particular department or operating area. The reason for the existence of any operating area can very neatly be expressed in the formula:

$$P = O - I$$

where P is purpose, O is output and I stands for input.

A third advantage of the systems approach is that it can sometimes be related to decision making. Forrester, for example, in his model for industrial dynamics (page 364), shows information flows controlling valves in material and money flows.[4]

Forrester, incidentally, develops this theme very well in demonstrating the effect of varying sales volume on inventory levels.

Disadvantage of the Total Systems Approach

The author's main quarrel with the approach is that many of the followers of systems theory seem to have translated *general* systems into total systems; they give the impression that if systems are omnipresent they must somehow, like

---

[3] Stanford L. Optner, *Systems Analysis for Business Management,* Prentice-Hall, pp. 3–15.

[4] From J. W. Forrester, *Industrial Dynamics,* John Wiley & Sons, New York, 1961, p. 67.

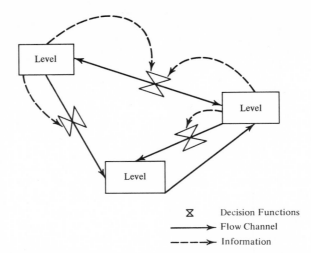

$\overline{\text{X}}$ Decision Functions

⟶   Flow Channel

----➤   Information

God, be omnipotent. General systems theory is a valid field of inter-disciplinary study. Those who profess general systems theory realize its limitations, which are not recognized by those who take the *total* systems approach. As an example of an understanding of the limitations of the approach, let's refer again to Hall. Following his definition of a system quoted on page 28 of this article he continues:

"Systems may consist of atoms, stars, switches, springs, wires, bones, gases, mathematical variables, equations, laws and processes." [5]

Nowhere in this list does he refer to businesses or people; nowhere in his book does he suggest the use of systems engineering models in business.

Bertalanffy remains conservative: "General systems theory in its present form is one—and still very imperfect—model among others." Even then, this organismic picture would not claim to be a 'nothing but' philosophy: it would remain conscious that it only presents certain aspects of reality . . . but never exhaustive, exclusive or final." [6]

In contrast is the Forrester definition quoted above. Later, in his book, he says: "Industrial dynamics models in their purpose and origin will be . . . similar to models of engineering systems . . . concentration must be on those factors that determine the characteristics of information feedback systems—structure, amplification and delays."

Even more ambitious is Wiener: "It is the thesis of this book that society can only be understood through a study of the messages and the communication facilities which belong to it. . . ." [7]

The Error in the "Total" Approach

In a nutshell the objection to the "totality" of systems approach is that there is

[5] Hall, *Ibid.,* p. 60.

[6] Bertalanffy, *General System Theory—A Critical Review,* Yearbook of the Society for General Systems Research, Vol. VII, 1962, p. 10.

[7] Norbert Wiener, *The Human Use of Human Beings—Cybernetics and Society,* Doubleday-Anchor, New York, 1954, p. 16.

an assumption that this approach is the most important one.[8] This assumption is translated into practice by writers who define the role of change agents such as systems analysts in terms of the total systems concept.

In terms of this concept, the role of the change agents is to design the business system in terms of *flows* of information, materials, money and people, and to persuade members of the enterprise to adopt the system or sub-system so designed. The author has never come across a situation where this has actually been achieved nor has he read an account of where this has been done. This may be coincidental or it may be because of the following:

1. The total systems approach in business makes no attempt to explain, predict or understand why the human members of the business system act the way they do. It is concerned with components of a business system in the same way as communication theory is concerned with electronic components in a communications system, but it offers little or no understanding of those components either as individuals or as members of business organizations.

2. If it cannot explain the way things are, the total systems approach cannot be expected to explain the way things are going to be. Insofar as the total systems approach is weak analytically with regard to the most significant aspects of the business system (viz., the people), it must also be weak in predicting future developments with regard to people.

Illustrations of the Myth

In order to demonstrate the points we have been making we are going to discuss two articles, both heavily influenced by the total systems concept.

The first is "Analyzing an Overall System" by Charles J. Berg.[9] Early in his article he defines a business system as a: *". . . set of policies, rules, and procedures which defines the actions, responsibilities, and authorities of all elements of a business organization in the day-by-day conduct of its normal activities."*

This is all-encompassing, and justifies us as classifying it as being an wholistic or total approach. How does Mr. Berg use it? The core of his article is concerned with the stepwise "analytical technique for defining our present position and for use as a systems reference point. Step One is the use of the conventional flow chart of the existing system, with each step analyzed and measured showing the amount of time, money and physical distance required in each processing component. It is not unusual to find at this stage that unnecessary transportation, time and money are incorporated into the system. Step Two relies on the information previously produced, but it is a modified form of the same information. This is the input-output analysis chart. This technique clearly depicts the multitudinous uses of various data. Generally it can be stated that where many inputs are used to devise many outputs, potential systems improvements are of a high order. Step Three is to relate the present system as described in steps one and two above into financial terminology. What lines on the statement are affected and what are the potential improvements available? Step Four is the allocation of people responsibility for the planned systems improvement, along with specific financial objectives to be attained. Step Five is to accomplish the improvements resulting

---

[8] The reason for the error lies in what the author calls the Magical Fallacy. See page 31.
[9] *Systems and Procedures Journal,* November–December, 1963.

from the analysis of the above information."

Diagramatically Berg expresses his approach as shown in Figure 1.

But the author does not fulfill his promise. In terms of his own definition

of a business system his analytical technique is mainly concerned with "procedures and actions." He refers to policies, rules, responsibilities and authorities *of all elements of a business organization in* his definition of a business system

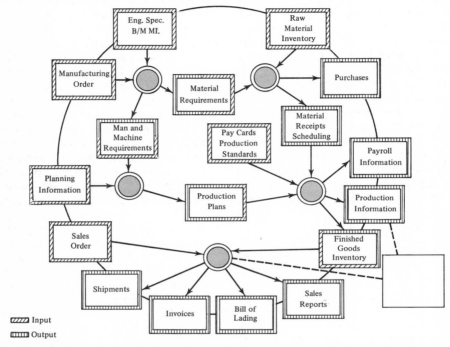

Figure 1. *The Stepwise Analytical Techniques Shown Here Are Too Narrow to Fulfill the Promise Evident in the Definition of Total Systems.*

One: If you have a manufacturing order and this is combined with an engineering specification, bills of material, and manufacturing information, these can be combined and materials information, manpower, and the facilities required can be determined.

Two: With material requirements being compared to raw material inventories, purchases and material receipts schedules can be derived.

Three: Returning now to the manpower and facilities requirements, combining and comparing this with planning information, we can evolve specific production plans.

Four: Material receipts schedules and pay cards, along with production standards and the production plans, can be integrated to produce payrolls, production data and finished goods inventory.

Five: Coordinating the information of a sales order with that of the finished goods inventory we can produce shipments, invoices, bills of lading and sales receipts.

Six: Finally, we can build management decisions into the system which are necessary to operate it most effectively.

quoted above, and says precious litle about them in his analytical technique. Under which of his stepwise analytical techniques could one consider the following problems which have to be considered in any business organization?

What business should we be in? For example, should we diversify our operations, or consolidate? Should our business be divisionalized along product lines, customer grouping, or geographic areas? Should our engineering function be centralized or decentralized or along some combination of both?

In fact these problems cannot be subsumed under the techniques proposed because they are too narrow. The promise of total systems—evident in the definition —remains unfulfilled in the proposals for its creation.

Similar objections come to mind with a second article by Dr. R. L. Martino.[10] But in this case the gap between promise and proposal is even more blatant. The promise lies in the title: "The Development and Installation of a Total Management System."

Most business people are inclined to accept the simple notion that management is concerned with governing and controlling of the activities of a company, somewhat analogous to the executive branch of the government of a state. To enlarge "management" to "total management system" emphasizes the pervasiveness of the phenomena and also its completeness and orderliness. This promise is not borne out by the following:

"*. . . The primary objective in developing a total management system should be the production of detailed up-to-the-minute summaries of the past and the use of these summaries to project future activity. In essence the functions of a total management system are: (1) To predict; (2) To compare the prediction with actual*

results; and (3) To produce the deviations between the predicted and the actual."

In other words, the total system conceptualizers, when they really get down to it, talk of designing flows of information to enable management to do its job better. Martino represents this diagramatically in Figure 2.

The figure shows what management does with various kinds of information. In Martino's model, management *itself* is not part of the total management system, for nowhere is there any phase where management looks at itself or the organization of which it is a part. It is as though management were something like the driver of a car, detached; as though, like a car driver, management made the decisions, the "system" carried them out.

Factories, warehouses and saleshouses and other industries, services, utilities— whatever the business exists for—consists of much more than information handling systems glorified into some state of "totality." Just as a map of a country may cover the whole of it, it is not a "total" depiction of it, because in a country there are other dimensions and features that cannot be shown on a map. Similarly, in a business there are other dimensions and features which cannot be subsumed under the kinds of total systems we have been discussing.

Requirements of a General Business Theory

What, then, are the theoretical requirements of change agents in business? The following thoughts are offered as criteria for basic theory:

A. UNDERSTANDING FOR ACTION

1. It must be capable of understanding current problems of business. Therefore,

---

[10] *Data Processing for Management,* April 1963, p. 31.

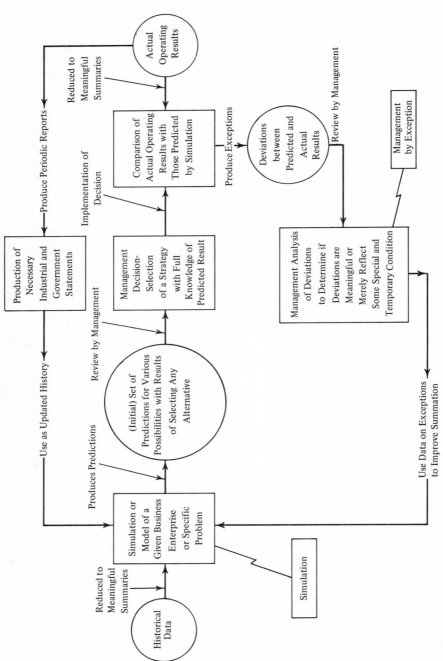

Figure 2. *This Figure Shows What Management Does with Various Kinds of Information.* Management itself, however, is not part of the total management system, for nowhere is there any phase where management looks at itself or the organization of which it is a part.

2. It should be capable of realistic predictions on consequences of proposed actions.

3. It should provide a basis for establishing direction for proposed change.

B. BASIS FOR THEORETICAL DEVELOPMENT

An acceptable basic theory should be broad enough to include other more specific theories. If, for example, we reject total systems theory as a basic tool, the basic tool we do adopt should be capable of covering the valuable aspects of such a theory.

Outline of a Basic Theory

What follows is a skeletal account of a theory which meets these requirements:

1. A business is primarily a social human group. The machines, however vast, are originated by and operated by human beings. Therefore, the theoretical basis should be human oriented.

2. There are three aspects of human groups which are important to the understanding of a business. They are objectives, or purpose; activities, or the actual work performed; and relationships which include cooperative and functional as well as the ever-present man/boss relationship. In addition, there are three corresponding concepts pertaining to the individual: values, status and activities.

3. The basis of the approach suggested is, first, that there are certain desirable or healthy conditions for these group and individual aspects, particularly in their relationship to one another. Second, it can be assumed that these conditions do not necessarily apply at all times. Third, it is suggested that the lack of desirable conditions applying will lead to the occurrence of certain effects or symptoms. Fourth, the approach envisages the use of various techniques to reveal these symptoms. Fifth, it is suggested that the symptoms can be used to identify the *causes* of malfunction, and sixth, that planning and executing projects which rectify causes are the proper work of systems analysts, or other change agents, in business.

4. The activities of business are only one of many aspects. Only when this aspect is viewed against its proper background of group purpose (or objectives) and structure, and individuals' values and status, should it be elaborated into a "totality" of system.

5. It is entirely possible to make use of the valuable aspects of systems theory (discussed in the early part of this article) within these other concepts, but then the systems aspect is no longer "total" but ancillary.

A Proposed Role for Systems Analysis

How can the role of the systems analyst be met in view of these criticisms? The senior systems man in a company may be analogous to a cabinet minister in charge of communications (embracing, for instance, tele-postal-road-rail and air-communications). A minister of communications is concerned with the development of channels for the transmission of information in whatever form. Similarly, the VP of communications with a firm should be concerned with the development and maintenance of communication networks which best achieve company, and divisional if necessary, purpose(s).

This is far reaching in that it would be extending throughout the whole but it is not wholistic or "total" in the Wiener or Forrester sense. Systems departments, therefore, are not analogous to the management of a *real* whole (e.g., a company, a plant or a division).

Let us again take a geographic analogy. All the cities in North America are connected by a system of roads, but urban development—as in the case of corporate development—means working with the wholes in the situation.

City management and development undoubtedly requires auxiliary and parallel development and modification in the road system, and occasionally cities have to adjust to a road development program under the control of a wider authority which constitutes a natural whole,[11] such as a state government.

Roads in this way are analogous to the communications networks of business. Corporations as natural wholes are composed of other, smaller wholes, (divisions, operating departments, staff functions, etc.), and the role of management is the continuous mutual adjustment of these parts to one another in order to achieve company goals. This process of continuous adjustment requires the continuous development of new communications transmittal, reception and storage, and it is the role of the systems analyst to carry out this development.

Sometimes, as in the case of a city having to adjust to the road development by a wider authority, the natural wholes (e.g., divisions, departments) within a company have to adjust to the communications system imposed upon them by the company as a whole.

The total systems concept implies—indeed some of its exponents, as we have seen, are quite explicit—that the communications system is the basis for understanding and changing society, or the micro-society that the corporation forms. This is not true; the systems concept is not that "total."

---

11 J. C. Smuts, *Wholism and Evolution,* Compass Books, New York, 1961.

B

SYSTEMS ANALYSES

40. Industrial Dynamics—After the First Decade

JAY FORRESTER

History

A decade has passed since the first work on organizing system concepts into the form which has come to be called 'industrial dynamics." [1] Four years before 1956, the Alfred P. Sloan School of Management at MIT had been started with the generous support of Mr. Sloan who believed that a management school in a technical environment would develop in new and important directions that would be different from management schools in other kinds of academic settings. When the author came to the School from his background in feedback control systems, computers, and practicing management, it was for the planned purpose of searching for and developing the linkages which might exist between engineering and management education. It was the expectation that these lay in the areas of

Reprinted from *Management Science,* Vol. 14, No. 7 (March, 1968), pp. 398–414, with permission of the author and the publisher. Jay Forrester is Professor of Management, Alfred P. Sloan School of Management, Massachusetts Institute of Technology.

Editor's Note: This article is a companion to the one by H. I. Ansoff and Dennis P. Slevin which appears in this same issue. Because of their relationship, the authors of each have consented to comment on the other article. Their comments are scheduled to appear in the May Issue of *Management Science: Theory.*

[1] This article assumes some familiarity with the basic material in [3].

operations research and the application of computers to processing management information.

The year 1956–57 was devoted to examining the national activity in operations research which was aimed at bringing mathematics and scientific method to bear on problems in industry. The study indicated that operations research was not dealing effectively with the broader, top-management problems. Most of the work was concentrated on individual decisions structured as open-loop processes, meaning that the inputs to the decision process were considered as unaffected by the decisions themselves. But decisions are made for the purpose of influencing the environment and thereby generating different inputs to succeeding decisions. Although the open-loop assumption simplified analysis, the assumptions underlying the analysis could be invalidated by the closed-loop structure surrounding the actual decision process.

Furthermore, the mathematical orientation of management science, the concentration on analytical solutions, and the optimization objectives could cope only with rather simple situations. They excluded treatment of the more complex management relationships and also forced neglect of most nonlinear phenomena. It appeared that management science as it then existed did pay its way by working on significant problems. However, there was no substantial body of opinion either inside or outside management science that believed that the problems being attacked were the major ones that made the difference between the companies that succeed and those that stagnate or fail.

The manager's task is to interrelate the separate functions of the company, to create the flows that cause the company and market mutually to support one another, and to interweave the tangible economic variables with the intangible variables of psychology and power structure.

None of these was being adequately reached by the management science activities which remained focused on the separate corporate functions and were thus being applied within sharply restricted areas of decision-making. Furthermore, the methods did not seem amenable to much broadening of scope. The manager's principal problems seemed not to lie in decisions taken as isolated events, but rather in policies that deal with streams of decisions and in the structure of the managerial system that interrelates information sources, policy, and action.

The first year of exploration pointed toward the concepts of feedback systems as being much more general, more significant, and more applicable to social systems than had been commonly realized. Feedback system analysis had been extensively applied by engineers in the design of technical devices. Cybernetics as another name for feedback processes was becoming a common word in the biological sciences. The elementary idea of feedback as a circular cause-effect phenomena could be traced back through centuries of economic literature. But even so, the implications, the importance, and the principles of feedback processes were only beginning to be understood. Rather than its having been exhaustively studied, it became increasingly clear that the systems frontier had only begun to open. Feedback processes emerged as universal in social systems and seemed to hold the key to structuring and clarifying relationships that had remained baffling and contradictory.

Aided by a grant from the Ford Foundation, a research program began to relate the elementary concepts of feedback systems, previously developed in the engineering fields, to the processes in social systems. Compatible with the overriding determination to avoid restriction to simple linear systems, analytical treatment was subordinated. One could for the first time turn away from mathematical solutions as the principal means of analysis because computers had reached the point where convenient low-cost system simulation was possible. With simulation available as a procedure for determining the behavior of a model system, it became fruitful to concentrate not on mathematical methods but on the fundamental nature of structure in systems. This work led to a simple and general structure that seemed capable of representing the interactions within any type of system. This generalized structure serves, not only as a framework for organizing observations and experience, but also expedites the simulation stage of system studies. The structure is discussed in a later section.

The past and immediate future of industrial dynamics divides into three periods:

Period One, 1956–1961, Structural Concepts and Steady-State Dynamics. The structure of systems was identified in terms of feedback loops and their component substructures. Examples of system formulation were developed. Applications of the concepts were made to "steady-state" dynamics which concentrate on the fluctuation about equilibrium conditions and which do not involve the processes of growth and decline. This was a period when "enterprise engineering," meaning corporate policy redesign, formed the focus of industrial dynamics. The first period ended with the publication of *Industrial Dynamics* [3].

Phase Two, 1962–1966, Growth Dynamics and General Systems Theory. This has been a period of consolidation and of clarifying the concepts about systems in the social sciences. Experimental educational programs have been tried for the teaching of system principles. It has been a time for reaching a better understanding of the educational materials and methods that will be required to make the concepts of dynamic systems accessible to the average student of management. During this period, examples of industrial dynamics modeling were extended into

situations where nonlinearity was of dominant importance. The positive feedback processes of growth in products, companies, and economies have been explored. During this period the view of industrial dynamics was enlarged not only to include the application to enterprise design but also to become a general systems theory to serve as a unifying framework capable of organizing behavior and relationships in areas as diverse as engineering, medicine, management, psychology, and economics. The literature as yet only inadequately conveys the industrial dynamics work of this period in growth and life cycle dynamics [4, 12, 13, 14], education [5, 6, 9], and systems theory [5, 7].

Phase Three, 1967–1975, Foundations and Bridges. The forthcoming period must provide the literature and educational materials necessary to make the theory and the art of dealing with systems more generally accessible. At the present time systems concepts are scattered and incomplete, feedback theory exists in an unnecessarily forbidding mathematical context, and the field lacks interpretation into the specifics of social systems. There needs to be developed a simplified interpretation of the mathematics of feedback processes. The principles of dynamic behavior in systems need to be identified and illustrated with practice exercises for the student. Bridging articles and applications from system theory to a variety of fields need to be presented both to demonstrate generality and to provide guides to the art of system identification and interpretation.

The Present

Industrial dynamics, described as the science of feedback behavior in social systems, is still in a very early stage of development. Many people have been exposed to an introduction to the subject, but, except by serving an apprenticeship in the development of the field, there as yet exists almost no educational opportunity for developing professional competence.

Industrial dynamics is seen very differently by different people. Some observers see it merely as a simulation technique, apparently thinking of industrial dynamics as synonymous with the DYNAMO compiler. The DYNAMO compiler is a computer program for simulating industrial dynamics models but certainly is not the only possible method for such simulation. Simulation, in turn, is not the essence of industrial dynamics; simulation is merely the technique, used because mathematical analytical solutions are impossible, for exposing the nature of system models. To those at the center of industrial dynamics activity, the subject is the interpretation and the extension of feedback system concepts to apply in the multiple-loop, nonlinear systems to which the social processes belong. Although still very incomplete, industrial dynamics is a body of theory dealing with feedback dynamics. It is an identifiable set of principles governing interactions within systems. It is a view of the nature of structure in purposeful systems.

At MIT the first-term subject in industrial dynamics is a popular management elective. Some 120 undergraduate and graduate students take the subject each year. A substantial fraction come from other departments. The subject is also presented to the hundred men in the Sloan Fellow and the Senior Executive Development Programs. But any single-term treatment is incomplete and somewhat superficial. It conveys the importance of structure in determining the behavior of systems. It opens to the student the hope of a better understanding of managerial systems. But it does not prepare the student to proceed by himself. The student exposure in a one-term subject succeeds and fails in much the same way as the book *Industrial Dynamics* [3]. It is probably fair to say that this book seems readable without any specialized training. However, it can be misleading. Many readers can read the book without

being aware of the extensive background in feedback systems underlying the presentation. The book does not attempt to convey the principles of feedback systems. The reader without a foundation in feedback dynamics can read the book without realizing that he does not have the conceptual and theoretical background necessary to carry on the work discussed in the book. After reading the book, and apparently understanding it, such a reader turns to the world around him and finds himself unable, without guidance, to apply successfully the industrial dynamics approach to systems. This difficulty reflects the inadequacy of the present literature and educational materials.

Because the literature is dominated by industrial dynamics applications to production and distribution processes, many people see only a usefulness to such areas and fail to see the generality and the extensions to such areas as marketing, finance, and competition. This deficiency in the literature can now be remedied. Time and effort should yield results.

The very widespread but shallow exposure to industrial dynamics has created acceptance beyond the availability of skilled practitioners to deliver on its hope and promise. Thirty or more universities are teaching industrial dynamics to some extent; in most places this is as part of another course, usually one in production emphasizing simulation methods and the dynamics of production processes. Many industrial organizations have some industrial dynamics activity, but most are in the early phases of self-education. There is widespread international interest in industrial dynamics. The Japanese are active and have translated parts of the American literature and have written a number of original articles. A German translation of *Industrial Dynamics* [3] is in process. Interest in Scandinavia, the United Kingdom, and France seems substantial.

Inquiries in a steady stream come from companies ready to establish industrial dynamics systems groups when competent personnel are available. However, it has become increasingly clear that management schools and social science departments are not training men with adequate depth in system dynamics to fill such openings successfully. The only class of person now having a high probability of success is the one who has studied the dynamics of feedback processes in an engineering curriculum and who then extends and generalizes these ideas in applying them to social systems. The supply of men with such training is much too small to create any significant impression on the demand. The present imbalance between opportunity on the one hand and supply on the other points clearly to the need for much more adequate literature and new and more intensive educational programs.

Status of Feedback System Theory

Because industrial dynamics is a feedback system view of social behavior, it is well to have some perspective on the status of feedback theory. The basic structure of a feedback system is a loop within which the system condition provides the input to a decision process that generates action which modifies the system condition. It is a continuously circulating process. Every decision—personal, corporate, national, international, or in nature—occurs within such a context.

Such an assertion of total generality sometimes generates the response that such a broad concept could have no usefulness because it would not divide the decision-making field into categories— that something which is all-encompassing is empty of meaning. But we do not con-

sider physics meaningless because all its phenomena are based on the atom, nor is biology without interest because of the pervasive presence of the cell. The word "decision" is used here to mean the control of an action stream. Such an action stream may be the time devoted to sleeping in response to one's physical state, the effort to improve products in response to market information about product acceptance, the change in interest rates in responce to money supply, the change of prices in response to a world-wide commodity shortage, or the rate of consumption of rabbits as a response to the size of the coyote population. As in these and all other decision streams, the action resulting from the decision stream affects the state of the system to which the decision stream itself is responding.

The feedback concept is found throughout the professional and also the public literature. However, only in the engineering fields is there a well organized body of theory dealing directly with the processes of feedback dynamics. Most of this material is written in the field of electrical engineering. One could probably assemble a forty foot shelf of books devoted to the subject. Consider what such a library would contain. To measure the scope of the existing literature, we might examine four dimensions or characteristics of feedback systems—order, direction of feedback, nonlinearity, and loop multiplicity.

SYSTEM ORDER

The order of a system can be expressed in a variety of ways. In physical systems the order is often defined in terms of the number of energy storage elements. In a system expressed as a differential equation the order is equal to the highest derivative. In a system expressed as a series of integrations the order is equal to the number of integrations. In a system expressed in first-order difference equations (which are integrations), the order is equal to the number of difference equations. The number of "levels" (which are first-order difference equations, i.e., integrations) in the industrial dynamics terminology is equal to the system order. In more practical terms, the order of the system is equal to the number of accumulations. In a managerial system one will increase the order of the system for each bank balance, each pool of machine tools, each group of employees, each information variable which measures *average* system activity, and each attitude or psychological state necessary to describe the system.

An examination of the feedback literature will show that most of the material deals with first and second-order systems. A small percent of the literature presses into the region of third and fourth-order systems and beyond. Yet even elementary managerial phenomena usually require a minimum of fifth to twentieth order for adequate representation. Any effort to represent realistically a comprehensive industrial system may carry one well up toward hundredth order. A ratio of ten or more exists between the solidly established literature and the models needed to exhibit the modes of behavior that dominate industrial and economic systems.

POLARITY OF FEEDBACK

A feedback loop is described as being positive or negative in its action. This refers to the polarity or algebraic sense of influence around the loop.

A positive feedback loop has a polarity around the loop such that action increases a system state to produce still more action. Positive feedback takes place in a build-up phase of an atomic explosion. It occurs in management where salesmen produce revenue to support still more salesmen. Positive feedback is the system description of the process in the multiplication of rabbits. The positive feedback loop

produces exponential departure from some reference or neutral condition, often that of zero activity. Positive feedback is an essential process in the growth of products, companies, or countries.

By contrast, the negative feedback loop is goal seeking. A departure from the reference point produces action tending to return the system toward the equilibrium position, that is, the goal. A negative feedback loop may approach its equilibrium position in a smooth, exponential, non-oscillatory manner; or it may approach equilibrium through a decaying series of oscillations; or it can be unstable and produce ever wider swings around the "equilibrium" position which is crossed but to which the system never settles.

Probably 99% of the literature on feedback systems deals with the negative feedback loop. The negative loop is more difficult and subtle than the positive loop. But all processes of growth are manifestations of positive feedback behavior. Positive feedback in the engineering literature is almost entirely omitted because the emphasis has been on steady-state control for maintaining equilibrium conditions. The same is mostly true in the mathematical literature of economics. Positive feedback must usually be omitted from analytical mathematical treatment of linear systems because, in linear systems, a positive feedback loop leads to infinite excursion and destructive consequences. It is in the social and biological systems that so much practical attention is focused on positive feedback behavior. Models of positive feedback processes are feasible when the nonlinearity of natural systems is included to limit the growth phase, or when simulation is used for system study and the time span is short enough that the normal growth phase is not exceeded.

DEGREE OF NONLINEARITY

Without attempting a rigorous definition, we can say that a system is nonlinear if it contains a multiplication or division of variables or if it has a coefficient which is a function of a variable. For example, the rate of sale in a market might be expressed as the product of the number of salesmen multiplied by the sales effectiveness, where the sales effectiveness may depend on such things as the price, quality, and delivery delay of the product. But if these latter are variables, the sales rate is a nonlinear function of the variables representing the number of salesmen and the sales effectiveness. Likewise, throughout our social systems, nonlinearity dominates behavior.

In a general sense we can speak of the degree of nonlinearity of a system. The degree of nonlinearity implies the number of policies in the system that are nonlinear and the extent to which the system modes of behavior arise only because of the existence of nonlinearity. The degree of nonlinearity, although not a well-defined concept, might be thought of as a scale extending to the right from an origin, which point of origin represents linear systems. Almost all of mathematical analysis lies within the end point at the beginning of the line. Most of the processes of life and society lie along the scale to the right. Probably not more than two per cent of the literature of feedback systems deals with nonlinear behavior, and that which does is limited to very special cases of nonlinearity.

The importance of nonlinearity is well put by Kovach [10]:

We have broken through the sonic barrier, we are well on our way to conquering the thermal barrier and we are now at the threshold of the nonlinear barrier. Of all three, this last seems the most insurmountable. Strange that these nonlinear phenomena that abound so widely in nature should be so intractable. It is almost as if Man is to be denied a complete knowledge of the universe unless he makes a superhuman effort to solve its nonlinearities. . . . In a way we have

been lulled into the belief that everything is ideal, homogeneous, uniform, isotropic, perfect as well as frictionless, weightless, but withal infinitely rigid. . . . We have, so to speak, located a few nonlinear zippers in the blanket of nonlinearity that covers us. Opening these zippers has allowed us to put our hand through and try to fathom the vast unknown in this way. . . . It seems entirely plausible that the qualitative habit of thought will eventually supersede the present quantitative one in mathematics. There are certain indications in science and many in mathematics which point to the analysis of structure as the mathematics of the future. In simple language, it is not things that matter, but the relations between them.

MULTIPLICITY OF LOOPS

The literature of feedback systems is mostly devoted to the single feedback loop. Only a small fraction of the literature deals with systems of two or more interconnected loops. Yet, to represent adequately managerial systems one must incorporate from two to twenty major loops, each of which may contain many minor loops. For example, a simple structure describing the growth in sales of a new product might contain three nonlinear loops—a positive sales-department loop of salesmen producing orders, leading to revenue to hire more salesmen; a negative market loop in which orders alter backlog to change delivery delay to modify the attractiveness of the product to change order rate; and a negative capital-investment loop where order backlog leads to expanding production to reduce the backlog.

MODELS OF INCREASED COMPLEXITY

As one moves toward systems of greater complexity in any one of the preceding dimensions—order, inclusion of positive feedback, nonlinearity, and multiple loops—he finds that system behavior changes in major qualitative ways. The more complex systems do not merely show extensions of behavior seen in the simpler systems. For example, the way in which system behavior can change as the order of a negative feedback loop is increased is well known. A first-order, negative feedback loop can show only exponential approach to its equilibrium position. A second-order loop introduces the possibility of an entirely new mode of operation—it can show fluctuation either as a damped oscillation or as a growing instability. A third-order system is the simplest one that is capable of showing fluctuations superimposed on exponential growth. More · comprehensive models can represent important modes of behavior that are recognized in actual systems but which have previously resisted analysis.

Nonlinearity can introduce unexpected behavior in a system. A nonlinear system can be unstable for small disturbances but stable with sustained oscillation for larger disturbances. Nonlinearity can cause a feedback loop to shift its fundamental character between positive feedback and negative feedback. Nonlinearity can cause dominance to shift from one loop in a system to another. For example, the positive feedback characteristic of growth of a new product can be suppressed and dominance shifted to a negative feedback loop which produces stagnation in product growth.

Multiple feedback loops produce system behavior not seen in the simpler systems. For example, in a multiple loop system containing nonlinearities, the system behavior becomes surprisingly insensitive to change in values of a majority of the system parameters. In some system models, 90% of the parameters can be changed individually by factors of as much as five without substantially affecting the system behavior. Partly this is due to the dilution caused by a single parameter being immersed in a large number of others. But even more importantly, it

arises from the intrinsic propensity of a multiple-loop nonlinear system to defeat changes in the system policy statements. A substantial change can be made in a particular policy. However, the system warps in such a way that the incoming information to that decision point shifts to new values which, when processed through the new policy statement, yield approximately the old result. Time after time the manager encounters this in actual practice where a major policy change aimed at correcting a corporate problem seems to produce almost no result. Within a model of a complex system one discovers orderly processes to explain how the system defeats attempts to change its behavior. But there are exceptions, and some of the most useful insights to come from industrial dynamics show which policies in a system have enough leverage so that by changing them one can hope to alter system behavior.

Industrial Dynamics as a Theory of Structure

It may be helpful to distinguish two aspects of a system investigation—that relating to structure, and that relating to dynamic behavior. The two are intimately interwoven because it is the structure which produces the behavior. However, one's interest in the two aspects is sequential. There must be structure before there is a system that can have behavior. It is in the absence of a unifying structure that management education and practice have been particularly weak. Bruner, in his perceptive book on the educational process [1], discusses with great clarity in the first several chapters the importance of structure for expediting learning.

Industrial dynamics is a philosophy of structure in systems. It is also gradually becoming a body of principles that relate structure to behavior. The structure which is codified in industrial dynamics has its counterpart in other fields and other bodies of literature. It is in industrial dynamics, however, that the structure has probably been given its sharpest definition and its most rigorous application.

Structure is seen as having four significant hierarchies:

> The Closed Boundary
> The Feedback Loop as the Basic System Component
> Levels (the integrations, or accumulations, or states of a system)
> Rates (the policy statements, or activity variables, or flows)
> Goal
> Observed Conditions
> Discrepancy between Goal and Observed Conditions
> Desired Action

At the first hierarchy, industrial dynamics deals with closed systems. This means that the behavior modes of interest are generated within the boundaries of the defined system. It does not mean that one believes that nothing crosses the boundary in the actual system between the part inside the boundary and that outside. Instead, it means that what crosses the boundary is not essential in creating the causes and symptoms of the particular behavior being explored.

Within the boundary, the system is seen as one composed of feedback loops. Every decision exists within one or more such loops. The loops interact to produce the system behavior. A model of a system is formulated by starting with the loop structure, not by starting with components of loops.

At the third hierarchy, loops are themselves composed of two classes of variables, called "levels" and "rates" in the industrial dynamics terminology. Levels are the variables, generated by integra-

tion, which at any moment define the state of the system. Rates are the flow variables that depend on the levels and which are integrated to produce the levels. This concept of the level and rate variables appears with different terminology in other fields. The level and rate variables are a necessary and sufficient substructure within the feedback loop.

At the fourth hierarchy, the level variables are generated by the process of integration and have no significant subsubstructure except for the rates flowing into them. The rate variables do have an identifiable subsubstructure. The rate variables are the policy statements of the system and within each there is explicitly or implicitly a statement of the goal of that decision-making point in the system, the observed condition, a discrepancy based on the relationship of goal and observed condition, and the desired action that results from the discrepancy.

THE CLOSED BOUNDARY

The feedback loop is fundamentally a closed process in which a decision, acting through time delay and distortion, influences the state of the system which, after further time delay and distortion, is detected as the observed state of the system. The focus of attention is on how this loop operates. Forces may impinge on the loop from the outside, but our interest is in how the characteristics of the loop itself cause it to amplify or attenuate disturbances or produce growth. The boundary encloses those elements necessary to give the system its intrinsic character. The boundary implies dynamic independence in the sense that any variable crossing the boundary from the outside is not itself a function of the activity within the boundary. Anything on the outside is essentially random or independent of anything on the inside. There are no closed loops of significance to the particular study going from inside the system to outside of the boundary and returning.

Where to draw the boundary depends intimately on the specific system behavior being studied. If one's interest is restricted to a particular mode of behavior, the boundary must necessarily include those elements which generate the mode. Focusing attention on a different behavior mode may well produce substantial changes in the boundary. For an industrial system model, the boundary should include those aspects of the company, the market, the competitors, and the environment which are just sufficient to produce the behavior being investigated. Anything not essential to producing the mode of behavior under study should be left outside the system boundary. Perhaps the point can be illustrated by a recurring example in our Industrial Dynamics Summer Session Programs. The participants go through all of the stages of defining a system, building a model of that system, and examining the dynamic behavior through computer simulation. The price and supply instability in a commodity market is often taken as a vehicle. The problem starts at the simplest level of showing how the supply and consumption responses to price can cause a recurring imbalance between supply and demand. Because government price support programs play a conspicuous part in many commodities, Summer Session participants often feel compelled to incorporate such government activity in the first model. But such a step should be guided by answering this question: "Is the government activity *essential* to *creating* the fluctuation of price and supply, the fundamental cause of which is being explored?" Of course it is not. Commodity prices have been unstable long before there were government price support programs. Price support programs may be helpful or harmful, but they are not necessary in demonstrating the classic and fundamental processes of price and supply instability.

The concept of the closed boundary seems elementary yet it is apparently hard to grasp. It asserts that exogenous variables are not the key to the character of the system. Test inputs to a system may be used for study, but they are for the purpose of causing the system to divulge its inherent nature.

THE FEEDBACK LOOP

The feedback loop is seen as the basic structural element of systems. It is the context within which every decision is made. Every decision is responsive to the existing condition of the system and influences that condition. This is a statement equally true for the forces that control the flow of electricity into a capacitor, for the conscious decisions of the individual or the manager, and for the selective decisions of nature that fit species to the environment by the processes of evolution. The skilled industrial dynamics analyst operates through an iterative process that cycles through the four hierarchies of structure. Yet the focus is always on the higher levels, until these have been satisfactorily established, before devoting much attention to the lower levels. In other words, establishing the system boundary comes first. The second stage is the identification of feedback loops and should come before the detailing of the level and rate substructure. It is here that the man without a solid background in the dynamic nature of feedback systems is at his greatest disadvantage. He is not able to correlate observed symptoms and behavior with probable loop structures. He does not see in the history of a real life situation the evidence that points toward the significance of the different positive and negative feedback loops and their interactions.

LEVELS AND RATES

The industrial dynamics structure recognizes two classes of fundamental system variables as being necessary and sufficient. (The auxiliary equations are algebraically part of the rate equations. The first-order smoothing equations can be decomposed into a simple level equation and two rate equations.) The level equations at any moment in time describe the condition or state of the system. The level variables carry the continuity of the system from the present toward the future and provide the information on which rates of flow are based. The rate variables are the activity or flow variables. The rates change the values of the levels. The level equations are integrations which accumulate the effects of the rates. The rate equations are algebraic expressions without reference to time.

The rate and level concepts are found in the literature of many fields. In economics, the levels are often referred to as stocks and the rates as flows or activity. In engineering feedback systems the "state variable approach" shows increasing prominence. Some quotations from engineering convey the same ideas that are associated with the industrial dynamics level variables. "The state variable approach aids conceptual thinking about these problems, and nonlinear system problems as well. Furthermore, it provides a unifying basis for thinking about linear and nonlinear problems . . . the state of the network is related to the memory of the network . . . heuristically, the state of a system separates the future from the past, so that the state contains all the relevant information concerning the past history of the system required to determine the response for any input . . . the manner in which a system reaches a present state does not affect the future output. The present state of a system and the present and future inputs to a system uniquely determine the present and future outputs . . . the outputs of the integrators in the simulation diagram are used as the components of the state vector . . .

although the outputs of the integrators in the simulation diagram form a natural state vector, these variables may not be physically measurable in a system," [2, Chapter 5].

In business, the financial accounting statement implicitly recognizes level and rate variables by separating these onto the balance sheet and the profit and loss statement. The balance sheet gives the present financial condition or state of the system as it has been created by accumulating or integrating the past rates of flow. The profit and loss variables (if one overlooks the fact that they do not represent instantaneous values but are instead averages over some period of time) are the rates of flow which cause the level variables in the balance sheet to change.

The same concept of level and rate variables, cast in a different terminology, can be found in the field of psychology where we might quote from the foreword by Cartwright to a book of papers by Lewin. "The most fundamental construct for Lewin is, of course, that of 'field.' All behavior (including action, thinking, wishing, striving, valuing, achieving, *etc.*) is conceived of as a change of some state of a field in a given unit of time . . . in treating individual psychology, the field with which the scientists must deal is the 'life space' of the individual . . . it is the task of the scientist to develop constructs and techniques of observation and measurement adequate to characterize the properties of any given life space at any given time and to state the laws governing changes of these properties . . . Lewin's assertion that the only determinants of behavior at a given time are the properties of the field at the same time has caused more controversy than any of his other systematic principles. This principle asserts that the life space endures through time, is modified by events, and is a product of history, *but only the contemporaneous system can have effects at any time,"* [11, Foreword]. The field or life space of Lewin seems clearly to correspond to the level variables which we here use. The "behavior" and the "laws governing changes of these properties" correspond to the rate variables.

POLICY SUBSUBSTRUCTURE

The rate equations are the policy statements in a system. There are the rules whereby the state of the system determines action. A policy statement is seen as having four components. The first is the goal of the decision-making process. It is the objective toward which this part of the system is striving. In the very broad sense used here, physical processes have goals just as do individuals in their decision making.[2] Second, the policy specifies certain information inputs on which the decision-making process is based. These are the apparent states of the system. Apparent state must be distinguished from true state. It is only the *available* information which governs a decision. A true system state may be delayed, distorted, biased, depreciated, and contaminated before making its appearance at the decision point as an apparent state. Both true and apparent states are system levels. Third, the policy describes a process for determining the discrepancy between goal and observed condition. Fourth, the policy defines a desired action which will result from the discrepancy. The preceding structure of a policy has been discussed in more detail elsewhere, [3, Chapter 10].

COMMENTS ON STRUCTURE

Some persons have criticized the industrial dynamics structure as being stylized or naive or oversimplified. Some seem to feel that the system concepts have been adjusted to fit the DYNAMO compiler rather than *vice versa*. We believe that the structure will come to be recognized as having simple elegance, universality, and a fundamental character common to a very broad range of systems running from physical devices through medicine and psychology to social and ecological systems.

Once one has come to have confidence in the generality of a system structure, that structure is a tremendous aid to organizing knowledge in a particular situation. One organizes knowledge for a purpose. The purpose may be to explain and perhaps to alter some specific mode of behavior. Without a purpose or objective there is no basis for defining a system. But once this objective is clear, he can then deal in terms of the closed boundary concept. Attempting to define the boundary focuses attention on what must be included to generate the symptoms and behavior mode of the system. Definition of the boundary is no doubt done while perceiving the next level of structure dealing with feedback loops. As the loops are defined, these become the paths through the real-life system which are to be represented in the specific model of that system. The loops represent the cross-sections out of reality which are to be recognized as important for the purposes of the particular study.

After establishing the boundary and the feedback loops, one begins to sort system variables into levels and rates. All variables that define the state of the system are levels and will be represented as integrations (first-order difference equations). All variables that define activity will be algebraic and belong to the class of rate equations. Levels determine rates, and

---

[2] The float and valve in a toilet tank have the goal of keeping the tank full. An identical conceptual structure describes a pail of water with a hole—the outflow (action) depends on the difference (discrepancy) between the water level (apparent condition) and the water level at the hole (the goal).

rates generate levels. Any path through a system structure will necessarily encounter alternating level and rate variables. The subsubstructure within a rate or policy statement focuses attention on the concepts which must be incorporated.

After one has practice in its use, a formal, dependable, and general structure reduces by as much as two orders of magnitude the time necessary to establish the significant relationships that are buried within the conflicting, inadequate, and irrelevant information found in an actual situation.

It is perhaps unnecessary to point out that an industrial dynamics structuring has almost no relationship to the normal corporate organization chart. The dynamic system structure deals with information flows and decision points that control specific action streams. The decision stream at one particular policy point in the system may represent contributions from a number of persons or levels in the actual organization. Conversely, any particular person is likely to be a part of several different decision points controlling quite different flow rates.

The levels in an industrial dynamics model are cast in terms of first-order difference equations. Because the solution interval is made sufficiently short, this is entirely equivalent to a system of integrations. One might comment then on the choice between a system of equations cast in the form of integrations versus a system of differential equations. Engineering systems are almost universally defined in terms of differential equations. But this seems artificial. It tends to focus attention on the wrong direction of causality. For example, if one is filling a tank from a garden hose, our perception of reality suggests thinking of the water in the tank as the integral (accumulation) of the stream from the hose. The alternate statement, built around differentiation rather than integration, would define the water

flow rate from the hose in terms of the derivative of water level in the tank. This derivative formulation comes close to implying that the water flows from the hose *because of* the change in water level. The differential equation formulation tends to obscure the direction of causality in systems.

One can go a step further in questioning the differential equation description of a system and call attention to the fact that nowhere in nature does the process of differentiation take place. No instrument measures derivatives. Devices which nominally measure rates of flow in fact measure average rates over some time span and operate on principles that involve integration. When a physical solution to a differential equation in engineering is to be obtained, as on a differential analyzer, the equation is first integrated enough times to eliminate derivatives. "Differential analyzer" is a misnomer; the machine is assembled from integrators.

In teaching system dynamics we have found it much easier and much more natural to the student to deal exclusively with the processes of integration and to make no reference to differentiation. Differentiation is seen as a mathematical artificiality which does not have a real life counterpart in the systems being represented.

The Task Ahead

The reader is, of course, correct if he observes that the available literature and educational materials do very little to help him achieve the understanding of systems implied by the preceding sections. The industrial dynamics literature suggests the promise of advantages which may accrue from a better understanding of systems, but it does not adequately convey the essential mathematics of the field, nor expose the principles which should guide judgment in modeling of systems, nor does it provide an adequate number of examples to be used as guides in system structuring.

If system structure and dynamic behavior are to form a thread that runs through a management education and integrates the functional areas into a cohesive whole, several gaps must be filled. There must be an appropriate treatment of the mathematics of system dynamics. There should be examples of the system structures that generate some of the principal modes of behavior seen in corporate and economic systems. There should be bridging articles to show how system concepts can be applied in the functional areas and to management policy.

MATHEMATICS OF FEEDBACK SYSTEMS

There are now numerous books on the mathematics of feedback systems, but most of these concentrate on obtaining analytical solutions. For this reason the mathematical techniques are pressed to the absolute limit. Even so, the systems dealt with are too simple to be of much managerial interest. While concentrating on the mathematical frontier, the existing treatments do not adequately stress the simple concepts of dynamic behavior with a primary aim of improving the individual's intuitive sense of how feedback systems function. At MIT we are now embarking on an interpretation of the existing mathematics to simplify, to expose more clearly the concepts, and to make the material a base from which intuitive judgments and simulation studies can be extended.

PRINCIPLES OF FEEDBACK BEHAVIOR

Besides a mathematical treatment of systems, there seems to be a need for a descriptive treatment which verbally identifies principles and illustrates these by examples. Such a treatment would depend heavily on simple problems and ex-

ercises aimed at making the concepts and the techniques part of the working skills of the student. The author is now writing such a book with an accompanying workbook of exercises.

SYSTEM EXAMPLES

A person applying the industrial dynamics approach to actual corporate problems seems to do so by drawing heavily on his mental library of the systems which he has previously studied. If others are to be able to do the same, such libraries of examples must be put in orderly written form. Such a series of structures would identify those relationships which are found repeatedly in industry. [References 8, 12, and 13 suggest the nature of this approach.] Such a treatment of systems should concentrate on the minimum structure necessary to create a particular mode of behavior. Along with such an identified structure would be presented the ensemble of data which in the actual situation indicates that the particular subsystem is apt to be dominant. Historical data are often decisive in distinguishing between the possible subsystems that might be causing a corporate difficulty.

BRIDGING ARTICLES

A series of articles is necessary to show how system structuring can be brought to bear on the problems that manifest themselves in various functional areas of management. Difficulties that appear in one functional area are apt to be caused by a system that cuts through several functional areas. Such articles would create ties between different fields which now are too highly compartmentalized.

MANAGEMENT EDUCATION

Management education has been without a foundation of theory to serve the function that physics provides to the technological professions. Although many academic programs in management treat economics as a discipline underlying management, we might better see both management and economics as systems having the same conceptual structure and exhibiting similar kinds of dynamic behavior. They differ in scale but not necessarily in nature or essential complexity. The physical size or scope of a system has but little to do with the complexity of the model necessary to represent that system adequately. The bigger the system, the greater can be the degree of aggregation. A model of an economy need not contain all component companies. A model of a company does not represent each person. A model of human behavior would not reach to the individual cell. A model of dynamics of a cell would aggregate to a much higher level than individual atoms and most molecules. In fact, the models needed in each of these systems would probably be of about the same complexity.

The nonlinear, multiple, feedback loop structuring of systems with associated dynamic principles should grow into a foundation and central core to unify management education. The same approach to organizing relationships should serve in each functional area, in economics, and in psychology. Linking between the areas would then become easy if they were cast in a common underlying structure.

As management education moves toward a greater emphasis on systems, the mathematical threads running through the academic material will change. The future will show less concentration on statistics and matrix algebra and more on the continuous variables of causal systems. There is a common foundation beneath statistics and the mathematics of continuous processes, but the two branches of mathematics seem to produce very different attitudes in students (or the paths are followed by students who previously had developed different attitudes). The branch of mathematics dealing with random events seems to be associated with a view of the world as being capricious and beyond control. The mathematical branch through differential equations (or the preferred integral formulation) emphasizes the cause-and-effect relationships and supports the attitude of an environment that can be altered and controlled. Statistics seems to concentrate on the deviation of processes from the mean, with insufficient attention to the ways of changing the mean. The approach through continuous variables lays first emphasis on the causal structure that controls the mean and, when this is understood, adds randomness to determine the influence of uncertainty on the system.

Industrial dynamics has more in common with the case study approach than with most other methods in management education. But it goes further than discussion of a case. Building a model of a process enforces more disciplined thought than does mere discussion, just as a written description usually leads to more careful thought than does a conversation. So model building leads to a better considered and more precise statement of the system description. After a model has been formulated, model simulation shows whether or not the agreed component assumptions can lead to the expected behavior. The simulation result is often not as expected. The degree to which the model behaves like the actual system that is being modeled is one measure of model validity. This check is never achieved in a mere case discussion of a management system problem.

Industrial dynamics should help fill in the management part of management education. Now much of management education serves the interests of the staff advisor but not of the line manager. The manager's viewpoint has traditionally been reserved for a policy course taken usually at the end as a capstone to a management education. But systems thinking and the ability to deal with dynamic interactions takes much longer to learn than the facts of the functional areas. In response to the system challenge, we should expect to see a core being developed through the entire management curriculum. This core will be a new ensemble of subjects that deal with the mathematics of systems, the dynamic principles of systems, the conversion of experience and descriptive knowledge to a precise structured form, policy design through simulation experiments, coordination of model systems and case discussions, and a policy course that builds descriptively and intuitively beyond a foundation of policy studies in the form of dynamic models.

Exploration of system dynamics by way of more comprehensive models is opening the door to a new understanding of feedback processes in social systems. The future will no doubt show that we now know only a fragment of what we need to learn about the principles, theory, and behavior modes of feedback structures.

References

1. Bruner, Jerome S., *The Process of Education,* Harvard University Press, 1960.
2. DeRusso, Paul M., Rob J. Roy and Charles M. Close, *State Variables for Engineers,* John Wiley & Sons, Inc., 1965.
3. Forrester, Jay W., *Industrial Dynamics,* The M.I.T. Press, 1961.
4. ———, "Modeling the Dynamic Processes of Corporate Growth," *Proceedings of the IBM Scientific Computing Symposium,* December 7–9, 1964. pp. 23–42.
5. ———, "The Structure Underlying Management Processes," *Proceedings of the 24th Annual Meeting of the Academy of Management,* December 28–30, 1964. pp. 58–68.
6. ———, "A New Avenue to Management," *Technology Review,* Vol. LXVI, Number 3, January, 1964.
7. ———, "Common Foundations Underlying Engineering and Management," IEEE *Spectrum,* September, 1964. pp. 66–77.
8. ———, "Modeling of Market and Company Interactions," *Proceedings of the American Marketing Association,* August 31–September 3, 1965.
9. Jarmain, W. Edwin, editor, *Problems in Industrial Dynamics,* Cambridge, The M.I.T. Press, 1963.
10. Kovach, Ladis D., "Life Can Be So Nonlinear," *American Scientist,* Vol. 48, No. 2, pp. 218–225 (June 1960), published by the Society of the Sigma Xi.
11. Lewin, Kurt, edited by Cartwright, Dorwin, *Field Theory in Social Science,* Harper, 1951.
12. Nord, Ole C., *Growth of a Product: Effects of Capacity-Acquisition Policies,* Cambridge, The M.I.T. Press, 1963.
13. Packer, David W., *Resource Acquisition in Corporate Growth,* Cambridge, The M.I.T. Press, 1964.
14. Roberts, Edward B., *The Dynamics of Research and Development,* New York, Harper and Row, Publishers, Inc., 1964.
    For a bibliography on industrial dynamics see the following:
15. ———, "New Directions in Industrial Dynamics," *Industrial Management Review,* Vol. 6, No. 1, Fall 1964, Alfred P. Sloan School of Management, M.I.T.

41. Management Development: A Systems View

PAUL S. GREENLAW

Before discussing managerial development in systems terms, it will be useful to present a systems view of the manager's role as an organizational member. Central to such a conception are two basic notions. The first of these is that the basic activity performed by the manager in any organization is that of decision making. Developing organizational policies, rules, procedures and methods, handling human problems, organization structuring, communicating information to subordinates— all involve managerial decision making in one way or another.

The second notion of central interest to our discussion is that his managerial decision-making process takes place within an organizational information-decision system. The organization, viewed as such a system, is comprised of six different kinds of systems *elements*: input, transformation, output, feedback, memory, and control. Let us now examine briefly the manager's role in the organization in terms of each of these.

What the manager essentially does as a decision maker is to transform information relative to his operations into specified courses of action to be taken by himself and/or other members of the organization. For example, when a first line production supervisor observes one of his men violating the plant's no smoking rule, he may decide to discipline the man. In

systems terms, this decision represents the *transformation* of an informational *input* (knowledge of the rule violation) by the supervisor into a performance *output* (the disciplinary action undertaken).

Two further observations are in order concerning the nature of system inputs and outputs. First, many elements of organizational behavior may be considered as representing either inputs or outputs, depending upon the vantage point from which they are viewed. Looking at the events described in the previous illustration from the point of view of the disciplined subordinate, rather than his supervisor, for example:

1. The rule violation would be considered as a performance output, and
2. The supervisor's communication of his disciplinary decision would represent an informational input to the subordinate.

What this observation points up is that the total organizational system is, in effect, comprised of a number of interdependent sub-systems (and sub-sub-systems), with the outputs of some serving as inputs to others. Whether one wishes to consider the individual members of an organization as constituting its sub-systems (as above); to view the organization's departments as sub-systems, and their members as sub-sub-systems; or to

Reprinted from *Personnel Journal,* Vol. 43, No. 4 (April, 1964), pp. 205–211, with permission of the publisher. Paul S. Greenlaw is Professor of Management, College of Business Administration, Pennsylvania State University.

focus attention on still other sub-organizational elements, will depend upon the purposes of his analysis.

Second, the input elements of the organizational system (or any of its sub-systems) may assume any one of at least four different forms:

1. A message communicated orally to a member of the organization,

2. A message communicated in written form to a member of the organization,

3. Human behavior observed by an organizational member—e.g., the rule violation in our above example, or

4. A non-human event or process observed by an organizational member, as when a foreman sees that a machine in his department has broken down.

All of these input types represent messages which may help provide the basis for making managerial decision transformations.

The manager's decision transformations also influence and are influenced by the other three types of systems elements indicated previously. In making decisions, the manager:

1. Draws on information about previous happenings as stored either (a) in his own human memory, or (b) in some external memory system—e.g., organizational data recorded in files, on punched cards, etc.,

2. Receives *feedback* as to the appropriateness of his behavior aimed at its improvement in the future, as when a manager's performance is appraised by his superior, and

3. Is guided by certain *control* elements within the organizational system. The control elements include those policies, objectives, models, procedures, decision rules, etc., which specify for the manager what shall be done with the input, memory and feedback in order to produce the output required.

These six types of systems elements and some of their interrelationships with respect to the managerial decision-making process are illustrated in Figure 1.

Drawing on the above discussion, several further observations are now in order to provide a basis for an examination of management development in systems terms. First, a major value of the systems approach is that it permits us to sharpen our analyis of the decision making process by breaking it down into its basic elements and examining each in relationship to the others rather than simply viewing this process as a gross phenomenon. Second, the ultimate objective of all managerial endeavor, including management development efforts, ought to be, in systems terms, that of improving the quality of the organization's *outputs*—i.e., arriving at more effective courses of action in terms of attaining organizational objectives. Third, the quality of any organizational output is conditioned by the quality of all other relevant systems elements—input, memory, transformation, control and feedback—and, hence if any of these other elements is inadequate, output too, will not be adequate. For example, some courses of action chosen by a manager may be ineffective largely because his *transformational abilities* are weak—i.e., he lacks skill in making decisions. In other cases, however, inadequate output may be generated primarily because the manager is not able to obtain the information needed to make an effective decision, or because the courses of action which he is permitted to choose are circumscribed by poorly programmed control elements—policies, rules, procedures or methods. Fourth, from the above it follows that if managerial development efforts are to be effective in improving the quality of the outputs produced by the manager as a decision maker, they must take into consideration *all* systems elements relevant to his performance within the organization.

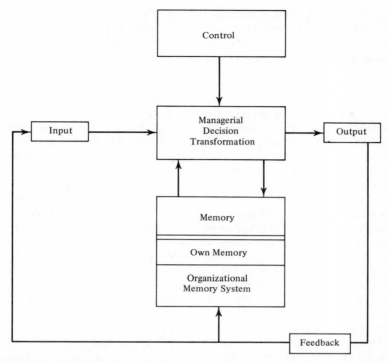

Figure 1. *Elements in the Organizational Information—Decision System.*

Let us now turn to the question: "To what extent have those responsible for managerial training and development taken such a systems view?"

Management Development: A Systems View

In attempting to answer this question, it will not be possible to give specific consideration to all of the many different kinds of managerial training and development programs being carried out by business (and other) organizations. Rather, the ensuing discussion will center around some observations about one major type of management development approach in wide use today—off the job training. Included in this category are in-company conferences, university executive development programs, and institutes and seminars sponsored by professional associations. Although the objectives and content of different programs of this type vary considerably, all are similar in that they take the executive away from the organizational system in which he normally functions, and attempt to induce improvement in his managerial abilities in one way or another—utilizing such approaches as the lecture or discussion methods, case studies, role playing, business gaming, etc.

In terms of our system view, these off-the-job programs generally focus primary attention on further developing either the manager's own *memory element* and/or his *transformational skills*, both of which, of course, are interrelated facets of the same personality system. That is, the manager:

1. May be furnished with information which hopefully will be stored in his mind for future utilization in making decisions—e.g., being familiarized with the company's new contract with its union, or

2. May be provided in the training conference with some form of synthetic experience in actually transforming certain types of inputs into outputs—e.g., assuming the role of a supervisor in a mock performance appraisal interview, or playing a business game.

On the other hand, it would appear that in the design of many off-the-job training programs, inadequate consideration is given to the other systems elements which have an important bearing on the outputs of those managers whom the organization is attempting to develop—i.e., *organizational* memory, input, control and feedback. As a number of observers have noted, certain kinds of human relations problems in the business firm seem to occur more because of the existence of stress situations which are largely a function of organizational design—work flow inputs on the job, types of interaction patterns required, etc.—than because of any major inadequacies in the human skills of the organizational members so involved. For example:

1. Chapple and Sayles in their book *The Measure of Management* have cited a case in which repeated arguments between a firm's sales manager and credit manager although "interpreted by management as a clash of personalities," were basically due to the fact the flow of certain work in the organization "was divided into separate pieces on the basis of functional similarities." [1]

2. In his "Parable of the Spindle," Elias Porter has indicated how a number of human problems existing in a restaurant operation were largely overcome when through the introduction of a spindle, it was no longer necessary for waitresses to give their orders verbally to the cook. [2]

Yet in designing, and in deciding on which managers are to participate in, many so-called "human relations" courses in industry today, concern is often given only to the modification of the human skills (transformational abilities) of the manager, without consideration of the impact that such other organizational system elements may be having on his performance output. For example:

The training director of one industrial concern was asked by the firm's plant manager to recommend a human relations training program for an industrial engineer who apparently was experiencing some difficulties in "getting along" with some of his colleagues in certain types of situations. In the discussion which ensued, sole consideration was given to which available program could best help the engineer more fully develop his interpersonal skills. No attention at all was given to the possibility that his human skills might have been quite adequate, and that the problem which existed might have been due largely to stresses created by inadequacies in other systems elements relevant to his job—e.g., his being required to follow certain organizational rules and procedures (control elements) which made it necessary for him

---

[1] Eliot D. Chapple and Leonard R. Sayles, *The Measure of Management* (New York: McGraw-Hill Book Co., Inc., 1961), pp. 23, 25.

[2] Elias H. Porter, "The Parable of the Spindle," *Harvard Business Review,* 40 (May–June, 1962), 58–66. The spindle, upon which the waitresses could place their *written* orders helped relieve tensions in a number of ways. For example: (1) serving as a memory element, it obviated the cook's need to remember the orders given him by the waitresses, and (2) as a queuing device it relieved the waitresses from the necessity of standing in line in order to give their orders to the cook.

to create unnecessary problems for his colleagues.

Further, the question may be raised: "In light of the considerable difficulty usually encountered in attempting to change the individual's basic personality structure once he has reached adulthood, might not it often be easier to improve the manager's output by modifying the organizational inputs, feedback and controls which affect his performance, rather than his own memory system and transformational skills?" As Chapple and Sayles have pointed out, considerable attention to managerial development has been devoted to the so-called "conversion" approach,

changing people through efforts to modify their attitudes, values, and feelings, that is, by "working on their personalities" . . . individual personalities can be changed only with the greatest difficulty, if at all . . . with rare exception . . . the most efficient way of accomplishing change is to modify the organization itself: the technology, systems and procedures, layout, controls, and the positioning of individual personalities within the organizational structure.[3]

These observers suggest, for example that:

If Supervisor A has a tantrum whenever situation X occurs, his job can be changed so the behavior that is difficult for him is not required. It is unlikely that he will ever learn to tolerate situation X.[4]

Or, to restate this suggestion, in systems terms: if information input X is consistently transformed into an inappropriate emotionally traumatic behavioral output by Supervisor A, it is much easier to modify the input element than the transformation element.

One should, of course, not infer from this suggestion that all attempts to develop the manager's transformational skills be abandoned, for within the constraints of his personality structure, these skills may often be improved considerably. Moreover, it is obviously not always possible to restructure the organization's input, feedback, memory and control elements to suit the personalities of its members. Rather, the view just described simply suggests that in attempting to improve managerial output, all systems elements be considered with the question in mind: "Which elements may be most easily modified so as to meet organizational objectives?"

Another point that seems to be of importance in viewing management development efforts is that in many cases if the manager's transformational skills are to be improved so also must certain other systems elements be modified. Evidence suggests that managers exposed to off-the-job development may fail to apply the knowledge and skills learned in such training when they return to their own jobs largely because the changes which they attempt to make in their own behavior are *not supported* by their own supervisors.[5] For instance, a manager who comes to the conclusion, through exposure to a human relations course, that

---

[3] Chapple and Sayles, *op. cit.*, p. 191.

[4] *Ibid.*, p. 202.

[5] For example, in a study of the effects of training in two divisions of the Detroit Edison Company, "it was found that there had been a loss of ground in one division, which was more than compensated for by gain in the other. . . . The researchers found that in the division where progress had been made, the foremen were led by a higher management which supervised them very much in line with the principles developed in the course. On the other hand, in the division which lost ground, the foremen were under supervisors who directed them in a manner which was entirely out of harmony with the program." William F. Whyte, *Men at Work* (Homewood, Ill.: The Dorsey Press, Inc., and Richard D. Irwin, Inc., 1961), p. 12.

he ought to be more "permissive" in his leadership style may find that any attempts taken to these ends will be ridiculed by his own boss. Or, in systems terms, he may fail to modify his transformational skills largely because of inappropriate *feedback* from his supervisor rather than because of any major inadequacies in the training program inputs or in his willingness to try out new patterns of behavior.

In recognition of this need to modify the supervisory feedback element as well as the trainees' own memory and transformational and training program input elements, a number of companies have followed the approach of exposing their management groups to various forms of training "from the top down." In one manufacturing plant with which this author is familiar, for example, the plant manager and general foremen were given courses in creative thinking and employment interviewing before these programs were instituted for the first line supervisors. Having been exposed first themselves to the new skills and concepts taught, the general foremen seemed to be more receptive to and to give more support to attempts by their subordinates —the supervisors—in trying out new patterns of behavior on the job than when such an approach was not followed.

A Broader Role for the Training Director

Now that a number of observations have been made about off-the-job training programs in systems terms, some concluding observations about the role of

the training director with respect to these programs are in order.

In spite of the many millions of dollars being spent each year on off-the-job developmental programs, an uncomfortably large number of these efforts seem not to have been as successful as hoped in effecting significant improvements in managerial output. In some cases, this probably has been due more to the utilization of inappropriate educational methodologies than to anything else—e.g., employing the lecture method to try to improve the manager's interpersonal skills. In many other cases, however, even developmental programs based on sound learning theory have not enjoyed the success which their designers had intended.

A central thesis of this article is that the effectiveness of off-the-job training programs has in many cases been limited because their designers—by conceiving of their role primarily as *educators* interested in improving the manager's memory and transformational abilities—have not given adequate consideration to the impact of other systems elements on performance output. The systems view suggests that for more effective developmental efforts the training director must conceive of his role more broadly—both as an educator and as a systems analyst.[6] In doing so, he must focus attention on a number of questions such as those indicated in Figure 2, concerning the need and feasibility of improving all types of systems elements relative to managerial performance. Only in this way can those responsible for managerial development contribute significantly to the betterment of organizational output.

----

[6] It should be noted that such a broader view of organizational learning has been taken by such enterprises as the RAND Corporation and the System Development Corporation with respect to military-oriented training. For numerous references to this type of endeavor, see: Robert M. Gagne, ed., *Psychological Principles in System Development* (New York: Holt, Rinehart and Winston, 1962).

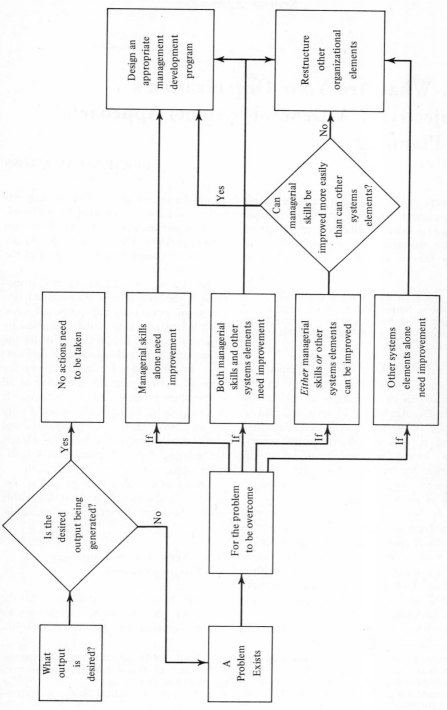

Figure 2. *Management Development: A Systems View.*

42. What Are Your Organization's Objectives? A General-Systems Approach to Planning

BERTRAM M. GROSS

There is nothing that managers and management theorists are more solidly agreed on than the vital role of objectives in the managing of organizations. The daily life of executives is full of such exhortations as:

'Let's plan where we want to go . . .'
'You'd better clarify your goals . . .'
'Get those fellows down (or up) there to understand what our (or their) purposes really are . . .'

Formal definitions of management invariably give central emphasis to the formulation or attainment of objectives. Peter Drucker's (1954) idea of "managing by objectives" gave expression to a rising current in administrative theory. Any serious discussion of planning, whether by business enterprises or government agencies, deals with the objectives of an organization.

Yet there is nothing better calculated to embarrass the average executive than the direct query: "Just what are your organization's objectives?" The typical reply is incomplete or tortured, given with a feeling of obvious discomfort. The more skillful response is apt to be a glib evasion or a glittering generality.

To some extent, of course, objectives cannot be openly stated. Confidential objectives cannot be revealed to outsiders. Tacit objectives may not bear discussion among insiders. The art of bluff and deception with respect to goals is part of the art of administration.

But the biggest reason for embarrassment is the lack of a well-developed language of organizational purposefulness. Such a language may best be supplied by a general-systems model that provides the framework for "general-systems accounting," or "managerial accounting" in the sense of a truly generalist approach to all major dimensions of an organization. It is now possible to set forth—even if only in suggestive form—a general-systems model that provides the basis for clearly formulating the performance and structural objectives of any organization.

Let us now deal with these points separately—and conclude with some realistic observations on the strategy of planning.

The Need for a Language of Purposefulness

Many managers are still too much the prisoners of outworn, single-purpose models erected by defunct economists,

Reprinted from *Human Relations*, Vol. 43, No. 4 (April, 1964), pp. 205–211, with permission from the publisher. Bertram M. Gross is Professor of Political Science at Maxwell Graduate School of Citizenship and Public Affairs, Syracuse University.
   Based on an address given before the Polish Association of Political Sciences, Warsaw, 22 April 1965.

engineers, and public administration experts. Although they know better, they are apt to pay verbal obeisance to some single purpose: profitability in the case of the business executive, efficiency in the case of the public executive.

If profitability is not the sole objective of a business—and even the more tradition-ridden economists will usually accept other objectives in the form of constraints or instrumental purposes—just what are these other types? If efficiency is not the only objective of a government agency—and most political scientists will maintain that it cannot be—what are the other categories? No adequate answers to these questions are provided by the traditional approaches to economics, business administration, or public administration. Most treatises on planning—for which purpose formulation is indispensable—catalogue purposes by such abstract and non-substantive categories as short-range and long-range, instrumental and strategic (or ultimate), general and specific. One book on planning sets forth thirteen dimensions without mentioning anything so mundane as profitability or efficiency (LeBreton & Henning, 1961). Indeed, in his initial writings on management by objectives, Drucker never came to grips with the great multiplicity of business objectives. In his more recent work Drucker (1964) deals with objectives in terms of three "result areas": product, distribution channels, and markets. But this hardly goes far enough to illuminate the complexities of purpose multiplicity.

Thus far, the most systematic approach to organizational purposes is provided by budget experts and accountants. A budget projection is a model that helps to specify the financial aspects of future performance. A balance sheet is a model that helps to specify objectives for future structure of assets and liabilities. Yet financial analysis—even when dignified by the misleading label "managerial accounting"—deals only with a narrow slice of real-life activities. Although it provides a way of reflecting many objectives, it cannot by itself deal with the substantive activities underlying monetary data. Indeed, concentration upon budgets has led many organizations to neglect technological and other problems that cannot be expressed in budgetary terms. Overconcentration on the enlargement of balance-sheet assets has led many companies to a dangerous neglect of human and organizational assets.

The great value of financial analysis is to provide a doorway through which one can enter the whole complex domain of organizational objectives. To explore this domain, however, one needs a model capable of dealing more fully with the multiple dimensions of an organization's performance and structure. To facilitate the development of purposefulness in each of an organization's subordinate units, the model should also be applicable to internal units. To help executives to deal with the complexities of their environment, it should also be applicable to external competitors or controllers.

The General-Systems Approach

As a result of the emerging work in systems analysis, it is now possible to meet these needs by developing a "general-systems model" of an organization. A general-systems model is one that brings together in an ordered fashion information on all dimensions of an organization. It integrates concepts from all relevant disciplines. It can help to expand financial planning to full-bodied planning in as many dimensions as may be relevant. With it, executives may move from financial accounting to "systems accounting." It can provide the basis for "managerial accounting" in the sense of the managerial use not only of financial data (which is the way the term has been recently used) but of all ideas and data needed to appraise the state of a system and guide it towards the attainment of desirable future system states.[1]

Before outlining a general-systems model, it is important to set aside the idea that a system is necessarily something that is fully predictable or tightly controlled. This impression is created whenever anyone tries to apply to a human organization the closed or non-human models used by physicists and engineers. A human organization is much more complicated.

Specifically, when viewed in general-systems terms, a formal organization (whether a business enterprise or a government agency) is

1. a man-resource system in space and time,
2. open, with various transactions between it and its environment,
3. characterized by internal and external relations of conflict as well as cooperation,
4. a system for developing and using power, with varying degrees of authority and responsibility, both within the organization and in the external environment,
5. a "feedback" system, with information on the results of past performance activities feeding back through multiple channels to influence future performance,
6. changing, with static concepts derived from dynamic concepts rather than serving as a preliminary to them,
7. complex, that is, containing many subsystems, being contained in larger systems, and being criss-crossed by overlapping systems,
8. loose, with many components that

may be imperfectly coordinated, partially autonomous, and only partially controllable,
9. only partially knowable, with many areas of uncertainty, with "black regions" as well as "black boxes" and with many variables that cannot be clearly defined and must be described in qualitative terms, and
10. subject to considerable uncertainty with respect to current information, future environmental conditions, and the consequences of its own actions.

The Performance-Structure Model

The starting-point of modern systems analysis is the input-output concept. The flow of inputs and outputs portrays the system's performance. To apply the output concept to a formal organziation, it is helpful to distinguish between two kinds of performance: producing outputs of services or goods and satisfying (or dissatisfying) various interests. To apply the input concept, a three-way breakdown is helpful: acquiring resources to be used as inputs, using inputs for investment in the system, and making efficient use of resources. In addition, we may note that organizational performance includes efforts to conform with certain behaviour codes and concepts of technical and administrative rationality.

These seven kinds of performance objective may be put together in the following proposition:

The performance of any organization or unit thereof consists of activities to (1) satisfy the varying interests of people and

---

[1] "General-systems theory" often refers to theories dealing broadly with similarities among all kinds of systems—from atoms and cells to personalities, formal organizations, and populations. In this context the term refers to a special application of general-systems theory to formal organizations—an application that deals not merely with a few aspects but generally with all aspects of formal organizations.

groups by (2) producing outputs of services or goods, (3) making efficient use of inputs relative to outputs, (4) investing in the system, (5) acquiring resources, and (6) doing all these things in a manner that conforms with various codes of behaviour and (7) varying conceptions of technical and administrative rationality.

In simplified form, the relations between these categories of performance may be visualized as follows:

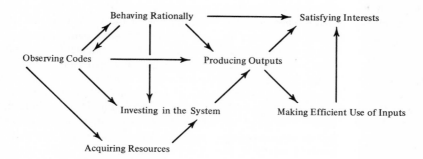

Let us now turn to system structure. The minimum elements in a machine system are certain physical components, including a "governor" (or "selector"), an "effector," a "detector," and lines of communication between them and the environment. For a formal organization these may be spelled out more specifically as subsystems in general, a central guidance subsystem, internal relations among the subsystems, and relations with the external environment. It is helpful at times to consider separately the people and the physical assets grouped together in the subsystems. It may also be helpful to give separate attention to the values held by individuals and the various subsystems.

These seven sets of structural objectives may be put together in the following proposition:

The structure of any organization or unit thereof consists of (1) people and (2) non-human resources, (3) grouped together in differentiated subsystems that (4) interrelate among themselves and (5) with the external environment, (6) and are subject to various values and (7) to such central guidance as may help to provide the capacity for future performance.

In the language of martix algebra, one can bring the two elements of system performance and system structure together into a 2×1 "nested" vector which may be called the "system state vector." Let P symbolize system performance and S system structure. Then the following sequence of vectors may symbolize changing system states over a period of time:

$$\begin{bmatrix} P \\ S \end{bmatrix}^1 \qquad \begin{bmatrix} P \\ S \end{bmatrix}^2 \qquad \ldots \begin{bmatrix} P \\ S \end{bmatrix}^n$$

The vector is "nested" because both the performance element and the structure element consist of seven subelements and are themselves 7×1 vectors. Each subelement, in turn, is a multidimensional matrix.

The performance vector, it should be noted, includes among its many components the basic elements in income statements and revenue-expenditure budgets. The structure vector includes all the assets (and claims against them) measured in a balance sheet. Indeed, the former may be regarded as a greatly enlarged performance budget, the latter a balance sheet that includes human and institutional assets as well as financial assets. The relations between the two are even closer than those between an income statement and a balance sheet. Almost any aspect of system performance will have some effect on system structure. Any important plans for future performance inevitably require significant changes in system structure. Changes in system structure, in turn, are invariably dependent upon some types of system performance. In everyday affairs, of course, executives often make the mistake of

—planning for major improvements in performance without giving attention to the structural prerequisites, and

—planning for major changes in structure (sometimes because of outworn or unduly abstract doctrines of formal organization) without considering their presumed connection with performance.

The skillful use of a performance-structure model may help to avoid these errors.[2]

The first elements in both structure and performance, let it be noted, are human: people and the satisfaction of people's interests. All the other elements and their many decisions—both financial and technological—are ways of thinking about people and their behaviour. An organization's plans for the future are always plans made by people for people—for their future behaviour and for their future relations with resources and other people. Financial and technological planners may easily lose sight of these human elements. Another virtue of general-systems analy-

sis, therefore, is that it helps to bring together the "soft" information of human relations people with the "hard" data of accountants and engineers.

Performance Objectives

Any one of the seven elements of system performance, as baldly stated above, may be used in a statement of "where we want to go" or a criterion of "doing an effective job." But none of them is meaningful unless broken down into its subelements. When this is done, indeed, the basic subelements may be rearranged in many ways. There is no magic in any one ordering.

Within the present space limits I shall merely touch upon some of the major dimensions of each element and subelement. Additional details are available in *The Managing of Organizations* (Gross, 1964, Pt. V, Chs. 20–29).

Some random illustrations for both an organization (an aircraft company) and a unit thereof (its personnel office) are provided in Table 1. Tables 2 and 3 provide more detailed illustrations in two areas of special complexity: output objectives and input-output objectives. In these tables "goal" refers to a specific type of subelement and "norm" to a more specific formulation of a goal. To save space, reference to the tables will not be made in the text.

1. SATISFYING INTERESTS

Although the satisfaction of human interests is the highest purpose of any organization, interest-satisfaction objectives (often referred to as *benefits, welfare,*

---

[2] This performance-structure model represents a major adaptation of what has long been known as "structural-functional" analysis. It is more dynamic than traditional structural-functional analysis, however, since it starts with action (performance) and works back to structure as the more regularized aspect of action. Also, instead of assuming a single function such as "system maintenance," it broadens the idea of function to cover the major dimensions of performance.

utility, value, or *payoff*) are the most difficult to formulate.

First of all, such objectives always involve a multiplicity of parties at interest
—or "interested." These include the
members of the organization, the organization's "clientele network," and other
external groups and individuals. They
vary considerably in visibility and in the
extent to which their interests are affected
by an organization's performance.

Second, their interests are usually multiple, often hard to identify, always divergent, and sometimes sharply conflicting.
In psychological terms these interests may
be described in terms of the human needs
for security, belonging, status, prestige,
power, and self-development. Many of
these needs are expressed in terms of services and goods designed to meet them
and the monetary income which, in a
market economy, is necessary to provide
such services and goods. They may also
be expressed in terms of the needs for
both employment and leisure. The terms
"public interest" or "national interest" are
ways of referring to the great multiplicity
of interests that many people and groups
throughout a society have in common.
There are always conflicting views concerning the nature of "public interests."

Third, is is immensely difficult to specify the extent of satisfactions desired or
attained. Satisfactions themselves are
locked in the hearts and minds of the
people whose interests are presumed to
be satisfied. They are inextricably associated with dissatisfactions and frustration. The most we can do is use certain
indirect indicators expressed in terms of
the observable behaviour of the behaviour
of "interesteds." Two of the most immediate forms of behaviour are the choices
they make (in participating in the organization or using its product) and money
they are willing to pay (in the form of
consumer purchases, taxes, or dues).
Other indicators are their expressed opin-

ions (complaints or praise) and their subsequent behaviour as a presumed result of
the satisfactions obtained. Such indicators
with respect to clientele satisfactions provide the most important measures of output quality.

2. PRODUCING OUTPUT

Output production objectives are much
easier to formulate. They may best be
expressed in terms of an "output mix" listing the types of services or goods supplied
to the organization's (or unit's) clientele.
For each type quality and quantity objectives may then be set.

Yet there are at least five major problems in this area. First of all, output quality has many dimensions. As already indicated, clientele satisfaction, the most
important dimension of output quality, is
exceedingly difficult to measure. Less direct indicators—such as product specifications, production processes, and the
quality of input factors—may also be
needed. The objective of higher quality
often conflicts with the objective of higher
quantity.

Second, although monetary aggregates
are the only way of measuring total output, they must be used with considerable
care. Important distinctions may be
needed between the total value of output
and value added, between marginal value
and total or average value, between different ways of allocating value to time
periods. For comparisons over time, adjustments for price changes may be
needed; for international comparisons,
adjustments in the value of international
currencies.

Third, in the case of services and goods
that are not sold (and this includes most
of the intermediate output within business
organizations) the only direct measure of
output quantity is physical units. In most
instances this means that there is no common denominator for the total quantity
of different kinds of unit. All that can be

TABLE 1

Performance Objectives: Some General Illustrations

Performance Objectives	Aircraft Company — Goals	Norms	Personnel Unit — Goals	Norms
1. Satisfying Interests				
(a) Members	Higher morale	Reducing labour turnover to 6%	Professional prestige	Leadership in professional organizations
(b) Clientele network	Meeting airlines' needs	5% rise in total sales / Maintaining 3% yield on common stock	Meeting needs of line	Fewer complaints
(c) Others	Investors		Serving all employees	Reducing labour turnover to 10%
2. Producing Output				
(a) Output mix	Adding short-range jets	End-product production schedule	New management training programme	End-product services
(b) Quantity	Increased market penetration	15% of industry sales	Greater coverage	150 'trainees' per year
(c) Quality	Safer planes	Wing improvements	Better designed courses	Better consultants
(d) Output flow	Work-flow	Detailed schedules	Work-flow	Detailed schedules
3. Making Efficient Use of Inputs				
(a) Profitability	Higher profits on net worth (or total assets)	20% on net worth	—	—
(b) Costs per unit	Lower engine costs	8% reduction	Total costs per trainee	$200 per week
(c) Partial input ratios	More output per man-hour	10% increase	Teacher costs	$150 per training-hour
(d) Portion of potential used	Reducing idle equipment-time	5% reduction	Full participation in training programme	No vacancies
4. Investing in the Organization				
(a) Hard goods	Re-equipment programme	Detailed specifications	New files	No vacancies
(b) People	Management training programme	50 trainees per year	'Retooling' of old-timers	Participation in 'refresher' courses
(c) Internal units	Reorganization of personnel unit	Higher status for training section	Maintenance of existing organization	Maintaining present status for training section
(d) External relations	More support in Congress	Support by specific senators	More support from 'line' executives	Support by specific executives
5. Acquiring Resources				
(a) Money	More equity	Selling securities	Larger budget	5% increase
(b) People	Better managers	Recruitment programme	More professional staff	Recruitment programme
(c) Goods	New machines	Procurement programme	New files	Procurement programme
6. Observing Codes				
(a) External codes	Obeying anti-trust laws	Competition within limits	Living within budgets	Controls on commitments
(b) Internal codes	Obeying company regs.	Control of deviations	Loyalty to unit	Social exclusiveness
7. Behaving Rationally				
(a) Technical rationality	Aeronautical research	Specific studies	Personnel research	Specific studies
(b) Administrative rationality	Formal reorganization	More decentralization	More 'democracy'	Monthly staff meetings

Output Performance Objectives: Some Detailed Illustrations

Output Production Objectives	Aircraft Company Goals	Aircraft Company Norms	Personnel Unit Goals	Personnel Unit Norms
A. Output Mix	Continued output of long-range jets / New short-range jet / Parts production / Research for government / Advisory services for users	Detailed production schedule	Maintaining personnel records / Recruitment services / Classification system / Job analysis and evaluation / Training programme	Operating programme
B. Output Quality				
1. Client satisfactions				
(a) Presumed results	Planes: Faster, safer flights	Specific speed and safety standards	Training programme: Better managers	Subsequent performance of trainees
(b) Choices made	Popularity among passengers	Prosperity of airline customers	Popularity of programme	Backlog of applications
(c) Payments given	Rising volume of airline sales	15% of industry sales	Budgets allocated	Specific budget figures
(d) Opinions expressed	Low complaint level	Decline in pilots' complaints	Trainees' opinions	Specific statements
2. Product characteristics	Conformance with specifications	Detailed specifications	Improved curriculum	Emphasis on decision-making skills
3. Production processes	Careful testing	Specific tests	Improved teaching methods	Use of field studies
4. Input quality	Outstanding productive personnel	Acquiring best designers	Outstanding teachers	Acquiring teachers of high repute
C. Output Quality				
1. Monetary value				
(a) Total sales value	Planes: 15% of industry sales	X million dollars	—	—
(b) Value added	Lower proportion of value added with more subcontracting	$\dfrac{X}{3}$	—	—
(c) Value added adjusted for price changes	20% beyond 1960	$\dfrac{X \cdot 9}{3}$ (price deflator)	—	—
(d) Imputed value of nonmarketed output	Advisory services: Input value	Specific cost figures	Input value	Specific cost figures
2. Physical volume	Planes: Number to be produced / Advisory services:	Detailed production schedule	Training programme:	—
(a) Tangible units		Specific figures		Specific figures
(b) Surrogates for intangible services				
(i) clients	More clients		More trainees	
(ii) duration	Longer periods		Longer courses	
(iii) intermediate or subsequent products	Memoranda produced		Field studies undertaken	
(iv) input value	Total costs		Total costs	

TABLE 3

Input-Output Performance Objectives: Some Detailed Illustrations

Efficiency (Input-Output) Objectives	Aircraft Company		Personnel Unit	
	Goals	*Norms*	*Goals*	*Norms*
A. Profitabilty				
1. Unit profits	Short-range jet: higher profits with rising volume	Specific figures	—	—
2. Total profits				
Before taxes	Higher profits	10% increase	—	—
After taxes	Higher profits	12% increase	—	—
Total profits	Lower (with replacement of debt by equality)	10% decrease	—	—
3. Net worth	Higher	10% increase	—	—
4. Total assets	Lower (with higher volume of sales)	10% decrease	—	—
5. Sales				
B. Costs per Unit	New short-range jets: Declining total costs with rising volume	10% decline per unit over first year	Training programme: Rising costs with longer duration and higher quality	20% more per trainee
C. Partial Input-Output Relations				
1. Labour-output ratios				
(a) Labour time	For a specific output unit: More output per direct man-hour	10% increase	More teacher-time per trainee	10% more per trainee
(b) Labour cost	No increase in direct costs	Same	Higher teacher fees	20% more per trainee
	Small increase in direct plus indirect labour costs	5% increase	Higher overhead costs	5% increase
(c) Output per $1 of labour cost	Lower total value	−6%	—	—
	Lower added value	−29%		
2. Capital-output ratio	For specific machines: fuller use of rated capacity	Specific figures	Low-cost residential facilities	Specific figures
D. Portion of Output Potential Used				
1. Waste	Less scrap material	Specific figures	Less waste	Elimination of unnecessary paperwork
	Better utilization of scrap	Reaching 80% in 2 shifts	Fuller use of computers (on personnel records)	Reaching 35% of capacity
	Fuller use of capacity			
2. Gap between actual and potential	Higher fulfilment of profit potential	8% on total assets	Higher fulfilment of service potential	Specific data on quality and quantity of end-products

TABLE 4

Structural Objectives: Some General Illustrations

Structural Objectives	Aircraft Company Goals	Norms	Personnel Unit Goals	Norms
1. People				
(a) Types	Fewer 'blue-collars'	Specific manning tables	More professionals	Specific manning tables
(b) Quantity	No overall increase	Specific manning tables	Larger staff	4 new positions
(c) Quality	Better-educated staff	90% college graduates above supervisory level	Better educational background	All college graduates with a few PhDs
2. Non-human resources				
(a) Physical assets	More modern plant	Specific re-equipment programme	More adequate space	5 more rooms
(b) Monetary assets	More liquid position	2:1 current liability ratio	Larger reserves	More transferable budget items
(c) Claims against assets	Higher ratio of equity to long-term debt	$10 million equity increase	—	—
3. Subsystems				
(a) Units	Improved divisional structure	Stronger jet-plane divisions	Improved internal structure	Stronger training group
(b) Committees	Improved committee structure	Inter-divisional task force on new jets	Better representation on committees	Participation in jet-plane task force
4. Subsystem relations				
(a) Cooperation-conflict	Settlement of inter-divisional disputes	Compromise on jet-plane design	Settlement of inter-unit disputes	Compromise on location of training division
(b) Hierarchy	Stronger central control	Fewer levels	Stronger unit position	Direct line to top manager
(c) Polyarchy	Dispersed responsibility	New clearance procedures	Dispersed responsibility	New clearance procedures
(d) Communication	Better communication among divisions	Weekly paper	Better communication with line executives	Liaison units in line divisions
5. External relations				
(a) Clients and suppliers	Better distribution channels for parts	Relations with specific distributors	More support from line executives	Supported by specific executives
(b) Controllers and controllees	More support in Congress	Support by specific Senators	More support by budget unit	Support for 4 new positions
(c) Associates and adversaries	Limits on competition	'Understandings' on division of markets	Rivalry with budget unit	Less budget opposition to training programme funds
6. Values				
(a) Internal-external orientation	Public service	Safer planes	Professionalism in personnel management	Advancement of unit's interests
(b) Conformity and individualism	Initiative	Proposing of company policy by divisions	Loyalty to unit	Subordination of external interests
(c) Activism-passivity	Progress	Faster planes	Progress	All-round improvement
7. System management				
(a) Higher level	More 'professional' approach	Specific planning and control methods	More 'human' approach	More emphasis on personnel management
(b) Lower level	More effective supervision	Participatory activation methods	More effective supervision	Better check of supervisors

done to aggregate quantity objectives is to use input costs or some administratively determined "price" (as in internal pricing systems) as an indirect quantity indicator.

Fourth, in the case of intangible services there are no physical units that can readily be identified. Here one can set objectives only in terms of such indirect indicators as the number of clients, the duration of services, certain intermediate products that are more tangible, and the volume or value of input factors.

Fifth, considerable confusion may develop between intermediate products and the end-products supplied to an organization's clientele. This readily happens with intangible end-product services that are provided on a non-sale basis to an intangible, unorganized, or reluctant clientele. More tangible intermediate products —particularly when supplied by hard-driving, ambitious units—may then receive disproportionate attention. One remedy is to formulate objectives in terms of work-flow—that is, a series of intermediate outputs leading to the production of the organization's end-products.

3. MAKING EFFICIENT USE OF INPUTS

When resources available for use as inputs are perceived as scarce, an organization or unit usually becomes interested in making efficient use of inputs relative to outputs. Since there are many ways of calculating input and output and of relating the two, there are many varieties of input-output performance.

Profitability is the most useful input-output relation, since it provides a common measure of value for both input and output. Profitability measures may be used in many ways, however, depending upon whether one (1) relates profits to net worth, total assets, or sales, (2) focuses on unit profits or total profits, or

(3) thinks in short- or long-range terms. Depending upon a variety of techniques for handling difficult accounting problems, they are subject to considerable statistical manipulation. They may also reflect an organization's monopoly power and its ability to obtain subsidies, as well as its efficiency. Nevertheless, in many circumstances—particularly over a long time period—profitability is the best single measure of efficiency, output quantity and quality, and interest satisfaction.

The most generally applicable efficiency objective is attaining the lowest possible total costs for a given unit of output. This cost-accounting measure is an essential instrument in attaining—even in formulating—profitability objectives. It is relevant to non-marketed products as well. In developing cost-accounting goals, however, it is essential not to neglect the quality dimensions of output. In the case of intangible services, as already indicated, the identification of the unit is extremely difficult. Where capital and material inputs are involved, it is necessary to make difficult—and sometimes arbitrary—decisions with respect to depreciation, the distinction between current and capital expenditures, and the value of withdrawals from inventories.

Partial input-output ratios are those relating some measure of input—usually either labour or capital—to some measure of total output. Such a ratio is particularly meaningful when the volume of other input factors may be presumed to remain unchanged. It will be very misleading, however, whenever there is any significant change in any other input factor—as when increased output per employee is counterbalanced, and in fact caused, by increased capital per unit of output.

Another efficiency measure is the proportion of potential actually used. This may be expressed in terms of a reduction in waste, a higher utilization of capacity (potential output), or profits in relation to potential profitability.

4. INVESTING IN THE SYSTEM

In addition to producing current output, an organization must invest in its capacity for future production. Investment objectives involve the expansion, replacement, conservation, or development of assets. They are essential not only for survival, but to prevent decline or promote growth.

The most obvious investment objectives relate to hard goods and monetary reserves. The hard goods may include land, buildings, equipment and machinery, and stocks of materials. The monetary reserves may include cash, deposits, securities, receivables, and any other funds that can be drawn upon.

Less obvious, although equally important, is investment in people, subsystems, subsystem relations, external relations, and the development of values. Investment in the guidance subsystem itself— that is, in the management structure—is particularly important.

In other words, investment performance may deal directly with any element of system structure. Accordingly, the specifics of investment objectives may be presented in the subsequent discussion of system structure.

In general, however, it should be pointed out that investment objectives often mean a diversion of resources from use in current output. Thus there are often important conflicts not only among different forms of investment but between investment and output production.

5. ACQUIRING RESOURCES

Neither output production nor investment is possible without resources that can be used as inputs. These must be obtained from the external environment or from within the organization. Under conditions of scarcity and competition this requires considerable effort. Thus resource-acquisition objectives usually receive high priority. Indeed, long-range planning is often oriented much more to acquiring resources than to utilizing them.

Organizations that sell their output may acquire external resources from the consumer market (through sales revenue), the capital market (through investment), and banks (through loans). Their sales, investment, and borrowing objectives are closely related to the extent of clientele satisfactions. Organizations and units that do not sell their output must depend mainly upon budgetary allocations.

In both cases monetary terms provide the most general expression of resource-mobilization objectives. But the monetary objectives are meaningful only when they reflect the specific resources to be acquired with money—people, information, facilities, goods, or organizations. In many circumstances it is also necessary to include (1) specifications for the resources desired, (2) specific terms and conditions, (3) selection methods, (4) the maintenance of supply lines, and (5) inspection of resources received.

The logical justification of an organization's "requirements" for additional resources is best provided by a set of objectives that moves back from (1) interest satisfactions and (2) output mix to (3) efficiency and (4) investment. In the budget-allocation process "acquisition logic" also requires efforts to appeal to the interests of those with most influence in the allocation decisions.

6. OBSERVING CODES

Every organization aims at doing things in the "right" way. To some extent the "right" way is set forth in external codes —laws, regulations, moral and ethical prohibitions and prescriptions, and professional principles. It is also determined by the codes of the organization—its written and unwritten rules and rituals.

Some may prefer to think of code observance as a restraint upon efforts to attain other objectives. None the less, a considerable amount of purposeful activity in organizations is involved in containing inevitable tendencies towards code deviation.

The greatest attention is usually given to internal codes. In the case of external codes that are not "internalized," the organization will often tolerate deviation. Indeed, the deception of external inspectors may itself become part of the internal code. Similarly, the deception of the organization's code-enforcement efforts may become part of the internal code of various units. These tendencies towards deviation are facilitated by the difficulty of understanding—or even keeping up with —complex regulations. They are promoted by recurring code conflicts.

These difficulties may be handled only in part by formal enforcement measures. Successful code observance also requires widespread internalization of codes and the continuing adjustment of conflicting and confusing codes.

7. BEHAVING RATIONALLY

An organization or unit also aims at doing things "rationally." This means the selection of the most satisfactory means of attaining a given set of objectives— from interest satisfaction and output production down to rational behaviour itself. Thus rationality is an all-pervasive instrumental objective.

Perfect rationality is an impossible objective. The instruments of rational calculation—information, knowledge, and skill—are always imperfect. The dimensions of rational behaviour—desirability, feasibility, and consistency—are themselves frequently conflicting. The more desirable objective will frequently be less feasible, the more feasible objective less consistent with other goals, the more consistent objective less desirable.

Technical rationality involves the use of the best methods devised by science and technology. With rapid scientific and technological progress, it is constantly changing. On the one hand, the rational methods of a few years ago may be irrational today. On the other hand, new techniques are often adapted on the basis of "technological faddism" rather than truly rational choice. In either case, there are usually serious disputes among technicians, disputes that cannot be entirely settled within the confines of technical rationality.

Administrative rationality is a much broader type of rationality. It involves the use of the best methods of guiding or managing organizations. This involves the interrelated processes of planning, activating, and evaluating with respect to all significant dimensions of both performance and structure. It provides the framework for resolving technical disputes. Yet administrative rationality, although highly developed on an intuitive basis, still awaits systematic scientific formulation. Many so-called "principles" of administration neglect the major dimensions of performance, deal formalistically with structure, and ignore the relation between the two. Management theory has not yet gone far enough in encouraging managers to think and communicate explicitly in connexion with such delicate subjects as the development and use of power and the management of internal and external conflict.

Structure Objectives

In thinking of system structure we should beware of images derived from the "non-human" structure of a building. The structure of an organization is based upon the expectations and behaviour of people and human groups. It has informal as well as formal aspects. It can never be understood (not even in its formal aspects) from an inspection of written decisions alone. It is never free from internal conflicts and inconsistencies. Unlike the frame of a building, it is always changing in many ways. Indeed, structure is merely the more stabilized aspect of activity. It consists of interrelations that provide the capacity for future performance and that can be understood only in terms of performance objectives. Some random illustrations of objectives for structural change are provided in Table 4.

1. PEOPLE

The people in an organization are the first element in an organization's structure. Thus structural objectives may be formulated in terms of the types of personnel, their quality, and their quantity.

Personnel may be classified in terms of specific positions with such-and-such titles, salaries, and perquisites; abilities, knowledge, and interests; experience; educational background; health; and various personality characteristics. Other characteristics relate to age, sex, race, religion, geographical origins. Some combination of these dimensions is usually employed in objectives for recruitment, replacement, and promotion.

The formulation of quality objectives involves consideration of the place of various people within a specific subsystem. Without reference to any subsystem, however, it also involves attention to people's capacity for learning and self-development. It involves objectives for promoting the utilization of such capacity.

The number of people in an organization is one of the simplest measures of its size. Larger numbers are often sought as a prelude to obtaining other assets, as a substitute for them, or as compensation for the lack of quality. Even with high-quality personnel and an adequate complement of non-human resources, larger numbers are often needed to supply essential reserves or the basis of major output expansion.

2. NON-HUMAN RESOURCES

With advancing science and technology, non-human resources become increasingly essential as instruments of human activity.

Certain natural resources—if only a piece of land—are an essential foundation of human activity. Physical facilities provide the necessary housing for human activity. Equipment and machinery, particularly when driven by electrical energy, make it possible for people to move or process things with little expenditure of human energy. Data-processing machinery replaces human labour in the processing of information. Thus investment objectives must deal with the structure of these physical assets.

As indicated in the discussion of investment performance, they may also include objectives with respect to monetary assets and—where balance-sheet accounting is used—to the structure of claims against them (liabilities).

3. SUBSYSTEMS

Within any organization people and non-human resources are grouped together in various subsystems. Each subsystem, in turn, is often subdivided still further. The smallest subdivision is the individual person.

Each subsystem is identifiable mainly by its role or function. The major element in role definition is the output expected from the subsystem. In larger organizations, particularly those based upon advancing technology, role differentiation tends to become increasingly specific and detailed. It also tends to undergo change —but at uneven and varying rates in response to recurring new environmental conditions, new technology, and adjustments in the quantity and quality of the organization's output mix. This means an internal restructuring of the subsystems. With growth of the organization as a whole, the subsystems change in a disproportional manner. Some expand, some decline, and some must be liquidated.

Important distinctions must be made between individuals and roles. People may come and go, while a role remains. Moreover, one person may play a number of roles—that is, "wear many hats." Some roles are substantially developed by the people who play them. Most people are substantially affected by the roles they play.

There are many kinds of subsystem. Some are hierarchically organized units; others are committees. Some are organized to perform functions peculiar to a specific organization; others provide certain kinds of services (personnel, budgeting, accounting, procurement, methods analysis, public relations) that are widely used by many organizations. Some are called "line," others "staff." Some are informal only. The most important subsystem is the management or guidance subsystem (discussed separately under 7 below).

4. INTERNAL RELATIONS

By itself subsystem differentiation is divisive. The system as a whole exists only to the extent that the parts are brought together in a network of internal relations.

The first element in internal relations is cooperation among and within the subsystems. This cooperation must be based upon certain commonly accepted objectives for future performance. Otherwise work-flows will not mesh. A large part of this cooperation may consist of routinized, habitual expectations and activity. At the same time cooperation is always associated with conflict relations within and among subsystems. If carried too far, conflict and tension may impair —even destroy—the internal structure. Within limits they may help to invigorate it.

Hierarchic relations are an indispensable element in the cooperation-conflict nexus. These consist of superior-subordinate relations, usually confined to certain spheres of behaviour. The lines of hierarchic authority provide formal channels of internal communication and ladders for career advancement. The upper positions in a hierarchy provide valuable points for conflict settlement and important symbols of organizational unity. At the same time, the growing role differentiation in modern organizations leads inevitably towards the subdivision of hierarchic authority and the growth of "multiple hierarchy" (see Gross, 1964, pp. 377-9).

Hierarchy is always accompanied by polyarchy—sometimes referred to as "lateral relations." One form of polyarchy is "joint authority." Thus committee members (often representing different units) may operate together as equals rather than as superiors and subordinates. Another is "dispersed authority." In budget procedures various units negotiate and bargain with each other—at least up to the point where hierarchic authority may be brought into play.

The communication network is an all-pervasive part of internal relations. A critical role in this network is always played by the various lines of hierarchic authority. But many other multi-directional channels and media—some of them informal—are also needed.

5. EXTERNAL RELATIONS

The immediate environment of any organization includes not only individuals but also various groups that may be classified as enterprises, government agencies, and various types of association. The relations between an organization and this immediate environment may be expressed in terms of the roles played by such individuals and groups:

(a) Clients and suppliers

The clients are those who receive, or are supposed to benefit from, an organization's output. The suppliers are those who supply the goods, services, information, or money acquired by the organization.

(b) Controllers and controllees

The controllers are the external regulators or "superiors." The controllees are the organization's regulatees or "subordinates."

(c) Associates and adversaries

The associates are partners or allies engaged in joint or cooperative undertakings. The adversaries include rivals for the same resources, competitors in producing similar outputs, and outright enemies interested in limiting or destroying the organization's performance or structure.

The same external organization often plays many—at times even all—of these roles. In so doing it will use many forms of external persuasion, pressure, or penetration.

Resistance to external influence usually involves an organization in preventive or counter measures of persuasion, pressure, or penetration. A more positive approach to external relations involves efforts to isolate, neutralize, or win over opponents and build up a farflung structure of external support through coalitions, alliances, and "deals." Such efforts may be facilitated by persuasive efforts aimed at unorganized publics.

6. VALUES

The individuals and subsystems in any organization are always guided by some pattern of values—that is, general attitudes towards what is desirable or undesirable and general ways of looking at the world. Some of the most important elements in this value structure may be defined in terms of the continua between

(a) Internal and external orientation

Internal orientation emphasizes the interests of members—in terms of their income, status, power, or self-development. External orientation emphasizes the interests of non-members; these may range from investors (owners) to clients to the society as a whole. Some organizations aim at integrating the two sets of values.

(b) Conformity and individualism

In many organizations conformity is a high value—sometimes to the point of the complete subordination of individual initiative. Nevertheless, highly individualistic values may be hidden behind a façade of superficial conformism.

(c) Passivity and activism

Among many members or organizations passivity is a highly cherished value. It leads to "playing it safe," "taking it easy," "following the book," and waiting for orders. Activist values, in contrast, lead to risk-taking, initiative, and innovation. Although apparently conflicting, the two are often intertwined.

Other values relate to freedom and control, authoritarianism and democracy, material and non-material interests, equity and equality, impersonality and particularism, and ascription and achievement.

7. GUIDANCE SUBSYSTEM

Some amount of coordinated action is always provided by the autonomous action—both routinized and spontaneous—of an organization's subsystems. But sufficient capacity for effective performance is not possible without the coordinating and promotional functions of a special subsystem with the responsibility for system guidance, or management. This guidance subsystem is composed of a network extending from a general directorate and top executives down through the middle and lower levels of managerial or supervisory personnel. At any level the members of this subsystem play various roles in decision-making and communication with respect to the making of plans, the activating of people and groups, and the evaluating of plans made and action taken. The interrelation among these roles helps to determine the structure of the guidance subsystem.

An important aspect of management structure is the balance between centralization and decentralization. Both centralization and decentralization may be thought of in terms of the distribution of responsibility and authority by (a) vertical levels, (b) horizontal levels, and (c) geographical location. The extent of centralization or decentralization in any of these dimensions can best be specified with reference to specific roles or functions. The prerequisite for effective decentralization of some functions is the centralization of other functions. With increasing size and complexity, it usually becomes necessary to delegate greater responsibility and authority to lower levels and to field offices. This, in turn, requires the strengthening of certain planning, activating, and evaluating functions *of* the "centre," as well as various horizontal shifts in the centralization-decentralization balance *in* the centre.

Another vital aspect of management structure is its power base. This includes the resource at its disposal. It includes the support it obtains from the membership and major points of internal influence. It includes the support obtained externally —from associates, from clients and suppliers, and from controllers and con-trollees. Top business executives need support from their boards of directors and banks; government executives from President or Governor, legislators, and external interest groups.

Other important dimensions of management structure relate to managerial personnel and tenure. Admission to the upper ranks of management may be dependent upon a combination of such factors as sponsorship, ability, education, personality characteristics, and social origins. Some top managers seek a self-perpetuating oligarchy, with little or no provision made for inevitable replacement. Others set as major objectives the development of career and recruitment systems that make for high mobility within managerial ranks.

The Strategy of Planning

Planning is the process of developing commitments to some pattern of objectives.

The preceding section set forth the major categories of objectives.

Let us now turn to some of the strategic considerations involved in deriving a pattern from these categories.

1. THE SELECTIVITY PARADOX

As specialists develop comprehensive ways of looking at systems, they often tend to overemphasize the role of comprehensive objectives in plannning. Thus economists often give the false impression that national aggregates of income, product, investment, and consumption are the major goals in national policy-making. In the process of "selling their wares," budgeteers and accountants often give the impression that comprehensive projections of budgets, income statements, or balance sheets can define an organization's major goals. If this approach should be automatically transferred to general-systems accounting, we should then find ourselves recommending that an organization's planners should formulate comprehensive objectives for all the elements of system performance and system structure.

Yet this would be a misleading position. The essence of planning is the *selection of strategic objectives in the form of specific sequences of action to be taken by the organization.* These critical variables must be selected in terms of:

(*a*) The major interest satisfactions that must be "promised" to obtain external and internal support.

(*b*) Present, imminent, or foreseeable crises or emergencies. These may require "contingency plans."

(*c*) Their decisive impact upon preceding, coordinate, or subsequent events.

(*d*) The long-range implications of action in the present or the immediate future. These are the critical considerations with respect to the "sunk costs" of investment programmes and the immediate steps in extended production processes (such as the building of houses, ships, or aircraft).

With these strategic elements selected, many elements of performance and structure may be detailed in subsystem plans or handled on the basis of current improvisation. A passion for comprehensive detail by either the organization or its subsystems may undermine selectivity. It may easily result in a loss of perspective, in document-orientation instead of action-orientation, and in an information supply that overloads communication channels and processing capacity. It may thus lead to serious waste of resources.

But—and here is the paradox of selectivity—strategic objectives can be selected rationally *only if the planners are aware of the broad spectrum of possible objectives.* Otherwise, objectives may be set in

a routinized, arbitrary, or superficial fashion. The very concept of selection implies the scanning of a broad range of possibilities.

The solution to this paradox may be found in the use of general-systems accounting to provide *a comprehensive background for the selection of strategic objectives.*

2. THE CLARITY-VAGUENESS BALANCE

There is no need to labour the need for clarity in the formulation of an organization's objectives. Precise formulations are necessary for delicate operations. They provide the indispensable framework for coordinating complex activity. They often have great symbolic significance.

Yet in the wide enthusiasm for "crystal-clear goals," one may easily lose sight of the need for a fruitful balance between clarity and vagueness. The following quotation is an effort to contribute to this balance through a "crystal-clear" statement on the virtues of vagueness:

If all the points on a set of interrelated purpose chains were to be set forth with precise clarity, the result would be to destroy the subordination of one element to another which is essential to an operating purpose pattern. The proper focusing of attention on some goals for any particular moment or period in time means that other goals must be left vague. This is even more true for different periods of time. We must be very clear about many things we aim to do today and tomorrow. It might be dangerously misleading to seek similar clarity for our long-range goals.

Apart from its role in helping provide focus, vagueness in goal formation has many positive virtues. It leaves room for others to fill in the details and even modify the general pattern; over-precise goals stifle initiative. Vagueness may make it easier to adapt to changing conditions; ultra-precision can destroy flexibility. Vagueness may make it possible to work towards many goals that can only be attained by indirection. Some of the deepest personal satisfactions from work and cooperation come as by-products of other things. If pursued too directly, they may slip through one's fingers; the happiest people in the world are never those who set out to do the things that will make them happy. There is something inhuman and terrifying about ultrapurposeful action proceeding according to blueprint and schedule. Only vagueness can restore the precious element of humanity.

Above all, vagueness is an essential part of all agreements resulting from compromise. When a dispute is resolved, some degree of ambiguity enters into the terms of settlement. Hence the wide-open language often used in the final language of statutory law. Similar ambiguities are found in most constitutions, charters, declarations of purpose, policy manifestos, and collective bargaining agreements. Certain anticipated situations are always referred to in terms that mean different things to different people, and are valuable because of, not despite, this characteristic. (Gross, 1964, p. 497.)

3. WHOSE OBJECTIVES?

Whose objectives are an organization's objectives?

The crystal-clear answers to this question point to (1) the people who wrote the charter (law or articles of incorporation) under which the organization operates, (2) the holders of formal authority over the organization (legislators or stockholders), (3) the members of the organization as a whole, (4) the organization's specialized planning people, or (5) the organization's top managers.

Yet each of these answers is incomplete. The charter-writers and the holders of formal authority can deal with only a small portion of an organization's objectives. The members, the subsystems, and the specialized planners have or propose many objectives that the organization never accepts. The manager's objectives may be accepted only in part by the rest of the organization. All of these

groups have many conflicting objectives.

A better, although vaguer, answer is one that defines an organization's objectives as those widely accepted by its members. These objectives may (to some extent, they *must*) reflect the objectives of charter-writers, the holders of formal authority, and other external groups. They must represent a common area of acceptance on the part of the organization's subsystems and members, albeit within a matrix of divergent and conflicting purposes. The technical planners play a major role in helping to formulate planning decisions. The top managers make (or legitimate) the decisions and play a major role in winning their acceptance throughout the organization. Whether recognized in formal planning procedures or not, the entire management structure is involved *de facto* in the daily operation of formulating and winning commitment to objectives for future performance and structure.

4. CONFLICT RESOLVING AND CREATING

As already indicated, the process of organizational planning involves dealing with many conflicting objectives and with divergent or conflicting parties at interest both inside and outside an organization.

Hence planning—rather than involving nothing but the sober application of technical rationality—is an exercise in conflict management. In this exercise systematic technical calculations are exceedingly valuable as a means both of narrowing areas of conflict and of revealing possibilities for conflict resolution. Yet technical calculations are never enough. Over-reliance upon them can lead to administrative irrationality.

Rational planning, in contrast, requires realistic attention to the power for and against alternative plans. It requires the resolution of conflicts through the use of power in various combinations of persuasion and pressure. It also requires the building of a power base through various methods of conflict resolution.

The most widespread mode of conflict resolution is compromise, through which some interests are sacrificed. A more creative—but more difficult—method is integration. This involves a creative readjustment of interests so that all parties may gain and none lose. In some cases, total victory may be obtained for one point of view, with consequent defeat for its opposition. To prevent defeat on some objectives, it is often necessary to tolerate deadlock or avoid an issue entirely. Any real-life planning process may be characterized as *a stream of successive compromises punctuated by frequent occasions of deadlock or avoidance and occasional victories, defeats, and integrations.* All these outcomes lead to new conflicts to be handled by the planners and managers.

Successful planning is often possible only when the key members of an organization see themselves threatened by an imminent crisis. In non-crisis conditions the subsystems tend to move in their own directions. They will most readily accept common objectives when the alternative is perceived as an onslaught of acute dissatisfactions, that is, a crisis. With crisis as the alternative, conflicts may be more quickly and effectively resolved. This is particularly relevant to subsystem resistance against plans for significant structural change.

In developing an organization's purposes, therefore, managers are frequently involved in crisis management. They try to anticipate crises around the corner. They try to respond promptly to crises that emerge. They may even try to create crises by setting high aspirations and accentuating fears of failure. These are delicate activities. For managers without a broad perspective on an organization's performance, structure, and environmental relations, they are dangerous undertakings—with much to be lost on one front as the price of victory on another. Even with such a broad perspective, they involve considerations that may not always be publicly discussed with complete frankness.

Hence a better-developed language of organizational purposefulness will not provide an outsider with a satisfactory answer when he asks a manager, "Just what are your organization's purposes?" The most it can do is help the managers themselves in the difficult and unending process of asking the question and finding workable answers.

References

Drucker, Peter F. (1954). *The Practice of Management.* New York: Harper.

Drucker, Peter F. (1964). *Managing for Results.* New York: Harper & Row.

Gross, Bertram M. (1964). *The Managing of Organizations* (2 vols). New York: Free Press.

LeBreton, Preston P. & Henning, Dale A. (1961). *Planning Theory.* Englewood Cliffs, N.J.: Prentice-Hall.

DISCUSSION QUESTIONS: PART V

1. Define the following terms: system, general system theory, management system theory. Describe the relationship between a general systems theory and a management systems theory.
2. How are traditional concepts of management related to systems concepts? In

what ways could the process, behavioral, and quantitative approaches be integrated into a management systems approach?

3. Explain how an organization can be viewed as a total system. How would you improve Professor Young's approach to management systems? Why?

4. Why are design criteria important in designing a management system?

5. Evaluate the arguments for and against a total systems concept. What position would you take with respect to a total systems concept? Defend your position.

6. What is industrial dynamics? How is it related to systems concepts? In what direction does industrial dynamics appear to be heading? Why?

7. Discuss the current status of feedback system theory. What was its status ten years ago? What will its status be ten years from now?

8. How are systems analysis and management planning related? How are systems analysis and information systems related?

9. What is the purpose of an information system? Why is such a system important? What steps would you take to design an information system? What impact do you feel an information system has on management? Why?

10. Describe briefly the role of systems analysis in management development. How could management development be improved through the use of systems analysis?

11. Using the performance–structure model, discuss the most important facets of the model. What objectives are sought in systems performance? Why? What structural objectives are considered in systems development? Explain.

12. Consider the possible research problems that could be carried out in the systems concepts and systems analyses areas. Discuss several major problems which you think are the most important and why.

13. After examining the general systems and management systems concepts, outline what you consider to be the major points in each. How would you improve these concepts? Why?

SELECTED REFERENCES: PART V

A. SYSTEMS CONCEPTS

Carzo, Rocco, Jr., and John N. Yanouzas, *Formal Organization: A Systems Approach.* Homewood, Ill.: Richard D. Irwin, 1967.

Forrester, Jay W., *Industrial Dynamics.* Cambridge, Mass.: The M.I.T. Press, 1961.
————, "The Structure Underlying Management Processes," *Academy of Management, Proceedings of the 24th Annual Meeting.* University Park, Pa.: 1965, pp. 58–68.

Graham, Richard W., Jr., "Total Systems Concept," *Management Technology,* Vol. 4 (June, 1964), pp. 1–6.

Hook, Harold S., "Bridging the Systems–Management Gap," *Systems and Procedures Journal,* Vol. 19, No. 2 (March–April, 1968), pp. 10–12.

Johnson, Richard A., Fremont E. Kast, and James E. Rosenzweig, *The Theory and Management of Systems.* New York: McGraw-Hill Book Co., Inc., 1963.

Millman, R. William, "A General Systems Approach to the Analysis of Managerial Functions," *Academy of Management, Proceedings of the 1962 Annual Meeting.* University Park, Pa.: 1963, pp. 133–138.

Pondy, Louis R., "A Systems Theory of Organizational Conflict," *Academy of Management Journal,* Vol. 9, No. 3 (September, 1966), pp. 246–256.

Spett, Milton, "Modern Systems Management and the Systems Game." *Systems and Procedures Journal,* Vol. 17, No. 6 (November–December, 1966), pp. 22–28.

B. SYSTEMS ANALYSES

Brown, Warren B., "Systems, Boundaries, and Information Flow," *Academy of Management Journal,* Vol. 9, No. 4 (December, 1966), pp. 318–327.

Cleland, David I. and Wallace Munsey, "Charting the Organizational System," *University of Washington Business Review,* Vol. 27, No. 1 (Autumn, 1967), pp. 37–57.

Hare, Van Court, Jr., *Systems Analysis: A Diagnosis Approach.* New York: Harcourt, Brace, and World, Inc., 1967.

Klein, S. M., "A Systems Approach to Behavior Modification and Attitude Change," *Proceedings of the 9th Annual Midwest Management Conference,* Carbondale, Ill.: Business Research Bureau, Southern Illinois University, 1966, pp. 43–52.

Lipperman, Lawrence L., "Advanced Business Systems," *Research Study No. 86.* New York: American Management Association, 1968, pp. 11–17.

Mockler, Robert J., "Developing a New Information and Control System," *Michigan Business Review,* Vol. XX, No. 2 (March, 1968), pp. 13–19.

Odiorne, George S., "A Systems Approach to Training." *Training Directors Journal,* Vol. 19, No. 10 (October, 1965), pp. 11–19.

Optner, Stanford L., *Systems Analysis for Business and Industrial Problem Solving.* Englewood Cliffs, N.J.: Prentice-Hall, Inc., 1965.

Young, Stanley, "Designing a Behavioral System." *Academy of Management, Proceedings of the 1963 Annual Meeting.* University Park, Pa.: 1964, pp. 76–83.

PART VI

Management
in the Future

Throughout this book an attempt has been made to examine the present and future problem areas in management. Since World War II, the field of management has changed significantly, and it will change even more dramatically in the next twenty-five years. At the end of the war a few contributions to the foundations of management had been made, but today substantial conceptual strides have been made toward a philosophy of management, toward theory construction in the different facets of management, and toward a profession of management.

One of the issues which has become increasingly important during the past decade is the management of multinational companies. With the advent of faster modes of transportation, newly developing nations, better educated societies, and new markets, the number of companies operating across international borders has increased tremendously. These expanded operations have called for critical appraisal of the management approaches in these companies which have different cultures, different levels of technology, and varying levels and quantities of quali-/ fied workers. In such companies, what type of approach should be utilized? Should one of the American management approaches be used directly, or should it be modified, or should a totally new approach for the multinational company be formulated? In the future, the interaction of the approaches taken by these multinational companies and those taken by managers in the United States may dramatically alter the entire field of management both conceptually and operationally.

In the first section, Professor Fremont Kast examines some of the management concepts and practices used in Europe and compares them to those of the

United States. In the next article, Mr. Thomas J. Murray discusses some of the ways in which American companies are operating on a multinational basis and how they are applying their ingenuity in solving their problems.

During the next twenty-five years, management will develop some startling innovations in concepts and practices to solve the problems facing executives. Some of the new approaches and techniques will assist the manager in solving problems which previously appeared to be unsolvable. For example, the behavioral sciences, mathematical techniques, and the computer certainly will become increasingly sophisticated and will aid in the solution of managerial problems. In the last section, Professor Dalton E. McFarland analyzes the future of organizations that are constantly changing, and Professor Harold Koontz examines the challenges of the future for managers and discusses the continuing importance of the manager from first-line supervision to the top-level executive.

A

MULTINATIONAL MANAGEMENT

43. Management Concepts and Practices: European Style

FREMONT E. KAST

Americans are generally aware of the accelerating economic growth in Western Europe over the past two decades, during which many of these countries have shown economic growth and expansion greater than that of the United States. Movements toward economic and social integration through the European Economic Community (Common Market) have increased speculation that Western Europe is moving towards integrated economic activities patterned after the United States. Unfortunately, Americans are only superficially aware of developing management concepts and philosophies throughout Western Europe. Although there have

been many comparisons of business philosophies, much that is written continues to reflect the stereotyped views that have become the American image of European business practices.

Changing Business Philosophies

Many of our current impressions of European business philosophies and practices are based upon observations made ten to fifteen years ago that fail to appreciate the current transitions. Immediately after World War II, and in the late 1940's and early 1950's, the wide gap in indus-

Reprinted from *Business Horizons,* Vol. 7, No. 4 (Winter, 1964), pp. 25–36, with permission of the author and the publisher, Indiana University. Fremont E. Kast is Professor of Management and Organization, Graduate School of Business Administration, University of Washington.

trialization and standards of living made Europeans very receptive to management ideas exported from the United States. Through the Organization for European Economic Cooperation (OEEC) in 1948, and its branch, European Productivity Agency in 1953, as well as through many direct business contacts, Americans and Europeans exchanged information. These agencies, designed to stimulate productivity, helped achieve an integration of philosophies and practices. In 1960 OEEC became the Organization of Economic Cooperation and Development, its role was expanded to include broader international obligations and relationships, and the flow of information has gradually changed direction. In the immediate postwar years most of the new ideas flowed from America to Europe, but now more new ideas are moving westward across the Atlantic. This has interesting implications for American businessmen and business educators and requires some adjustments in thinking.

AN AMERICAN BUSINESS PHILOSOPHY

Many misleading comparisons of European and American business philosophies assume a unique American business ethic that can be utilized as a standard of comparison. But in the United States a transition in business philosophies has taken place because of many factors—basic religious and moral beliefs, economic concepts, scientific management, and more recently sociology, psychology, and other behavioral sciences. Joseph McGuire comments:

Modern business philosophies are conglomerate. Like children's toys discarded haphazardly on the playroom floor, some business beliefs have fallen upon others and have tended to build vertically upon the foundation of earlier ideas; others lie side by side on the floor. Some concepts have their corners chipped off; others have their sides stove in; a few are intact. However these ideas appear, they still exist; and they form a heterogeneous mound. Occasionally someone pulls an idea from the mass, and perhaps refurbishes it (although not always), and it enjoys a more prominent position in society for a brief period. In the long run, though, it is the mass of ideas that counts rather than any one.[1]

In addition to the differences in philosophies, important divergencies appear in business concepts and practices between industrial segments. Railroads, retail distribution, and space technology are not likely to be governed by the same basic management concepts and practices. These divergencies suggest comparable differences between European managements of different industries. There are probably fewer differences in management practices between two large international firms such as General Electric and Philips' Lamps, than between General Electric and other firms in the United States.

NATIONAL DIFFERENCES

Unfortunately, Americans often think of European business operations as a unique entity without recognizing important national differences. The current development of the Common Market tends to emphasize this assumption of homogeneity. But this view fails to recognize the different cultural and social systems within which business operations take place in the various European countries. The business enterprise is a subsystem operating as a component of the broader environmental and social system of each country. Many concepts in management in Britain, for example, are more similar to American concepts than to those of continental Europe. This is logical because Britain and the United States share

---

[1] Joseph W. McGuire, *Business and Society* (New York: McGraw-Hill Book Co. Inc., 1963), p. 71.

many cultural and social values that set the framework for business. Generally, the Netherlands and Belgium show more similarity to American management concepts than do France and Italy. Depending upon the particular characteristic or practice under consideration, important national differences can be found within the European business community as well as between the United States and Europe. Many others have suggested that appropriate business philosophies differ by country. Winston Oberg states:

An important issue is whether or not the requirements for managerial success and the ground rules under which managers operate are quite similar from country to country or whether they differ so significantly as to make any attempt to generalize meaningless and futile. . . . My own experience in international management leads me to believe that cultural differences from one country to another are more significant than many writers now appear to recognize.[2]

Many forces tend to create similarity in managements between Europe and America. They are not only due to the exchange of information on management processes, but are related to current trends toward similarities in social and cultural environments. Over the long run, these trends will be more important than the mere copying of management tools, techniques, and approaches.

A Management Elite. Throughout Europe many highly intelligent and dynamic business leaders in the upper ranks have the broad wisdom and skills necessary for directing the activities of their enterprises. They are not inwardly directed but are well aware of the broad social and cultural changes occurring in their countries and are attempting to work within these frameworks; they do not appear to be backward, conservative, nor lacking in competitive drive. Many European businessmen are well informed on international relationships, and often have profound knowledge and insight about the United States. This top and high middle management group compares favorably to American business management.

But they are an elite. The gap between the knowledge, skills, and value orientation of this group and the lower levels in their organization is much greater than in the United States. This elite is found in other European professions. For example, a full professor has substantially greater prestige and status in European countries than in the United States. But, there is a great gulf between the professor and the instructors and assistants. Innovations and ideas rarely come from someone other than the professor, although in the United States it is often the bright young assistant or associate professor who comes up with the truly innovative ideas and pushes his older colleagues intellectually.

One of the factors creating this management elite is the continued family ownership and control of many European enterprises, particularly in the medium-sized business, although this is less prevalent in the larger firms that have become international in their operations. Ownership control provides the basis for a management elite and precludes the rise of others in the business to top management positions. However, there is evidence that the strong owner-manager business is losing its place, particularly among larger concerns and medium-sized firms that have not been sufficiently viable in meeting the new economic environment. Nevertheless, the family business is still important in Europe and encourages a clearly defined management elite.

---

[2] Winston Oberg, "Cross-Cultural Perspectives on Management Principles," *Journal of the Academy of Management* (June, 1963), pp. 129–30.

Centralizing of Decision Making. Traditionally highly centralized decision-making occurs in small and medium-sized owner-manager concerns, even in the United States, but limited delegation is apparent throughout larger European business organizations as well. The favoring of centralization and lack of delegation has several causes. The desire on the part of top management to maintain control, and influence over-all operations is a factor in Europe as it is in the United States, but a major contributing factor appears to be the actual differences in skills and abilities of top management compared to lower levels. The gap is greater in Europe than in the United States because the traditional European educational system encourages differentiation between those who will be leaders in business and professions and those who will remain at lower levels. The class system is relatively rigid, and in European concerns the subordinate levels frequently do not have sufficient training or necessary skills for effective delegation.

Paternalistic Attitudes. Rigidity of social class structure demonstrates itself subtly in the attitude of management toward subordinates. Many European managers have high regard for their workers' interests and devote time and money in their interest. But this relationship often has a strong paternalistic flavor and a wide social distance remains between management and subordinate levels. Yet, European workers do not appear to be dissatisfied with these relationships; one explanation may be that they are content with their greatly improved wages and the number of consumer goods they are able to buy.

While an observable difference exists between the authoritarian-centralization concepts of business in Europe and the

more participative-decentralized forms in the United States, concern is growing over means for effective motivation and the need for increased delegation and participation in many progressive European firms. On the other hand, there is some reaction to the concept of total democracy in business in the United States.

Utilization of Specialists and Staffs. A comparison of the organization of the medium-sized or large firm in America and in Europe reveals a substantial difference in the utilization of specialists and staff personnel. The European company usually has a streamlined organization with a clear line authority from top management down, in contrast to the American firm with many more management specialists and staff departments that influence and have functional authority over specific activities. The fundamental cause of the difference is the European executive's attitude toward management.

To understand these differences it is useful to look more completely at the staff concept. Pfiffner and Sherwood state that staff work is basically an intellectual activity; the staff member's function is to gather data, reflect, and come up with solutions arrived at through intellectual processes. He is the thinking and planning arm of the organization.[3] Technology and the complexity of knowledge has made it increasingly difficult for the generalist to develop plans and make decisions in all the activities of the firm. Thus, in the United States, top management has come to rely increasingly upon the aid of specialists in the decision-making and controlling processes. The use of specialists in accounting, engineering, personnel, organizational analysis, design, advertising, market research, and more recently in such areas as operations research and systems analysis is indicative of the recog-

---

[3] John M. Pfiffner and Frank P. Sherwood, *Administrative Organization* (Englewood Cliffs, N.J.: Prentice-Hall, Inc., 1960), pp. 172–73.

nition that specialized knowledge is important for the successful operations of the organization. In the European management philosophy, the top manager often views his own role as providing the major intellectual activities in the firm to be practiced with an art and skill based upon his own experience, training, and background.

The use of the committee system reflects a fundamental difference in the approaches of the European and American top executive. The successful committee serves as a basis for getting ideas from subordinates and as a means for communicating decisions and reasons to lower levels. The European executive generally does not see the need for this type of participation nor the need to communicate his reasoning back down the line.

Executive Mobility. The lack of executive mobility in Europe compared to the United States is due in part to restrictions of nationality and language, which narrow the talent market for the European executive. But a more important reason is a fundamental difference in attitude. In America, value is placed upon a young man having wide experience, and a background of employment in several companies or even in different industries is no disadvantage; in fact, the fastest means of promotion may be through company change. In Europe, greater value is placed upon the stability of the individual and the slow growth and maturing of mangement personnel within the firm. This philosophy was clearly stated by a prominent Belgian businessman, the president of N.V. Kredietbank, Brussels:

When a candidate for a managerial job produces a curriculum vitae with a number of job changes, this would generally involve an unfavorable impression. It is considered a proof of inconstancy in the character of the candidate. Furthermore there is a suspicion that the services rendered by the candidate are not satisfactory because otherwise he would have preferred to stay in the place where he was.

In short, in Europe we do not yet believe that promotion can be obtained through job change. Whatever might be the situation in the U.S.A. I am convinced that there is much sense in the European attitude. It is my personal experience that the hiring of people from another firm is seldom a good solution to staff problems. . . . Really good talent, even very young talent, is seldom available in the market. It is really an exception if the firm in which they work is prepared to let them leave. In any case it is much more easy to make a mistake by hiring a man from outside than by promoting one of the firm's employees.[4]

This attitude certainly reflects a different concept from that prevalent in the United States, where job pirating and executive mobility are accepted and even encouraged.

This different attitude may stem from the concept that management is to be learned slowly and nurtured through company experience in the European firm. Also, it reflects differences in utilization of specialists in management. The staff specialist within the American business firm is often a professional in his field (accountant, economist, operations researcher, personnel specialist, and so on) whose talents extend beyond his specific operational experiences within the firm. He usually develops professional allegiances that vie with firm loyalty, and he has professional relationships with his counterparts in different firms. He has job mobility because his specialized knowl-

---

[4] F. Collin, *Industry and Education for Managers, Experiences of a Business Man,* Eighth I.U.C. Conference in Ghent, Belgium (Delft, the Netherlands: International University Contact for Management Education, July, 1961), pp. 16–17.

edge and skills transcend the individual company and he knows the market for his services.

Attitudes Toward Change and Leisure. Many people have suggested that European businessmen are more conservative and show more restraint in instituting change than does the American businessman. Otto H. Nowotny observed:

Though neither continent can claim to have a monopoly on vitality or wisdom, it is reasonably true to say that American management philosophy is, in general, more vital than wise, while Europe's is more wise than vital.[5]

This generalization is difficult to prove, and the remarkable vitality and progress of European firms over the past ten years casts some doubt upon it. Recent trends suggest a difference in emphasis rather than in vitality and receptiveness to change. In America, the trend has been toward an increasing emphasis upon distribution while still retaining production efficiency; in Europe, with the relatively high level of consumer demand and low saturation for consumer items, the emphasis is properly on technical innovations to increase production. However, there is some evidence of innovations and changes in marketing and distribution.

The observer certainly does not get the impression that management lacks vitality or fails to recognize the necessities for change. However, subtle differences within the business organization tend to reduce pressures for innovation. In American business staff groups with specialized projects and interests are often the chief innovators within the organization and create pressures for change. Innovation is the primary means by which the staff earns its way in the organization and influences organizational activities. The lack of elaboration of the staff functions and the higher level of centralization in European business firms create less internal pressure for change and adaptation.

Europeans are often thought to have more leisure and to know how to utilize it more effectively, but the hardworking and dynamic European businessman does not seem to have more leisure than his American counterpart. Even the much discussed two-hour lunch is succumbing to the demands of technical and social change in some countries. But there does seem to be a different attitude toward leisure. Many Americans approach leisure activities with a compulsion and determination equal to their professional endeavors, often pursuing the weekly golf game as relentlessly as the job. The European appears to have the ability to relax and enjoy his leisure activities to a much greater extent than the American. With the prospect of more leisure resulting from the growing productivity of the American economic system, European values concerning leisure may be one of our most valuable imports.

Social Responsibilities. The social responsibilities of business leadership has been of increasing concern in America, where it is widely felt that the pure rational profit motive should be restricted by other organizational objectives and by responsibilities to various interest groups. European business leaders do not appear to be much concerned about this issue. Is it because they are less socially responsible than Americans? Do they have less regard for various internal participants and outside interest groups? This is certainly not true. Throughout Europe many examples show highly paternalistic employee relationships and a true feeling of responsibility toward the participants in the company. However, the controversy

---

[5] Otto H. Nowotny, "American vs. European Management Philosophy," *Harvard Business Review* (March–April, 1964), XLII, p. 103.

over the question of business responsibilities does not seem to be as strong in Europe as in America. This reflects a fundamental difference in the attitude of business management concerning the specific roles of business, government, and labor. Generally, there is greater willingness to allow the government to meet social responsibilities and to regulate economic activity in Europe than in the United States. The European businessman has accepted the government functions in determining social responsibilities and in balancing various social objectives and he operates his business within these restraints. Although the continual power struggle between government, business, and labor apparent in the United States is not so evident in Europe, the European executive feels more restricted by outside forces in his employee relationships than does the American executive.

Role of Labor Unions. In most European countries the role of the labor organization is quite different than in the United States. Certainly the labor unions are strong and there are reports of strikes and work stoppages, but the primary objectives of many unions are to represent workers as a class and to achieve broad social and economic changes. In contrast, although American labor unions operate within the established framework, they demand more and more from the system. Most major European strikes and work stoppages are directed against governmental policies rather than against a given company or industry. The recent doctors' strike in Belgium is typical; it was directed against the policies of the government. Throughout Europe the governments have a stronger role in determining pay and other conditions of employment than in the United States. Where true collective bargaining exists, it is generally on an industrywide basis between unions and employer representatives. The role of the union at the plant

level in terms of conditions of employment, handling grievances, and day-to-day activities is generally less influential than in America.

In many European countries, governmental policy has restrained wage increases in order to keep costs down and to maintain favorable trade relationships. Coincidental with these restraints on wages has been full employment of labor. In Europe the pressure to keep labor costs down has often resulted in the utilization of marginal workers with low training and skill levels who might not be employable at higher wages. There is little incentive to replace this low cost, marginal labor with labor-saving devices. Thus, some of these countries, may have minimized their unemployment problems at the cost of lower productivity and output.

Educational System

The previous sections have outlined some differences in management concepts and practices between European countries and the United States. Many can be traced to important differences in educational systems: first, in basic educational programs, and second, in education for management.

GENERAL EDUCATION

Throughout Western Europe the education system tends to be much more rigidly structured and differentiated between classes of students than in the United States. European educational programs stress a quality education for an elite group of students, whereas the United States is geared to a broader education for a much larger segment of student population. In Europe an academic secondary education is available for the few and is the avenue for future entrance to the universities and for later achievement. At the university age level, this differentiation is even more extreme. In a recent study of higher education in England the following conclusion was drawn:

There is a basic distinction between large and comprehensive arrangements such as found in the United States of America, where rather over a third of the age group now enter higher education of extreme diversity in content and level, and smaller hierarchial systems such as those of Western Europe, where universities tend to be sharply distinguished from other institutions and where the proportion of the age group in full-time higher education is usually less than a third of the proportion in the United States. In this respect Britain is to be classed with Europe.[6]

The following table taken from the same study illustrates these differences.

Comparisons on Higher Education in Selected Countries

Country	Per Cent of Age Group Entering Higher Education, 1958–59	Per Cent of Age Group Completing Higher Education, 1961–62
Great Britain	12.5	9.8
France	9.0	5.0
Germany (West)	7.0	4.0
Netherlands	7.0	4.0
Sweden	13.0	7.0
United States	35.0	17.0

It is difficult to compare these statistics for various countries because of different classifications of programs in higher education and because of part-time students. Moreover, it is impossible to assess the quality of these various programs. For example, the average university student in the Netherlands studies between six and seven years to receive his university degree compared to four years in the United States. Nevertheless, higher education in the United States, even when incomplete, is much more general and provides a broader basis of skill than is typical in Europe. Incidentally, this report specifically points out the similarity in breadth of coverage of higher education in the United States and Russia:

The Systems in the United States and the Soviet Union present a sharp contrast to the foregoing [Britain and Western Europe]. Much as they differ from each other, they share a more variegated pattern of institutions. Professional training is provided within both systems in far more forms than in Europe. This variety is no doubt in part to be attributed to the individual history of each country, but in part also it seems to be a function of the scale on which higher education is provided.[7]

Many of the differences in concepts and practices between European and American managements can be traced to the differences in education and training of the management elite and the subordinate levels. These wider differences tend to create a more highly centralized and narrow management structure in European enterprises, whereas the basis of managerial talents and skills is much broader in the United States.

EDUCATION FOR MANAGMENT

In professional management education the differences are even more apparent. In Europe the older, more traditionally oriented universities adhere firmly to their pursuit of knowledge for its own sake and only grudgingly admit practical and vocational studies into their programs. Furthermore, the rigid structuring of faculties

---

[6] *Higher Education,* Report of the Committee Appointed by the Prime Minister Under the Chairmanship of Lord Robbins, 1961–63 (London: Her Majesty's Stationary Office, 1963), p. 35.

[7] *Higher Education,* pp. 36–37.

and courses of study in European universities makes it quite difficult to develop new programs in business management, which, to be effective, demand the integration of knowledge from a broad range of academic subjects.

On the other hand, European business has not generally encouraged the development of programs in management education within universities. They fear that the university will not really meet the requirements for training future managers but will continue their traditional concern with the advancement of knowledge and its communication, turning out scholars and not men well-suited for management. The universities, they believe, have traditionally downgraded applied knowledge and competence. Furthermore, many European businessmen believe that management cannot be taught, but view it as an art acquired through the development of an individual style, not as a science. But there is evidence that these views are changing.

Forces of Change

This has been an observer's impression of current concepts and practices in European business management and has suggested contrasts with the United States. To stop here would give a misleading static, historical picture, for European business is dynamic and is changing rapidly. Many forces—economic, social, educational, and organizational—are causing innovations in these concepts. In many ways the changes are leading European managers closer to their American counterparts. This is already true of the large international firms such as Unilever and Royal Dutch Shell. It is impossible to describe all of these factors of change; however, some of the most important will be set forth in the next pages.

SCIENCE AND TECHNOLOGY

Management concepts and practices in the United States have been greatly influenced by science and technology. Business management has been instrumental in translating the growing scientific and technological achievements into practical programs and applications. This close association has had a direct impact upon management concepts; management usually applies scientific approaches to decision-making processes, organization structure, the size and integration of firms, and the physical aspects of operations. Historically, European management has been more of an art than a science. Certainly, the effect of science and technology has been important in Europe, but to a lesser extent than in the United States. In the postwar period this impact has increased, and significant transitions have been made in management practices within European industries most affected by advancing technology, such as electronics, aeronautics, and nuclear power, where there is generally greater use of staff specialists with less centralized decision making and fewer authoritarian practices. These industries demand participants with higher education and skill level. These people have greater job mobility because of their specialized skills.

The continuing forces of advancing technology will accelerate within American society, and they will have an increasing impact upon European management. As a result, some of the differences in management between the United States and Europe will disappear.

COMPETITION

Many of the differences in management practices stem from the divergent attitude on competition and the different market environments within which businesses operate. Historically, national boundaries with tariff and other restrictions have protected the European businessman from the rigors of competition. The development of a political and economic union within Western Europe has resulted ·in major changes. As Emile Benoit states:

The European Common Market represents the emergence of a new economic unit in the world, almost as populous as, and with nearly half the productive output of, the United States.[8]

Of course, many difficulties remain in the establishment of a truly viable and effective common market in Western Europe. Nevertheless, some form of co-operation, permitting broader free markets and large-scale industries, seems inevitable if Europe is to advance economically and compete in world markets.

Since the formulation of the Common Market in 1958, many companies have moved to rationalize their production and distribution. Increasingly, they have adopted management practices similar to those of large-scale American enterprises. Much more emphasis is being placed upon long-range planning, utilization of staff specialists, and management training to develop a broad base of effective management talent. Increasingly, it is recognized that effective management, rather than physical equipment, location, or political advantage, may be the most important factor in a highly competitive market.

DISTRIBUTION

Since the end of World War II, European industry's primary concern has been to rebuild and expand productive capacity to meet the large backlog of latent demand for many products, especially consumer durables. This production orienta-

tion represents one of the differences between the European and United States business environments. Nevertheless, growing interest in distribution will undoubtedly have an impact upon management practices. The distribution function will become significantly more important in industries that have been traditionally dominated by production and engineering philosophies. Many large multinational companies are aggressively pushing distribution with increased emphasis upon advertising, market research, and promotion, and a revitalization of distribution channels. This market orientation will probably help to bring United States and European management concepts and practices into closer accord.

DECENTRALIZATION OF CONTROL

Although earlier European management was characterized as more autocratic and centralized than American management, external and internal forces are causing a change toward greater participation and decentralization. It is difficult to determine whether this trend is due to greater insights into effective motivation and leadership by top management, or whether these changes are being forced upon management by circumstances. With the growth of size and complexity of business operations it is no longer possible to have the high degree of centralization typical under the smaller, limited market-oriented, and often family-owned company. Furthermore, the need for functional specialization of many managerial skills forces decentralization of authority to the people with these skills. The growing need for active, intelligent participation by middle and lower management is causing a reevaluation of past management concepts. Leadership and positive motivation is stressed increas-

---

[8] Emile Benoit, *Europe at Sixes and Sevens* (New York: Columbia University Press, 1961), pp. 4–5.

ingly rather than the authority of position in the organizational hierarchy. The position of Slater and Bennis bears out these observations:

We will argue that democracy has been so widely embraced not because of some vague yearning for human rights, but because under certain conditions it is a more 'efficient' form of social organization. . . . Democracy is the only system which can successfully cope with the changing demands of contemporary industrial civilization.[9]

Obviously, greater delegation and participation is not only dependent upon the desires of top management or the necessity of circumstances. To be effective there must be a high degree of education, skill, and capability on the part of the lower level participants within the organization. Here too, significant changes have taken place.

EDUCATIONAL LEVELS

Throughout Europe one senses a revolution in views on education. Traditionally, higher education has been available for a top few—a well-educated elite. Furthermore, the importance of education for professional business management has not been appreciated. In many European countries consideration is being given to upgrading the level of education with increased emphasis upon large-scale programs at the university level. For example, the Robbins Report on Higher Education recommends that the number of places in higher education in Britain be increased from 216,000 to 560,000 by 1980. More widespread education for the population will have an impact upon management practices. With a higher level of education and training of lower management and employees, greater delegation and increaesd participation will be pos-

sible. Furthermore, a higher educational level for a broad base of people will increase social and job mobility. Education rather than family or social position will eventually become the important factor in determining entry into professional management.

The growth in education and skill levels will have further impacts. It will accelerate the trend of decreasing differentials in economic and living standards between various classes. This not only influences internal operations of the business, but also its market environment. Throughout Europe there is a growing demand for many products by the working classes that were previously only available to the wealthy. People at all levels are developing new aspirations in their employment and professional opportunities and also as consumers in the market place.

SOCIAL PRESTIGE OF BUSINESS MANAGERS

In Europe, as contrasted to the United States, professional business management has not been regarded with social esteem as high as that accorded to government and military service and the traditional professions. But there is a growing awareness of the importance and influence of professional management in an industrial society and of the social contributions that can be made by those who hold these positions. Not only are external environment and internal organzational relationships changing, but attitudes and values related to management are adapting to the new situations. There is a discernible trend in Europe to integrate professional management education with the university systems. Thus, for the first time in many countries, management education is gaining the esteem of association with the prestige universities.

---

[9] Philip E. Slater and Warren G. Bennis, "Democracy is Inevitable," *Harvard Business Review* (March–April, 1964), XLII, pp. 51–52.

Important differences remain in European and American management concepts and practices, but many forces, such as advancing technology, changing social concepts, and increasing educational levels are causing these differences to diminish. Harbison and Myers suggest:

As the industrial society continues to lay stress upon scientific discovery, technological innovations, and economic progress, patrimonial and political managements tend to be displaced by the professionals. The successful organization builders tend to become the self-conscious practitioners of the arts of leadership, direction, coordination, delegation, and control. Decision-making is no longer based upon intuitive judgment; it depends increasingly upon objective analysis, the reports of specialists, the advice of consultants, and carefully directed collective thinking. Positions within the managerial hierarchy are more precisely defined; goals are more formally established, and criteria for successful performance more explicitly stated.[10]

The increasing commercial and intellectual contacts between businessmen and business educators from different countries tend to create uniformity of practices. In the United States, current management concepts have evolved over several generations. European management philosophers are changing much more rapidly. There will never be total uniformity of management concepts and practices—too many basic cultural and social differences divide the countries. Yet, the pressures of technology, industrialization, and social adaptation encourage similarity in many managerial practices.

Many conflicts will occur between these changing managerial approaches and the social environment within which the manager must operate and a variety of adaptations are possible. In meeting the demands of industrialization and change, European managers have willingly accepted American ideas. Increasingly, the United States business manager and business educator should be willing to learn, understand, and accept new ideas from a dynamic Europe.

---

[10] Frederick Harbison and Charles A. Myers, *Management in the Industrial World* (New York: McGraw-Hill Book Co., 1959), p. 120.

44. Organizing the Global Company in a Changing World

THOMAS J. MURRAY

When New York's First National City Bank a few weeks ago named Walter B. Wriston as its new president, much of the business world was greatly surprised. There had been at least eight contenders for the post, and the guessing game played no favorites. But for the shrewd few who have closely followed Citibank's surging international growth, the appointment was no surprise. Hemmed in by state laws that prohibit New York City banks from expanding outside the

---

Reprinted from *Dun's Review*, Vol. 90, No. 2 (August, 1967), pp. 27–30; 64–66, with permission of the publisher. Copyrighted by Dun and Bradstreet Publications Corp. Thomas J. Murray is a Senior Editor of *Dun's Review*.

metropolis, Citibank has become the largest overseas operator of all U.S. banks; and as head of the international operation for the past seven years, Wriston was in a key spot.

In the months ahead, more up-and-coming managers can expect the world to intrude on their own working lives. For today the more farsighted U.S. corporations and banks are becoming increasingly global-minded and are beginning to use the whole world as a training ground for their executives-to-be. Such companies as American Express Co., Armco Steel and Chase Manhattan Bank, among others, lately have named men in their thirties or early forties to highly responsible positions in Europe. Even with recessions still gripping several parts of Europe, many a promising young man now making his mark in Dallas or Duluth may yet find himself in Duesseldorf or Danzig on his way to the executive suite.

The basic reason for this mounting two-way traffic between the U.S. and the rest of the world is the growing lure of foreign markets as competition and profits at home tighten. Says Wriston: "The potential for U.S. industry abroad is just enormous. The overseas market is growing twice as fast as the domestic, and it should double or triple in the years just ahead. With some 3 billion people in the world and only 200 million in the U.S., it is most important that every corporation structure itself to get on that escalator."

Yet it is getting harder these days to climb aboard. For even as U.S. companies step up their outlays on overseas production and marketing—some $50 billion in all—vexing problems persist in doing business abroad. Long-established companies on the spot naturally have no intention of yielding meekly to an invasion from the U.S. Moreover, in many countries a rising tide of economic nationalism threatens the vast private in-vestment that U.S. corporations have built up there over the years. And sporadic drops in foreign economies keep adding to the complexities.

From all the foregoing, two inescapable conclusions emerge. First, from now on top management must be just as closely involved in its international operations as it is with the domestic. Second, it can achieve that balance only by toppling the artificial corporate barriers that now screen it from day-to-day contact with activities abroad. In practical terms, this means that the separate international division, as it is now set up in most U.S. companies, is dead.

As President Donald P. Kircher of internationally minded Singer Co. puts it: "We know that the failure of a business enterprise to attune its strategy and practices to fundamental environmental change will in the end prove fatal."

But the kind of tuning needed pits top management against some of the toughest questions it has ever faced: What is the right structure to handle operations on a worldwide scale? When is the right time to set it up? And how is the thinking of all the key people to be lifted to a global level?

No less a corporate powerhouse than General Electric Co. found it was on the wrong track abroad only this past June. Obviously dissatisfied with top management's control in this critical area, GE disbanded its separate international group organization. Now all foreign divisions report directly to group executives in the U.S.

Many another blue-chip corporation (among them: Caterpillar Tractor, Union Carbide and Celanese Corp.) recently has moved to tighten its control over its own international activities. The details naturally differ from company to company. Lee L. Morgan, executive vice president of Caterpillar Tractor, second largest exporter in the U.S., is quick to point out that no single corporate design—so far—is the ultimate.

Consider Caterpillar's own attempts to internationalize. When foreign volume in 1956 rose to 37% of a $650-million total, the company formed a Foreign Trade Group—in effect, a separate international division—to handle three overseas subsidiaries.

By 1959, however, group head William Blackie (now chairman of the company), realized that the division setup gave the company a "split personality." This was both inefficient and duplicative, considering that one of the company's strengths was a product line that could be manufactured in the same way both here and abroad.

This interchangeability became the keystone of a new corporate structure. A general staff was created with worldwide responsibility. Operating out of company headquarters in Peoria, Illinois, departments such as engineering and research, manufacturing, marketing, parts and service, and finance were given the task of supporting line operations anywhere on the globe. The rationale was simple: Since Cat's products and components were basically the same in Australia or Brazil as in Peoria or Joliet, the same staff man could service any plant location.

Not so simple, however, was the organization that began to evolve for foreign line operations. The separate international unit was dissolved and a regional approach adopted. Dividing its overseas world into three areas—Australasia, Canada-Latin America and Europe-Africa-Middle East—the company placed in charge of each, with full responsibility for marketing and manufacturing, a vice president directly accountable to top management in Peoria. This company-wide restructuring, Blackie asserts, has given top management more effective control of worldwide planning while allowing oper-ating heads almost complete independence in execution.

In practice, the process has been aided enormously by a device that dates back to 1954: a President's Office, in which two executive vice presidents relieve President William H. Franklin of some of his day-to-day burdens. All operating heads report directly to this three-man office. But, as Lee Morgan points out, the arrangement is flexible. If an executive vice president rather than the president can handle a matter, he does. "The classic thing," Morgan explains, "is to have sharp lines defining who reports to whom. But we mean it when we say, 'Report to our secretaries.' "

The top command is thus freed for overall policy decisions. Line vice presidents get swifter response to reports and requests for action decisions. And the President's Office helps free the chief executive from having to cover the world personally.

The integration of all Cat activities around the world has also helped to improve the flow of internal communications, says Morgan. "Take our foreign operations in Africa. Our man in Geneva is responsible for all marketing and manufacturing there, whether in Johannesburg or Nigeria. He's the man they all must deal with, and he in turn deals with us. If we organized along functional or product lines over there as we do in the United States; there would be a risk of jurisdictional complexities and overlaps."

"We also try to establish a tone of informality in our communications," Morgan continues. "Our top man in Geneva does not have to transmit all the information he gets, either up or down. There are literally dozens of people in his area communicating with peer groups, with superiors and subordinates, with staff groups and other operating groups, and they are well-coordinated."

Cat's evolution into a multinational

company has been rewarding financially as well as operationally. Foreign volume climbed to $628.4 million in 1966, some 41% of the total. "At this rate," notes Morgan, "we will soon be deriving more than 50% of our volume abroad. In fact, there may be more potential for us abroad than here."

Along the way, the organization will probably undergo further changes. "I don't know of anyone here who is convinced that this is the ultimate form," Morgan declares. "But the organization has made it easier for us to think in global terms."

Realizing the Potential

The same mental stretch has become equally important to Union Carbide Corp., which now garners 30% ($765 million in 1966) of its total volume from operations outside this country. "As for potential," says Chairman Birny Mason Jr., "we expect a faster rate of growth overseas than in the U.S."

Like General Electric, Carbide not long ago dissolved its foreign operating division. It then established five wholly owned U.S. subsidiaries to manage all overseas operations. Each of the five geographical units is headed by a group vice president who reports directly to Carbide's top management. Each group represents a vast area of the world and a huge chunk of company operations.

The group head, besides administering all manufacturing and marketing in his area through several regional directors, also sits on Carbide's General Operating Committee. This is a top-level unit charged with reviewing major capital investment proposals and the business planning of all operating groups in the U.S. and abroad. Its members meet regularly in the company's New York office, a procedure that is facilitated by having all the

men headquartered there. "For the first time," says Mason, "we now have in one place all the people who are contributing to management planning."

Carbide, like Caterpillar, also has its President's Office, consisting of Mason, the chief executive; Kenneth Rush, the chief operating officer; two executive vice presidents and the corporate secretary. They meet at least once a week. "With the increasing complexity of the company," explains Mason, "coherence was becoming more difficult to achieve. The chief executive was the only bridge between operations, and this was just not adequate."

Today, operating heads report to President Rush, who decides what matters are to be brought before the Office. Says Mason: "We have achieved a flow of information far superior to anything in the past."

Yet there is, as noted, no one master plan for organizing the multinational company. In the early 1960s, for example, Celanese Corp., the huge fiber and chemical company, created a worldwide organzation that differs substantially from that of either Caterpillar or Carbide. For one thing, all line operations are organized by products; there are two broad product groups, each headed by an executive vice president whose stewardship is worldwide. For another, Celanese ventures abroad are mostly on a minority-interest basis.

Celanese management decided to organize by product line because most of the company's operations were then in the Western Hemisphere. Moreover, its production technology was so complex and its products and markets so diverse that it was felt they would overburden a geographic structure.

The domestic divisions thus became the nuclei for product groups now operating around the world. Each division is headed by its own president. The division presidents report to one of the two corporate executive vice presidents, and the latter, in turn, report to top management. Operations abroad are further coordinated by both line and staff personnel who support the foreign units.

"We don't exercise direct control over these foreign units," explains Frank J. Pizzitola, the executive vice president in charge of chemicals, plastics and coatings. "When we go into a country, we prefer to ask local people to put up the money to back our technology. We tell them we'll show them how to do it."

The resulting company is usually locally managed and highly decentralized. But Celanese influence makes itself felt through the presence of Pizzitola or another corporate officer on the board. "In this way," says Pizzitola, "we have top-level operational and financial representation in these companies."

At the top, two corporate committees coordinate the whole global apparatus. The management committee (Chairman Harold Blancke, President John W. Brooks, two vice chairmen and the executive vice presidents) sets corporate policy and direction. An eight-man operations committee serves as a high-level conduit for communications and as coordinator of decisions on current operating problems.

The new structure at Celanese has, says Pizzitola, greatly improved communications between top management and local operations around the globe. Intermediate layers of executives have been sliced away, enabling the company to arrive at vital decisions more quickly.

The corporate balance sheet happily reflects this streamlining. Since 1962, volume has nearly doubled from $504.5 million to $1 billion in 1966. Foreign sales have even outsizzled that pace, soaring from $110 million to $228 million. More than half of all Celanese plants are now located outside the U.S.

Singer Shrinks Its Universe

The far-reaching changes taking place at Celanese, Union Carbide and Caterpillar will undoubtedly prompt comparable realignments at many other companies in the years ahead. A fortunate few, however, thanks to good fortune or foresight, will escape most of the painful tugging and hauling. Take the case of Singer Co. A big international operator for decades, Singer has slowly been evolving a management structure to handle its worldwide operations.

A year ago, Singer announced organizational changes keyed mainly to simplifying top management's role in a global market. It grouped eleven operating divisions (including five foreign units) under five group vice presidents, each reporting to President Kircher, the chief executive.

The chain of command today deploys one group vice president over all consumer product activities in Europe, another over the underdeveloped nations in Africa, Latin America, the Near East and the Far East, and a third over Canada and the U.S. In the U.S., Singer is organized along product lines (other than consumer), with each of three basic groups given worldwide manufacturing and marketing responsibilities.

To Kircher, the principal advantages of the group concept lie in its centralizing influence on what had been, from a planning viewpoint, a highly decentralized company. "This building," he explains, referring to New York headquarters, "is now the nerve center of the whole corporation."

Not only are division heads able to swap information and views at headquarters, centralized staff functions have also generated company-wide benefits, says Kircher. "Much of our product development capability is now centralized in the U.S.," he declares. "And our personnel people from all areas meet twice a year, still another centralizing influence as corporate policy is imposed on a particular area."

One often overlooked benefit of operating a worldwide company lies in the personal gratification it affords a top executive. As Kircher sees it: "It is just more fun to act one's role on a larger stage, to deal with the added complexities and subtleties of foreign operations and to feel that one is participating in a broad and historic movement that is undoubtedly the most important economic development of our generation."

Whatever the strength of that movement, it can safely be said that there is as yet no such thing as a truly global company. Ideally, the worldwide corporation would not only produce and sell in every corner of the globe; its management would be completely international, its board would include citizens of many nations, and its stockholders would be scattered all around the world. That goal, as First National City's Wriston is quick to point out, is still many years away.

But at least some forward-looking corporations are moving in that direction, experimenting with various forms of organization in quest of optimum results. To be sure, they still have riddles to solve: What are the best ways to finance foreign operations? How do you avoid the impact of purely national recessions? How do you deal with the multiplicity of laws and regulations affecting overseas activities?

In any case, the evolution of the multinational company has begun. What remains is to grapple with each major question, try various solutions, discard the unworkable, and try once again. "And by so doing," says President John Powers of Chas. Pfizer & Co., "establish direction for the tomorrow of the 1970s and 1980s."

B

THE 1970'S AND BEYOND

45. Organizations in Ferment

DALTON E. McFARLAND

Today, as never before, our business enterprises are organizations in a state of ferment. Organizational turbulence is not exactly new, but it is always interesting. To the concern of the private citizen, the government official, and the business executive, we may now add the aroused attention of the behavioral scientist. How has this come about, and what are the implications for the actions and decisions of managers?

At first our image of the huge monolithic corporation or the tightly-knit, owner-dominated small business enterprise is one of system, order, and stability. This is the intended image of the bureaucratic form of organization structure. It emphasizes the perpetual existence of the organization itself. Positions and tasks endure, although persons come and go. A hierarchical network of authority binds the positions together laterally and vertically. Systems of rewards and punishments reinforce the hierarchical layers. Symbols emerge to identify and support the status and authority of individuals. Everyone has a boss and knows his place. The bureaucracy demands discipline, loyalty, hard work; it gets these demands in reasonable degree and in return yields stability and a highly efficient out-put.

It is true that bureaucratic organization does not guarantee company survival. Some businesses fail; others find it necessary to drastically alter their objectives or modes of operation. Studebaker, Inc., for example, abandoned the production of automobiles. Some firms merge with

Reprinted from *Arizona Business Bulletin*, Vol. 14, No. 4 (April, 1967), pp. 94–97, with permission of the publisher. Dalton E. McFarland is Professor and Chairman, Department of Management, College of Business Administration, Michigan State University.

others out of weakness, some out of strength, but changes of this kind highlight rather than negate the enduring qualities of bureaucratic organizations.

Not only does bureaucratic organization provide stability, but it provides efficiency and expansibility as well. The bureaucracy is the most efficient system of organizing for the production of goods and services ever discovered by man and is capable of infinite expansion. Its patterns accommodate growth in many forms —number of employees, volume or output, amount of sales, etc. Also, contrary to general opinion, bureaucracy has demonstrated the capacity to adapt to change, and even to innovate. The vast amount of change within large-scale business organizations is clearly visible, and it has occurred within the bureaucratic framework.

Despite all these advantages, the bureaucratic forms of organization design and their accompanying management assumptions and precepts are undergoing extensive modification, the outlines of which are just barely becoming noticeable. This is the kind of change that can be referred to as organizational ferment. The bureaucratic form has experienced incipient breakdowns, and shows signs of major and minor changes. Managements that do not recognize the symptoms and adjust their styles and philosophies accordingly can be expected to encounter serious difficulty.

Bureaucratic Costs

We can look at the problems associated with bureaucratic forms of organization as costs of obtaining the advantage of bureaucracy, and the changing expectations indicate that we are no longer sure of our willingness to pay these costs. Therefore, we have sought ways of organizing and managing that will eliminate or reduce the problems without unduly sacrificing efficiency. A large part of the responsibility for making the bureaucracy work better has been allocated to the personnel management function. But personnel managers have restricted their views, philosophies and methods to those of the bureaucracy. They have accepted its basic assumptions and promised much by way of eliminating or mitigating its inhuman effects. Delivery on these promises has in the views of some fallen short.

The bureaucracy exacts a heavy discipline in terms of its inhuman effects. It erects an authority system which at many points appears to be incongruent with the needs of a healthy, mature personality. It provides a hierarchy that must be climbed to attain success, often at great personal sacrifice. But the effort to climb induces frustrations and tensions, and even worse, failure leads to more intensive psychological disorientations. The bureaucracy promises advancement and reward by merit and fairness, but punishment and threats are ever-present tools of the supervisor. The bureaucracy demands conformity, subservience, and docility of its employees; authority and status become important for their own sake, and the means for accomplishing work become ends in themselves.

Lost in the large-scale organization, the individual feels helpless in the face of its power, and so he turns to less desirable ways of meeting his personal needs. He derives his satisfactions not from his work or his job, but from his outside roles in his profession, family, or recreational activities. Within the organization, he may withdraw from active engagement with its needs, or do just enough to get by and stay employed, or occasionally blow off steam in hostile incidents. Another alternative for some individuals is to play the game of politics and power as the organization structures it. They see the organization as a giant arena in which opportunism, favoritism, nepotism and adroitness in advancing their own interests over those of the company or fellow employees become paramount.

Personnel dicta to communicate, to practice good human relations, and to accept organizational goals lose their force when matched against the power and aggrandizement structure described above. Efforts to teach managers how to produce good human relations in their work groups are perceived as unrealistic.

Changing Expectations and the Business Enterprise

Organizational ferment has its roots in several conditions—rapid growth, the accelerating pace of social and technological change, and the increased expectations of an ever more affluent society. Of these three sets of factors, the increased expectations are the most influential for problems of organization; and they are the least recognized and least studied. It is still a question whether the bureaucratic form will meet the increased range of expectations with which it is now being confronted.

It seems clear that over the years society has greatly increased its expectations of the business enterprise. At first we were content that the corporation be efficient. But we have come to expect much more than this. We are not against efficiency, but we want companies to attain some additional goals. We want companies to be good citizens of the community; we ask that they provide clean, healthy, safe places to work, and indeed we pass laws to assure it. We demand that companies accept a share of the responsibility for the social and economic problems of unemployment, technological displacement, employee obsolescence, and other social ills. We ask that executives take an active part in politics. We demand that compa-

nies bargain collectively with recognized unions. Most important of all, we insist that corporations provide maximum job satisfaction and adequate career opportunities for its employees at all levels. And not only are these objectives multiple ones, but often they are in mutual conflict. The bureaucratic organization encounters trouble not in its ability to handle the technology of industry or the problems of productivity and efficiency, but rather in its ability to cope with the enlarged demands going beyond the sphere of efficiency.

Management History

The unfolding flow of managerial history lends support to my views on these questions. When we were content for the corporation to be only efficient, we tolerated and even greatly rewarded tycoons, moguls and exploiters as agents of public benefit. They located, processed and distributed our great natural resources in the form of products and services highly beneficial to society. They were active, virile pragmatists. Human considerations, although they were present, were secondary to efficiency and subject to whim, caprice, and the personal philosophies of the great leaders.

These "captains of industry" were men of genius—capable of exercising strong personal leadership, but they were destined to be replaced by the great organizers, such as Alfred P. Sloan, Jr. These organizers elaborated new management concepts that developed and strengthened the bureaucratic form, making possible the uses and benefits of large-scale organization. They developed ideas of coordination and control, and designed mechanisms by which organizations are self-perpetuating through creating their own bureaucratic leaders. They coupled decentralization of responsibility with centralization of planning and control, thus enlarging the sphere within which efficiency could flourish. In short, they discovered, extended and utilized the bureaucratic concepts to a degree unparalleled in the past.

The Human Relations Movement

In the next stage of management history we find that human relations concepts were widely adopted. Within the bureaucratic form we have tried to eliminate or minimize human problems. We have tried to curtail sandbagging, soldiering on the job, employee disloyalty, high grievance rates, absenteeism, unionization, low morale, poor motivation, job dissatisfaction, job monotony, and employee boredom and restlessness. But we have done all this in the name of efficiency, and during this time we did not recognize the enlarging expectations becoming endemic in society.

The contributions of human relations thinkers were and still are substantial. They shifted our attention from large organizations to small groups. We learned much about leadership, communications, group dynamics, sensitivity, interaction, training, motivation, and job satisfaction. Personnel managers really went for this body of knowledge, selling it to top, middle and supervisory management as the route to greater efficiency and productivity. Although these bodies of knowledge made worthwhile contributions, they have not provided a lasting solution to the continuing disparity between satisfaction, acceptable organizational experiences on the one hand and our extended expectations on the other.

Further progress in human relations and personnel management depends on a greater harmonizing of organization theory with the objectives and methods of

managerial decision and action. So far the field of personnel management has given little cognizance to organization research. Personnel executives seldom participate in organization planning and design, despite the fact that organization structure is certainly one of the most central elements influencing the objectives claimed by personnel management.

The Challenge of Organization Theory

"Organization theory" may be described as the findings of a vast and growing body of research designed to explain both the behavior of organizations and the behavior of people within organizations. Organization research represents the third and current stage of inquiry in which the large organization, substantially neglected by human relations investigators, has been rediscovered. There are definite signs coming out of this research that the methods and assumptions of the bureaucratic form of organization is undergoing some basic modifications that signify much for managerial styles in the years ahead. For example, such concepts as "one boss and only one for every person" are giving way to ideas about loosely structured, fluid work groups organized around processes and team tasks. Members are brought into such groups to apply their special knowledge and skills. When they are no longer needed, they move to another assignment. Thus their careers depend more on individual technical and organization participation skills and less on conformist, boss-oriented behavior. Evaluations by a single boss on a personal basis would give way to evaluations of groups by numerous independent evaluators who would be the persons most interested in or affected by the results of the team effort. Evaluations would be based on results rather than the personalities or behaviors of individuals.

Job descriptions and organization charts predicated on bureaucratic assumptions, already so widely criticized, would disappear or undergo great modifications. Selection criteria and training efforts would change to meet the new ideas on organization design. Discipline would be generated within the group rather than imposed by the top. The commonality of aims and efforts so difficult to develop under traditional organization concepts would be more readily attainable. If meaningful participation were induced by the looser structures, more reliance would be placed on the capacity of individuals to be creative and innovative. This in turn might lead to greater maturity and self-realization by organization members.

This necessarily brief overview indicates that we must expect rather sweeping innovations in organization design and in production systems. Personnel management predicated on structuralized organizational forms carrying out bureaucratic assumptions would be unable to

continue. There may be a time lag in the process by which personnel management acquires an organization research framework more adequate to its objectives and more appropriate to the changed expectations we have concerning organizations and their work. The computer is greatly speeding up the coming revolution in personnel management by reason of its ability to change the forces by which organization itself changes.

Reading List

Etzioni, Amitai, *Modern Organization* (Englewood Cliffs, N.J.: Prentice-Hall, Inc., 1964).

Likert, Rensis, *New Patterns of Management* (New York: McGraw-Hill Book Company, 1961).

McGregor, Douglas, *The Human Side of Enterprise* (New York: McGraw-Hill Book Company, 1960).

Thompson, Victor A., *Modern Organizations* (New York: Alfred A. Knopf, Inc., 1961).

46. Management and Challenges of the Future

HAROLD KOONTZ

The task of the manager is usually thought of as getting things done through people. While it is something akin to this, there is always the danger that this will be interpreted by some as implying a kind of manipulation of people by a manager attempting to be an amateur psychiatrist. To avoid this misguided and hopeless approach, it appears to make more sense to regard the central role of the manager as one of effective and efficient operation of *individuals* working together in groups.

While there are many essential elements in an environment for performance, the more important appear to be the following:

(1) An environment involving a commonality of understood purpose; to be effective people must work toward and contribute to something specific, verifiable, meaningful, actionable, attainable (with some "stretch") and widely understood.

(2) An environment involving an intentional structure of roles since people fill roles (as every athletic coach has learned); this structure of roles, synonymous with formal organization in its broadest sense, requires not only a statement of major duties and an understanding by individuals of areas of their discretion through authority delegation, but also an understanding of goals and of authority and informational relationships with others.

(3) An environment that induces people to perform, preferably because they wish to, often because they simply find it worth their while to in the sense that things can be accomplished best a certain way, and, in some cases, where they must.

(4) An environment in which every superior actively assumes the responsibility for removing obstacles from the performance of his subordinates; he may do this himself, but if it is beyond his power he has the obligation to press upwards—with constructive recommendations for action—to get these obstacles removed.

(5) An environment of clarity, hopefully not clarity obtained through spelling out tasks in detail because of the danger of putting a straightjacket around roles where discretion, imagination, and creativity are desired; rather what is meant is meaningful clarity in objectives or goals, plans, authority delegations, relationships with others, and those matters which a person must know to comprehend his role in a team effort.

Reprinted from *Advanced Management Journal*, Vol. 33, No. 1 (January, 1968), pp. 21–30, with permission of the author and the publisher. Harold Koontz is Mead Johnson Professor of Management, Graduate School of Business Administration, University of California, Los Angeles. Much of the material used in this paper will appear as the final chapter in H. Koontz and C. O'Donnell, *Principles of Management*, 4th edition, to be published by McGraw-Hill Book Company in April, 1968.

Managing Is an Art

Managing is an art and like any good art—whether engineering, medicine, accountancy, or football—succeeds best when the practitioner understands underlying knowledge, the science of his art, and can apply it to reality to gain results. This application almost invariably involves compromise, or blending, taking into account realities and designing, in much the same way an engineer designs an instrument, an approach which will work best in a given set of circumstances.

We have long known in intellectually based arts that the best designer or practitioner is one well grounded in basic knowledge. This is true in electronics. It is true in medicine. It is likewise true in managing. Despite admitted crudities in the science—organized knowledge—of management, the fact is that a growing science is developing. Likewise, managerial techniques and tools are evolving rapidly, borrowing, as many have, from the systems approach long applied with benefit in the physical sciences. And insights from researches of the behavioral scientists are slowly beginning to have their effect on management understanding of people and groups.

Managing is perhaps the most complex of all arts. Growing knowledge, plus the spurs of world-wide super competition and rapid change, mean that those who manage increasingly face the problem of becoming obsolete.

So long as managing was a task only learned from experience, obsolescence was unimportant. But now experience has been distilled into meaningful and useful principles and theory, inadequate as they may be. These are furnishing structures on which both distilled experience and new findings in management and related sciences can be arranged and made meaningful for the practitioner so that now there is no time for individuals to reach a state of managerial excellence required for his job through trial and error.

Management Must Be for Reality

There is ever the danger that management knowledge will not be used to obtain results in practice. It must be operational and it must be for reality since managing, as an art, is a matter of using knowledge to solve real problems, to develop operating systems or environment in which people can perform. This means several things. Knowledge of management is not enough. There is always the danger in any field of developing a science aimed at elegance or polish, rather than results. Every science has its "educated derelicts" who know but cannot apply this knowledge to gain useful results.

Moreover, the reality with which a manager must deal is always tomorrow. As it has been well said, reality is a moving target. In looking at management for tomorrow, it may be well to identify a few of the major challenges which managers face, as well as what this future means to managers, and to call specific attention to the urgent need for intellectual leadership in management.

The Need to Meet Change with Flexibility

It may be stated that the most effective management is flexible management. In other words, since the environment in which an enterprise operates is certain to change and since the attitudes and motivations of people likewise vary, it can be no exaggeration to emphasize the importance of flexibility in managing. To be sure an effective manager must be able to recognize change but, preferably, so that he will have time to meet it, he should be able to anticipate change. Likewise, the internal environment of the enterprise which he develops, if it is to remain consistent with an responsive to the external environment, must be flexible.

The problem of managerial flexibility is made even more challenging and difficult by a number of inflexibilities which tend to be built into the system of an enterprise. One finds too often enterprises regarding their policies as something written on stone rather than guides to thinking for future decision making. Likewise, almost all enterprises find themselves enmeshed in procedures, which have usually grown up like Topsy, and which tie up action and stultify thinking.

In addition, inflexibilities are likely to be imposed upon an enterprise by stubbornly resistant government regulations and labor rules and customs frozen into union contracts and thinking. But perhaps the greatest element of inflexibility is the natural human resistance to change. The space scientist, Edward Teller, once declared that, in all of his scientific explorations, the most inert material he had ever encountered was the human mind, with one exception, a group of human minds.

A Balanced Environment for Creativity and Conformity

One of the major problems facing every manager is that of designing and maintaining a balanced environment for creativity and conformity. Perhaps there is, as William Whyte pictured in his *The Organization Man*,[1] too much conformity, too much belongingness, too much togetherness, and too little individual responsibility. Perhaps there is too much reliance on group operations and committees. Perhaps there is some foundation to the charge of the many psychol-

ogists who decry tendencies toward conformity and stultification of individuality and creativity.

However, one can grant the underlying thesis of Whyte and many other management critics that people rarely think or create as groups, but rather as individuals. One can agree that the want satisfactions of people go far beyond the paycheck, without casting any necessarily damaging criticisms of formalized management, particularly as exercised by intelligent practitioners in many of our outstanding enterprises. The question is not conformity, but the degree; no one can operate as a member of a group without some conformity. Any effective group activity implies some structure of roles, some limitations, some consistent patterns of behavior.

This is not a question of looking upon all formalized management as one wherein an authoritarian hand suppresses the needs and wants of intelligent human beings. It is rather one of whether a manager is utilizing his formal organization structure, formal plans, or formal controls, as environmental devices that make desired performance possible.

What is needed, of course, is balanced design. The creation of a role or the establishment of goals or plans does not, by any means, imply a detailed, narrow role or objectives which cannot stretch the imagination and creativity in anyone. In other words, the total environment should provide for a role allowing and encouraging creativity and imagination where it is wanted. There are also many cases where complete conformity is required.

There are times, for example, when basic accounting records must be prepared in a precise way in order to assure accurate financial statements, or where billing on a government contract must

---

[1] New York: Simon and Schuster, Inc., 1956.

follow in strict conformity the requirements of the contract if the company is to be paid. Likewise, there are many areas in a typical company where chemicals create an explosive atmosphere and when a rule against smoking means exactly that. What is often forgotten is that the conformity necessary for people to live and work together may be unbending in one area of activity and yet there can be provided ample opportunity for innovation and creativity in another.

Preserving the Carrot and the Stick

One of the major problems facing the manager of the future is that of balancing for best results the carrot and the stick. Some two decades ago, the British *Economist* pointed out that "The human donkey requires either a carrot in front or a stick behind to goad it into activity." Perhaps, in modern society, there has been a tendency to overemphasize the carrot and forget the stick. Perhaps what is even worse, we have tended to whittle away both the carrot and the stick. The passion for equality may have removed much of the stick. Such practices as promotion by seniority, level pay, automatic merit increases, executive bonuses not based on individual performance, and guaranteed wages, while having a desirable sound, may have, in some instances, removed much of the stick.

Perhaps, also, much of the carrot has been taken away. Progressive income taxation, increased government regulations which may dull enterprise, and even growing social insurance, may have removed much of the carrot. This is nowhere more evident than in the action of a misguided United States Congress which, apparently misunderstanding the motivating factors involved in executive stock options, shortened the option period

from ten years to five and increased the period an executive must hold options to qualify for capital gains from six months to three years.

As any informed corporate shareholder knows, a fair and well-administered stock option plan which gives executives the same motivation as owners, has long proved to be in the interest of those who own the company. It is overlooking the fact that, not only do executives, like other people, react to a carrot but, in this case, the carrot can also be sweet for the public shareholders.

There are questions in this area of great importance to the future manager. How can he maintain incentive, either through the carrot or the stick, without abandoning the aims of equality of economic opportunity? How can a society have the worthwhile goals of social security and still maintain motivation for accomplishment? As the famous editorial said, "How can the carrot and the stick be combined with a pleasant life for the donkey?" That this requires managerial ingenuity for finding means of sharpening the appropriate sticks or sweetening the right carrots is both obvious and challenging.

One of the major problems facing the manager of the future is that of coping with increased sophistication in all aspects of managing. Of particular importance has been the introduction of newer techniques in the areas of management planning and control. These, based upon the systems approaches brought over from the physical sciences, include applications of such important techniques as operations research, network analysis, and the new information technologies. Likewise, there have been the many findings of the behavioral sciences which, if they are applied to managing, can improve personal efficiency.

But evidence exists that practice has been slow to adopt many of these new techniques and findings. There appears to be far too much talk and too little action. In most cases, it is the author's opinion that practicing managers have not adopted them simply because they are not understood and what individuals in a responsible position do not understand, they are not likely to trust or to use. Much of this has arisen from the fact that experts in these fields seem to thrive on a kind of a mysticism and jargon which protects their image as experts but which becomes unintelligible to most managers.

For example, in the area of operations research, there has appeared to be too much emphasis on the mathematics of models and too little recognition that the model is a "little black box," the internal working of which a manager need not understand. The need, of course, is for emphasizing the key importance of conceptualizing problem relationships and leaving the model to the specialist. Likewise, experts in the field should realize that, if their findings are to be useful, they must engage in fewer gymnastics and less self-gratification from complexity and have more realization that there are practical problems which can be solved.

There are still a great many management techniques not of great sophistication which are too little used or too ineptly applied. When one looks at such "cloud one" level areas as authority delegation, variable budgeting, formalized product planning, market-oriented organization, and appraisal of managers by results, one can see that these are not based upon highly sophisticated concepts.

Likewise, in the control area, the approach of tailoring control to plans and individuals, as well as organization structure, is another example where managing might be made far more effective. Even though these and other tools are relatively simple in concept, they are admittedly difficult to apply in practice. But those managers who have earnestly tried to apply them have reaped tremendous benefits.

New Information Vistas

Another challenge to the manager and one changing his role materially is that related to new vistas of information and new ways of systematizing it. It has been well said that the reach of an executive is determined by the information at his command. This, in turn, implies information, preferably of a forecast nature, material to a manager's task, weighed against goals, and analyzed to determine why and where actions are missing goals.

What has not been as widely recognized as desirable, is that the spectrum of information has been widening considerably. Financial data themselves have been widened through direct costing, a program of accounting which altogether too few companies have adopted and which is virtually unknown in non-business enterprises. Likewise, the alert manager of today will insist upon considerable information inputs from social, economic, and technical sources to supplement the necessary limitations of financial or physical input or output data.

Another problem is the need for information design. Data are only a raw material until designed and produced to make information. What is often forgotten is that, despite the tremendous potentials of electronic data processing equipment, no one can expect a useful end-product unless he knows what product he wishes and develops and utilizes the raw materials to make the product.

In fact, it can be well understood that the long-promised information revolution is still much further away than most people suspect. Likewise, it can hardly be made a fact unless the highest order of intelligence and analysis is applied to the basic tools at hand.

Absorbing New Findings

As is indicated above, one of the most interesting challenges facing the manager of today and tomorrow is how to absorb the methods and findings of the physical and behavioral sciences into the fundamental scheme of management. Even though it may be unfairly argued that the outpouring of behavioral research has offered limited practical help to managers, one can agree that this research has not been integrated into the theory and structure of management thought or utilized to a material extent by practitioners

One of the most exciting phenomena of our times is the conscious attempt to utilize the methods of the physical sciences to solve managerial problems. One can certainly see the relevance and value to management of the methodologies of the physical sciences—such as simulation, the systems approach, symbols, models, approximation, and other tools of mathematical analysis, the logic of rationality and optimization, and the need for balance in design. But, one may ask a question as to whether they have really been adequately absorbed in the operational science of management.

Perhaps the greatest challenge lies in finding methods of integrating these new findings and approaches into the basic theory of an operational management science. What is needed even more is for the specialists in these fields to adopt more thoroughly than has yet been the case an attitude of making their findings operational. One of the ways this can be done is for more of these specialists to understand the total of the manager's task and the total theory underlying it.

Another need is for some of these specialists to undertake *applied* research and

development in their field. As one of the leading behavioral scientists said, "I think the thing we do not have is any meaningful applications from behavioral research at the basic level to practice." [2]

Assuring Managerial Quality

Despite remarkable advances in the quality of managers in the past quarter-century, the needs for assuring the quality of managers are greater than ever before. The most direct of all control is to control the quality of managers. Even though tremendous advances have been made in management appraisal and training, needs tend to outdistance action. In the first place, many appraisal programs still do not aim at measuring what the manager does rather than what people think of him. Many appraisers do not know what to appraise or how. Too many appraisal systems are involved in a maze of forms, systems, records, and marks.

While a huge step has been taken in the fast growing programs of appraisal by results against verifiable objectives, these are still subject to inadequacies. Goals are difficult to establish and, by necessity, tend to be short-range. Also, managers sometimes succeed or fail in their performance through factors beyond their control. To offset these deficiencies, it is hoped that, in the near future, appraisal by results may be supplemented by appraisal of the quality of managing itself. The need is for performers, to be sure. But long-term needs are better filled by managers who can both manage and obtain performance.

Once adequate appraisal systems are developed and utilized, the next step is logically to tie programs of management development into the gaps disclosed and

---

[2] As stated by Professor Mason Haire in H. Koontz (ed.), *Toward A Unified Theory of Management* (New York: McGraw-Hill Book Company, 1964), p. 224.

to the need for individual managers to acquire new knowledge and techniques.

Developing Managers for the Future

There is certainly ample evidence that the nature of the managerial task is changing greatly and that competition for success is becoming more sharp. In addition, the role of the manager is and will continue to require ever increasing sophistication. This emphasizes the urgent importance of an accelerated program of management development.

Perhaps the first requirement of so doing is willingness of managers to learn. They must be aware that experience alone is not only a costly teacher but may even be a dangerous one. Undistilled experience can lead an individual to assume that approaches or programs of the past will or will not work in a future certain to be different. To be willing to learn and take advantage of new knowledge and techniques requires a humble approach to a manager's successes and limitations. It demands a recognition that there is no finishing school or terminal degree for management education.

One of the major problems of developing managers for the future is the need for compressing growing management knowledge and transmitting it to those on the firing line of practice in as simple and useful a way as possible. Every field of art based on a burgeoning science has this problem. No field has solved it although certain areas, such as specialized aspects of medicine, have made considerable progress.

There is no easy or readily available answer for this problem. It does appear that those on the management faculties of our universities have an obligation to practicing managers to do much of the task of compressing and transmitting available knowledge as easily and quickly as possible. There is still inadequate evidence that many university professors see the social importance of this role.

Also, one might expect a greater contribution from various management associations, as well as the management consultants who can certainly greatly improve their value to clients by doing this. Perhaps something can be done through intelligent digesting of articles and books, although this does not appear too hopeful since those who probably know what is significant to managers and how to transmit it to them are not likely to be in the position of digesters.

It is entirely possible that a series of special management clinics might be regularly established in which managers at all levels in alert companies would spend a day every two weeks or so to be brought up-to-date on a specific area of the new knowledge and technique. But more and better techniques must be found if the widening gap between knowledge and practice is to be narrowed.

Need for Research and Development

One of the greatest needs for the future, and perhaps one of the most challenging, is that of obtaining more real research and development on management tools and techniques themselves. The level of research effort and support in the field of management is woefully low. It is also not particularly great in the disciplines underlying management, and, for that matter, in the entire area of social science. Nevertheless, it is probable that research in underlying disciplines far outpaces that in the central area of management.

There are many reasons for this. General management research is a difficult field, exceedingly complex and dynamic.

It is one where facts and proved relationships are hard to come by and where the controlled experiment of the laboratory is difficult to use without dangerous oversimplification. Likewise, management research is expensive and the funds that have gone into it are abysmally inadequate.

It has been estimated that not more than two per cent of the total being spent annually for all research in this country, or approximately one-twentieth of one per cent of Gross National Product, goes into research in *all* social sciences. In turn, if funds spent on management and management-related research are more than one-tenth of this, or one-two-hundredth of one per cent of Gross National Product, the author would be surprised.

Still another reason for the low state of management research is that there is a lack of clinical analyses, despite a considerable volume of clinical experience. Consulting efforts of both professional consultants and individual academics, extensive management case collections, and studies and analyses made internally in business, government, and other enterprises, almost certainly encompass a huge mass of undigested, largely unsummarized, and generally useless information. If this clinical experience could be given a kind of analytical and summarizing work so common in the health sciences, there might be now considerable useful evidence of what is workable in practice and where deficiencies exist.

In undertaking this research, a high order of patience and understanding is needed. Perfection of truth and analysis is a laudable goal for the researcher. But, particularly in the field of management, a little light can be a massive beam in a hitherto dark area of knowledge. We must often settle for small advances so that cumulatively, and over time, we may gain larger ones.

But research without application is inadequate. One of the major challenges for the manager of the future is the need for developing more managerial inventions. It is an interesting thing how so much creative talent has been channeled into the invention of physical designs and chemical compositions and how so little into social inventions.

The GANTT chart has sometimes been regarded as the most important social invention of the first half of the twentieth century. Other management inventions include the variable budget, rate-of-return-on-investment analysis, linear organizational charts, and PERT (Program Evaluation and Review Technique). Mere reference to these inventions underlines the fact that they are perceptive tools developed from a basis of principles on one hand and needs on the other. Reference to them indicates also that they are useful devices in improving the art of management.

Inventions tend to reflect the cultural level of an art. There are few of them in management. Surely even the present inadequate cultural level can be coupled with urgent management needs to give rise to many more management innovations, particularly if those concerned are willing to spend some time and money to direct their energies toward inventions. It is very easy to see that one significant management invention, such as those mentioned in the previous paragraph, can make considerable contributions to management effectiveness and economy of operation.

Need for Intellectual and Creative Leadership

That intellectual and creative leadership in management is urgently needed can hardly be denied. Managing can no longer require only native intelligence and experience. The rapid growth of underlying knowledge and the obvious need for even more, particularly that knowledge which is organized and useful for improvement of practice, are requirements which have tremendous social significance.

It is not difficult to anticipate a five per cent rise in productivity in the American economy due to improved management, or an effort, in sheer economic terms, worth some forty billion dollars per year. Yet even these dramatic data give no direct recognition to the rise in human satisfactions involved in such improvement.

This means that key elements in any society would do well to give the area of managerial scientific research and development a high priority. Our college and university administrators and scholars —leaders in what former President Clark Kerr of the University of California has called the "knowledge industry"—should take the lead by giving management research and teaching the support their social importance deserves. Private foundations have an obligation as instruments of social betterment to support meaningful research in the field.

Likewise, there can hardly be a more important area of research for a government to support. Every part of society would do well to seize the opportunity to support management research and development with the same vigor they have pursued such goals as new products, improved physical health, defense, and public welfare. In short, what is needed is an awareness that the intellectual and creative requirements of management are urgent, manifold, and socially important.

The challenges for a better society through improved management practice in every type of enterprise and those involved in intellectual and creative leadership in the field are impressive. History teaches us that when needs exist and are recognized and when the cultural level reaches the point of ability to meet these needs, leadership usually arises to inspire solutions.

The challenging needs are here. The cultural level appears to be rising to the point where many answers are feasible. The question is simply where and how this leadership can be developed.

DISCUSSION QUESTIONS: PART VI

1. Compare management in the United States and Europe. How do they differ? How are they similar? In what ways do you think management will change in Europe during the next decade? Why?
2. After examining the four major approaches of this book, what type of approach would you take to management in a multinational company? Explain.
3. Develop a new approach to management for use in a multinational company. Is it related to the present approaches used in the United States? Why or why not?
4. What are some of the challenges of the future for managers? Would you balance the "new" with the "old" as suggested by Professor Koontz? Why or why not?
5. Describe several of the major problems facing managers in the next decade (you may use the entire book, not just this section in answering this question). Establish a set of criteria upon which to judge whether or not the problem is a major problem before you answer the question.

6. What advancements would you predict in the development of a philosophy for management, a science of management, and profession of management in the next decade? Explain each prediction.

7. Formulate an eclectic approach to management which could be used by executives. Be sure to consider the major approaches to management.

SELECTED REFERENCES: PART VI

A. MULTINATIONAL MANAGEMENT

Benge, Eugene J., "Managers Abroad—They're Different," *Advanced Management Journal*, Vol. 33, No. 2 (April, 1968), pp. 31–36.

Farmer, Richard N. and Barry M. Richman, "A Model for Research in Comparative Management," *California Management Review,* Vol. 7, No. 2 (Winter, 1964), pp. 55–68.

Kolde, Endel and Richard E. Hill, "Conceptual and Normative Aspects of International Management," *Academy of Management Journal,* Vol. 10, No. 2 (June, 1967), pp. 119–128.

McKenzie, C., "Incompetent Foreign Managers?" *Business Horizons,* Vol. 9, No. 1 (September, 1966), pp. 83–90.

Negandhi, A. R. and B. D. Estafen, "A Research Model to Determine the Applicability of American Management Know-How in Differing Cultures and/or Environments," *Academy of Management Journal,* Vol. 8, No. 4 (December, 1965), pp. 309–318.

Oberg, Winston, "Cross-cultural Perspectives on Management Principles," *Academy of Management Journal,* Vol. 6, No. 2 (June, 1963), pp. 129–143.

Prasad, S. B. (ed.), *Management in International Perspective.* New York: Appleton-Century-Crofts, Inc., 1967.

B. THE 1970's AND BEYOND

Ansoff, Igor H., "The Firm of the Future," *Harvard Business Review,* Vol. 43, No. 5 (September–October, 1965), pp. 162–178.

Bennis, Warren G., *Changing Organizations.* New York: McGraw-Hill Book Co., Inc., 1966.

Close, Frederick J., "A Look Back from the Year 2010," *Advanced Management Journal,* Vol. 32, No. 1 (January, 1967), pp. 6–14.

Farmer, Richard N., *Management in the Future.* Belmont, California: Wadsworth Publishing Co., Inc., 1967.

Hodge, Billy J., "Contemporary Management in a Dilemma," *Business Review,* Vol. 13 (Summer, 1966), pp. 28–44.

Knight, Kenneth E., "A Behavioral View of Tomorrow's Organization . . . Its Men . . . Its Machines . . . Its Managers," *Stanford Graduate School of Business Bulletin,* Vol. 35, No. 1 (Summer, 1966), pp. 14–19.

Smiddy, Harold F., "Theory and Research for the Improvement of Management Practice," *Academy of Management, Proceedings of the 1962 Annual Meeting.* University Park, Pa.: 1963, pp. 188–196.

Suojanen, Waino W., *The Dynamics of Management.* New York: Holt, Rinehart, and Winston, Inc., 1966.

INDEX

451